12th IADIS International Conference Information Systems 2019

Utrecht, The Netherlands
11 – 13 April 2019

Editors:

Miguel Baptista Nunes
Pedro Isaias
Philip Powell
Pascal Ravesteijn
Guido Ongena

ISBN: 978-1-5108-8902-6

Printed from e-media with permission by:

Curran Associates, Inc.
57 Morehouse Lane
Red Hook, NY 12571

Some format issues inherent in the e-media version may also appear in this print version.

Printed by Curran Associates, Inc. (2019)

For permission requests, please contact International Association for Development of the Information Society (IADIS) at the address below.

International Association for Development of the Information Society (IADIS)
Rua Sao Sebastiao Da Pedreira
No. 100, 30, 1050-209
Lisbon, Portugal

Phone: 351 21 3151373
Fax: 351 21 3151244

secretariat@iadis.org

Additional copies of this publication are available from:

Curran Associates, Inc.
57 Morehouse Lane
Red Hook, NY 12571 USA
Phone: 845-758-0400
Fax: 845-758-2633
Email: curran@proceedings.com
Web: www.proceedings.com

PROCEEDINGS OF THE 12th IADIS INTERNATIONAL CONFERENCE

INFORMATION SYSTEMS 2019

UTRECHT, THE NETHERLANDS

11 - 13 APRIL, 2019

Organised by

iadis

international association for development of the information society

Co-organised by

UNIVERSITY OF APPLIED SCIENCES UTRECHT

Edited by Miguel Baptista Nunes, Pedro Isaías, Philip Powell, Pascal Ravesteijn and Guido Ongena

Associate Editor: Luís Rodrigues

TABLE OF CONTENTS

FULL PAPERS

SHORT PAPERS

REFLECTION PAPERS

POSTER

FOREWORD

These proceedings contain the papers and poster of the 12th IADIS International Conference Information Systems 2019, which was organised by the International Association for Development of the Information Society and co-organised by the University of Applied Sciences, in Utrecht, The Netherlands, 11 - 13 April 2019.

The IADIS Information Systems Conference 2019 aims to provide a forum for the discussion of IS taking a socio-technological perspective. It aims to address the issues related to design, development and use of IS in organisations from a socio-technological perspective, as well as to discuss IS professional practice, research and teaching. A set of key areas has been identified. However, these do not aim at being prescriptive, or set in stone, and any innovative contributions that do not fit into these areas have also been considered.

The following main tracks have been object of paper submissions:

- IS in Practice, Technology Infrastructures and Organisational Processes
- IS Design, Development and Management Issues and Methodologies
- IS Professional Issues
- IS Research
- IS Learning and Teaching

The IADIS Information Systems Conference 2019 had 149 submissions from more than 27 countries. Each submission has been anonymously reviewed by an average of 3 independent reviewers, to ensure the final high standard of the accepted submissions. Out of the papers submitted, 28 got blind referee ratings that published them as full papers, which means that the acceptance rate was 19%. Some other submissions were published as short and reflection papers, poster and tutorial format. Extended versions of the best papers will be selected to be published in the Journal of Electronic Commerce in Organizations (JECO) journal (ISSN: 1539-2937) and also in the IADIS Journal on Computer Science and Information Systems (ISSN: 1646-3692) indexed by Emerging Sources Citation Index by Thomson Reuters.

The conference, besides the papers' and poster's presentations, also includes a keynote presentation from an internationally distinguished researcher. We wish to thank Professor Hajo Reijers, Department of Information and Computing Sciences of Utrecht University (UU), The Netherlands, for accepting our invitation as keynote speaker. In addition, we would like to thank Dr. Ilia Bider for the Tutorial.

As we all know, a conference requires the effort of many individuals. We would like to thank all members of the Program Committee for their hard work in reviewing and selecting the papers that appear in the book of the proceedings. We would also like to thank all the authors who have submitted their papers to this conference. We wish to thank all members of our organizing committee.

Last but not the least, we hope that everybody will have a good time in Utrecht, and we invite all participants for the next year edition of the IADIS International Conference of Information Systems 2020.

Professor Philip Powell, Executive Dean, University of London, UK
Pascal Ravesteijn, University of Applied Sciences, Utrecht, The Netherlands
Guido Ongena, University of Applied Sciences, Utrecht, The Netherlands
Conference Co-Chairs

Miguel Baptista Nunes, School of Information Management, Sun Yat-sen University, Guangzhou, China
Pedro Isaias, The University of Queensland, Australia
Program Co-Chairs

Utrecht, The Netherlands
April 2019

PROGRAM COMMITTEE

CONFERENCE CO-CHAIRS

Professor Philip Powell, Executive Dean, University of London, UK
Pascal Ravesteijn, University of Applied Sciences, Utrecht, The Netherlands
Guido Ongena, University of Applied Sciences, Utrecht, The Netherlands

PROGRAM CO-CHAIRS

Miguel Baptista Nunes, School of Information Management, Sun Yat-sen University, Guangzhou, China
Pedro Isaias, The University of Queensland, Australia

COMMITTEE MEMBERS

Abdelkrim Meziane, Cerist, Algeria
Adam Wojtowicz, Poznan University of Economics and Business, Poland
Amelia Badica, University of Craiova, Romania
Andrea Kienle, University of Applied Sciences Dortmund, Germany
Andrea Ko, Corvinus University of Budapest, Hungary
Andreas Oberweis, Karlsruhe Institute of Technology (KIT), Germany
Andreja Pucihar, University of Maribor, Slovenia
Betim Cico, Epoka University, Albania
Carlos Blanco, Universidad de Cantabria, Spain
Christos Kalloniatis, University of the Aegean, Greece
David G. Rosado, University of Castilla-la Mancha, Spain
Dimitar Trajanov, Ss Cyril and Methodius University, Macedonia
Dimitris Karagiannis, University of Vienna, Austria
Dimitris Kardaras, Athens University of Economics and Business, Greece
Eddie Soulier, Université de Technologie de Troyes, France
Edward Bernroider, Vienna University of Economics and Business, Austria
Eleutherios A. Papathanassiou, Athens University of Economics and Business, Greece
Euripides Loukis, University of the Aegean, Greece
Faiez Gargouri, Institut Superieur D'informatique et de Multimedia, Tunisia
Farshad Badie, Aalborg University, Denmark
Francisco Jose Silva Mata, Cenatav, Cuba
François Bergeron, TELUQ, Canada
Hans-Peter Steinbacher, University of Applied Sciences, Austria
Haralambos Mouratidis, University of Brighton, United Kingdom
Hepu Deng, RMIT University, Australia
Iraklis Varlamis, Harokopio University of Athens, Greece

KEYNOTE LECTURE

INFORMATION TECHNOLOGY ON THE WORK FLOOR: ADVANCES AND CHALLENGES

by Professor Hajo Reijers,
Department of Information and Computing Sciences of Utrecht University (UU),
The Netherlands

Abstract

People have always been looking for ways to apply technology to do less work. Recent technological advances have considerably extended the range of human work that may be automated: from routine, low-complexity activities to tasks that involve cognition, exploration, and collaboration. In this talk, I will give an overview on how various information technologies are being used in work processes to carry out the work that was once done by people. I will also discuss current research at Utrecht University that aims at establishing the affordances of information technology, in particular Robotic Process Automation (RPA). Finally, I will show that the use of information technology on the workfloor is not unproblematic and leads to many new research challenges.

TUTORIAL

BUSINESS PROCESS CANVAS AND ITS USAGE IN IS TEACHING AND LEARNING

by **Ilia Bider**
DSV, Stockholm University, Sweden

Abstract

The tutorial introduces a new type of canvas called Business Process Canvas (BPC), and discusses experience of its usage in an IS course related to Business Process Modeling/Management (BPM). BPC represents a model of a business process in a nutshell that covers the most important aspects of the process, including its place in the organization, resources that it uses, and how it is driven. The canvas could be used in practice for decision making on a higher level when particular details are not important for the decision. It can also be used by process mapping experts for a pre-modeling phase to gather and systematize basic data about the process before diving into details; this could be especially useful for new, less experience process modelers. However, the primary motivation behind the development of BPC was to have a tool that facilitates both the students' understanding of the concepts related to BPM and their learning of how to model a process given a text description, or interviewing people engaged in the process. The tutorial introduces the structure of the
canvas, discusses the experience of its usage, and devotes some time for exercises where the participants fill the canvas based on process descriptions.

KEYWORDS

Business Process, Business Process Modeling, IS Teaching and Learning, Canvas

1. MOTIVATION

While teaching students formal notations for business process modeling is relatively easy, teaching them how to actually analyze available information to build a model is more difficult. This is even harder when the available information is vague or not covering all issues involved, and the students need to fill the gaps by finding more information or using common sense. Facing these difficulties in a Business Process Management (BPM) course at our university (Koutsopoulos & Bider, 2017), we devised a Business Process Canvas (BPC)

(Koutsopoulos & Bider, 2018) to be used in a pre-modeling phase for analyzing and systemizing information about a process before starting process modeling using a particular notation. The canvas was introduced in the autumn 2018 round of the course and proved to be useful not only for pre-modeling phase, but also for students getting understanding of the basic concepts of BPM. We conducted a small survey among the students, and found that the canvas was considered as a useful tool in the course, even by the students who were exposed to BPM before the course.

Though the main motivation for BPC development was educational, the usefulness of the canvas is not limited to teaching and learning BPM. BPC can be used by experts for practical tasks. In particular, we envision that it can be used (a) by professional process modelers at the phase of gathering and systemizing information before diving into details; (b) by high level of managers when making decisions that do not require knowledge on the details of a particular process(es).

The distinguishing feature of BPC is that it is not connected to any specific type of process modeling, and can be used for workflow, state-oriented and other non-traditional types of process modeling. This also can be seen as a limitation, as some properties that are natural to a particular business process modeling technique, e.g. order of activities, cannot be represented in the canvas. In other words, BPC should be considered as a starting point for process modeling, and should not be overloaded with too many details.

2. BUSINESS PROCESS CANVAS - A PROCESS MODEL IN A NUTSHELL

The canvas layout to be presented is shown in Fig.1. The layout uses colors to differentiate three distinct sections called:

1. *Outside* – upper part of the canvas marked with the orange color. *Outside* refers to the essential
   characteristics of a business process type, e.g. why this process type exists, how it is connected to other processes in the organization, etc.
2. *Inside* – left bottom part of the canvas marked with the blue color. *Inside* refers to how instances of the given type are run, e.g. what are main milestones and activities, etc.
3. *Resources* – right bottom part of the canvas marked with the green color. *Resources* refer to human and non-human resources used for driving business process instances, people, technological devices, methods/methodologies, etc.

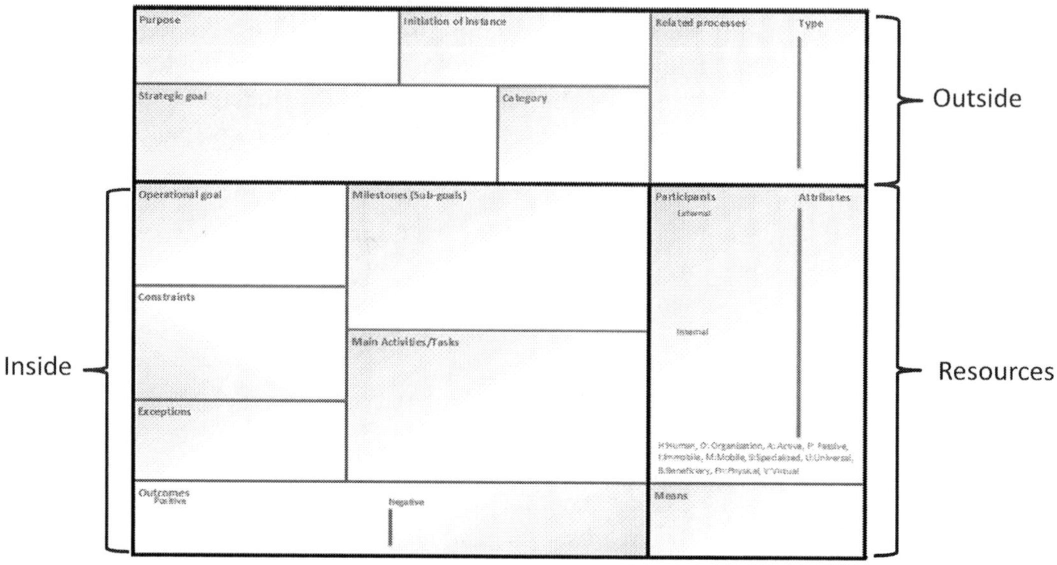

Figure 1. A layout of Business Process Canvas

3. TUTORIAL DISPOSITION

The tutorial will cover three topics (a) introduction of BPC; (b) experience of using it in teaching (c) exercises for using BPC for pre-modeling phase in order to systemize the available material. As one of the exercises, the participants will be filling BPC for a business process used in the exams.

REFERENCES

Koutsopoulos, G. & Bider, I., 2017. Teaching and Learning State-Oriented Business Process Modeling. Experience Report. In *Enterprise, Business-Process and Information Systems Modeling, LNBIP, Vol. 287*. Springer, pp.171-85.

Koutsopoulos, G. & Bider, I., 2018. Business Process Canvas as a Process Model in a Nutshell. In *Enterprise, Business-Process and Information Systems Modeling, LNBIP, Vol. 318*. Springer, pp.49-63.

Full Papers

METHODOLOGICAL FOUNDATIONS OF MHEALTH DESIGN STUDIES: A CONTENT ANALYSIS OF LITERATURE

Ahmet Faruk Acar and Sevgi Özkan Yıldırım
METU
Ankara, Turkey

ABSTRACT

Despite the pervasiveness of mobile devices and the number of available mobile health (mHealth) apps, a scaled nationwide mHealth solution for supporting continuous healthcare is lacking in many developing countries. Systematic reviews in mobile health field show various barriers to explain the lack of scalability and sustainability among mHealth interventions. However, little is known about the methodological soundness of mHealth app design studies. We conducted a literature review to investigate the theoretical foundations of mHealth design studies, which are essential to inform design and content of the solution. The purpose of this paper is to evaluate and classify the mHealth studies in terms of their methodological soundness for the design, development process of smartphone application (app) through content analysis.

KEYWORDS

mHealth, Methodology, Design, Development, Evidence-Based

1. INTRODUCTION

mHealth stands out as a promising intervention method to provide medical consultancy, social support, and evidence-based information. Despite the obvious need and benefits of mHealth systems for self-management, behavior change and provider consultancy; sustainable, scaled and well-adopted mHealth systems are lacking in many developing counties. Literature review studies brings different aspects regarding the barriers and facilitators towards design, development and implementation of mHealth applications (app) such as financial issues, policies, privacy and security concerns, individual and organizational readiness.

Alvarado et al. categorize the barriers of remote health interventions as patient barriers, technology access barriers, design barriers, provider barriers, and system barriers (Alvarado *et al.*, 2017). According to review of Matthew-Maich et al., organizational and system readiness, financial resources, policies, and workplace culture all play a key role in the successful adoption of mHealth technologies. Also their review refers to the inertia and resistance to change that can exist within organizations (Matthew-Maich *et al.*, 2016). Kim et al. also refer to organizational readiness by the fact that current healthcare systems are not adequately designed to meet the long-term management needs of individuals, instead, suited better for the acute management (Kim et al., 2017).

Factors such as the cost of implementing the system, increased clinical workload and workflow, maintaining up-to-date records, and concerns about being supervised and depending too much on technology are also given as the main concerns regarding implementation of mHealth adherence interventions (Hamine *et al.*, 2015). Steinhuble et al. emphasize the current fee-for-service reimbursement model in healthcare as a major financial barrier due to lack of financial incentive for practitioners to implement such mHealth systems. They propose value-based care instead of fee-for-service but the former is not likely to replace the other very soon (Steinhubl *et al.*, 2015).

The mHealth field is relatively new and the main assumption of this paper is that mHealth studies may lack the methodological rigor. Therefore, mHealth studies need further investigation in terms of their theoretical and methodological soundness besides the various aspects given in the reviews above. In this study, we conducted a literature review and analyzed mHealth studies in terms of theoretical and other systematic approaches that substantiates their design, development and implementation methods. Our content analysis shows that mHealth studies may have evidence-based and/or design-based theoretical basis while some of them possess none. Following sections have the details of literature review's results.

2. METHODOLOGY

We conducted a literature review to find mHealth studies, which has at least one of design, development and implementation phases of an mHealth application. The key eligibility criteria were a smartphone application (or at least a prototype with high or low fidelity) should be developed within the scope of study. Furthermore, we aim only for peer-reviewed journal articles which are expected to have more rigorous methodology for the design, development phases and exclude review studies, conference papers and other studies from grey literature. Smartphone applications become ubiquitous in the last 10 years and even mobile phones were common before 2009, mHealth studies mostly focused on SMS and text-based intervention and lacked the design, development process of smartphone apps and complex interaction of its users. Therefore, journal articles which are published in the last 10 years are particularly sought for.

2.1 Identification

Medline, Scopus and Web of Science are chosen as scientific databases to have optimum coverage for our search results. Keywords and Boolean representation of the search query is formulated (Table 1) and run within the title field of studies that are published in the last 10 years.

Table 1. Keywords and boolean representation of search query

Keywords	Boolean Representation
design, development, implementation, mhealth, mobile health, m-health, mobile app, mobile application, smartphone application	((design OR development OR implementation) AND (mhealth OR mobile health OR m-health OR mobile app OR mobile application OR smartphone application))

List of the search criteria used for all three digital libraries are as follows:

- Publication date is between '2009/01/01 – 2019/01/01'
- Publication type is 'Journal Article'
- Publication language is 'English'
- Full text and abstract is available

Medline, Scopus and Web of Science database searches yield 306, 100 and 241 results respectively. After the duplications were removed, 429 articles left for screening. Based on the PRISMA guidelines (Moher, 2009), literature review is conducted as in the following section.

3. RESULTS

3.1 Screening

The researcher (corresponding author of this paper) screened the titles and abstracts of 429 articles to check the focus of the studies and filtered down the related ones based on the eligibility criteria. Author names and publication year of the articles are hidden during this procedure to prevent bias. Articles which are excluded from final evaluation can be described as:

- Purely social or psychological studies which doesn't have mobile application design phase
- Technical studies that focus on only algorithm or hardware design for mHealth
- Literature review studies

- Study protocols which describes how the mHealth design will be conducted but doesn't involve the actual design and development process.
- Studies that use an existing mobile health app for evaluation but doesn't involve any of the design, development and implementation phases
- Qualitative studies which only does requirement elicitation for mHealth but doesn't involve any of the design, development and implementation phases
- mHealth studies which focus solely on content/text/message design

Screening phase yields 123 articles for eligibility.

3.2 Eligibility

Relevant 123 journal articles are reviewed and analyzed by the researcher for their theoretical soundness and methodological rigor. Analysis is done in an iterative fashion. In the first iteration, the researcher read the 123 articles and write keywords about the frameworks, methodological approaches, tools and theoretical basis that substantiate the design, development phases of each mHealth study such as "focus-group discussion", "interdisciplinary team approach", "Theory of Planned Behavior (TPB)", "use of clinical guidelines", "workshops", "agile development", "pilot phase" and "interview" etc. Accumulated list of keywords was then used to group articles into the following classifications for their methodological approach:

- 'Design-based studies' is used to annotate articles which comprise theories and frameworks that are mostly originated from software engineering or other Information Systems (IS) related fields to inform the design, development and implementation processes of mHealth study
- 'Evidence-based studies' is used to annotate articles which comprise theories, existing behavior change techniques (BCTs), and guidelines that is mostly rooted in behavioral, clinical science to inform the content and intervention components of mHealth study
- 'None' is used to annotate articles which doesn't have any theoretical basis or systematic approach to design, development and implementation of their mHealth app design

3.3 Included

In the second iteration, 123 articles were coded with one of these three codes. Consequently, 47 (39%) studies are coded with 'None' which means they lack any kind of systematic approach for the design phase and they also lack refer to evidence from literature to initiate the content for the mHealth app they developed. Remaining 76 (61%) is coded with one or two of the codes and only 12 (9%) studies reports the use of both evidence-based and design-based approaches in their methodology. Also, 35 (28%) articles adopts design-based approach without referring to evidence-based and 29 (23%) articles comprise only evidence-based information without any design-based approach. Details of the results and implications are discussed in the following section.

4. DISCUSSION

4.1 Design-based mHealth Studies

Among the 123 articles, 35 (28%) studies adopt at least one systematic approach to inform the design stage of mHealth app. Design-based frameworks commonly have roots in software engineering or other Information Systems (IS) related fields. List of frameworks and theories on which mHealth app design studies grounded is given in Table 2.

Table 2. Frameworks and Theories that inform the mHealth Studies Design

Theory & Framework	# of Study
User-center design	18
Participatory design	5
Analysis Design Development Implementation Evaluation (ADDIE)	4
Design Science Research	3
Medical Research Council (MRC) Framework	3
Web-Roadmap Methodology	1
Formative Evaluation Framework	1
Validated Learning	1
Grounded Theory	1
ICT Implementation Framework	1
Consolidated Framework for Implementation Research	1
IDEAS Framework	1
Rapid Application Development (RAD) Framework	1
Waterfall Model	1

Not all the frameworks and theories mutually exclusive in their use, since some of the studies prefer to use more than one approach in their study. User-centered design (UCD) is the most common approach for mHealth app design process. Eighteen articles report the use of UCD principles, methods and materials such as focus-group discussions, interviews, and surveys. Even UCD approach provides certain principles for the involvement of end users in the design process, it still lacks the systematic approach to structure overall study or evaluate the mHealth intervention besides usability. However, usability is merely one of many concerns for mHealth design, development and evaluation. For instance, (Goyal *et al.*, 2016) follows the literature research, iterative developing and piloting phases of the of the Medical Research Council's (MRC) model along with UCD methods to assist with the development and evaluation of health technology interventions.

Participatory action research design is the second most common approach among the design-based studies. Involvement of stakeholders during workshops and focus-groups are common methods used during the design, development of mHealth apps. Having interdisciplinary teams, which consists of professionals from technical, clinical and organizational backgrounds for the co-design efforts is the key feature of the participatory design research (Ravn et al., 2018; Revenäs et al., 2015). Lin *et al.*, which also adopts participatory design, highlights the importance of adaptive intervention design (AID) approach to be able to update an intervention throughout a trial while assuring the delivery of the same intervention to every participant (Lin *et al.*, 2015).

Four studies use the standard life cycle of system development steps: analysis, design, implementation, and evaluation (ADDIE) to structure their mHealth design phase. López et al. use ADDIE steps to create their "MyNutriCart" app to improve food selection in the grocery stores based on dietary guidelines (López et al., 2017). In Analysis step, studies extracted system requirements from various resources such as literature review (López *et al.*, 2017), clinical guidelines (Jeon and Park, 2015; Jo and Park, 2016) but none of these studies involve end users into Analysis step.

Software development frameworks such as ICT Implementation Framework and Waterfall model inform the design and development of mHealth studies (Mehmood *et al.*, 2017; Thinnukool *et al.*, 2017). Additionally, the study of Ithnin *et al.,* adopts an agile methodology for the design and development phases (Ithnin *et al.*, 2017).

Only three articles refer to Design Science Research (DSR) as a comprehensive framework to structure their design process. Schnall et al. employs the framework as an overarching theoretical foundation of the mHealth study (Schnall et al., 2016). Based on DSR framework's 3 cycles: they conducted focus groups with end-users in the Relevance cycle; performed a review to identify technology-based interventions for meeting the health prevention needs in the Rigor cycle and they employed usability evaluation methods to iteratively develop and refine mock-ups for a mHealth app in the Design Cycle. Alharbi et al and Alnosayan et al also align their design methodology with the DSR framework's three cycles (Alharbi et al., 2018; Alnosayan et al., 2017).

4.2 Evidence-based mHealth Studies

Thirty-one (24%) of 123 studies report at least one evidence-based method such as BCT and guidelines for determining content and components of mHealth intervention. Evidence-based approaches are mostly derived from one of Behavior Change Techniques, clinical guidelines and some studies create their own customized technique by blending several BCTs and guidelines to achieve optimized content, algorithm, and intervention components. The list of the BCTs and guidelines used for evidence-based mHealth studies is given in Table *3*.

Table 3. Evidence-based Theories and Guidelines

BCT/Guideline	#	Name
Behavior Change Techniques (BCTs)	35	Social Cognitive Theory (SCT), Self-determination Theory (SDT), Information-Motivation-Behavioral Skills Model, Theory of Planned Behavior (TPB), Cues to Action, The Cognitive-Behavioral Model, Stress-vulnerability Model, The Early Intervention Model, Brief Behavioral Activation Treatment for Depression (BATD), Self-regulation Model, Strength Model of Self-control, Self-efficacy Theory, Social Exchange Theory, Motivational Interviewing (MI) principles, Dietary Approaches to Stop Hypertension (DASH), Persuasive Techniques, Behavioral Activation Treatment, Goal Setting Theory, The Knowledge to Action (KTA)...
Guidelines	6	CAIDE Dementia Risk Score, Swedish Web-based Quality of Recovery (SwQoR) questionnaire, Food Pyramid and Mediterranean Diet guidelines, Dietary Guidelines for Americans...

Social Cognitive Theory (SCT) is the most common theory among behavioral change techniques to inform the mHealth intervention. For example, Choo et al. derived theoretical basis for their mHealth study from SCT by adopting key mediators such as; self-regulation skills, goal setting and self-monitoring of behaviors (Choo *et al.*, 2016). Other studies (Lubans *et al.*, 2014; Zhu *et al.*, 2017; Lau *et al.*, 2018) create their own blended theoretical basis by making use of multiple frameworks. In addition, six studies use guidelines to create the intervention component or algorithm of the mHealth intervention (Gabrielli *et al.*, 2017; López *et al.*, 2017).

4.3 Other Studies and Descriptive Statistics

While 47 studies (39%) did not mention any systematic approach for the design phase or ground their intervention development with evidence-base, only 12 (9%) studies adopted both evidence-based and systematic design approaches. Overall distribution of the articles according to years is given in **Error! Reference source not found.**

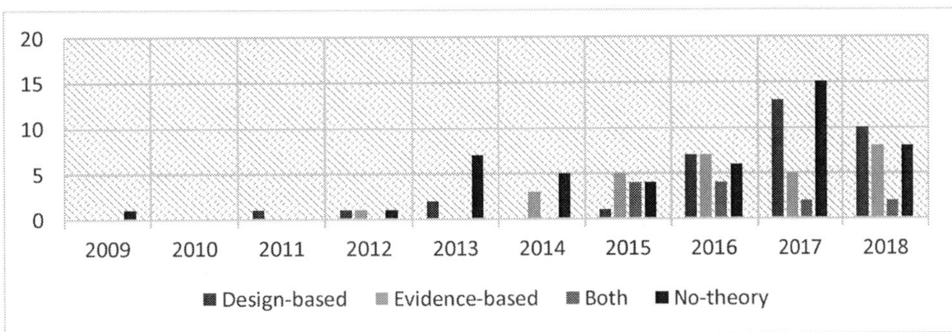

Figure 1. Distribution of mHealth studies based on the existence of theoretical approaches

Total number of mHealth studies that comprise design and development phases of a smartphone application is increasing since 2008. Only after 2012, design-based and evidence-based studies have emerged and upsurge in numbers. However, mHealth design studies without any theoretical foundations or systematics approaches have risen in numbers too. This recent rise in the number of publications are indicators for a need of rigorous methodology for future mHealth studies. The studies, which have both design-based and evidence-based techniques in their methodology are summarized in Table *4*.

Table 4 Summary of mHealth studies that have both design-based and evidence-based methodology

Author, Year	**Methodology**	
	Design-based	Evidence-based
(Jeon and Park, 2015)	The study was conducted in the order of analysis-design-implementation-evaluation (ADDIE) according to the standard lifecycle of system development	Obesity-related knowledge and functional requirements were extracted from clinical practice guidelines.
(Lin *et al.*, 2015)	Initial intervention development utilized focus groups and iterative, participatory design. Intervention testing employed adaptive intervention design.	Active interventions are designed based on social cognitive theory and incorporated techniques.
(Revenäs *et al.*, 2015)	Qualitative data is collected using multiple methods in four workshops via participatory design.	Correlations between the system requirements and the established behavior change techniques (BCTs) is explored.
(Tregarthen *et al.*, 2015)	Validated learning is established through two processes: inclusion of feedback fields into the app and measuring utilization metrics to assess the additive value of new features.	The concept of the application is defined with the intention to target aspects of Cognitive Behavioral Therapy (CBT) treatment that require behavioral activation and assimilation into the user's everyday life.
(Goyal *et al.*, 2016)	The Knowledge to Action and Medical Research Council provides a framework for the development of intervention.	Self-monitoring, providing actionable knowledge and behavior change is aligned with the constructs of social cognitive theory (SCT)
(Mayberry *et al.*, 2016)	Intervention is developed through user-centered design and iterative testing	Study employs techniques from Goal Setting Theory
(Mummah *et al.*, 2016)	App development follows phases outlined by the IDEAS framework.	Study include 18 behavior change techniques (BCTs) such as goal setting, feedback, social comparison, prompts/cues.
(Gabrielli *et al.*, 2017)	Design sessions is hold with a team of Behavioral Change experts, working with 2 nutritionists and 3 pediatricians	Content is derived from knowledge founded on the Food Pyramid and Mediterranean Diet Guidelines
(López *et al.*, 2017)	App developed follows the ADDIE (analysis, design, development, implementation, and evaluation) model.	List of healthy food is created based on Dietary Guidelines for Americans
(Backman *et al.*, 2018)	Study follows a user-centered design process integrated with a modern agile software development methodology to iteratively codesign the app.	Paper-based Path to Home workbook.
(Direito *et al.*, 2018)	The intervention mapping (IM) framework comprises six fundamental steps that guide the design, implementation, and evaluation of an intervention.	Using the IM framework, study selects theoretical constructs (e.g., perceived social norm, intention, and competence) from the Integrated Behavior Change Model (IBCM) and maps them to specific BCTs to define intervention content.
(Giunti *et al.*, 2018)	Study identifies needs, barriers, and facilitators for the app for following UCD.	Design decisions were evidence-driven and guided by behavioral change models (BCM)

As the table indicates, mHealth studies with design-based and evidence-based methodology had only emerged after 2015. There are several implications of this summary. Using clinical guidelines is a concrete way to develop evidence-based mHealth interventions as long as they correspond to intervention requirements (Gabrielli *et al.*, 2017; López *et al.*, 2017; Jeon and Park, 2015). However, single BCT or clinical guideline may not suffice all the requirements for an mHealth intervention thus blended approaches can also be adopted (Lin *et al.*, 2015; Revenäs *et al.*, 2015; Mummah *et al.*, 2016).

Furthermore, many mHealth researches are long-period efforts and requirements can change during that period. Users can receive the final product as archaic at the end of study or the mHealth application can fall short for satisfying recent requirements due to fast changing nature of mobile technologies. In order to keep pace with fast changing user needs and technologies, agile software development practices along with iterative and incremental design techniques can be preferred. In this regard, minimal viable product (MVP) and validated learning is good practices originated from the "Lean Startup" philosophy to eliminate wasteful practices by incorporating user feedback into early stage of development (Tregarthen *et al.*, 2015).

Apparently, mHealth interventions are growing in technical complexity as well as in behavioral change techniques used within them. Therefore, it becomes essential to use specific frameworks, which obliges study to be evidence-based and to structure the design process in a systematic manner at the same time. MRC, DSR, IDEAS, and intervention mapping are some of favorable frameworks that is discovered within the literature review and recommended for future mHealth studies to guide their overall study.

5. CONCLUSION

This paper investigates methodological foundations of mHealth studies regarding the app design and content development processes and investigates the current situation in the field by reviewing articles published in last 10 years. Unlike the previous literature reviews, we emphasis understanding theoretical grounds and methodological rigor before understanding the success and failure reasons of mHealth interventions. The content analysis shows that even user-centered design (UCD) is a common approach for mHealth design studies, only few of them adopts a systematic approach (e.g. DSR Framework) to guide design process or content development. However, complex mHealth interventions requires both evidence-based and design-based approaches to go beyond initial adoption and cover socio-technical aspects of intervention such as scalability, long term engagement, financial sustainability. Therefore, lack of methodological rigor in mHealth design studies can be another factor to explain lack of scaled and sustainable mHealth interventions. This study investigates and quantitatively analyze theoretical approaches within mHealth studies and recommends utilization of frameworks tailored to mHealth intervention. Future studies can investigate not only the design, development but also evaluation methodologies of mHealth applications.

REFERENCES

Alharbi, I. et al. (2018) 'Big Data Based m-Health Application to Prevent Health Hazards: A Design Science Framework', Telemedicine and e-Health, p. tmj.2018.0063. doi: 10.1089/tmj.2018.0063.

AlJaberi, H. (2018) 'Social Interaction Needs and Entertainment Approaches to Pregnancy Well-Being in mHealth Technology Design for Low-Income Transmigrant Women: Qualitative Codesign Study', JMIR mHealth and uHealth, 6(4), p. e61. doi: 10.2196/mhealth.7708.

Alnosayan, N. et al. (2017) 'Design and Usability of a Heart Failure mHealth System: A Pilot Study', JMIR Human Factors, 4(1), p. e9. doi: 10.2196/humanfactors.6481.

Alvarado, M. M. et al. (2017) 'Barriers to Remote Health Interventions for Type 2 Diabetes: A Systematic Review and Proposed Classification Scheme', Journal of Medical Internet Research, 19(2), p. e28. doi: 10.2196/jmir.6382.

Backman, C. et al. (2018) 'Development of a Path to Home mobile application for the geriatric rehabilitation program at Bruyere Continuing Care: A protocol for user-centered design and feasibility testing studies (Preprint)', JMIR Research Protocols. doi: 10.2196/11031.

Choo, S. et al. (2016) 'Development of a Weight Loss Mobile App Linked With an Accelerometer for Use in the Clinic: Usability, Acceptability, and Early Testing of its Impact on the Patient-Doctor Relationship', JMIR mHealth and uHealth, 4(1), p. e24. doi: 10.2196/mhealth.4546.

Direito, A. et al. (2018) 'Using the Intervention Mapping and Behavioral Intervention Technology Frameworks: Development of an mHealth Intervention for Physical Activity and Sedentary Behavior Change', Health Education & Behavior, 45(3), pp. 331–348. doi: 10.1177/1090198117742438.

Gabrielli, S. et al. (2017) 'Design of a Mobile App for Nutrition Education (TreC-LifeStyle) and Formative Evaluation With Families of Overweight Children', JMIR mHealth and uHealth, 5(4), p. e48. doi: 10.2196/mhealth.7080.

Gagnon, M.-P. et al. (2016) 'm-Health adoption by healthcare professionals: a systematic review', Journal of the American Medical Informatics Association, 23(1), pp. 212–220. doi: 10.1093/jamia/ocv052.

Giunti, G., Mylonopoulou, V. and Rivera Romero, O. (2018) 'More Stamina, a Gamified mHealth Solution for Persons with Multiple Sclerosis: Research Through Design', JMIR mHealth and uHealth, 6(3), p. e51. doi: 10.2196/mhealth.9437.

Goyal, S. et al. (2016) 'The Systematic Design of a Behavioural Mobile Health Application for the Self-Management of Type 2 Diabetes', Canadian Journal of Diabetes, 40(1), pp. 95–104. doi: 10.1016/j.jcjd.2015.06.007.

Hamine, S. et al. (2015) 'Impact of mHealth chronic disease management on treatment adherence and patient outcomes: A systematic review', Journal of Medical Internet Research, 17(2), pp. 1–15. doi: 10.2196/jmir.3951.

Ithnin, M. et al. (2017) 'Mobile App Design, Development, and Publication for Adverse Drug Reaction Assessments of Causality, Severity, and Preventability', JMIR mHealth and uHealth, 5(5), p. e78. doi: 10.2196/mhealth.6261.

Jeon, E. and Park, H.-A. (2015) 'Development of a Smartphone Application for Clinical-Guideline-Based Obesity Management', Healthcare Informatics Research, 21(1), p. 10. doi: 10.4258/hir.2015.21.1.10.

Jo, S. and Park, H.-A. (2016) 'Development and Evaluation of a Smartphone Application for Managing Gestational Diabetes Mellitus', Healthcare Informatics Research, 22(1), p. 11. doi: 10.4258/hir.2016.22.1.11.

Kim, K., Gollamudi, S. S. and Steinhubl, S. (2017) 'Digital technology to enable aging in place', Experimental Gerontology. Elsevier Inc., 88, pp. 25–31. doi: 10.1016/j.exger.2016.11.013.

Kruse, C. S. et al. (2018) 'Evaluating barriers to adopting telemedicine worldwide: A systematic review', Journal of Telemedicine and Telecare, 24(1), pp. 4–12. doi: 10.1177/1357633X16674087.

Laidlaw, R. et al. (2017) 'Using participatory methods to design an mHealth intervention for a low income country, a case study in Chikwawa, Malawi', BMC Medical Informatics and Decision Making, 17(1), p. 98. doi: 10.1186/s12911-017-0485-6.

Lau, Y. et al. (2018) 'Development of a Healthy Lifestyle Mobile App for Overweight Pregnant Women: Qualitative Study', JMIR mHealth and uHealth, 6(4), p. e91. doi: 10.2196/mhealth.9718.

Lin, P.-H. et al. (2015) 'Adaptive intervention design in mobile health: Intervention design and development in the Cell Phone Intervention for You trial', Clinical Trials: Journal of the Society for Clinical Trials, 12(6), pp. 634–645. doi: 10.1177/1740774515597222.

López, D. et al. (2017) 'Development and Evaluation of a Nutritional Smartphone Application for Making Smart and Healthy Choices in Grocery Shopping', Healthcare Informatics Research, 23(1), p. 16. doi: 10.4258/hir.2017.23.1.16.

Lubans, D. R. et al. (2014) 'Development and Implementation of a Smartphone Application to Promote Physical Activity and Reduce Screen-Time in Adolescent Boys', Frontiers in Public Health, 2. doi: 10.3389/fpubh.2014.00042.

Matthew-Maich, N. et al. (2016) 'Designing, Implementing, and Evaluating Mobile Health Technologies for Managing Chronic Conditions in Older Adults: A Scoping Review', JMIR mHealth and uHealth, 4(2), p. e29. doi: 10.2196/mhealth.5127.

Mayberry, L. S. et al. (2016) 'The Design, Usability, and Feasibility of a Family-Focused Diabetes Self-Care Support mHealth Intervention for Diverse, Low-Income Adults with Type 2 Diabetes', Journal of Diabetes Research, 2016, pp. 1–13. doi: 10.1155/2016/7586385.

Mehmood, A. et al. (2017) 'Development of an mHealth trauma registry in the Middle East using an implementation science framework', Global Health Action, 10(1), p. 1380360. doi: 10.1080/16549716.2017.1380360.

Moher, D. (2009) 'Preferred Reporting Items for Systematic Reviews and Meta-Analyses: The PRISMA Statement', Annals of Internal Medicine, 151(4), p. 264. doi: 10.7326/0003-4819-151-4-200908180-00135.

Mummah, S. A. et al. (2016) 'Iterative development of Vegethon: a theory-based mobile app intervention to increase vegetable consumption', International Journal of Behavioral Nutrition and Physical Activity, 13(1), p. 90. doi: 10.1186/s12966-016-0400-z.

Pereira-Azevedo, N. et al. (2017) 'Rotterdam Prostate Cancer Risk Calculator: Development and Usability Testing of the Mobile Phone App', JMIR Cancer, 3(1), p. e1. doi: 10.2196/cancer.6750.

Ravn Jakobsen, P. et al. (2018) 'Development of an mHealth Application for Women Newly Diagnosed with Osteoporosis without Preceding Fractures: A Participatory Design Approach', International Journal of Environmental Research and Public Health, 15(2), p. 330. doi: 10.3390/ijerph15020330.

Revenäs, Å. et al. (2015) 'Development of a Web-Based and Mobile App to Support Physical Activity in Individuals With Rheumatoid Arthritis: Results From the Second Step of a Co-Design Process', JMIR Research Protocols, 4(1), p. e22. doi: 10.2196/resprot.3795.

Schnall, R. et al. (2016) 'A user-centered model for designing consumer mobile health (mHealth) applications (apps)', Journal of Biomedical Informatics, 60, pp. 243–251. doi: 10.1016/j.jbi.2016.02.002.

Steinhubl, S. R., Muse, E. D. and Topol, E. J. (2015) 'The emerging field of mobile health', Science Translational Medicine, 7(283), p. 283rv3-283rv3. doi: 10.1126/scitranslmed.aaa3487.

Thinnukool, O., Khuwuthyakorn, P. and Wientong, P. (2017) 'Pharmacy Assistant Mobile Application (PAMA): Development and Reviews', International Journal of Interactive Mobile Technologies (iJIM), 11(3), p. 178. doi: 10.3991/ijim.v11i3.6757.

Tregarthen, J. P., Lock, J. and Darcy, A. M. (2015) 'Development of a smartphone application for eating disorder self-monitoring', International Journal of Eating Disorders, 48(7), pp. 972–982. doi: 10.1002/eat.22386.

Vorrink, S. N. et al. (2016) 'A Mobile Phone App to Stimulate Daily Physical Activity in Patients with Chronic Obstructive Pulmonary Disease: Development, Feasibility, and Pilot Studies', JMIR mHealth and uHealth, 4(1), p. e11. doi: 10.2196/mhealth.4741.

Zhu, J. et al. (2017) 'Development of a mobile application of Breast Cancer e-Support program for women with breast cancer undergoing chemotherapy', Technology and Health Care, 25(2), pp. 377–382. doi: 10.3233/THC-161292.

THE PREDICTING SUCCESS FACTORS OF MOBILE APPLICATIONS DEVELOPMENT: ORGANIZATIONAL PERSPECTIVES

Chinedu Wilfred Okonkwo and Magda Huisman
North-West University, Unit for Business Mathematics and Informatics
Private Bag X6001, Potchefstroom, South Africa, 2520

ABSTRACT

Mobile applications (mobile apps) development is one of the fastest evolving technological innovations across the globe. The immense growth of mobile apps development can be attributed to the incredible rate of growth of mobile technology and its propagation into every facet of modern life. The success of these applications lies within some predicting success factors with respect to stakeholders' expectations and perceptions. Researchers have attempted to identify the factors influencing mobile apps development. However, these researches were mostly conducted from the individual software developers' perspective. This paper presents an empirical investigation of the significance of these predicting factors of mobile apps development from different organizations' perspectives. A survey was conducted among different organizations that are involved in one way or another in the development of mobile apps. The findings showed that individual development skills, functionality, mobile devices specifications, use of a software development kit, back-end integration, portability, web and network integration, and the use of a system development methodology are the predicting success factors of mobile apps development whereas open source technology is not. Furthermore, different types of organizations have different perceptions of how important a predicting success factor is in the development of mobile apps.

KEYWORDS

Mobile Applications Development, Predicting Success Factors, Organizations, Perception, Mobile Applications

1. INTRODUCTION

In the past couple of years, there has been tremendous growth in the development of mobile applications (mobile apps). The entry of mobile devices into the market has triggered the development of various kinds of mobile apps. Mobile technologies have created a major shift in the way we perform our daily activities. In today's fast-paced world, mobile services are the engine that powers virtually all activities including education, communications, economics, commerce, banking, politics, healthcare, agriculture and social activities (Qiang et al. (2011), Murugesan (2013), Hellstrom and Troften (2010), El-Hussein and Cronje (2010)).

Mobile apps development is the procedure by which application software is designed and created to facilitate the operations of mobile technologies services (Qiang et al. (2011), McNamara (2009)). The rapid growth of the mobile phone market and technological advancements has resulted in a high demand for mobile apps. Consequently, the advancement in the mobile apps development field is unprecedented.

The search for success factors is not new in information systems research. Several studies have been conducted to discover the factors that are significant to be considered for the development of mobile apps (Wasserman (2010), Siau et al. (2010), He and Xu (2014), Corral et al. (2013), Capretz and Ahmed (2010), Ahmed et al. (2013)). These authors have emphasized the need to identify the predicting success factors (PSFs) that can be used to develop successful mobile applications.

Every software project has a unique purpose and unique features, thus the developmental process and factors to be considered may vary with the regards to the stakeholder's expectations and purposes. There are different perceptions about a project's success, as well as how and when the success is measured (Toor and Ogunlana (2009)). The design and development of a mobile app depend on the stakeholder's requirements and expected services. There exist several kinds of mobile apps with different functionalities including mobile learning, mobile health, mobile agriculture, mobile commerce, mobile government, mobile banking and mobile social activities (Qiang et al. (2011), Murugesan (2013), Hellstrom and Troften (2010), Mutula and Mosterd (2010), GMSA (2015)). These mobile apps are developed by or for different organizations with their respective objectives. The measurement of their successes are also different. It is, therefore, observed that most of the studies that identified the PSFs are context-specific and fragmented. The obtained results are based on a specific kind of mobile app like the PSFs of developing mobile banking (Noor (2011)), mobile learning (Papanikolaou and Mavromoustakos (2006)), mobile commerce (Feng et al. (2006)), and mobile health (Chatterjee et al. (2009)) applications.

Although, most of the identified PSFs are important, what is a valued PSF to one organization might not be valued by the other organization. Each of these organizations operates on a different contextual environment with unique objectives and their mobile apps are uniquely designed to support their operational services. It is necessary to bring all these PSFs together to examine their degree of significance to the different kinds of mobile apps as it concerns different organizations.

There is a need for more studies on this area; hence, this paper intends to address two major issues, 1) to capture all the generally identified PSFs and 2) to investigate and find the level of importance of each PSF from the perspective of different types of organizations including educational institutions, financial institutions, telecommunication companies and software development companies.

2. BACKGROUND INFORMATION

Software application development has been steadily growing and is of great importance to the advancement of information systems and communication technology. The development of mobile apps involves formalized methods or system development methodologies which is the combination of a software development approach, method, process and techniques (Huisman and Iivari (2006), Holzer and Ondrus (2011)). Mobile app development provides a platform for creating applications that combine the functionality of the mobile telephone as a traditional communication device with the information systems' functionality of computing which include data collection, data processing, information access, transmission of text, voice and chatting (Murugesan (2013)). This has indeed led to the increased usage of mobile apps and hence the need for the everyday development of applications to meet the needs of mobile phone users. It, therefore, became imperative for application developers to concentrate on creating mobile apps that provide similar applications that used to be run on PCs for mobile devices.

Currently, mobile apps development is significantly higher than ever before. As a result, software development companies are constantly seeking a suitable development platform for mobile apps development which can support the current and future needs of their projects (Olavsrud (2012)). The creation of a successful mobile app requires a proper consideration of some predicting success factors which are discussed in the next section.

2.1 Predicting Success Factors (PSFs) for Mobile Application Development

The term PSFs implies certain necessary elements that contribute positively towards the success of any project (Toor and Ogunlana (2009), Hwang and Lim (2012)). These elements must be vital, beneficial and connect to the plan of achieving the project goal. Thus, to attain success in any project, one must first discover the significant factors that affect a project positively or negatively. In other words, the important factors to be considered for a project to be successful, otherwise failure will occur. A good understanding of the project, its environment and the development strategy will help to identify the PSFs. Besides the IT domain, research on the PSFs concept has been extensively conducted in other fields including medicine, construction and production industry (Toor and Ogunlana (2009)). Some of the predicting success factors identified for investigation under this study will be discussed next.

2.1.1 Open Source Technology

Open source technology enables the environment for peer programming by the collaboration of public developers, making the source code free to be used, modified and improved on. Open source is a critical component to achieve agility in mobile apps development (Rodrigues et al. (2010), Holzer and Ondrus (2011), Hesselman et al. (2009)).

2.1.2 Individual Development Skills

It requires innovative skills (Huntley (2011)), teamwork (Licorish and MacDonell (2017), interactive ability (Capretz and Ahmed (2010)), cognitive reasoning (Ahmed et al. (2012)), and good mental representation (Ahmed et al. (2013)) to develop successful software. Hence, mobile apps created by a team of software experts and a team staffed with skilled individuals will be more successful (Siau et al. (2010)).

2.1.3 Software Development Kit

A software development kit (SDK) provides tools for the development community and the required resources to developers during mobile apps development. Therefore, SDKs is a predicting success factor of mobile apps development (Wasserman (2010), Rodrigues et al. (2010), Gavalas and Economou (2011), Dalmasso et al. (2013), Charland and Le Roux (2011)).

2.1.4 Portability

The fact that mobile apps can be ported successfully from one device to another using a common platform makes it easily accepted by the community of users; hence portability has an effect on mobile apps development (Wasserman (2010), Gavalas and Economou (2011), Mahesh et al. (2012), Ahern (2009)).

2.1.5 Functionality

The functionality of a mobile app requires that it must meet the functional requirements of the users (Wasserman (2010, Gavalas and Economou (2011), Ally and Tsinakos (2014), Zhou et al. (2011)). If a mobile app does not meet the needs and expectations of the users, it will not be adopted into use; hence functionality is a factor to be considered in the mobile apps development.

2.1.6 Back-end Integration

The development of a mobile app requires the integration of the new application with the organization's existing applications and database infrastructure to produce similarly efficient, effective, user-friendly implementation of the existing systems. Hence back-end integration is considered to be a success factor of mobile apps development (He and Xu (2014), Unhelkar and Murugesan (2010)).

2.1.7 System Development Methodology (SDM)

The development of mobile apps requires the use of a systems development methodology (Okonkwo and Huisman (2018)). To achieve success in mobile apps development, it is important to adopt an SDM that best suits the need and requirements of the organizational project (Wasserman (2010), Corral et al. (2013), Partsch (2012), Huisman and Iivari (2006)).

2.1.8 Mobile Device Specification Issues

Mobile app developers are faced with very strict boundaries of mobile devices' specifications. In developing a mobile app, the specifications of the mobile devices specifications must be considered (Wasserman (2010), Unhelkar and Murugesan (2010), Vidas et al. (2011), Nosrati et al. (2012), Dehlinger and Dixon (2011)).

2.1.9 Web and Network Integration

Web-based mobile apps allow the usage of online applications on mobile devices. One of the ways to distribute the mobile app software is through the websites, which allow users to retrieve information or access services via their handheld devices, therefore web and network integration are considered to be a success factor of mobile app development (Ahern (2009), Zhou et al. (2010), Perez (2010)).

The above success factors of mobile apps development will be measured in this study to determine their degree of importance to the success of mobile apps' development as perceived by the different types of organizations.

3. RESEARCH METHODOLOGY

To achieve the goal of the study, a survey was conducted with a questionnaire as an instrument for data collection. The questionnaire comprised of three sections: background information, mobile apps development and success factors. With background information, we gained more insight into the respondent's core business area. The mobile apps section investigates how mobile apps development (MAD) is performed especially in South Africa. The last section of the questionnaire covered the success factors of MAD. We listed some success factors obtained from literature with some explanatory statements in relation to each factor. The participants were asked to rate the importance of these success factors and their explanatory questions accordingly. The questionnaire contained mostly closed-ended questions with a 5-point Likert scale rating of 1 (totally disagreed) to 5 (totally agreed).

Using a convenience sample, our targeted audience was mobile apps developers from various organizations. The organizations involved in this study were software development companies, financial companies, telecommunication companies, educational institutions and engineering companies. The organizations used for the research study were selected when they were 1) Software companies that are fully into the business of software development and 2) Other companies that develop their respective mobile apps for their operational services, hence they have in-house developers and ICT professionals that develop, maintain and sustain their mobile apps. The questionnaires were sent to the IT department and were completed by the software developers and the ICT professionals in each respective organization. Drop off and electronic methods were used to distribute the questionnaire. A total of 392 questionnaires were distributed to different respondents and 152 (38.8%) responses were returned within May to August 2015 in South Africa. The responses comprise 131 drop off and 21 electronically completed questionnaires.

The participants who participated in the survey were from an extensively diverse background in IT services and were mostly software developers. They were comprised of 17 (11.2%) managing directors, 23 (15.1%) chief information officers, 21 (13.8%) IT managers, 79 (52%) software developers, 5 (3.3%) system administrators and 7 (4.6%) system analysts. Their respective organizations have been into mobile application development ranging from 1-5 years to above 10 years including 23 (15.1%) of 1-5 years, 51 (33.6%) of 5-10 years, 66 (43.4%) of above 10 years and 12 (7.9) indicated that they have not be involved in mobile application development. Also, these participants have developed or were involved with the development of a number of mobile apps ranging from 1-10 apps to above 100 apps including 66 (43.7%) of 1-10 apps, 34 (22.5%) of 10-50 apps, 18 (11.9%) of 50-100 apps, 30 (19.9%) of above 100 apps, 3 (2%) indicated that they have not yet developed a working mobile app and one did not respond at all.

4. RESULTS

All the responses were thoroughly examined to extract the data and statistical analysis was performed to determine the PSFs of MAD. On the part of PSF, multiple items were used to examine the research variables.

A descriptive analysis was performed to describe the frequency and percentage of responses from the study population. Cronbach alpha reliability analysis was used to compute reliability coefficients for each of the examining factors. The criterion for Cronbach's coefficient alpha for reliability is $\alpha \geq 0.6$ (Sethi and King (1991), Nunally and Bernstein (1978)). That is if the obtained $\alpha \geq 0.6$ then the data obtained of that item is reliable.In addition, the data were categorized and analysis of variance (ANOVA) was performed to determine if there is any difference or similarity between the categories in order to determine organizational perceptions on the relevance of each of the PSFs (Creech (2003)). The mean comparison was done according to Cohen's effect sizes (Cohen, 1988)) and the guidelines for interpreting the effect sizes (d values) are as follows: $d = 0.2$ (small effect); $d = 0.5$ (medium effect) and $d \geq 0.8$ (large effect or practical significant).

The first objective of this study is to determine the perceptions of various organizations on the identified PSFs towards the development of mobile apps. The PSFs were examined using one general question and some explanatory questions to test the participant perception regarding the importance of each particular PSF. A 5-point Likert scale was used for measurement ranging from 1 (totally disagreed) to 5 (totally agreed). Factor analysis was performed on the individual items to minimize the number of data points. This resulted in 9 factors which corresponded with the identified PSFs. Testing the reliability of the identified factors, the Cronbach alpha coefficients range from 0.73 to 0.98 indicating that the identified predicting success factors were reliable. The results obtained from descriptive statistics and reliability analyses are shown in Table 1.

In Table 1 the results are ranked in descending order according to mean for each PSF. The rating of the importance of the predicting success factors shows that if a mean value is ≥ 3 then the respondents agree that the factor has a significant influence on the success of mobile apps development. The findings indicate that 8 out of 9 identified predicting success factors emerged as important regarding mobile apps development (minimum response mean ≥ 3.68), while one did not. The three most important PSFs are individual development skills, functionality, and mobile devices specifications. The respondents did not perceive that the use open source technology is an important PSF for mobile application development success.

The results compare well with the report of the previous researches (Wasserman (2010), He and Xu (2014), Capretz and Ahmed (2010), Ahmed et al. (2013), Siau et al. (2010), Perez (2010)) even though the investigations were conducted in different environments. That is, this study agreed with the previous studies performed in a different context that the 8 factors are important predicting success factors of mobile apps development.

Table 1. Perceived Importance and Ranking of PSF for Mobile Application Development

PSF	Mean N=152	Std. Dev.	Scale rating					Cronbach alpha	PSF Rank
			1	2	3	4	5		
Individual development skills	4.60	0.99	0	0	0	61 (40.1%)	91 (60%)	0.83	1
Functionality	4.55	0.57	0	1 (0.7%)	3 (2%)	59 (38.8%)	89 (58.6%)	0.96	2
Mobile devices specifications	4.20	0.62	0	0	17 (11.2%)	87 (57.2)	48 (31.6%)	0.93	3
Software development kit	4.00	0.76	0	0	1 (0.7%)	61 (40.1%)	90 (59.2%)	0.98	4
Back-end integration	3.89	0.71	0	3 (2%)	38 (25%)	83 (54.6%)	28 (18.4%)	0.95	5
Portability	3.84	0.80	0	9 (5.9%)	36 (23.7%)	78 (51.3%)	29 (19.1%)	0.97	6
Web and network integration	3.76	0.79	0	9 (5.9%)	42 (27.6%)	77 (50.7%)	24 (15.8%)	0.98	7
System Dev. methodology	3.68	0.63	0	4 (2.6%)	49 (32.5%)	89 (58.9%)	9 (6%)	0.93	8
Open source technology	2.89	0.99	13 (8.6%)	38 (25.2%)	58 (38.4%)	36 (23.8%)	6 (4%)	0.91	9

The second objective of this study is to investigate whether there are differences between the different types of organizations' perceptions regarding the importance of the identified PSF of the development of mobile apps. The organizations were divided between 4 groups, namely software development companies (Group 1), financial companies (Group 2), educational institutions (Group 3) and telecommunication companies (Group 4). ANOVA was performed the test whether there are differences between these different types of organizations' perceptions regarding the importance of the identified PSF. The results obtained are shown in Table 2.

Table 2. ANOVA Analysis of Core Business Area and Perceived Importance of PSF

PSF items	**Core business area (Grp 1-4)**	**No. of respondents**	**Mean**	**Std. dev.**	**F-value**	**p-value**	**Tukey significance and d – value for the Groups**			
							1	2	3	4
Individual developer skills	Grp. 1	85	4.49	0.47				0.28	-.0.04	-0.03
	Grp. 2	18	4.65	054	0.54	0.6532			-0.32	-
	Grp. 3	21	4.48	0.51	(3:136)					.0.30
	Grp. 4	16	4.48	0.56						0.01
Functionality	Grp. 1	85	4.37	0.48				0.39	-0.58	0.53
	Grp. 2	18	4.56	0.47	5.26	**0.0018**			-0.98	0.15
	Grp. 3	21	4.10	0.30	(3:136)					1.17
	Grp. 4	16	4.63	0.45						
Mobile devices specifications	Grp. 1	85	4.17	0.54				0.34	0.18	0.79
	Grp. 2	18	4.42	0.73	2.94	**0.0353**			-0.18	0.24
	Grp. 3	21	4.29	0.62	(3:136)					0.49
	Grp. 4	16	4.59	0.49						
Software development kit	Grp. 1	85	4.10	0.70				-	-0.90	0.03
	Grp. 2	18	3.81	0.68	5.15	**0.0021**		0.41	-0.50	0.39
	Grp. 3	21	3.48	0.60	(3:136)					0.82
	Grp. 4	16	4.13	0.79						
Back-end integration	Grp. 1	85	3.80	0.75				0.69	0.18	0.88
	Grp. 2	18	4.31	0.58	5.97	**0.0008**			-0.66	0.25
	Grp. 3	21	3.94	0.55	(3:136)					0.90
	Grp. 4	16	4.46	0.58						
Portability	Grp. 1	85	3.82	0.81				0.55	0.15	0.20
	Grp. 2	18	4.26	0.64	1.66	0.1788			-0.41	-0.36
	Grp. 3	21	3.94	0.78	(3:136)					0.05
	Grp. 4	16	3.98	0.78						
Web and network integration	Grp. 1	85	3.58	0.70				0.57	-0.01	1.04
	Grp. 2	18	4.07	0.85	6.13	**0.0006**			-0.58	0.28
	Grp. 3	21	3.57	0.87	(3:136)					0.85
	Grp. 4	16	4.31	0.56						
System development methodology	Grp. 1	85	3.61	0.61				0.60	0.64	0.29
	Grp. 2	18	3.97	0.61	3.82	0.115			0.05	-0.32
	Grp. 3	21	4.00	0.45	(3:136)					-0.38
	Grp. 4	16	3.78	0.58						
Open source technology	Grp. 1	85	3.17	0.69				0.17	0.05	0.02
	Grp. 2	18	3,29	0.56	0.53	0.80			-.0.09	0.06
	Grp. 3	21	3.21	0.84	(3:136)					0.15
	Grp. 4	16	3.34	0.85						

Table 2 indicates some statistically significant differences in the perceived importance of five of the PSF (functionality, mobile device specifications, software development kit, back-end integration, and web and network integration) from the perspectives of the different types of organizations. When one considers *functionality*, there is a practical significant difference between the perceptions of financial companies and educational institutions, and also between educational institutions and telecommunication companies. Considering *mobile device specifications*, there is a practical significant difference between the perceptions of software development companies and telecommunication organizations. There is a practical significant difference in the perception of the importance of the use of a *software development kit* in mobile apps development between software development organizations and educational institutions, and also between educational institutions and telecommunication companies. Regarding *back-end integration*, there is a practical significant difference between the perceptions of software development companies and telecommunication organizations, and also between educational institutions and telecommunication companies. Considering *web and network integration*, there is a practical significant difference between the perceptions of software development companies and telecommunication organizations, and also between educational institutions and telecommunication companies.

No statistical difference in the perception of the other PSFs like individual development skills, portability, use of a system development methodology and open source technology were found.

Although the PSFs are important in mobile apps development (excluding the use of open source technology), the different types of organizations value them differently. This may be because of the nature of their business and their need for mobile apps.

5. CONCLUSION

This study determined the predicting success factors and the degree of importance of these factors from the perspectives of various organizations on mobile apps development in South Africa. Through a survey, quantitative data was collected, empirically evaluated and the necessary results were obtained. The findings showed that individual development skills, functionality, mobile devices specifications, use of a software development kit, back-end integration, portability, web and network integration, and the use of a system development methodology are the predicting success factors of mobile apps development whereas open source technology is not. Although these factors are general and have been proven to be important in other context or countries, this study justified their importance in a different contextual environment of South Africa. Depending on their objectives and purposes, different organizations have different perceptions of the relevance of these factors. In terms of applications, mobile apps developers and organizations will use these factors as the baseline to know the most appropriate factors to be considered to achieve success in any mobile apps development project. Further study will be oriented towards the identification of new factors that may emerge as technology advances and expand the scope of the research.

REFERENCES

Ahern, K., 2009. Critical success factors for commercial mobile application. http://www.slideshare.net/keithahern/critical-success-factors-for-commercial-mobile-applications-or-how-to-put-big-ideas-into-small-devices.

Ahmed, F. et al. 2012. Evaluating the demand for soft skills in software development. *IT Professional*, Vol. 14, No. 1, pp. 44-49.

Ahmed, F., et al., 2013. Soft Skills and Software Development: A Reflection from Software Industry. *International Journal of Information Processing and Management*, Vol. 4, No. 3, pp. 171-191.

Ally, M. and Tsinakos, A., 2014. *Increasing access through mobile learning*. Commonwealth of Learning, Vancouver.

Capretz, L.F. and Ahmed, F., 2010. Making sense of software development and personality types. *IT professional*, Vol. 12, No. 1, pp. 6-13.

Charland, A. and Le Roux, B., 2011. Mobile application development: web vs. native. *Communications of the ACM*, Vol. 54, No. 5, pp. 49-53.

Chatterjee, S., et al., 2009. Examining the success factors for mobile work in healthcare: A deductive study. *Decision Support Systems*, Vol. 46, No. 3, pp. 620-633.

Cohen, J., 1988. *Statistical power analysis for the behavioural sciences (2nd ed).* Hillsdale, NJ: Erlbaum.

Corral, L., et al., 2013. Software development processes for mobile systems: Is agile really taking over the business? *1st International Workshop on the Engineering of Mobile-Enabled Systems (MOBS).* 10.1109/MOBS.2013.6614218.

Creech, S., 2003. *Statistically significant.* http://www.statisticallysignificantconsulting.com/Anova.htm.

Dalmasso, I., et al. 2013. Survey, comparison and evaluation of cross platform mobile application development tools. *9th IEEE International Wireless Communications and Mobile Computing Conference (IWCMC)*, July 1-5, 2013, Cagliari, Italy.

Dehlinger, J. and Dixon, J., 2011. Mobile application software engineering: Challenges and research directions. *Workshop on Mobile Software Engineering.* https://pdfs.semanticscholar.org/3ffc/4f867e45f8c8e9019726b351172ed77aca4f.pdf

El-Hussein, M.O.M. and Cronje, J.C., 2010. Defining Mobile Learning in the Higher Education Landscape. *Educational Technology & Society*, Vol. 13, No. 3, p p. 12-21.

Feng, H., et al., 2006. Exploring the critical success factors for mobile commerce. *ICMB'06. International Conference on Mobile Business,* Copenhagen, Denmark.

Gavalas, D. and Economou, D., 2011. Development platforms for mobile applications: Status and trends. *IEEE software*, Vol. 28, No. 1, pp. 77-86.

GSMA, 2015. The mobile economy Sub-Saharan Africa 2015. *GSMA Intelligence*. Regional report https://gsmaintelligence. com/research.

He, W. and Xu , L., (2014). Integration of distributed enterprise applications: A survey. *IEEE Transactions on Industrial Informatics*, Vol. 10, No. 1, pp. 35-42.
Hellström, J. and Tröften, P.E., 2010. *The innovative use of mobile applications in East Africa*. Swedish international development cooperation agency (Sida).
Hesselman, C., et al., 2009. Interactive TV Together: An Open Service Infrastructure for Enhancing Interactive TV Experiences. *Social Interactive Television: Immersive Shared Experiences and Perspectives*. IGI Global. pp. 30-49.
Holzer, A. and Ondrus, J., 2011. Mobile application market: A developer's perspective. *Telematics and informatics,* Vol. 28, No. 1, pp. 22-31.
Huisman, M. and Iivari, J., 2006. Deployment of systems development methodologies: Perceptual congruence between IS managers and systems developers. *Information & Management*, Vol. 43, No. 1, pp. 29-49.
Huntley, C.L., 2011. Onshore Mobile App Development: Successes and Challenges. *Computer*, Vol. 44, No. 9, pp. 102-104.
Hwang, B.G. and Lim, E.S.J., 2012. Critical success factors for key project players and objectives: Case study of Singapore. *Journal of Construction Engineering and Management*, Vol. 139, No. 2, pp. 204-215.
Licorish, S.A. and MacDonell, S.G. 2017. Exploring software developers' work practices: Task differences, participation, engagement, and speed of task resolution. *Information & Management*, Vol. 54, No. 3, pp. 364-382.
Mahesh, B.R., et al. 2012. Portability of mobile applications using phonegap: A case study. *International Conference on Software Engineering and Mobile Application Modelling and Development (ICSEMA 2012), pp.* 1-6. 10.1049/ic.2012.0156.
McNamara, K.S., 2009, Mobile Applications in Agriculture and Rural Development–Framing the Topic, and Learning from Experience. *World Bank Workshop on Mobile Innovations for Social and Economic Transformation*.
Murugesan, S., 2013. Mobile apps in Africa. IT Professional, Vol. 15, No. 5, pp. 8-11.
Mutula, S.M. and Mostert, J., 2010. Challenges and opportunities of e-government in South Africa. The Electronic Library, Vol. 28, No. 1, pp. 38-53.
Noor, M.M., 2011. Determining critical success factors of mobile banking adoption in Malaysia. Australian Journal of Basic and Applied Sciences, Vol. 5, No. 9, pp. 252-265.
Nosrati, M. et al., 2012. Mobile computing: principles, devices and operating systems. World Applied Programming, Vol. 2, No. 7, pp. 399-408.
Nunally, J.C. and Bernstein, I.H., 1978. Psychometric theory. McGraw-Hill, New York.
Okonkwo, W.C. and Huisman, M., 2018. The Use of System Development Methodologies in the Development of Mobile Applications: Are they Worthy of Use? IEEE 42nd Annual Computer Software and Applications Conference (COMPSAC), Tokyo, Japan, pp. 278-283.
Olavsrud, T., 2012. 10 Top Mobile Application Development Platforms. Network World. http://www.networkworld.com/article/2286706/4g/10-top-mobile-application-development-platforms.html.
Papanikolaou, K. and Mavromoustakos.,S., 2006. Critical Success Factors for the Development of Mobile Learning Applications. EuroIMSA, Innsbruck, Austria.
Partsch, H.A., 2012. Specification and transformation of programs: a formal approach to software development. Springer Science & Business Media.
Perez, S., 2010. 10 distribution channels for mobile applications. http://readwrite.com/2010/11/17/10-distribution-channels-for-mobile-apps.
Qiang, C.Z., et al., 2011. Mobile applications for agriculture and rural development. World Bank, Washington, DC.
Rodrigues, J.J. et al, 2010. New trends on ubiquitous mobile multimedia applications. EURASIP Journal on Wireless Communications and Networking, No.1, pp. 1-11.
Siau, K. et al. 2010. Important characteristics of software development team members: an empirical investigation using Repertory Grid. Information Systems Journal, Vol. 20, No. 6, pp. 563-580.
Sethi, V. and King, W.R., 1991. Construct measurement in information systems research: An illustration in strategic systems. Decision Sciences, Vol. 22, No. 3, pp. 455-472.
Toor, S.-u.-R. and Ogunlana, S.O., 2009. Construction professionals' perception of critical success factors for large-scale construction projects. Construction Innovation, Vol. 9, No. 2, pp. 149-167.
Unhelkar, B. and Murugesan, S., 2010. The enterprise mobile applications development framework. IT professional, Vol 12, No. 3, pp. 33-39.
Vidas, T. et al., 2011. Toward a general collection methodology for Android devices. Digital investigation, Vol. 8, pp. 14-24.
Wasserman, A.I., 2010, Software engineering issues for mobile application development. Proceedings of the FSE/SDP workshop on Future of software engineering research, FoSER 2010, November 7-8, 2010, Santa Fe, New Mexico, USA.
Zhou, T. et al. 2010. Integrating TTF and UTAUT to explain mobile banking user adoption. Computers in human behavior, Vol. 26, No. 4, pp. 760-767.
Zhou, Y., et al. 2011. Taming information-stealing smartphone applications (on Android). Trust and Trustworthy Computing. Trust 2011. Lecture Notes in Computer Science, vol 6740. Springer, Berlin, Heidelberg.

A COMPANY'S LONG-TERM INNOVATION CAPACITY WHEN INTRODUCING ENTERPRISE SOFTWARE: SOCIOLOGICAL ASSESSMENT OF HYBRID CLOUD-PLATFORMS

Marek Holze
University of Duisburg-Essen
Universitätsstraße 2, 45141 Essen, Germany

ABSTRACT

While the cloud emerged as an economic successful model compared to Application Service Provider (ASP), it is now a prerequisite for ever shorter innovation cycles in networked companies; risks and opportunities arise for companies using enterprise systems. Startup companies are positioned to implement innovations and build up the company, as well as its further components, while taking innovation into account. Established companies have to deal with the integration of these innovations into their existing business system. This paper studies the aspects that must be considered when software is introduced to bring about a stable innovation capability for the company. A case study is therefore presented in which a medium-sized retail company introduces new POS (point-of-sale) software with the help of a cloud platform. The case study assessed the relevance of various aspects, which must be considered during implementation. The relevance of complexity reduction was, among others, rated as highly relevant while uncertainty absorption, in contrast to other literature, was rated as less relevant.

KEYWORDS

Complexity Reduction, Uncertainty Absorption, Platform, Ecosystem, Standard Software, Cloud

1. INTRODUCTION

Brown and Vessey (2008) have already indicated that better managing the complexity of enterprise systems reduces the risk of failure and the costs involved. For the second "Wave of Enterprise Systems" a reduction of sociological complexity is therefore strategically important for a company. When it comes to implementing enterprise software, complexity becomes an important issue for academic researchers and practitioners around the world as Hwang (2005) stressed. In Europe it stressed Hanseth et. al. (2001); in Asia it stressed Liang et. al. (2004) and Martinsons (2004). If the core performance's complexity increases, for example by integrating new software products into an existing IT landscape, complexity must be reduced elsewhere. If this is not considered, new resources are required in the first step, for example for managing new IT systems. This paper must realize that not only the time expenditure, but also the necessary understanding of the associated components increases in order to forecast the long-term consequences of changes – in summary, qualitative and quantitative expenditure increases. In the following, the qualitative effort is referred to as complexity. While the quantitative effort can be dealt with almost without limitations – with sufficient capital –, the manageable complexity is limited by the intelligence of the employees or consultants. This complexity can hardly be dealt with by using a larger number of IT staff; this is often even counterproductive. When integrated innovations are introduced into the enterprise system, another part of the system should simultaneously be relieved of complexity. Cloud platforms can possibly reduce the enterprise system's complexity. As a rule, no new IT system is created for an organization – a digital core ERP is used onsite, which is supplemented by functionalities via a cloud platform. The leaner the core ERP (enterprise resource planning) is, the less complexity has to be handled in the company – this is widely known as standard software implementation. Furthermore, uncertainty absorption is mostly promoted by integrated and software-based introductions. In the latter, decisions are linked to previous decisions.

This encourages workflow efficiency and effectiveness in the company, as Hwang (2005) stressed. This paper studies the following research question via a case study:

How can a hybrid cloud-platform approach promote the long-term innovation capability of enterprise systems?
What aspects must be considered in such an introduction?

When complexity is reduced in companies using enterprise systems, they remain innovative with less effort, which prevents displacement by competitors. In other words: Companies that use enterprise systems perceive the network effects, which software manufacturers are striving for, as pressure to innovate. These companies will thus become more digital and less technical – a prerequisite for the ever-shorter innovation cycles. This paper uses a case study to research the introduction of new standard software to replace individual software. A hybrid cloud-platform approach is used for introducing new software.

In order to answer the research question, the second chapter introduces basic technological terms, for further study, based on a historical overview of ERP systems. The third chapter explains the structure of the case study and presents the results. This is followed, in the fourth chapter, by a discussion of the case study's results. This paper concludes with a summary of the research results.

2. HISTORY OF ERP AND ONGOING CHANGES

The history of ERP (enterprise resource planning) systems is significant for understanding enterprise systems, their ability to innovate, and some of the problems associated with them. For this reason, this paper presents a broad historical review in the following. In the 1960s, when computers were first used in business operations, application systems were developed for production planning and control purposes, as discussed by Görtz and Hesseler (2007). Individual companies usually developed these application systems into an individual software package to meet specific requirements (Kurbel 2016). However, with ever increasing hardware performance, the application scope of the systems expanded, which was also expressed by the name Manufacturing Resource Planning Systems (MRP II) (Schütte & Vering 2011). The term Enterprise Resource Planning (ERP) was coined by the Gartner Group (Jung-Elsen 2013).

The Application Service Provider (ASP) concept, which is known since 1997, represents a further development of IT outsourcing in the direction of today's SaaS. Hess and Wolf (2008) cite customer-specific infrastructure as the main reason for ASP's lack of profitability. Hess et. al. (2009) looks into this problem by means of a study and deals with the change from ASP to SaaS or ERPaaS (enterprise resource planning as a service). This study determines the demand for SaaS (software as a service), especially for users with low complexity and criticality.

Gottwald (2013) highlights the aspiration of companies to anchor ERP solutions deeply in their own corporate structure and to use them for a correspondingly long time. From the user's point of view, the focus is not on being up-to-date, but rather on purpose and function. In order to represent these aspects in the ERP system, they are usually highly individualized. Elsewhere, a less holistic stance is taken towards onsite ERP systems: While Josefiok (2014) concludes that it seems unlikely to realize a holistic solution with the current offer of ERPaaS and the SaaS providers' orientation towards less individualized products, Jung-Elsen (2013) shows that ERPaaS is mostly used as an addition to existing ERP systems –these additions are usually included in areas such as CRM (customer relationship management), collaboration, and HR (human resource management). There, the advantages of a cloud – such as location-independent access – would be particularly noticeable. This paper confirms that this statement is true for retailers. Furthermore, it shows that very few providers offer traditional ERP via a public cloud service. In most cases it concerns hosting company-specific needs in the cloud infrastructure.

3. CASE STUDY

A qualitative case study presents the results of interviews with a medium-sized retail company during a five-month software introduction in the summer of 2018. The study was carried out by the author of this article and is organized as Oates (2005) described. The following two chapters present the case study and examine the results of the interviews.

3.1 The Case Study

The company chosen for the case study, has approximately 300 stores in Germany. In 2013, the company had a turnover of 130 million euros. The current ERP system is hosted in a cloud. This is not ERPaaS, because the software as such is completely and separately available. A hybrid cloud-platform approach was chosen for introducing the new POS software. The hosted version is also selected for the standard POS software. When the software is introduced, the branch stores will be equipped with new cash registers. All functions, which a store must perform, such as cashing up daily or receiving new goods, are newly implemented. This results in process and ERP system changes. Two new software solutions are introduced in the stores: The POS software itself and a so-called "portal" on a separate computer in which functionalities are provided independently of the actual sales process. Both the new POS software and the ERP system are standard software. The previous POS software was developed by the retail company itself. Three parties are involved in the implementation of the project: The retail company itself, a consultant of the POS software manufacturer, and an independent consulting company. The independent consulting firm also advised on the ERP implementation. Eighteen interviews were conducted with all three parties for the case studies. The interview partners are broken down into the project roles as shown in Table 1.

Table 1. Case Study Setup

	Project Leader	Consultan	Specialist Department	IT Department
Retail company	1	2	3	3
POS software manufacturer	1	2	-	-
Consultancy firm	1	2	-	3

Unstructured interviews were conducted so that, over a period of five months, a direction of questioning could be determined without, as far as possible, leaving out any facets of the software introduction and without determining the focus in advance. For the case study, concepts for introducing the new software, as well as concepts of the ERP project and the old POS software were analyzed. During the software introduction, processes were identified, which could not be handled in the standard POS software. The ERP manufacturer's app platform was used to develop the lacking functionalities. For example, certain reports could be used; certain apps had to be re-developed by using the tools, which were made available in the cloud platform to create mockups and programming. The classic consulting concept was used here, in which consultants work together with the specialist department to develop a concept for the apps. The retail company's IT department then collaborates with the technical consultants of the independent consulting company to implement these, which are not available on the platform.

3.2 Case Study Results

Next, this paper presents the interview results. Figure 1 shows the topics resulting from the document analysis on the y-axis, subdivided according to the survey groups. The x-axis shows the number of interview partners who consider the respective topic as important. It becomes clear that complexity reduction plays an important role when it comes to introducing the new standard software. The topic in the interviews related to a "close-to-standard software introduction." This means that as few new developments as possible were made so that the maintenance complexity was reduced and innovations or new releases could be implemented more quickly. This topic is indirectly linked to lower implementation costs. The topic of uncertainty absorption is given less priority when it comes to introducing POS software. The interviews clearly showed that this characteristic for introducing the ERP system is rated almost on the same level as complexity reduction. The reason for this is that uncertainty absorption is primarily driven by ERP systems. With the new POS software, this topic plays a relatively minor role. The other topics were evaluated in the interviews, but with less relevance for the software introduction project and are not considered further in this paper.

While Sontow and Kleinert (2010) emphasize the relatively high dependence on service providers and the very consistent standardization of the software, the interviews in this case study show otherwise. Becker and Ortmann (2010) already pointed out that ERP systems are in use for more than 10 years on average in small and medium-sized enterprises, as well as in large enterprises. Under this premise, the hosted version of an ERP system was chosen. This, of course, makes it less likely that the service performance will be rated as good overall, since only one of the two service providers –namely the software manufacturer or the hosting service provider – needs to work unsatisfactorily. In the interviews, the question about the fear of lock-in effects was answered by the fact that it would be very difficult for a medium-sized company to provide comparable services in a short time as a cloud operator would do. This includes technical aspects, as well as personnel. In addition, an internally-hosted system could also be described as a lock-in effect, since employees need to be trained. Switching to another system would hardly be less complicated.

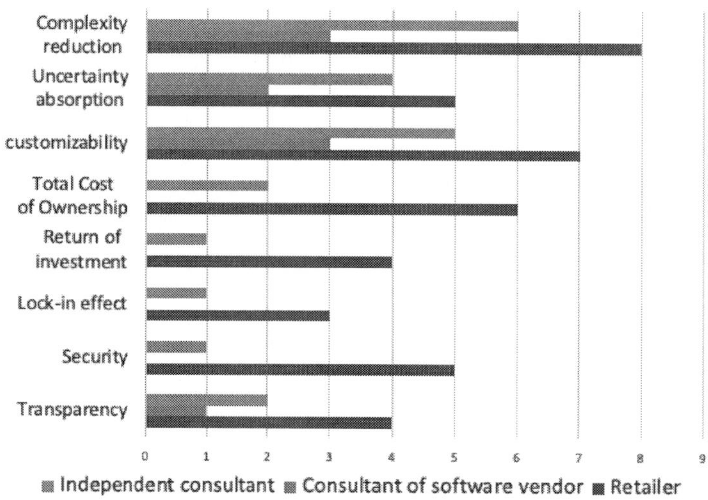

Figure 1. Rating of Importance of Factors for Hybrid Cloud- platform Software Implementation

4. EFFECTS OF A HYBRID CLOUD-PLATFORM ARCHITECTURE

Next, this paper discusses the decision, which was made in the introductory project, to adopt a hybrid cloud platform, taking into account various aspects; these are shown in Figure 2. Complexity reduction and uncertainty absorption are investigated analogously to the results of the interviews. While preparing for the following discussion, the sociological complexity theory – in the context of a cloud platform –will be inferred; this gives rise – almost incidentally – to a sociological legitimation of SaaS providers with which the retail company's decision can be placed in a scientific context.

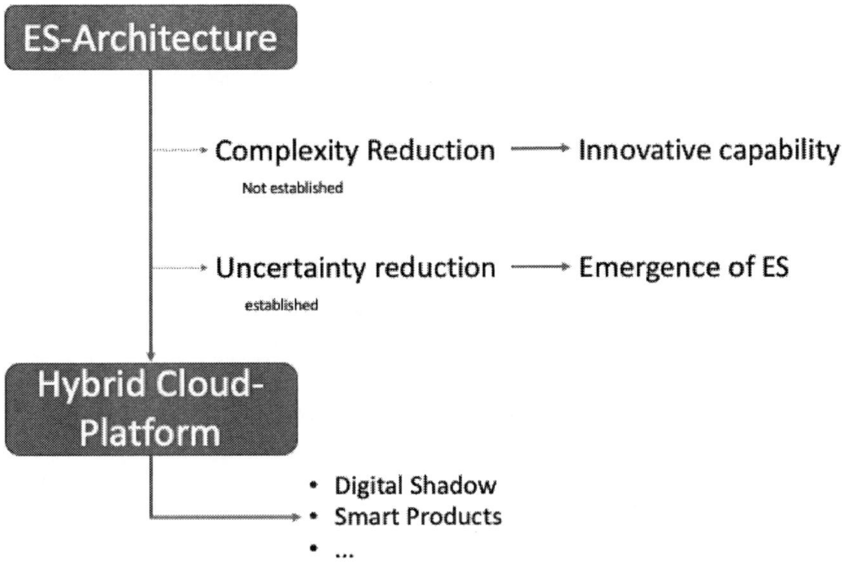

Figure 2. On-going changes of ES-Architecture

4.1 Social Legitimacy of SaaS Providers

In general, a system is a dynamic entity with certain characteristics and behaviors (Ropohl 2009). It consists of interconnected parts. No part is independent of all the other parts and the behavior of the unit is influenced by the interaction of all parts. Subsystems must fulfill two tasks for a form of system differentiation: A subsystem recognizes the essence of another subsystem, and the subsystem is defined according to this difference (Luhmann 1997). Subsystems differ in that they diagnose a social problem and use their processing and solution functionalities. Companies are subsystems related to this work. As an enterprise, the subsystem tries to legitimize society as a whole in order to differentiate itself further; the subsystem does this by adopting a certain function and by providing a service.

The modern economy often contains a differentiation, which is brought about by the increasing complexity of individual tasks and areas. In this paper, Software-as-a-Service is considered as a consequence of the technological world's increasing complexity. SaaS providers solve the high-complexity problem of software and its necessary infrastructure. This socially legitimizes SaaS providers. The previous chapter already stated that, according to Hess et. al. (2009), the ASP model was not ecologically successful, due to customer-specific infrastructure. The complexity, which was previously created at individual companies in the form of infrastructure, was identically reproduced in the ASP. This does not lead to any reduction in complexity and can therefore only achieve ecological advantages with difficulty. Only when a cloud is introduced can complexity be reduced, thereby legitimizing the CSP (cloud solution provider).

4.2 Complexity Reduction

The previous chapter discusses the legitimacy of SaaS providers as a process of social differentiation. The complexity argument is used; this is discussed in more detail below. Two possible ways of reducing complexity are investigated.

Operational closure means that the system's behavior affects itself and becomes the starting point for further behavior. Operational consistency in small systems reduces the complexity of each individual system. This can explain why a decentralized IT landscape is often created – almost automatically –in companies. Designing an integrated application system for the entire enterprise is usually a much more complex task. The trend is to outsource such ventures to an external software manufacturer in the form of standard software. In accordance with the previous chapter's argument, software vendors can – in addition to SaaS providers –also be socially legitimized in this way.

Second, in their environment, communication systems only perceive what is appropriate to their subject; what is associated with the "Sinn" (meaning) of earlier communication. For Luhmann, meaning is a mechanism for reducing complexity. In the infinitely complex environment, only a small part is filtered out according to certain criteria; the boundary of a social system thus marks a difference in complexity from the outside to the inside. The legitimization of software manufacturers is thus not only determined by their ecological use of network effects –that is, they supply many companies with the same or similar software. According to Luhmann, the complexity, and thus the controllability, of a task decreases, also when systems are distinguished from each other according to meaning. This cannot happen within a company, because the entire company usually has a single meaning – for example, to sell food inexpensively. Overhead cost calculations represent an attempt to break down this meaning within a company. Nevertheless, it remains difficult to link the success or failure of a company to the IT department.

Based on interviews, Johansson and Ruivo (2013) have already reported a decline in the complexity of implementing an ERP in the cloud. According to the interviews of this work, the reduction of complexity played an important role both in the introduction of the new POS software and in the previous ERP projects. The interviews drew attention to the following points on choosing a strategy for introducing the software when it comes to complexity: In the long run, ERP systems will have to be modified time and again. This emerged from the theory of Orlikowski (1992), in which human agents change or influence technology. This is a critical point when it comes to complexity, because resources must be available at all times to anticipate how software changes will impact on the complete enterprise system. As the systems interact with each other in a more integrated way, so the complexity, which needs to be managed, increases. Many software projects still fail due to this – even years after the software introduction. The availability of resources must be taken into account when introducing software. For example, employees can leave the company or a new consultancy company can be appointed. In most cases, the long-term availability of knowledge should be ensured through concepts. Analogous to the point of changes, effects must be understood if a subsequent innovation is to be integrated.

4.3 Uncertainty Absorption

Luhmann adopted the term uncertainty absorption from March and Simon (1958). According to Luhmann (2000) and Simon (2007), uncertainty arises when knowledge and lack of knowledge occur simultaneously. It, therefore, arises due to this balance between knowledge and lack of knowledge. Uncertainty absorption occurs when a decision is made after evidence had been gathered, and the conclusions – instead of the evidence– are communicated. This is exactly what usually occurs when an enterprise system is introduced; where decisions are supported by, for example, an ERP system with the help of data or data evaluations. For example, in the following query of a marketing manager to an ERP system, there is no identity between data entry and query: Which advertising campaigns help reduce underutilization in production capacities? The answer to this question consists of marketing data and production data; the sales figures of the product in individual sales areas, as well as the corresponding advertising campaign of the last months are shown to the marketing manager on the basis of this data linking. This means that there is no longer any identity between data input and information retrieval (Mormann 2016). By linking decisions like this, Luhmann succeeds in explaining–from an organizational theory perspective–how the organization establishes itself as a developing order and social system (Luhmann 2000). In the present case study, uncertainty absorption was assessed as rather insignificant in the new software implementation. This may be due to the fact that uncertainty absorption is mainly relevant for decision makers and therefore less important when it comes to introducing a new POS software. Figure 2, therefore, deals with uncertainty absorption.

5. CONCLUSION AND FUTURE WORK

This paper presents a case study in which the introduction of a hybrid cloud platform was examined. The results of this case study showed a clear trend towards the importance of complexity reduction. The topic related to a "close-to-standard software introduction." Uncertainty absorption was assigned a lesser importance in the new POS software introduction. This is attributed to the ERP system, which was already implemented. Thus, uncertainty absorption seems to depend on the contextual circumstances of a software introduction, and complexity reduction seems to be significant across the board–at least for ERP and POS software introductions. Subsequently, this paper provides a sociological justification for the legitimacy of SaaS. Possible approaches, which could be used to reduce complexity, were explained. In the case study, the relevant aspects for reducing complexity were identified via interviews. Uncertainty absorption was assessed as less relevant for the implementation project. This paper has established how uncertainty absorption relates to the cloud platform topic.

Overall, the issue of complexity reduction continues to be regarded as relevant for both research and practice. Because the relevance of reduction absorption has been identified as dependent on the particular introductory context, this paper expects that interest for research and practice will decline.

REFERENCES

Becker, M., & Ortmann, J. (2010). ERP-Studie. Hamburg: mondula GmbH.

Brodocz, A. (1997). Niklas Luhmann: Die Gesellschaft der Gesellschaft. MEDIENwissenschaft: Rezensionen| Reviews, (4), 441-441.

Brown, C. V., & Vessey, I. (2008). Managing the Next Wave of Enterprise Systems: Leveraging Lessons from ERP. MIS Quarterly Executive, 2(1), 6.

Ciborra, C., Hanseth, O., & Braa, K. (2001). The control devolution: ERP and the side effects of globalisation. Database for Advances in Information Systems, 32(4).

Gottwald, M. (2013). ERP Trend Report 2013 Prozessindustrie. München: Infor Deutschland GmbH.

Görtz, M., & Hesseler, M. (2007). Basiswissen ERP-Systeme: Auswahl. Einführung & Einsatz betriebswirtschaftlicher Standardsoftware, W3I.

Hwang, Y. (2005). Investigating enterprise systems adoption: uncertainty avoidance, intrinsic motivation, and the technology acceptance model. European journal of information systems, 14(2), 150-161.

Hess, T., & Wolf, C. M. (2008). Software as a service 1.0 and beyond. Software as a Service: Strategische Perspektiven und praktische Bedeutung, München, 8-14.

Hess, T., Benlian, A., Wolf, C. M., & Buxmann, P. (2009). ERP-as-a-Service: Zukunft oder Sackgasse?. Controlling & Management, 53(3), 14-17.

Johansson, B., & Ruivo, P. (2013). Exploring factors for adopting ERP as SaaS. Procedia Technology, 9, 94-99.

Josefiok, M., Göring, M., & Rohde, J. (2014). ERP as a Service Potenziale und Hemmnisse. ERP Management, 10.

Jung-Elsen, S. (2013). Sind ERP-Systeme geeignet für die Cloud?. In ERP Management, 9.

Kurbel, K. (2016). Enterprise Resource Planning und Supply Chain Management in der Industrie: von MRP bis Industrie 4.0. Walter de Gruyter GmbH & Co KG.

Liang, H., Xue, Y., Boulton, W. R., & Byrd, T. A. (2004). Why Western vendors don't dominate China's ERP market. Communications of the ACM, 47(7), 69-72.

Luhmann, N. (2000). Die Paradoxie des Entscheidens. In Organisation und Entscheidung (pp. 123-151). VS Verlag für Sozialwissenschaften.

Luhmann, N. (2000). Vertrauen: Ein mechanismus der reduktion sozialer komplexität (Vol. 2185). Grove/Atlantic, Inc.

March, J. G., & Simon, H. A. (1958). Organizations.

Martinsons, M. G. (2004). ERP in China: one package, two profiles. Communications of the ACM, 47(7), 65-68.

Mormann, H. (2016). Das Projekt SAP: Zur Organisationssoziologie betriebswirtschaftlicher Standardsoftware. transcript Verlag.

Oates, B. J. (2005). Researching information systems and computing. Sage.

Orlikowski, W. J. (1992). The duality of technology: Rethinking the concept of technology in organizations. Organization science, 3(3), 398-427.

Ropohl, G. (2009). Allgemeine technologie: Eine systemtheorie der technik (p. 363). KIT Scientific Publishing.

Schütte, R., & Vering, O. (2011). Erfolgreiche Geschäftsprozesse durch moderne Warenwirtschaftssysteme: Produktübersicht marktführender Systeme und Auswahlprozess. Springer-Verlag.

Simon, F. B. (2007). Einführung in die systemische Organisationstheorie (Vol. 1). Heidelberg: Carl-Auer.

Sontow, K., & Kleinert, A. (2010). Software as a Service–Die schlanke Zukunft für ERP-Lösungen? Ergebnisse eine Anwenderbefragung. ERP Management, 6(4), 24-27.

SUCCESS FACTORS OF COLLABORATION IN THE CONTEXT OF DEVOPS

Michiel van Belzen, Dave de Kruijff and Jos Trienekens
Open University, The Netherlands

ABSTRACT

Context: Collaboration is an important aspect of DevOps. However, researchers continue to report problems with collaboration between development and operations.
Objective: We aim to contribute to a better understanding of collaboration in the context of DevOps, especially to aid in adopting DevOps.
Method: We conducted a literature review on collaboration and corresponding success factors. For practice we classified the factors into factors influencing the likelihood of collaboration and factors influencing the performance of collaboration, to aid in the adoption of DevOps. We will validate the factors of collaboration in a DevOps context using an inductive approach, i.e. semi-structured interviews and document studies.
Results: We developed an initial framework of success factors and classified the found success factors. Subsequently we conducted two interviews. We learned that most factors are considered as important, however few factors could be confirmed and no more factors are added. We will interview the other respondents to prove the applicability of the framework. Which may identify promising avenues for further development of the framework.
Conclusions: This is study is not finalized yet, therefore we cannot fully answer the main research question.

KEYWORDS

DevOps, Adoption, Success Factors, Collaboration, Performance

1. INTRODUCTION

Organizations that can release software early and with a high frequency have a higher capability to compete in the market (Erich, Amrit, & Daneva, 2017). Software producers need to deliver products and new features to customers as fast as they can (Colomo-Palacios, Fernandes, Soto-Acosta, & Larrucea, 2018). The notion of software development agility (i.e. a software team's ability to efficiently and effectively respond to user requirement changes) is at the heart of agile development approaches (Lee & Xia, 2010). At the same time it is important to be aware of drawbacks using incremental and agile practices, which are mainly related to increased complexity when scaling agile (Petersen & Wohlin, 2009). DevOps, a compound of "development" and "operations," is a software development and delivery approach designed for high velocity (Sebastian et al., 2017). Companies are building continuous delivery (i.e., DevOps) into their digital services backbones to facilitate speed (Ross et al., 2016). DevOps adoption proves able to improve cycle times and quality (Colomo-Palacios et al., 2018). It appears that as, over time, DevOps capabilities (e.g. high velocity of software delivery and quality of IT services) will become a competitive necessity (Sebastian et al., 2017), it becomes important to know what DevOps is. However DevOps is not a precisely defined concept, organizations have to find their own way of implementing it which might slow down the rate of adoption (Erich et al., 2017). Moreover the authors did not found any quantitative data to show the effectiveness of DevOps. Erich et al (2017) consider DevOps as an interaction between development and operations personnel. Also other researchers (Claps, Berntsson Svensson, & Aurum, 2015; Ebert, Gallardo, Hernantes, & Serrano, 2016; Hüttermann, 2012; Wiedemann, 2018) consider DevOps as a set of practices that advocate the collaboration between software developers and IT operations, where the aim is to shorten the feedback loop while aligning the goals of both the development and IT operations departments. IS development and IT operations have to pursue the objective of establishing a relationship that ensures that high-quality IT services are being delivered to the business (Iden, Tessem, & Paivarinta, 2012). IS development and IT operations in practice have to cooperate effectively on a number of topics and activities during a system development project (Iden et al., 2012). Thus it appears that collaboration is an important aspect of DevOps. However, researchers continue to report problems with collaboration between development and operations, e.g. poor communication (Iden et al., 2012; Lwakatare, Kuvaja, & Oivo, 2015), cultural and organizational gaps (Wettinger, Breitenbücher, Falkenthal, & Leymann, 2017), knowledge boundaries (Colomo-Palacios et al., 2018; Nielsen, Winkler, & Norbjerg, 2017) and overcoming the Dev versus Ops mentality and Dev and Ops toolset clashes (Ghantous & Gill, 2017). Experts with long and relevant industry experience agree that they do not cooperate effectively in development projects (Iden, Tessem, & Päivärinta, 2011). Thus the topic of integrated corporate functions (e.g. DevOps) appear to be especially relevant (Rodríguez et al., 2017). To aid in adopting DevOps (De Feijter, Overbeek, Van Vliet, Jagroep, & Brinkkemper, 2018) propose a DevOps competence model and a DevOps maturity model. However the case study was conducted in one organization, which poses a limitation on the generalizability of the case study results. And it is not clear whether all respondents were real DevOps experts.

Therefore we aim to contribute to a better understanding of collaboration in the context of DevOps, especially to aid in adopting DevOps. As existing literature has paid little attention to different contexts and success factors of collaboration (Yoon, Lee, Yoon, & Toulan, 2017), we focus on the identification of success factors of collaboration and subsequently validate them empirically in a DevOps context. Our main research question is: What is successful collaboration in the context of DevOps? The sub questions are: (SQ1) What is collaboration? (SQ2) What are critical success factors of collaboration? (SQ3) How are these factors addressed by DevOps? First we conducted a systematic literature review (Kitchenham et al., 2010) on collaboration and success factors of collaboration. These concepts are elaborated in chapter 2. Based on the findings we developed an initial framework and classified the success factors (chapter 3). Subsequently we conducted two interviews and learned that most factors are considered as important, however few factors could be confirmed. Chapter 4 reveals our plan to conduct more interviews and to prove the applicability of the framework.

2. THEORETICAL BACKGROUND

In a comprehensive study on collaboration, (Bedwell et al., 2012) define collaboration as "An evolving process whereby two or more social entities actively and reciprocally engage in joint activities aimed at achieving at least one shared goal". Collaboration cannot be treated as a hardened structure, a "done deal"-in theory or in practice (Mintzberg, Jorgensen, Dougherty, & Westley, 1996). Other researchers define collaboration also as a joint effort towards a group goal, e.g. (Kolfschoten, de Vreede, Briggs, & Sol, 2010). Collaborative success depends on willingness of its participants, therefore it has an intrinsic unpredictable element which makes it a complex activity or task (Kolfschoten et al., 2010). The authors consider collaboration as both a process and a system.

On a firm level technological collaboration in small and medium-sized firms can impact product- and process innovation, while vertical collaboration (with suppliers and clients) has the greatest impact on firm innovativeness (Nieto & Santamaria, 2010). The impact of collaboration, in a DevOps context, on innovation is confirmed by scholars, e.g. DevOps lower barriers for immediate and continuous delivery of new services and features (Airaj, 2017). Systematic managing social interaction between developers and IT operations staff (Iden & Bygstad, 2018) is another example. According to the authors this will lead to important business improvements, including improved quality of software in operation, improved IT service quality. However a clear performance measurement and regulation must be set to accelerate the process innovation through collaboration (Yoon et al., 2017).

Bedwell et al. (2012) developed an overarching theoretical framework based on the Input-Mediator-Output-Input-framework (Ilgen, Hollenbeck, Johnson, & Jundt, 2005), which has been used to describe phenomena related to performance. They consider the individual/entity characteristics as inputs, whereas the output is labeled 'distal collaborative output' to signify the achievement of a shared goal that motivated the collaborative initiative. They also include mediators that comprise the collaborative performance cycle: cognitive and affective emergent states, defined as "properties of the team that are typically dynamic in nature and vary as a function of team context, inputs, processes, and outcomes" and collaborative behaviors. They emphasize that the emergent states also influence one another and reciprocally influence collaborative behaviors enacted during a collaborative performance episode. This creates essentially a feedback loop, which incorporates initial collaborative performance outcomes back into the collaborative cycle until the distal collaborative outcome is achieved. In addition to these inputs, mediators, and outputs, their collaborative framework considers the moderating impact of contextual factors.

DevOps adoption drives a challenging cultural shift towards collaboration and knowledge-sharing between software development, quality control and operations (Colomo-Palacios et al., 2018). All effective collaborative efforts require varying levels of coordination, depending on task and the size of the entities involved (Bedwell et al., 2012). Tessem and Iden (2008) consider collaboration, coordination and co-decisions as forms of cooperation (Tessem & Iden, 2008). However, Bedwell et al (2012) define cooperation as an attitude or predisposition held by the involved parties to be concerned about the overall collaborative goal rather than their own individual goal. They consider cooperation as a requirement for effective collaboration, not as a description of collaboration itself. Some authors (Iden & Bygstad, 2018; Söderlund, 2011) consider cooperation and coordination as the two main problems that must be solved when personnel with different professional profiles and organisational affiliations are to interact in a project.

In the early stages of research on collaboration Mattessich & Monsey (1992) review and summarize existing research literature on factors which influence the success of collaboration. They identified nineteen success factors and grouped them into six categories (which have no research significance according to the authors). They confirmed the factors in 2001 and add an additional factor: An appropriate pace of development (Mattessich, Murray-Close, & Monsey, 2001). (Mohr & Spekman, 1994) studied the relationship between a computer dealer and one of its suppliers (i.e., manufacturers) at which both partners have jointly aligned goals to accomplish mutually beneficial end (which we consider as collaboration). They found the key characteristics of successful vertical collaboration to be confidence, adaptation, devotion, quality of communication, degree of participation, and the methods of solving common problems. (Mintzberg et al., 1996) noted that the nature of a particular collaboration may depend on impinging factors, e.g. task and the goal, the parties involved, and its evolution over time. The contexts surrounding the performance situation influences collaborative inputs, processes, and outcomes (Bedwell et al., 2012). (Marek, Brock, & Savla, 2015) examined for distinctiveness and comprehensiveness, all factors and categories found by Mattessich & Monsey (1992) that were linked to coalition success, and confirmed the original six categories identified by Mattessich and Monsey (1992). They also generate additional ones, introducing seven interrelated factors: context, members, process and organization, communication, function, resources and leadership. De Feijter et al. (2018) noticed that the organization itself should be in place to perform work, i.e. interdisciplinary professionals should communicate, share knowledge, have trust and respect for one another, work in teams, and there should be release alignment (some form of alignment between internal and external dependencies in order to timely deploy software). Kotlarsky & Oshri (2005) mentioned human-related issues/factors in the form of social ties, in particular rapport and transactive memory, and organizational mechanisms that create and maintain social ties between dispersed team members. Tsanos et al. (2014) identified comparable factors: trust, commitment, mutuality and reciprocity.

3. TOWARDS A FRAMEWORK OF SUCCESS FACTORS FOR COLLABORATION

We started with the work of (Mattessich & Monsey, 1992) and (Mohr & Spekman, 1994), which are well-known publications. And applied forward snowballing to search for further peer reviewed research (described in section 2) on this topic. We found additional success factors in (Marek et al., 2015; Patel, Pettitt, & Wilson, 2012; Tsanos et al., 2014; Yoon et al., 2017). However, the search missed five relevant papers of which we were aware: (Bedwell et al., 2012; De Feijter et al., 2018; Kolfschoten et al., 2010; Kotlarsky & Oshri, 2005; Lwakatare et al., 2015). We only found additional factors in Bedwell et al. (2012). We put all the found success factors into one table and add the corresponding definitions, which forms the basis of our framework.

To search for confirmation of the found success factors in a DevOps context, we conduct a systematic literature review (Kitchenham et al., 2010). We searched two digital libraries in December 2018: Web of Science and Business Source Premier. All searches were based on title and the period between 2009 (the emerge of DevOps (Dornenburg, 2018; Hüttermann, 2012)) and 2018. For all the sources we used the following search string: (collaboration OR cooperation OR coordination) AND factor. We undertook an initial screening of the 554 papers found. The screening was based on excluding papers that were obviously irrelevant, duplicates, not written in English, not peer reviewed or not in the field of Business/Management or Computer Science. The remaining 81 papers were then assessed to identify papers that could be rejected based on abstract and title on the basis that they did not include success factors of collaboration between Development and Operations (DevOps). We found no other papers which confirmed the success factors in our initial framework.

The next step we took was classification of the found factors. As our research goal is to aid in adopting DevOps, we would like to classify the found factors in line with the process of evolving collaboration. De Feijter et al. (2018) classify in their maturity model five focus areas (which are part of the perspective of culture and collaboration) gradually in terms of capabilities. I.e. capabilities in levels 1 to 5 mention a situation where an organization is not yet adopting DevOps, capabilities in levels 5 and 6 mention a situation transitioning to a DevOps situation and capabilities in levels 5 to 10 mention a situation in which DevOps is already adopted to a more mature extent. However the success factors we found were of a different abstraction level and not fine grained. In addition the maturity model of De Feijter et al. (2018) does not take into account all the factors we found. Therefore we classify the found success factors into a more coarse way: factors influencing the likelihood of collaboration and factors influencing the performance of collaboration, which is a widely used classification method (Yoon et al., 2017). Yoon et al. (2017) add five success factors to the planning stage perspective, which we consider as success factors influencing the likelihood of collaboration (table 1). Tsanos et al. (2014) identified four factors that are recurrently mentioned as antecedents of collaboration: trust, commitment, mutuality and reciprocity. The authors mentioned that complicated pairings of concepts exist (e.g. trust and commitment). These factors are also part of the definition of collaboration of (Bedwell et al., 2012). Although trust and commitment are not explicitly mentioned, we consider them as prerequisites of mutuality and reciprocity. Therefore we add the four factors found by (Tsanos et al., 2014) to table 1. All other found success factors will be considered as factors influencing the performance of collaboration. Comparable success factors will obtain the same classification. We applied this classification in order to organize the analysis of the empirical data (e.g. new factors) as well.

Table 1. Success Factors influencing the likelihood of Collaboration (Tsanos et al., 2014; Yoon et al., 2017)

Success factor	Content and operational definition
Setting of clear goals	- Setting of clear goals at the planning stage. - Supplementary purposes.
Distribution regulation for collaboration results	Prescribe issues related to distribution in advance, and prevent technical knowhow from leaking out.
Methods of solving common issues	Refrain from using harsh methods such as persuasion, domination and arbitration to solve conflicts.
Governance: clear role-setting	Main agents and strategies about role-setting of collaboration.
Governance-defining performance measurement methods	Main agents about methods to measure performance of collaboration.
Trust	Professionals trust each other.
Commitment	The belief of a partner that the exchange is so important it merits the maximum effort to maintain it.
Mutuality	Belief about the inherent value of cooperating for mutual gain.
Reciprocity	Degree to which individuals expect cooperative action (as opposed to forced interaction) within a relationship.

This leads us to the theoretical framework with success factors of collaboration (table 2). If a respondent confirmed a success factor we added to table 2 examples of practices and if applicable how they measure collaboration.

Table 2. Theoretical Framework with Success Factors of Collaboration

Classification	Success factor	Operational definition	Confirmation
Success factors influencing the likelihood of collaboration	Concrete attainable goals and objectives	Setting of clear goals (at the planning stage), supplementary purposes (Patel et al., 2012; Yoon et al., 2017) and feasible (Mattessich & Monsey, 1992), based on key community issues, agreed upon (Marek et al., 2015).	-
	Shared vision (agreed goals)	With clearly agreed upon mission, objectives and strategy. May exist at the outset of collaboration or may develop in time (Mattessich & Monsey, 1992; Patel et al., 2012).	-
	Unique purpose	Mission and goals or approach differ (at least in part) from the mission and goals or approach of the member organizations (Mattessich & Monsey, 1992).	-
	Distribution regulation for collaboration results	Prescribe issues related to distribution in advance, and prevent technical knowhow from leaking out (Yoon et al., 2017).	
	Clear rules and	The need for clear rules and procedures in order to structure	-

Classification	Success factor	Operational definition	Confirmation
	procedures	collaboration (Marek et al., 2015). The methods of solving common problems (Mohr and Spekman, 1994). Error management: the procedures to identify and manage errors and violations (Patel et al., 2012). Refrain from using harsh methods such as persuasion, domination and arbitration to solve conflicts (Yoon et al., 2017).	
	Clear roles and responsibilities	The need for roles and responsibilities in order to structure collaboration (Marek et al., 2015; Patel et al., 2012). Main agents and strategies about role-setting of collaboration (Yoon et al., 2017).	-
	Governance-defining performance measurement methods	Main agents about methods to measure performance of collaboration (Yoon et al., 2017). Performance relevant to collaborative working includes: keeping to project budgets and deadlines, profits, time saved, meeting or improving required quantity and quality of product/service, improving work processes, innovation, achieving goals, meeting requirements, improving relationships, extending professional networks, generating new business, learning, individual and team satisfaction and wellbeing, improving trust and commitment, reducing errors, high level of safety, low levels of absenteeism and staff turnover (Patel et al., 2012).	-
	Mutual respect, understanding, and trust (social ties). Conflict.	Understanding and respect for each other and their respective organizations: how they operate, their cultural norms and values, limitations, and expectations (Kolfschoten et al., 2010; Mattessich & Monsey, 1992), confidence (Mohr & Spekman, 1994), professionals trust each other, respect (De Feijter et al., 2018; Tsanos et al., 2014) and human-related issues (Kotlarsky & Oshri, 2005). Conflict (Patel et al., 2012).	Developers are higher educated, the perception of developers on Ops is that they only execute and maintain. There is still a large gap between operations and development, they are not seen as one team at the moment.
	Members see collaboration as in their self-interest	Mindset where collaboration is seen as contribution to the quality of tasks and outcomes (Marek et al., 2015; Mattessich & Monsey, 1992). Commitment, i.e. the belief of a partner that the exchange is so important it merits the maximum effort to maintain it (Tsanos et al., 2014).	Lack of social skills, mindset and background are obstacles as well as hesitation of older employees.
	Members share a stake in both process and outcome	Members feel 'ownership' of the way the group works and the results or product of its work (Mattessich & Monsey, 1992). Devotion (Mohr & Spekman, 1994). Incentives which emphasize team goals rather than individual goals (Patel et al., 2012).	-
	Mutuality	Belief about the inherent value of cooperating for mutual gain (Tsanos et al., 2014).	-
	(Shared) resources	Reciprocity, i.e. the degree to which individuals expect cooperative action (as opposed to forced interaction) within a relationship (Tsanos et al., 2014), sharing time, effort, knowledge, interaction channels, physical resources (Kolfschoten et al., 2010)(Marek et al., 2015), monitoring information (Lwakatare et al., 2015). Resources, training, team building, relationships, shared knowledge/awareness, common ground, constraints (Patel et al., 2012).	-
Success factors influencing the performance of collaboration	History	Exists in the community, offers partners an understanding of, and trust in, the collaboration process (Mattessich & Monsey, 1992).	Feedback received by the software integration team is more useful and detailed.
	Leadership	The collaborative group is perceived as a leader, at least related to the goals and activities it intends to accomplish (Mattessich & Monsey, 1992).	Have the status of being the specialist in this field.
	Political/social climate favorable	Stakeholders support (or at least do not oppose) the mission of the collaborative group (Mattessich & Monsey, 1992).	Hierarchic organization is an obstacle for other

Classification	Success factor	Operational definition	Confirmation
			factors (e.g. feeling responsible), however there is freedom without resistance from higher management e.g. to create capacity to support Ops. Exists social pressure that solutions have to be found. It seems that DevOps is being pushed bottom-up.
	Task characteristics	Types of tasks that is performed (Bedwell et al., 2012; Patel et al., 2012). Demands: task differ in the demands they make on individuals, teams and processes. In times of high demand, successful teams employ 'back-up behaviours' (Patel et al., 2012).	Different types of work are recognized, needs overlap in competences.
	Environmental characteristics	Degree of risk prevalent in the environment, the level of autonomy that members have in their work, stressors (e.g. dangerous work conditions, or uncertainty), different cultures which result in a different manner to approach the collaboration (Bedwell et al., 2012), culture, environment and business climate (Patel et al., 2012).	Freedom without resistance from higher management e.g. to create capacity to support Ops.
	Temporal characteristics	Including team lifespan, performance episode duration, performance episode frequency, and continuity of membership (Bedwell et al., 2012). Time limits, cycles of activity, work rhythms, events when a team is first formed and how their goals and tasks are communicated and discussed. Temporary versus long-term teams, individuals' power sources may vary over time (e.g. with age, experience, time on the job and by expanding their professional and personal networks) and can alter interpersonal dynamics and their capacity to influence the context within which collaboration takes place (Patel et al., 2012).	-
	Structural characteristics	Including structure of leadership, communication structure and division of work and roles among members, distribution (physical and temporal) of members (Bedwell et al., 2012), organizational structure and task structure (Patel et al., 2012). Coordination (Bedwell et al., 2012) which involves goal setting, managing and integrating people and information etc. (Patel et al., 2012).	Internal Ops and Dev are closely situated, which reduces the complexity of communication. The communication with external Ops is a bit more difficult.
	Ability to compromise	Partners are able to compromise, since the many decisions within a collaborative effort can not possibly fit the preferences of every member perfectly (Mattessich & Monsey, 1992). Group decision making (Patel et al., 2012).	-
	Appropriate cross-section of members	Representatives are included from each segment of the community who will be affected by its activities (De Feijter et al., 2018; Mattessich & Monsey, 1992). Team composition, skills, experience, psychological factors, wellbeing (Patel et al., 2012).	-
	Members view the benefits of collaboration as outweighing the costs	Believe that the benefits of collaboration will offset costs such as loss of autonomy and 'turf' (Mattessich & Monsey, 1992).	-
	Multiple layers of decision-making and participation	Every management level within each organization participates in decision-making (Mattessich & Monsey, 1992), degree of participation (Mohr & Spekman, 1994; Patel et al., 2012), release alignment (De Feijter et al., 2018).	-
	Flexibility	Open to varied ways of organizing and accomplishing work (Mattessich & Monsey, 1992).	Some teams continuously focus on goals they need to reach.

Classification	Success factor	Operational definition	Confirmation
	Adaptability	Ability to sustain itself in the midst of major changes, even if it needs to change some major goals, members, etc., in order to deal with changing conditions (Mattessich & Monsey, 1992), adaptation (Mohr & Spekman, 1994).	Employees quickly adopt new technology in order to deal with changing conditions.
	Appropriate pace of development	The structure, resources, and activities of the collaborative group change over time to meet the needs of the group without overwhelming its capacity, at each point throughout the initiative (Mattessich et al., 2001).	
	Knowledge Management	The sharing of knowledge (as a resource) (De Feijter et al., 2018; Kotlarsky & Oshri, 2005; Patel et al., 2012). Training, learning, skills and team building (Patel et al., 2012).	Knowledge is partially shared by a shared platform.
	Formal and informal communication	Channels of communication and information flows, personal connections (De Feijter et al., 2018; Kolfschoten et al., 2010; Mattessich & Monsey, 1992; Patel et al., 2012), networks (Patel et al., 2012).	Formal communication mainly focus on risk management.
	Open, frequent and clear communication	Frequent, open and clear interactions, conveying all necessary information (Mattessich & Monsey, 1992; Patel et al., 2012). Set meeting times (Marek et al., 2015), quality (De Feijter et al., 2018; Mohr & Spekman, 1994). Group processes (social and psychological interactions) (Patel et al., 2012).	-
	Sufficient funds	Adequate, consistent financial base (Marek et al., 2015; Mattessich & Monsey, 1992) and resources (Patel et al., 2012).	Budget cuts in recent years put engineering research below a critical level.
	Skilled leader/Management	Convener with organizing and interpersonal skills, carries out the role with fairness, is granted respect or legitimacy (Mattessich & Monsey, 1992). Support from management e.g. providing clear direction, guidance, inspiration of collaborative project management (Patel et al., 2012).	-
	Tools	Technologies for collaborating, e.g. email, conferencing, scheduling tools and knowledge management tools (Patel et al., 2012).	-

To validate this framework in a DevOps context, we will use an inductive approach, i.e. carrying out semi-structured interviews and document studies (cross sectional). This approach enables us to achieve depth, elaboration and soundness (Verschuren & Doorewaard, 2010), which is important as we aim to contribute to a better understanding of collaboration in the context of DevOps. We will conduct approximately twelve interviews in two IT Service Provider organisations (ISP's) which serve 12,000 (ISP1) respectively 60,000 (ISP2) employees. Both have different maturity levels of DevOps implementation, ISP1 experience DevOps for one year, ISP2 have several years of experience with DevOps. We will interview managers of Development-, Operations- or DevOps-teams, advisors and managers (on tactic/strategic levels) which are closely involved at the introduction and evolvement of DevOps. We ask them whether they recognize the success factors and if they know additional factors. To obtain more soundness and to explore if we can find any (quantitative) data to show the effectiveness of DevOps (to close the gap mentioned by Erich et al. (2017)), we ask for examples based on own experiences and facts and ask how they measure success. Collaboration performance measurement can be broadly classified into quantitative (e.g. the degree of improvement in productivity and profitability) and qualitative (e.g. perceived satisfaction, status of goal accomplishment) performance (Yoon et al., 2017). Bedwell et al. (2012) mentioned six behaviors to measure collaborative performance: adaptive, extra-role, information processing, leadership, sensemaking and task execution. We consider these six behaviors as less abstract for our respondents, therefore we will use them as examples to support the question about how they measure success. But we will ask the respondents whether they measure any additional quantitative or qualitative performance aspects. After making an appointment with the respondents and before the interviews started, we share the definition of collaboration, the six behaviors of Bedwell et al. (2012) and the found success factors (table 2), and we share a short summary of the research project with the respondents.

At this moment we conducted two semi-structured interviews. We started with a pilot interview at ISP1 to test our interview guide (Yin, 2012). We learned that we have to add an explanation to the six behaviors of Bedwell et al. (2012). No more improvements were necessary. After the pilot interview we conducted the second interview at ISP1. Although the respondents recognized the importance of several factors, they could not confirm them in terms of how the factors are measured (indicated in table 2). In addition they mentioned no other/new success factors. We will interview the other respondents in the coming months. Each respondent will have the opportunity to amend the transcription of the interview before we analyse the data by open coding.

4. CONCLUSIONS AND FUTURE WORK

We conducted a literature review on collaboration and developed an initial framework of success factors. To aid in the adoption of DevOps, we classified the factors into factors influencing the likelihood of collaboration and factors influencing the performance of collaboration. Subsequently we conducted two interviews. We learned that most factors are considered as important, however few factors could be confirmed and no more factors are added. Thus the preliminary results confirmed in part the initial framework (table 2).

We will interview the other respondents to prove the applicability of the framework. Which may identify promising avenues for further of the framework, e.g. distinctions between factors in terms of different maturity levels of DevOps implementation and possible ranking (regarding the impact) of success factors. Regarding the quality of the case study we will address internal-, construct- and external validity and reliability aspects.

REFERENCES

Airaj, M. (2017). Enable cloud DevOps approach for industry and higher education: Enable cloud DevOps approach for industry and higher education. *Concurrency and Computation: Practice and Experience*, *29*(5), e3937. https://doi.org/10.1002/cpe.3937

Bedwell, W. L., Wildman, J. L., DiazGranados, D., Salazar, M., Kramer, W. S., & Salas, E. (2012). Collaboration at work: An integrative multilevel conceptualization. *Human Resource Management Review*, *22*(2), 128–145. https://doi.org/10.1016/j.hrmr.2011.11.007

Claps, G. G., Berntsson Svensson, R., & Aurum, A. (2015). On the journey to continuous deployment: Technical and social challenges along the way. *Information and Software Technology*, *57*, 21–31. https://doi.org/10.1016/j.infsof.2014.07.009

Colomo-Palacios, R., Fernandes, E., Soto-Acosta, P., & Larrucea, X. (2018). A case analysis of enabling continuous software deployment through knowledge management. *International Journal of Information Management*, *40*, 186–189. https://doi.org/10.1016/j.ijinfomgt.2017.11.005

De Feijter, R., Overbeek, S., Van Vliet, R., Jagroep, E., & Brinkkemper, S. (2018). DevOps Competences and Maturity for Software Producing Organizations. In J. Gulden, I. Reinhartz-Berger, R. Schmidt, S. Guerreiro, W. Guédria, & P. Bera (Eds.), *Enterprise, Business-Process and Information Systems Modeling* (Vol. 318, pp. 244–259). Cham: Springer International Publishing. https://doi.org/10.1007/978-3-319-91704-7_16

Dornenburg, E. (2018). The Path to DevOps. *IEEE Software*, *35*(5), 71–75. https://doi.org/10.1109/MS.2018.290110337

Ebert, C., Gallardo, G., Hernantes, J., & Serrano, N. (2016). DevOps. *IEEE Software*, *33*(3), 94–100. https://doi.org/10.1109/MS.2016.68

Erich, F. M. A., Amrit, C., & Daneva, M. (2017). A qualitative study of DevOps usage in practice: A Qualitative Study of DevOps Usage in Practice. *Journal of Software: Evolution and Process*, *29*(6), e1885. https://doi.org/10.1002/smr.1885

Ghantous, G. B., & Gill, A. (2017). DevOps: Concepts, Practices, Tools, Benefits and Challenges. *PACIS 2017 Proceedings*. Retrieved from http://aisel.aisnet.org/pacis2017/96

Hüttermann, M. (2012). *DevOps for developers*. Apress.

Iden, J., & Bygstad, B. (2018). The social interaction of developers and IT operations staff in software development projects. *International Journal of Project Management*, *36*(3), 485–497. https://doi.org/10.1016/j.ijproman.2017.12.001

Iden, J., Tessem, B., & Päivärinta, T. (2011). Problems in the interplay of development and IT operations in system development projects: A Delphi study of Norwegian IT experts. *Information and Software Technology*, *53*(4), 394–406.

Iden, J., Tessem, B., & Paivarinta, T. (2012). IS development/IT operations alignment in system development projects: a multi-method research. *International Journal of Business Information Systems*, *11*(3), 343–359.

Ilgen, D. R., Hollenbeck, J. R., Johnson, M., & Jundt, D. (2005). Teams in Organizations: From Input-Process-Output Models to IMOI Models. *Annual Review of Psychology*, *56*(1), 517–543. https://doi.org/10.1146/annurev.psych.56.091103.070250

Kitchenham, B., Pretorius, R., Budgen, D., Pearl Brereton, O., Turner, M., Niazi, M., & Linkman, S. (2010). Systematic literature reviews in software engineering – A tertiary study. *Information and Software Technology*, *52*(8), 792–805. https://doi.org/10.1016/j.infsof.2010.03.006

Kolfschoten, G. L., de Vreede, G.-J., Briggs, R. O., & Sol, H. G. (2010). Collaboration 'Engineerability'. *Group Decision and Negotiation*, *19*(3), 301–321. https://doi.org/10.1007/s10726-010-9192-8

Kotlarsky, J., & Oshri, I. (2005). Social ties, knowledge sharing and successful collaboration in globally distributed system development projects. *European Journal of Information Systems*, *14*(1), 37–48. https://doi.org/10.1057/palgrave.ejis.3000520

Lee, G., & Xia, W. (2010). Toward Agile: An Integrated Analysis of Quantitative and Qualitative Field Data. *MIS Q.*, *34*(1), 87–114.

Lwakatare, L. E., Kuvaja, P., & Oivo, M. (2015). Dimensions of devops. In *International Conference on Agile Software Development* (pp. 212–217). Springer.

Marek, L. I., Brock, D.-J. P., & Savla, J. (2015). Evaluating Collaboration for Effectiveness: Conceptualization and Measurement. *American Journal of Evaluation*, *36*(1), 67–85. https://doi.org/10.1177/1098214014531068

Mattessich, P. W., & Monsey, B. R. (1992). *Collaboration--what makes it work: a review of research literature on factors influencing successful collaboration*. St. Paul, Minn: Amherst H. Wilder Foundation.

Mattessich, P. W., Murray-Close, M., & Monsey, B. R. (2001). *Collaboration What Makes It Work* (Vol. 2nd.). Saint Paul, MN: Fieldstone Alliance.

Mintzberg, H., Jorgensen, J., Dougherty, D., & Westley, F. (1996). Some surprising things about collaboration—Knowing how people connect makes it work better. *Organizational Dynamics*, *25*(1), 60–71. https://doi.org/10.1016/S0090-2616(96)90041-8

Mohr, J., & Spekman, R. (1994). Characteristics of partnership success: Partnership attributes, communication behavior, and conflict resolution techniques. *Strategic Management Journal*, *15*(2), 135–152. https://doi.org/10.1002/smj.4250150205

Nielsen, P. A., Winkler, T. J., & Norbjerg, J. (2017). Closing the IT Development-Operations gap: The DevOps knowledge sharing framework. *16th International Conference on Perspectives in Business Informatics Research. BIR 2017. CEUR.*

Nieto, M. J., & Santamaria, L. (2010). Technological Collaboration: Bridging the Innovation Gap between Small and Large Firms. *Journal of Small Business Management*, *48*(1), 44–69. https://doi.org/10.1111/j.1540-627X.2009.00286.x

Patel, H., Pettitt, M., & Wilson, J. R. (2012). Factors of collaborative working: A framework for a collaboration model. *Applied Ergonomics*, *43*(1), 1–26. https://doi.org/10.1016/j.apergo.2011.04.009

Petersen, K., & Wohlin, C. (2009). A comparison of issues and advantages in agile and incremental development between state of the art and an industrial case. *Journal of Systems and Software*, *82*(9), 1479–1490. https://doi.org/10.1016/j.jss.2009.03.036

Rodríguez, P., Haghighatkhah, A., Lwakatare, L. E., Teppola, S., Suomalainen, T., Eskeli, J., … Oivo, M. (2017). Continuous deployment of software intensive products and services: A systematic mapping study. *Journal of Systems and Software*, *123*, 263–291. https://doi.org/10.1016/j.jss.2015.12.015

Ross, J. W., Sebastian, I. M., Beath, C., Mocker, M., Moloney, K. G., & Fonstad, N. O. (2016). Designing and Executing Digital Strategies (pp. 1–17). Presented at the Thirty Seventh International Conference on Information Systems, Dublin.

Sebastian, I. M., Ross, J. W., Beath, C., Mocker, M., Moloney, K. G., & Fonstad, N. O. (2017). How Big Old Companies Navigate Digital Transformation. *MIS Quarterly Executive*, *16*(3), 197–213.

Söderlund, J. (2011). *Theoretical Foundations of Project Management*. Oxford University Press. https://doi.org/10.1093/oxfordhb/9780199563142.003.0003

Tessem, B., & Iden, J. (2008). Cooperation between developers and operations in software engineering projects (pp. 105–108). ACM Press. https://doi.org/10.1145/1370114.1370141

Tsanos, C. S., Zografos, K. G., & Harrison, A. (2014). Developing a conceptual model for examining the supply chain relationships between behavioural antecedents of collaboration, integration and performance. *The International Journal of Logistics Management*, *25*(3), 418–462. https://doi.org/10.1108/IJLM-02-2012-0005

Verschuren, P., & Doorewaard, H. (2010). *Designing a Research Project* (2nd edition). Eleven International Publishing.

Wettinger, J., Breitenbücher, U., Falkenthal, M., & Leymann, F. (2017). Collaborative gathering and continuous delivery of DevOps solutions through repositories. *Computer Science - Research and Development*, *32*(3–4), 281–290. https://doi.org/10.1007/s00450-016-0338-z

Wiedemann, A. (2018). IT Governance Mechanisms for DevOps Teams - How Incumbent Companies Achieve Competitive Advantages. Presented at the Hawaii International Conference on System Sciences. https://doi.org/10.24251/HICSS.2018.617

Yin, R. K. (2012). *Applications of case study research* (3rd ed). Thousand Oaks, Calif: SAGE.

Yoon, C., Lee, K., Yoon, B., & Toulan, O. (2017). Typology and Success Factors of Collaboration for Sustainable Growth in the IT Service Industry. *Sustainability*, *9*(11), 2017. https://doi.org/10.3390/su9112017

DEVELOPING FORMATIVE EVALUATION FOR COMPLEX INTERACTION

Chris Roast and Elizabeth Uruchurtu
Department of Computing and Computing & Communication Research Centre
Sheffield Hallam University, Sheffield, United Kingdom

ABSTRACT

This paper reports on the development, refinement and use of a design instrument for supporting the exploration of interactive tool design. The distinctive focus of the instrument is that it is intended for interactive tools that go beyond the aim of enabling direct interaction. It is intended to tools that by necessity mediate access to rich complex functionality. We argue that the majority of evaluative instruments that HCI designers have at-hand are not particularly useful in this context. We proposed that alternative concepts are of more relevance, specifically the concepts developed in the Cognitive Dimensions Framework. We have developed an instrument to enable and support the critical assessment of alternative complex interaction designs that is motivated by these concepts. Having described the origins of the tool, the paper then describes how it has been applied in three real world design and development settings. The paper concludes with reflections upon how best to refine, encapsulate and further improve the instrument.

KEYWORDS

Interaction Design, Ease of Use, Evaluation, Cognitive Dimension

1. INTRODUCTION

Approaches to evaluating interactive systems are wide and varied and can be broadly judged in terms of the value of their outputs and the effort required in obtaining such an output. Hence, the continued popularity of discount usability techniques, as first proposed by Nielsen (1994), where evaluation outputs can be easily managed, and the skills required perform evaluation are easily developed. Other more design led approaches have also gain credibility, as discussed in McCarthy and Wright (2004) where evaluation is an integrated element of a continuous collaborative process. Despite the success of these user experience and usability focused approaches they are limited in their domain of application. They are commonly applied in context where the functionality accessed is of a relatively limited scope, when compared with the functional power offered by information systems in general.

The technique described in this paper is formative and lightweight in character, and specifically developed to address the usability of a class of interactive system that are intrinsically challenging for users. The challenge arises when users are given access to a wealth of functionalities that imply a range of task beyond those that any individual user is likely to have. In general, the functionality and features of a system are a product of user needs that have informed it, and what can easily designed and developed. Hence the overall functional may not always match what is explicitly needed.

An over simplified example would be a user need to see a say select a file within a group, and also a user need to see a file's details. Faced with these two, a solution may fulfil both and also both in combination (selecting and showing the file details at the same time). Technically offering both is relatively simple their combination may never have been validated with users. A more substantive illustration would be a contemporary WYSIWYG word processor – its functionality may be relatively easily scoped by different contexts of use. However, the impact of complexity can be illustrated when we consider the provision of user defined macro facility in a word processor. According to good design practice, such a feature would be a response to a user need. However, it is unlikely that a user need will have defined the macro language with the level of detail that the feature requires. It is more than likely that the extent of the marco language, its concepts and its control features will be been developed with limited consideration of specific user needs. When treated as whole, the needs that could be fulfilled by the language exceed those ever evidenced. Evaluating the word processor's support for user tasks, becomes impractical when the macro facility is considered: (i) the scope of user tasks working with macros would be difficult to establish, and (ii) in general user performance would be influenced dynamically by which ever macros are already defined.

Hence, the challenge of evaluating complex interaction is one of having to assess the quality of interaction when the functionality offered is beyond that established through the principle of good user centred design. In this context the Cognitive Dimensions Framework is of value since it is a framework designed to examine human factors associated with human tasks such as programming and thus the tools and environments designed to enable programming. The factors focused upon by the framework are evident but rarely addressed by traditionally in user interface design (Green, 1989 and Blackwell et al, 2001). The framework captures features of complex interaction by characterizing recurring features of interaction when it is unrealistic to define a set of realistic user tasks. Although the dimensions, as such, do not offer an objective means of measuring or assessing the quality of interactive behaviours, they do indicate how common issues are inter-related and have been addressed in other systems. Blackwell (2006) summarizes the range of contexts in which the framework has been used. (For concrete cases, the series psychology of programming workshops (see PPIG n.d.) provide many examples.)

Because of the higher-level perspective adopted by the Cognitive Dimensions, they are designed to be applicable across levels and systems, such as: they are presented in a concise and accessible manner; they are un-biased in the sense of not promoting specific styles of solution. Nine of the dimension concepts are summarized in table 1.

Table 1. A brief summary of some of the dimensions used to motivate the method developed in the paper

Dimension name	Explanation
Abstraction	Ability to introduce new abstractions, degree to which the notation requires abstractions in order to work
Consistency	Internal consistency of notational elements
Error Proneness	Susceptibility of users' to error when using the notation
Hard Mental Operations	Requirement for users to perform complex operations 'in the head'
Premature commitment	Degree to which the notation imposes a particular order of working
Provisionality	Ability to 'sketch' things out
Secondary notations	Ability to make notes to self, add comments
Viscosity	Ease or difficulty of making changes to previous work
Visibility	Ease or difficulty of finding parts of the notation and comparing them

In the rest of this paper we analyze the concept of complex interaction in more detail, along with the rationale for our approach to operationalizing an analysis method motivated by the Cognitive Dimensions Framework. The method developed, termed the tabular approach, is then described. We go on to describe how the approach has been used and refined in three real world case studies. The work concludes with reflections upon how best to ensure the such instruments can be employed effectively and productively in interaction design.

2. COMPLEX INTERACTION AND USABILITY

The concept of complex interaction outlined in the introduction is of interest because of the number of systems, such as enterprise systems, that in principle provide access to extensive functionality and the wide range of users exposed to that functionality. A simple characterisation of complex interaction is when the functional space that the designer makes available to users is sufficiently broad that the designer resorts to offering the users intermediate (mediating) notations for controlling the functional space. In the introduction, we treated a macro language as such a mediating notation. Alternatively, a configuration panel on a desktop app represents a similar mediating notation. In simple user interfaces, such notations could be viewed as a case of designers wrongly discharging their responsibility by exposing a user to new concepts that are indirectly relevant to their tasks. In general, it would be argued that a good user interface would hide users from that detail.

However, when the functionality supported prevents a coherent and bounded set of user goals to be identified and directly supported, the appropriateness of a mediating notation becomes a reasonable option. Despite best intensions, such notations may never have a corresponding "user need" during design, or "user story" during development. As a consequence, it will be likely that the notation will be novel to a user. This naturally represents a tension for traditional user centred design since the introduction of "un-needed" notations and concepts is presumptive and risks introducing unwarranted complexity.

From a user perspective such intermediate notations demand that they use new concepts beyond that of their primary task (see figure 1). More often than not, an intermediate notation exposes the user to new concepts of controlling information, processes or a computation. In addition, there is the risk of mistakes with such notations having significant unwanted impacts. For instance, in the case of a macro facility, an arbitrary macro is capable of radically altering a document in unintended ways.

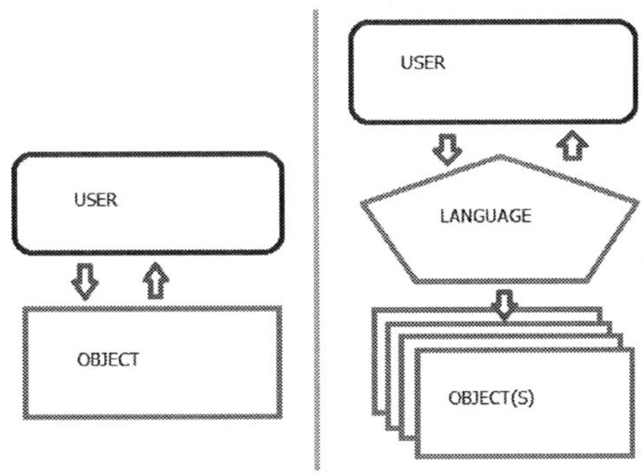

Figure 1. Becoming complex, a conceptual illustration of the impact of moving to a complex interaction view

2.1 Assessing Complex Interaction

Conventional evaluation methods tend to be oriented to user feedback and behavior gathered as a product of conducting realistic tasks that a system is designed to support. For complex interaction this is an unrealistic model since:

- The scale of realistic tasks that the mediating language entertains is extensive. The task space implied by a mediating notation could not be assessed by traditional methods.
- The mediating notation becomes the entity the user manipulates; as such it needs to be a focus for usability evaluation itself along with its constructs, abstractions, etc., it offers.
- With the presence of a mediating notation, knowledge and experience with a notation becomes an important factor.

Together these factors undermine conventional evaluation techniques. By contrast the Cognitive Dimensions Framework has motivated evaluation methods that are in principle are better suited for complex interaction, such as API design (Clarke, 2001) and formal specification notations (Triffitt and Khazaei, 2002). Blackwell (2006) offers one systematic method for employing the framework is assessing an existing system. It involves identifying elements of the system assessing each in terms that relate to the dimensions and then iteratively assessing interactive components of a system. More generally, the frameworks common informal use is predominantly analytic and abductive, helping draw associations between different interaction designs. The popularity of this informal speculative use of the dimensions is to some extent evidenced in a recent review of Cognitive Dimensions research (Hadhrawi, et al. 2017).

3. INSTRUMENT DESIGN

In contrast to traditional methods, our approach was motivated by the desire to encourage the exploration of the different perspectives that the framework encourages and thus provide more formative feedback. Both of these points implicitly promote opportunity for the framework to expose designers and users to new ideas and new perspectives. The governing principles for the instrument design were:

- to maintain the generality and reduce the risk of the approach being considered inapplicable;
- to ensure a lightweight flexible process that can be easily managed and adopted;
- to support formative assessment through a descriptive process capable of encouraging reflection.

Our approach has been led by ensuring that the problem owner frames the context for the evaluation in their own terms. Clearly considering the range of potential settings where complex interaction may become important or evident, an untailored generic framework risks appearing irrelevant. To support this we use framing concepts to contextualise the assessment. The framing concepts are developed in collaboration with the problem owner.

To encourage reflection, and minimize implicit bias, the framing concepts are used to instantiate a number of questions. Permuting the use of the concepts the instantiated questions presents a number of comparable and thought provoking cases. As a toy example, if the evaluative question were, say:

"How easy is it to find the **A** for a specific **B**?"

and the scoping concepts were "time" and "train", both of the following questions should be considered:

"How easy is it to find the time for a specific train?"

and

"How easy is it to find the train for a specific time?"

For convenience these permutations of evaluative questions are presented in a tabular format, this helps convey the simple focus upon exploring and contrasting answers to questions, and thus encourage reflection.

The evaluative questions were derived from a series of questions corresponding to the different dimensions developed in Blackwell and Green (2007) and used in Roast and Khazaei (2006).

By considering permutations of framing concepts, the number of question instances to be presented can grow rapidly. To ensure the approach was lightweight the number of scoping concepts was limited to only three. While this weakens the reach of the evaluation, it does reduce the risk of temporal evaluation bias.

> *Temporal evaluation bias*: when evaluation procedures are sufficiently resource demanding that the consistent performance of activities overtime becomes unrealistic.

Over all there are 21 tabular form questions addressing nine of the cognitive dimensions. Eight of the questions are 'binary' in style (concerning the inter-relationship between framing concepts) as illustrated in figure 2. Notice that the framing concepts are indicated by placeholders A, B and C. The other main type of question is 'unary' in the sense that they do not concern the explicit relationship between framing concepts but they do implicitly encourage comparative assessment of some concept, illustrated in figure 3. In this case the same concept placeholders A, B and C are used, but there is the opportunity to consider them singularly or as collections. The other four questions are general and cannot be easily associated with the framing concepts. One example of such as question is: "What's the best way of preparing to use the tool?". We summarise the range of questions, their tabular form and associated dimensions in table 2.

The current form of the tabular assessment framework is publicly available Roast and Uruchurtu (2019).

What are the dominant / common ways in which these concepts are shown together or reached from one another?

to / from	A	B	C
A			
B			
C			

Figure 2. A generic tabular question to examine how easy it is for the user to navigate (Corresponding to "Visibility" in the Cognitive Dimensions Framework)

Indicate the relative ease of changing or editing instances?

A(s)	B(s)	C(s)

Figure 3. A unary generic tabular question to examine ease of change (Corresponding to "Viscosity" in the Cognitive Dimensions Framework)

Table 2. A collation of the Cognitive Dimension based questions and their question types

Dimension name	Single questions	Unary questions	Binary questions
Abstraction	-	2	2
Consistency	-	2	-
Error Proneness	1	-	-
Hard Mental Operations	2	1	1
Premature commitment	1	-	2
Provisionality	-	2	-
Secondary notations	-	1	-
Viscosity	-	1	1
Visibility	-	-	2

4. USE AND REFINEMENT

Here we summarize the uses of the approach and its refinement using three real world case studies

4.1 A Rule Based System for Media Production Management

The initial application of the tabular approach was in a software development company working in digital media management. They were developing a media production management tool to reduce the effort and errors encountered with the bespoke crafting of media assets for when they are localized for individual languages and regions. When performing localization, assets (such as posters, blu-ray box covers, blu-ray menus, etc.) are re-designed to reflect regional requirements and sensitivities. Hand crafting such re-designs is time consuming and requires extensive quality control. The tool developed by our collaborator focused upon improving the efficiency of this process by allowing layout rules to be defined, so from one original, localized versions could be generated in a consistent and approved form. For example, a rule might be to scale a film title to fit the space available on a poster, if its translation lengthens it. The rule based approach was similar in capability that of web technology style sheets (CSS), but presented and manipulating through a GUI interface.

Despite the power and promise of the tool, the principle challenge for users was that the rules constituted a new intermediate notation. In keeping with our notion of complex interaction, the rules distanced users from their traditional design domain.

A comparative assessment of the rule base tool was conducted contrasting two versions of it. The versions differed in terms of how rules were presented: *version A* was asset oriented showing the rules that influenced asset components when they were selected; and *version B* presented all the rules highlighting those influencing any selected asset component.

In keeping with our proposed tabular approach, we initially established framing concepts. Following interviews with users and stakeholders, we settled upon: "asset components", "styling rules" and "target language". Using these, the tabular form was used with developers and product owners within the company to contrast the two versions.

The outcomes highlighted the core importance of rules and issues focused around: the differentiation between rules; the abstract level of rules; and, the inability to annotate rules with their intended purpose. Overall the outcomes identified version B as being more fit for purpose.

Post engagement reflection on the use and appropriateness of the tabular form was conducted with academic peers. The tractability of the tool as a means of gaining coverage of a number of views of potential usability issues was seen as a benefit. However, the limit of three scoping concepts clearly biased stakeholder engagement. Despite that it was noted that the framing concepts limited scale of the activity although respondents used the concepts flexibly.

4.2 Authentication Monitoring and Management

A second case study employing the tabular form concerned a tool for the monitoring of online resource authentication within higher education. The context was one of overseeing and analysing the numerous differing online library subscription services. By way of illustration, a library manager may wish to identify whether, say, computing students use the ACM Digital library (www.acm.org/dl) on a comparable basis to IEEE Explore (ieeexplore.ieee.org), or whether Sciencedirect (www.sciencedirect.com/) is used in preference to both. Since such services are individually paid for analyzing their use and value is important for financial planning and management.

The complexity of such monitoring arises from: the different service subscription models used, the different authentication protocols used by them, and interpreting the data in terms value for money. The tool evaluated, called RAPTOR, was designed to support such monitoring activity by integrating authentication service logs, providing aggregate views of accesses over time.

The decision to employ the tabular approach in assessing this tool came from a cursory review of RAPTOR. One of the main functionalities on offer was the ability build a search specification, using a number of given types-of-search. Within each search-type parameters could be set by the user, such as: authentication-type; the date range; filters and data presentations.

Based on discussions with the tool developers and prospective users, tailored searches were judged to in effect be a novel intermediary notation demanding a significant change of perspective if they were to be used effectively by intended end users.

The tabular form approach was adopted to analyse and evaluate the tool's user interface collaboratively with a group of intended end users. As with the previous case study, scoping concepts were established through initial discussions and then used to instantiate questions to lead subsequent discussions. The relative novelty of the tool for the end users resulted in the scoping concepts being more domain based than tool based. In this case: "search specification", "data set" and "publisher service" were the chosen concepts.

Limited experience with the tool meant that the mode of discussion was often more about the users' needs than the appropriateness of specific tool functionality. The outcomes were collated reported to the developers. A number of issues were sufficiently specific to be recorded in an issue tracking system. Over the subsequent months many of issues raised were addressed by the development team.

Reflection upon the use of the tabular form in this case study focused upon how it could be used more effectively when engaging end users. An intrinsic feature of complex interaction is that end users may lack confidence and familiarity with complexities that are the motivation for this type of evaluation. Compared with the initial case study the outcomes were closer to user requirements, than formative design improvements. This insight was used to help inform how best to prepared and engage different types of evaluators when using the tabular form.

4.3 Data Replication Management

The final case study concerns the design and configuration of a comprehensive distributed big data replication and management service. The commercial service is founded on unique intellectual property for governing replication management and is highly integrated with existing data and cloud computing services, such as AWS, Hadoop, Azure, Google Cloud, etc..

The company was aware of issues that customer encountered during installation and management of their product. Despite the technical context of the product, technical staff tasked with installing and managing the service still required significant support. Specifically, the company's customers generally worked in sectors where service interruptions could have significant financial implications.

Based on our experience with previous case studies the prospect of conducting an evaluation was judged to be appropriate for the tabular approach due to the domain's complexity. The configuration and operation of the data replication is reliant upon integrating and linking numerous services to data nodes, and specifying the replication rules across groups of nodes for different data and differing geographic jurisdictions.

In contrast to the previous case studies, groups of staff teams including designers, developers and customer staff were encouraged to engage by the company. This resulted in three half-day workshops with largely different cross disciplinary groups. Groups involved between eight and ten people. To support this more collective use of the instrument, the workshops were planned to involve: individual introductions; an introduction user centred evaluation concepts, and; then using the tabular form. With each workshop framing concepts were established collaboratively and thus they differed between each workshop.

Analysis and reporting was a challenge simply because the authors were insufficiently familiar with the product and related services. As the participants were highly familiar with the product, the tabular form questions frequently led to discussions of product history and detailed aspects of its functionality. Within this context participants were encouraged to record their findings and observations. The company has reported that a number of innovations from the workshop have been recorded for inclusion in future versions of the product.

As a workshop the analysis and evaluation activity was less focused and demanded additional effort to keep participants focused and "on board". The relatively open format of the tabular approach needed to be more structured and supportive of participants. This led to consideration of pre-tailoring the instrument in future uses so as to prioritize the questions likely to be more productive.

5. CONCLUSIONS

The evaluation approach discussed in this paper is a lightweight reflective method motivated by concepts taken from the Cognitive Dimensions Framework. We have motivated the specific approach and described its development. It use in a three case studies of design that vary in nature and character has been described and the lessons learnt summarized. Overall the experience with the tabular method has informed our way of working with it in different context - the general tabular form has not varied.

Future work with the instrument will include more accurately documenting ways of working with it and, more significantly, attempting to develop a means of pre-assessing an evaluation context in order to prioritize specific evaluative questions from the instrument.

ACKNOWLEDGEMENT

This work was partially supported by the Technology Strategy Board, JISC and European Regional Development Funds. We are indebted to the organizations involved and their staff for their cooperation.

REFERENCES

Blackwell, A.F., Britton, C., Cox, A. Green, T.R.G., Gurr, C.A., Kadoda, G.F., Kutar, M., Loomes, M., Nehaniv, C.L., Petre, M., Roast, C., Roes, C., Wong, A. and Young, R.M. (2001). Cognitive Dimensions of Notations: Design tools for cognitive technology. In M. Beynon, C.L. Nehaniv, and K. Dautenhahn (Eds.) Cognitive Technology 2001 (LNAI 2117). Springer-Verlag, pp. 325-341.

Blackwell, A.F. (2006). Ten years of cognitive dimensions in visual languages and computing. Journal of Visual Languages and Computing, 17(4), 285-287.

Blackwell, A.F. & Green, T.R.G. (2000). A Cognitive Dimensions Questionnaire optimised for users. In A.F. Blackwell & E. Bilotta (Eds.) Proceedings of the Twelth Annual Meeting of the Psychology of Programming Interest Group, 137-152.

Blandford, A.E., Green, T.R.G. and Connell, I.W. (2004). Formalising an Understanding of User-system Misfits. Proceedings of EHCI-DSVIS 2004, the 9th IFIP Working Conference on Engineering for Human-Computer Interaction (Jointly with the 11th International Workshop on Design, A and Verification of Interactive Systems), Hamburg, 11-13 July 2004.

Blackwell A. and Green, T. (2007) A Cognitive Dimensions Questionnaire. https://www.cl.cam.ac.uk/~afb21/CognitiveDimensions/CDquestionnaire.pdf. Accessed Jan 2019.

Clarke, S. (2001). Evaluating a new programming language. In G. Kadoda (Ed.) Proceedings of the Thirteenth Annual Meeting of the Psychology of Programming Interest Group, 275-289.

Green, T. R. G. (1989). Cognitive dimensions of notations. In People and Computers V, A Sutcliffe and L Macaulay (Ed.) Cambridge University Press: Cambridge., pp. 443-460.

Mohammad Hadhrawi, Alan F. Blackwell, Luke Church (2017) A Systematic Literature Review of Cognitive Dimensions. PPIG 2017: 3 (see PPIG).

McCarthy, J. and Wright, P. (2004) Technology as Experience, The MIT Press, ISBN: 9780262633550

Nielsen, J. 1994. Usability inspection methods. In Conference Companion on Human Factors in Computing Systems (CHI '94), Catherine Plaisant (Ed.). ACM, New York, NY, USA, 413-414. DOI: https://doi.org/10.1145/259963.260531

PPIG The Psychology of Programming Interest Group. Workshop archive: http://www.ppig.org/ (Last accessed: December 2018).

Roast, C. and Khazaei, B., (2006) An Investigation into the validation of formalised Cognitive Dimensions. Design, Specification and Verification of Interactive Systems (DSVIS), Springer Verlag.

Roast, C. and Uruchurtu, E. (2019). A tool for the mediated exploration of complex digital interaction design. SHU Research Data Archive (SHURDA). http://doi.org/10.17032/shu-180010.

Triffitt, E. and Khazaei, B. (2002). A Study of Usability of Z Formalism Based on Cognitive Dimensions. In J. Kuljis, L. Baldwin and R. Scoble (Eds), Proceedings of the Fourteenth Annual Meeting of the Psychology of Programming Interest Group, pp. 15-28.

ADOPTION FACTORS OF HEALTH MONITORING SYSTEMS FOR SMART HEALTHCARE: A SYSTEMATIC REVIEW

Halil Cicibas and Sevgi Ozkan Yıldırım[1]
Department of Information Systems
Middle East Technical University, Ankara, Turkey
[1]Prof.

ABSTRACT

Although there have been several studies that focus on technical aspects of health monitoring systems, adoption of these systems remains largely unknown. A limited number of researches has explored the factors influencing users' adoption of these systems that provide successful system implementation. In this study, we reviewed articles addresses the adoption of health monitoring systems. We extract criteria that influence the adoption decision that has been made at some stage to use health monitoring systems. Then group these criteria into nine categories in terms of cost, ease of use, environment, knowledge, management, security, social influence, subjective norm, technical, usefulness, and enjoyment. By using these criteria, we develop an adoption model for health monitoring systems.

KEYWORDS

Health Monitoring Systems, Smart Health, Technology Acceptance

1. INTRODUCTION

By the technological advances; "smart healthcare" has become a commonly used term in the healthcare domain. Internet of Things, Cloud Computing, Artificial Intelligence, Big Data, and High-Speed Networking are some of the enabling technologies of the smart healthcare concept. Recent advances in these technologies facilitate developing of new health monitoring systems which areas which are the main application areas in smart healthcare concept.

Health monitoring system can be explained by the devices that sense, collect and process the health status of the users and send it to health professionals and central systems for taking preventive actions and making an advanced analysis. These devices can be wearable, mountable or implantable. In the literature, some of the products designed for non-health purposes can be also used as health monitoring systems, since they can deliver healthcare services with the help of their sensing and networking capability. These technologies can be listed as wellness technologies (Misra et al., 2015), smart home applications (Townsend, Knoefel and Goubran, 2011), smart wristbands (Nelson, Verhagen and Noordzij, 2016), robots (Dagioglou et al., 2014).

While health monitoring systems are being deployed in hospitals, houses, and workplace; adoption of these technologies should be addressed for effective use of these systems. All stakeholders in terms of physicians, nurses, technicians, managers, and patients should adopt these systems to leverage the benefits of them. Previous studies show that slow adoption rates of potential users may lead to operation and project failures in healthcare while high adoption rates increase the accuracy and usefulness of health data. Therefore, studies that examine the influencing factors on the adoption of health monitoring systems are needed. In "healthcare information systems" perspective, we found some review studies that synthesize and interpret influencing factors on the adoption of health information systems. However, we are not able to find any systematic review that analyzes and summarize influencing factors more specifically in "health monitoring systems" area.

The purpose of our study is; 1) to review facilitators and barriers to the adoption of health monitoring systems, 2) investigate if there is a trend in the occurrence of the adoption criteria 3) identify most and least addressed adoption criteria among others 4) categorize adoption criteria.

To achieve this aim, we surveyed articles that focus on adoption of health monitoring systems and summarized the criteria addressed in these studies. In our study, we extract criteria mentioned in these studies and classify the criteria into nine categories in terms of cost, ease of use, environment, knowledge, management, security, social influence, subjective norm, technical, usefulness, and enjoyment. We also propose an adoption map that can help to understand the impact of criteria on behavioral intention and usage behavior.

We believe that our findings will show state-of-art of the adoption criteria in health monitoring systems area which is one of the main applications of smart healthcare. Furthermore, this review may help decision makers and academic researchers, working on “smart healthcare”, “digital transformation in health monitoring” or “acceptance of patient monitoring systems” fields, to prioritize levels of effort.

2. ADOPTION CRITERIA OF HEALTH MONITORING SYSTEMS

2.1 Adoption Criteria Listed in the Reviewed Studies

We found 135 criteria in our literature survey. We found that some criteria address the same concepts although they are defined by different terms. Therefore, we applied a refining procedure to eliminate this repetition regarding similarity and simplicity. In similarity perspective; terms that address similar meaning, are converged to a generic term while maintaining their meanings. In simplicity perspective; adjectives are removed from the terms. After the refining process, the number of criteria is decreased to 74. Refined criteria are listed in Table 1.

Table 1. Adoption Criteria of Health Monitoring Systems

Refined Criteria	Reference
Post-adoption efforts, technical knowledge, common vision, leadership, organizational support, project management, technical knowledge	Yu, Gandhidasan and Miller, 2010
Social influence, usefulness, ease of use, time-saving	Giger et al., 2015
Security, personal attitude, social influence, usefulness, ease of use, behavioral control	Ermakova *et al.*, 2015
Device performance, ease of use, reliability, confidentiality, economic feasibility	Holekamp, 2017
Technical knowledge, awareness, need, social influence, ease of use, age, gender	Ziefle, Röcker, and Holzinger, 2011
Cost, life quality, ease of use, performance expectancy, social influence	Alaiad and Zhou, 2015
Confidentiality, facilitating conditions, ease of use, performance expectancy	Patrick Ndayizigamiye, 2016
Authentication, user fatigue, cybersecurity, privacy, simplicity, gamification	Bae *et al.*, 2017
Ease of use, usefulness, reliability	Su, Tsai and Chen, 2012
Technical complexity, privacy, relative advantage, compatibility, data quality, interactivity	Jing, 2016
Initial costs, maintenance costs, return on investment, privacy, technical knowledge	Wallace *et al.*, 2017
Human interaction	Dagioglou et al., 2014
Technical knowledge, privacy, trust	Dhukaram et al., 2011
Social influence, technical capability, manuals, privacy, ease of use, gender, technical knowledge	Schaar and Ziefle, 2011
Design, data interpretation	Korhonen, Mattila and Vam Gils, 2010

Compatibility, self-efficiency, technical support, technical knowledge, usefulness, ease of use	Su and Gururajan, 2010
Confidentiality, authentication, integrity, access control, security	Acharya, 2010
Privacy, autonomy	Townsend, Knoefel and Goubran, 2011
Integration to daily life, privacy, design	Young Mi Choi et al., 2013
Usefulness, interoperability	Jimenez-Fernandez, De Toledo and Del Pozo, 2013
Legality, organizational support, trust, return on investment, security, safety, improved medical process, real-time data access, time-saving, cost-saving, medical support, resource utilization	Yao, Chu and Li, 2010
Battery life, physical design, technical capability, configurability, data analysis, cost saving, improved medical process, resource utilization	Misra *et al.*, 2015
Technical capability, ease of use, technical knowledge, terminology, security, privacy, interoperability, portability, ownership, motivation	Alyami and Song, 2016
Interference, effectiveness, standardization, cost, privacy	Yao, Chu and Li, 2010
Motivation, ease of use, performance expectancy, financial risks, technology anxiety, resistance to change, privacy, security	Krishnan, Dhillon and Lutteroth, 2015

2.2 Most Addressed Criteria

Yao, Chu and Li 2010, Alyami and Song 2016, Krishnan, Dhillon and Lutteroth 2015 and Misra et al. 2015 contributed to the greatest number of criteria to the literature. Regarding refined criteria, our analysis showed that most addressed criteria are ease of use, cost, ease of use, environment, knowledge, management, security, social influence, technical, usefulness, and enjoyment. The number of occurrences of these criteria is shown in Table 2.

Table 2. Most addressed Criteria

Criteria	# of Oc.	Criteria	# of Oc.
Ease of use	11	Technical knowledge	5
Privacy	10	Usefulness	5
Security	5	Training	4

2.3 Barriers and Facilitators

Criteria, presented in Table 1, influence the adoption of health monitoring systems positively or negatively in any stage of usage of these systems. While many of the studies directly classified criteria as "facilitators" or "barriers", some studies identify them by using as "influencing factor" without addressing their impact direction. However, we believe that to understand the impact of criteria on technology adoption, it is required to define them as "facilitator" or "barrier".

We categorize each criterion by using metrics such as "good", "complex", "high", "low" and "positive". Although these metrics are unmeasurable, they indicate the direction of impact. By the assistance of this categorization, we can show the main facilitators and barriers in the adoption of health monitoring systems.

Barriers against the adoption of health monitoring systems are depicted in Table 3, whereas the facilitators are listed in Table 4.

We don't use any metric for age and gender criteria since there are so many conflicted findings of the impact of age and gender in literature. Based on these findings, age and gender can be considered as both facilitator and barrier. We believe that the context and personal characteristics are the main variables that determine the impact of gender and age on technology adoption.

Table 3. Barriers

Metric	Criteria
Complex	Manuals, terminology
High	Cost, financial risks, initial costs, interference, maintenance costs, resistance to change, security, standardization, technical complexity, technology anxiety
Low	Authentication, confidentiality, cybersecurity, effectiveness, legality, organizational support, post-adoption efforts, privacy, return on investment, security, technical capability, technical knowledge, training, trust

Table 4. Facilitators

Metric	Criteria	Metric	Criteria
Good	Data interpretation, Design, Physical design, Project management	High	Access control, authentication, autonomy, awareness, battery life, behavioral control, compatibility, confidentiality, configurability, cost saving, data analysis, data quality, device performance, ease of use, economic feasibility, facilitating conditions, human interaction, improved medical process, integration to daily life, integrity, interactivity, time-saving, training, interoperability, leadership, life quality, medical support, motivation, need, organizational support, ownership, performance expectancy, portability, real-time data access, relative advantage, reliability, resource utilization, safety, security, self-efficiency, simplicity, technical capability, technical knowledge, technical support, usefulness
Positive	Common vision, Personal attitude, Social influence		
Without Metric	Gamification		

2.4 Grouping of Criteria

To facilitate understanding of the influencing factors; we grouped adoption criteria under nine categories based on their similarity. These groups are cost, ease of use, environment, knowledge, management, security, social influence, subjective norm, technical, usefulness, and enjoyment. We believe that the level of abstraction and segmentation is balanced by using such a grouping methodology. Detailed information about the groups are described as follows:

Cost: It includes the factors related to expenditure during owning, delivering and maintaining the system and savings after installation. In our study, economic feasibility, cost expectancy, perceived financial risk, return on investment, cost saving, initial costs, maintenance costs are grouped under "cost" construct group. Factors listed under the "cost" group are addressed 10 times (mentioned %7 of the time) in the reviewed studies.

Ease of use: It includes the factors that make use of the required features of a system with less effort. In our study; perceived ease of use, simplicity, complexity, terminology, portability, integration to daily life, design, manuals, human interaction are grouped under "ease of use". Factors listed under the "cost" group are addressed 20 times (mentioned %15 of the time) in the reviewed studies.

Environment: In our study, facilitating conditions and legality are grouped under "environment". Members of the group are listed only 2 times (mentioned less than %2 of the time) in the reviewed studies.

Knowledge: Knowledge refers to the information and skills of a user which are acquired through experience or education. In our study; training, awareness, and vision are listed in this group. Members of the group are listed 10 times (mentioned %7 of the time) in the reviewed studies.

Management: It can be related to organizational efforts, attitudes of the managers or the initiatives of decision-makers in an organization. In our study; post-adoption efforts, leadership, organizational support, project management, ownership, and technical support are grouped under "management". Members of the group are listed 8 times (mentioned %6 of the time) in the reviewed studies.

Security: Factors that can raise security concerns in users and managers are group under this category. Theft of user records, cyber-attacks, authentication qualifications of the system or any threat that make the system unfunctional may be the reasons for these concerns. In our study; privacy, confidentiality, authentication, legality, safety, cybersecurity criteria are grouped under "security". Members of the group are listed 22 times (mentioned %16 of the time) in the reviewed studies.

Social Influence: Views, attitudes, and behaviors of the individuals in the neighborhood on the use of system have impacts on system users. Therefore, any factor that may be the source of this impact is classified under "Social Influence" group. Common vision, word of mouth, social contacts, social pressure are grouped under "social influence". Members of the group are listed 6 times (mentioned less than %5 of the time) in the reviewed studies.

Subjective Norm: Factors mentioned in this group are related to the characteristics, values, knowledge level and other personal features of a user. Lack of vision, training, attitude, norms, interest, awareness, age, gender, motivation, technology anxiety, resistance to change, digital skills, expertise, and technical knowledge are grouped under "subjective norms". Members of the group are listed 22 times (mentioned %16 of the time) in the reviewed studies.

Technical: Most of the criteria listed in the reviewed articles belong to the technical group. Performance, reliability, simplicity, technical complexity, compatibility, data quality, interactivity, interference, effectiveness, standardization, trust, real-time data access, battery life, design, technical capability, configurability, data analysis, capability, terminology, interoperability, portability, autonomy, integration to daily life, manuals, authentication, integrity, access control, data interpretation and human interaction level are grouped under "technical". Members of the group are listed 37 times (mentioned more than %27 of the time) in the reviewed studies.

Usefulness: Perceived usefulness, time-saving, need for medical operations, life quality expectancy, performance expectancy, improvement of medical operations, resource utilization and usability are grouped under "usefulness". Members of the group are listed 17 times (mentioned %13 of the time) in the reviewed studies.

Enjoyment: Factors mentioned in this group are related to the impacts to which the users deem the technology used as a fun experience regardless of outcome (Davis et al). User fatigue, Gamification and Motivation are listed under "Enjoyment".

The number of occurrence of criteria per group and the percentage of the groups is depicted in Table 5. It is shown that technical, security and personnel are the most addressed groups in literature. Least-mentioned groups are environment and social influence.

Table 5. Number of Occurrence of Criteria Per Group

	2010		2011		2012		2013		2014		2015		2016		2017		Total	
Criteria	# of Oc.	%	# of Oc.	%	# of Oc.	%	# of Oc.	%	# of Oc.	%	# of Oc.	%	# of Oc.	%	# of Oc.	%	# of Oc.	%
Cost	3	8	-	-	-	-	-	-	-	-	3	12	-	-	4	25	10	7
Ease of use	2	5	2	11	-	-	1	20	1	100	-	-	-	-	1	6	7	5
Enjoyment	-	-	-	-	-	-	-	-	-	-	1	4	1	4	2	13	4	3
Environment	1	3	-	-	-	-	-	-	-	-	-	-	1	4	-	-	2	1
Knowledge	3	8	3	16	-	-	-	-	-	-	1	4	3	11	1	6	11	8
Management	6	16	-	-	-	-	-	-	-	-	-	-	1	4	-	-	7	5
Security	8	22	4	21	-	-	1	20	-	-	3	12	4	14	5	31	25	19
Social Influence	-	-	2	11	-	-	-	-	-	-	2	8	1	4	-	-	5	4
Subjective Norm	1	3	4	21	-	-	-	-	-	-	1	4	3	11	-	-	9	7
Technical	6	16	1	5	1	33	1	20	-	-	5	19	8	29	2	13	24	18
Usefulness	7	19	3	16	2	67	2	40	-	-	10	38	6	21	1	6	31	23
Total	37	100	19	100	3	100	5	100	1	100	26	100	28	100	16	100	135	100

2.5 Barriers and Facilitators

It is revealed that most of the barriers shown in Table 3 are related to cost and security issues. The percentage of security-related criteria among barriers is %48, while the percentage of security-related criteria is %16 among all type of criteria. Similarly, the percentage of cost-related criteria among barriers is %19, while the percentage of cost-related criteria is only %7 among are all type of criteria. In addition, none of the criteria listed under the social influence are mentioned as a barrier in the reviewed studies.

It is found that the positive impact of criteria listed under the usefulness and technical is higher than the other groups. In addition, the percentage of the criteria belongs to these groups is %55 among facilitators, while the percentage is %12 among all barriers. Note that, the analysis described in this study may change if the metrics of the criteria would have defined in opposite direction. Our analysis is shown in Table 6.

Table 6. Percentage of Groups as Barrier and Facilitator (* Age and gender are not defined as barrier or facilitator)

	Barrier		Facilitator		Total	
Criteria	#	%	#	%	#	%
Cost	7	17	3	3	10	7
Ease of use	2	5	5	6	7	5
Enjoyment	1	2	3	3	4	3
Environment	1	2	1	1	2	1
Knowledge	4	10	7	8	11	8
Management	1	2	6	7	7	5
Security	20	48	5	6	25	19
Social Influence	-	-	5	6	5	4
Subjective Norm	1	2	5	6	9	7
Technical	4	10	20	22	24	18
Usefulness	1	2	30	33	31	23
Total	42	100	90	100	135	100

3. ADOPTION MAP FOR HEALTH MONITORING SYSTEMS

Based on the criteria mentioned above, we developed an adoption map that presents the potential relations between factors. The adoption map is presented in Figure 1. Although much research has been done on developing technology adoption models such as TAM (Davis, 1989), TAM-2 (Venkatesh and Davis, 2000) and UTAUT (Venkatesh et al., 2003), our adoption map is a conceptual representation of the adoption factors mentioned in surveyed articles addressing health monitoring.

Arrows, depicted in the adoption map, show the potential impacts between factors, behavioral intention, and usage behavior. Arrows are shown as bi-directional since each criterion is a potential influencer of another one. "+" and "-" symbols depicted on the arrows indicate "positive" or "negative" impacts of criteria. Although most of the factors generally influence use behavior indirectly, some of the factors may influence use behavior directly. This relation is shown by the relation between the two "influence" point.

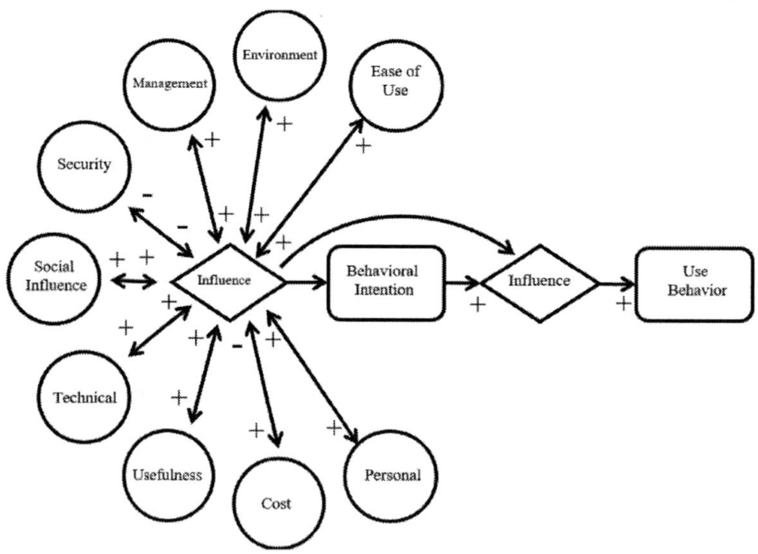

Figure 1. Conceptual Adoption Map for Health Monitoring Systems

4. DISCUSSION AND CONCLUSION

In this study, we reviewed articles that address adoption of health monitoring systems. We extracted criteria from the articles, summarized them as barrier and facilitator and classified them into nine categories. Usefulness, technical and security were found as the most addressed criteria in the articles. On the other hand, environment criteria were found as the least addressed article in our study. It was found that cost is not the main barrier while technical and security-related issues remain as the main factors that influence technology adoption in healthcare information systems, which was also mentioned in (Cicibas and Yildirim, 2018)

In this research, an adoption map is developed for the health monitoring system. We believe that such a map would assist to understand the factors that influence technology acceptance and usage decision. The findings of this study would serve as a guideline for solution developers while understanding the state-of-art of technology acceptance in health monitoring systems.

ACKNOWLEDGMENT

The views and conclusions contained herein are those of the authors and should not be interpreted as necessarily representing the official policies or endorsements, either expressed or implied, of any affiliated organization or government.

REFERENCES

Abreu, C., Ricardo, M. and Mendes, P. M. (2014) 'Energy-aware routing for biomedical wireless sensor networks', Journal of Network and Computer Applications. Elsevier, 40(1), pp. 270–278. doi: 10.1016/j.jnca.2013.09.015.

Acharya, D. (2010) 'Security in pervasive health care networks: Current R&D and future challenges', Proceedings - IEEE International Conference on Mobile Data Management, (figure 1), pp. 305–306. doi: 10.1109/MDM.2010.38.

Alaiad, A. and Zhou, L. (2015) 'Patients' Behavioral Intentions toward Using WSN Based Smart Home Healthcare Systems: An Empirical Investigation', 2015 48th Hawaii International Conference on System Sciences, pp. 824–833. doi: 10.1109/HICSS.2015.104.

Alyami, M. A. and Song, Y.-T. (2016) 'Removing barriers in using personal health record systems', 2016 IEEE/ACIS 15th International Conference on Computer and Information Science (ICIS), pp. 1–8. doi: 10.1109/ICIS.2016.7550810.

Bae, J. et al. (2017) 'CloudConnect: Evaluating the use of precision medicine in treatment of Type 1 Diabetes', 2017 Systems and Information Engineering Design Symposium (SIEDS), pp. 138–143. doi: 10.1109/SIEDS.2017.7937704.

Cicibas H., Yildirim S.Ö. (2018) 'Adoption of Internet of Things in Healthcare Organizations', In: Sezgin E., Yildirim S., Özkan-Yildirim S., Sumuer E. (eds) Current and Emerging mHealth Technologies. Springer, Cham

Dagioglou, M. et al. (2014) 'Human-Robot Interaction Strategies for Unobtrusively Acquiring Health-Related Data', Proceedings of the 4th International Conference on Wireless Mobile Communication and Healthcare - 'Transforming healthcare through innovations in mobile and wireless technologies', pp. 3–6. doi: 10.4108/icst.mobihealth.2014.257363.

Davis, F. D. (1989). 'Perceived usefulness, perceived ease of use, and user acceptance of information technology', MIS Quarterly, 319-340.

Dhukaram, A. V. et al. (2011) 'End-User perception towards pervasive cardiac healthcare services: Benefits, acceptance, adoption, risks, security, privacy and trust', 2011 5th International Conference on Pervasive Computing Technologies for Healthcare (PervasiveHealth) and Workshops, (June), pp. 478–484. doi: 10.4108/icst.pervasivehealth.2011.246116.

Ermakova, T. et al. (2015) 'Antecedents of health information privacy concerns', Procedia Computer Science. Elsevier Masson SAS, 63(Icth), pp. 376–383. doi: 10.1016/j.procs.2015.08.356.

Field, F. T. H. E. (2017) 'Virtual Rehabilitation with Children', (December), pp. 3–5.

Giger, J. T. et al. (2015) 'Remote patient monitoring acceptance trends among older adults residing in a frontier state', Computers in Human Behavior. Elsevier Ltd, 44, pp. 174–182. doi: 10.1016/j.chb.2014.11.044.

Holekamp, N. M. (2017) 'Moving From Clinic to Home: What the Future Holds for Ophthalmic Telemedicine', American Journal of Ophthalmology. Elsevier Inc., pp. 1–8. doi: 10.1016/j.ajo.2017.11.003.

Jimenez-Fernandez, S., De Toledo, P. and Del Pozo, F. (2013) 'Usability and interoperability in wireless sensor networks for patient telemonitoring in chronic disease management', IEEE Transactions on Biomedical Engineering, 60(12), pp. 3331–3339. doi: 10.1109/TBME.2013.2280967.

Jing, F. (2016) 'An empirical study on the features influencing users' adoption towards personal health records system', 2016 13th International Conference on Service Systems and Service Management, ICSSSM 2016. doi: 10.1109/ICSSSM.2016.7538554.

Korhonen, I., Mattila, E. M., and vam Gils, M. (2010) 'Personal health systems - Opportunities and barriers for adoption', 2010 Annual International Conference of the IEEE Engineering in Medicine and Biology, 2010, pp. 5272–5272. doi: 10.1109/IEMBS.2010.5626309.

Krishnan, S. B., Dhillon, J. S. and Lutteroth, C. (2015) 'Factors influencing consumer intention to adopt Consumer Health Informatics applications an empirical study in Malaysia', 2015 IEEE Student Conference on Research and Development (SCOReD), pp. 653–658. doi: 10.1109/SCORED.2015.7449419.

Misra, V. et al. (2015) 'Self-powered wearable sensor platforms for wellness', 2015 International Conference on Compilers, Architecture and Synthesis for Embedded Systems, CASES 2015, p. 187. doi: 10.1109/CASES.2015.7324559.

Mital, M. et al. (2016) 'Adoption of Internet of Things in India: A test of competing models using a structured equation modeling approach', Technological Forecasting and Social Change. Elsevier Inc., pp. 1–8. doi: 10.1016/j.techfore.2017.03.001.

Nelson, E. C., Verhagen, T. and Noordzij, M. L. (2016) 'Health empowerment through activity trackers: An empirical smart wristband study', Computers in Human Behavior, 62, pp. 364–374. doi: 10.1016/j.chb.2016.03.065.

Patrick NDAYIZIGAMIYE;Manoj MAHARAJ (2016) 'Applying Bridges Framework to Investigate Challenges to the Adoption of mHealth in Burundi', IST-Africa 2016 Conference Proceedings, pp. 1–8.

Sezgin, E. and Yıldırım, S. Ö. (2014) 'A Literature Review on Attitudes of Health Professionals towards Health Information Systems: From e-Health to m-Health', Procedia Technology. Elsevier B.V., 16, pp. 1317–1326. doi: 10.1016/j.protcy.2014.10.148.

Shaygan, A. et al. (2017) 'Adoption Criteria Evaluation of Activity Tracking Wristbands for University Students', 2017 Portland International Conference on Management of Engineering and Technology (PICMET), pp. 1–7. doi: 10.23919/PICMET.2017.8125443.

Su, S. P., Tsai, C. H. and Chen, Y. K. (2012) 'Applying the technology acceptance model to explore intention to use telecare system in Taiwan', Proceedings - 13th ACIS International Conference on Software Engineering, Artificial Intelligence, Networking, and Parallel/Distributed Computing, SNPD 2012, pp. 353–356. doi: 10.1109/SNPD.2012.113.

Su, Y. and Gururajan, R. (2010) 'The determinants for adoption of wearable computer systems in traditional Chinese hospital', APWCS 2010 - 2010 Asia-Pacific Conference on Wearable Computing Systems, pp. 375–378. doi: 10.1109/APWCS.2010.102.

Tan, J. et al. (2010) 'Gateway to quality living for the elderly: Charting an innovative approach to evidence-based e-health technologies for serving the chronically ill', Proceedings - 2010 13th IEEE International Conference on Computational Science and Engineering, CSE 2010, pp. 146–159. doi: 10.1109/CSE.2010.27.

Townsend, D., Knoefel, F. and Goubran, R. (2011) 'Privacy versus autonomy: A tradeoff model for smart home monitoring technologies. BT - Proceedings of Engineering in Medicine and Biology Society, EMBC, Annual International Conference of the IEEE';, pp. 4749–4752.

Venkatesh, V., & Davis, F. D. (2000). 'A theoretical extension of the technology acceptance model: Four longitudinal field studies', Management Science, 46(2), 186-204.

Venkatesh, V., Morris, M. G., Davis, G. B., & Davis, F. D. (2003). 'User acceptance of information technology: Toward a unified view', MIS Quarterly, 425-478.

Wallace, E. L. et al. (2017) 'Remote Patient Management for Home Dialysis Patients', Kidney International Reports. Elsevier Inc, 2(6), pp. 1009–1017. doi: 10.1016/j.ekir.2017.07.010.

Yao, W., Chu, C.-H. and Li, Z. (2010) 'The use of RFID in healthcare: Benefits and barriers BT', 2010 IEEE International Conference on RFID-Technology and Applications, RFID-TA 2010, June 17, 2010 - June 19, 2010, (June), pp. 128–134.

Young Mi Choi et al. (2013) 'Potential barriers in adoption of a medication compliance neckwear by elderly population', 2013 35th Annual International Conference of the IEEE Engineering in Medicine and Biology Society (EMBC), pp. 4678–4681. doi: 10.1109/EMBC.2013.6610591.

Yu, P., Gandhidasan, S. and Miller, A. A. (2010) 'Different usage of the same oncology information system in two hospitals in Sydney-Lessons go beyond the initial introduction', International Journal of Medical Informatics. Elsevier Ireland Ltd, 79(6), pp. 422–429. doi: 10.1016/j.ijmedinf.2010.03.003.

Ziefle, M., Röcker, C. and Holzinger, A. (2011) 'Medical technology in smart homes: Exploring the user's perspective on privacy, intimacy and trust', Proceedings - International Computer Software and Applications Conference, pp. 410–415. doi: 10.1109/COMPSACW.2011.75.

GATHERING RESEARCHERS' REQUIREMENTS TO DEVELOP A LEARNING TECHNOLOGIES DASHBOARD

Miguel Alonso Canizares Mena and Pedro Teixeira Isaias
The University of Queensland
St Lucia, Queensland - Australia

ABSTRACT

The learning technologies area has expanded incredibly fast due to the growing and acceptance of technology in the classrooms. As a result, the data produced by students is vast and is growing in each of the learning technologies used, leading to a possibility of discovering patterns that can help to enhance the student experience. However, a clear research regarding the adoption of learning technologies and how to spread this research is limited and almost inexistent. Most of the research revolves around students or teachers disregarding the researcher's standpoint. All the tools and artefacts such as dashboards that have helped to improve both students and teachers' knowledge are absent for researchers. Hence, this paper is aimed on finding and defining the most common learning technologies platforms and tools as well as the user requirements to build a dashboard to display this information considering the researchers' objectives. In this regard, an online survey was created and sent to both researchers interested in the learning technology area and learning technologies designers. The responses were analysed with quantitative tools such as exploratory factor analysis, analysis of variance, t-tests and graphical means. The results led to the user requirements for developing a dashboard.

KEYWORDS

Learning Technologies, Learning Analytics, Dashboard Design, Quantitative Research

1. INTRODUCTION

The massive consumption of technology is a growing area as new generations are more connected to technology than ever before. Resources, such as laptops and mobile phones, are available to them from an early age (Glenn, 2008). Devices and connectivity are entering every aspect of human life, including education. During the latest boom, technology has brought huge changes to the learning methodology used in classrooms. These changes affect students, teachers, institutions and researchers—almost every actor in the learning environment (Bothma & Cant, 2011). The inclusion of technology has changed the traditional pedagogy used in educational institutions and modified the centre of learning, moving from a teacher-centred classroom to a student-centred classroom (Ariso, 2017).

The tools created specifically for the learning environment to enable active pedagogy methodologies are called 'learning technologies'. These are technologies created to improve, enhance and support the student's learning (Aleven, Beal & Graesser, 2013).

Information and communication technology (ICT), is the technical section of the tools that involves the programming of the software that is going to be used in the classroom. The ICT enables humans to achieve goals that would have been impossible to accomplish before technology (Cerri, 2012). Although the rapid development of technology and internet is one of its great qualities, it also poses one of its great challenges.

The psychological section mainly involves the pedagogy behind the development and use of specific learning technology characteristics, such as student's motivation, enjoyment, engagement, expectations and values (Jackson & McNamara, 2013). One of the major changes to the traditional pedagogy is its transformation from a passive to an active method. This encourages teachers to develop more practical and challenging activities, rather than the traditional lecture format (Paquette, Randall-Schab & Busacca, 2015).

The introduction of learning technologies tools and platforms have increased interest in other research areas, such as learning analytics. Learning analytics have come to the forefront of researchers' focus as these tools are enablers of techniques and are a source of data for future studies.

While the learning analytics tools and frameworks are still evolving, one of the biggest challenges of analytics techniques is how to report the findings. There is more information than ever, which becomes more complex to analyse, leading to the use of more complicated analytics techniques. The raw outcomes can overwhelm a person. To tackle this limitation, visual analytics is used to report statistical outcomes. This provides clean and understandable results that are easy to communicate to stakeholders (Keim et al., 2008). Within the visual analytics framework, one of the leading tools used to report information is the dashboard.

One of the biggest challenges of creating a dashboard is finding the correct requirements of the users and the purpose of the tool (Few, 2007). This is considerably difficult as sometimes not even the final users know exactly what they need and so what they want can be misunderstood. The most useful techniques to tackle this issue are surveys and interviews (Bethlehem, 2009). Even once the requirements are established, there is still the design of the dashboard that must be considered. The presentation of the dashboard is important as it can amplify human cognition, performance and support (Card, Mackinlay & Shneiderman, 1999).

As stated previously, the learning technologies and analytics fields are new, being active for less than a decade. Additionally, research so far is spread around the world with no commonality. Although some papers have begun to analyse and compile previous research to present the path that the area is taking, there is still a lack of tools to share this information with the wider research community. Papers such as those by Schwendimann et al. (2017) and Verbert, Duval, Klerkx, Govaerts and Santos (2013) have marked the trend to present the results and the current state of the research. Consequently, there is a need among learning technologies researchers to receive current updates on the state of the research to provide them with the opportunity to drill down in the information and find what has been done and how it can be implemented.

This paper outlines the process of finding research on the current state of learning technologies and dashboard design. The literature review was used to determine what the most important learning technologies around the world are and which platforms are the most popular.

2. LITERATURE REVIEW

2.1 Learning Technologies

Learning technologies are defined as technologies that support and improve teaching and/or learning that may include virtual platforms or learning environments (Kumar & Daniel, 2016; Sife, Lwoga & Sanga, 2007). Learning technologies is broad and can include hardware, software and online applications. The inclusion of technology in classrooms has increased in the last decade for two main reasons: positive learning outcomes and low cost. Research has demonstrated that the use of learning technologies can increase the quality of learning and the student experience (Karasavvidis & Kollias, 2014) and the ease of access to powerful computational devices at the cheapest price (Zoya & Valeriy, 2016). According to Drent and Meelissen (2008), students can benefit from learning technologies in developing skills such as collaboration, communication and problem-solving. Teachers can improve their pedagogy, resulting in a better quality of teaching (Levin & Wadmany, 2008; Mends-Brew, 2012). The newest devices are becoming smaller and more powerful, leading to a tendency that has mobility and reachability as main characteristics (BenMoussa, 2003; Camponovo & Pigneur, 2003; Ng-Kruelle, Swatman, Rebne & Hampe, 2002). This has resulted in efficiency and effectivity in teaching and learning (Maginnis, White & Mckenna, 2000). All of the characteristics of learning technologies have led to its rapid development (Fernández-Ferrer & Cano, 2016). As such, there is disorganisation as a consequence of learning technologies being created by different sources. Some literature has defined the different tools available within the learning technologies framework: learning management systems, mobile learning tools, social networks, video conferencing, collaboration tools, gamification tools, active-learning tools, virtual augmented reality platforms and MOOCs (Bothma & Cant, 2011; Harley, Lajoie, Frasson & Hall, 2017; Kasapoglu-Akyol, 2010).

2.2 Dashboard Design

A dashboard is defined as a visual interface that provides critical information in the form of visualisations for stakeholders (Wolf, 2016). It can also be added that the information provided must be in real-time (Wexler, Shaffer & Cotgreave, 2017). The idea of a dashboard is to simplify critical information into a single screen, providing an overview of the data (Key et al., 2012). There are researchers who argue that a dashboard leaves out important data in its objective to simplify the information. Opponents to dashboard argue that simplifying the information leads to problems such as misaligned, incorrect and imposed indicators (Allio, 2012). The premise of the opponents is that 'complex scenarios cannot be simplified into few indicators' (Allio, 2012). Supporters of dashboard argue that providing few critical indicators in a clear and concise form results in an increase in the human cognition and processing of information (Card et al., 1999). This is supported by several human cognition studies that demonstrate that a visual material is easier for the human brain to process (Ware, 2004) due to its inherent analytical and intuitive qualities (Patterson, Pierce, Bell, Andrews & Winterbottom, 2009). The human brain is skilled in perceiving patterns, the relationship between different domains, deduction and logical conclusions and storing information in the long-term section of the brain (Patterson et al., 2014). According to Patterson, Pierce, Bell and Klein (2010), the combination of these characteristics leads to better decision-making due to the robust activities performed by the human brain while processing this information. To create effective visualisations, the human cognition literature recommends focusing on a three-stage hierarchical framework (Ware, 2004). The first stage is a lower stage that processes basic elements of the visualisation, such as shape, colour and texture. The second stage is a middle stage that processes complex information within objects such as patterns and motion. The third stage is a higher stage that processes relations between the objects (Patterson et al., 2014). To create effective visuals to be included later in dashboards, guidelines have been created by some researchers (Fisher, Green & Arias-Hernandez, 2011; Thomas & Cook, 2006). According to Patterson et al. (2014), six leverage points can be defined that will increase the efficiency of visualisations; the first three are regarding the lower and middle-stage processes in which information about the object is processed. The final three considers the relationships of the objects or decision-making.

3. MODEL AND HIPOTHESIS

The research method selected to develop this thesis is conceptual design science research (CDSR) due to the limitation of the empirical testing of the artefact created. This research method was described by Gleasure (2014) as the foundation for research that develops an artefact based on theory or user requirements.

Gleasure (2014) proposes the following guidelines for developing CDSR.

First, the behavioural outcomes of the design must be identified. The behavioural outcomes will act as meta-requirements for guiding the design. The purpose of meta-requirements is to provide a broad specification in terms of scale and scope of the user's needs (Ceccarelli, Mori, Lollini & Bondavalli, 2015).

Second, the existing artefacts with a similar set of behavioural outcomes must be identified. The platforms were identified using the paper by Schwendimann et al. (2017). In this paper, the platforms that were selected were those in which the target users included researchers.

Third, the key differentiating design features must be analysed in each artefact. The main differences that were found were the platform used to provide access to the artefacts, the tools used to develop the artefacts in specific data collection and the grouping and interactivity of the visualisations. Table 1 provides a clear picture of the relationship between the behavioural outcomes and the design features.

Table 1. Matrix Relationship

Existing Artefacts	Data Integration	Visualizations Grouping	Data Processing	Access	Data Collection	Visualizations Interactivity
EngAGe	High	High	High	**Web**	APIs	Medium
TFM	Medium	Medium	High	Web	APIs	Low
moocRP	Low	Low	Medium	App	**Manual**	High
eMUSE	High	Medium	Medium	Web	APIs	**Low**
SCALE	Medium	Low	High	Web	APIs	Low

4. METHODOLOGY

To build an effective information system, it is essential to find the correct user requirements (Nuseibeh & Easterbrook, 2000). Although the requirements are usually focused on the user, other factors—such as the technical, cultural and social environments—must be considered to develop an information system (Sawyer & Kotonya, 2001). While these factors must be studied, only the user requirements involve a human factor. Thus, these are the ones that require deeper research. Sommerville (2007) found three main difficulties while working with humans: users usually do not know exactly what they need, the language they use to describe the requirements is often too related to the domain and different users may have different requirements. To tackle these limitations, this paper designed a questionnaire that comprehensively analysed the literature in the learning technologies area along with existing surveys that found the popularity of each platform in the education industry that might be of interest for researchers. Table 2 describes the principal learning technologies and platforms discovered in the literature review and its respective popularity (Hart, 2018).

Table 2. Learning Technologies Global Popularity

Group Name	Learning technology	Group Popularity	Global popularity
LMS	Moodle	1	16
	Google classroom	3	54
	Blackboard	4	55
	Edmodo	9	85
Social network platform	YouTube	1	2
	Wikipedia	2	13
	Twitter	3	15
	Facebook	4	17
Video conferencing	Zoom	2	10
	Skype	3	26
	Adobe Connect	4	28
	Google Hangouts	6	50
Collaboration tools	Padlet	1	7
	Slack	2	31
	G Suite	5	40
	Microsoft SharePoint	10	101
Active learning tools	Kahoot!	1	6
	Quizlet	3	23
	Pool Everywhere	4	29
	Socrative	7	56
MOOCs	Coursera	6	101
	edX	8	101
	Udacity	10	101
	Future Learn	11	101
Mobile learning tools	All	N/A	N/A
Gamification tools	All	N/A	N/A
Virtual/augmented reality tools	All	N/A	N/A

Despite the extensive research done to gather information of all the learning technologies specified, a popularity index for technologies such as mobile learning tools, gamification tools, and virtual/augmented reality was not found. Therefore, the selection of the technologies was based only on existing literature.

In order to find the constructs needed for the development of the dashboard, it was taken the design criteria stated by Marx et al (2011). Table 3 shows the constructs and its respective design criteria.

Table 3. Constructs and Questionnaire Design Criteria

Construct	Design Criteria
Learning technologies	Scope of information
Individual platforms in each learning technology	Scope of information
Dashboard visualizations	User interface
Dashboard aggregations	System functions
Dashboard maintenance	Information management

5. DATA COLLECTION

The foundation for this project is a thorough literature review, which will provide the first learning technologies insights. The main characteristics were obtained, in addition to the most frequently used tools in classrooms worldwide. This information was transformed into an online survey following the criteria by Marx et al. (2011), using the platform, Qualtrics, and was sent via email to a testing group composed of eight people. Four participants were related to the information systems field and four were not. The purpose of the testing was to provide insights regarding the construction of the survey, including poorly structured questions or if there was more information required to complete the questionnaire successfully and to consider respondent fatigue. After one week of being deployed, the survey gathering process was stopped and six answers were received, providing the following feedback: most of the participants agreed that more information was required to complete the questionnaire. Terms such as learning technologies and platforms were unknown. The level of fatigue described by participants was described as low. Half of the participants agreed that the instructions or the platform did not provide clear guidance for answering the questions. The default ranking order was not accepted as an answer by the platform. One participant noted that the demographic question about gender should be more inclusive and allow a third option for people who identify as non-binary. Another respondent detected several grammatical errors in some questions and in a set of instructions. To improve the survey and to address the most common issues raised by the group's participants, a website was created on a free platform called 'Wix'. The website contained a description of each learning technology as well as a description of each of the platforms proposed in the survey. The final survey was sent via email and were gathered 109 responses.

6. ANALYSIS AND RESULTS

Questions that were considered the most important in the statistical analysis were chosen due to the low quantity of answers obtained that limited the number of variables that could be analized. The remaining questions were analysed using graphs to show the trends of the answers. The statistical method used was an exploratory factor analysis. This was used because of the absence of models in the learning technologies area, with a focus on researchers. The statistical results given by the exploratory factor analysis were not strong enough to provide a robust fit. Although there were relationships between learning technologies and dashboard design sections that have a high correlation and covariance, the model did not reach the minimum required to be considered significant. As a consequence, an ANOVA (analysis of variance) analysis and t-tests were used to check the relationships between elements within these groups (Law, 2016).

6.1 Analysis of variance: ANOVA

ANOVA is a powerful tool for checking the interaction between variables or factors. ANOVA leads to the decision of whether or not to reject the null hypothesis; that is, if the variable's mean is statistically different. This analysis does not specify what variable is the one that has a statistically different mean (Smalheiser, 2017b). To discover further insights, t-tests must be performed between variables to discover what variables are statistically different. A t-test compares the means between two variables to discover if there is a statistically significant difference (Smalheiser, 2017a). To check the previous relationships found in the exploratory factor analysis, three ANOVAs were performed on the observations.

The first ANOVA addressed the learning technologies variables as, according to the exploratory factor analysis, these variables were grouped into one factor. The analysis resulted in a rejection of the null hypothesis [$F = 119.68 > F_{crit} = 1.88$]. To check what variable or variables have this difference a t-test was performed. The results showed that five pairs of variables were not statistically significant ($p\text{-value} > 0.05$). A p-value, or reference, of 0.05 was used for all the tests as it is a standard used. Table 4 describes what pair of variables were not statistically significant and their p-value.

Table 4. Learning Technologies t-test Results (p-value > 0.05)

Variable 1	Variable 2	P - Values
Mobile learning tools	Collaboration tools	0.630
Mobile learning tools	Active learning tools	0.183
Social networks	Video conferencing tools	0.782
Collaboration tools	Active learning tools	0.225
Gamification tools	MOOCs	0.976
Virtual/augmented reality	MOOCs	0.051

The second ANOVA addresses the types of visualisation variables as, according to the exploratory factor analysis, these variables were grouped into one factor. The analysis resulted in a rejection of the null hypothesis [F = 108.21 > Fcrit = 2.39]. To check which variable or variables have this difference a t-test was performed. The results showed that three pairs of variables were not statistically significant (p-value > 0.05). Table 5 describes what pair of variables were not statistically significant and their p-value.

Table 5. Visualizations Type t-test Results (p-value > 0.05)

Variable 1	Variable 2	P - Values
Line graphs	Pie charts	0.753
Line graphs	Network diagrams	0.903
Pie charts	Network diagrams	0.700

The third ANOVA addresses the aggregations variables as, according to the exploratory factor analysis, these variables were grouped into one factor. The analysis resulted in a rejection of the null hypothesis [F = 195.33 > Fcrit = 2.39]. To check what variable or variables have this difference, a t-test was performed. The results showed that two pairs of variables were not statistically significant (p-value > 0.05). Table 6 describes what pair of variables were not statistically significant and their p-value.

Table 6. Aggregations t-test Results (p-value > 0.05)

Variable 1	Variable 2	P - Values
Region	Country	0.086
User	Educational institution level	0.751

To gain a better understanding of the needs of the researchers, all of the questions were analysed graphically by aggregating responses according to the level of importance and adding weights according to their ranking. Each answer was weighted with 10 points if was ranked first and with 1 point if it was ranked last. The comparison between learning technologies is shown in Figure 1.

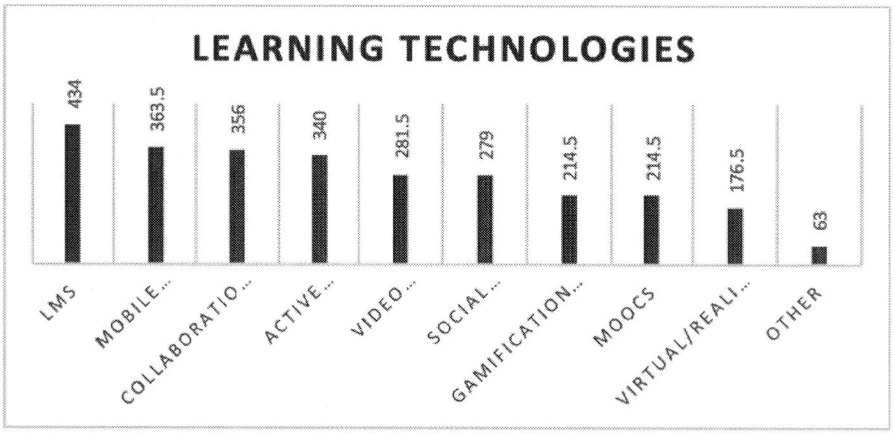

Figure 1. Weighted Learning Technologies Importance Ranking

As shown in Figure 1, the most important learning technology for researchers is LMS. This is followed by mobile learning tools and collaboration tools. It is important to mention that, according to the results of the t-tests, mobile learning tools, collaboration tools and active-learning tools do not have a statistical difference, resulting in a possible grouping of technologies that will fall second in importance.

A comparison was conducted between learning technologies platforms or tools most used. This information is used to describe what platform or tools is considered most important in each section. According to the results, the most popular platforms were as follows: Learning management systems – Moodle, Mobile learning tools – Laptops, Social network platforms – YouTube, Video conferencing technologies – Skype, Collaboration tools – Google suite, Gamification tools – Classcraft, Active learning tools – Kahoot!, MOOCs platforms – Coursera. The most popular type of visualization was bar charts and the second one pie charts. However, according to the t-tests results, there is no statistical mean difference between pie charts, line graphs, and network diagrams. Thus, for the design can be chose the second most popular option. The same occurred with the aggregations. The most popular options were active users and educational institutional level. Even though according to the t-tests there is no statistical mean difference between these two, both of them have higher values than its followers.

7. CONCLUSION

The learning technologies field requires further research, categorisation, a more structured way to grow and different standpoints. Almost all of the research in this area is focused on the advantages and effects of these tools on students and teachers. Due to the impressive growth of learning technologies, researchers require support and resources in which they can find meaningful information to increase the efficiency of their research. In this sense, the dashboards that, for many years, have improved decision-making in fields such as business, health and transportation, can provide support to researchers and improve decision-making before beginning a new project. One of the most difficult steps to beginning research is finding and describing the problem, in addition to finding a starting point from which to gather useful information (Alvesson & Sandberg, 2011). To address this issue, this paper focused on providing insights about learning technologies, in addition to tools or platforms that are considered most important by researchers. Responses from the survey provide strong foundations of the characteristics required in a dashboard for researchers in the field of learning technologies. Although a clear factorial analysis was not possible due to lower KMO test results, there is evidence that a relationship exists between learning technologies and design characteristics. While the categorisation that was used was comprehensive, some similarities were found. This can reduce the amount of learning technologies to combine technologies for broader research. The t-tests results showed that some learning technologies have no statistical mean difference leading to a possible grouping reducing the learning technologies categories. In this regard the learning technologies shown in Table 4 are the ones that have a p-value higher than 0.05, resulting in a no statistical mean difference. As a result, table 7 depicts the possible grouping and its label according to the characteristics shared among the technologies of the group.

Table 7. Learning Technologies Factors

Mobile online tools	Social network communication tools	Online presence tools
Mobile learning tools	Social networks platforms	MOOCs
Collaboration tools	Video conferencing tools	Gamification tools
Active learning tools		Virtual/augmented reality

This grouping can be helpful for further research that may focus on a specific tool to study its effects on students or teachers and provide insights regarding the current state of the research. For example, the most studied learning management system is Blackboard. However, according to the results of the survey, this platform is falling behind Moodle and Google Classroom. Additionally, the studies focusing on Google Classroom are minimal, meaning that more research must be done that focuses on Google Classroom to adequately understand the advantages and disadvantages of this platform.

The results of the dashboard design section can be used as a starting point in different research fields as these can be standardised to define researchers' requirements and to provide insights about the characteristics of a dashboard. In this regard, the results of the survey showed that the most important type of visualisation is bar charts and that there is no clear second choice for researchers. It can be concluded that a dashboard should at least contain a bar chart visualisation. To some extent, this result highlights the importance of bar charts in both the statistical and the graphical analysis and might indicate that this type of visualisation is the most important. It can be tested in other research areas to establish if the results are similar or not. The results of the survey indicated the need for a portal characteristic embedded in the dashboard. This is a useful insight as it can be determined that as the users of the dashboard are researchers and so, for this type of user, a descriptive information section is required.

This paper was limited by time as it was completed in a short period of time. As a consequence, the dashboard could not be tested. This would be the next step of this project, the evaluation of the prototype and further improvements to the dashboard. To proceed with the evaluation, it would be necessary to apply for an extension of the human ethics approval and submit a new questionnaire for evaluation. To accomplish the evaluation task, the best model to follow would be the technology acceptance model (TAM). Although the model is simple, it is an adequate starting point for a first evaluation. The prototype can be improved by the creation of a panel of experts to provide initial feedback about the tools and to encourage other researchers and learning technologies designers to continue to provide more feedback and information for the dashboard.

REFERENCES

Aleven, V., Beal, C. R. & Graesser, A. C. (2013). Introduction to the special issue on advanced learning technologies. *Journal of Educational Psychology*, 105(4), 929–931.

Allio, M. K. (2012). Strategic dashboards: designing and deploying them to improve implementation. *Strategy & Leadership*, 40(5), 24–31.

Alvesson, M. & Sandberg, J. (2011). Generating research questions through problematization. *The Academy of Management Review*, 36(2), 247–271.

Ariso, J. (2017). *Augmented Reality (Vol. 11)*. Berlin, Germany: De Gruyter.

BenMoussa, C. (2003). Workers on the move: New opportunities through mobile commerce. *Paper presented at the UKAIS Conference*, University of Warwick.

Bethlehem, J. (2009). *Applied survey methods: A statistical perspective*. Hoboken, NJ: Wiley.

Bothma, C. H. & Cant, M. C. (2011). Adopting learning technologies: From belief to practice. *Educational Studies*, 37(4), 375–389.

Camponovo, G. & Pigneur, Y. (2003). Business model analysis applied to mobile business. *Paper presented at the 5th International Conference on Enterprise Information Systems (ICEIS)*, Angiers, France.

Card, S., Mackinlay, J. & Shneiderman, B. (1999). *Readings in information visualization: using vision to think*. San Francisco, CA: Morgan Kaufmann Publishers.

Ceccarelli, A., Mori, M., Lollini, P. & Bondavalli, A. (2015). Introducing meta-requirements for describing system of systems. *Paper presented at the IEEE International Symposium on High Assurance Systems Engineering*.

Cerri, S. A. (2012). Advanced learning technologies. In N. Seel (Ed.), *Encyclopedia of the Sciences of Learning (pp. 154-157)*. New York: Springer.

Drent, M. & Meelissen, M. (2008). Which factors obstruct or stimulate teacher educators to use ICT innovatively? *Computers & Education, 51*(1), 187–199.

Fernández-Ferrer, M. & Cano, E. (2016). The influence of the internet for pedagogical innovation: Using twitter to promote online collaborative learning. *International Journal of Educational Technology in Higher Education*, 13(1), 1–15.

Few, S. (2007). Dashboard confusion revisited. (2007, March) *Perceptual Edge Visual Business Intelligence Newsletter*.

Fisher, B., Green, T. M. & Arias-Hernandez, R. (2011). Visual analytics as a translational cognitive science. *Topics in Cognitive Science*, 3(3), 609–625.

Gleasure, R. (2014). Conceptual design science research? How and why untested meta-artifacts have a place in IS. *Paper presented at the International Conference on Design Science Research in Information Systems*, Karlsruhe, Germany.

Glenn, M. (2008) The Economist Intelligence Unit. *The Future of higher education: How technology will shape learning* [White paper]. Retrieved from http://graphics.eiu.com/upload/the%20future%20of%20universities.pdf.

Harley, J. M., Lajoie, S. P., Frasson, C. & Hall, N. C. (2017). Developing emotion-aware, advanced learning technologies: a taxonomy of approaches and features. *International Journal of Artificial Intelligence in Education*, 27(2), 268–297.

Hart, J. (2018). *12th Annual Digital Learning Tools Survey.* Retrieved 03/03/2019, from Centre for Learning & Performance Technologies.

Jackson, G. T. & McNamara, D. S. (2013). Motivation and performance in a game-based intelligent tutoring system. *Journal of Educational Psychology*, 105(4), 1036–1049.

Karasavvidis, I. & Kollias, V. (2014). Technology integration in the most favourable conditions: Findings from a professional development training program. In C. Karagiannidis, P. Politis & I. Karasavvidis (eds) *Research on e-Learning and ICT in education*. Springer (pp. 197–224). New York, NY: Springer.

Kasapoglu-Akyol, P. (2010). Using educational technology tools to improve language and communication skills of ESL students. *Novitas - Research on Youth and Language (ROYAL)*, 4(2), 225–241.

Keim, D., Andrienko, G., Fekete, J. D., Görg, C., Kohlhammer, J. & Melançon, G. (2008). Visual analytics: Definition, process, and challenges. In A. Kerren, J. T. Stasko, J. D. Fekete & C. North (eds.) *Information Visualization. Lecture notes in computer science*, Vol 4950. (pp. 154–175). Berlin, Heidelberg: Springer.

Key, A., Howe, B., Perry, D. & Aragon, C. (2012). VizDeck: Self-organizing dashboards for visual analytics. *Paper presented at the 2012 ACM SIGMOD International Conference on Management of Data*, Arizona, USA.

Kumar, S. & Daniel, B. (2016). Integration of learning technologies into teaching within Fijian polytechnic institutions. *International Journal of Educational Technology in Higher Education*, 13(1), 1–17.

Law, J. (2016). *A Dictionary of Business and Management (6th ed.)*: Oxford, United Kingdom: Oxford University Press.

Levin, T. & Wadmany, R. (2008). teachers' views on factors affecting effective integration of information technology in the classroom: Developmental scenery. *Journal of Technology and Teacher Education, 16*(2), 233–263.

Maginnis, F., White, R. & Mckenna, C. (2000). Customers on the move: m-Commerce demands a business object broker approach to EAI. *eAI Journal*, 58–62.

Marx, F., Mayer, J. & Winter, R. (2011). Six principles for redesigning executive information systems-findings of a survey and evaluation of a prototype. *ACM Transactions on Management Information Systems (TMIS)*, 2(4), 1–19.

Mends-Brew, E. (2012). Enhancement of ICT in polytechnics for accelerated development. *Natural and Applied Science, 3*(3), 99–107.

Ng-Kruelle, G., Swatman, P., Rebne, D. & Hampe, F. (2002). The price of convenience: Privacy and mobile commerce. *Quarterly Journal of Electronic Commerce*, 3(3), 273–285.

Nuseibeh, B. & Easterbrook, S. (2000). Requirements engineering: A roadmap. *Paper presented at the IEEE International Conference on Software Engineering*, Limerick, Ireland.

Paquette, L., Randall-Schab, M. & Busacca, J. (2015). *Teaching political science to undergraduates: active pedagogy for the microchip mind*. Warsaw/Berlin: De Gruyter Open.

Patterson, R., Blaha, L., Grinstein, G., Liggett, K., Kaveney, D., Sheldon, K. & J. Moore. (2014). A human cognition framework for information visualization. *Computers & Graphics*, 42(1), 42–58.

Patterson, R., Pierce, B., Bell, H., Andrews, D. & Winterbottom, M. (2009). Training robust decision making in immersive environments. *Journal of Cognitive Engineering and Decision Making*, 3(4), 331–361.

Patterson, R., Pierce, B., Bell, H. & Klein, G. (2010). Implicit learning, tacit knowledge, expertise development, and naturalistic decision making. *Journal of Cognitive Engineering and Decision Making*, 4(4), 289–303.

Sawyer, P. & Kotonya, G. (2001). Software requirements. In P. Bourque & R. Fairley (Ed.), *Guide to the Software Engineering Body Knowledge (pp. 30–55)*. Washington, United States: IEEE Computer Society.

Schwendimann, B., Rodriguez-Triana, M., Vozniuk, A., Prieto, L., Boroujeni, M., Holzer, A. & Dillenbourg, P. (2017). Perceiving learning at a glance: A systematic literature review of learning dashboard research. *IEEE Transactions on Learning Technologies*, 10(1), 30–41.

Smalheiser, N. R. (2017a). *Chapter 9 - Null Hypothesis Statistical Testing and the t-Test Data Literacy (pp. 127–136)*: Academic Press.

Smalheiser, N. R. (2017b). *Chapter 11 - ANOVA Data Literacy (pp. 149-155)*: Academic Press.

Sommerville, I. (2007). *Software engineering*. Harlow, England.

Thomas, J. & Cook, K. (2006). A visual analytics agenda. *IEEE Computer Graphics and Applications*, 26(1), 10–13.

Verbert, K., Duval, E., Klerkx, J., Govaerts, S. & Santos, J. (2013). Learning Analytics Dashboard Applications. *American Behavioral Scientist*, 57(10), 1500–1509.

Ware, C. (2004). Information visualization: *Perception for design (2nd ed.)*. San Francisco, CA: Elsevier.

Wexler, S., Shaffer, J. & Cotgreave, A. (2017). *The big book of dashboards: visualizing your data using real-world business scenarios*. Hoboken, NJ: Wiley.

Wolf, R. (2016). Dashboard design. *Strategic Finance*, 97(12), 20–27.

Zoya, H. & Valeriy, S. (2016). Factor of competitiveness of universities under globalization of educational markets. *USV Annals of Economics and Public Administration, 16*, 106–110.

SPAGHETTI VS. MODULAR CODE – THE CHOICE OF NOVICE PROGRAMMERS

Ilana Lavy and Rami Rashkovits
Yezreel Valley College
Yezreel Valley, Israel

ABSTRACT

Code modularity is one of the criteria for testing software quality. Nevertheless, novice programmers often tend to avoid writing modular code. In this study, we aim to explore the circumstances in which novice programmers choose to write modular code. To address this aim, two student groups, twenty in each, were given a programming task, each in different configuration. Group-1 was given the task in several phases, each add complexity to the previous one, while Group-2 was given the entire task at once. The entire task was rather complex and its modular solution requires the definition of few classes and methods, each responsible to one of the problem's aspects. The students' solutions were analyzed using the dual-process theory, cognitive dissonance theory and content analysis methods to explore the extent of code modularity. The analysis revealed the following: (1) as regards to Group-1, a minor increase in the number of modular solutions was found while they progressed along the phases; (2) The number of modular solutions of Group-2 was higher than of Group-1. Analysis of students' justifications for lack of code modularity in Group-1 revealed the following. The first phase of the problem was perceived as rather simple hence many students did not find any reason to invest in designing a modular solution. When the task got complex in the following phases, some students realized that a modular solution would fit better, hence a cognitive dissonance was raised. Nevertheless, many of them preferred to continue their course of non-modular solution instead of re-designing a modular new one. In order to decrease the dissonance they claimed that this decision saved time. Students of both groups also attributed their non-modular code to lack of explicit criteria for the evaluation of the code quality that lead them to focus on functionality alone.

KEYWORDS

Code Modularity, Novice Programmer, Program Design, Cognitive Dissonance Theory, Dual-Process Theory

1. INTRODUCTION

Modular programming refers to a technique design that separates the functionality of a code into independent, extendible, reusable, maintainable and interchangeable modules, each responsible for one aspect of the desired behavior of the program (Parnas, 1972). Modular programming is a core issue in programming studies (Topi et al., 2010).

Code modularity supports gradual development and easy maintenance. In order to provide a modular code, one needs to possess abstract thinking capabilities enabling her to decompose the solution into small logical parts, and then integrate them to create the whole solution. The main challenge of this process is to define the 'right' and the 'right' functions with the 'right' parameters, allowing efficient integration. Modular design necessitates recursive decomposition of the problem into subcomponents, until the components are sufficiently simple and each responsible for a single operation.

Upon graduation, novice programmers are familiar with modularity principles and are aware of its importance to software quality; however, they often tend to avoid modular programming (Bollinger et al., 1999; Stamelos et al., 2002). Many students adapt 'bad programming habits' during their studies. These habits are the result of focusing on functionality only, while neglecting the structure and quality of the code. As far as they are concerned, if the program does what it should, its structure is not important, and hence it is not necessary to invest in design.

In order to demonstrate their programming abilities novice programmers are focused mainly on being productive. Novice programmers assume that they are expected to provide the solution in the shortest possible time in order to prove their professionalism. To achieve this goal, they often skip the design phase that would bring them closer to a modular code. The result is what is called spaghetti code, with many repetitions of similar code snippets. We believe that in cases where novice programmers will recognize that they are facing a complex problem, such that modular design may shorten the coding time, they will choose to invest in it.

The aim of this study is to explore the conditions in which novice programmers choose to program modular or non-modular code and to understand the reasons underlying their choices.

To address this aim, two student groups, twenty in each, were given a programming task, which included repetitive components, each in different configuration. Group-1 was given the task in several stages, each add complexity to the previous one, while the Group-2 was given the entire task at once.

2. BRIEF THEORETICAL BACKGROUND

Modularity in software systems was widely discussed in the research literature and it was found that software systems with low degree of modularity have costly maintenance (Baldwin et al., 2000; Sullivan et al., 2001; MacCormack et al., 2007). On the other hand, researchers found that modular programming raises the quality of software packages by improving the software's readability and understanding, facilitates maintenance and increases the reuse of the software components (Sullivan et al., 2001; MacCormack et al., 2007).

In attempting to explain why novice programmers avoid modularity in spite their awareness to its importance we turned to the Dual-Process and Cognitive Dissonance theories. The Dual-Process theory deals with the distinction between intuitive and analytical modes of thinking. It suggests that human cognition and behavior operate in two different modes, in parallel, called System 1 and System 2 (Leron & Hazzan, 2006; Kahneman, 2002). These modes are similar to our perception of intuitive and analytical modes of thinking (Fischbein, 1987); are activated by different parts of our brain, and have different evolutionary history. The Dual-Process theory refers to S1 thinking processes as being automatic and fast. They are perceived as unconscious, effortless, and inflexible. S2 thinking processes on the other hand, are being effortful and slow. In addition, they are perceived to be flexible, conscious, and expensive in terms of working memory resources. S1 and S2 systems differ mainly on the level of accessibility referring to the easiness and rapidness thoughts come to our mind.

While probing in the students' reflections expressed during the interviews, we noticed an underlying motive referring to a cognitive dissonance they experienced. Hence, we turned also to the cognitive dissonance theory to find answers. The cognitive dissonance theory refers to the mental discomfort that might occur to an individual who at the same time holds two or more incongruous beliefs, ideas, or values (Festinger, 1957; Cooper, 2011). Cognitive Dissonance theory refers to human tendency to strive for internal psychological consistency, in order to be able to function mentally. A person experiencing internal inconsistency becomes psychologically uncomfortable, and is tries to reduce the dissonance. This can be achieved by altering the stressful behavior, either by adding new information to the cognition causing the psychological dissonance to reduce the dissonance, and/or by actively avoiding contradictory information likely to increase the degree of the cognitive dissonance.

3. THE STUDY

3.1 The Study Participants and Task

Forty participants took part in the study, all were third (and final) year Information Systems students in an academic college, in the 2017-2018 years.

The participants were randomly assigned into two groups (20 students in each). They were given a programming task, which was presented to each group in a different way. The students were asked to address the following problem: (1) input of a polynomial coefficients and a certain point x; (2) compute the polynomial value at x; (3) repeat the previous step for the first, second and third derivatives of the polynomial. Group-1 were provided with the task divided into three successive phases each was given after the completion of the previous. The first phase refers to steps 1-2. The second phase refers to step three with the first derivatives, and the last phase refers to the rest of the derivatives. Group-2 had to address the same task, presented as a whole. Both groups were given no specific guidelines other than the requirement to provide a solution in any programming language they deem fit.

3.2 Data Gathering and Analysis

The research data included the students' solutions to the given tasks and the transcripts of the conducted interviews. Using content analysis methods (Neuendorf, 2002) the students' solutions were classified into three main categories: (1) non-modular; (2) partial-modular; and (3) full-modular. In the first category, we classified solutions in which the entire code was written in one or two functions. In the second category, we classified solutions in which several functions were defined, each responsible for small functionality, however, only one class exists representing both the program and the polynomial computations. In the third category, we classified modular solutions including at least two classes, one represents the program and the interaction with the user, and the second represents the polynomial. Moreover, each class includes several simple functions, each dealing with one functionality.

After classifying the students' solutions to the above categories, to understand the underlying reasons behind the students' choices of solution courses, we conducted open interviews with a representative group of students (three students from each category and each phase). The interviews transcripts were analyzed using te Dual-Process and the Cognitive Dissonance theories.

4. RESULTS

The results shown in Figure 1 demonstrate the evolution of modular solutions across the phases of Group-1. As shown, the number of non-modular solutions decreases from one phase to the next. However, it remains high even after the third phase in which the entire problem was revealed.

Figure 2 demonstrates the difference between the results of the final phase of Group-1 in which the entire problem was revealed, and Group-2 that had to address the entire problem right from the beginning. Comparing group-1-phase 3 with Group-2 distributions reveals that although at this point both groups had the entire problem, there is a significant difference between the numbers of non-modular solutions between groups.

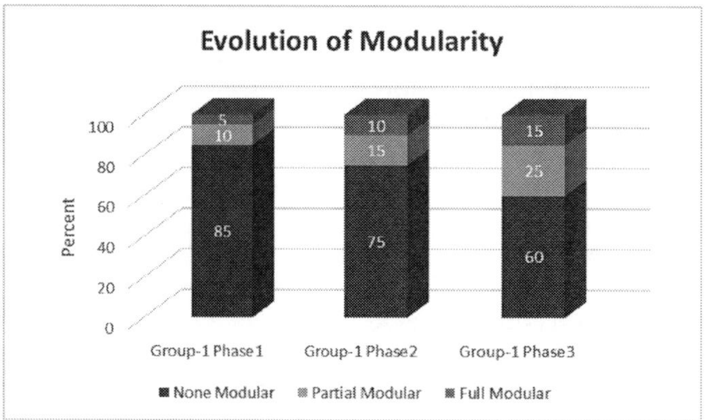

Figure 1. Evolution of Modularity across Phases (Group-1)

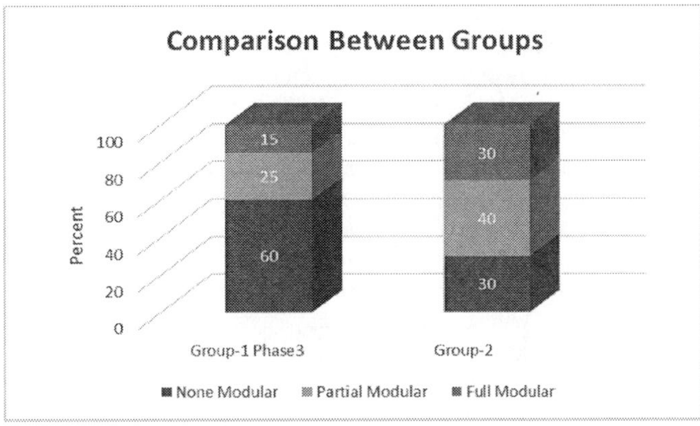

Figure 2. Comparing Group-1 and Group-2

5. DISCUSSION

As to phase-1 solutions, the high percentage of non-modular solution of phase-1 (Figure 1) may be attributed to the students' perception of the problem. The problem provided in the first phase was rather simple, without any repetitive structures. Hence, the students, being novice programmers, did not recognize the advantages of investing efforts in designing classes and functions that would not be used more than once. The following explanation was provided in similar words by these students: "*Why not use a modular solution?.. I did not really think about it. This looks like a very simple task... If I knew there were follow-up tasks with repetitive structure, I might have done better.*" In terms of the dual-process theory (Gilovich, et al., 2002; Stanovich, & West, 2000; Kahneman, 2002), we may say that the students who provided a non-modular solution acted in an intuitive manner (activating S1). On the other hand, those who have provided modular code introduced additional considerations related to the quality of the solution (activating S2), as some of these students uttered in similar words: "*The task was very simple, so I figured out that you examine not only the solution but also its quality.*"

As to phase-2, some repetitive structures are revealed (i.e., the computation of the polynomial and its first derivative at point x). The students were provided with their previous phase solutions after we took a snapshot of them. As can be seen from figure 1, non-modular solution are still in high percentage (75%). In fact, they proceeded the first phase course of solution, adding the needed code to the main method, including code duplications. However, two students had improved their solution. One of them rewrote his solution and built a separate class to represent the polynomial function, and the other changed the code structure by separating the main method into several ones.

The students who provided non-modular solution to the phase-2 problem uttered in similar words: "*In fact, it occurred to me that the code for the evaluation of the derivative polynomial is identical to part of the code I wrote earlier. However, since I already had a solution to the previous stage, it seemed a waste of time to rewrite the solution. Therefore, I decided to continue without changing the code from earlier stage.*" The above utterance imply on buds of understanding as regards to the need for modular solution. We may say that at this stage, a cognitive dissonance (Festinger, (1957; Cooper, 2011) regarding the effectiveness of their course of solution was emerged. To overcome this dissonance, they justified their adhering phase-1 course of solution claiming that it would save time compared to the idea of starting the solution from the beginning. In terms of dual-process theory (Gilovich, et al., 2002; Stanovich, & West, 2000; Kahneman, 2002), we may say that although they became aware to the need to change their course of solution, the temptation not to activate S2 was stronger since it saved investment of cognitive efforts.

In phase-3 the students were asked also to calculate all the remaining derivative polynomials of the original polynomial and compute their values at the given point x. The percentage of non-modular solutions was still high (60%) (Figure 1). However, three additional students redesigned their solutions at this phase and provided modular (or partial-modular) solutions. Still, the tendency to invest minimal efforts in solving the task and avoid redesigning the entire solution was dominant.

During the interviews, one of the few students that changed their solution from non-modular to partial-modular uttered: "*At this stage I noticed that repeated actions of polynomial derivation had to be done for the second time and I saw that the code I wrote for the previous stages began to be cumbersome with many repetitions. Therefore, I decided to write a function that calculates the derivative and avoid some of these repetitions. If I would get the entire problem from the start, I might design and implement the derivative method from scratch*". As to these few students, we may say that to deal with the cognitive dissonance they experienced, they decided to abandon their intuitive thinking (activating S1) and adopt analytical thinking (activating S2).

As to the students of Group-1 who adhere their non-modular solution provided the following explanation in similar words: "*At this stage it was obvious to me that the continuing with the same course of solution will lead to many code repetitions. However, I did not consider redesigning since I wanted to complete the task as fast as possible, having in mind that the most important goal is to solve the problem.*" At this phase, in which the entire problem was revealed to Group-1, most of the students who solved the previous phases in a non-modular way came to realization that their course of solution was problematic (code repetitions, unclear). We may say that they experienced a cognitive dissonance. To solve the dissonance, they decided to adhere the same course of non-modular solution (activating S1). They justified their choice claiming that redesigning the solution at this stage would take long time, more than to keep the same course.

Group-2 students were given the entire task, which was composed of all the three phases handed to Group-1. As can be seen in Figure 2, only 30% of the solutions were non-modular. The students, who provided a full-modular solution, uttered in similar words: "*When I read the problem it occurred to me right away that many calculations of polynomials are required. Hence, I created a polynomial class to contain all the necessary methods, just as we learned in object-oriented programming course. It was not a difficult task for me.*"

As to the Group-2 students who provided non-modular solution, they justified their choice in similar words: "*As I progressed with my solution, I saw that it contains many code repetitions. But you* [the researchers] *didn't specified any criteria as regards to the quality of the solution, so I decided to invest the minimal efforts to solve the problem... to provide a modular solution, it would have taken me longer time to achieve.*"

From the above utterances, we can conclude that though the students had to address the same problem, each of them interpreted it differently according to their capabilities and skills. Approximately Third of them were able to identify the problem components, define appropriate classes and methods and provide a full-modular solution. The first utterance can imply on the internalizing of the importance of early planning of the solution by third of the students, which eventually led to a full-modular solution. Yet, it was also important for these students to provide a solution in a short time. They understood that investing time in planning the solution would lead to saving in coding time and result in a short and clear solution. The internalization of the importance of the designing phase before coding can indicate on abstraction capabilities and planning skills. We may infer that the planning stage has become an integral part of the student's cognitive toolbox. In terms of dual-process theory (Gilovich, et al., 2002; Stanovich, & West, 2000; Kahneman, 2002), we may say that for these students, full-modular solution is achieved by activating S1.

Figure 2 shows that more than a third of Group-2 students provided partial-modular solutions. They justified their course of solution uttering in similar words: "*When I read the problem, I identified repeated elements such as the polynomial derivation and the calculation of its value. However, it was difficult for me to design a perfect solution that included many classes and methods. I did my best to finish the task successfully.*" We learn from the above utterance that these students understand the advantages of modular design but encounter difficulties in its implementation. In terms of the dual-process theory (Gilovich, et al., 2002; Stanovich, & West, 2000; Kahneman, 2002), we might infer that modular design did not become completely an integral part of their intuitive thinking (S1).

As to the Group-2 students who provided a non-modular solution (30%), we may infer that they were not able to grasp the problem as a whole, and instead they view it as a collection of sub-problems each to be addressed separately and successively, similar to the situation of group-1. In terms of dual-process theory

(Gilovich, et al., 2002; Stanovich, & West, 2000; Kahneman, 2002), we might infer that these students were not able yet to integrate modularity into their S1. This may be attributed to several reasons such as lack of solution planning before coding; not enough exposure to the consequences of non-modular code. As a result, the modularity principle was not completely internalized; and did not become an integral part of their cognitive toolbox.

6. CONCLUSIONS

In this study, we explored the circumstances in which novice programmers decide to design their course of solution before they start to code. The research data revealed that when a problem is simple, they tend to provide a quick solution, which lacks modularity. Even if they have to add to this solution a code that includes repetitive components, they adhere to the course of solution they had started with (Group-1 task). However, when the problem is handed to them as a whole (Group-2 task), approximately two-thirds of the students, invested efforts in planning and designing before coding their solutions and handed full or partial modular ones although it was not easy for them. To be able to design the solution before its implementation one has to possess abstraction and generalization skills. This is especially difficult when referring to novice programmers. The students behavior might be explained via dual-process theory (Gilovich, et al., 2002; Stanovich, & West, 2000; Kahneman, 2002) referring to the natural tendency of people to invest minimal efforts while coping with cognitive tasks (activating S1). We also found that even after they understand that a modular solution would fit better, a situation, which evokes cognitive dissonance (Festinger, 1957; Cooper, 2011), they adhere the original course of the solution. To overcome the cognitive dissonance, many of them say that it seems ineffective and a waste of time to "throw away" what they have done so far and start all over again.

To raise students' awareness to the importance of code modularity and add this principle to their professional toolbox, we recommend the following action: (1) Include programming tasks that present two implementations of a given solution, one modular and the other non-modular. The students will be asked to put changes in the code, addressing new requirements. In such activities, students would appreciate the easiness of adding or changing functionalities to a modular code in contrast to the complexity of doing the same changes in the non-modular code; (2) Include tasks in which students will be required to reuse parts of code they provided in previous tasks. The aim of such activity is to raise the student's awareness to the crucial role of modularity in software reuse ;(3) Include tasks composed of several stages, in which each successive stage has to be handled by a different student. The student has to continue the solution of the next stage using the previous stage solution done by another classmate. The purpose of such activity it to confront students with the consequences of non-modular solutions.

In order to gain further refined insights, this study should be repeated with larger groups of students separating them according to academic achievements, and compare their performances to products of experienced programmers.

REFERENCES

Baldwin, C. Y. & Clark, K. B. 2000. *Design rules: The power of modularity* (Vol. 1). Cambridge: The MIT Press.

Bollinger, T., Nelson, R., Turnbull, S. & Self, K. 1999. From the editor-response: open-source methods: peering through the clutter. *IEEE Software*, vol. 16, no. 4, pp. 6-11.

Cooper, J. 2011. *Cognitive dissonance theory. Handbook of theories of social psychology*, vol. 1, pp. 377-398.

Festinger, L. 1957. *A Theory of Cognitive Dissonance*. California: Stanford University Press.

Fischbein, H. 1987. *Intuition in science and mathematics: An educational approach* (Vol. 5). Springer Science & Business Media.

Gilovich, D. Griffin, & D. Kahneman, (Eds.). 2002. *Heuristics and biases: The psychology of intuitive judgment*. Cambridge university press.

Kahneman, D. 2002. *Maps of bounded rationality: A perspective on intuitive judgment and choice*. Nobel Prize lecture, vol. 8, pp. 351-401.

Leron, U. & Hazzan, O. 2006. The rationality debate: Application of cognitive psychology to mathematics education. *Educational Studies in Mathematics*, vol. 62, no. 2, pp. 105-126.

MacCormack, A, Rusnak, J. & Baldwin. 2007. The impact of component modularity on design evolution: Evidence from the software industry, *Harvard Business School Working Paper*.

Neuendorf, K.A. 2002. *The Content Analysis Guidebook*. Thousand Oaks, CA: Sage Publications.

Parnas, D.L. 1972. On the criteria to be used in decomposing systems into modules, Communications of the ACM, vol. 15, no. 9, pp. 1053-1058.

Stamelos, I., Angelis, L., Oikonomou, A. & Bleris, G. L. 2002. Code quality analysis in open source software development". *Information Systems Journal*, vol. 12, no. 1, pp. 43-60, 2002.

Stanovich, E. & West, R. 2000. Individual differences in reasoning: Implications for the rationality debate. Behavioral and brain science, vol. 23, pp. 645-726.

Sullivan, K.J., Griswold, W. G., Cai, Y. & Hallen, B. 2001. The structure and value of modularity in software design, *In the Proceedings of the 8th European Software Engineering Conference*, Vienna, Austria.

Topi, H., Valacich, J. S., Wright, R. T., Kaiser, K., Nunamaker Jr, J. F., Sipior, J. C., & de Vreede, G. J. 2010. IS 2010: Curriculum guidelines for undergraduate degree programs in information systems. *Communications of the Association for Information Systems*, 26(1), 18.

DATA MODEL DESIGN - THE CASE OF THREESOME

Rami Rashkovits and Ilana Lavy
Yezreel Valley College
Yezreel Valley, Israel

ABSTRACT

Information systems students encounter difficulties in understanding and implementing ternary relationships when designing a data model. The aim of this study is to explore the origins of these difficulties and to suggest didactical guidelines to overcome these difficulties. This research examines the data model produced by students in which a ternary relationship is required, and looks for errors. The students reflect on their solution via open interview and unfold the underlying reasons to their erroneous design. The issue is analysed using the cognitive complexity theory. The data of this research includes the students' responses to a questionnaire with a design problem and the transcripts of open interviews conducted with representative group of the study participants. The obtained data was analysed using content and inductive analysis methods. The research is qualitative yet some quantitative data are presented as well. The study shed light on the underlying reasons causing erroneous data model design by novice data modelers, referring to ternary relationships, and suggest ways to teach the issues involved more effectively. The findings are used to classify the difficulties involved in designing ternary relationships and the underlying reasons, which lead novice data modelers to err. The insights gained from the research findings enabled us to come with useful didactical suggestions for educators that might help them improve their teaching as regards to the ternary relationships modeling. The research findings might enrich the data body research on data model design from the students' perspective. Novice data modelers may perform better and avoid beginners' errors, which perhaps lead to better information systems quality.

KEYWORDS

Data Model Design, Ternary Relationships, Abstract Thinking Abilities

1. INTRODUCTION

Novice data designers encounter various difficulties when designing a data model addressing given users' requirements (Dey et al., 1999) and identification of ternary relationships are one of them (Hitchman, 2003; Batra, 2007). The research literature attributes these difficulties mainly to cognitive complexities; among them, lack of immediate feedback, no flexibility for errors, and information overload (Batra, 2007). As a result, models designed by novice are often poor, and the source for many faulty behaviors of information systems.

Novice modelers are often graduates of colleges and universities in the computing field (e.g., Information Systems, Computer Sciences, etc.) and as part of their curriculum they take several database courses (Topi et al., 2010). They learn how to design a relational database schema addressing given business requirements, and how to control the schema using SQL commands.

As part of the design phase, the modeler identifies the major model constituents using Entity Relationships Diagram (ERD) (Chen, 1976). The modeler sketch entities and relationships between them, and then transform them into a relational model using a set of predefined rules. Each entity becomes a table, and each table includes a set of attributes, from which a subset is chosen to be primary key. Binary relationships are transform into separate table in the case of N:M multiplicity constraints, or into foreign keys in one table holding the value of the primary key in the other table, in cases of multiplicity of 1:N or 1:1.

There may be various relationship cardinalities in a data model. The most common one is a binary relationship connecting two entities. For example, **employee** *works-in* **company** matches a pair of <*employee, company*>. But binary relationship does not always address a business requirement and high-order relationship is sometimes needed. For example, to model an **employee** *assigned* to a **project** in a certain **role**, assuming that one can play different roles in different projects, one has to connect the threesome <*employee, project, role*>. Replacing the above ternary relationship with two binary relationships would result in a loss of information. Suppose we connect **employee** to a **project** and **project** to **role**, then we cannot tell the role an employee plays in a project. Similarly, if we connect **employee** to **role** and **role** to **project**, we will not be able to track the specific role an employee plays in a project, and same if we connect **employee** to **role** and **employee** to **project**. Setting three binary relationships instead of one ternary relationship would suffer from the same problems, hence would not be appropriate as well. In this case, only the ternary relationship would keep all required information.

Batra (1994) found that novice designers have difficulties to identify ternary relationships much more then binary ones. He found that often they tend to use two binary relationships to connect the threesome instead of one ternary relationship. As shown above, applying such a solution on some examples would lead to loss of information and erroneous information system.

Existing research is mainly focused on theoretical rather than empirical aspects of data design. That is, there has been little exploration of empirical data gathered from novice data modelers. We believe that such empirical findings might shed light on the causes of the difficulties novice data modelers encounter during the design phase, and help instructors improve their practice. Therefore, in this research we focus on empirical data gained from students who are considered novice data modelers.

2. THEORETICAL BACKGROUND

The entity-relationship model (Chen, 1976), is frequently used to model relational database schemas (Lenzerini & Nobili, 1990). ERD consists of entity-sets and relationships between them, representing real-world objects and their connections. Entity-sets include attributes of the objects, and specify an identifying key. Relationships connect two or more objects and may have attributes of their own. The relationships-sets connecting between the entity-sets represents real-world associations between the objects, important to the users.

The cardinality of a relationship can be binary or n-ary. A binary relationship connects two objects, while an n-ary relationship connects three or more (n) objects. In this study we focus on the understanding of novice data modelers regarding ternary relationship (n=3)

Binary relationships have multiplicity constraints representing limitations on the participation of an object in the relationship. Multiplicity constraints can be of type 1:1, 1:N, or N:M. Ternary relationship also have multiplicity constraints of type: N:M:K or N:M:1. While the first enables each object to participate in many threesomes, the latter forces the first pair to participate in only one threesome. For example, if <*employee, project, role*> are connected in a multiplicity of N:M:1 accordingly, then an employee in a project can play only one role. Relationships of any cardinality may include additional attributes describing the relationship (e.g., weekly hours an employee spend in each project for each role she plays).

The transformation rules of ERD constituents into relational schema (Chen, 1976) are concerned with turning entities into tables, and relationships into foreign keys holding the key value of the other entity in case of 1:1 or 1:n multiplicity constraints, or dedicated table, with a primary key composed of both foreign keys holding the key values of the connected entities. In case of ternary relationships, a separated table is set, with three foreign keys, and a primary key composed of all three foreign keys in case of N:M:K multiplicity constraint or two foreign keys in case of N:M:1).

Both cardinality and connectivity errors are found frequently in novices' models and novices are unable to decide which entities participate in a relationship (Batra & Antony, 1994). A protocol study by Batra and Antony (1994) found that novice designers are satisfied if the entities in an application are somehow related to each other; they rarely consider the consequences of their design. For example, a heuristic commonly used in ER design is that if there is a sentence relating two entities, then there is a relationship in the solution. However, an indiscriminate use of this heuristic can lead to errors.

3. THE STUDY

3.1 The Study Participants

The study participants are eighty-two second year students studying for a B.Sc. degree in Information Systems. The research was conducted at the end of the 'Introduction to Data Bases' course. The participants were provided with a task in which they were asked to provide a database schema addressing a given business scenario. The task requires an entity-relationship diagram sketch and the corresponding table model, as well as SQL query based on their data model.

3.2 The Task

The study participants had to address two problems designed by the researchers, aiming at shedding light on the perception of ternary relationships by novice modelers. The problems refer to three entities and their relationships. Both problems discuss business firms who market various **products** to different **countries** and use **distributors** who sell the products around the globe. The study participants were directed to keep their relational model simple and normalized, and avoid redundant tables, attributes and keys.

The first problem describes a company in which each distributor is permitted to sell the company's products everywhere around the globe allowing multiple distributors to act simultaneously in the same country, each may set different price for the same product. The second problem describes a company in which **distributors** are allowed to distribute the company's **products** in many **countries**, however, in a specific country, only one distributor is allowed to sell, exclusively. The distributor may set different prices for the same product in each country.

In addition, in both problems the students were asked to query their tables and list the prices of all products. If a product has multiple prices, all prices, sorted alphabetically by countries and distributors, should be displayed, including product name, distributor name, country and price.

The solution of the first problem requires a ternary relationship between product-distributer-country, as shown in Figure 1, whereas the solution of the second problem requires the use of two binary relationships, one between country and product and another one between country and distributor, as shown in Figure 2.

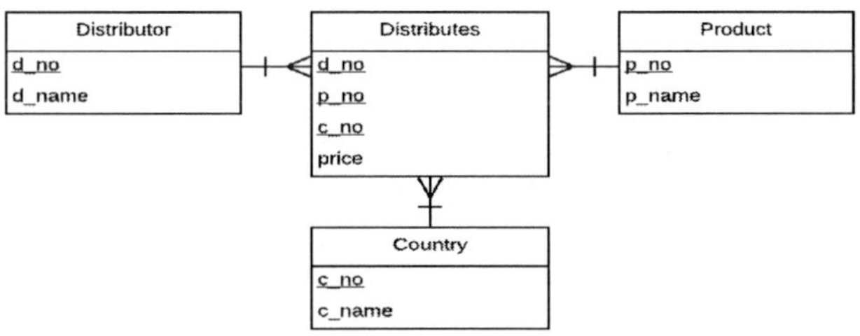

Distributor (**d_no**, d_name)
Country (**c_no**, c_name)
Product (**p_no** p_name)
Distributes (**c_no, p_no, d_no**, price)

Figure 1. Data Model - Solution to Problem-1

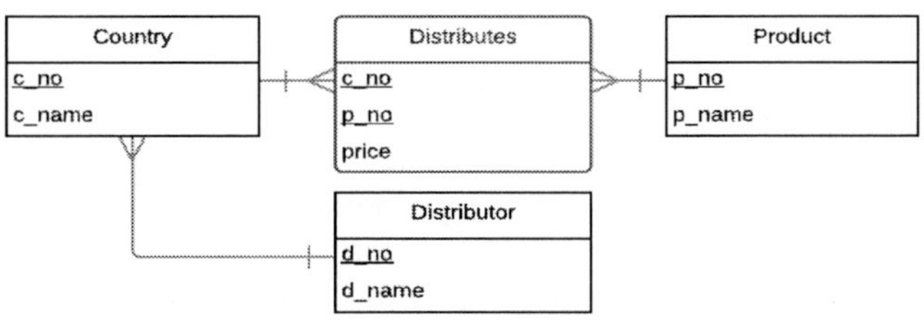

Distributor (**d_no**, d_name)
Country (**c_no**, c_name, d_no)
Product (**p_no**, p_name)
Distributes (**c_no, p_no**, price)

Figure 2. Data Model - Solution to Problem-2

The difference between the solutions of both problems may be found in the relationships between the tables, represented by foreign keys. As shown in Figure 1, the distributes table primary key includes the three keys of the connected entities. In Figure 2 only country and product keys compose the primary key of the Distributes table, since only one distributor is allowed in a country anyway, hence its key is redundant. The relationship between the country and the one distributor allowed to sell there is found on the foreign key of the distributor at the country table.

As to multiplicity constraints, the solution to the first problem has one ternary relationship with N:M:K constraint (Figure 1), and the solution to the second problem has two binary relationships, one with a N:M relationship, and another one with 1:N.

Figures 3-4 show the query solutions for problem-1 and problem-2 respectively. The solutions are quite similar, but the join operations for the distributor is not based on the distributes table, but on the country table. The purpose of the query was to provide some kind of immediate feedback to the designer, to test their model.

```
SELECT c_name, p_name, d_name, price
FROM   country c JOIN distributes di ON c.c_no = di.c_no
             JOIN Product p ON di.p_no = p.p_no
             JOIN Distributor d ON di.d_no = d.d_no
ORDER BY c.c_name, p.pname, d.d_name
```

Figure 3. Query - Solution to Problem-1

```
SELECT c_name, p_name, d_name, price
FROM   country c JOIN distributes di ON c.c_no = di.c_no
             JOIN Product p ON di.p_no = p.p_no
             JOIN Distributor d ON c.d_no = d.d_no
ORDER BY c.c_name, p.pname, d.d_name
```

Figure 4. Query - Solution to Problem-2

3.3 Data Collection and Analysis Tools

The solutions were analysed and classified according to the error types we found. We also conducted interviews with a representative group of the study participants, and asked the them to reflect on their solutions, and classified the underlying reasons led them to provide erroneous solutions. Using analytic induction (Taylor & Bogdan, 1998) and content analysis (Neuendorf, 2002) we classified the interviews' transcripts into categories and discussed their meanings.

3.4 Results and Discussion

3.4.1 Problem-1

Figure 5 shows the distribution of correct vs. faulty solutions referring the first problem. As shown only 48% of the students provided correct solutions, while the rest of the students provided faulty ones. The majority of the students who provided faulty solutions used two binary relationships instead of the desired ternary relationship, similar to the model presented in Figure 2. The model presented in Figure 2 is not properly addressing problem-1 since each pair <*country*, *product*> has only one price, contradicting the requirement that multiple prices can be set in each country by various distributors. Another variation of faulty solution has one relationship between *distributor* and *product*, and another one between *product* and *country*. In this variation the distributor of a product in a country is untraceable.

Few students constructed three binary relationships between all entities, as shown in Figure 6. From this solution one can extract which products are distributed by each distributor, and which products are sold in each country. However, one cannot extract the price each distributor set for a product, as only one price per <*product*, *country*> exists, contradicting the requirements.

As to multiplicity constraints, surprisingly though, all the students who provided correct solutions, had provided the correct N:M:K constraints. Maybe if the given problem would require N:M:1 multiplicity constraints had we seen other percentage.

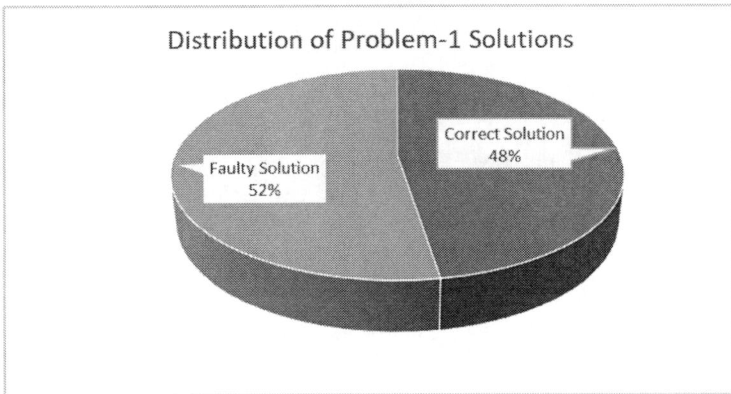

Figure 5. Distribution of Solutions - Problem-1

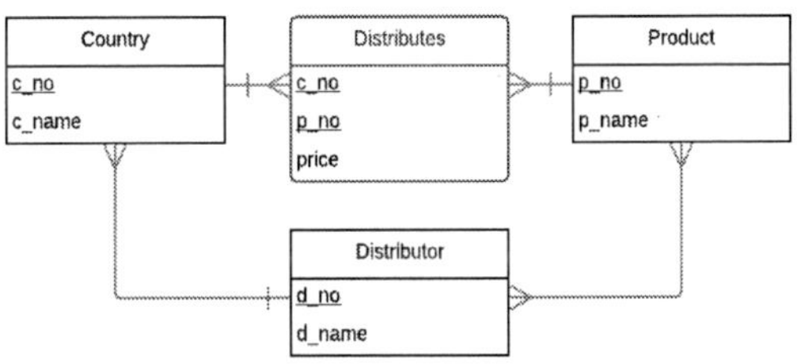

Distributor (**d_no**, d_name)
Country (**c_no**, c_name, d_no)
Product (**p_no**, p_name)
Distributes (**p_no, d_no**, price)
ProductDistributor (**d_no, p_no**)

Figure 6. Faulty Data Model – Three Binary Relationships

3.4.2 Problem-2

Figure 7 shows the distribution of correct vs. faulty solutions referring the second problem. As shown only 41% of the students provided correct solutions, while the rest of the students provided faulty ones. The majority of the students who provided faulty solutions used ternary relationships instead of the desired binary relationships, with N:M:1 multiplicity constraints as shown in Figure 8. The 1 constraint near country means that for every pair of <*distributor*, *product*> only one country is possible, which is obviously contradicting the requirement allowing a distributor to sell in many country and set different prices. Few other students provided a solution with three binary relationships similar to the one presented in Figure 6.

As to multiplicity constraints, the vast majority of the students who provided correct solutions, had provided the correct constraints, 1:N between country and distributor, and N:M between country and product.

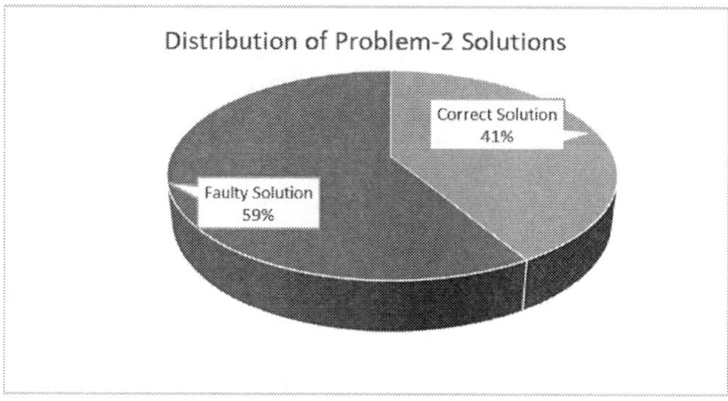

Figure 7. Distribution of Solutions - Problem-2

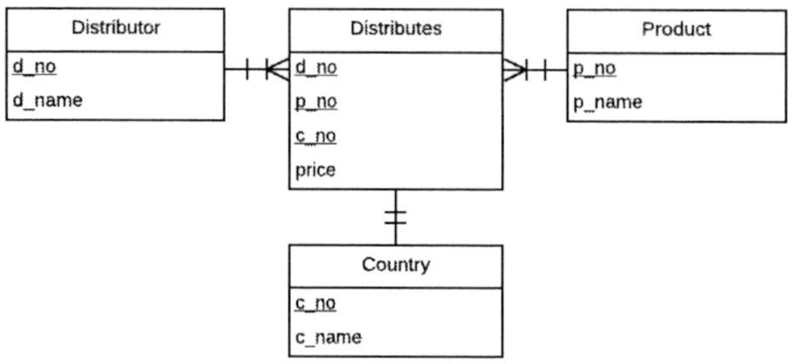

Distributor(**d_no**, d_name)
Country(**c_no**, c_name)
Product(**p_no**, p_name)
Distribute (**p_no, d_no, c_no**, price)

Figure 8. Faulty Data Model – n:m:1 Ternary Relationships

4. DISCUSSION

Following the solution analysis and classification we conducted interviews with a representative group of the study participants. The students were asked to reflect on their solution, and the reasons lead them to choose erroneous solution. In what follows, we present representative excerpts from these interviews, and analyse them.

'*My solution was created gradually, after reading each sentence, I added elements to the ERD chart addressing the requirements came up…For instance, when I came across a distributor who distributed products, I created two entity-sets for distributors and products, and constructed a binary relationship between them. Then it was said that the distributor could distribute in any country, and I added entity set for the countries, and a binary relationship between distributor and country*'. From this excerpt, it can be seen that some students solved the problem step by step, one sentence at the time. However, they continued without reflecting on the obtained results. They did not look back to re-examine the solution in light of the problem requirements to verify its correctness and integrity.

'*…I find it difficult to implement ternary relationship. …we were less exposed to n-ary relationships, although they are more difficult to understand. …the cardinality issue is quite confusing, and I'm not sure why my solution with two binary relationships is incorrect…*'. From the first part of the above excerpt we can learn about the reason underlying the students' difficulties in identifying ternary relationships, which stems from too few examples and a non-exhaustive discussion of the differences between the types of relationships. The second part of the excerpt shows that the students did not internalize the fact that the problem of designing a schema has a single solution (Batra, 2007). This may be attributed to the fact that in math and computer science problems, there is usually more than one way to solve a problem, and students are asked to look for more than one method of solution and examine its implications.

'*If I had the chance to run the query I wrote against real data I believe I would immediately get the design error and fix it. But when the solution is on paper it's harder for me to detect such errors*'. Although the students were expected to formulate a query based on their data model, they still were not confronted with their faulty design because they could not view the query output. This is in line with Batra (2007), who referred to time delay as one of problem solving principles influencing cognitive complexity in data modeling.

Batra (2007) presents four major sources of complexity. We believe that there is an additional source, experience in data design. From both excerpts, we may learn that students feel that they are not sufficiently experienced in designing a data model, since it requires skills that are gained only via experience acquired over time while working in the field. Being novice data modelers they use naïve heuristics that may lead them to an erroneous design. Experienced designers use advanced heuristics gained via engagement in similar problems (Purao, Storey & Han, 2003).

'*I thought the purpose of the second problem was to check if my solution is consistent with the first one. I thought that both problems have similar solution although they were phrased differently*'.

From the above excerpt, we learn that sometimes students make prior assumptions before they try to solve a given problem. In this case, since this problem was given to them after they solved the first problem, in which a ternary relationship was used, some students who solved correctly the first problem assumed that the second problem was a variation of the first one. As a result, they tried to adapt the previous solution to fit the new requirements by changing the cardinality constraints of the ternary relationship instead of starting the design from scratch. They actually used a naive heuristic that results in an erroneous solution (Polya, 1985).

5. CONCLUSION

Four major sources for cognitive complexity: problem-solving principles, design principles, information overload, and systems theory (Batra, 2007). We found professional experience to be the fifth source. Gaining professional experience in data modeling means, among other things, confronting the consequences of erroneous models. This process usually leads to the understanding that continual reflection on the built model must be carried out, and that the obtained model should be examined against the data and queries. Professional experience also means the developing of problem solving and critical thinking abilities, as well as being sensitive to the nuances embedded in various situations.

In this study, we found that many students, do not reflect on their solution process. In the absence of reflection, students avoid confronting the solution they have reached so far with additional requirements ahead. Also, at the end of the solution process, the students rarely examine their solution against the problem full requirements.

In the process of solution providing, students do not always approach the problem free of extraneous. They try to figure out the hidden researcher's motives, and try to address them. This results in biased solutions. In addition, they tend to believe that similarly to math and programming, there may be various correct solutions to a problem (Batra, 2007), which is incorrect as regards to data modelling.

To improve students' ability to recognize and incorporate ternary relationships in data modeling we suggest the following recommendations for data modeling instruction: (1) The students should engage with different types of modeling problems. Namely, not only the standard problems they usually get, which involve the modeling of a given situation, but also different kinds of tasks. For example, to provide them with an erroneous model, and ask them to check the model's 'quality' through examining its derived relational model and the execution of different queries; (2) The students should carry out comparison tasks in which they will have to examine two data models, one correct and the other erroneous, against the problem's requirements in order to develop their awareness of the meaning of each requirement in the problem; (3) The students should be provided with tasks involving peer work. That is, one student has to design the data model and hand it to a classmate. The classmate has to construct a relational model and run queries using it. In case of encountering difficulties due to erroneous modeling, that classmate has to provide feedback to the original student; (4) All the above recommendations should be followed by class discussions in which students are exposed to problems their classmates encountered, so as to avoid them in the future.

In order to examine the contribution of our recommendations stated above, we recommend on repeating the process by implementing these recommendations and examining the future results against the results gained in the current study. In addition, the research population should be extended and the impact of this action on the findings should be examined.

REFERENCES

Batra, D., Hoffer, J.A., & Bostrom, R.P. 1990. Comparing representations with the relational and extended entity relationship models, *Communications of the ACM* 33, 126–139.

Batra, D., & Antony, S. 1994. Novice errors in database design, *European Journal of Information Systems* 3(1), 57–69.

Batra, D. 2007. Cognitive complexity in data modeling: Causes and recommendations. *Requirements Engineering* 12(4), 231–244.

Chen, P. P. S. 1976. The entity-relationship model—Toward a unified view of data. *ACM Transactions on Database Systems* 1(1), 9–36.

Dey, D., Storey, V. C., & Barron, T. M. 1999. Improving database design through the analysis of relationships. *ACM Transactions on Database Systems* 24(4), 453–486.

Hitchman, S. 2003. An interpretive study of how practitioners use entity-relationship modelling in a ternary relationship situation. *Communications of the Association for Information Systems* 11(1), 451–485.

Lenzerini, M., & Nobili, P. 1990. On the satisfiability of dependency constraints in entity-relationship schemata. *Information Systems* 15(4), 453–461.

Neuendorf, K. A. 2002. The Content Analysis Guidebook. Thousand Oaks, CA: Sage Publications.

Polya, G. 1985. How to Solve It. Princeton University Press.

Purao, S., Storey, V., & Han, T. 2003. Improving reuse-based design: Augmenting analysis patterns reuse with learning. *Inform Syst Res* 14, 269–290

Taylor, S.J. & Bogdan, R. 1998. Introduction to Qualitative Research Methods. New York: John Wiley & Sons.

Topi, H., Valacich, J. S., Wright, R. T., Kaiser, K., Nunamaker Jr, J. F., Sipior, J. C., & de Vreede, G. J. 2010. IS .2010: Curriculum guidelines for undergraduate degree programs in information systems. *Communications of the Association for Information Systems*, 26(1), 18.

RESEARCH-ORIENTED PRACTICAL PROBLEM SOLVING AS A LEARNING GOAL FOR THESIS COURSES

Ilia Bider and Paul Johannesson
DSV, Stockholm University, Sweden

ABSTRACT

The paper is devoted to the topic of introducing practically oriented thesis writing in the Department of Computer and Systems Sciences of Stockholm University. The paper considers both legal and practical aspects of introducing practically oriented thesis. The material is based partly on the literature study, and partly on the experience of supervising practically oriented BS and MS thesis in the department. The research presented in this paper is of the Action Research type. The paper introduces a rough classification of practically oriented thesis, and discusses problems that need to be solved, such as proper disposition, grading, and method-related courses.

KEYWORDS

Dissertation, Thesis, Education, Information Systems, Problem Solving

1. BACKGROUND AND MOTIVATION

The paper reports on ongoing practical and research work at the Department of Computer and Systems Sciences (abbreviated to DSV in Swedish) with several Information Technology (IT) and Information Systems (IS) related Bachelor and Master programs (not counting Doctoral programs). The work aims at facilitating our students to acquire skills of using contemporary research for solving practical problems. The needs for these skills arise from the fact that the majority of our students, both from BS and MS programs, pursue a professional career in private, non-profit or public sector after their graduation; only a small minority chooses an academic carrier. For the university in general and DSV in particular, it is important that the graduates get lasting scientific knowledge useful for their future practice. Otherwise, there is a risk that all scientific theories they studied will be soon and well forgotten.

That there actually are needs to give our students theoretical knowledge useful for practice have been confirmed in a recent survey conducted among our alumni. A number of students forwarded complaints that the theories they learned were not connected to practice, and wished this connection to be established. Some complaints were even more serious: some students stated that if they had had a chance to make their choice once more, they would have chosen a professional education, rather than an academic one.

In regards to our goal of facilitating students to acquire skills for research-oriented problem solving, two questions need to be answered:

1. What should be taught to the students, e.g. which kind of theories and methods?
2. How should it be taught, e.g. in which kind of courses?

In regards to the first question, we refer to the work of (Lee, 2010). Written in 2010, it gives a retrospective view on the IS discipline in the previous 25 years and tries to draft its path for the next 25 years (a third part of which has already passed). The main conclusion of this article is that there is a discrepancy between what IS is trying to achieve in the real world and in the university world. In the real world, IS is trying to establish itself as a profession based on the science of artificial, in the sense of (Simon, 1969). In the university world, however, IS is trying to establish itself as a discipline based on the natural science. The difference reveals itself in what kind of theories (models, methods, etc.) are in the focus for these two contradictory directions. While the university world is focused on theories that are aimed to *explain and predict*, in the categorization of (Gregor, 2006), the real world needs the theories of *design and action*, also in the categorization of (Gregor, 2006). The paper also suggests that the IS discipline needs to take the same path as medicine, engineering and architecture to become useful and relevant to the real world.

The findings of (Lee, 2010) are in full accordance to what our students do after their graduation. The large majority of them never do any social science type of investigations; instead, their tasks include, diagnostics, analysis, problem solving and design (which is apparent from what positions they take after their graduation according to our alumni survey). Thus, the theories they need are the theories of *design and action*. That said, teaching the latter just as theories is not enough to attain our goal of students acquiring skills of research-oriented practical problem solving. Some of the students' complaints were not about the theories themselves, but about not getting knowledge on applying them to practice. Teaching the latter is much more difficult than just teaching the theories, as it requires the students acquiring tacit knowledge (Polanyi, 1969), or Ways of Thinking and Practicing (McCune & Hounsell, 2005), and this type of knowledge is difficult to transfer remaining in the classroom environment.

To answer our second question, about how the theories of design and actions should be taught, we need to analyze our programs. As Sweden has adopted the Bologna recommendations, now, the department has three years BS (bachelor) programs and two years MS (master) programs. Adopting Bologna resulted in a substantial change in the programs, as before the adoption, the department had four-year candidate programs, and one year magister programs. The transfer from the Swedish candidate to BS programs resulted in losing one full year (two terms) of studying. The transfer from the Swedish Magister to Master programs was accompanied with enrolling bachelor students with less IT and IS education (including none), which makes the additional year received in the transition to Bologna used for catching up, i.e. giving courses that before belonged to the candidates programs.

Both BS and MS programs are concluded with a thesis (dissertation) course, which is mandatory. For BS programs, this course is a half term long, while for MS programs, this course is one term long (a quarter of the whole education length). Not all students complete this course in time, and many work on their theses after finishing their education and finding a job. Having thesis courses is mandated by the university, thus the department cannot remove them or substitute with some other courses, e.g. a capstone project. This situation, we believe, is typical not only for Sweden, but also for other European countries, but may not be typical for other regions, e.g. U.S. (Karsten et al., 2015) investigated IS master programs all over the world, and found that most of the European programs included a thesis course.

The short length of the programs does not allow introducing an additional course with just one learning goal *research-oriented problem solving*. Thus, we need to find an already existing course(s) to introduce this goal. Analyzing our programs, we concluded that the primary candidate for this end was the thesis courses in both BS and MS programs. Firstly, these courses are long enough to accommodate such a goal. Secondly, the students are supposed to do field work outside the university walls in these courses. The basic idea here is that the students do some actual work in an organization (private, nonprofit, or public) of the type they will be doing after their graduation, e.g. problem diagnostics, analysis or design.

One issue that needs to be resolved with the idea of using thesis courses is to fulfill the requirement of the Swedish legal framework related to higher education (Higher Education Ordinance), which prescribes the education having both a scientific base, and being related to practice. The risk of the thesis work becoming a consultant work, and the thesis – a consultant report needs to be mitigated. A traditional way of satisfying the requirement on scientific base in a thesis is asking the student to complete a mini-research project, e.g. a short empirical research based on surveys and/or interviews. However, the requirement on scientific base does not limit the ways in which it could be satisfied; other options are open for exploitation. One option that could be satisfactory for both requirements on scientific base and being related to practice is using contemporary research for solving practical problems in an organization to which a thesis work is attached, rather than employing standard solutions already accepted in practice. One can envision various ways of using research in problem solving. For example, one can review several scientific approaches suggested in the literature, choose one, and then report how well it worked in practice. Alternatively, one can pick a new innovative, but not tested in practice, theory or method, and try to apply it to a practical problem.

One question is whether the Swedish organizations are willing to accept the students using research-based solution, instead of more established in practice methods. In our practice, we found that Swedish organizations fully understand the needs for students fulfilling the requirements of a scientific base, and they are content to leave them to test new theories and ideas. This, probably, can be attributed to the fact that the managers, being former university students themselves, perfectly well understand the students' needs to pass their exams. We believe, that there are no hinders to encourage the students to do their thesis work as research-based practical problem solving at an industrial, public, or not-profit organization.

The goal of our current project is creating methodological support for practically oriented BS and MS thesis work. It aims at designing a set of logical templates and guidelines on selecting among these to be used by supervisors and students whose theses are aimed at solving concrete problems in practice. Under logical template, we understand a thesis report outline with suggestions on sections and subsections headings together with detailed explanations on what should be included in each section/subsection, as well as examples. A template serves as a guideline for both: how to do the work, and how to format the thesis report.

There is a large body of literature devoted to methodological support for thesis writing, including books dedicated to this purpose (Biggam, 2008). However, most of this literature is focused on the thesis being a small research project, rather than research based solving of practical problems in organizations or other societal setting. The literature devoted to practically oriented thesis writing is relatively rare, and mainly concerns doctoral thesis (Archbald, 2010). The recommendations from such literature, though useful, cannot be directly applied to BS and MS theses due to the different time frames for BS, MS and PhD thesis writing. So far, we have not found works related to BS and MS theses that include not only principles, but also logical templates of different kinds that would be suitable for our programs.

Methodologically, our work fits the action research paradigm (Baskerville & Myers, 2004; Kolb, 1984), as we deal with a problem found in a local (teaching) practice, and we are testing a solution in the same practice. Our research can also be categorized as Design Science (DS) research (Hevner et al., 2004), as we aim at designing a solution (or artefact) in the form of a set of logical templates and rules of how to choose the one that suits best particular business settings.

The rest of the paper has the following structure. We start with literature review. Then, we describe the main ideas of our project. After that, we describe the current state of the project, plans for the future and potential impact of our work on the society in case of success, including accomplishing the third mission.

2. LITERATURE REVIEW

2.1 General Literature on Thesis Writing and Supervision

The literature on the topic of writing and supervising theses is vast. The literary review (Svärd, 2013) has found more than 200 research articles related to the theme; this number does not include numerous books and manuals with prescriptions on writing thesis and thesis structure. The reviewed literature covers a wide range of topics, such as motivation (including legal issues), completion, disposition, grading criteria, supervision, etc. The conclusion that (Svärd, 2013) draws is that the area is quite researched, but lack of systematization. However, it also underlines that not all areas related to BS/MS thesis are investigated in the same depth. Some relevant for our work areas that lack consensus, or are less investigated are highlighted below.

The research on thesis work is mostly related to professional education, especially in such areas as teaching (see also the next section) and nursing. Some other professions that have research on thesis writing include engineering, business and psychology. (Svärd, 2013) does not mention any works related to Information Systems Education, or Computer Science. This corresponds to our own experience of trying to find research papers on thesis writing in IS.

There is no consensus on the motivation of the thesis work. There are two opinion on the motivation: one is that thesis work should be regarded as preparation for research activity, the second is that the thesis work should aim at preparing students for work outside academia. The discussion on which motivation should prevail is going for several decades without reaching a consensus. The more spread opinion is the research-oriented motivation, though the professional preparedness motivation is also discussed in the literature. For example, (I'Anson & Smith, 2004), among other rationales for thesis work, include:

- To help the students' ability to define and analyze a complex business problem
- To help students integrate academic knowledge and practical applications

These rationales are in full agreement with our opinion on the thesis work aim.

From the legal perspective, the Swedish legal regulation is considered as not very restrictive, see for example (Gustafsson, 2008) that analyzes the history of regulation in this area. This "elasticity" of regulations is compensated by each Swedish university department choosing to interpret the regulation in different ways dependent on the subject matter, and own preferences. (Gustafsson, 2008) also makes an observation that though the regulation does not prohibit practically-oriented thesis, they are not very common, at least in the teachers education. The main reason for this is considered not the regulation as such, but academics themselves "who have an academic tradition and who want to protect the degree project as an academic product." We believe that this also explains the fact that the literature related to practically oriented thesis is not that extensive compared with the literature related to research-oriented thesis.

From the disposition perspective, (Svärd, 2013) states that most common type of thesis is a mini-doctoral dissertation, though alternative forms are also discussed in the research literature. One of this form is a Patchwork Text (Maisch, 2003), or Portfolio (Meeus et al., 2004) where a dissertation consists of an assortment of texts written at different times and connected together in the end. Though this form could be of interest in some fields, we do not believe that it would be beneficial for the practically oriented thesis in our discipline.

As far as books and manuals for conducting thesis work are concerned, they are numerous. However, as (Svärd, 2013) concludes, the great majority of them consider only a research-oriented work formed as a mini PhD dissertation. This observation corresponds to our own experience when trying to find a proper disposition for practically oriented BS/MS thesis.

2.2 Literature Relevant to the Topic of Practical Oriented Thesis

In this section, we review the works which are directly related to our topic, and which discuss not only the needs and ideas of practically oriented theses, but also practical experience of introducing this kind of thesis writing. The best works that we have found that are related to the topic belong to the educational domain (Archbald, 2008; Archbald, 2010; Belzer & Ryan, 2013). Though these works concern doctoral education, insights from them are highly relevant to undergraduate theses as well.

A seminal work in this area (Archbald, 2008) starts with:

"*Although many doctoral mentors doubtless have misgivings about training someone to do research who is not going into professional research, such misgivings have not translated into organized efforts at change or even much public deliberation on the subject*"

The paper continues with discussing the four important issues related to doctoral theses: (a) developmental efficacy, (b) community benefit, (c) intellectual stewardship, and (d) distinctiveness in form and function. During this discussion, the paper underlines the difference between the research-oriented and practically oriented dissertations in regard to these issues. For example, while the goal of efficacy with research-oriented dissertations is training in being a researcher, this goal for the practically oriented dissertations is training for the practical purpose, for educational leadership in the particular case taken in the paper. The paper proceeds with pointing out five areas where research and practically oriented dissertation differs:

1. Pragmatic problem, not theoretical question
2. Multiple questions, not a single hypothesis or research question
3. Persuasion, not proof
4. Recommended actions, not conclusions
5. Professional report, not a research monograph

The following work of the same author (Archbald, 2010) discusses the experience of having practically oriented doctoral programs. It points out four major changes that need to be done for transiting from research-oriented to practically oriented dissertations, noting that these changes are not small adjustments, but a radical change that results in breaking the current tradition:

1. Research studies begin with theory, curiosity, and questions. The topic and research question is based on studying the literature and identifying a gap in theories. In real-world practice, problems do not present themselves to the practitioner as givens. The candidate must construct a problem definition, defining a gap between an existing state in an organization and a preferred goal state.
2. The literature review in a traditional thesis is presented in a chapter. In a practically oriented thesis, according to (Archbald, 2010), it should be used in any place of the text as needed.
3. In a research thesis, the epistemology and methods of science govern the collecting, reporting, and interpretation of evidence. The new type of theses reflects an epistemology of decision-making. This statement corresponds to the difference between usage of theories for *explaining and predicting* on the

one hand and theories for *design and actions*, in the categorization of (Gregor, 2006) on the other hand, which was discussed in the previous section.

4. A research dissertation is aimed at generation of new knowledge to be presented to the examination committee, which serves as a proxy for the larger scholarly audience. The new thesis compiles scholarly narrative along with documents for organizational audiences and other artifacts generated as part of the problem solving initiative.

(Belzer & Ryan, 2013) summarizes the experience of practically oriented dissertation programs at School of Education at Rutgers focusing on which kind of problems are to be handled in the practically oriented dissertations. In their practice, the three types of practical questions are most common: "(1) questions that evaluate an initiative or policy that is already in place, (2) questions that ask what happens when the student implements an initiative to solve a problem and improve outcomes, and (3) questions that seek to describe current conditions as a way to generate appropriate and contextualized solutions to problems". All three correspond to the recommendations in a handbook they created for the program.

(Mason et al., 2015) presents an experience of making dissertation relevant in Lamar University. Besides the issues discussed in other works, this paper discusses support the university provides in offering doctoral candidates opportunities to team with organizations throughout the world in order to affect change and impart relevant impact on education and communities.

3. OUR APPROACH

The literature reviewed in the previous sections gives insights in the issues to be resolved when transiting from research-oriented to practice-oriented dissertations. However, the experience presented in this literature cannot be directly applied to our BS and MS programs without adaptations. Firstly, our programs are in another domain in which the students work with both organizational and technological issues, and often a combination of both. Thus, practical problems can be connected to system design and implementation in organizational practice. Secondly, and more important, the time frame of a BS and even MSc thesis course radically differs from the PhD study.

In principle, the easiest way of introducing practically-oriented thesis in the IS discipline while formally remaining in the research domain would be forming the work according to the Action Research (AR) (Baskerville & Myers, 2004) or Design Science (DS) (Hevner et al., 2004) paradigm. The latter was what we tried in our department by creating a template for DS based theses. However, due to the short time frame even for the MS thesis work, this template did not work well, as it required to address all parts of the DS process, while a student, usually, could be able to complete only one or few of them. The template created unnecessary formalities that distracted and confused the students. We did not try to make an AR template, as the chances that a student can complete even half of the AR cycle are slim. Based on the experience of using the DS template, we decided to create a set of less bureaucratic templates, each of which covers a specific type of the thesis projects.

For developing new templates, we assume that the settings for a practically oriented BS or MS thesis are as follows. The work is connected to an organization that provides the student with access to the information related to the organization's business and its technological infrastructure. Such access consists of possibility to interview the staff of the organization and/or conduct a small-scale survey, read internal documentation, including documentation on their IT systems, observe how the staff works, e.g. by being present at the internal meetings. We also assume that the students have a possibility to present the results of their work to the management and other workers involved in the area of thesis work, and get feedback on the usefulness of these results.

To satisfy the requirement on having both scientific and practical content, we consider two dimensions in order to create a general classification of thesis work: (1) business dimension and (2) theoretical dimension. The business dimension is related to whether the organization wants the student to deal with a particular problem they want to solve, or challenge to meet, or they allow him/her to freely choose what to focus one. This dimension is about the problem uncertainty. The theoretical dimension is related to whether the student has a preference to certain theories, methods, modeling techniques, etc. that s/he wants to test, or these need to be found during the work on the thesis. This preference can come from the student's own interests, advice from the supervisor, or even from the organization to which the student work is attached. Combining the two dimensions, we get a classification of the thesis works as represented in Fig. 1. Note that term theory in this picture is interpreted in a broad way; a theory can be a specific modeling technique, or some kind of a method.

The classification in Fig.1 defines a starting point for the student work, which can be of three types, explained below:

1. Testing a specific theory, method, modeling technique, etc. for solving a specific problem or meeting a challenge. The task here could be to identify the underlying cause of the problem (diagnostics) and/or suggest a solution. The outcome can be both positive, the theory has been found suitable or not suitable for solving this kind of problems. The theory, method, or modeling technique used should be somewhat innovative, e.g. new, or not much tested for this specific problem-solving.
2. Finding a theory method, modeling technique, etc. for solving a specific problem or meeting a specific challenge. The focus here is to complete the task of the same kind as in quadrant one while finding a suitable way of doing so. The outcome is to be positive, i.e. the task completed is by the end of the thesis.
3. Having an interesting, and innovating theory, method, modeling technique, etc. find out what can it be used for in an organization. It could be a completely new theory, or a student will try to find an unusual usage of the known theory.

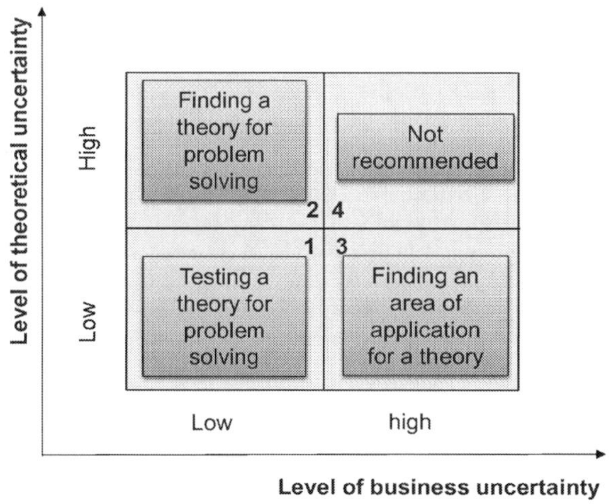

Figure 1. Classification of Thesis Types

The fourth type is not recommended due to the short timeframe for completing the work; a student needs to have a more definite starting point for his/her work then just having an organization to be attached to. Also, the starting point does not preclude changing to another quadrant after the work has already been started. For example, a student starting in quadrant one can discover at an early stage that the original theory does not suit the task, and transits to quadrant 2 in order to complete the task, not just report on the unsuitability of the original theory. As another example, a student starting in quadrant 3 can early in his/her work find a particular problem to work on and switches to quadrant 1 to continue his/her work.

To illustrate Fig. 1, below, we give one example of MS thesis for each of the recommended quadrants:

1. Business context is an IT consulting company. Business problem is to analyze external and internal communication in the frame of a business process and find areas for improvement. Theoretical foundation is a LAP-based (LAP = Language Action Perspective) methodology developed for analyzing communication capabilities of business process support systems (Bider, 2015). This framework had never been tried for analysis of communication as such. The thesis work included adjusting the framework to the new task, conducting interviews, completing analysis of communication in one of the processes and presenting the findings to the management. The findings included a list of areas for improvement and some suggestions.

2. Business context is a manufacturing company. Business problem is a dysfunctioning business process of producing a sample of a new material on the request of an existing customer. The company discovered that the time for completing such a request started to grow, which was not appreciated by the customers. The work included finding the cause and suggesting a way to optimizing the process. First, the company wanted the student to use a specific method for the task, but agreed to allow the student to freely choose any method(s) that would be found suitable. The students conducted a field study and applied several methods for analyzing and interpreting the material, two of which were taken from the latest research publications (on the advice of the supervisor). The main problem with the process was defined as the process not having dedicated resources, e.g. people, machines, materials, but using resources dedicated to the production process in an ad hoc manner. One of the technique used for interpreting the material showed exactly what resources where shared between the processes, and what was lacking. The results were presented to the company management, who said that they had had some suspicion that there is a managerial problem, but did not now it for sure.
3. Business context is an IT solutions provider. Theoretical background is a new technique for enterprise modeling (Bider et al., 2017). The task is to discover new areas of application for the technique. An approach taken in the thesis project was to build a model that would cover some important parts of the enterprise, and then to present it to the employees with different roles and ask these for what purpose(s) the model could be used. The company agreed to provide resources (people to interview and observe, documentation, etc.) for the study, even though it was not aimed at solving a specific problem. The model was built and presented, and very interesting for farther research feedback was obtained.

4. CURRENT STATE, PLANS FOR THE FUTURE AND POTENTIAL IMPACT

Our work on methodological support for practically oriented theses started at the end of 2015 and was completed on the basis of an individual initiative in spare time. We created a set of logical templates and short guidelines for how to choose a suitable one base on the case in question in the form of a decision table (Bider, 2016). The templates were published on the thesis course website with recommendation for the supervisors to use them when the thesis is related to a case in practice. The templates and guidelines were used in our own practice and by some other teachers who considered them useful. Besides using the templates to organize the students work and the structure of the thesis, the templates were used as a means for communication between the teaching staff engaged in the thesis work: Supervisor-Reviewer-Examiner.

As the project had been started based on personal initiative, there were no dedicated resources attached to it. Templates and guidelines, though useful, have never been modified/extended/streamlined based on the practice of their usage. Also, designing the templates was not coordinating with adjusting the grading criteria and methodological courses, of which we had more than one. This resulted in the templates we created having historical traits of the old thinking – considering a thesis as a mini research. The historical traits and the old-style methodological courses resulted in some confusion among students, which created an additional burden for the supervisors. In addition, no investigation of the impact of the new thesis types on the students learning has been made, and no efforts to promote them among all supervisors have been undertaken.

For the future, we plan actions aimed at moving the project beyond being the individuals' initiative to becoming part of the strategy of improving the education in the department. In particular, the activities listed as not completed at the end of the previous section need to be completed, e.g.:

- Based on the outline presented above and experience of template usage correct, streamline and extend the existing set of templates. Classification from Fig. 1 could be employed for this end.
- Investigate the impact on students learning through surveys/ interviews with current and former students.
- Adapt grading criteria and scientific writing and methodology courses to include the new type of thesis.
- Introduce a new method course aimed at preparing the students for writing practically oriented thesis. The decision on this issue has already been taken and the work is about to start in spring 2019.

These activities are aimed at making the theses of the *research-oriented problem solving* type well established in the department.

Besides attaining our main goal stated above, we believe that introduction of the practically oriented type of thesis can assist in accomplishing the university's third mission: (a) targeted use and transfer of academic knowledge to help resolve diverse societal challenges, and (b) transfer of technologies and innovations in the form of cooperation with public and private enterprises. Firstly, the academic staff, as students' supervisors, will be directly involved in solving practical problems advising the students on what theories and methods to choose, including those that are worked out by the supervisors themselves. Secondly, the students who have acquired the research-oriented problem solving skills during the thesis course will be able to use these skills after graduation, if not immediately, then after achieving a more independent senior position in their future careers. This can multiply the efforts of our academic staff, and, hopefully, lead to the usage of research-oriented problem solving becoming a norm in practice, rather than an exception.

REFERENCES

Archbald, D., 2008. Research Versus Problem Solving for the Education Leadership Doctoral Thesis: Implications for Form and Function. *Educational Administration Quarterly*, 44(5), pp.704-39.

Archbald, D., 2010. "Breaking the Mold" in the Dissertation: Implementing a Problem-Based, Decision-Oriented Thesis Project. *The Journal of Continuing Higher Education, 58*, 58(2), pp.99–107.

Baskerville, R. & Myers, M.D., 2004. Special Issue on Action Research in Information Systems: Making IS Research Relevant to Practice—Foreword. *MIS Quarterly*, 28(3), pp.329-35.

Belzer, A. & Ryan, S., 2013. Defining the Problem of Practice Dissertation: Where's the Practice, What's the Problem? *Planning and Changing*, 44(3/4), pp.195–207.

Bider, I., 2015. Analyzing communication capabilities of CM/ACM systems with the help of Language/Action perspective. In L. Fischer, ed. *Thriving on Adaptability: Best practices for knowledge workers*. Future Strategies Inc. pp.88-99.

Bider, I., 2016. *Choosing Template.* [Online] Available at: http://bit.ly/2TfPice [Accessed February 2019].

Bider, I., Perjons, E., Elias, M. & Johannesson, P., 2017. A fractal enterprise model and its application for business development. *Software & Systems Modeling*, 16(3), pp.663–89.

Biggam, J., 2008. *Succeeding with Your Master's Dissertation. A step-by-step handbook.* Open University Press.

Gregor, S., 2006. The Nature of Theory in Information Systems. *MIS Quarterly*, 30(3), pp.611-42.

Gustafsson, C., 2008. Degree Project in Higher Education. In M. Mattson, I. Johansson & B. Sandström, eds. *Examining Praxis*. Rotterdam: Sense Publishers. pp.7–34.

Hevner, A.R., March, S.T. & and, P.J., 2004. Design Science in Information Systems Research. *MIS Quarterly*, 28(1), pp.75-105.

I'Anson, R.A. & Smith, K.A., 2004. Undergraduate Research Projects and Dissertations: issues of topic selection, access and data collection amongst tourism management students. *Journal of Hospitality, Leisure, Sport & Tourism Education*, 3(1), pp.19–32.

Karsten, H. et al., 2015. Master's Degree Programs in Information Systems: A Global View. In *SIGED: IAIM Conference*. AIS.

Kolb, D.A., 1984. *Experiential learning: Experience as the source of learning and development*. Englewood Cliffs, NJ, US: Prentice-Hall.

Lee, A.S., 2010. Retrospect and prospect: information systems research in the last and next 25 years. *Journal of Information Technology*, 25, pp.336–48.

Maisch, M., 2003. Restructuring a Master's Degree Dissertation as a Patchwork Text. *Innovations in Education and Teaching International*, 40(2), pp.194–201.

Mason, D., Shelton, S. & Saltsman, G., 2015. Making the doctoral dissertation relevant. In *The meeting of the National Council for Professors of Educational Administration (NCPEA)*. Washington, DC.

McCune, V. & Hounsell, D., 2005. The development of students' ways of thinking and practising in three final-year biology courses. *Higher Education*, 49(3), pp. 255-289.

Meeus, W., Van Looy, L. & Libotton, A., 2004. The Bachelor's thesis in teacher education. *European Journal of Teacher Education*, 27, pp.299–314.

Polanyi, M.S., 1969. *Knowing and Being.* Chicago: University of Chicago.

Simon, H., 1969. *The Sciences of the Artificial.* Cambridge, MA: MIT Press.

Svärd, O., 2013. *Examensarbetet i högre utbildning: En litteraturöversikt*. Pedagogical Research in Uppsala, No 165. Uppsala : Uppsala University Institutionen för pedagogik, didaktik och utbildningsstudier.

THE ACCEPTANCE OF COMPULSORY USE OF IPAD MINI: "ORIGINAL" UTAUT PERSPECTIVE

Samiaji Sarosa
Atma Jaya Yogyakarta University, Jl. Babarsari 43 Yogyakarta, Indonesia 55281

ABSTRACT

Faculty of Economics, Atma Jaya Yogyakarta University (FEUAJY) since 2015 has decided that new undergraduate students have to purchase iPad Mini and e-books as part of intake package. This study is looking at the acceptance of compulsory iPad Mini usage and purchase for supporting academic activities when the students are required to purchase instead of voluntary. This study used the "original" UTAUT model by using Self-Efficacy and Computer Anxiety variables and dropping Voluntariness moderating variable. A survey was employed to gather data from class intake of 2015 and 2016 FEUAJY undergraduate students. The result of the survey was analysed using PLS-SEM. The result shown that the original UTAUT model could explain the acceptance of iPad Mini and consistent with findings of previous study on the same population with some different result.

KEYWORDS

UTAUT, iPad Mini, Acceptance, Compulsory

1. INTRODUCTION

The use of technology for teaching and learning has been common for quite sometimes. Different technologies such as personal computers and laptop, computer projectors, multimedia devices, computer networks, the Internet, etc. have been used to enhanced, supplement, and even provide a new mode of learning such in case of online classroom. Recent development in mobile device, electronic content (including e-books), and e-learning platforms has also been adopted quite extensively and intensively. Few research into the use and development of technology in the classroom has been made such as Brill and Galloway (2007), Mandl, Kohane, McFaden .(2014), Raaij and Schepers (2008), Halonen, Acton, Golden and Conboy, (2009) among others.

Faculty of Economics, Atma Jaya Yogyakarta University (FEUAJY) in Indonesia has been requiring new undergraduate students to purchase a set of English language textbooks (mostly from US publishers and authors) when they enrolled in the university. The books are intended for five first-year subjects for all undergraduate students from three departments within FEUAJY (namely accounting, management, and economics). The subjects are Introduction to Business, Introduction to Accounting, Introduction to Information Systems, Business Mathematics, and Introduction to Economic Theory. This practice has been implemented since early 2000's. Since 2015, FEUAJY changed the policy and adopting e-books to replace physical books. Along with the change, FEUAJY also made it compulsory for undergraduate students to buy Apple iPad Mini Wifi 16 GB (iPad Mini) for delivering the e-books. The policy means an increase in the fee paid by new undergraduate students to cover both e-books and iPad Mini, whereas previously new undergraduate students only hadto pay for printed textbooks.

The compulsory iPad Mini policy is not accepted by all, some lecturers especially those who teach Introductory Financial Accounting subject complained that the usage of iPad Mini disrupt the way they usually deliver the lectures and tutorials. Some complaints also emerged from the applicants who had been accepted at FEUAJY but withdrew their applications due to higher cost of admission. The additional cost of iPad Mini is about US$ 365 on top of admission fee and other fees (Pramudita 2017).

A follow up research (Sarosa 2017) on the same population as Pramudita (2017) was conducted in the middle 2017 using UTAUT (Venkatesh et al. 2003; Venkatesh, Thong & Xu 2016). The result was that the UTAUT could explain the acceptance of involuntary iPad Mini used among two groups of first year students at FEUAJY (Sarosa 2017). The result also showed that the moderating variables of Gender and Experience are not supported by the findings. Age as moderating variable was eliminated considering the fact that the participants were from the intake of 2015 and 2016. They are only having less than 2 years of age difference among them. The age difference was deemed as not significant enough to show any impact. Voluntariness of Use as moderating variable was eliminated due to the fact the use of iPad Mini was and is mandatory for new students at FEUAJY.

This research was conducted with few reasons. First reason is based on the R^2 of the previous result using UTAUT was quite low. The result of UTAUT model with moderating variables Gender and Experience only showing that Behaviour Intention (BI) have 26.2% R^2 (Sarosa 2017). Therefore 73.8% of Use is explained by other variables which are not included in the UTAUT Model. UTAUT was claimed to have been able to explain up to 70% of the variance in intention to use technology (Venkatesh et al. 2003). The claim of 70% was criticised by Raaij and Schepers (2008) by arguing that is only achieved when moderating key relationships with up to four variables. In previous study, the moderating variables used was only two.

This study tries to use additional variables with the UTAUT, which are Attitude Toward Using, Self-Efficacy, and Anxiety. The additional variables are expected able to explain factors influencing the acceptance and use of iPad Mini.

2. ACCEPTANCE OF MOBILE LEARNING TECHNOLOGY

Unified Theory of Acceptance and Use of Technology (UTAUT) formulated by has been used extensively for information technology acceptance such as (Akbar 2013; Kohnke, Cole & Bush 2014; Marchewka, Liu & Kostiwa 2016)

This section would provide theoretical basis for the use of UTAUT and the use of mobile device (tablet) for learning in university environment. The discussion started with the use of mobile technology for teaching and learning. The second part is discussing the UTAUT and justification on using "original" model. This section would be ended by the development of hypotheses.

Using mobile technology for teaching and learning

The use of information and communication technology for learning has been studied quiet extensively. For example, Yuen, Law, and Wong (2003) found that ICT innovation adopted by schools in Hong Kong has been affected by schools' objectives, perception of ICT's role in education as well as the understanding of teaching and learning and the part played by teachers and students. The impact of ICT adoption toward first year university students has been studied and the findings showed that familiarity with ICT is one of the keys to successful adoption (Verhoeven, Heerwegh, & De Wit, 2010). Akbar (2013) confirmed that familiarity with ICT is influencing the success of adoption of ICT for students.

As part of adopting ICT into teaching and learning, various elements have been adopted such as e-learning systems, Learning Management Systems (LMS), and even mobile learning. Mobile learning is defined as the delivery of learning to students anytime and anywhere through the use of wireless Internet and mobile devices such as computer tablet (Wang, Wu, & Wang, 2009). Siau, Lim, and Shen (2001) explained some of the limitation of using mobile devices such as small screen size, resolutions, underperformed compared to personal computers, battery life, and graphical limitation. Arguably some of the limitations of mobile device currently has been overcomed (for example battery life, screen size, and screen resolutions), yet the performance of computer tablet such as iPad Mini is still far away from the personal computers. For example, a scan of Apple App Store in iPad Mini could not find the equivalent of statistical package such as SPSS for tablet. Looking at the common usage tablet among FEUAJY students, the use of iPad Mini for teaching and learning is currently limited to information gathering (including e-books and web browsing) and communications and collaborations (email, chat, instant messaging, social media). For serious data analysis and report writing, students still need a personal computer (desktop or laptop).

Limited capability and capacity of iPad Mini along with relatively expensive price (therefore low price to performance ratio compared to some laptop) make the decision to adopt seemed problematic. The price of iPad Mini is equivalent with some laptop having Intel Core i3 processors, 4 GB RAM, and 1 TB storage. A laptop has lower mobility score compared to iPad Mini but have much bigger raw computing power. Pramudita (2017) started his study into the net benefit of using iPad Mini among FEUAJY students based on the premises of iPad Mini has higher price tag and lower raw computing power. Pramudita (2017) investigate the use of e-books and iPad Mini using DeLone and McLean Information Systems Success Model (W. H. DeLone & McLean, 2003; Halonen et al., 2009). DeLone and McLean model assess the success of an information systems (in this case the e-books and iPad Mini) by the proxy of net benefit. Net Benefit is influenced by Use and User Satisfaction which in turn influenced by Systems Quality, Information Quality, and Service Quality (W. H. DeLone & McLean, 2003). Pramudita conducted a survey to 253 students of the 2015 and 2016 classes. The results are Information Quality influenced both Use and User Satisfaction, Systems Quality influenced both Use and User Satisfaction, Service Quality influenced User Satisfaction, Service Quality did not influence Use, Use influenced User Satisfaction and Net Benefit, and User Satisfaction influenced Net Benefit.

DeLone and McLean model only look at the actual use, user satisfaction, and net benefit of an information systems to judge the success. It does not look into the acceptance of the information systems itself. This article reports the findings of study into the acceptance of iPad Mini by FEUAJY undergraduate students from the class of 2015 and 2016. The study is deemed necessary to look into the acceptance of FEUAJY policy where new undergraduate students have to pay additional fee on top of other entrance fees for buying iPad Mini. The study use the unified theory of acceptance and use of technology (UTAUT) originally proposed by Venkatesh, Morris, G. Davis, and F. Davis (2003).

2.1 UTAUT

UTAUT was originally proposed by Venkatesh, Morris, G. Davis, and F. Davis (2003) as refinement and improvement of various previous user acceptance of technology models. The UTAUT model can be seen in Figure 1 below.

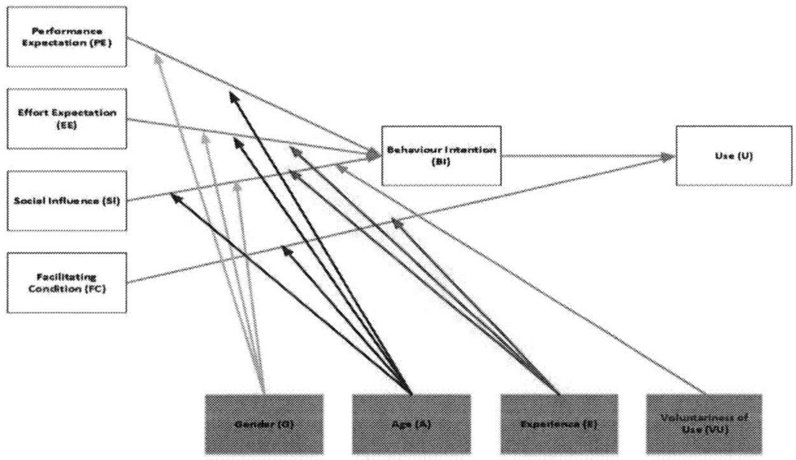

Figure 1. The original model of Unified Theory of User Acceptance of Technology or UTAUT (Venkatesh et al., 2003)

The acceptance of a technology is shown by the use of the technology (U). U is influenced by Behavioural Intention (BI) and Facilitating Conditions (FC). BI itself is influenced by Performance Expectancy (PE), Effort Expectancy (EE), and Social Influence (SI). UTAUT also use moderating variables for the relationship between variables. Gender (G) is moderating variable for PE, EE, and SI influences toward BI. Age (A) is moderating variable for PE, EE, SI influences toward BI and FC influence toward U. Experience (E) is moderating variable for EE, SI influences toward BI and FC influence toward U. Voluntariness of Use (VU) is moderating variable for SI influence toward BI.

UTAUT is an integration of eight different models of technology acceptance theory (Venkatesh et al., 2003). UTAUT use four core constructs to explain and predict user acceptance of a new technology: PE (equivalent to perceived usefulness), EE (equivalent to perceived ease of use), FC, and SI (Raaij & Schepers, 2008). UTAUT has been extensively used for various research such as to investigate mobile banking adoption (Tan & Lau, 2016), investigating students' acceptance of technology in Qatar (Akbar, 2013), acceptance of course management software (Marchewka, Liu, & Kostiwa, 2016), and acceptance of hospital information systems (Sharifian, Askarian, Nematolahi, & Farhadi, 2014) among others.

In the previous study (Sarosa 2017), the UTAUT model was slightly modified by eliminating Age and Voluntariness of Use, which can be seen on Fig 2. Age as moderating variable is eliminated due the fact that the participants were from the class of 2015 and 2016. They are only having less than 2 years age difference. The age difference is deemed as not significant enough to show any difference. Voluntariness of Use as moderating variable is eliminated due to the fact the use of iPad Mini is mandatory for new students at FEUAJY. Therefore, the moderating variables are only Gender (G) and Experience (E) in using or owning tablet computers and not only iPad Mini (Brill & Galloway, 2007; Mandl et al., 2014; Venkatesh et al., 2003).

The result of UTAUT model with moderating variables Gender and Experience only showing that Behaviour Intention (BI) have 26.2% R^2 (Sarosa 2017). Therefore 73.8% of Use is explained by other variables which are not included in the original UTAUT Model used in this research. The UTAUT was claimed to have been able to explain up to 70% of the variance in intention to use technology (Venkatesh et al. 2003). The claim of 70% was criticised by Raaij and Schepers (2008) by arguing that is only achieved when moderating key relationships with up to four variables. In previous study (Sarosa 2017), the moderating variables used was only two.

In the original UTAUT article (Venkatesh et al. 2003), there are three additional variables in UTAUT that were excluded from the final version of UTAUT. The variables are Attitude Toward Using (ATU), Self-Efficacy (SE), and Computer Anxiety (ANX) (Akbar 2013; Venkatesh et al. 2003). The three variables were dropped since it was deemed as did not have any direct effect on intention to use the technology. In this study, we tried to see if ATU, SE, ANX has any effect toward either Behaviour Intention (BI) to use iPad Mini.

We have the data from previous study that include three moderating variables, which are Gender, Experience, and Age. We exclude Age since we deemed it was not much difference between the users since they were only 2 years apart. In this study we include Age as moderating variables as suggested by Raaij and Schepers (2008). The model used in this study could be seen in Figure 2 below.

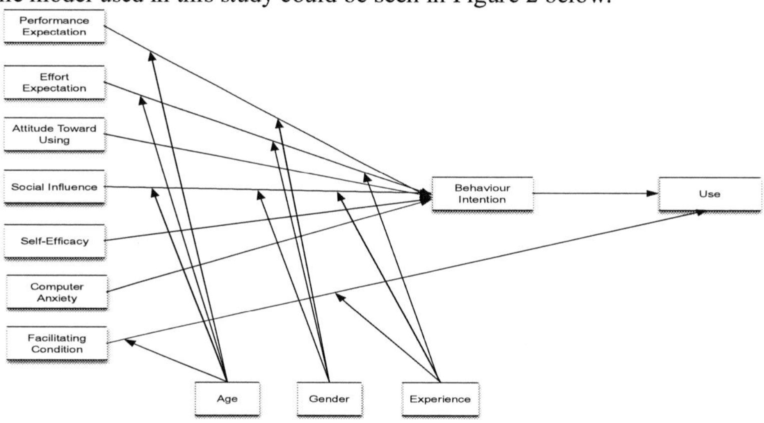

Figure 2. The original model of Unified Theory of User Acceptance of Technology or UTAUT (Venkatesh et al., 2003)

2.2 Hypotheses Development

The original UTAUT model consist of seven constructs. There are:

Table 1. "Original" UTAUT Constructs (Akbar 2013; Venkatesh et al. 2003)

Construct	Definition
Performance Expectancy (PE)	The degree to which an individual believes that using the system will help him or her to attain gains in learning performance.
Effort Expectancy (EE)	The degree of ease associated with the use of the system.
Attitude towards using technology (ATU)	An individual's overall affective reaction to using a system.
Social Influence (SI)	The degree to which an individual perceives that important others believe he or she should use the new system.
Facilitating Conditions (FC)	The degree to which an individual believes that an organizational and technical infrastructure exists to support use of the system.
Computer self-efficacy (SE)	Judgment of one's ability to use a technology to accomplish a particular job or task. (adapted from the Social Cognitive Theory)
Computer anxiety (ANX)	Evoking anxious or emotional reactions when it comes to performing a behaviour (i.e. using the technology)

PE is the extent of a student believes that the task performance would be improved by using particular technology (Venkatesh et al., 2003). In this study, PE is measured by asking students their perception on how the iPad Mini would help them in their lectures/classes, finishing their assignments faster, increasing their productivity, and as the result gaining better marks (Akbar 2013; Marchewka, Liu & Kostiwa 2016; Venkatesh et al. 2003) Therefore:

H1 PE would influence BI to use iPad Mini and would be moderated by Age or A (H1a) and Gender or G (H1b)

EE is the extent of effort needed by a student to use iPad Mini for their academic activities (Tan & Lau 2016; Venkatesh et al. 2003). Therefore:

H2 EE would influence BI to use iPad Mini and would be moderated by A (H2a), G (H2b), and Experience or E (H2c)

SI is the degree of perception of a student on how the other students, lecturers, faculty, and other people think that the students should use the iPad Mini (Akbar 2013; Brennan & Johnson 2000; Venkatesh et al. 2003). SI is the subjective norm that might influence the intention of use a particular technology (Tan & Lau 2016). Therefore:

H3 SI perception would influence BI to use iPad Mini and would be moderated by A (H3a), G (H3b), and E (H3c)

FC is the degree to which a student believes that an organizational and technical infrastructure exists to support use of the system (Venkatesh et al. 2003). In this study, FC is measured by looking at resources to support students in using iPad Mini, iPad Mini compatibility with the other gadgets owned by students, students' knowledge, and technical support provided by the faculty and vendor (Akbar 2013). Therefore

H4 FC would influence Use of iPad Mini (U) and would be moderated by A (H4a) and E (H4b)

SE is defined as judgment of one's ability to use a technology (e.g., computer) to accomplish a particular job or task (Compeau & Higgins 1995a, 1995b; Venkatesh et al. 2003). Therefore

H5 SE would influence BI to use iPad Mini

ANX is defined as evoking anxious or emotional reactions when it comes to performing a behaviour (Bandura 1986; Bozionelos 1996; Fagan, Neill & Wooldridge 2003; Hong et al. 2012; Venkatesh 2000). Therefore

H6 ANX would influence BI to use iPad Mini in a negative way

ATU is defined as an individual's overall affective reaction to using a system (Akbar 2013; Venkatesh et al. 2003). Therefore

H7 ATU would influence BI to use iPad Mini

BI would influence the use of technology (Marchewka, Liu & Kostiwa 2016; Raaij & Schepers 2008; Venkatesh et al. 2003). Therefore

H8 BI would influence Use of iPad Mini (U)

3. RESEARCH METHOD

The survey was developed based on the "original" UTAUT model (Akbar 2013; Venkatesh et al. 2003) and modifying it by eliminating Voluntariness questions. The survey used Likert Scale with range of 1 to 5, where 1 is represents strongly disagree and 5 represents strongly agree. The population of FEUAJY students who have to purchase iPad Mini is 1400 from the intake year 2015 and 2016. We prepared a survey questionnaire adopted from the "original" UTAUT. The survey was conducted in the second half of 2016-2017 academic year. We distributed the questionnaires to Introduction to Financial Accounting 2 classes for class of 2016 and Information Systems Management Classes for class of 2015. As many as 450 questionnaires were distributed. We were asking the lecturer for each class to distribute the questionnaires to their students and also to gather the responses. We received 371 filled questionnaires, but further examination revealed that only 349 were usable. The respondents' profile could be seen in table 2.

For data analysis, we used Structural Equation Modelling or SEM using Partial Least Square or PLS (Kline, 2011; Westland, 2015). We utilised SmartPLS software by SmartPLS version 3 (Ringle, 2015).

Data Analysis

For SEM, the analysis using SmartPLS version 3 started by examining Outer Model (Kline 2011; Ringle 2015; Westland 2015). Outer Model Output for SmartPLS consist of evaluating Convergent Validity, Discriminant Validity, Composite Reliability, Average Variance Extracted (AVE), and Cronbach's Alpha.

Table 2. Respondents' Profile

		Number	Percentage
Gender	*Male*	120	35%
	Female	229	66%
Previous tablet ownership	*Yes*	131	38%
	No	218	62%
Department	*Accounting*	161	46%
	Management	103	30%
	Economics	6	2%
	No Answer	79	22%

As a rule of thumbs Convergence Validity value should be greater than 0.7, AVE greater than 0.5, and Cronbach Alpha should be greater than 0.6. Therefore, we decided to delete Q14 and Q18 which has Outer Loading value less than 0.7. All variables shown Cronbach Alpha greater than 0.6, therefore we decided to keep all the variables.

We tested the hypothesis by using SmartPLS's Bootstrapping. The result can be seen in table 3 below.

Table 3. Path Coefficient

	Original Sample (O)	Sample Mean (M)	Standard Deviation (STDEV)	T Statistics (|O/STDEV|)	P Values
Age -> Behaviour Intention	-0,040	-0,022	0,092	0,431	0,667
Age -> Use	0,028	0,030	0,071	0,398	0,691
Anxiety -> Behaviour Intention	-0,126	-0,123	0,043	2,943	0,003
Attitude Toward Using -> Behaviour Intention	0,292	0,290	0,071	4,118	0,000
Behaviour Intention -> Use	0,515	0,522	0,047	10,907	0,000
Effort Expectation -> Behaviour Intention	0,131	0,129	0,061	2,156	0,031
Experience -> Behaviour Intention	0,023	0,023	0,045	0,508	0,612
Experience -> Use	0,000	0,000	0,045	0,006	0,995
Facilitating Conditions -> Use	0,143	0,149	0,055	2,619	0,009
Gender -> Behaviour Intention	0,059	0,057	0,046	1,275	0,202
Gender -> Use	0,057	0,054	0,043	1,304	0,192
Moderating Effect 1 -> Behaviour Intention	-0,024	-0,010	0,255	0,096	0,924
Moderating Effect 10 -> Behaviour Intention	-0,002	0,001	0,056	0,044	0,965
Moderating Effect 2 -> Behaviour Intention	-0,055	-0,072	0,175	0,311	0,756
Moderating Effect 3 -> Behaviour Intention	-0,003	-0,004	0,087	0,037	0,970
Moderating Effect 4 -> Use	-0,165	-0,152	0,096	1,718	0,086
Moderating Effect 5 -> Behaviour Intention	0,019	0,011	0,045	0,420	0,674
Moderating Effect 6 -> Behaviour Intention	-0,031	-0,031	0,049	0,638	0,523
Moderating Effect 7 -> Use	0,017	0,022	0,047	0,365	0,715
Moderating Effect 8 -> Behaviour Intention	-0,018	-0,016	0,059	0,304	0,761
Moderating Effect 9 -> Behaviour Intention	-0,071	-0,063	0,056	1,273	0,203
Performance Expectation -> Behaviour Intention	0,034	0,036	0,078	0,433	0,665
Self Efficacy -> Behaviour Intention	0,156	0,158	0,055	2,832	0,005
Social Influence -> Behaviour Intention	0,060	0,057	0,062	0,964	0,335

By looking at the result we can determined the result of hypotheses testing. A hypothesis would be supported if the original sample value is in the same way as the hypothesis and T Statistics value greater than 1.64 (two tailed test) and P Values less than 0.05 (Kline 2011; Ringle 2015; Westland 2015). The hypotheses testing result are:

- Based on data analysis result, the supported hypotheses are H2, H4, H5, H6, H7, and H8.
- Based on data analysis result, hypotheses H1 and H3 are not supported
- All moderating variables hypotheses are not supported by result of data analysis.

Table 4 showing the result of Adjusted R Square which shows the ability of the independent variables to explain dependent variables.

Table 4. Adjusted R^2

	R Square	R Square Adjusted
Behaviour Intention	0,396	0,337
Use	0,369	0,349

The result of original UTAUT model with moderating variables Age, Gender, and Experience only showing that BI have 39.6% R^2, therefore 60.4% of Use is explained by other variables which are not included in the original UTAUT Model used in this research.

4. CONCLUSION AND FURTHER WORKS

The hypotheses testing for original UTAUT model to test the acceptance of involuntary iPad Mini used among two group of first year students at FEUAJY has shown that the "original" UTAUT model can explain the acceptance. The hypotheses testing also showed that the moderating variables of Age, Gender, and Experience are not supported by the findings. The result is consistent with the previous research (Sarosa 2017).

The difference this time is PE and SI are not supported by findings, while SE, ANX, and ATU are supported by findings. Performance Expectation is not supported probably because the students do not see any difference in learning performance and result in the classroom with the use of iPad Mini. The conclusion is made based on comparation of students result in classes that used iPad Mini and classes that did not used iPad Mini. Social Influence is not supported probably because the compulsory nature of iPad Mini. Some lecturers, especially where e-books and other learning technology were used extensively, required the students to bring and use iPad Mini in classroom. Self-Efficacy is found to be influencing the behaviour intention to use iPad Mini unlike the original UTAUT (Akbar 2013; Venkatesh et al. 2003). It is likely due to the popularity of smartphone among participants. All the students surveyed have at least one smartphone, either Android or iOS. From interview with them, mostly said it was not difficult to use iPad Mini due to similarity in usage with their smartphone, especially those who own iOS devices. Anxiety is also influencing behaviour intention in negative way. It means the higher level of anxiety the more difficulties faced by user in utilising technology. This is consistent with previous studies in Computer Anxiety (Fagan, Neill & Wooldridge 2003; Hong et al. 2012). Attitude Toward Using is influencing behaviour intention. The result is actually consistent with the original TRA and TPB where ATU originated (Ajzen 1991; Fishbein & Ajzen 1975).

Overall, the result of this study is complementing and consistent with the result from Pramudita's (2017) and Author's study (2017). The same population has been tested using two different tools, which are DeLone and McLean IS success model (DeLone & McLean 2003; Halonen et al. 2009; Pramudita 2017) and the original UTAUT (Akbar 2013; Raaij & Schepers 2008; Venkatesh et al. 2003). Both studies shown that iPad Mini is accepted and perceived as success (by providing Net Benefit) to FEUAJY students.

For future works, we are planning to address low R^2. Our result is higher (39.6%) than the previous study (26.2%). An increase of 13.4%. Although many would argue that low R^2 is not a problem, we are intrigued by the phenomenon. From interview conducted to the students who participated in the study, some showing some indications that they were influenced by the reputation of Apple Inc. and its product like the iPad Mini. There were also indications that iPad Mini was seen as a life style gadget rather than productivity tool. We are currently devising a study to enhanced UTAUT with life style and brand influence in the next study as suggested by Venkatesh et al. (2016).

REFERENCES

Ajzen, I. 1991, 'The Theory of Planned Behavior', *Organizational Behavior and Human Decision Processes*, vol. 50, no. 2, pp. 179-211.

Akbar, F. 2013, 'What affects students' acceptance and use of technology? A test of UTAUT in the context of a higher-education institution in Qatar', Carnegie Mellon University, USA.

Bandura, A. 1986, *Social foundations of thought and action: A social cognitive theory*, Prentice-Hall, Englewoods Cliffs, NJ.

Bozionelos, N. 1996, 'Psychology of Computer Use: XXXIX. Prevalence of Computer Anxiety in British Managers and Professionals', *Phychological Reports*, vol. 78, no. 3, pp. 995-1002.

Brennan, L.L. & Johnson, V.E. 2000, 'Learning Technology While Teaching Technology Management: A Trial of Distance Learning in Higher Education', in M. Khosrowpour (ed.), *Organizational Achievement and Failure in Information Technology Management*, IDEA Group Publishing, Hershey, pp. 39-60.

Brill, J.M. & Galloway, C. 2007, 'Perils and promises: University instructors' integration of technology in classroom-based practices', *British Journal of Educational Technology*, vol. 38, no. 1, pp. 95-105.

Compeau, D.R. & Higgins, C.A. 1995a, 'Application of Social Cognitive Theory to Training for Computer Skills', *Information Systems Research*, vol. 6, no. 2, pp. 118-43.

Compeau, D.R. & Higgins, C.A. 1995b, 'Computer Self-Efficacy: Development of a Measure and Initial Test', *MIS Quarterly*, vol. 19, no. 2, pp. 189-211.

DeLone, W.H. & McLean, E.R. 2003, 'The DeLone and McLean Model of Information Systems Success: A Ten-Year Update', *Journal of Management Information Systems*, vol. 19, no. 4, pp. 9-30.

Fagan, M.H., Neill, S. & Wooldridge, B.R. 2003, 'An empirical investigation into the relationship between computer self-efficacy, anxiety, experience, support and usage', *Journal of Computer Information Systems*, vol. 44, no. 2, pp. 95-104.

Fishbein, M. & Ajzen, I. 1975, *Belief, Attitude, Intention, and Behavior: An Introduction to Theory and Research*, Addison-Wesley, Reading, MA.

Halonen, R., Acton, T., Golden, W. & Conboy, K. 2009, 'DeLone & McLean success model as a descriptive tool in evaluating the use of a virtual learning environment', *International Conference on Organizational Learning, Knowledge and Capabilities (OLKC 2009),*, Amsterdam.

Hong, J.C., Han, C.J., Dai, C.Y., Hwang, M.Y., Lin, P.H. & Lee, C.C. 2012, 'Technology Anxiety and Implicit Learning Ability Affect Technology Leadership to Promote the Use of Information Technology at Elementary Schools', *12th International Educational Technology Conference - Ietc 2012*, vol. 64, Elsevier Science Bv, Amsterdam, pp. 555-63.

Kline, R. 2011, *Principles and Practice of Structural Equation Modeling* 3rd edn, Guilford.

Kohnke, A., Cole, M.L. & Bush, R. 2014, 'Incorporating UTAUT Predictors for Understanding Home Care Patients' and Clinician's Acceptance of Healthcare Telemedicine Equipment', *Journal of Technology Management and Innovation*, vol. 9, no. 2, pp. 29-41.

Mandl, K.D., Kohane, I.S., McFadden, D., Weber, G.M., Natter, M., Mandel, J., Schneeweiss, S., Weiler, S., Klann, J.G., Bickel, J., Adams, W.G., Ge, Y.R., Zhou, X.B., Perkins, J., Marsolo, K., Bernstam, E., Showalter, J., Quarshie, A., Ofili, E., Hripcsak, G. & Murphy, S.N. 2014, 'Scalable Collaborative Infrastructure for a Learning Healthcare System (SCILHS): Architecture', *Journal of the American Medical Informatics Association*, vol. 21, no. 4, pp. 615-20.

Marchewka, J.T., Liu, C. & Kostiwa, K. 2016, 'An application of the UTAUT model for understanding student perceptions using course management software', *Communications of the IIMA*, vol. 7, no. 2, pp. 93-104.

Pramudita, K.E. 2017, 'Penilaian Kesuksesan Penerapan Apple iPad Mini Menggunakan Model DeLone and McLEan 2003 pada Fakultas Ekonomi Universitas Atma Jaya Yogyakarta', Atma Jaya Yogyakarta University, Yogyakarta.

Raaij, E.M.v. & Schepers, J.J.L. 2008, 'The acceptance and use of a virtual learning environment in China', *Computers and Education*, vol. 50.

Ringle, C.M., Wende, Sven, and Becker, Jan-Michael 2015, 'SmartPLS Release: 3', SmartPLS GmbH, Boenningstedt, Germany <www.smartpls.com>.

Sarosa, S. 2017, 'I Have to Buy iPad Mini: The UTAUT Perspective', *The 18th Asian Academic Accounting Association Annual Conference 2017*, Asian Academic Accounting Association, Bali, Indonesia, pp. 121-9.

Tan, E. & Lau, J.L. 2016, 'Behavioural Intention to Adopt Mobile Banking Among the Millenial Generation', *Young Consumers*, vol. 17, no. 1, pp. 18-31.

Venkatesh, V. 2000, 'Determinants of Perceived Ease of Use: Integrating Control, Intrinsic Motivation, and Emotion into the Technology Acceptance Model', *Information Systems Research*, vol. 11, no. 4, pp. 342-65.

Venkatesh, V., Morris, M.G., Davis, G.B. & Davis, F.D. 2003, 'User Acceptance of Information Technology: Toward A Unified View', *MIS Quarterly*, vol. 27, no. 3, pp. 425-78.

Venkatesh, V., Thong, J.Y.L. & Xu, X. 2016, 'Unified Theory of Acceptance and Use of Technology: A Synthesis and the Road Ahead', *Journal of the Association for Information Systems*, vol. 17, no. 5, pp. 328-76.

Westland, J.C. 2015, *Structural Equation Modeling: From Paths to Networks*, Springer, New York.

BUILDING A REFERENCE ARCHITECTURE FOR VIRTUAL RESEARCH ENVIRONMENTS

Keith G Jeffery[1], Carlo Meghini[2], Cesare Concordia[2] and Francesco Furfari[2]
[1]*Keith G Jeffery Consultants*
[2]*ISTI - CNR, Italy*

ABSTRACT

Virtual Research Environments (VREs) aim to support multidisciplinary research and collaboration between researchers, but face great challenges from data heterogeneity, user experience issues, and fast changes to datasets. This complicates research on multidisciplinary societal challenges. The objective of this paper is to present a reference architecture and components that can be (re)used to construct a general, domain-specific or cross-domain enhanced VRE (e-VRE) that enhances FAIR-ness of data and process interoperability across research infrastructures. The e-VRE makes it easier to conduct multidisciplinary research by assisting the researcher in accessing and utilising the assets of research, commonly stored in digital Research Infrastructures. The reference architecture also reduces complexity by interfacing with research management systems.

KEYWORDS

Virtual Research Environment, IS Design and Development, Distributed Computer Systems

1. INTRODUCTION

VRE4EIC (A Europe-wide Interoperable Virtual Research Environment to Empower Multidisciplinary Research Communities and Accelerate Innovation and Collaboration) is a three-year project funded by the European Commission in the context of the H2020 Program, under the topic EINFRA-9-2015 e-Infrastructures for virtual research environments. The major goals of the VRE4EIC project are the design of a Reference Architecture (RA) for VREs and the development of a Canonical Prototype that implements the RA. Generally speaking a Reference Architecture presents a description of a system in terms of its components and their relationships; it can be viewed as a sort of template that can be used to implement systems in a family of applicative domains. The components of the VRE4EIC RA have been designed to be used to build a general, domain-specific or cross-domain VREs that enhances FAIR-ness of data and process interoperability across research infrastructures. A VRE built using the VRE4EIC RA components is called *enhanced VRE* (e-VRE). The VRE4EIC RA has been designed to meet five main requirements:

- Increase VRE usability in different interdisciplinary domains by closely involving user communities and real-world use cases.
- Increase the quality of VRE user experiences by providing user centered, secure, privacy compliant, sustainable environments on searching data, composing workflows and tracking data publications.
- Increase the deployment of the VRE on different clusters of research infrastructures by abstracting and reusing building blocks and workflows from existing VREs, infrastructures and projects.
- Improve the contextual awareness and interoperability of the metadata across all layers of the resources in the VRE.

This paper presents the VRE4EIC RA, by first illustrating the methodology followed in defining the Reference Architecture and the derivation of a technical architecture from it.

2. VIRTUAL RESEARCH ENVIRONMENTS

Sharing research data is a critical activity to improve global collaboration on contemporary scientific research (Kim, 2017). A large diversity of datasets is already becoming available from various sources, including government data, geographical data, structured media data and life sciences data (Musto, Basile, Lops, de Gemmis, & Semeraro, 2017). Many research challenges span multiple scientific disciplines and both cross-domain and generic solutions need to be developed (Khan et al., 2017). Such solutions require the availability and integration of data, publications, software and other resources from multiple disciplines. VREs encourage multidisciplinary research by facilitating a research environment for the provision and (re)use of research data and other resources (Terras et al., 2016). They can be used to provide researchers with heterogeneous data, presented in a homogenous and user-friendly way. VREs provide researchers with access to research resources of a multiplicity of underlying e-research infrastructures minimizing much of the underlying complexity (Zuiderwijk, 2018).

3. DESIGN APPROACH AND METHODOLOGY

The development of a software architecture involves different points of views: the user, the system (the IT infrastructure), and the business goals. For each of these areas, the key scenarios/requirements should be identified as well as quality attributes. Then requirements should be refined into architectural functions and mapped into specific architectural components or modules. In the last 10 years different approaches for architecture specification have been proposed, largely inspired from the Software Development Life Cycle, SDLC [ISO/IEC 12207]. A typical SDLC includes different activities such as: understanding of business needs and constraints; elicitation and collection of requirements; functional architecture design; architecture design; implementation; testing; deployment; maintenance. The order in which these activities are to be executed is usually defined into a specific software development process such as Waterfall model, incremental model, RUP, V-model, iterative model, Agile model, Prototype model, to mention just a few. In the development of the VRE4EIC Reference Architecture, an incremental software development process largely inspired by the RUP process (RUP 2003) has been followed. In this Section, the main characterization of the process to the specific exigencies of the project constraints and activities are schematized. In particular, the Section provides details about activities concerning the software architecture specification and design that are: elicitation and collection of requirements; functional architecture design; architecture design. Elicitation and collection of requirements is a fundamental stage in the VRE4EIC RA, from a technical point of view, it involves different stages such as [ISO/IEC/IEEE 29148]:

1) High-level use case definition: a representative of the stakeholder community presents the business/mission drivers for the VRE4EIC RA considering also quality attributes, security aspects.

2) Use case definition: Stakeholders express scenarios representing their concerns about the system prioritizing when possible the main ones.

3) Specification VRE4EIC RA requirements: the main use cases are analysed and refined in more detail. The focus is on specifying what a system should do (the functional requirements) and on how the system should function (the non-functional, or quality, requirements) [ISO/IEC 25010, ISO/IEC 25030].

Figure 1 presents a class diagram where these entities are related to one another and to the entities subsequently derived in analysing the requirements to derive the Reference Architecture. The analysis of requirements is explained in the next Section, with reference to Figure 1.

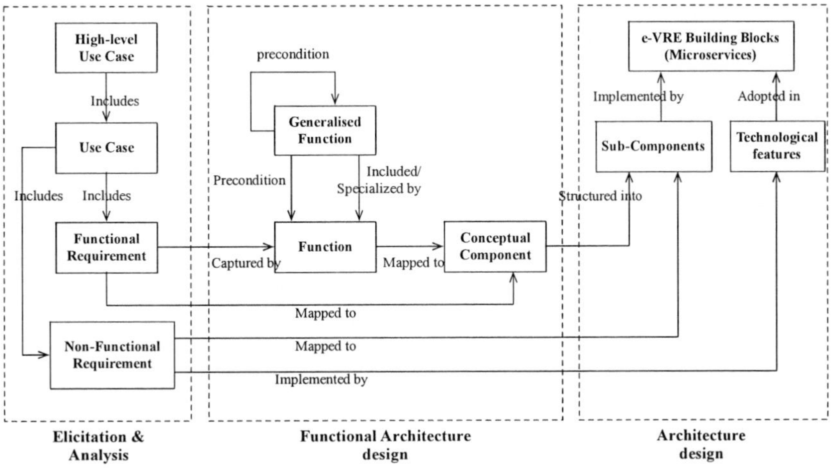

Figure 1. The Reference Architecture Derivation Process

The analysis started from the **Functional Requirements**. Each requirement has been considered individually, and the **Functions** required for its implementation have been derived. In order to ease the specification of functions, a set of **Generalised Functions** has also been derived, which are included or specialised by functions, or which may be used as preconditions by functions. During the execution of this phase, several design guidelines have been followed [RUP, https://msdn.microsoft.com/en-us/library/ee658124.aspx]. A synthesis of the most important ones is provided below.

- *Separation of functions*: Isolate from the requirements different functions with as little overlap in functionality as possible. The important factor is minimization of interaction points to achieve high cohesion and low coupling.
- *Aggregation of functions:* Identify possible generalization or composition relations between the isolated functions to improve the organization and readability of the functional architecture design.
- *Learn from similar projects:* analyze similar projects and documentation so to derive a high conceptual-level architecture description focusing mainly on high view of modules/components and communications and interactions between them.
- *Reduce Responsibility:* Assign to each component or module the responsibility for only a specific functionality or aggregation of cohesive functionality.
- *Minimal Knowledge:* Each component or module should be unaware of the internal details of other components.

This analysis of requirements into functions has been used for the assessment of the Reference Architecture. Overall, the approach has allowed maintaining the relationship between use cases, requirements and components, thereby realizing the traceability of the Reference Architecture. The **Components** that are required for the implementation of functions have finally been derived. The first step to derive components have been to refine and further decompose the Components into **Sub-Components** so that the identified functional and *non-functional* requirements are completely satisfied. Also for carrying out this step several design guidelines have been followed. Here below a synthesis of the most important ones is provided.

- Assess minimal knowledge: verify that each component does not rely on internal details of other components. In particular check that each component method is called from at least another object or component. Verify also that the method has information about how to process the request and, if appropriate, how to route it to appropriate subcomponents or other components.
- Avoid overloading of the functionality of a component: Avoid to overloaded components with many functions and applying the single responsibility and separation of concerns principles.
- Focus on communication between components: Understand the deployment scenarios and determine if all components will run within the same process, or if communication across physical or process boundaries must be supported—perhaps by implementing message-based interfaces.
- Define a clear contract for components: Components and modules should define a contract or interface specification that describes their usage and behavior clearly. The contract should describe

how other components can access the internal functionality of the component, module, or function; and the behavior of that functionality in terms of preconditions, postconditions, side effects, exceptions, performance characteristics, and other factors.

Components are detailed in next section.

4. THE VRE4EIC REFERENCE ARCHITECTURE

There is no common definition of a VRE system. Some scholars refer to the complete stack of software, data, computing resources, and sensors available to a researcher through a GUI. Others use the term VRE to refer only to an integrating 'hub', composed of a user interface component, a metadata catalogue and an integrating system (e.g., Zuiderwijk et al., 2016). In the second definition the integrating system assembles and provides components which access (via metadata) assets such as datasets, services, software components, workflows, computing facilities and sensors (we call these assets VRE resources). The Research Infrastructures (RIs) then provide access to the datasets, services and other resources. In this second definition, the 'hub' also assists the researcher in constructing and deploying workflows to meet the need, together with providing access to facilities for office functions, peer communication, publication, management of educational material and assistance with routine management tasks. Here we use the second definition because it reflects better the requirements of multidisciplinary researchers while also catering for domain-specific research. Considering the multi-tiers view approach, used in the design of distributed information systems (Schuldt, 2009), we can individuate three logical tiers in a VRE system:

- The *Application* tier, which provides to researchers and e-scientists functionalities to execute their experiments, to manage the system and to *expand* it, by plugging on it new components or tools.
- The *Interoperability* tier, which deals with interoperability aspects by providing functionalities for: i) enabling application tier components to discover and use VRE resources that may be stored in different locations and may be created according to different data models; ii) publishing VRE functionalities (e.g. using a Web Service API); and iii) enabling VRE applications and tools to interact with each other.
- The *Resource Access* tier, which implements actual integration functionalities, to enable VRE components to access RIs resources and services using the correct interaction protocol.

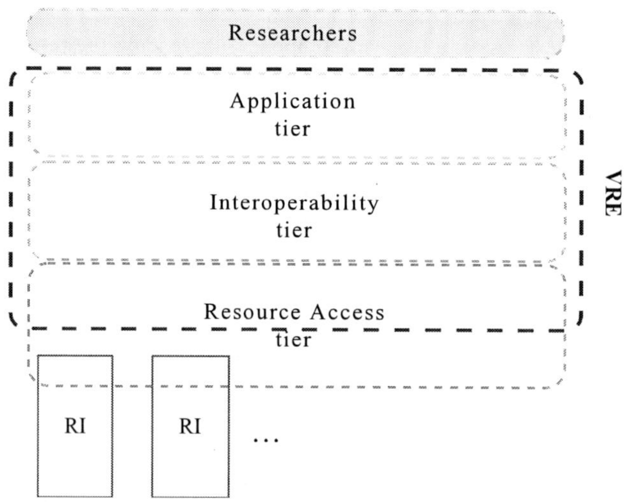

Figure 2. Architectural Tiers in a Virtual Research Environment

Figure 2 depicts the logical tiers of an VRE and shows their placement in an ideal space between the researchers that use the VRE and the RIs that provide the resources to the VRE. The VRE4EIC RA has been designed by distributing the implementation of the functional requirements in a number of conceptual components and by logically *placing* each component in the tiers defined above. In particular the functional architecture design activity has identified six conceptual components:

- The RA management is implemented in the System Manager component. The System Manager can be viewed as the component enabling Users to use the core functionalities of an e-VRE: access, create and manage resource descriptions, query the e-VRE information space, configure the e-VRE, plug and deploy new tools in the e-VRE and more.
- The Workflow Manager enables users to create, execute and store scientific workflows and business processes.
- The Linked Data (LD) Manager is the component that publishes the information space using the LOD (Linked Open Data) paradigm, based on the RDF (Resource Description Framework) data model. Essentially this component provides functionalities to access the metadata concerning the e-VRE and the RIs in a form suitable for end-user browsing in a SM (Semantic Web)-enabled ecosystem.
- The Metadata Manager (MM) is the component responsible for storing and managing resource catalogues, user profiles, provenance information, preservation metadata used by all the components using extended entity-relational conceptual and object-relational logical representation for efficiency.
- The Interoperability Manager (IM) provides functionalities to implement interactions with RIs resources in a transparent way. It implements services and algorithms to enable the VRE to: communicate synchronously or asynchronously with RIs resources, query the RIs catalogues and storages, map the data models. The Interoperability Manager is also responsible for efficiently managing the integration of third-party software, enabling the e-VRE to virtually acquire any desired functionality that is not directly offered by any component.
- The Authentication, Authorization, Accounting Infrastructure (AAAI) component is the responsible for managing the security issues of the VRE system. It provides user authentication for the VRE and connected e-RIs, authorisation and accounting services, and data encryption layers for components that are accessible over potentially insecure networks. The AAAI component interfaces with external identity providers to enable single sign-on across the various connected infrastructures. For any authenticated user, it provides authorization services by using attributes provided by the external identity provider (if any). This includes user authorisations (role-based access) and accounting and billing of resources for which payment is required, both based on CERIF (euroCRIS, 2018) metadata provided by the metadata manager component.

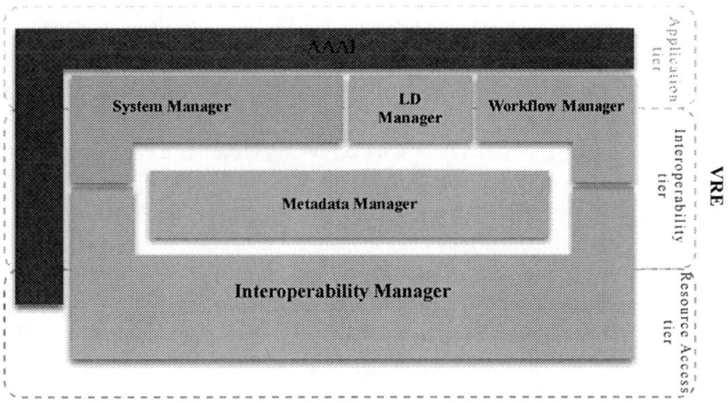

Figure 3. VRE4EIC RA Conceptual Components and VRE Logical Tiers

5. DERIVING A TECHNICAL ARCHITECTURE

The first step in designing the RA has been to refine the modularity of the system at functional level, by analysing functionalities implemented in every conceptual. The Figure 4 shows an overview of the sub-components in which every component has been structured, criteria adopted for this process has been various. For instance, the Workflow Manager has been structured in three sub-components following the typical structure of a workflow engine: the Configurator that implements workflows definition functionalities, the executor implementing execution functionalities and the Repository implementing storage management. The same approach has been followed for LD Manager.

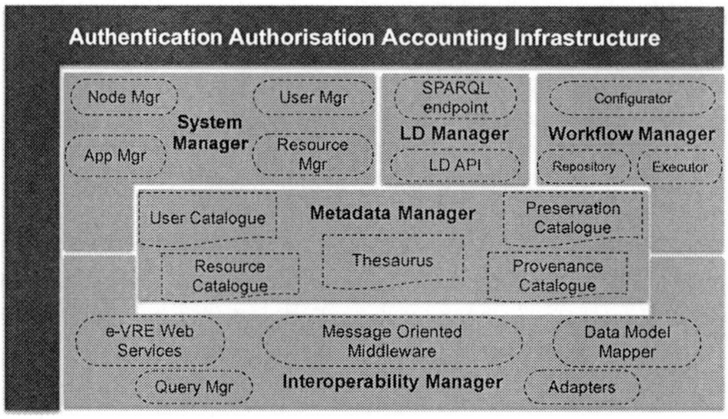

Figure 4. The designed Reference Architecture

The structure of the System Manager instead, depends from the consideration that managing a complex distributed system requires to deal with various kind of data and entities, for instance user *status* must be maintained across sessions, resources description data must be accessed, application life-cycle information must be monitored and managed, distributed configuration must be implemented etc. The functionalities of the System Manager has then been partitioned in four homogenous subsets and a subcomponent has been defined for every subset. A similar approach has been followed to define sub-components for the Interoperability Manager and for the Metadata Manager. The second step in the derivation of the technical architecture, has been to consider the FURPS+[1] (Ottinger, T., Langr, J. 2001) non-functional requirements, collected during the elicitation steps of the project and during the Gap Analysis, a survey conducted after the definition of the functional architecture to identify the most needed components in existing e-RIs and VREs. E-VRE Non-Functional Requirements can be synthesized as follows.

a) The e-VRE must be a dynamic system, it should be easily expandable by adding new software modules or replacing existing software components.

b) The e-VRE should reuse and integrate existing VRE tools, services, standardized components and workflows where appropriate, and develop new innovative ones where needed.

c) The e-VRE should be applicable to multidisciplinary domains, and it can be potentially used in every research domain.

d) The e-VRE functionalities should be exposed as services in a standardized way to enable developers to easily use them to develop new software that can be used in VREs.

e) The e-VRE must provide innovative standard software services to be *retro-fitted* to existing VREs to enhance them for their own domain purposes and for interoperability.

To implement these requirements, an approach based on Microservices[2] has been chosen. The two key concepts of Microservices architecture [Newman] *loose coupling* and *high cohesion* of components, perfectly respond to the above requirements. Every e-VRE microservice, called e-VRE building block, is an autonomous component that encapsulates al components that are needed for the implementation of its functionalities. Figure 5 shows the resulting micro-services, highlighting the functional components included in it, each characterized by the color relative to the tier where the component belongs.

---

[1] the FURPS+ acronym, devised by Robert Grady of HP, refers to the non -functional requirements categories named Functionality (Generality of Feature Set, reusability, security), Usability, Reliability, Performance, Supportability, and the constraints(+) on design, implementation, interface and physical properties, of the system.

[2] https://martinfowler.com/articles/microservices.html

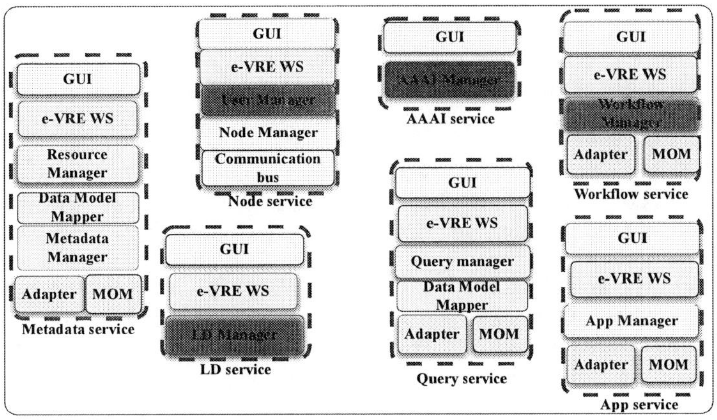

Figure 5. The Services in the Technical Architecture of e-VRE

As shown in the figure, changes has been made with respect to the structure of functional architecture. The main difference is that there is not a specific building block for the Interoperability Manager (IM). The IM is a crucial component to implement the cross domain capabilities of e-VRE, it is involved in every use-case where an e-VRE component needs to access or use assets (datasets, services, facilities, sensors etc) belonging to RIs. The IM sub-components can be divided according to the *integration level* they provide (Aloia N.; Concordia C.; Weinbach G 2002): ad-hoc Adapters, e-VRE Web Services and MOM component, provides integration at application level, Query Manager and the Data Model Mapper are used for integrating RIs at and at *data level.* A possible implementation of the IM could be to create a specific building block for the IM sub-components and call it from other building blocks. However, this approach will introduce dependencies when retro-fitting an e-VRE component or integrating distributed search functionalities into an existing VRE (requirements *e* and *f*). Application level integration sub-components (Adapters, MOM, e-VRE WS) have then been *distributed* in the various e-VRE Microservices, this means that these sub-components have been replicated and embedded into the building blocks using them. This solution helps developers in implementing requirements *d* and *e*.. Data level integration components (Query Manager, Data Model Mapper) have been implemented in a specific building block called the Query Service, this building block can be easily retrofitted in existing VREs and this implements requirements. In order to fully implement the non-functional requirements, the following technical solutions have been adopted in the e-VRE architecture:

- **Use event-driven communication to avoid component coupling.** The event-driven model is not blocking and is highly decoupled: every event is mapped into a *message*, messages are exchanged *asynchronously*. This approach removes direct dependencies between architecture components, and is a fundamental choice to implement the non-functional requirements listed above.
- **Using a distributed configuration service and synchronization service to manage coexistence of different endpoints**. An important feature provided by microservices architectures is that different services can be installed on different servers and also that different version of the same service can coexist on the same system. This has required the implementation of a distributed configuration service, synchronization service, and naming registry.

The assessment process has been performed by relating the VRE4EIC RA and vision to the ongoing work in the area of VRE, and then by validating the most significant Generalized Functions thereby showing the adequacy of the Reference Architecture from a functional point of view. The e-VRE building blocks are currently being developed, a repository has been created on GitHub to host the source code of e-VRE (VRE4EIC project, 2018). A live prototype of an e-VRE system is available[3], the main goal of the prototype is to collect feedbacks in order to individuate design errors and weaknesses of the reference architecture.

[3] http://v4e-hub.isti.cnr.it:8099/#!/login

6. CONCLUSIONS

The objective of this paper is to present a reference architecture and components that can be (re)used to construct a general, domain-specific or cross-domain enhanced VRE (e-VRE) that enhances the Findability, Accessibility, Interoperability and Reusability (FAIR) of data and process interoperability across research infrastructures. The purpose is to assist researchers and others in finding, accessing, interoperating and re-using data resources concerning global challenges such as global warming, climate change, pollution, food crises, refugees and natural disasters. The research problems behind those challenges are essentially interdisciplinary. Requirements for the e-VRE were elicited from 2VRE-related projects, 10 user interviews, a survey with 76 end-users and a characterization of 7 Research Infrastructures. A Reference Architecture for an enhanced Virtual Research Environment (e-VRE) was designed to particularly handle the above-mentioned requirements and limitations.

ACKNOWLEDGEMENT

The research leading to these results has received funding from the European Union Horizon 2020 Programme, Topic: e-Infrastructures for virtual research environments, Research and Innovation action VRE4EIC (A Europe-wide Interoperable Virtual Research Environment to Empower Multidisciplinary Research Communities and Accelerate Innovation and Collaboration), grant agreement n 676247.

REFERENCES

Aloia N.; Concordia C.; Weinbach G (2002) EAI: Concept and trends, ICSSEA 2002, Paris 2002.

euroCRIS. (2018). Main features of CERIF. Retrieved March 15, 2018, from https://www.eurocris.org/cerif/main-features-cerif

ISO/IEC 12207 International Organization for Standardization, "ISO/IEC/IEEE 12207:2008 - Systems and software engineering -- Software life cycle processes," ISO/IEC, Mar. 2008.

ISO/IEC 25010 International Organization for Standardization, "ISO/IEC 25010 - Systems and software engineering — Systems and software Quality Requirements and Evaluation (SQuaRE) — System and software quality models," ISO/IEC, Mar. 2011.

ISO/IEC 25030 International Organization for Standardization, "ISO/IEC 25030 - Software engineering — Software product Quality Requirements and Evaluation (SQuaRE) — Quality requirements," ISO/IEC, June 2007.

ISO/IEC/IEEE 29148 International Organization for Standardization, "ISO/IEC /IEEE 29148:2011 - Systems and software engineering — Life cycle processes — Requirements engineering," ISO/IEC/IEEE, Nov. 2011.

Khan, S., Liu, X., Shakil, K. A., & Alam, M. (2017). A survey on scholarly data: From big data perspective. *Information Processing & Management, 53*(4), 923-944. doi: https://doi.org/10.1016/j.ipm.2017.03.006

Musto, C., Basile, P., Lops, P., de Gemmis, M., & Semeraro, G. (2017). Introducing linked open data in graph-based recommender systems. *Information Processing & Management, 53*(2), 405-435. doi: https://doi.org/10.1016/j.ipm.2016.12.003

Ottinger, T., Langr, J. (2011). Agile in a Flash.

RUP (2003) Rational Unified Process Best Practices for Software Development Teams, Rational Software White Paper TP026B, Rev 11/01, July 2003

Schuldt, H. (2009). Multi-Tier Architecture. In L. Liu & M. T. Ozsu (Eds.), *Encyclopedia of Database Systems*: Springer.

Sommerville, 2011. Software Engineering. 9th Edition, Addison-Wesley 2011

Terras, M., Warwick, C., & Ross, C. (2016). Building Useful Virtual Research Environments: The Need for User-led Design. In P. Dale, J. Beard & M. Holland (Eds.), *University Libraries and Digital Learning Environments* (pp. 151). London: Routledge.

Zuiderwijk, A., Jeffery, K., Bailo, D., & Yin, Y. (2016). *Using Open Research Data for Public Policy Making: Opportunities of Virtual Research Environments*. Paper presented at the Conference for E-Democracy and Open Government, Krems an der Donau, Austria.

Zuiderwijk, A. (2018). Analysing open data in virtual research environments: New collaboration opportunities to improve policy making. *The International Journal of Electronic Government Research, 13*(4), 76-92. doi: 10.4018/IJEGR.2017100105

THE ADOPTION OF M-COMMERCE APPLICATIONS: RURAL DWELLERS' PERSPECTIVES

Chinedu Wilfred Okonkwo, Estelle Taylor and Magda Huisman
North-West University, Unit for Business Mathematics and Informatics
Private Bag X6001, Potchefstroom, South Africa, 2520

ABSTRACT

In recent years, mobile applications (mobile apps) have gained widespread acceptance. Mobile apps services have effectively encircled most of the human activities, with the purpose of improving the living standard of the entire public. The adoption and diffusion of a mobile app are influenced by its characteristics. This study examines the adoption and diffusion of mobile commerce among the people living in a remote area of South Africa to determine the relationship between the characteristics of innovations and the adopters' attitudes. Through a survey that used diffusion of innovation as the basic framework, the opinions of the participants living in Mbongolwane in the Uthungulu District Municipality in the KwaZulu-Natal province of South Africa were gathered. A total of 120 out of 300 questionnaires distributed, were returned, giving a response rate of 40%. It was found that the perceived attitudes of the rural dwellers are closely related to the characteristic of innovations as well as the adoption of mobile commerce. Also, the findings indicate that though the people are very keen to receive a new technological invention, they are still late adopters. This research work offers a support in improving the adoption and diffusion of mobile apps among the rural inhabitants.

KEYWORDS

Mobile Applications, Adoption and Diffusion, Rural Dwellers, Characteristics of Innovations, M-commerce, Attitudes

1. INTRODUCTION

The introduction of mobile devices like mobile phones, personal digital assistants, computers etc., has triggered the development of various kinds of mobile apps. It's a common belief that an owner of a mobile device is also an adopter and user of mobile apps. For instance, every mobile phone can be used to send an SMS message. Mobile technology services have seen extensive growth in many aspects of life activities including education, economic, government and social (Murugesan (2013), Hellstrom (2011), GSMA (2017)). In developing countries like Africa, mobile technology diffusion has seen the highest growth-rate between 2012-2017 (ITU (2017)). Mobile apps are created to be used by the public covering the urban and rural dwellers. The global economic development, in particular, the African continent, is mainly propelled by the mobile technologies (Murugesan (2013), Qiang et al. (2011)) and extending these life-changing innovations to the remote areas is highly needed. The major challenges in deploying mobile apps to rural environments include technology infrastructural costs, computer costs and internet fees and the dwellers' low computer literacy (Liu et al. (2014)).

Several studies have been conducted on the adoption and diffusion of mobile technologies (Nickerson et al. (2014), Chang (2010), Brown et al. (2003)). Most of these studies centered on the opinions of the urban dwellers. Urban areas include town and cities which are characterized by their advanced civic amenities, better education opportunities, improved transport facilities, business and social interaction and generally improved standard of living. On the hand, rural areas include villages and hamlets which are characterized by lack of overall amenities and poor standard of living. There is rapid penetration of mobile phones, especially smartphones among the rural dwellers and this has improved the adoption of mobile apps among them. In a study on the diffusion of mobile apps among rural dwellers in China, Liu et al. (2014) noted that there is a lack of empirical research on the perceptions of the rural dwellers to adopt mobile apps in the developing countries like India, China and Africa. Rogers (2003) proposed some characteristics of innovations and stated that individuals' perceptions of these characteristics predict the rate of adoption of innovations. Also, it was suggested that the perceptions of the characteristics of a new mobile app and other technologies (Mannan and Nordan (2014)) influence the adoption rate.

However, the relationship between the perceptions of these characteristics and the adopters' attitudes (positive, negative and nervousness) towards the adoption of mobile apps is not clear. To our knowledge, there is no study to substantiate such a relationship and it is important to conduct such a study. In this light, this study seeks to investigate the relationship between the rural dwellers' attitudes and the characteristics of innovations towards the adoption of m-commerce apps. Based on the diffusion of innovations framework, a research model was developed and used for this study. Through a survey, quantitative data was collected and empirically evaluated.

2. BACKGROUND INFORMATION

Mobile apps are the mobile technological innovation of computer programs that run on mobile devices enabling users to perform their economic, political, educational and social activities irrespective of the location and context of the user. Mobile apps are developed to facilitate the functionalities of various mobile technology devices for the purpose of data gathering, information dissemination, and other activities (Okonkwo and Huisman (2018), Mc Namara (2009)). There are different types of mobile apps including mobile commerce (Bhatti (2007), Abdelkarin and Nasereddin (2010)), mobile learning (Hwang and Chang (2011)), mobile governance (Poblet (2011)), mobile agriculture (Murugesan (2013), Hellström and Tröften (2010)) and mobile health (Kumar et al. (2013)). These mobile apps are widely adopted and used in various contexts and activities across the globe (Wang et al. (2013)). This study centers on the adoption and diffusion of mobile commerce among rural dwellers.

2.1 Mobile Commerce (M-commerce)

M-commerce involves any commercial transaction performed through different kinds of mobile devices over a wireless network connection or telecommunication (Bhatti (2007), Joubert and Van Belle (2013), Chong (2013)). According to Bhatti (2007), there are two categories of m-commerce namely content delivery m-commerce and transactions m-commerce. The former involves reporting, notification and consultation while the later covers data entry, purchasing and promotions. GSMA (2015) reported that m-commerce is on a rise in African region due to rising growth of internet penetration and that 20% of South African internet users have made purchases online and another 48% are expected to do so in the future. M-commerce is important to economic growth in Africa because of ubiquitous and unison access to information and services, and the likelihood of a unique and personalized exchange of information (Bhatti (2007), San Martin et al. (2012)). The significant of m-commerce has resulted in the establishment of digital commerce sites across the African region. In 2012, Jumia was launched in Nigeria with funding from Rocket Internet. The company has expanded beyond its original base, with local sites across many other African countries including Cameroon, Senegal, Kenya, Tanzania, Ghana and Uganda. It is also in partnership with MTN and Millicom to drive future growth and facilitates the efficiency of m-commerce among increasing mobile users (GMSA (2015)). Hellström and Tröften (2010) point out some key drivers of m-commerce as including: Increased diffusion and penetration of mobile phones; falling prices of mobile phones and services; cost-effectiveness of mobile solutions; strong branding of easy to use mobile apps; user demand and needs; need for banks to reach out and get more customers; need for operators to keep customers (loyalty); scalable agent distribution for cash-in cash-out; and fast and simple customer registration process.

There are many m-commerce apps developed and functioning actively in Africa. These include all online shopping mobile apps like Zando, Ackerman, Spree online shopping apps and many others. The purpose of this study is to investigate the association between the attitudes and perceptions of the rural dwellers on the adoption of m-commerce apps in South Africa using the people living in Mbongolwane in the Uthungulu District Municipality in the KwaZulu-Natal province as the sample population.

The use of mobile-phone-based business transaction services offers a lot of benefits including but not limited to these; long distance coverage, consumer deals, savings and easy to use and on-time service delivery (Kim (2006), Siau et al. (2003)).

2.2 Adoption

Rogers (2003) defined adoption as a choice of complete acceptance and usage of a mobile technological innovation such as mobile apps. GSMA (2015) stated that adoption is acceptance and making use of a new invention. It is the user's acceptance (Lule et al. (2012)) and usage (Taylor et al. (2011)) of an innovative product such as mobile apps. Therefore, we defined adoption as the acceptance and usage of an idea or product that is perceived to be new by the adopters.

2.3 Diffusion of Innovation Theory

Rogers (2003) proposed a framework that has been using to measure the adoption and diffusion of technological innovations. The framework consists of four key components of the diffusion of innovations including innovation, communication channels, time, and social system. In addition, there are five categories of adopters centered on time to adoption: innovators, early adopters, early majority, late majority, and laggards. He went further to determine that adopters were unevenly spread in these categories. Also, the framework involves five characteristics of innovation that influence the rate of innovation adoption including relative advantage, compatibility, complexity, trialability and observability. Finally, he described the processes involved in innovation decision-making including knowledge, persuasion, decision, implementation and confirmation.

3. METHODOLOGY

Moore and Benbasat (1991) developed an instrument used to measure user's perceptions of adopting an IT innovation with diffusion theory as its basis. They noted that relative advantage and complexity are like usefulness and ease of use: hence they changed complexity to ease of use. In conclusion, they added two extra characteristics, which they believed to be significant in the adoption decision including image and voluntariness. Tan and Teo (2000) integrated the decomposed theory of planned behavior and diffusion of innovations theory to develop a framework that identified factors that may influence the adoption of internet banking. In conclusion, they included some factors to innovations characteristics which they believed to be important factors in the adoption decision including subjective norms, facilitating conditions, perceived risk and self-efficacy. Brown et al. (2003) applied the diffusion of innovations theory to determine the predictors of cell phone banking. They concluded that relative advantage, trialability, banking needs and perceived risk are the major predicting factors of cell phone banking adoption in South Africa.

The above factors were derived from the diffusion of innovation theory. These characteristics measured the adoption and diffusion of technologies in relation to the user's perception which in effect cause the perceived attitudes of the adopters. Drawing from the above previous studies, the relevant innovation characteristics which may be used to determine the relationship between the characteristics of innovations and rural dwellers adopters' attitudes on the adoption of mobile commerce include: *relative advantage, compatibility, ease of use, voluntariness, facilitating conditions, self-efficacy, subjective norms and perceived risk.*

A questionnaire was used as an instrument of data collection. The questionnaire contained closed-ended questions with 5-point Likert scale rating of 1 (strongly disagree) to 5 (strongly agree). The sections of the questionnaire included: Background information, mobile applications, adoption and diffusion of mobile apps, innovation characteristics, and adopter's category.

The target audience is mobile apps users residing in the rural area of Mbongolwane, a town in Uthungulu District Municipality in the KwaZulu-Natal province in South Africa. The questionnaire was administered to the participants through a self-approach system (drop off) whereby the participants were approached and convinced to complete the questionnaire. To achieve validated responses to the survey, 2 persons from that area were employed to assist us to collect responses from the participants. Also, they served as interpreters used to explain the questions in their local language to some of the participants who do not understand the English language very well. A total of 300 questionnaires were distributed to different participants and 120 (40%) responses were returned. This research was conducted between February and March 2018. The final sample population comprises of 72 (60%) males and 48 (40%) females. Concerning the level of education, 88 (73.33%) of the participants have grade 12, 18 (15%) have a diploma, 13 (10.83%) are university degree holders and 1 (0.83%) has a master's degree. Most of the participants are within the age range of 31-40.

4. DATA ANALYSIS

A descriptive analysis was performed to describe the frequency and percentage of responses from the study population. A Pearson correlation analysis was performed to determine if linear relationships exist between the research variables. Cronbach alpha reliability analysis was used to compute reliability coefficients for each of the examining variables. The criterion for Cronbach's coefficient alpha for reliability is $\alpha \geq 0.6$ (Sethi and King (1991), Nunally (1978)). That is if the obtained $\alpha \geq 0.6$ then the data obtained from that particular item is reliable. In addition, multiple linear regression analysis was performed to test the relationship between the characteristics of innovation and the rural dwellers' attitudes' towards adopting mobile apps with 0.05 as significant level criteria.

4.1 Reliability

A reliability analysis was performed on the construct items. Cronbach's alpha indicates that the used questions reach acceptable reliability, $\alpha = 0.72$. This showed that the instrument of measurement is reliable. Also, the correlation scores of all the items are identical ($r=1$) which indicates that the construct items correlate with each other. This is possible because the study was conducted in a unique domain where the perceptions and attitudes of the participants are similar. The reliability results are: Compatibility ($\alpha = 0.68$), Relative advantage ($\alpha = 0.67$), Voluntariness ($\alpha = 0.64$), Subjective norms ($\alpha = 0.64$), Ease of use ($\alpha = 0.72$), Perceived risk ($\alpha = 0.64$), Facilitating conditions ($\alpha = 0.8$) and Self-efficacy ($\alpha = 0.69$).

4.2 Survey Results

The obtained results from the collected data are presented as follows:

Mobile apps – this section tested the knowledge of, and the use of mobile apps. A larger percentage of the participants agreed to know about mobile apps and have used them in various activities including 120(100%) for SMS, social networking and entertainment, 10% for agriculture, 40% for education and 20% for commerce.

Adoption and diffusion of mobile apps – this section tested the participants' attitudes towards a new mobile app. With regards to the individual reaction whenever he/she heard of a new mobile app, 60 (50%) are positive, 13 (10.8%) are negative and 47 (39.2%) are indifferent. Concerning nervousness on adopting a new mobile app, 61 (50.8) are not nervous, 26 (21.6%) are nervous and 33 (27.5%) are neutral. 93 (77.5%) of the participants strongly agreed that their main purpose of using mobile apps is for easy communications while 44 (36.6%) used mobile apps for other activities including online shopping. Also, 96 (80%) agreed that, from the time they get to know about a new mobile app, it takes them between 1-3 months to adopt and use it.

Innovation characteristics – this section tested the perceptions of the participants on the characteristics of innovations.

Relative advantage – is the extent to which an innovation is observed to be better than the existing ones. The obtained results are: 47 (39.2%) of the participants agreed that the relative advantage of a mobile app influences their adoption of that mobile app, 49 (40.8%) are neutral about the impact of this factor and 24 (20%) disagreed on this factor.

Compatibility – is the degree to which the innovation fits well with the existing values, experiences, and needs of possible adopters. The obtained results are: 57 (47.5%) of the participants agreed that the compatibility of a mobile app influences their adoption of that mobile app, 45 (37.5%) are neutral about the impact of this factor and 18 (15%) disagreed on this factor.

Ease of use – is the extent to which the innovation seems easy to be used. The obtained results are: 57 (47.5%) of the participants agreed that the ease of use of a mobile app influences their adoption of that mobile app, 39 (32.5%) are neutral about the impact of this factor and 24 (20%) disagreed on this factor.

Voluntariness – is the degree to which use of the innovation is perceived as being of free will. The obtained results are: 59 (49.1%) of the participants agreed that the voluntariness of a mobile app influences their adoption of that mobile app, 37 (30.9%) are neutral about the impact of this factor and 24 (20%) disagreed on this factor.

Facilitating conditions – are the supports provided by service providers and the government. The obtained results are: 63 (52.5%) of the participants agreed that the facilitating conditions of a mobile app influence their adoption of that mobile app, 33 (27.5%) are neutral about the impact of this factor and 24 (20%) disagreed on this factor.

Self-efficacy – is the individual ability to use an innovation. The obtained results are: 87 (72.2%) of the participants agreed that the self-efficacy of a mobile app influences their adoption of that mobile app, 11 (9.2%) are neutral about the impact of this factor and 22 (18.4%) disagreed on this factor.

Subjective norms – is the individual perception that most people who are important think that he/she should perform a behaviour. The obtained results are: 61 (50.9%) of the participants agreed that the subjective norms of a mobile app influence their adoption of that mobile app, 48 (40%) are neutral about the impact of this factor and 11 (9.2%) disagreed on this factor.

Perceived risk – is the danger involves in using an innovation. The obtained results are: 49 (40.8%) of the participants agreed that the perceived risk of a mobile app influences their adoption of that mobile app, 49 (40.8%) are neutral about the impact of this factor and 22 (18.4%) disagree on this factor.

Adopter's category – this section determines the types of adopter each of the participants is.

Innovators – they are the set of adopters that are willing to experience a new innovation irrespective of the profit, loss or risk involved. The obtained results are: 22 (18.3%) of the participants agreed to be in this category of adopters, 11(9.2%) are neutral about the category and 87 (72.5%) are not in this category.

Early adopters – they are leaders and advisers of the social system and their actions are limited within the boundaries of the social system. The obtained results are: 11 (9.2%) of the participants agreed to be in this category of adopters, 11 (9.2%) are neutral about the category and 98 (81.6) are not in this category.

Early majority – they are non-leaders with good interpersonal networks, deliberate in adopting an innovation and they are neither the first nor the last to adopt the innovation. The obtained results are: 49 (40.8%) of the participants agreed to be in this category of adopters, 35 (29.2%) are neutral about the category and 36 (30%) are not in this category.

Late majority – they are the set of adopters that are skeptical about adopting an innovation and wait for most people to adopt it first. The obtained results are: 83 (69.2%) of the participants agreed to be in this category of adopters, 13 (10.8%) are neutral about the category and 24 (20%) are not in this category.

Laggards – they are the most localized group in the social system with traditional view and very much skeptical about adopting a new idea. The obtained results are: 71 (59.2%) of the participants agreed to be in this category of adopters, 38 (31.7%) are neutral about the category and 11 (9.2%) are not in this category.

4.3 Adopters Attitudes

For this research, attitude is defined as an individual's beliefs and feelings over an innovation. The attitudes of an adopter may be positive, negative and nervousness towards the adoption and rejection of an innovation. Wang et al. (2008) suggested that attitudes are a major predicting factor influencing the adoption of a new product, therefore there is a need for more understanding of attitudes in a well-defined manner. Attitudes are considered to be a three-factor concept comprising of cognitive, affective and conative covering thoughts and beliefs, feelings and actions respectively (Prislin and Crano (2008)).

This study seeks to determine the relationship between the characteristics of innovations and adopters' attitudes among rural dwellers on the adoption of m-commerce. Applying regression analysis to the research model whereby the characteristics of innovations are the independent variables and the perceived attitudes are the dependent variable, the results obtained are shown in Table 1 – Table 3.

Table 1 indicates that relative advantage, voluntariness, subjective norms, perceived risk, facilitating conditions and self-efficacy characteristics showed statistical significant predictive capability. This means that these characteristics have an impact on the positive attitudes of the rural dwellers towards the adoption of m-commerce apps.

Table 1. Positive Attitudes

Model		Unstandardized Coefficients B	Std. Error	Standardized Coefficients Beta	t	Sig.
1	(Constant)	2.190	.614		3.565	.001
	Compatibility	-.200	.121	-.137	-1.646	.103
	Relative advantage	.569	.127	.527	4.475	.000
	Voluntariness	-.792	.175	-.641	-4.519	.000
	Subjective norms	1.839	.213	1.018	8.615	.000
	Ease of use	-.115	.100	-.077	-1.143	.255
	Perceived risk	.314	.157	.220	1.998	.048
	Facilitating conditions	-.579	.108	-.357	-5.356	.000
	Self-efficacy	-.694	.115	-.643	-6.029	.000

Table 2. Negative Attitudes

Model		Unstandardized Coefficients B	Std. Error	Standardized Coefficients Beta	t	Sig.
1	(Constant)	3.160	.673		4.697	.000
	Compatibility	-.054	.133	-.052	-.406	.686
	Relative advantage	-.660	.139	-.858	-4.739	.000
	Voluntariness	.531	.192	.603	2.764	.007
	Subjective norms	-.371	.234	-.288	-1.588	.115
	Ease of use	.157	.110	.147	1.423	.158
	Perceived risk	.028	.172	.027	.162	.871
	Facilitating conditions	.112	.118	.097	.943	.348
	Self-efficacy	.015	.126	.020	.123	.903

Table 2 indicates that relative advantage and voluntariness characteristics showed statistical significant predictive capability. This means that these characteristics have an impact on the negative attitudes of the rural dwellers towards the adoption of m-commerce apps.

Table 3. Nervous Attitudes

Model		Unstandardized Coefficients B	Std. Error	Standardized Coefficients Beta	t	Sig.
1	(Constant)	3.493	.364		9.606	.000
	Compatibility	.182	.072	.150	2.535	.013
	Relative advantage	-1.380	.075	-1.538	-18.327	.000
	Voluntariness	1.240	.104	1.208	11.950	.000
	Subjective norms	-1.438	.126	-.957	-11.377	.000
	Ease of use	.332	.059	.268	5.580	.000
	Perceived risk	.846	.093	.712	9.082	.000
	Facilitating conditions	.092	.064	.068	1.438	.153
	Self-efficacy	-.060	.068	-.067	-.882	.380

Table 3 indicates that compatibility, relative advantage, voluntariness, subjective norms, ease of use and perceived risk characteristics showed statistical significant predictive capability. This means that these characteristics have an impact on the nervous attitudes of the rural dwellers towards the adoption of m-commerce apps.

5. INTERPRETATION OF THE RESULTS

Generally, the results indicated that the rural dwellers have a good knowledge of what mobile apps are about, though not familiar with using all. For instance, all the participants are users of the SMS app. This is because they are using mobile phones for telephony and messages communications. With regards to m-commerce, a little portion (20%) of the sample population has knowledge of it and has used it. This implies that there is a lack of awareness-knowledge of m-commerce apps among the rural inhabitants and there is a need to create more awareness-knowledge about m-commerce and other related mobile apps.

A larger number of the rural dwellers perceived m-commerce app to be a good technological innovation and are willing to adopt and use them without being nervous at all. In addition, the results revealed that the rural dwellers show positive attitudes when they hear of a new mobile app. Therefore, it implies that they are willing, ready to accept, learn how to and practically use an innovation that get to their reach. They adopt and use mobile apps mostly for communications purposes like SMS, social networking and entertainments. Although they have limited awareness-knowledge of m-commerce apps, they demonstrated to have a high rate of interest in adopting and using m-commerce apps such that it takes an average range of 1-3 months for them to adopt and use a new mobile app.

Eight characteristics of innovations were used to examine the perceptions and attitudes of the rural dwellers on the adoption and diffusion of m-commerce including relative advantage, compatibility, ease of use, voluntariness, facilitating conditions, self-efficacy, subjective norms and perceived risk. The obtained results revealed that the rural dwellers perceived the innovation characteristics to be significant factors in their decision-making either to accept or reject m-commerce. Thus, the characteristics of innovations influence the attitudes of the rural dwellers towards decision-making on the adoption and diffusion of m-commerce apps.

The rural dwellers demonstrated a good intention of embracing a new technological innovation but still, they fall in the late majority and laggards categories. Probably because they live in a remote area and extension of the knowledge about a new innovation comes late. This suggests that if the information about an innovation like m-commerce apps is being disseminated to the rural areas in due time as it is done in the urban areas, there is the possibility that some rural dwellers will be in the early adopters and innovators categories.

Multiple linear regression analysis was performed to investigate the relationship between the characteristics of innovations and the rural dwellers' attitudes. The obtained results indicated that all the 8 tested characteristics of innovations have statistical significant capabilities of influencing the rural dwellers' attitudes (positive, negative or nervous) towards the adoption of m-commerce.

Concerning positive attitudes, the relative advantage, voluntariness, subjective norms, perceived risk, facilitating conditions and self-efficacy characteristics have significant influences towards the positive attitudes of the rural dwellers' adopters. This suggests that changes to these characteristics result in changes to the adopters' attitudes. With respects to the negative attitudes, the relative advantage and voluntariness characteristics have significant influences towards the negative attitudes of the rural dwellers' adopters. In relation to nervous attitudes, the compatibility, relative advantage, voluntariness, subjective norms, ease of use and perceived risk characteristics have a significant influence on the nervous attitudes of the rural dwellers' attitudes.

The analyses show that there exists a clear relationship between the perceived attitudes of the rural dwellers and the characteristics of innovations. From the perspectives of the rural dwellers, the adopters of mobile apps believe that an innovation should have a relative advantage over the existing ones, fits well into their lifestyle, be easy for them to learn and use, and with necessary support both from the innovators and the government. Furthermore, with the acquisition of the required knowledge and free decision to use the innovation, it must be in line with their societal norms and with reduced risk. Moreover, the rural dwellers exhibit positive interest whenever they get to know about a new mobile app which activated their enthusiasm to adopt and use the mobile app without panic.

REFERENCES

Abdelkarim, A. and Nasereddin, H., 2010. Mobile commerce. *Journal of Mathematics and Technology*, Vol. 4, No. 1, pp. 51-56.

Bhatti, T., 2007. Exploring factors influencing the adoption of mobile commerce. *The Journal of Internet Banking and Commerce*, Vol. 12, No. 3.

Brown, I., et al., 2003. Cell phone banking: predictors of adoption in South Africa—an exploratory study. *International journal of information management*, Vol. 23, No. 5, pp. 381-394.

Chang, H., C., 2010. A new perspective on Twitter hashtag use: Diffusion of innovation theory. *Proceedings of the American Society for Information Science and Technology*, Vol. 47, No. 1, pp. 1-4.

Chong, A.Y.-L., 2013. Mobile commerce usage activities: The roles of demographic and motivation variables. *Technological Forecasting and Social Change*, Vol.80, No. 7, pp. 1350-1359.

GSMA, 2017. The Mobile Economy Sub-Saharan Africa 2017. https://www.gsmaintelligence.com/research/?file=7bf3592e6d750144e58d9dcfac6adfab&download.

GSMA, 2015. The mobile economy 2015, GSMA, Editor. GSM Association. p. 1-62.

Hellström, J.,2011. Mobile governance: Applications, challenges and scaling-up. *Mobile Technologies for Conflict Management*, Springer. pp. 159-179.

Hellström, J. and Tröften, P.-E., 2010. The innovative use of mobile applications in East Africa. *Swedish international development cooperation agency (Sida).*

Hwang, G.-J. and Chang H.-F., 2011. A formative assessment-based mobile learning approach to improving the learning attitudes and achievements of students. *Computers & Education*, Vol 56, No. 4, pp. 1023-1031.

ITU, 2017. ITU releases 2017 global information and communication technology facts and figures. http://news.itu.int/itu-releases-2017-global-information-and-communication-technology-facts-and-figures/

Joubert, J. and Van Belle, J., 2013. The role of trust and risk in mobile commerce adoption within South Africa. *International Journal of Business, Humanities and Technology*, Vol. 3, No. 2, pp. 27-38.

Kim, S.H., 2006. Impact of mobile-commerce: benefits, technological and strategic issues and implementation. *Journal of Applied Sciences*, Vol. 6, No. 12., pp. 2523-2531.

Kumar, S., et al., 2013. Mobile health technology evaluation: the mHealth evidence workshop. *American Journal of Preventive medicine*, Vol.45, No. 2, pp. 228-236.

Liu, Y., et al., 2014. An empirical investigation of mobile government adoption in rural China: A case study in Zhejiang province. *Government Information Quarterly*, Vol. 31, No. 3, pp. 432-442.

Lule, I., et al., 2012. Application of technology acceptance model (TAM) in m-banking adoption in Kenya. *International Journal of Computing and ICT Research*, Vol. 6, No. 1, pp. 31-43.

Mannan, S. and Nordin, S.M., 2014. The Influence of Innovation Attributes on New Technologies Adoption by Paddy Farmers. *International Review of Management and Business Research*, Vol. 3, No. 3, p. 1379.

Mc Namara, K.S., 2009. Mobile Applications in Agriculture and Rural Development–Framing the Topic, and Learning from Experience. *World Bank Workshop on Mobile Innovations for Social and Economic Transformation.*

Moore G.C. and Benbasat I., 1991. Development of an instrument to measure the perceptions of adopting an information technology innovation. *Information Systems Research,* Vol. 2, No. 3, pp. 192-222.

Murugesan, S., 2013. Mobile apps in Africa. *IT Professional*, Vol. 15, No. 5, pp. 8-11.

Nickerson, R., et al., 2014. Mobile Technology and Smartphone Apps: A Diffusion of Innovations Analysis. *Proceedings of the 20th Twentieth Americas Conference on Information Systems*, Savannah, USA, pp. 1-12.

Numally, J.C.,1978. *Psychometric theory.* NY: McGraw-Hill, 1978.

Okonkwo, W.C. and Huisman, M., 2018. The Use of System Development Methodologies in the Development of Mobile Applications: Are they Worthy of Use? *IEEE 42nd Annual Computer Software and Applications Conference (COMPSAC).* Tokyo, Japan, pp. 278-283.

Poblet, M., 2011. Rule of Law on the Go: New Developments of Mobile Governance. *J. UCS*, Vol.17, No.3, pp. 498-512.

Prislin, R. and Crano, W.D., 2008. *Attitudes and attitude change.* New York: Psychology Press.

Qiang, C.Z., et al., 2011. *Mobile applications for agriculture and rural development.* World Bank, Washington, DC.

Rogers, E., 2003. *Diffusion of Innovations (5th ed).* New York: Free Press.

San Martín, S., B., et al., 2012. Factors determining firms' perceived performance of mobile commerce. *Industrial Management & Data Systems*, Vol. 112, No. 6, pp. 946-963.

Sethi, V. and King, W.R., 1991. Construct measurement in information systems research: An illustration in strategic systems. *Decision Sciences,* Vol.22, No.2, pp. 455-472.

Siau, K., et al., 2003. Mobile commerce: Current states and future trends. *Advances in mobile commerce technologies,* IGI Global. p. 1-17.

Tan, M. and Teo, TSH, 2000. Factors influencing the adoption of Internet Banking. *Journal of the Association for Information Systems,* Vol.1, Issue 1, Article 5. https://aisel.aisnet.org/jais/vol2/iss1/5

Taylor, D.G., et al., 2011. Mobile application adoption by young adults: A social network perspective. *WCOB Faculty Publications.* Paper 1. http://digitalcommons.sacredheart.edu/wcob_fac/1

Wang, H.-Y., et al., 2013. What affects mobile application use? The roles of consumption values. *International Journal of Marketing Studies*, Vol. 5, No. 2, p. 11.

Wang, G., et al., 2008. Consumption attitudes and adoption of new consumer products: a contingency approach. *European Journal of Marketing*, Vol. 42, No. 1/2, pp. 238-254.

ONLINE BRAND COMMUNITIES IN SOCIAL COMMERCE: IDENTIFYING FACTORS AFFECTING CUSTOMER ENGAGEMENT

Pelin Bayraktar and Sevgi Özkan Yıldırım
Middle East Technical University
Dumlupınar Bulvarı No:106800 Ankara/Turkey

ABSTRACT

Social commerce is defined as a new wave of e-commerce in which traditional e-commerce is mediated by social media and social networking services in order to promote online transactions and shopping-related information exchanges. One of the main application of social commerce is 'online brand communities'. Although utilization of social media in order to advance customer brand engagement has proliferated significantly in recent years, most of the companies do not meet the expected level of engagement of their customers. Overall, the key factors that could explain customer engagement are not yet thoroughly identified. Therefore, the current study develops a conceptual customer engagement model that aims to explain customer engagement in online brand communities. Customer engagement in brand social media is related to interactions and communications with the brand and other customers. In this study, the antecedents and outcomes of customer engagement dimensions will be investigated. As different dimensions of engagement can be influenced by factors from different aspects, it is important to cover as many categories as possible. Therefore, the model includes various factor categories including social, brand related, self-oriented and contend related factors drawn from relevant literature. The research instrument was designed, and a pilot study was conducted with 75 participants to assure content validity and to test reliability. The paper contributes to understanding the factors influencing each dimension of customer engagement to brand communities.

KEYWORDS

Customer Engagement, Brand Communities, Engagement Dimensions, Brand Loyalty

1. INTRODUCTION

The emergence of social media has changed the way that the customers and companies communicate. Relations based on one way information flow have given their place to more participatory and interactive communication. This structure has strengthened the customer's position in the communication and gave them a more active role in influencing the company (Brodie et al., 2011). Social media is an effective tool for the companies in understanding their customers and their expectations, communicating with their customers, presenting their identity, products or services, receiving feedback from their customers to enhance their performance (Guesalaga, 2016). Therefore, companies should invest time and money to social networks in order to establish engagement with customers (de Castro, 2017).

Consumer engagement has become a popular research area after it was specified as a key research priority for future research. Brodie et al. (2011) defined consumer engagement as a psychological state that occurs through customer experiences having cognitive, emotional, and behavioral dimensions. However, there is a lack of consensus on its definition, conceptual domain and dimensionality. Customer engagement is ahead of similar concepts participation and involvement by requiring an active interactive relationship with the engaged object (Marbach et al., 2016). Although customer engagement can occur in brand generated platforms such as brand social media channels, a great deal of engagement take place on consumer generated platforms governed by individuals such as Facebook groups. With the emergence of online technologies, online brand communities have been started to serve as an additional channel for the organization to communicate with and receive feedback from customers (Chan et al., 2014).

In the literature, several studies aimed to find the significant factors affecting customer engagement in brand communities (Jayasingh and Venkatesh, 2015; Carlson et al., 2017; Guo et al., 2017). They focused on various factor types including social factors such as tie strength, trust, social identity, trust and reciprocity (Chahal et al., 2017; Kang et al., 2016; Carlson et al. 2017; Tsai et al., 2017; Bohari, 2016), content based factors such as perceived usefulness and perceived enjoyment (Guo et al., 2017; Carlson et al, 2017; Dessart et al., 2015; Chahal et al., 2017), brand related factors such as satisfaction ore brand image (Dessart et al., 2015; Carlson et al., 2017) and customer related factors such as self image enhancement and altruism (Simon et al., 2016; Jahn et al., 2012; Luarn et al., 2016; Marbach et al., 2016). Heinonen (2017) focused on the effect customer based factors on behavioral, emotional and cognitive dimensions of customer engagement. Kuzgun and Josiassen (2016) investigated the relationship between different engagement dimensions and revealed the effect of cognitive dimension on emotional dimension and emotional dimension on behavioral dimension.

In order to provide strategic guidelines to companies for increasing customer engagement and developing communication strategies, it is important to determine the factors that the customers value the most for interacting with the brand and other community members. Although customer engagement is defined as a multi-dimensional concept including cognitive, emotional and behavioral dimensions, there is no comprehensive study investigating which factor influences which engagement dimension. The relationship between engagement dimensions has been investigated in a small number of studies; however, the mediating effect of these dimensions between the factors and other dimensions has not been examined. Loyalty has emerged as a consequence of customer engagement in a various studies, but the relationship between loyalty dimensions and engagement dimensions has not been investigated. The purpose of this study is to identify the factors that affect cognitive, emotional and behavioral engagement of customers in brand related social media. Also, relationships between customer engagement dimensions and loyalty dimensions will be investigated.

2. CONCEPTUAL MODEL

The aim of this research is to determine the factors influencing the cognitive, emotional and behavioral dimensions of customer engagement in online brand communities. Therefore, proposed model should include the factors representing social, brand related, self-oriented and content based factors in order to gain a wider perspective and increase explanation power of the model. The conceptual model, *Customer Engagement Evaluation* Model *(CEEM) in Online Brand Communities,* is given in Figure 1.

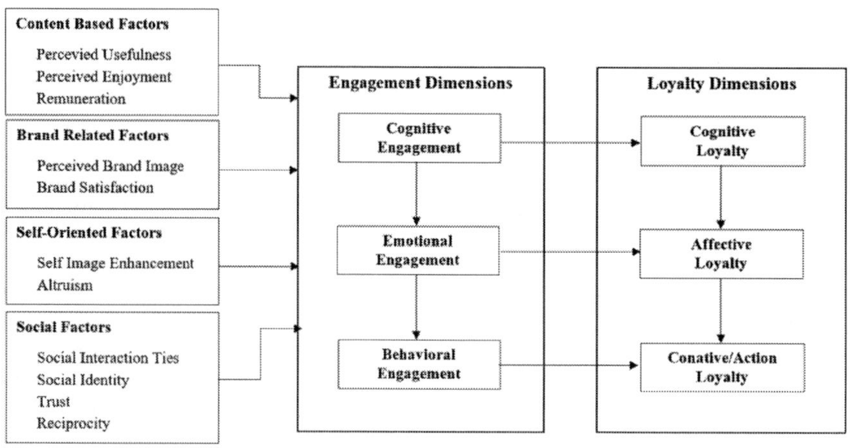

Figure 1. The proposed Customer Engagement Evaluation Model (CEEM) in online brand communities

2.1 Customer Engagement

In terms of dimensionality several authors suggested that customer engagement includes cognitive, emotional and behavioral dimensions (Brodie et al., 2011). Although many other studies used different concepts to represent the dimensionality, those dimensions correspond to the generic cognitive, emotional and behavioral nature of engagement. Cognitive engagement represents the processing, concentration and interest in an object (de Castro, 2017) and refers to being immersed in the content of the brand social platform. Emotional engagement is expected to occur through recurrent feeling of these emotional responses after certain time of satisfying cognitive immersion in brand social networks (Kuzgun et al., 2016) and refers to consumer' level of excitement, interest, pleasure and happiness derived from engaging in brand related content and interactions with brand community and its members. Behavioral engagement refers to the willingness to devote time and effort to the brand social platform. This level of engagement is considered as the strongest engagement level. Kuzgun et al. (2016) found that cognitive engagement has a direct effect on emotional engagement and emotional engagement has a direct effect on behavioral engagement in virtual brand communities.

2.2 Brand Loyalty

Brand loyalty is defined as "a deeply held commitment to rebuy or repatronize a preferred product or service consistently in the future" (Oliver, 1997, p. 392). Oliver (1997) specified dimensions of loyalty as cognitive, affective, conation and active loyalty. Cognitive loyalty is based on the beliefs of customers that the brand is preferable to its alternatives. Those beliefs may result from prior knowledge of or experiences with the brand. After these cumulative satisfying experiences, positive attitude toward the firm has developed which brings the customer into affective loyalty phase. Affective loyalty reflects deeper level of commitment than cognitive level. Conative loyalty refers to intention of repurchase influenced by repeated positive affect toward the brand. Various studies on engagement propose loyalty as a consequence of customer engagement (Dessart et al., 2015; de Castro, 2017; Harrigan et al., 2017).

2.3 Antecedents of Customer Engagement

Various social factors have been proposed as drivers of customer engagement (Simon et al., 2016; de Castro, 2017; Luarn et al., 2016; Carlson et al., 2017; Chahal et al., 2017; Huang et al., 2013). Also, Jahn et al. (2012) suggested that one most prominent needs of customers is related to content-oriented area which is based on functional and hedonic values. As one of the main objects of customer engagement is brands, factors such as the perception of the customers about the brand and perception that the brand meet their expectations will affect the level of engagement. Jahn et al. (2012) stated that customer engagement is driven by particular needs of individuals such as achieving status or need for diversion. Therefore, we include social, content based, brand related and self-oriented factors in our model as antecedents of customer engagement.

2.3.1 Social Interaction Ties

With its interactive nature, social media supports two-way communication between customers and brands as well as between customers and customers. Social interaction ties refer to the intensity of interaction and closeness of relationships between community members in a social network. Chang et al. (2011) stated that the strong connections and direct ties between community members increase the intensity and sustainability of knowledge exchange in virtual communities. Various studies depicted that tie-strength and social interaction influence customer engagement on social networks (Chahal et al., 2017; Luarn et al., 2016; Jahn et al., 2012).

2.3.2 Trust

Since social media are interactive channels, the users not only follow what the brand is saying, but also joining in conversation with the brands and other community members. The communication in virtual communities exists between a customer and other unfamiliar community members or the brand. Community trust refers to relying on the honesty, reliability and trustworthiness of other community members and it is a crucial factor for interactions in brand-related social media (Kang et al., 2016). Trust has been offered as an antecedent of customer engagement in various studies (Chahal et al., 2017; Youssef et al., 2018).

2.3.3 Social Identification

Identification refers to customer's sense of emotional belongingness and shared representation of his/her self with a social group (Simon et al., 2016). Customers who feel sense of belongingness to a brand community and feel them as important and valuable part of the community tend to engage in community activities and maintain committed relationships with the community (Chiu et al., 2006). Also, customers identify more with the brands matching their self-image and use social media to present their self-image by expressing their belongingness to the community. Identification with the brand and the community deepen community engagement by enhancing group and oriented attitudes and motivation to exchange knowledge and also deepen customer brand relationships (Simon et al., 2016). Prior studies on customer engagement revealed social identity to be significant predictor of brand social media engagement (Chahal et al., 2017; Simon et al., 2016).

2.3.4 Reciprocity

Community members expect reciprocity to balance their investments and gains from the community (Mathwick et al., 2007). Their expected future returns could be exchanges in-kind or alternate form of aid. Previous studies indicated that norm of reciprocity is a significant driver of information exchange and knowledge sharing behaviors in online environments (Bohari, 2016; Chiu et al., 2006).

2.3.5 Perceived Usefulness

Perceived usefulness is defined as "the extent to which an individual believes that using an information system will enhance their productivity" (Davis, 1989). Accessing quality content promotes customers to follow brand social media more closely and feel involved (Guo et al., 2017). It will not be possible to ensure the sustainability of continued use and engagement in brand social media activities unless the customer perceive the usefulness of brand social media. Perceived usefulness has been found as an important factor affecting customer engagement to social media (Chahal et al., 2017; de Castro, 2017). Reitz (2012) hypothesized that perceived information quality positively influence all customer engagement dimensions.

2.3.6 Perceived Enjoyment

Perceived enjoyment is defined as "an intrinsic motivation that emphasizes the usage process and reflects the pleasure and enjoyment associated with the using a system" (Praveena and Thomas, 2014, p.25). Calder and Malthouse (2005) stated that customers engage in online activities regarding not only utility or quality of the content but also hedonic or emotional factors such as interestingness and enjoyment of the content. Various studies demonstrated the effect of enjoyment on customer engagement in brand related social media (Guo et al., 2017; Chahal et al., 2017; Tsai et al., 2017; Yesiloglu, 2018). Reitz (2012) and Huang et al. (2017) investigated the effect of enjoyment on dimensions of customer engagement and both studies revealed that perceived enjoyment positively predicted all engagement dimensions.

2.3.7 Remuneration

Remuneration refers to expectations of customers in gaining rewards and economic incentives (Yesiloglu, 2018). Companies suggest large amounts stimuli including rewards, promotions, discounts, and coupons to increase the motivation of their customers to encourage engagement in their social media (Guo et al., 2017). Earlier studies concluded that economic benefits drive customers to maintain relationships with the brand and engage in brand related social networks (Guo et al., 2017; Yesiloglu, 2018; de Castro, 2017; Hussain at al., 2018). Chan et al. (2014) stated that the customers will feel obliged to devote themselves and the level of engagement will increase when they perceive rewards from the brand community. Dessart et al. (2015) indicated that benefits from participating in brand community including explicit monetary incentives enhance affect, cognition and behaviors of the community members.

2.3.8 Perceived Brand Image

Brand image refers to subjective perceptions of a customer about a particular brand (Nandan, 2005). Customers combine impressions about the brand that they received from various sources to form a perceived brand personality. When a brand has strong image, it will increase the attractiveness of the brand and willingness of customers to associate with the brand to gain social prestige. Previous works suggested that high reputation and prestige companies are likely to cause higher levels of customer engagement (Goldsmith et al., 2012; Andonova, 2016).

2.3.9 Brand Satisfaction

Tse and Wilton (1988) defined brand satisfaction as "the consumer's response to the evaluation of the perceived discrepancy between prior expectations and the actual performance of the product as perceived after its consumption" (p. 204), and it is a key factor for the stability of customer-brand relationships (Ling and Pedersen, 2006). Satisfaction arises when customers perceive that the benefits provided by the company exceed customers' expectations (Carlson et al., 2017). It is considered as a key factor affecting customer engagement behaviors in previous studies (Carlson et al., 2017; Dessart et al., 2015). When the customers are satisfied with the brand and its products or services will be likely to engage in brand related social media.

2.3.10 Self-Image Enhancement

Social enhancement is defined as the perceived value of being recognized or approved by other members of the social network on account of one's contributions to and relationships with the brand (Dholakia et al., 2004). By engaging in community activities, customer can present their self-concept, create perception about themselves, and gain recognition and reputation from others and those induce a strong motivation to customers for community participation (Simon et al., 2016). Previous studies shown the effect of self-image enhancement value on customer engagement to brand fan pages (Simon et al., 2016; Jahn et al., 2012).

2.3.11 Altruism

Altruism refers to concerning for others without expecting compensation (Luarn et al., 2016). Through social networks, customers can reach a large number of people and share their brand related knowledge and experiences to help them in reaching the necessary information or in making purchasing decisions. In prior studies, it was found that altruism enhances customer engagement behavior such as sharing their knowledge or brand generated content with others that they concern, writing reviews or creating brand related posts or eWOM (Luarn et al., 2016; Hennig-Thurau at al., 2003). Marbach et al. (2016) proposed that altruism is positively related to cognitive, emotional and behavioral dimension of engagement.

2.4 Instrument Development and Pilot Study

To develop the instrument, the conceptual definitions of each construct of the model were defined. To measure the constructs in the model, an item pool was generated using the established measures from prior literature and minor modifications were made to the items to fit them to the context of customer engagement.

Table 1. Brief of Questions of the Survey Instrument

Construct	Sample Question	Reference
Brand Satisfaction	Brand [X] has lived up to my expectations.	Solem (2015)
Brand Image	Brand [X] is reliable.	Chahal et al. (2017)
Trust	I feel safe in my postings with the [X] brand community.	Chahal et al. (2017)
Altruism	I feel good when I can help answer other community members' questions.	Casas et al. (2016)
Reciprocity	I believe that members in the [X] brand community would help me if I need.	Chiu et al. (2006)
Perceived Enjoyment	The content of the [X] brand community is exciting.	Carlson et al. (2017)
Perceived Usefulness	The content of the [X] brand community is useful for me.	Jahn et al. (2012)
Remuneration	I follow [X] brand community because of incentives I receive.	Guo et al. (2017)
Self-Image Enhancement	I follow [X] brand community because I can present others who I am.	Jahn et al. (2012)
Social Interaction Ties	I know some members in the [X] brand community on a personal level.	Chiu et al. (2006)
Social Identity	The [X] brand community's identity is reflection of my self-image.	Chahal et al. (2017)
Cognitive Engagement	Time flies when I am interacting with the [X] brand community.	Huang et al. (2013)
Emotional Engagement	I pay a lot of attention to anything about the [X] brand community.	Huang et al. (2013)
Behavioral Engagement	I devote lots of energy to the [X] brand community.	Huang et al. (2013)
Cognitive Loyalty	Overall quality of brand [X] is the best.	Yuksel et al. (2010)
Affective Loyalty	I like brand [X] more than other brand.	Yuksel et al. (2010)
Conative Loyalty	I consider brand [X] to be my first choice.	Yuksel et al. (2010)

In order to ensure content validity, expert review procedure was conducted with three experts from scale development domain. They evaluate the survey items according to their conformance of the related construct definition. Also they assisted in making corrections on the wording and semantic structure of the questionnaire. The final survey items have been selected from the item pool considering their representativeness of the construct's conceptual definition. As a result, the item pool including 63 items was formed. Then, in order to test the instrument in terms of reliability and construct validity, a pilot study was conducted. The brief of questions of the instrument including one sample for each construct is given in Table 1.

2.4.1 Demographics of the Participants

The questionnaire reached 141 participants but only 75 of them stated that they follow a brand community (53.2%). 57% of the respondents are female and 43% are male. Most of the participants (%73.3) were between 20-39 years. Over 89% of the respondents had bachelors or upper degrees. 76% of the respondents were employed and 12% of them were students. 40% of the respondents use social media between 30 minutes-1 hour a day and %33.3 use it 1 to 3 hours a day. 26.7% of the respondents spent more than 3 hours a day using social media. The most widely used social media platform is Instagram. 90% of the respondents use the brand community for consuming type behaviors such as reading product reviews or product ratings, viewing the dialogues of other customers, 37% of them use it for contributing type behaviors such as rating products or brands, commenting on brand related content and media and only 20% of them use it for creating type behaviors such as publishing brand related content or making recommendations. 75% of the participants that perform contributing or creating type behaviors in their brand community are also found to be engaged in the brand community. 67% of the participants that use social media more than 1 hour a day and 89% of the participants in unemployed or retired occupation status are engaged in the brand community that they join.

2.4.2 Reliability Analysis

Since the pilot study was conducted in smaller scale, not all the reliability and validity measures would be applicable. Reliability analysis was performed using IBM SPSS Statistics v25. The Cronbach's Alpha values were examined. In terms of reliability analysis, Cronbach's alpha loadings would be above .70 (Hair, 1998) and all the constructs of our model fulfill the condition. Total reliability was found as 0.974. The Cronbach's Alpha values for each construct (ranged between 0.724 and 0.967) are given in Table 2.

Table 2. Cronbach's Alpha values of constructs

Construct	Cronbach's Alpha	Construct	Cronbach's Alpha	Construct	Cronbach's Alpha
Brand Satisfaction	0.967	Altruism	0.963	Social Interaction Ties	0.936
Perceived Brand Image	0.914	Reciprocity	0.724	Social Identity	0.888
Cognitive Loyalty	0.881	Perceived Enjoyment	0.916	Cognitive Engagement	0.967
Affective Loyalty	0.866	Perceived Usefulness	0.949	Emotional Engagement	0.909
Conative Loyalty	0.890	Remuneration	0.899	Behavioral Engagement	0.941
Trust	0.880	Self-Image Enhancement	0.929		

Also, Cronbach Alpha if item deleted, item total correlation and inter item correlation values were analyzed. As a result, all the items were decided to be included into the questionnaire since all the constructs have Cronbach Alpha value greater than 0.7. Also, according to the Cronbach Alpha if item deleted values, there is no significant change in construct based Cronbach Alpha values when any item deleted from the questionnaire.

3. CONCLUSION

Given the brands' increasing use of social media for engaging their customers, there is a need to better understand the factors that affects customer engagement in brand related social platforms. Currently, consumer engagement has become a popular research area. Customer engagement with its multidimensional structure having cognitive, emotional and behavioral dimensions, is a complex process where various factors are expected to affect it. The aim of the study is to identify the factors that can influence the dimensions of customer engagement to brand related social platforms. Therefore, a model including various factors that represent different aspects of customer engagement is proposed: *Customer Engagement Evaluation* Model *(CEEM) in Online Brand Communities.* It also includes relationships between engagement dimensions, loyalty dimensions and the relationships between engagement dimensions and its corresponding loyalty dimensions.

The factors were determined based on a systematic review of the established literature. The proposed model consists of social factors (social interaction ties, social identity, trust, reciprocity), content based factors (perceived usefulness, perceived enjoyment, remuneration), brand related factors (perceived brand image, brand satisfaction) and self-oriented factors (self-image enhancement, altruism). Those constructs are considered as relevant influencers of each dimension of customer engagement in brand related social platforms. The proposed model (*Customer Engagement Evaluation* Model *(CEEM) in Online Brand Communities)* represents a starting point for understanding the antecedents and outcomes of each dimension of customer engagement. In this paper, empirical validity and reliability tests of the proposed model are presented. Future work will involve further validation of the model via various brand communities. For that, the questionnaire is planned to be applied to the members of brand communities from automotive, technology and retail sectors.

REFERENCES

Andonova, Y., 2016. Customer Engagement: Perceived Benefits and Effect of Individual and Brand Personality on Engagement Behaviors (Doctoral dissertation, Isenberg School of Management).

Bohari, A. M. B., 2016. Knowledge Contribution Determinants through Social Network Sites: Social Relational Perspective. *International Review of Management and Marketing*, 6(3).

Brislin, R. W., 1986. Research instruments. *Field methods in cross-cultural research*, 8, 137-164.

Brodie, R. J. et al, 2011. Customer engagement: Conceptual domain, fundamental propositions, and implications for research. *Journal of Service Research*, 14(3), 252-271.

Calder, B. J., and Malthouse, E. C., 2005. Managing media and advertising change with integrated marketing. *Journal of Advertising Research*, 45(4), 356-361.

Carlson, J. et al, 2017. Go with the flow: engineering flow experiences for customer engagement value creation in branded social media environments. *Journal of Brand Management*, 24(4), 334-348.

Časas, R. et al, 2016. The Links Between Social Motivational Engagements, Brand Community Commitment and Repurchase Intention Across Online Brand Communities. *Organizations & Markets in Emerging Economies*, 7(2).

Chahal, H., and Rani, A., 2017. How trust moderates social media engagement and brand equity. *Journal of Research in Interactive Marketing*, 11(3), 312-335.

Chan, T. K. et al, 2014. Antecedents and consequences of customer engagement in online brand communities. *Journal of Marketing Analytics*, 2(2), 81-97.

Chang, H. H., and Chuang, S. S., 2011. Social capital and individual motivations on knowledge sharing: Participant involvement as a moderator. *Information & management*, 48(1), 9-18.

Chiu, C. M. et al, 2006. Understanding knowledge sharing in virtual communities: An integration of social capital and social cognitive theories. *Decision support systems*, 42(3), 1872-1888.

de Castro, A. P. R., 2017. Customer engagement in virtual social network brand communities: drivers and impact on brand loyalty (Master Dissertation, University of Porto).

Davis, F. D., 1989. Perceived usefulness, perceived ease of use, and user acceptance of information technology. MIS quarterly, 319-340.

Dessart, L., 2015. Consumer engagement in online brand communities: a social media perspective. Journal of Product & Brand Management, 24(1), 28-42.

Dholakia, U. M., 2004. A social influence model of consumer participation in network-and small-group-based virtual communities. International Journal of Research in Marketing, 21(3), 241-263.

Goldsmith, R. E., and Goldsmith, E. B., 2012. Brand personality and brand engagement. American Journal of Management, 12(1), 11.

Guesalaga, R., 2016. The use of social media in sales: Individual and organizational antecedents, and the role of customer engagement in social media. Industrial Marketing Management, 54, 71-79.

Guo, L. et al, 2017. Transforming followers into fans: a study of Chinese users of the WeChat Official Account. Online Information Review, 41(7), 1029-1045.

Hair, J.F., 1998. Multivariate Data Analysis, 5th Edition. Upper Saddle River, NJ: Prentice Hall.

Harrigan, P. et al, 2017. Customer engagement with tourism social media brands. Tourism Management, 59, 597-609.

He, H. et al, 2012. Social identity perspective on brand loyalty. Journal of Business Research, 65(5), 648-657.

Heinonen, K., 2017. Positive and negative valence influencing consumer engagement. Journal of Service Theory and Practice.

Hennig-Thurau et al, 2003. Electronic word-of-mouth: Motives for and consequences of reading customer articulations on the Internet. International journal of electronic commerce, 8(2), 51-74.

Huang, R. et al, 2013. Social capital in QQ China: Impacts on virtual engagement of information seeking, interaction sharing, knowledge creating, and purchasing intention. Journal of Marketing Management, 29(3-4), 292-316.

Hussain, S. et al, 2018. Consumers' online information adoption behavior: Motives and antecedents of electronic word of mouth communications. Computers in Human Behavior, 80, 22-32.

Jahn, B., and Kunz, W., 2012. How to transform consumers into fans of your brand. Journal of Service Management, 23(3), 344-361.

Jayasingh, S., and Venkatesh, R., 2016. Determinants of Customer Brand Engagement in Social Media Sites: A Conceptual Framework. International Business Management, 10(15), 2802-2807.

Kang, M. et al, 2016. The role of personalization, engagement, and trust in online communities. Information Technology & People, 29(3), 580-596.

Kuzgun, E., and Josiassen, A., 2016. Brand Loyalty States as an Antecedent of Customer Engagement in Virtual Brand Communities.

Ling, R., and Pedersen, P. E., 2006. Mobile communications: Re-negotiation of the social sphere (Vol. 31). Springer Science & Business Media.

Luarn, P. et al, 2016. Motivations to engage in word-of-mouth behavior on social network sites. Information Development, 32(4), 1253-1265.

Marbach, J. et al, 2016. Who are you and what do you value? Investigating the role of personality traits and customer-perceived value in online customer engagement. Journal of Marketing Management, 32(5-6), 502-525.

Mathwick, C. et al, 2007. Social capital production in a virtual P3 community. Journal of consumer research, 34(6), 832-849.

Men, L. R., and Tsai, W. H. S., 2013. Toward an integrated model of public engagement on corporate social networking sites: Antecedents, the process, and relational outcomes. International Journal of Strategic Communication, 7(4), 257-273.

Nandan, S., 2005. An exploration of the brand identity–brand image linkage: A communications perspective. Journal of Brand Management, 12(4), 264-278.

Oliver, R. L., 1999. Whence consumer loyalty?. Journal of Marketing, 33-44.

Praveena, K., and Thomas, S., 2014. Continuance intention to use Facebook: A study of perceived enjoyment and TAM. Bonfring International Journal of Industrial Engineering and Management Science, 4(1), 24.

Reitz, A. R., 2012. Online consumer engagement: Understanding the antecedents and outcomes (Doctoral dissertation, Colorado State University).

Simon, C. et al, 2016. The impact of external social and internal personal forces on consumers' brand community engagement on Facebook. Journal of Product & Brand Management, 25(5), 409-423.

Solem, B. A. A. (2015). The process of customer brand engagement in interactive contexts: Prerequisites, conceptual foundations, antecedents, and outcomes (Doctoral dissertation, Norwegian School of Economics and Business Administration).

Tsai, W. H. S., and Men, L. R., 2017. Consumer engagement with brands on social network sites: A cross-cultural comparison of China and the USA. Journal of Marketing Communications, 23(1), 2-21.

Tse, D. K., and Wilton, P. C., 1988. Models of consumer satisfaction formation: An extension. Journal of marketing research, 204-212.

Yesiloglu, S., 2018. To post or not to post: examining motivations of brand/product-related engagement types on social networking sites (Doctoral dissertation, Bournemouth University).

Youssef, Y. M. A. et al, 2018. A customer engagement framework for a B2B context. Journal of Business & Industrial Marketing, 33(1), 145-152.

Yuksel, A. et al, 2010. Destination attachment: Effects on customer satisfaction and cognitive, affective and conative loyalty. Tourism management, 31(2), 274-284.

DIALOGUE SYSTEM FOR ELDERLY PEOPLE CONSIDERING IMPRESSION FORMATION AND USER'S CHARACTER

Hiroshi Yajima, Huta Takeda, Jyunpei Kawaguchi and Manabu Kurosawa
Tokyo Denki University, 5 Asahi-cho Adachi-ku Tokyo Japan

ABSTRACT

In recent years, lacks of conversation among elderly people are becoming a serious problem accompanying an increase in elderly living alone. For this trend, dialogue systems for solving the lack of conversation by elderly people have received attention. As elderly people are thought to like to talk, current dialogue systems for elderly people are specialized in listening to the story. However, it will be difficult for elderly people to speak positively to the dialogue systems from the beginning. In this paper, we propose a dialogue system that considers psychological factors such as communication process and user's character. In the proposed method, communication between elderly people and the dialogue system is divided into two stages. In the initial dialogue, an agent talks positively to make elderly people easy to talk. In the late dialogue, we propose two kinds of agents that adopt different dialogue methods according to the character of the user. Finally, we conducted experiments on the formation of impressions in the initial dialogue and verified the effectiveness of the proposed method.

KEYWORDS

Dialogue System, Elderly, Character, Impression Formation, Primacy Effect

1. INTRODUCTION

In recent years, Japan is entering an aging society. The proportion of elderly people aged 65 or over in Japan's total population is 27.3% (Cabinet Office, 2017). As the aging progresses, the proportion of elderly people is expected to become 33.3% in 2025. In other words, it is said that one out of every three people will become an elderly person. With the progress of the aging population, the proportion of lonely elderly people is increasing. The proportion of elderly living alone in the elderly population was 4.3% for males and 11.2% for females in 1980. Thereafter, in men in 2001 the number increased to 13.3% for men and 21.1% for women. Senior citizens tend to be lacking in communication. We conducted a survey on the frequency of conversation among elderly people aged 60 and older. We analyzed those who were elderly people living alone and who responded that the frequency of conversation (including telephone and e-mail) was less than once every two or three days. As a result, the corresponding elderly people were 28.8% for males and 22.0% for females (Cabinet Office, 2016).

It is said that the risk of dementia is high in elderly people with poor communication. According to Saito et al. 'S research, the risk of dementia for elderly people whose frequency of conversation is less than once a week is 1.4 times that of elderly people who often talk (Dementia Forum, 2018).

In recent years, many chat dialogue systems for the elderly have been studied to solve the lack of communication of the elderly with aging (Aoyanagi et al., 2018), but the conventional system has the following problems: (1) system does not take into consideration factors such as the process of communication of the elderly and the character of the elderly, and (2) Because the system is not used to the elderly, it is difficult for the elderly to talk with the system that they first met.

The aim of this research is as follows. The first aim is to propose a system that is easy for the elderly to use, which has no dialogue experience with the dialogue system. The next aim is to propose a system that conducts dialogue in consideration of elderly personality. The effect of the proposed system is as follows: (1) the system eliminates the lack of communication of the elderly, and (2) the elderly has a good impression on the characters in the proposed system through conversation. Due to the effect of (2) above, higher elderly people can obtain higher degree of dialog satisfaction

2. RELATED RESEARCH

Dialogue system research can be divided into two types. (1) a task - oriented dialogue system that achieves a goal, (2) a non - task - oriented dialogue system aimed at talking itself (Saito et al., 2015).

In recent years, a dialogue system research to solve the lack of communication among elderly people was proposed (Takuwa et al., 2017, Shin Nakakarumai et al., 2014). This system aims at conversation itself such as chatting and counseling for the elderly. Therefore, this system is classified as a non-task-oriented dialog system (Inaba et al., 2014).

The chat dialogue system for the elderly generally considers the characteristics of elderly people (Torishima et al., 2017, Kamiyama, 2018). Many of these systems are studied based on the reminiscence method which is psychotherapy (Yokoyama et al., 2006). The reminiscence is a psychotherapy advocated for American psychiatrist Robert Butler in the 1960s. An important element of the reminiscence method is that elderly persons will share memories of the past and others through speaking; the mental state of the elderly becomes stable.

It is well known that the retrospective method is effective for communication between the elderly and the system (Kamiyama 2018). For this reason, many chatting systems for the elderly listen to the remarks of the elderly, and adopt a system of striking the remarks of the elderly (in this paper, the interactive system is referred to as a listening interactive system) (Kurati et al., 2018,). In the listening interactive system, the response of the system consists of questions about elderly people's remarks or striking to the elderly's remarks. In other words, in the listening interactive system, the conversation between the elderly and the system progresses mainly by the elderly (Shitaoka et al., 2017).

However, elderly people do not always have a personality talking to the system. In order for the elderly to relax and talk themselves, it is also advisable for the system to provide an interesting topic. However, there are few studies on systems that voluntarily provide topics to elderly people. Also, there are many studies focusing on some characteristics of conversation. However, there is no research on the effect of the whole conversation.

3. ISSUES OF LISTENING INTERACTIVE SYSTEM FOR THE ELDERLY

As mentioned in Chapter 2, many researches on interactive dialogue for elderly people are research of chat dialogue system. The conventional interactive dialogue systems have the following three problems.

Issues (1): The process of communication is not considered in designing interactive dialogue system. In the case of dialogue between humans, there is a clear difference between the dialogue with the partner for the first time and the dialogue with a close friend. Also in the design of dialogue between the discourse system and the elderly, consideration of the communication process is important. Also, it is important for the discourse system to use the optimal dialogue method in each process to realize natural communication. However, in the conventional research, communication process is hardly considered in construction of discourse system.

Issues (2): It is difficult for the elderly to talk to the discourse system for the first time. In the case of an interactive dialogue system, the response of the system is composed primarily of incompatibility and questions. Therefore, it is necessary for the elderly to speak to the discourse system by themselves, but most elderly people do not have experience to dialogue with the discourse system. For this reason, when the elderly speaks for the first time with the discourse system, there may be a case of embarrassment on the part of the elderly, or elderly can not recognize the discourse system as a partner according to the character of the elderly. It is difficult for the elderly to speak to the discourse system autonomously when the initial dialogue between the elderly and the discourse system has begun.

Issues (3): There are elderly persons with a personality whose discourse system is difficult to talk to. For elderly people who prefer to talk about themselves, interactive methods of listening interactive systems are effective. However, there are some elderly people who do not like to talk about themselves. The conventional interactive dialogue system without considering the character of such elderly persons, is doubtful in effectiveness for all elderly people if the system uniformly respond to elderly. Also, it is sometimes necessary to change the conversation scenario of the dialogue system according to the mood of the elderly on the day.

4. PROPOSED METHOD

4.1 Purpose of Research

In this paper, we propose a dialogue system incorporating a psychological point of view on the analysis of the communication process and the character of the elderly in order to solve the problem of the current state-of-the-art dialogue system described in Chapter 3.

4.2 Outline of the Proposed System

In this section, we present a proposed system to solve the three problems mentioned in Chapter 3 (Figure 1).

In order to solve the issue (1), the proposed system divides the communication process between the elderly and the discourse system into two stages. Specifically, the interaction process between the elderly and the discourse system is divided into two stages, "Initial Dialogue" and "Middle and Late Dialogue". And we developed a dialogue method suitable for each of these two stages.

In order to solve the issue (2), we developed an "initial dialog agent" to be used in the early stage of dialogue between the elderly and discourse system. Initial dialog agent adopts a dialogue form easy for the elderly to use a discourse system for the first time. This interactive format is constructed based on psychological knowledge. The aim of the initial dialog agent is to form a favorable impression on the discourse system for the elderly.

In order to solve the issue (3), we developed agents that consider the character of the elderly for discourse at the middle and late stages. Specifically, we developed two types of agents. These are "speech agents" who spontaneously talk to elderly, and the "listening agent" who listens frequently to elderly people. In the dis course of the middle and late stages, these two agents are selected according to the character of the elderly. In the proposed system, by switching such a discourse scheme, we provide a dialogue of a form that fits the elderly personality.

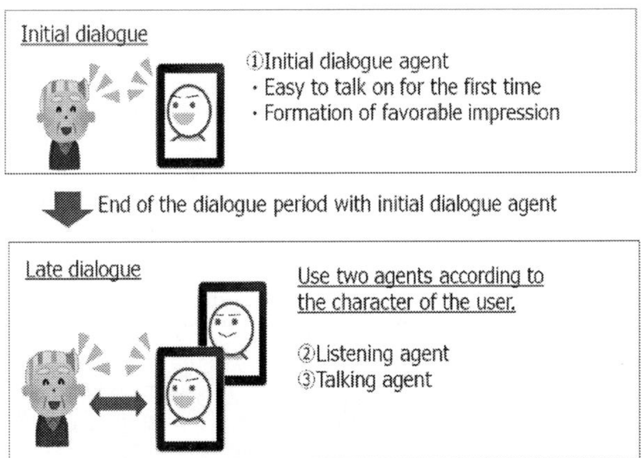

Figure 1. Image of the Proposed System

4.3 Basic Policy of Initial Dialog Agent Development

The purpose of the initial dialog agent is to provide an easy-to-talk environment for elderly people who are not accustomed to dialogue with the discourse system. Therefore, in the early stage discourse, basically, agent-based episode talk (hereinafter referred to as scenario response) is the main subject.

In the scenario response, the proposed system basically advances the dialogue in accordance with the scenario prepared in advance, so that the elderly will talk to the topic provided by the discourse system and answer the questions. In this way, dialogue will proceed. Through this initial discourse, even elderly people who are not used to dialogue with discourse system can easily adapt to dialogue with discourse system.

As an agent in the discourse system, we adopted "children in elementary school" because elderly people are naturally familiar with children. The scenario response has the following structure. First of all, the topic in discourse was an event in school. For elderly, the timings of dialogue with agent are twice in the morning and night in the day. In the morning dialogue, the agent makes simple greetings. In the evening dialogue the agent speaks to the elderly episodes about events at school.

4.4 Change Method of Agent Scenario Response Using Elderly Input

Basically, the scenario response of the initial dialog agent does not depend on the input contents of the elderly. However, if the input content of the elderly is different from one that is assumed in advance, the discourse system changes the response content of the agent according to the input contents of the elderly.

In this case, the agent's response corresponding to the case where the supposed input content matches the input contents of the actual elderly person is set in advance. With this setting, the agent can respond to the input contents of the elderly. In the case where the input content of the elderly does not exactly correspond to the input content assumed in advance, the discourse system classifies the input intention of the elderly into "other responses". Then, in that case, a reply with no sense of incompatibility is made regardless of the input contents of the elderly. For example, in the case where breakfast is the topic, agent replies "The doctor said that it is important to eat breakfast".

In addition, the discourse system not only uses the input contents of the elderly for the immediately following reply as described above, but also applies to the dialogue of the following day.

For example, if the agent makes a question saying "Have you eaten breakfast yet?", and the elderly answer is judged to be "not eating", the discourse system will record the responses of the elderly. Then, in the next morning, agent ask elderly "You seem to have not eaten breakfast yesterday, but did you eat today?"

By making such a response, the agent gives the elderly people the impression that the agent understands and remembers the elderly's talk answer.

4.5 Gentleness Expression Function

In order to realize improvement the satisfaction degree of dialogue which is one of the object of this research, ingenuity to improve the impression that the elderly holds against the agent is indispensable. Therefore, the initial dialog agent has a function to express gentleness, which is based on psychological knowledge.

Studies on interpersonal perception have revealed that there is a phenomenon called initial effect. Due to this phenomenon, the information presented at the initial stage of impression formation is found to have greater significance for the formation of impressions than the information given at a later time.

Various characteristics exist as personality characteristics of a human being as an element of impression formation. Among them, it has been clarified that characteristics having a central function exist in forming impressions such as "warmth", "cold", etc.

To summarize such findings, it can be said that a favorable impression is easily formed in the subsequent impression formation by giving the impression "gentle" at the beginning of impression formation.

Based on such knowledge, in order to improve the impression that the elderly has against the agent, we made the initial dialogue agent handling the initial dialogue function to express " gentleness ". " Gentleness " in this paper is defined as "compassion for others." Example of gentleness expression is to apply care-of words to others who are in trouble or sadness or make actions of gentleness.

As the method of initial dialog agent, there are two ways of expressing the gentleness expressed by the agent: "(1) expression of gentleness to the elderly" and "(2) expression of gentleness to other than the elderly." In (1) case, the agent responds such as worrying words when the elderly are in bad condition. In (2) case, the agent expresses gentleness by telling the elderly about the behavior to person other than the elderly such as "I helped a friend".

5. AGENTS CONSIDERING THE CHARACTER OF THE ELDERLY

5.1 The Purpose of the Discourse Agent in the Latter Period of Discourse

As shown in Section 4.2, the proposed system uses different dialogue methods in the early dialogue and the mid-latter term dialogue. In the middle-and-later term dialogue, the discourse system changes the dialogue method according to the character of the elderly.

5.2 The Purpose of the Discourse Agent in the Latter Period of Discourse

There are various methods to classify the personality of elderly people, but in this paper "aggressiveness to dialogue" is used for character classification of the elderly. The grounds for this selection is made by the following two considerations.

(1) Other Personality Characteristics Classification affects emotional expression and change of ending in agent response.

(2) On the other hand, in the case of "aggressiveness to dialogue", the response of the agent affects the interactive form and the amount of dialogue. Therefore, influence on dialogue is strong using this method.

Specifically, using the utterance tendency scale which is a psychological measure, we classify the character of the elderly into "speaking liking" and "discreetness".

When using the proposed system, questionnaires are given to elderly subjects before system use, and elderly people are classified.

5.3 Agent Classification

We classified the elderly into two in terms of aggressiveness towards dialogue. In other words, we developed two types of agents in consideration of compatibility with individual elderly people: concretely, "listening agent" who makes dialogue with elderly people who are "talkative", and "Talking agent" that makes dialogue with "conservative" elderly people.

5.4 The Purpose of the Discourse Agent in the Latter Period of Discourse

The listening agent takes an interactive form suitable for the elderly with talkative character. Specifically, the listening agent performs utterance mainly about repetition and striking a match.

The flow of listening agent dialogue is shown below. 1) The elderly talks to the agent first. 2) The agent responds. 3) After the agent 's response, there are sometimes times when elderly people cannot find the topic of an appropriate conversation. At that time, when a certain period of time elapses, the agent automatically issues new questions related to the topic of the past to the elderly. 4) If there is a remark from the elderly and the previous system response is a new question, agent asks deep question such as "Why is that?" 5) Next, when the content of the elderly's speech is a question, the agent responds in an ambiguous manner to the question, and then a new question is subsequently made by agent. The reason why the agent responds ambiguously is that many questions from the elderly tend to be irrelevant to the current topic. As an agent, it is difficult to respond to everything to the remarks of elderly people irrelevant to topics.

Next, when the elderly's input matches a response rule including a specific word such as "I like AA", agent performs a parrots such as "You like AA". In addition, if the input of the elderly does not include a noun, etc., the agent makes a new question related to the topic in order to broaden the talk.

5.5 Talking Agent

The talking agent takes an interactive form suitable for elderly persons of modest character. Therefore, responses of agents are basically centered on scenario-like responses that do not depend on the input contents of elderly people.

As a dialog flow, firstly, the talking agent has performs processing of ambiguous response to the timer processing and makes the question like the listening agent. As a function other than that, the talking agent makes an utterance concerning the topic according to the scenario.

The scenario has a branch point. If the elderly 's response to the agent' s question matches the rule prepared in advance at that branch point, the agent responds to express empathy, self - disclosure, etc., and changes the topic.

6. CONFIGURATION OF THE PROPOSED SYSTEM

This chapter describes the proposed system configuration (Figure 2). The proposed system uses MMD Agent from Nagoya Institute of Technology MMD Agent is a tool kit for spoke n dialogue system integrating speech recognition, speech synthesis, 3D model display.

The feature of MMD Agent is that description of response rules in discourse and change of model can be easily performed. The proposed system uses MMD Agent as an interface. And we developed our own dialogue control system .using complicated response rules in cooperation with MMD Agent.

The dialogue control system consists of "initial dialogue agent", "talking agent", and "listening agent".

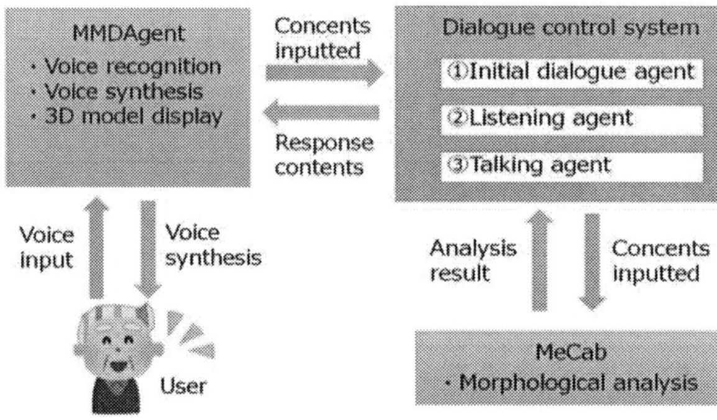

Figure 2. Configuration of the Proposed System

7. EXPERIMENT

7.1 Purpose of Experiment

The dialogue system proposed in this paper covers two kinds of dialogue between the elderly and discourse system (agent), that is, the initial dialogue and the middle and latter term dialogue. In this proposal, different dialogue methods are used for two kinds of dialogue. In this paper, we conducted experiments to verify the effectiveness of the initial dialogue agent used for the initial dialogue among the two types of dialogue. In the experiment, in particular, we verified that the "tenderness expression function" of the initial dialog agent influences the impression formation for the agent from the viewpoint of the elderly.

7.2 Comparison System

The purpose of the experiment is to verify the effectiveness of the gentleness expression function possessed by the initial dialog agent. For this reason, we used a typical conventional dialogue agent system (Kurati et al., 2018) as a comparison system.

7.3 Experimental Procedure

Eight people in their twenties who never used a dialogue system were taken as subjects. Subjects were divided into groups A and B. Group A used the proposed system and group B used the comparative system. The experimental period is 5 days and we conduct daily dialogue between morning and night. The average number of utterances in one dialog is 5 and the average dialog time is 1 minute 55 seconds. And we add three people in their eighties for our reference.

We conducted a questionnaire (Daibo edit, 1989, Hori edited, 2001) on the impression of the dialogue system for the subjects after the end of the dialogue on the first day night and the fifth day night of the experiment. The effectiveness of the proposed system is verified by comparing questionnaire results for each group and correlation analysis.

Table 1. Analysis Result of the Questionnaire correlation analysis

Question items	Median of evaluation		Correlation coefficient
	A	B	
1: The agent is gentle	5	3	
2: Conversation is fun	4.5	4	0.548
3: Conversation can be relaxed	4	3.5	0.287
4: The agent is friendly	5	4	0.523
5: The agent understands a dialogue	3	3	0.333
6: Interaction is easy to talk	3.5	3	0.738
7: I'd like to talk to the agent more	4	4.5	0.076
8: The agent can be trusted	3.5	3	0.491
9: I am attached to the agent	4.5	4.5	0.746

7.4 Experimental Result

The results of the questionnaire were tabulated for each group (Table 1). Questionnaires were also analyzed by the following procedure.

(1) Impression analysis on the tenderness of agent response. First, by using the gentleness expression function, it is necessary to verify whether the subject evaluated the character of the agent as gentle. We compared the effectiveness of gentleness expressions in groups A and B by "1" item of .table 1 (Subject thinks the agent is a gentle personality). As a result, the evaluation value of group A using the proposed system was median value 5, and the evaluation value of group B using comparison system was median value 3. From this result, by using the gentleness expression function, we found that subject could feel agent more gentle.

(2) Correlation analysis of gentleness and other impression formation rank correlation analysis was carried out to verify the correlation between the impression of the agent and the impression of other factors. The definition and calculation method of the two variables used in the analysis are shown below.

[Variable 1]: Evaluation of the gentleness that subject felt during the dialogue period [Calculation method]: With respect to the evaluation of question 1, the average value (value by subject) on the first day and the fifth day.

[Variable 2]: Improvement degree of each impression evaluation during the experiment period [Calculation method]: For questions other than question 1, the difference between day 1 and day 5 (value by subject).

As a result of the questionnaire, it was found that questions 6 and 9 had a strong correlation, and questions 2, 4 and 8 had a strong correlation.

8. DISCUSSION

As a result of the impression evaluation questionnaire, the proposed system was gained high overall evaluation. From the interview after the questionnaire, it became clear that the subject recognized the agent as a gentle character in the initial dialogue. Based on this recognition, it is considered that favorable impressions were formed as a whole discourse in subjects.

Even in the experiment, as a result of the correlation analysis, it was found that giving the impression that the agent is a gentle character at the beginning of the dialogue has a strong correlation with ease of talking and attachment formation.

The index of ease of talking is a very important index for users without dialogue experience with the dialogue system. In addition, the index of whether or not you can afford attachment is also very important in considering long-term communication with the dialogue system. So, It is considered that the usefulness of the "gentleness expression function" proposed in this paper is high. As the evaluation of items 6, 8, 9 was high, it became clear that issue 1 was solved. From items 1 and 4, it became clear that the division of the communication process was effective. From items 2, 3, 5, and 7 it became clear that issue 3 was solved.

9. CONCLUSION

In this paper, we proposed a discourse system for conversation closely to the elderly in order to solve the problem of the current dialogue system for elderly people. Specifically, we proposed a system to promote dialogue with emphasis on the feelings of elderly people. Specifically, the communication was divided into two. The initial phase is the initial dialogue phase impressing the tenderness of the agent.

From the experimental results, it became clear that 1) subjects received an expression of the gentleness of the agent, and a familiar relationship was born between the subject and the agent in the initial conversation, 2) the continuation of the conversation became smooth.

Future tasks are as follows.

1) Confirming the effectiveness when subjects are elderly
2) To clarify the individual effects with regard to the introduced multiple functions
3) Realize communication using scenarios considering emotion of elderly people.

REFERENCES

Aoyanagi, S. et al., 2018, Analysis of user's utterance to reduce inappropriate response of chat robot, proceeding of JSAI2018, pp. 234-238

Breuer, H. et al., 2008, A Mobile Pattern Discourse System, IEICE MoMuC 107(446), pp. 7-12

Cabinet Office, 2016, Aged Society White Paper http://www8.cao.go.jp/kourei/whitepaper/w-2015/html/zenbun/index.html (Last accessed date: Feb. 11 2019)

Cabinet Office, 2017, elderly society white paper, http://www8.cao.go.jp/kourei/whitepaper/w-2017/html/zenbun/index.html (Last accessed date: Feb. 11 2019)

Daibo, I. edit, 1989: "Social Psychology Perspective 1", SeiShin Shobo, Tokyo.

Dementia Forum, 2018, https://www.ninchisho-forum.com/knowledge/iryou/008.html (Last accessed date: Feb. 11 2019)

Hori, Y. edited, 2001, "Psychometric Measure Scale I", Science,Tokyo.

Inaba, M. et al., 2014, Candidate Utterance Acquisition Method for Non-task-oriented Dialogue Systems from Twitter, Journal of Artificial Intelligence Society, Vol.29, No.1, pp. 21-31

Kamiyama, T. 2018, Conversation service so much by heart, practical report of Information processing society of japan, 9(2), pp. 437-453.

Kurati, Y. et al., 2018, Chatbot Conversation Techniques, Fujitsu Journal 69(4), pp. 57-62.

Saito, M. et al., 2015, Criteria for social isolation based on associations with health indicators among older people. A 10-year follow-up of the Aichi Gerontological Evaluation Study, Japan Public Health Magazine, Vol.62, No.3, pp. 95-105

Shin, N. et al., 2014, Development of voice conversation system to automate response for elderly living alone: Prediction of response timing using multiple regression analysis based on prosodic information and power, utterance interval, IEICE technical report, 113(481), pp. 19-23

Shitaoka, K. et al., 2017, Active listening system for a dialogue robot", Natural language processing, Vol. 24, No.1, pp. 3-47

Takuwa, H. et al., 2017, A Study on Utterance Method Considering User's Hobby in Chat Dialogue System, proceeding of JSAI2017, pp. 212-217,

Torishima, M. et al., 2017, A Study on Chat Bot-based Communication, *IEEJ Technical Report*, Tottori Japan pp. 7- 9

Yokoyama, T. et al., 2006, Lessons learned from student 's visit activities for welfare, the Japanese association of rural medicine, 55(0), pp. 129-130.

APPLICATION OF MACHINE LEARNING FOR ESTIMATING KENYAN MOTOR VEHICLE INSURANCE PREMIUM

Fidelia Pamba and Lucy Waruguru
KCA University
P.O. Box 56808 – 00200 Nairobi, Kenya

ABSTRACT

Motor vehicle damage insurance is the most common type of insurance in the world and one that generates the largest amount of loss for most insurance companies. In Kenya especially, the challenge faced by insurers is to balance the growth of the motor vehicle insurance business by increasing the customer base while also maintaining the profitability of this sector. It is crucial to identify the main causes of motor vehicle damage, its impact on revenue for insurers and factors that contribute to high motor claims to enable more accurate estimates of risk versus premium paid. In recent years the interest has increased in the use of information technology (IT) and statistical machine learning methods, supported by increasing computing capabilities, data availability and the trend towards automation. Statistical regression models have numerous applications in this regard. This paper explores applicability of new machine learning techniques such as tree-boosted models to optimize the proposed premium of prospective policy holders. It proposes two machine learning models for pricing motor vehicle damage insurance (decision trees and regression). The aim is to identify sources of risks in motor vehicles and the variables for motor vehicle premium determination. Data from insurance companies has been used, which is made up of the premium rates and compensations, and other variables such as age, driver's experience, etc. Results will be used to advise the insurance companies on how to charge premiums dynamically.

KEYWORDS

Premium Estimation, Insurance, Machine Learning, Nairobi Kenya

1. INTRODUCTION

Motor vehicles in Kenya are the largest cause of accidents, damage and destruction of property (Peters et al., 2016). However, due to a low and uneven development of insurance in the developing society, companies rely on standardized measures for determining which premium to pay. The study carried out by IFAA in 2011 indicate, "out of the total 309,361 vehicles populated in Kenya only about 35% or 106,765 were insured voluntarily whereas the remaining 65% were dependent on their financial resources if liability arose". Many insurers have been suffering losses after charging inadequate statutory premiums, problems in premium rate determination and monitoring, lack of integrated data and co-operation between the insurance industry, increased fraud and malpractice.

Although the insurance industry has grown rapidly in the industrialized countries, its growth in developing countries like Kenya has neither been satisfactory nor in tandem with the growth of other sectors of the economy. A key issue is how to price an insurance contract, which is also known as rate making. As the Insurance industry continues to grow in Kenya, research by the Association of Kenya Insurers (AKI) has shown that customers often pick an insurance company as purely based on the premium to be paid (AKI Annual Report, 2015). If the price is too high, customers will turn to other insurance companies, and if the price is too low, the insurance company will not receive enough premiums to cover the insureds' claim costs.

1.1 Background

The insurance sector in East Africa is steadily developing, with its gross premiums totaling to $2.35b across the region. Kenya's premiums form 75% of the total, and it leads the region with a 3% penetration (AKI annual report, 2015). However, insurance in the region is still underdeveloped as compared to the rest of the world.

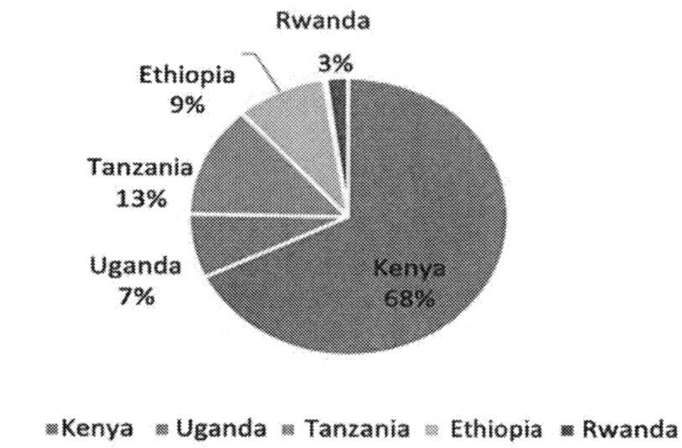

Figure 1. Gross written Premium in East Africa (From AKI Report 2015)

Although Kenyan insurance companies are the most well performing on almost the entire East Africa (See Figure 1), not all insurance products are generating high profits for the insurers. It has been discovered that motor vehicles generate losses every year because the amount of premium paid is very low compared to the cost of compensating damages from accidents. Transport plays a crucial role in facilitating socio-economic development.

1.2 Problem Statement

The high hazard of motor risk makes insurance companies to adopt various strategies to minimize motor insurance adverse effect and maximize their profitability. Different premiums or tariffs are applied depending on degree of risk that is highlighted within the insurance portfolio price (Mihaela, 2015). The main problem is that the level of premiums charged to a customer does not depend on statistical data about the state of road, age of vehicle, age and experience of the driver etc. (Dominique-Ferreira, 2017). The underwriting process involves investigation into various factors and analysing them through statisticians called actuaries. In many cases the actuaries are not accurate.

Recently, more sophisticated machine learning models such as logistic regression models and tree-based decision models have been developed, but their usage in the insurance industry is not widespread (Frees et al., 2014; Frees et al. 2016; Pozzolo, 2010) To the researchers' knowledge, a comparison of machine learning techniques to predict insurance premium at the local level is still lacking in the literature and will hence be explored here.

2. MOTOR VEHICLE PREMIUM DETERMINATION

As the Insurance industry continues to grow in Kenya, research by the Association of Kenya Insurers (AKI) has shown that customers often pick an insurance company as purely based on the premium to be paid (AKI Annual Report, 2015). This has made the need for accurate ratemaking more important than ever. The SAS Institute, (SAS, 2011) stated that multiple factors can be used to determine premium rates, and that as competition increases, insurers are introducing new and innovative rate structures. The critical question in ratemaking is, "What risk factors or variables are important for predicting the likelihood, frequency and severity of a loss?" Although there are many obvious risk factors that affect rates, subtle and nonnutritive relationships can exist among variables that are difficult, if not impossible, to identify without applying more sophisticated analyses.

Traditional univariate analysis methods are outdated, and insurers have turned to multivariate statistical techniques such as generalized linear modelling to understand the relationships between multiple risk variables. Finally, insurers need to consider marketing costs, conversion rates and customer buying behavior in accurately pricing insurance products. It is becoming more evident that the key to gaining an edge in today's competitive market is the ability to quickly and efficiently explore, understand and act on the data to improve price competitiveness.

2.1 Traditional Risk Estimation

Common traditional methods include the centrally determined price option and the free market priced option as discussed below.

2.1.1 Centrally Determined Price Option

Most regulators have placed various restrictions on insurance policy coverage and rates, particularly for non-life motor vehicle insurance. Statutory tariffs are commonly imposed on compulsory insurance and strictly regulated by national legislation due to its sensitive nature. They prevent unsustainable price wars (Ernst & Young, 2011). Unlike mature markets, prices are free and only subject to tough competition in most developing countries, compulsory premiums are statutory, and subject to government oversight, either directly or through some more complex governance process. In this case, the government is in charge of setting statutory in the form of setting of minimum and maximum or only maximum prices (Gönülal, 2010). The premium is calculated according to the risk + office expenses + other charges (Ben-Shahar & Porat, 2016).

Different countries have pursued motor insurance tariff liberalization at different times and in different ways. In most countries statutory tariffs do not reflect claims costs and necessarily involve an element of cross subsidy and sometimes inhibit innovative pricing. As a result, this is an area where knowledge of the distinctive features is important and the trained of future market evolution will be a move towards partial de-tariff of MTPL insurance premium rating and full risk-based pricing typically correlates to market profitability and stability (Ernst & Young, 2011).

2.1.2 Free Market Priced Option

In many developed and mature markets, prices are free and only subject to tough competition. In general, insurance risks can be very volatile, and the cost of meeting claims is constantly under pressure from inflation and other upward trends as a result the premium rating are very sensitive issue in insurance market. Most insurance policies are normally issued on a one-year renewable basis as a result in a competitive environment, an insurer can lose good business or gain bad business very quickly if its rates become out of line with the rest of the market. In this case, it is of vital importance for an insurer to keep rates under constant review and to amend them as necessary (Gönülal, 2010).

Competitive pricing will bring innovative product, new business idea, cheaper rates and variable discounts. However, the lower premiums force the insurer to be more selective to underwriting, and to accept only the better risks. It will also keep costs down and had economy administration and stricter claims procedures. This will have an impact on the general objectives of motor insurance (Einav et al., 2010).

2.2 Insurance Prediction with Information Technology

Different estimation techniques have been proposed in the past to be used to estimating the level of risk vs premium payment. From table 1 below, machine learning methods such as tree-based classification techniques are the best for predicting insurance premium. Several reasons explain their popularity: First, they are very easy to interpretable and communicate to a nontechnical audience. Second, they can handle both numeric and categorical predictors without any pre-processing. Third, they perform feature selection and can handle missing values explicitly, and any missing value is used as another level/numeric value (Kuhn and Johnson 2013).

Table 1. Various methods for estimating risk level for insurance premium determination

Technique	Methods		
	Econometric Model	**Regression Model**	**Tree-based Classification**
Description	A system of interdependent regression equations to describe economic sales or profit activity. Parameters of the equations are determined simultaneously. These models predict quite accurately but are relatively expensive to develop	Relates risk to other economic, competitive or internal variables and estimates an equation using least squares method. Relationships are analyzed statistically. They predict quite accurately, especially in short and medium term	Consist of tree-like nested if-then statements for predictors that partition data. This approach generates a structure of "nodes" and terminal "leaves", within which a model is used to predict the outcome. They predict very accurately, especially in short and medium term
Accuracy Short term (0-3 months)	Good to very good	Good to very good	**Very good to excellent**
Medium term (3 months – 2 years)	Very good to excellent	Good to very good	**Very good to excellent**
Long term (above 2 years)	Good	Good	**Very good**
Data Required	Monthly or quarterly history to obtain meaningful relationships. To have more observations than the no of independent variables	Same as in econometric models	Same as in econometric models
References	Evans (1969)	Clelland et al. (1966)	Quinlan (2004)

3. METHODOLOGY

3.1 Data Collection

Data collection was carried out by physically moving from organization to organization. Pre-established salient points and semi-structured questionnaires were used to uncover deeper meanings through a qualitative research design method using a multiple case study. The criteria and methods utilized for respondents' selection and contact are as follows:

- Insurance company's branch offices, which has been in operation to underwrite motor insurance since September 2011 are selected proportionally.
- Insurance officers directly involved in motor policy underwriting and/or claims handling are randomly selected from proportionally chosen insurance companies' branch office.
- Anyone who buys motor insurance policy and met accidentally at proportionally selected insurance company's branch office counter during the month of November 2016.

3.2 Study Variables

The study's independent variables included driver's experience, age, motorvehicle attributes, age and previous claims. The dependent variable was the level of risk, i.e. the probability for compensation.

3.3 Analysis Strategy

The data analysis method applied for this study comprises both quantitative and qualitative methods. Quantitative method was used with a view to properly address the research questions and qualitative analysis method was employed to analyzed response on open-ended questionnaires. The data collected through close-ended questionnaires were analyzed with descriptive statistics. The data are presented using tables and charts. The researcher also utilized various descriptive statistical techniques such as mean, percentage and frequency distribution tables. The Waikato Environment for Knowledge Analysis (Weka) was used to conduct decision trees classification. For modeling the regression analysis, SPSS version 16.0 software tool was used.

To determine the variation between premium payment and motor vehicle risk factors, a regression model was applied in the form:

$$y = \beta_0 + \beta_1 x_1 + \beta_2 x_2 + \beta_3 x_3 + \beta_4 x_4 + \beta_5 x_5 + \beta_6 x_6 + \beta_7 x_7 + e$$

Where β0 is the intercept of the regression, β1 to β5 are the slopes representing the expected y value, and e represents the errors that should be normally distributed with mean 0 and equal variance. The independent variables are Policyholder (or driver) Experience (x1), Age (x2), Education (x3), Previous History (x4), Vehicle Type (x5), Vehicle Age (x6) and Lease Condition (x7).

4. RESULTS

This this section we provide results from the statistical analysis and interpretation of the data. In addition to descriptive analysis, we also provide results of machine learning through decision trees regression modeling using the sampled data.

4.1 Demographic Outlook

Demographic findings were based on the age and gender of respondents who completed the survey, the number of years of experience in driving, the employment status and frequency of driving a motor vehicle.

The largest age groups of respondents were aged between 18 years and 30 years, making up more than half of the survey participants. 31 to 40 years had the second largest number of survey participants. These are also usually the age groups where most drivers belong. Only 3% of the survey participants were 51 years and above.

On years of driving experience, most of the participants had less than 1-year experience making up 43%. Most of these people filled the questionnaire on their way to take or renew their insurance policy. The next largest group had up to 3 years' experience (22%). This group is important because they can share solid experience about insurance premium payment and claiming. Drivers with 3-5 years' experienced were the smallest group, making up 9%. This group is also important for experience.

Luxury and sports cars received the highest compensation, either because of their high value or the likelihood to crash during a race. Private saloon cars and the truck and utility vehicles were almost similar in trends but also received high compensation. Minivans had the lowest compensation rate, especially in 2016 when less than 2M Kenyan shillings was paid out to compensate them.

4.2 Classification Results

The next part of the analysis was to develop a predictive model to predict the probability of claim given some possible risk factors on the occurrence of claims from the insurance industry. One of the ways to model insurance risk is through classification with Decision Trees. According to Duncan (1979), an advantage of the Decision Tree is that it is easy to interpret. The Decision Tree also works even if there is nonlinear relationship between variables. Finally, it does not require linearity assumption and it is not sensitive to outliers.

Figure 2 shows the output from the classification for policyholders. The significant nodes ($p \leq 0.05$) were displayed with the root of the decision tree being divided by the most important variable being the compensation amount. The policyholder experience highly determines compensation amount. Policyholders who had over 3 years driving experience are less likely to receive compensation because of an accident where PolicyHolder.Experience > 3.1 Years (215, with 173 Yes and 43 No). Age is also a good determinant, but on the negative side of risk. Younger drivers with less than a diploma for education, are the most likely to require high compensation amount where PolicyHolder. Age ≤ 31 Years (198, with 133 Yes and 65 No).

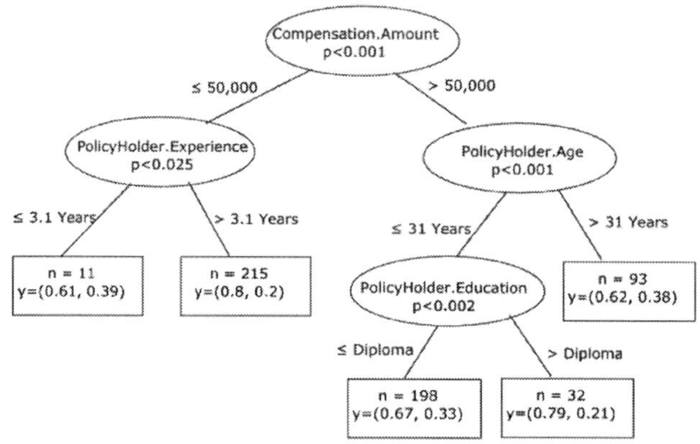

Figure 2. Classification output by Policyholder's characteristics

Figure 3 shows the output from the classification for motorvehicles. The significant nodes ($p \leq 0.05$) were displayed. The root of the decision tree is divided by the most important variable being the compensation amount. Motorvehicles with no previous accident history were less likely to need high compensation as a result of accidents where Previous.History ≤ 0 (203, with 142 Yes and 61 No). Motorvehicles such as sports cars had the highest risk of getting accidents and receiving high amount of compensation, especially for vehicles driven for not more than 1 year where Vehicle.Type ≤ 2 and Vehicle.Age ≤ 1 Year (76, with 51 Yes and 25 No).

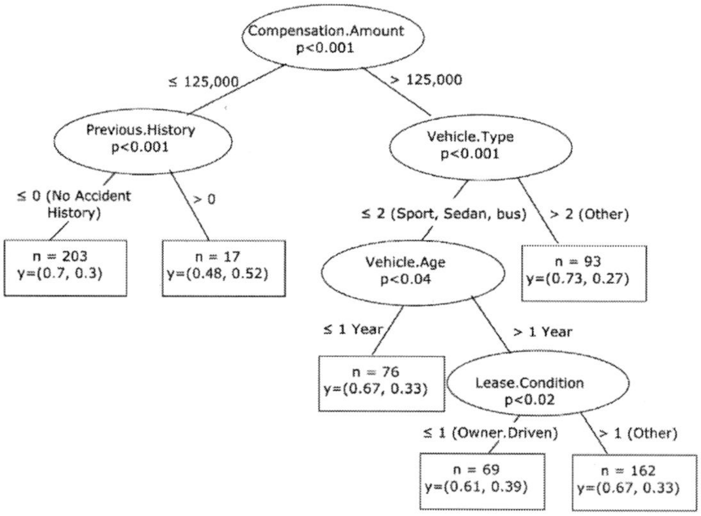

Figure 3. Classification output by Motorvehicle's characteristics

4.3 Results from Regression

Using results from the decision tree as guidance of which variables were good determinants for compensation, a regression model was created to test the dependent variable (Compensation) side by side with 7 independent variables: Policyholder Experience, Policyholder Age, Policyholder Education, Previous History, Vehicle Type, Vehicle Age and Lease Condition. Table 4.8 shows the estimation results. The previous history is the most significant variable with a t-statistic of 6.121 and p-value of 0.000. Policyholder's (or driver's) experience was negative to the probability for claim, meaning that the longer the policyholder had driven the motor vehicle, the less he/she was likely to be involved in an accident. The same with Motor vehicle's age. It seems that older vehicles were less involved in an accident than newer vehicles. According to the regression results, all variables were significant except the policyholder's education level which was found not to be significant to the likelihood of being involved in an accident and claiming from the insurance company.

Table 2. Estimates from regression analysis of motorvehicle risk

Variable	Coefficient	Standard Error	t-statistic	p-value	95% confidence interval	
P.EXP	-0.022	0.002	4.123	0.000**	0.013	0.031
P.AGE	0.139	0.094	3.110	0.023*	0.060	0.218
P.EDU	0.307	0.105	1.977	0.061	0.139	0.581
HIST	0.358	0.198	6.121	0.000***	0.290	0.426
V.TYPE	0.128	0.057	2.844	0.021*	-0.096	0.354
V.AGE	-0.012	0.003	3.258	0.010**	-0.018	-0.006
L.COND	0.417	0.126	3.315	0.002**	0.398	0.421
n	260					
R^2	0.745					
Adjusted R^2	0.691					

5. CONCLUSION

This paper has suggested a strategy for estimating motorvehicle insurance premium using statistical methods and information systems strategies. This section offers the theoretical and industrial implications of the study, with its limitations and propositions for future direction.

5.1 Discussion

The primary objective of this study was to establish machine learning models for regulating motor vehicle premiums among insurance companies. Results from this primary objective and associated specific objectives can help to investigate consequences of action by policyholders in a buyer-seller relationship in the car insurance market.

On average, policyholders pay KSh.3, 950 per month, about KSh.50, 000 per year. The highest standard deviation is on duration of vehicle ownership, which is almost the same as the mean indicating a lot of variation. These findings have been discovered in other studies such as Desalegn (2014) and Poposki et al. (2015). This shows that in general insuring a motor vehicle is an expensive investment. It is important for policyholders to get value for their money, and understanding how key variables influence their ability to receive compensation can help a lot. Other key findings were that the newly registered vehicles of 0-12 months had the highest number of compensation from theft or accident and that Luxury and sports cars received the highest compensation. These two findings are also similar with findings from other researchers (e.g. Müller and Te, 2017; Stevenson et al., 2017; Lesmana et al, 2018) and shows that drivers of such vehicles should be charged a much higher premium than any other groups.

All the results from the first three specific objectives were agreeing with each other, and the results from both decision trees and regression model were quite similar in identifying the most influencing variables. As based on the specific objective 4 which was to test the models, it can be reported that all the models were quite accurate. For example, analysis of covariance was done for age against the amount compensated in KSh. This was done separately for male and female participants but both genders showed the same pattern.

People were more likely to need compensation between 25 and 35 years old. Younger people also required high compensation, but after 60 years the compensation rate was very low.

The general observation from the results of this study is that several factors are important for determining risk in addition to the motor vehicle insurance premium value.

5.3 Limitations and Future Research Areas

Although the results from this study are encouraging, further work is needed before the procedures are used in practice. First, analysis using a larger sample of data is necessary as the study has used a limited sample. Secondly particular attention should be made to how well the assumptions behind the credibility model are fulfilled and whether improved variables for the model can be found.

Finally, the results of using the procedures described here should also be compared with present practice, where estimates of risk premium from the identified variables are, in effect, subjectively combined. It is expected that a dramatic improvement will be discovered, and that the proposed procedures described in this thesis will enable the process of motor vehicle insurance classification to be put on a more objective footing.

REFERENCES

AKI Annual Report 2015. *Association of Kenya Insurers Annual Report*, 2015

Ben-Shahar, O., & Logue, K. D. 2016. *The perverse effects of subsidized weather insurance*. Stan. L. Rev., 68, 571.

Dal Pozzolo, A. 2010. *Comparison of Data Mining Techniques for Insurance Claim Prediction*. SAS 2011. SAS Institute Inc., Cary, NC, USA.

Desalegn, A. 2014. *Assessment of Motor Insurance Business on Financial Performance of Insurance Company, The Case of Awash Insurance Company*. PhD diss., St. Mary's University.

Dominique-Ferreira, S. 2017. *How important is the strategic order of product attribute presentation in the non-life insurance market?*. Journal of Retailing and Consumer Services, 34, 138-144.

Duncan, R. 1979. *What is the right organization structure? Decision tree analysis provides the answer*. Organizational Dynamics, 7(3), 59-80.

Einav, L., Finkelstein, A., & Levin, J. 2010. *Beyond testing: Empirical models of insurance markets*. Annu. Rev. Econ., 2(1), 311-336.

Evans, M. K. 1969. *Macroeconomic activity: Theory, forecasting, and control; an econometric approach*. Harper & Row.

Farrell, D., Wheat, C., & Mac, C. 2017. *Paying a Premium: Dynamics of the Small Business Owner Health Insurance Market*.

Frees, E.W., G. Meyers, and R.A. Derrig. 2016. *Predictive Modeling Applications in Actuarial Science*: Volume 2, Case Studies in Insurance. International Series on Actuarial Science. Cambridge University Press.

Gönülal, S. 2010. *Motor third-party liability insurance*.

Kuhn, M., and K. Johnson. 2013. *Applied Predictive Modeling*. Springer

Lesmana, E., Wulandari, R., Napitupulu, H., & Supian, S. 2018. *Model estimation of claim risk and premium for motor vehicle insurance by using Bayesian method. I*n IOP Conference Series: Materials Science and Engineering Vol. 300, No. 1, p. 012027. IOP Publishing

Mihael, D. 2015. *A review of theoretical concepts and empirical literature of non-life insurance pricing*. Procedia Economics and Finance, 20, 157-162.

Müller, D., & Te, Y. F. 2017, December. *Insurance premium optimization using motor insurance policies—A business growth classification approach*. In Big Data (Big Data), 2017 IEEE International Conference on (pp. 4154-4158). IEEE.

Peters, J. A. J., Ferguson, D., Madigan, R., & McKenna, T. 2016. *U.S. Patent Application* No. 14/607,433.

Stevenson, M., Harris, A., Mortimer, D., Wijnands, J. S., Tapp, A., Peppard, F., & Buckis, S. 2017. *The effects of feedback and incentive-based insurance on driving behaviours: study approach and protocols*. Injury prevention, injuryprev-2016.

Temesgen, Z. B. 2004. *Determinants for Effective Application of Software in Computer Assisted Auditing Techniques* (CAATs).

Yang, Y., Qian, W., & Zou, H. 2018. *Insurance premium prediction via gradient tree-boosted Tweedie compound Poisson models*. Journal of Business & Economic Statistics, 36(3), 456-470.

THE TECHNOLOGY MATRIX – A TOOL-BASED METHOD FOR TECHNOLOGY SCOUTING

Marco Peter, Stella Gatziu Grivas, Daniel Horn, Florian Rüegg, Renato Barba and Manuela Graf
School of Business, University of Applied Sciences and Arts Northwestern Switzerland
Riggenbachstrasse 16, 4600 Olten, Switzerland

ABSTRACT

The digital transformation of businesses is crucial when initiating business model innovations and using technology as added value. The difficulty today for businesses is to keep track of emerging technology trends that are relevant and could significantly support their digitalization process. Especially for small and medium-sized enterprises, which often do not have the resources for a proper investigation of emerging technologies. This research paper presents the technology matrix, a new tool-based method of scouting technology trends, based on the relevant factors business impact, project size, and feasibility of the incorporation of the technologies. Existing technology scouting tools on the markets where analyzed on their strength and weaknesses and best practices were incorporated into the developed technology matrix. Furthermore, expert interviews have led to important inputs when designing the technology matrix.

KEYWORDS

Technology Trends, Technology Scouting, Digital Transformation

1. INTRODUCTION

According to the latest data analysis from the federal office for statistics in Switzerland, almost 99.7% of all enterprises in Switzerland are small and medium-sized enterprises (SMEs) (Bundesamt für Statistik BFS 2017). Therefore, SMEs have a huge impact on the Swiss economy, consequently also in terms of digital transformation. To digitally transform an established business, the companies often have to change their current organization fundamentally. Needed resources, a good holistic understanding, and a clear strategy are necessary to be successful (Kreutzer et al. 2018). Moreover, digital transformation means changing existing business models and most of the time also enable new ones by applying digital technologies.

Quite often SMEs are struggling with the digital transformation. As a study of 1'854 Swiss-based companies has shown, many companies are not satisfied with the outcome of initiatives in the field of digital transformation (Peter 2017). Especially since there are limited resources. SMEs usually cannot invest enough time to tackle the problems of a transformation on their own. Despite the fact that there is a lack of resources, according to the study, they can overcome these obstacles by applying frameworks, which are tailored to their specific needs. As well as working together with external partners to kick-start a transformation project.

There are a lot of frameworks already established on the market but most of them are not suitable for SMEs (Peter et al. 2018). An aspect to be able to foster SMEs with useful tools for digital transformation is to provide a method of how they can analyze the wide range of new technologies for their individual use cases. Even though there are many well-known methods, such as the SWOT-Analysis (Pelz 2004), the PESTEL-Analysis (Theobald 2016), the Porter's Five Forces-Analysis (Chan Kim & Mauborgne 2005), or the Force Fields Analysis (Baulcomb 2003), which tackle the topic of external analysis, many of them lack to consider the impact of new technologies on a company or industry. A well-defined framework or tool that uses visual representation to support SMEs when defining their digital transformation strategy would be an efficient method. Nevertheless, such a method has not yet been published.

This research project followed the Design Science approach by Hevner et al. (2004). Accordingly, the five phases of problem awareness, suggestion, development, evaluation, and conclusion were carried out. Regarding the awareness phase, the goal of the work was properly outlined by defining research questions and a literature review was carried out in order to investigate the knowledge base. Besides the literature review, four expert interviews regarding technology management were conducted. This helped to cover the questions regarding the behavior of Swiss SME. After collecting sufficient information on existing technology radars or similar methods as wells as gaining insight on the preferences and behavior of Swiss SMEs, a newly adapted technology matrix was designed. Nevertheless, an objective of this research project from the very beginning has been that this newly developed tool is usable not only for Swiss SMEs but for any SMEs. The phases suggestion, development, and evaluation were done in an iterative manner, in order to bring the insights from the evaluations into the final tool. The evaluations were carried out in collaboration with experts, where the artifact was presented and discussed in a semi-structured interview form.

2. OVERVIEW AND COMPARISON OF EXISTING TECHNOLOGY MATRIX'S

There are different approaches to scouting new technologies, which could help SMEs to find relevant tools to support their digital transformation. To get the key parts and takeaways over the existing frameworks, the available and most relevant ones on the market were analyzed by three different aspects *Intended use*, *Strength,* and *Weakness*, as shown in Table 2.

Table 1. Comparison of Existing Technology Matrixes

Name of the framework	**Intended use**	**Strength**	**Weakness**	**Key parts and takeaways**
Technology Portfolio Analysis (Gatzweiler 2013)	Strategic Technology Management	Long-term strategic view. Simple Matrix	Complex dimensions. Hard to define technology attractiveness.	Simple output but hard to get the input
The Technology Radar (Rohrbeck et al. 2006)	Transparent internal communication and vision	Is meant to be updated periodically (agile)	Specific for a technology-based company	Good criteria's inside the paper
Technology Radar (Parsons et al. 2018)	Complete overview from a Technology perspective	Big picture of all the Technologies	Specific for a technology-based company	A good approach to classify the technologie

The technology portfolio analysis from Gatzweiler (2013) supports strategic technology management. It uses a graphical representation of a two-dimensional matrix in which actual and future situations are displayed. In doing so, external (not influenceable by the company) and internally (influenceable by the company) parameters are combined with a view of future technology development. From the resulting constellations, recommendations for the allocation of R&D funds as well as the company's technology strategy can be derived. The goal of the technology portfolio analysis is to evaluate new, used, or alternative technologies to support strategic decision-making. This approach passes through four consecutive steps: technology identification, determining the current state (technology attractiveness and resource strength), the temporal transformation of the technology portfolio and the selective strategy recommendations. As part of technology identification, the technologies already used in the company are identified. These form the subject of the valuation or comparison. In a two-dimensional matrix, the technologies used in a company or in a particular product or service are mapped individually. The matrix corresponds to the technology portfolio and uses the dimensions of technology attractiveness and resource strength.

The technology portfolio analysis can help to compare the company's own technologies with known alternatives. From this, it is possible to deduce how attractive it is to pursue the current technology strategy in comparison with investing in another, more attractive future technology. If the matrix of a particular technology is supplemented with the identified complementary or substitution alternatives, this gives an overview of how attractive your own technology portfolio will be in the future in comparison to possible alternatives. This comparative assessment can serve as the basis for further strategic decisions. Finally, recommendations for action on the specific design of R&D programs are given. For this purpose, the so-called standard strategies or selective strategy recommendations are derived from the portfolio. The standard strategies differentiate between investment and divestment strategies.

The method from Rohrbeck et al. (2006) uses a similar approach. It goes through different steps: identification of potential technologies, selection, assessment, and dissemination of the generated information to the stakeholder inside the company. Deutsche Telekom AG and Cisco already successfully used this approach. Boe-Lillegraven and Monterde (2015) mention that there are three steps in the scouting process: identification step, selection step, and a verification step. Within the identification step, new technologies are submitted by an international network of technology scouts. Moreover, the company itself can define its scouts, which are collecting inputs together with customers, partners, academia, and other stakeholders. As part of the selection phase, a radar team, as well as a panel of senior technical experts on a quarterly basis, review the submissions. The selection is built upon the concepts of technology, impact, and novelty. In the verification step, the selection undergoes a more detailed analysis led by a technology scout. A short technology profile is written for an executive audience, where the technology is put in a business context. The criteria business and technical rank the relevance of each derived technology for the company. The assessment criteria are based on two factors: market opportunity and implementation risk. Finally, the company's Technology Radar gets published frequently with updated technologies along with their maturity, their place in the value chain and their relevance rated by the assessment.

There are also technology radars from companies, such as the open source technology radar from ThoughtWorks (Parsons et al. 2018). Zalando has already put it into practice and adapted it to stay aware of new technologies and tools, which would support their software development team the most. The Radar consists of quadrants, which divide the so-called blips (a blip is a technology or technique that is changing in the field of software development) into the following four categories: programming languages and frameworks, tools, platforms, and techniques. After the blips are assigned to their corresponding quadrant or topic area, they need to be aligned with the rings, which are: adopt, trial, asses, and hold. The closer a blip is to the center of the radar, the sooner it can be adopted. The blips, which are assigned to the most inner ring (adopt) are technologies, tools, or platforms that already should be adopted within the company by now. The trial ring represents the blips that can be used on a trial basis but are not completely proven as the ones in the adopt ring. The technologies, which should be analyzed more closely are placed within the assess ring. Unless they fulfill the company's criteria, those blips do not reach the trial phase. In the outer area of the radar, the hold ring, new technologies introduced to the industries, which yet are not mature enough to use, are placed. These tools have the potential to become relevant in the future.

All three frameworks define different steps or phases, which describe a technology's level of acceptance within a company. To gather information about new technologies, there still need to be scouts or experts involved, in the process of looking out for new tools. If a „radar team" exists, the phase of technology identification starts with a definition of technology or business needs within the company.

With that input, a technology exploration can be started, either externally or existing ones within the company could be analyzed, whether they still cover the company's needs. For a tool assessment, a graphical depiction could help to structure the findings. Some existing frameworks rank their findings in either concept of Technology, Impact, and Novelty, or dimensions of technology attractiveness and resource strength. Dimensions for supporting and fulfilling the needs of SMEs will be defined further in the document. In all frameworks, experts need to be called in for assessing the result of the findings. In this phase, the rewards and risks of the potential technology need to be further investigated and how the future technology portfolio will differentiate from the current one.

Finally, strategies for investments and divestments for technologies and tools need to be defined. A final graphic could illustrate the company's current state of digitalization with the derived technologies, which can be placed in different phases that express the level of adoption.

3. THE TECHNOLOGY MATRIX

The aim of our research and the focus of this paper is a technology matrix which supports through visualization of the impact of different technologies on a company. The following subsections describe the approach and the research results for the developed technology matrix.

3.1 Requirements for the Technology Matrix

In order to develop the technology matrix, requirements, a technology matrix should incorporate, were defined, as listed in Table 2. Thus, the goal of this artifact takes various factors from the applying SME into consideration and in return deliver a clear output showing the most relevant technologies for the company.

Table 2. Requirements for the Artifact Technology Matrix

Requirement	Description
Usability	As the company should be able to do the assessment by itself, the process of the tool should be self-explanatory. Thus, a clear structured and easy-to-use process is an essential requirement for the technology matrix. In addition, the questions leading through the process should be meaningful for the applying company and the process should be done within a reasonable period.
Validity of the results	The technologies shown in the technology matrix can be traced back and the reason for their result can be reenacted.
Comparability	Also, the results have to be comparable. Hence, the same input data will always lead to the same result. This will also make the model behind the tool comparable to similar models in that field.
Self-developing	The tool should evolve over time as numerous SMEs are applying it. Hence, factors that are static at the beginning (e.g. project size) can be adapted in the future, based on learnings gained during the process.
Sector-relation	One of the most important factors that have come up during the literature review was that the tool has to consider the different needs of sectors. As for example, the ICT sector has other needs for technologies as the hotel industry.
Multidimensional	As several important factors need to be displayed in the visual tool, the selected format should be able to show at least three dimensions.

3.2 Development of the Technology Matrix

After the conduction of an expert interview, it has been decided that the visualization tool needed to support multiple dimensions, in order to fulfill the need of SMEs in their technology trend exploration. The dimensions used are described as the *feasibility* of a possible technology project and the *business impact* caused by such a project. In addition, the *project size* of a possible implementation project is displayed by the size of the respective 'bubble'. As more than one dimension needs to be represented, a radar was deemed not the most suitable option, which usually is used for technology visualization. Instead, a matrix has been selected. An example of the resulted visualization output from the technology matrix is shown in Figure 1.

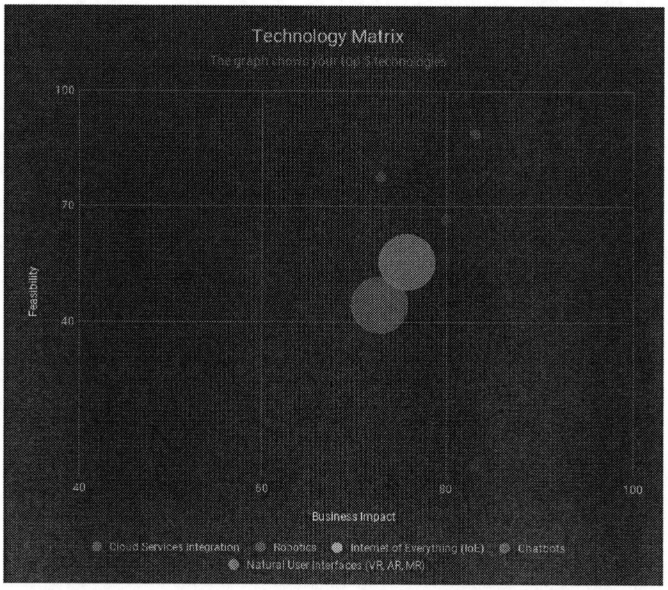

Figure 1. Example of the Technology Matrix, a Technology Trend Visualization

3.2.1 Feasibility

The feasibility is shown on the X-axis and is composed of the factors *maturity* (of the technology), the *complexity* (of a possible implementation), and the *internal know-how*.

A technology's maturity is evaluated with external sources and rated using the numbers 1 (Adolescent), 2 (Early Adoption), or 3 (Mainstream). The ratings are adopted from an article that was published in the year of 2016 by Atos, a big IT service provider, about tech trends with technologies that will impact businesses (Atos Societas Europea 2016). In combination with that, another more extensive report about digital disruption called 'Digital Shockwaves in Business' was published as a part of the Journey 2020 by Atos (2017). Furthermore, the very famous and popular Hype Cycle for Emerging Technologies from Gartner (Panetta 2017) was taken into account by deciding how mature a technology really is. In addition, the article about emerging technology trends from EY (Kimber et al. 2015) was considered as another source.

An external expert, such as a consultant, evaluates the second factor. By completing a predefined form, the expert can indicate if the individual technologies are complex when incorporating within the business. The expert can choose between *low*, *medium*, or *high* related to the complexity.

The last factor, the internal know-how, is assessed by various questions, which have to be answered by the company. For each technology, the company can choose its level of knowledge (e.g. 'training sessions planned', 'technology already in use', 'no knowledge', etc.). Depending on the chosen knowledge level, the internal know-how is rated with either 1, 2, or 3 points.

As all the three factors are rated with numbers from 1 to 3, the maximum score per technology is 9. An extract from the tool regarding the feasibility weighting is shown in Figure 2.

		Feasability Weighting (1 - 3)		
Technology	ref	Maturity (Source)	Complexity (Expert)	Internal knowledge (questionnaire)
Natural User Interfaces (VR, AR, MR)	Sector Weighting / Q9	2	1	1
3D Printing	Sector Weighting / Q10	2	1	3
Mobile Apps	Sector Weighting / Q11, Q6, Q7	3	3	2

Figure 2. Feasibility weightings

Next, the feasibility needs to be calculated. The formula is as follows:

Key table:
$score\ i = reached\ score$
$score\ n = score_{max}$

$$\frac{100 \times \sum_{n}^{1}(\text{score i})}{\text{score n}}$$

100, representing the maximum score, is divided by the maximum possible feasibility score (9), and multiplied with the reached score of all factors ([1 to 3]+[1 to 3]+[1 to 3]). For reasons of simplicity, the feasibility is visually split up into three parts within the technology matrix representing a low feasibility, a medium feasibility, and a high feasibility.

3.2.2 Business Impact

On the Y-axis of the technology matrix, the business impact is shown. The value for this dimension stems from two factors: the sector the company operates in and the result from the questionnaire, which is filled in by the company. The formula for the calculation of the business impact is as follows:

Key table:
$sector\ score\ i = reached\ score, based\ on\ sector$
$sector\ score\ n = sector\ score_{max}$
$questionnaire\ score\ i = reached\ score, based\ on\ questionnaire$
$questionnaire\ score\ n = questionnaire\ score_{max}$

$$Business\ Impact = \frac{50}{sector\ score_n \times sector\ score_i} + \frac{50}{questionnaire\ score_n \times questionnaire\ score_i}$$

The score for the sector is based on a pre-defined weighting determining the importance of each technology for the respective sector. Initially, this weighting is backed with sources for each sector. In general, all sectors are heading to similar goals, such as automation of processes, using robotics and artificial intelligence to derive more efficient business models and using cloud-based services and analytics to in order to cope with big data. Nevertheless, each sector has special needs regarding technologies. The ICT sector, as the most digitalized sector, strives especially for digital workplaces, development, and usage of more complex technologies such as cognitive computing and the internet of everything (Ewaldsson 2016). Hotels, on the other hand, need to focus on providing better customer services which can be realized through technologies such as chat bots, social media platforms, and automation in form of the internet of things to enable automated check-in and payment processes for instance (Marques 2017). Technologies such as autonomous vehicles could significantly change the industry of manufacturers and retailers into more efficient ways to distribute products. Also, more efficient production processes could be shaped thanks to the combination of robotics and artificial intelligence (Paine 2018).

For a productive version of the technology matrix, this weighting could also be defined by the different inter-trade organizations and be either statically or dynamically. The score per technology is defined by the numbers 1 (low) to 5 (high) and adds 50% to the total value of the business impact, as the literature review showed the difference between the various sectors. The other half of the business impact is determined by a questionnaire, which is filled in by the company.

For each technology, an ideal response (benchmark) is defined, which can be described as a pattern. The respective questionnaire answers are compared to these technology patterns and the deviations from this ideal response are determined. Eventually, the technology with the least deviation ranks first. The means for the different deviations of each technology are calculated with a weighted arithmetic mean. For every response, there can be an absolute deviation value between zero and maximum four. Furthermore, the total of every deviation is multiplied by a different weight. Each answer with a deviation of zero (which means the perfect match) is multiplied by 8. The ones with deviation 1 by 4, deviation 2 by 1 and all the answers with a deviation higher than 2 are multiplied by zero, which means they get ignored. The formula for this calculation is as follows:

Key table:
$weighted\ arithmetic\ mean\ \bar{x} = mean\ of\ all\ deviations\ for\ a\ technology$
$weight\ w_n = weight\ of\ a\ deviation$
$deviation\ d_n = deviation\ of\ an\ answer\ to\ the\ pattern$

$$\bar{x} = \frac{w_0 * d_0 + w_1 * d_1 + w_2 * d_2 + w_3 * d_3 + w_4 * d_4}{w_0 + w_1 + w_2 + w_3 + w_4}$$

If every answer is the perfect match for one technology, there is a possible maximum weighted arithmetic mean. Which then also means the highest business impact. This is calculated as follows:

Key table:
$maximum\ possible\ weighted\ arithmetic\ mean\ \max \bar{x} = maximum\ possible\ mean\ for\ a\ technology$
$number\ of\ questions\ (answers)\ with\ zero\ deviation\ i = number\ to\ calculate\ the\ maximum\ mean$

$$max\ \bar{x} = \frac{i}{w_0 + w_1 + w_2 + w_3 + w_4}$$

Summarizing, with these two numbers the business impact can be calculated with the following formula:

$$Business\ impact = 50 * \frac{\bar{x}}{max\ \bar{x}}$$

3.2.3 Project Size

The third dimension is the size (or effort) of a possible implementation project. Values for this dimension can be 1 (small), 2 (medium), or 3 (large). These values are static and are based on assumptions for this paper. Ideally, SMEs who have applied this tool will give feedback on their implemented projects afterward. Thus, in a productive version, the numbers regarding the project size are dynamically adapted based on experience. Thus, the matrix is self-developing as the number of applying users is growing.

3.2.4 Interpretation of the Technology Matrix

The matrix is roughly divided into 9 fields, representing a low, medium, or high business impact of a technology or feasibility in regards to potential implementation projects. Thus, a company applying the matrix should focus on technologies placed in the upper right corner. On the other hand, technologies located on the bottom left have a low impact on the respective business and are difficult to implement. Due to this, it is recommended to avoid these technologies at current.

In addition to the above factors, the size of the bubble has to be considered as it reflects the size of a possible implementation project. For example, an easy to implement technology with medium business impact could cause a quick win and therefore create momentum for a digital transformation initiative within the company. Small bubbles with relatively high impact can be considered as so-called 'low hanging fruits'.

3.2.5 Walkthrough of the Tool Technology Matrix

The exploration process starts with a questionnaire, which needs to be filled out by the SME. It assesses the current situation within the company in terms of internal data concerning the company structure, client data, and data related to the offering. The results of the questionnaire will influence the dimension business impact later on. In order to have a sector-based output, the company needs to fill in their company's sector.

After the questionnaire is filled out, the results are listed in the deviation calculation, where the difference between the as-is situation within the company is compared to the optimal situation in order to incorporate the listed technologies per each deviation. In the meantime, the feasibility weightings need to be assessed. Since the maturity of each technology is set statically, only the complexity and internal knowledge need to be filled out for each technology listed. Experts do this part. The data needed to show relevant technologies in the matrix is now complete and the results are shown within the technology matrix.

4. EVALUATION

To evaluate the developed technology matrix as part of this research project, seven tests were performed with SMEs acting as pilots. These pilots were guided through the technology scouting process. By observation technique, the results were noted and later on integrated into the technology matrix tool. The observation was used to evaluate the tool on four key performance indicators (KPI): usability, meaningfulness of the questions, the validity of the results, and the elapsed time. The KPI's are listed in Table 3. The described technology matrix in section 3 is the final outcome of this research project.

Table 3. Evaluation Key Performance Indicators

KPI	Description	Measure
Usability	The process is self-explanatory and easy to use	Level of support needed
Meaningful questions	Questions asked during the process were suitable in the context of the desired result	Pilot feedback
Validity of result	The delivered results make sense and are comprehensive	Pilot feedback
Elapsed time	How much time was spent from start to end	elapsed time in minutes

5. CONCLUSION

The goal of this research paper is to analyze possibilities for scouting and evaluating current technology trends, which could be relevant particularly for SMEs. SMEs would especially profit from such a tool-based method since they usually do not have the financial resources to hire experts such as consultants. Furthermore, current technology scouting tools are providing support rather for major companies than for SMEs that rely on uncomplicated processes, which do not cause high costs and time efforts. After the analysis of existing methods and frameworks, a technology scout has been designed in the form of a matrix, which weights technologies visually according to their business impact and feasibility in terms of business integration and depicts the project size for each technology. The evaluation of the technology matrix showed a successful and simple usage for SMEs as well as an added value compared to current technology scouting tools when scouting for new technology trends, which could play a relevant role for businesses. Thus, this research shows clear benefits for any SMEs when using this technology matrix tool: easy to use, transparency of the output and its process to reach those outputs, the tool can be reused in the future by the SME, and sector specifics are taken into consideration. Concluding, this tool can be applied by any SME in order to facilitate or improve its technology scouting capabilities.

REFERENCES

Atos, 2017. Journey 2020 - Digital Shockwaves in business. *ascent*. Available at: https://atos.net/content/mini-sites/journey-2020/index.html [Accessed October 20, 2018].

Atos Societas Europea, 2016. Technologies that will Impact your Business. *ascent*, p.28. Available at: https://de.scribd.com/document/367974180/ALO2016-Trends [Accessed October 25, 2018].

Baulcomb, J.S., 2003. Management of change through force field analysis. *Journal of Nursing Management*, 11(4), pp. 275–280.

Boe-Lillegraven, S. & Monterde, S., 2015. Exploring the cognitive value of technology foresight: The case of the Cisco Technology Radar. *Technological Forecasting and Social Change*, 101, pp.62–82. Available at: http://dx.doi.org/10.1016/j.techfore.2014.07.014.

Bundesamt für Statistik BFS, 2017. Struktur der Schweizer KMU 2015. *Statistik der Schweiz*.

Chan Kim, W. & Mauborgne, R., 2005. *Blue Ocean Strategy: How to Create Uncontested Market Space and Make Competition Irrelevant* 1st ed., Harvard Business Review Press.

Ewaldsson, U., 2016. Five trends: Shaping innovation in ICT. *Ericsson Review*, 93(2), pp. 30–41.

Gatzweiler, A., 2013. Technologie Portfolio Analyse., p. 15.

Hevner, A.R. et al., 2004. Design Science in Information Systems Research. , 28(1), pp. 75–105.

Kimber, A. et al., 2015. Emerging technology trends - The road to the bank of the future. *Emerging technology trends The road to the bank of the future*, p. 8.

Kreutzer, R.T., Neugebauer, T. & Pattloch, A., 2018. *Digital Business Leadership*, Berlin, Heidelberg: Springer Berlin Heidelberg. Available at: http://link.springer.com/10.1007/978-3-662-56548-3.

Marques, M., 2017. 5 tech trends revolutionising the hospitality industry. *Medium*. Available at: https://medium.com/hijiffy/5-tech-trends-revolutionising-the-hospitality-industry-76b734c961b7 [Accessed September 30, 2018].

Paine, J., 2018. Don't Miss these 5 Retail Tech Trends in 2018. *Inc.* Available at: https://www.inc.com/james-paine/top-retail-tech-trends-to-watch-in-2018.html [Accessed September 30, 2018].

Panetta, K., 2017. Top Trends in the Gartner Hype Cycle for Emerging Technologies. *Gartner Inc.* Available at: https://www.gartner.com/smarterwithgartner/top-trends-in-the-gartner-hype-cycle-for-emerging-technologies-2017/ [Accessed September 30, 2018].

Parsons, R. et al., 2018. Technology Radar Vol. 19. *thoughtworks.com/radar*, 19. Available at: https://www.thoughtworks.com/radar [Accessed October 30, 2018].

Pelz, W., 2004. *Strategisches und Operatives Marketing: Ein Leitfaden zur Erstellung eines professionellen Marketing-Plans* 1st ed., Norderstedt. Available at: http://www.wpelz.de/swot-analyse/SWOT-Analyse.pdf.

Peter, M. et al., 2018. Die ABILI-Methodik : Inspiration und Navigation bei der Digitalen Transformation mit Fokus auf KMU. *Arbeitsberichte der Hochschule für Wirtschaft FHNW*, (36).

Peter, M.K., 2017. *KMU-Transformation: Als KMU die Digitale Transformation erfolgreich umsetzen.* 1st ed., Olten: Marc K. Peter.

Rohrbeck, R., Heuer, J. & Arnold, H., 2006. The Technology Radar - An instrument of technology intelligence and innovation strategy. *ICMIT 2006 Proceedings - 2006 IEEE International Conference on Management of Innovation and Technology*, 2(June), pp. 978–983.

Theobald, E., 2016. PESTEL-Analyse: Die Wichtigsten Einflussfaktoren der Makroumwelt. *Management Monitor*, pp. 1–7.

CO-CREATING AN ICT ARTEFACT WITH WOMEN IN SOUTH AFRICA

Ronel Smith[1,2], Marita Turpin[2] and Marlien Herselman[1]
[1]*CSIR, Meraka, P.O. Box 395, Pretoria, South Africa*
[2]*Department of Informatics, University of Pretoria, Private Bag X20, Hatfield, Pretoria, South Africa*

ABSTRACT

The active involvement of rural women in ICT4D initiatives is essential to ensure that they benefit from the initiative in general, and the technology artefact in particular. Usually ICT4D projects are male centered and the relevance of ICTs to the women within their contextual realities are not always considered. The purpose of this paper is indicate how an ICT artefact was co-created with rural women in South Africa in a resource constrained context. Participatory approaches like co-creation are important when implementing ICT4D initiatives aimed at rural women. Through the application of Design Science Research as the methodology an ICT artefact was co-created in a specific context in South Africa with rural women only. It is a longitudinal study that is still evolving. The lessons learnt and process that was followed will be shared. The main finding was that the active participation and feedback of the users of a system are essential when aiming to address their immediate and long term needs. If this is not the case the ICT artefact will not be used and it will yet again become part of the statistics of why Information Communication Technology for Development (ICT4D) projects fail.

KEYWORDS

Co-Creation, Rural Women, ICT4D, Design Science Research Methodology

1. INTRODUCTION

When conducting technology-based projects in rural communities in developing countries it is important to remember that ICTs are socio-technical systems(Moens, Broerse, Gast & Bunders, 2010; Stillman, 2010). Western culture, typically unsuited to local requirements, is embedded in the design of technology, and when projects are ICT vendor or donor driven, this culture must be adapted to fit the community (Moens *et al.*, 2010; Morales-Gomez & Melesse, 1998). For ICT4D projects to be successful, context specific requirements and interpretations must be taken into account during the design process, with local community members afforded the opportunity to articulate their requirements, needs and demands (InfoDev, 2003). To maximise the value of co-creation, and avoid a top-down technology push, a bottom-up approach embedded in community participation is vital (David, Sabiescu & Cantoni, 2013). Co-creation or a participatory approach allows for the incorporation of the social values, perspectives and knowledge of the communities thereby producing a product or solution, which bridges Heeks' design-reality gap (Khumalo & Pather, 2018; Heeks, 2008; Puri, 2007). All this being said, community participation in an ICT4D context is always more complex than what has been reported in the literature ((Bailur in de la Harpe, 2014)), and even experienced ICT4D researchers and practitioners can find themselves with 'burnt fingers'. If ICT is exploited (like cultural capital), it can influence the way people will use technology as well as the value they give to the use of the ICT. This is even more the case in rural areas (Singh, Díaz Andrade & Techatassanasoontorn, 2018).

The label of co-creation has been associated with various topics like developing new services, collaborating with users and innovators, adapting a product to the needs of users, participation of stakeholders in a community, creating new knowledge, networks and exchanging services (Ramaswamy & Ozcan, 2018). Despite this diversity, however, there is surprisingly little consensus on what "co-creation" is. The research question that will be addressed in this study is: How can rural women benefit from a co-creation process that addresses their requirements and needs with relation to an ICT artefact?

2. CONCEPTUALISING CO-CREATION

The term 'co-creation', which has its origin in the innovation domain, is increasingly being used in the development context along with terms such as 'user-driven innovation', 'co-production' and 'collaborative innovation' to describe the intended beneficiaries' involvement in the design of solutions that are relevant to their needs (Smith, 2015). Co-creation refers to a situation in which research participants collaborate with the research team in order to add value to the research process and to create something of value (Humphreys & Grayson, 2008).

Co-creation can take place when the researcher and research participants are in contact with one another for a specific reason and/or to achieve a specific result. This contact creates the opportunity for the parties to influence each other's thinking and processes. Interaction must be mutual and reciprocal and should generally be beneficial for both parties, resulting in shared value creation (Grönroos, 2011; Windisch, 2011). Co-creation enables and empowers research participants to interact and collaborate with the researcher in order to create an artefact that has value for both parties (Edvardsson, Tronvoll & Gruber, 2011). The production of the co-created artefact can be viewed as the generation of potential value, whereas use of the artefact is viewed as generation of real value (Grönroos, 2011).

Many papers apply the term "value co-creation" but do not define "co-creation", and then add the term "value". Attention is then distracted from "creation (Vargo & Lusch, 2016). This resulted in comparing "co-production" and "value-in-use". Ranjan and Read Ranjan and Read (2016) have found that of the 149 papers they investigated, 71 papers focus on "co-production" and only 46 addressed "value-in-use". A focus on "value co-creation" was only indicated in 32 papers.

After investigating all concepts relating to co-creation Ramaswamy and Ozcan (2018:200) provides the best definition for co-creation pertaining to this study:

"Co-Creation is the enactment of interactional creation across interactive system-environments (afforded by interactive platforms), entailing agencing engagements and structuring organizations".

Ramaswamy and Ozcan Ramaswamy and Ozcan (2018) postulate that the real value of creation does not only apply to co-creating artefacts but rather lies with the value that the new co-designed artefact can have for them within their own contexts based on their involvement in their own networks. This is particularly relevant for this study as the rural women co-create an ICT artefact based on their needs and they get value out of this co-creation process as it improves the quality of their lives.

Ramaswamy and Ozcan (2018) also highlight the relation between co-creation and Giddens' structuration theory Giddens (1984), when they note the concepts of human agency and structure in their definition above. They also indicate that the test is to understand the role of both structure and agency and that these two concepts should not be juxtaposed but the value of both should be recognised as the interplay between them takes place. The idea is that agency and structure constitute responses that shape their orientations towards their contexts. This is also supported by Booyens, Hart and Ramoroka (2018) when they indicate that in South Africa agency has a role to play in innovation in developing contexts but that the involvement of the government is not very prominent to promote this. That is why some ICT4D studies do not acknowledge the innovation that takes place at an individual level as they develop products that are rooted in specific socio-cultural contexts (Jiménez & Zheng, 2018). In South Africa this is a challenge as the National Innovation System has to involve local communities when innovating (Booyens *et al.*, 2018).

As one collaborates during co-creation, people from various levels in society join one another to share their visions, in the quest to co-design and co-implement refined products and services that focus on deprived communities' needs (Ranjan & Read, 2016). This can ensue in socio-economic prosperity and a specific challenge in a community is addressed (Ruhl, Richter, Lembke & Allert, 2014). Therefore Hood (Hood, 2018) argues that when we scale we consider not only to identify the right innovation to implement, but also how best to adapt it to individual contexts. Fundamental to this work are two components: (1) the robust deployment of continuous improvement methods to promote iterative innovation, and sustained learning and progress; (2) and a systemic approach to collaboration through the creation of powerful and well-designed networks.

Traditionally ICT4D research focuses on women as users and beneficiaries, not as co-creators. In response the World Bank (2009:3) emphasise the importance of involving women in projects by stating that various studies have "highlighted the need to ensure greater continuity between design and implementation to integrate women more fully into mainstream development activities". This is further supported by Jagtap and

Larsson (2018) when they indicate that women living in poverty suffer many problems as compared to men living in poverty, as women have different needs and perspectives on problems they encounter. This implies that design research in this field can benefit from developing gender sensitive co-design approaches. This can result in more involvement of women in co-design activities.

3. MODELS OF CO-CREATION TO CONSIDER

In some community-based models of co-creation, a central issue is the lack of power of community members who are involved. This is found especially when co-designing with technology, as well as in value co-creation. In each case, there are inherent power differentials, and this should be carefully managed in order to allow all involved to participate meaningfully in the co-creation process (Greenhalgh, Jackson, Shaw & Janamian, 2016). Value also lies in empowerment especially when you develop an artefact during collaboration as the participant's motivation and ambitions are enhanced (Novani, Putro & Hermawan, 2015).

Various models of co-creation exist (Edvardsson *et al.*, 2011; Andreu, Sánchez & Mele, 2010; Gebauer, Johnson & Enquist, 2010; Zwass, 2010; Payne, Storbacka & Frow, 2008; Zwick, Bonsu & Darmody, 2008; Prahalad & Ramaswamy, 2004), but according to Durugbo and Pawar (2014) and supported by Ramaswamy and Ozcan (2018) most of these focus on the dynamics between a supplier, customer and encounter domains during the co-creation process. Value is derived from value in exchange as well as value in use. Durugbo and Pawar (2014), however developed a unified model of co-creation (Figure 1) and they explicitly define the key role of existing value and technique selection during co-creation (unlike other studies on co-creation). This research proposes a 'unified model' when you formalise the process in co-creation.

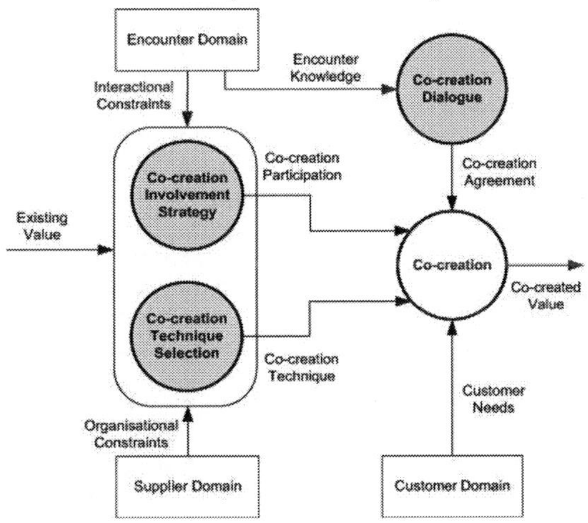

Figure 1. A Model for co-creation (Durugbo & Pawar, 2014)

This model adds a new perspective on collaboration during co-creation and it includes themes like capability-, customer-, governance-, intelligence-, value-, role-, process-, service-, and community-focused. This model has particular reference to this study as co-creation within a specific community is all about dialogue, participation, knowledge sharing, sense making, needs and to create value to the community in the end, in use and in their context.

Various authors (De Koning, Crul & Wever, 2016; Putro, 2016; Novani *et al.*, 2015; Kijima, Rintamki & Mitronen, 2012) indicate that a co-creation process should include specific steps like identify, analyse, define, design, realize and evaluate or listen, identify, ideate, collaborate, evaluate and experiment. However, according to Kijima *et al.* (2012) and supported by Suryana, Mayangsari and Novani (2017), for co-creation to have real value your co-creation process steps should rather be: *co-experience, co-definition, co-elevation, and co-development*. When applying co-experience, the client and supplier should share their understanding of the nature of the problem, process and to comprehend each other's preferences, capabilities, and expectations so that they may co-define and share a common internal model (Putro, 2016). Co-elevation has to do with the process of understanding the expectations of customers and abilities of the providers. The higher the expectation the greater the value. Thus, co-development addresses co-innovation that is the result of people who collaborate (Novani *et al.*, 2015).

True participatory design is more than just getting the users involved in the 'how' of implementation. They should also be involved in setting the agenda and deciding on the approach (Moens *et al.*, 2010). Full and active participation of the end users and local community in the design of an ICT artefact is crucial to ensure its usefulness at local level by directly addressing local needs, as well as promoting buy-in and the development of local champions (Booyens *et al.*, 2018; David *et al.*, 2013; Gurnstein, 2003).

4. THE ICT ARTEFACT

The ICT artefact in this paper stems from a project coined the Digital Doorway that has been in existence since 2002 and was developed with the main purpose of promoting digital literacy skills in deep rural areas. It has adapted the idea of 'The Hole in the Wall project' from India(Gush, 2018).

At the time of writing, sites are deployed throughout the nine provinces of South Africa and consist of 60 weatherproof walk-in containers with a built-in solar panel. To date more than 300 units have been deployed throughout South Africa, mostly in deep rural settlements. Internationally 30 Digital Doorways have been deployed in Uganda, four in Australia and one each in Lesotho, Ethiopia, and the Solomon Islands. The Digital Drum, a Digital Doorway in a 20 gallon drum developed with UNICEF for use in Uganda, was nominated by the Time Magazine as one of the top 50 inventions in the world for 2011 (Smith & Turpin, 2017). Most of the sites support VSAT Internet connectivity enabling them to transmit near-real-time data (comprised of many parameters) back to a monitoring server and support desk. There is thus a large amount of raw data on the who uses the machines and for what purposes available (Gush, 2018).

The current DDs include a satellite downlink and GPRS backhaul to access content and to log file retrieval. A Bluetooth dongle and GUI application allow a user to save files from the DD to a personal device. A user can create a personal account and enter their information (age, gender, home language). This data, as well as specific application usage is hosted on a server. A webcam allows users to create a personalised profile and they receive incentives for logins. This ensures the validation of demographic data. The system is based on Open source software, employing a modified Ubuntu Linux OS with the Xfce display. The Linux security mechanisms prevent unauthorised modification to essential folders and files (Gush, 2018).

The DD was selected as ICT artefact for this research project because it has proven itself to be very reliable and uniquely suited to the harsh environment of the rural areas in which the project will be conducted. The researcher's on-going involvement with the DD was useful when hardware and software modifications based on the middle-aged women's feedback needed to be made.

The DD was first installed at the Setsong Community Centre in August 2013, in a community consisting mostly of rural women over the age of 64 years. Currently the Setsong Centre is a place where the older women gather to work on projects such as sewing, beadwork, reed work (e.g. making brooms and baskets) and farming on a communal farm. The ICT artefact was co-created by through 7 site visits (*cf* Table 1) and refining the artefact based on feedback from the women and by applying the co-creation model as well as processes described in section 3 of this paper.

5. RESEARCH METHODOLOGY

A pragmatist research philosophy is adopted. Pragmatists are concerned with solutions to problems that work, and knowledge is viewed as a way to improve the world (Cresswell & Sheikh, 2013). This view aligns well with the Design Science Research (DSR) aim of changing the current situation into a desired one (Goldkuhl, 2012). In fact, some authors contend that DSR is essentially pragmatic in nature (Hevner, 2007).

The reason for choosing Design Science as a research methodology was to co-create the ICT artefact with the rural women by applying the specific DSR process of Peffers(Peffers, Tuunanen, Rothenberger & Chatterjee, 2007) (Figure 2).

DSR is used as the research strategy. DSR is a creative problem solving methodology that focuses on the production of innovative and new knowledge in order to solve a problem. DSR researchers are concerned with relevance and making an impact(Baskerville, Baiyere, Gregor, Hevner & Rossi, 2018).

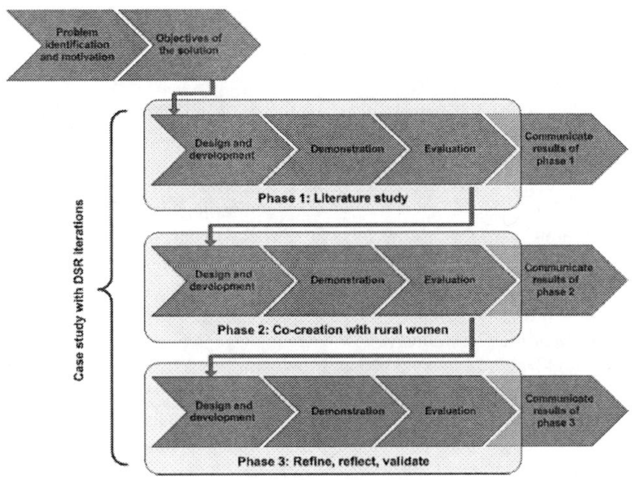

Figure 2. Design Science Research Methodology as applied in this study (Adapted from (Peffers *et al.*, 2007) and (Herselman & Botha, 2014))

The focus of this paper is on Phase 2 of the process where the ICT artefact was designed, developed and demonstrated as well as evaluated to improve it, by the rural women in Limpopo Province of South Africa.

6. RESULTS AND DISCUSSIONS

The ICT artefact was co-created during 7 site visits ranging from April 2013 to October 2016. Visit 7 constituted an assessment and the building of a new site for the ICT artefact in order for the project to continue, since the building where it was hosted was severely damaged by a storm. The project is still in progress at the time of writing. The design activities that occurred during the site visits are summarized in Table 1. Note that 'RURAL WOMEN' is an abbreviation of 'Elderly Rural Women', the participant group for the co-design study.

Table 1. Design Activities during Co-creation of ICT Platform

RURAL WOMEN design activities	RURAL WOMEN activities	Site visit #	CSIR team activities	CSIR team design activities
Listen	Mma C (leader of the rural women) agrees to participate and involves the other 21 rural women	Prior	Prior learning from rural DD projects Identify need for RURAL WOMEN study Identify Mafarafara site Establish relationship with Mma C	Identify
Listen Evaluate	Rural women share contextual information and evaluate desirability of the project	1	Introduce project Obtain ethical consent	Listen Ideate
		1a	Pre-installation site inspection	Identify
Collaborate Experiment	Help install ICT artefact Participate in training and share information on livelihoods	2	Install ICT platform Give training Interview RURAL WOMEN on livelihoods First update of ICT platform	Collaborate Listen
Collaborate Experiment Identify	Assist each other with use Maintain and clean venue Share info on use and further needs	3	Assess use of ICT platform Identify further needs	Evaluate Listen Identify
		3a	Upgrade solar panels Update information base	
Collaborate Experiment	Share use experiences and info on further needs	4	Evaluate use of ICT artefact Identify further needs	Evaluate Listen

RURAL WOMEN design activities	RURAL WOMEN activities	Site visit #	CSIR team activities	CSIR team design activities
Identify	Assist each other with use			Identify
Collaborate	Share use experiences and info	5	Evaluate use of ICT artefact	Evaluate
Experiment	on further needs		Identify further needs	Listen
Identify	Assist each other with use			Identify
		5a	Remove ICT artefact for maintenance and updates	
Collaborate	Share enthusiasm for returned	6	Re-install ICT artefact	Evaluate
Experiment	ICT artefact		Install new printer	
Define	Use updated ICT artefact and give feedback			
	Plan to upgrade Community center and lapa			
Collaborate	Share plans and activities towards new building	7	Assess storm damage	Listen
			Arrange temporary safekeeping of ICT artefact	Identify
	Progression with new building	After		

From site visits 3 to 5, there is a lot of repetition of activities: continued use of the ICT artefact on the rural women's side, and continued evaluation and further needs assessment on the CSIR's side. As time progressed and the rural women became familiar with the ICT artefact, they could provide more informed inputs related to further needs.

The CSIR team installed existing technology that was refined with and for the rural women who had unique user needs, in the process. As such, their design activities consisted mainly of evaluating use, listening to the users and identifying further needs. Because it was an existing product, not much ideation needed to happen.

The rural women's main activities consisted of trying out the technology that was totally new to them, thus they were experimenting. Throughout the project they did so in a collaborative manner, assisting each other to use the ICT artefact. Their use of the ICT artefact became integrated with their other collaborative activities at the community centre, such as sewing and weaving. Their continued use of the ICT artefact enabled them to better identify additional needs related to the information base and use of the ICT artefact.

7. UNEXPECTED FINDINGS

The women's feedback on the benefits of the ICT platform held some surprises. The first one was the pride that especially the illiterate rural women took in being able to type their name (their login username was their own name). The illiterate rural women could not use the ICT platform extensively, but they could perform some tasks such as playing games and watching videos. One of them reported that the training on the ICT platform enabled her to use an ATM for the first time in her life; previously she always required someone else to do her ATM banking for her. Activities such as these were a major accomplishment for some of the rural women that believed they were too old to learn, and would never be able to use computers because of being illiterate.

A second surprise was the pleasure they derived from playing games, many of which were educational. They did not only enjoy the games but believed that the games took away their stress as it made them forget about their worries. This is a major benefit to people who are in survivalist mode and who are regularly stressing about the next meal and other basic livelihood concerns.

There was a further unexpected benefit the rural women shared during feedback sessions, of exercising their bodies and fingers when moving between screens and having to type on the keyboard.

Lastly, from the interview data and site visit reports it became clear that visiting the community centre on a regular basis to use the ICT platform gave especially the retired women a sense of purpose.

The unexpected benefits were in a sense unique to the rural women: as a group they had high levels of illiteracy, a number of survivalist stresses and concerns, the retired person's loss of sense of purpose to their life, and age related ailments such as arthritis. Hence, the ICT platform project could be said to benefit the rural women in a unique manner, due to their unique composition but also due to the success of the project, without which they would not have adopted and regularly used the ICT platform.

8. CONCLUSION

ICT4D strategies and initiatives aimed at improving the situation rural women find themselves in, must place more emphasis on local realities such as power structures and indigenous sources of knowledge than has been done to date. For the women to benefit from 'new' knowledge such as that gained from ICTs, it must be integrated with their local knowledge within the context they are intimately familiar with. To make new technologies work for, rather than against women in rural areas it is important to take into consideration that they have different needs, capacities and skills than men. Consulting women when co-designing and co-creating with ICT is essential as this can empower them towards capacity building. Specific steps in the process of co-creation during the design process are crucial to follow as well as a specific co-creation model. Soliciting the views of RURAL WOMEN on new technology and involving them in the design can make the development of the technology more user-oriented and will improve the likelihood that they will adopt it.

ACKNOWLEDGEMENT

This paper acknowledges the support of the CSIR in South Africa for using the Digital Doorway project for the purpose of co-creation with rural women, the Department of Science and Technology for their funding and the University of Pretoria for supporting the project through research.

REFERENCES

Andreu, L., Sánchez, I. & Mele, C. 2010. Value co-creation among retailers and consumers: New insights into the furniture market. *Journal of Retailing and Consumer Services,* 17(4):241-250.

Baskerville, R., Baiyere, A., Gregor, S., Hevner, A. & Rossi, M. 2018. Design Science Research Contributions: Finding a Balance between Artifact and Theory. *Journal of the Association for Information Systems,* 19(5):358-376.

Booyens, I., Hart, T.G. & Ramoroka, K.H. 2018. Local innovation networking dynamics: evidence from South Africa. *The European Journal of Development Research,* 30(4):749-767.

Cresswell, K. & Sheikh, A. 2013. Organizational issues in the implementation and adoption of health information technology innovations: An interpretative review. *International Journal of Medical Informatics,* 82(5):e73-e86.

David, S., Sabiescu, A.G. & Cantoni, L. 2013. Co-design with Communities. A Reflection on the Literature Public and private access to ICTs in developing regions. Proceedings of the 7th International Development Informatics Association Conference, 1-3 November. Bangkok, Thailand.

De Koning, J.I., Crul, M.R. & Wever, R. 2016. Models of co-creation. Service Design Geographies. Proceedings of the ServDes. 2016 Conference.

de la Harpe, R. 2014. The level of participation during the development of a mobile application for home-based healthcare data in a developing context: An actor-network theory perspective. *SACJ,* 54:20-33.

Durugbo, C. & Pawar, K. 2014. A unified model of the co-creation process. *Expert Systems with Applications,* 41(9):4373-4387.

Edvardsson, B., Tronvoll, B. & Gruber, T. 2011. Expanding understanding of service exchange and value co-creation: a social construction approach. *Journal of the Acadamy of Marketing science,* 39:327-339.

Gebauer, H., Johnson, M. & Enquist, B. 2010. Value co-creation as a determinant of success in public transport services: A study of the Swiss Federal Railway operator (SBB). *Managing Service Quality: An International Journal,* 20(6):511-530.

Giddens, A. 1984. *The constitution of society : outline of the theory of structuration.* Berkeley: University of California Press.

Goldkuhl, G. 2012. Pragmatism vs interpretivism in qualitative information systems research. *European Journal of Information Systems,* 21(2):135 - 146.

Greenhalgh, T., Jackson, C., Shaw, S. & Janamian, T. 2016. Achieving research impact through co-creation in community-based health services: literature review and case study. *The Milbank Quarterly,* 94(2):392-429.

Grönroos, C. 2011. Value co-creation in service logic: a critical analysis. *Marketing theory,* 11(3):279-301.

Gurnstein, M. 2003. Effective use: a community informatics strategy beyond the digital divide. *First Monday,* 8(12):1 - 14.

Gush, K. 2018. An open-source tool-set for meaningful monitoring and visualisation of rural ICT projects. 2018 IST-Africa Week Conference (IST-Africa).

Heeks, R. 2008. ICT4D 2.0: The next phase of applying ICT for international development. *Computer,* 41(6):26-33.

Herselman, M. & Botha, A. 2014. *Designing and implementing an Information Communication Technology for Rural Education Development (ICT4RED) initiative in a resource constraint environment: Nciba school district, Eastern Cape, South Africa.* Pretoria, South Africa: CSIR.

Hevner, A.R. 2007. A three cycle view of design science research. *Scandinavian Journal of Information Systems,* 19(2):4.

Hood, N. 2018. The quest for scale: Achieving system-wide innovation and improvement in education.

Humphreys, A. & Grayson, K. 2008. The intersecting roles of consumer and producer: a critical perspective on co-production, co-creation and prosumption. *Sociology compass,* 2(3):963-980.

InfoDev 2003. ICT for Development. Contributing to the Millenium Development Goals: Lessons learnt from seventeen InfoDev projects. Washington DC, USA: InfoDev.

Jagtap, S. & Larsson, T. 2018. Design and Frugal Innovations: Three roles of resource-poor people. Design 2018.

Jiménez, A. & Zheng, Y. 2018. Tech hubs, innovation and development. *Information Technology for Development,* 24(1):95-118.

Khumalo, C. & Pather, S. 2018. Investigation of a Co-Design Approach for a Civic Engagement Mobile Application. 2018 IST-Africa Week Conference (IST-Africa).

Kijima, K., Rintamki, T. & Mitronen, L. 2012. Value orchestration platform: model and strategies. *Advances in the Human Side of Service Engineering*:433.

Moens, N.P., Broerse, J.E.W., Gast, L. & Bunders, J.F.G. 2010. A Constructive Technology Assessment Approach to ICT Planning in Developing Countries: Evaluating the First Phase, the Roundtable Workshop. *Information Technology for Development,* 16(1):34.

Morales-Gomez, D. & Melesse, M. 1998. Utilising information and communication technologies for development: The social dimensions. *Information Technology for Development,* 8(1):1-12.

Novani, S., Putro, U.S. & Hermawan, P. 2015. Value orchestration platform: promoting tourism in batik industrial cluster solo. *Procedia-Social and Behavioral Sciences,* 169:207-216.

Payne, A.F., Storbacka, K. & Frow, P. 2008. Managing the co-creation of value. *Journal of the Academy of Marketing Science,* 36(1):83-96.

Peffers, K., Tuunanen, T., Rothenberger, M.A. & Chatterjee, S. 2007. A design science research methodology for information systems research. *Journal of management information systems,* 24(3):45 - 77.

Prahalad, C.K. & Ramaswamy, V. 2004. Co-creation experiences: The next practice in value creation. *Journal of interactive marketing,* 18(3):5-14.

Puri, S.K. 2007. Integrating scientific with indigenous knowledge: constructing knowledge alliances for land management in India. *MIS Quarterly,* 31(2):355 - 379.

Putro, U.S. 2016. Value Co-creation Platform as Part of an Integrative Group Model-Building Process in Policy Development in Indonesia. *Systems Science for Complex Policy Making.* Springer.

Ramaswamy, V. & Ozcan, K. 2018. What is co-creation? An interactional creation framework and its implications for value creation. *Journal of Business Research,* 84:196-205.

Ranjan, K.R. & Read, S. 2016. Value co-creation: concept and measurement. *Journal of the Academy of Marketing Science,* 44(3):290-315.

Ruhl, E., Richter, C., Lembke, J. & Allert, H. 2014. Beyond methods: Co-creation from a practice-oriented perspective. Proceedings of Design Research Society Biennial International Conference, Umeå, Sweden.

Singh, H., Díaz Andrade, A. & Techatassanasoontorn, A.A. 2018. The practice of ICT-enabled development. *Information Technology for Development,* 24(1):37-62.

Smith, R. 2015. Women, participation and design in ICT4D: Addressing barriers using a co-creation approach.

Smith, R. & Turpin, M. 2017. Design Science Research and Activity Theory in ICT4D: Developing a Socially Relevant ICT Platform for Elderly Women in Remote Rural South Africa. International Conference on Social Implications of Computers in Developing Countries.

Stillman, L. 2010. Technologies of care in community-based organisations: agency and autheticity. *AI and Society,* 25:309-320.

Suryana, L.A., Mayangsari, L. & Novani, S. 2017. A Virtual Co-Creation Model Of The Hijab Fashion Industry In Indonesia. *International Journal of Business & Society,* 18.

Vargo, S.L. & Lusch, R.F. 2016. Institutions and axioms: an extension and update of service-dominant logic. *Journal of the Academy of Marketing Science,* 44(1):5-23.

Windisch, K. 2011. *Co-Creation and the ethics of stakeholder engagement for value creation.* Arhus University.

World Bank 2009. Information and Communications for Development: extending reach and increasing impact. Washington DC: World Bank.

Zwass, V. 2010. Co-creation: Toward a taxonomy and an integrated research perspective. *International journal of electronic commerce,* 15(1):11-48.

Zwick, D., Bonsu, S.K. & Darmody, A. 2008. Putting Consumers to Work: Co-creationand new marketing governmentality. *Journal of consumer culture,* 8(2):163-196.

EXTENDED THE SAM MODEL - PROPOSED A SYNCHRONIZE MODEL –

Kawtar Imgharene[1], Salah Baina[1] and Karim Doumi[2]
[1]*ENSIAS, University Mohamed V Rabat, Morocco*
[2]*FSJES, ENSIAS, University Mohamed V Rabat, Morocco*

ABSTRACT

Integration between business and information technology (IT) has become one of the top priorities for today's organizations, known as "strategic alignment", which has resulted in several models. The model that has attracted the most attention in this area is the Strategic Alignment Model (SAM) proposed by (Henderson and Venkatraman, 1993a). Any organization needs to be flexible and dynamic to support internal activities and external exchanges. The SAM model does not convene several points on this dynamic integration.

Our article will result in giving the limits and weakness of the SAM model by propagating the studies impeded by the model and concluding with a proposal of the revisited SAM model which will lead to the part of the implementation of the business and IT strategy and the infrastructure part, which must meet the requests to strategic and operational objectives with a synchronization that anticipates each time if there is a verification to do or to renew again the strategy and realign the business IT in a constantly evolving and dynamic way.

KEYWORDS

Business IT Alignment, SAM Model, Synchronization, Agility and Dynamism

1. INTRODUCTION

Today's businesses need flexible and adaptable information systems (IS) to support their strategies and business processes, as well as to facilitate the organization's adaptation to environmental requirements. Dynamic adaptations of the information system resulting from changes in strategy or environment are part of the problems addressed by the strategic alignment of information systems.

Like any business, to grow and prosper, managers must be able to anticipate, recognize and respond to changes in the internal and external environment. This study examines the limitations and gaps of Henderson and Venkatraman's SAM model, which will lead to a synchronous model between strategy and information system. The model will hinder the implementation of the strategy that will change the processes for changing information technology and therefore to achieve agile and synchronous strategic alignment. Since managers spend significant resources on consultation and training in the hope of creating smart strategies very often, these smart strategies do not translate into smart performance(Verweire, 2014).

The researchers examined the difficulties encountered by organizations in achieving a high degree of homogeneity across domains, i.e., the alignment of strategy with IT infrastructure and processes. The main challenges are: a strategy that is often unknown and ambiguous or difficult to implement. (Baets, 1992; Reich and Benbasat, 1996a) identified that high management does not understand the importance of alignment or contribution that IT can make to the business (Henderson and Venkatraman, 1993a), (Campbell and al., 2005) say that the business environment is dynamic and changing rapidly. A number of consequences have been observed as a result of these challenges. When the company's strategy is unknown, ambiguous or static, the computerized level is random rather than determined, resulting in inefficiency (Baets, 1992). When there is a disconnection between the IT team and the strategy team (a group often without an IT specialist), the strategic potential of IT is poorly understood (Campbell and al., 2005). And in environments characterized by dynamism and hyper-competition, it is a great challenge, a mission to align IT capabilities with an evolving strategy. Despite previous research and the identification of challenges for cross-domain areas, mechanisms to align business strategy with IT infrastructure and processes remain insufficiently studied, neither the above-mentioned studies on the discovery of important alignment factors nor the research that led Henderson and Venkatraman to the strategic alignment model (SAM) (Henderson and Venkatraman, 1993a).

In the following chapters, we will elaborate the strategic alignment globally, then the work that has extended the SAM model to acquire a specific need by elaborating if agility is between its empirical work, from this work we will determine the limits of the SAM model to lead to a revised and synchronous SAM model.

2. RELATED WORK

2.1 Strategic Alignment

Since the early 1990s, the alignment of activities with information technology has improved organizational performance and has received considerable attention in the literature (Bharadwaj and al., 1999) (Etien, 2006) (Thevenet, 2009) (Doumi and al., 2013). Alignment of Business Strategy and Information Technology (now referred to as Strategic Alignment) has many synonyms such as Alignment (Silvius, 2007), Harmony (Luftman and Brier, 1999), Linking (Reich and Benbasat, 1996b) and Business-IT Alignment (Maes and al., 2000) ...

In the literature, we identify many definitions of strategic alignment : Business IT alignment refers to the alignment between business and information technology Strategies and between organizational information systems and infrastructures (Henderson and Venkatraman, 1993b). It is defined as "the extent to which the mission framework, objectives and support plans, and are supported by the organization's mission, objectives and plans" (Hirschheim and Sabherwal, 2001). This alignment creates an integrated organization where each function, unit, and person is focused on the organization and its competitiveness. (Tallon and Kraemer, 2003) define strategic alignment by the extent to which the Information System strategy supports and is supported by corporate strategy, according to (Reich and Benbasat, 1996b) strategic alignment refers to the level at which the mission, objectives and plan contained in the business strategy are shared and supported by the IT strategy. (Luftman, 2003) reports that strategic alignment refers to the application of information technology in an appropriate and timely manner, consistent with business strategies, objectives and needs. (Chung and al., 2003) find a strong correlation between the agility of the IT infrastructure and alignment of the IT enterprise strategy. They conclude that the IT strategy needs to be closely aligned with the organizational strategy in view for IT infrastructures to be able to facilitate the agility of the business. This tight alignment means that IT infrastructures need to be flexible because the agility of the IT infrastructure allows the company to develop new processes and quickly applications. (Oosterhout and al., 2005) have developed a conceptual model that describes the conditions under which the specific attributes of the IT architecture and business governance mechanisms are viewed as the agility of the business by enabling and leading to better organizational performance. Operational IT alignment refers to the alignment between business and information technology strategies and between information systems and organizational infrastructures. This approach aims to increase the use value of the information system and make it an advantage for the company.

The main challenges of business IT alignment are to make the information system an advantage in support of the company's strategy. The information system emerges as a quality and creates a source of competitive advantage, only if it is ensured to coincide with the company's needs by strategic alignment.

"Strategic alignment" has resulted in several models. The model that has retained the most attention in this area is the strategic alignment model proposed by (Henderson and Venkatraman, 1993a). We will present the model by mentioning its limits concerning the misalignment of uses and the non-interconnection of the different types of domains of the SAM model.

2.1.1 SAM Model

The model that has attracted more attention in this area is the strategic alignment model proposed in the article written by Henderson and Venkatraman in 1993, SAM is the most cited. According to the literature review developed in (vargas and al., 2007). The SAM model has received empirical support and has conceptual and practical value (Avison and al., 2004; Maes and al., 2000; vargas and al., 2007). This model is based on the need to achieve alignment between internal and external domains as well as functional integration in the business and IT domains (Bomarius, 2005). Strategic alignment is a process in which the company's strategy aims to improve its activities compared to its competitors. The concept of strategic alignment is based on two elements, as shown in Figure 1.

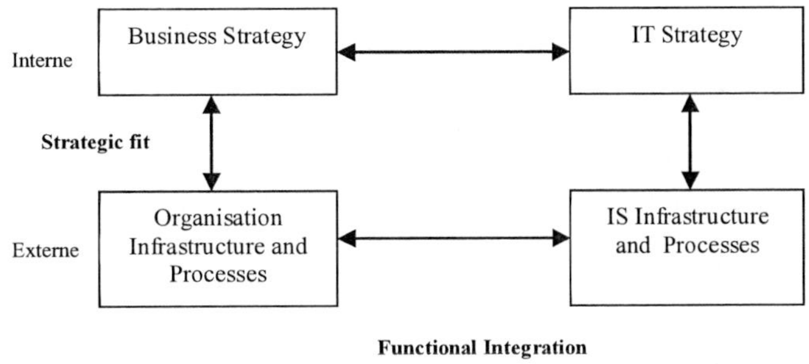

Figure 1. Strategic Alignment Model -Henderson & Venkatraman 1993

Model SAM is comprised of four strategic alignment perspectives. Henderson & Venkatraman (1993) classify alignment perspectives under two categories: business strategy driven perspectives, which consists of strategy execution and technological potential, and IT strategy driven perspectives, which encompasses both competitive potential and service level (Table 1).

Table 1. Alignment perspectives -Henderson & Venkatraman-

Business strategy driven	Business strategy driven
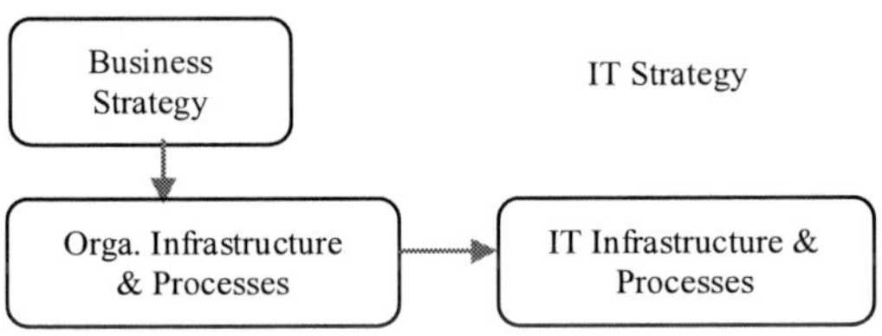	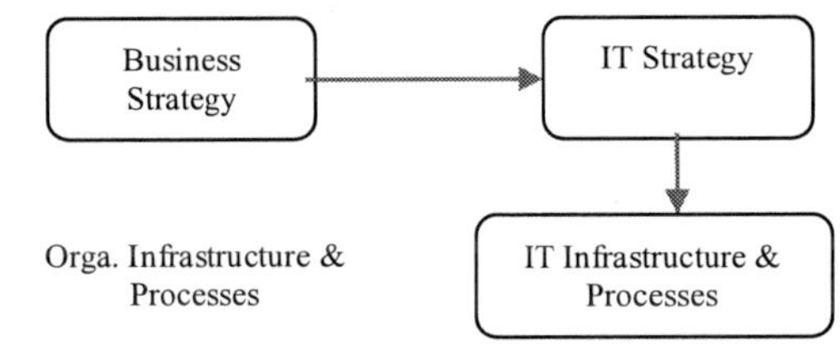
This perspective is consistent with the traditional top-down strategy approach.	This perspective focuses on the development of strategies adapted to information technology.
IT strategy driven	**IT strategy driven**
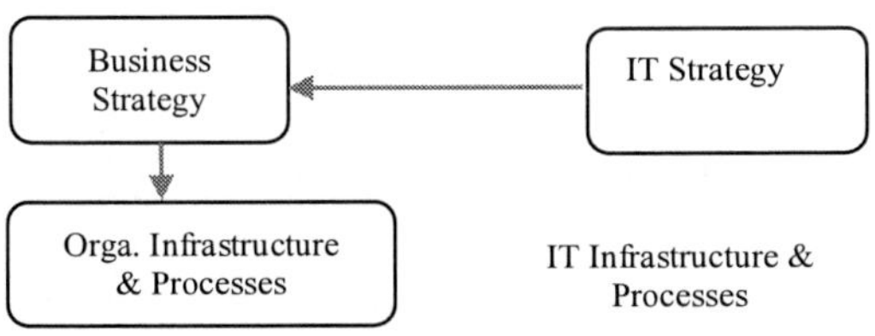	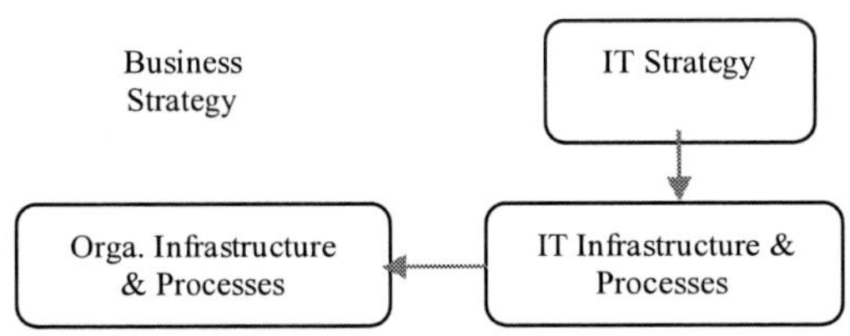
This perspective reflects the exploitation of new information technology capabilities to influence or enable a new strategy and therefore create a competitive advantage for companies.	This perspective emphasizes strategic complementarily that creates the capabilities required to satisfy IT needs.

We must realize that the real challenge for an organization is not to achieve static alignment between the four areas at any given time, but to ensure continuous assessment of trends in these four areas to enable the organization to review and reposition itself in the external environment, while reorganizing its internal infrastructure. The researchers determined that management must recognize the need to move from one perspective to another, based on the changing internal and external business environment. Quoting a quote: "The most important lesson to learn is that strategic alignment is a journey and not an event".

Henderson and Venkatraman (1990) also emphasized the need to understand the dynamic characteristics of this model. They claim that the numbers of strategic planning methods established in the previous decades have failed not because of the weakness of their logic, but because of their inability to realize the dynamic nature of the strategy, and therefore of the alignment.

The SAM model has received empirical support and is considered to have both practical concepts and values (Avison and al., 2004). The vast majority of tracking models and alignment consulting practices are based on the original strategic alignment model. Even today, it is considered to be the most fundamental work in business-IT alignment, and is cited in the majority of relevant academic work. Several specialists have developed and extended the SAM model, this part will be elaborated in the next section.

2.2 Extended SAM Model

Several studies have extended the SAM model to validate or evaluate strategic alignment or to create a new aligned enterprise architecture framework (Avison and al., 2004; Chen and al., 2005; Hinkelmann and al., 2017.)... Few researchers attack the SAM model by mentioning its limitations or its relationship with business and IT agility. In this chapter, we will develop different works obtained from the SAM model in Table 2:

Table 2. Extended Sam Model

Sources	Extend SAM Model
(Avison & al. 2004)	Validated the strategic alignment model and found that it had conceptual and practical values, Therefore, (Avison and al., 2004) proposed a more practical approach using a strategic framework based on the SAM model that "allows management and individuals in management and technology to determine current alignment levels" and to track and modify future alignment as required to determine the extent to which business strategies and IT are aligned...
(Gerow & al., 2015)	Gutierrez and Serrano also discover the strategic alignment of a theoretically useful model (Henderson and Venkatraman, 1993b) but it should be noted that the initial research provides little guidance on how to achieve the proposed strategic perspectives. (Gutierrez and al., 2009) indicate that the most recent alignment measurement tools are specific to each organization and that there is little data to validate their applicability to small businesses (Gutierrez and al., 2009).
(Wegmann & al., 2007)	The paradigm "SEAM" has been proposed as a systemic paradigm for improving existing environmental assessments framework methodologies and finding explanations for practical problems faced by enterprise architects (Wegmuller and al., 2000).
(Hinkelmann and al, 2017)	Proposed a new paradigm in the context of enterprise information systems for business continuity and IT alignment for the agile enterprise. (Jansen, 2017) explored how the alignment of the system based on "ArchiMate" The enterprise architecture model can be controlled using Semantic Web technology. Despite this important work, each of the above-mentioned studies is nevertheless limited.
(Fimbel, 2007)	Introduces a model by highlighting a double necessity. On the one hand, it would be necessary to have an operational model for professionals. On the other hand, it would be necessary to take into account the latest theoretical developments in management sciences. To do this, the author carries out an empirical study of 150 companies and then identifies seven success factors for the adjustment of the information system, which he describes as a "strategic manoeuvre". Thus, the authors develop a set of twelve steps to control, detect and correct misalignments between the "Business" architecture and the IT architecture. It is, in a way, the representation of a process that consists of twelve steps to complete the management, detection and correction of misalignment.

Finally, we conclude that most of the work reviewed by the SAM model gives us the opportunity to say that few have developed the limits of the SAM model and that they mention some tasks that can be discussed or validated with the SAM model such as the change in internal or external environment, as well as the fact that the SAM model perspectives are not uniform in 4 abstraction levels.... the work mentioned focuses on the validation of the SAM model, or the maturity of the SAM model, the others on issues related to enterprise architecture modeling and the others on strategic reorganization. It is our turn to determine the limits of the SAM model by projecting this meaning into the dynamism and determining the principle of agility, this part will be developed in the next section.

3. LIMITS OF SAM MODEL

The model shows its limits outside the "classical" alignment but today it is confronted with the uncertainties and complexity of the external environment, strategic alignment alone is not enough. In this chapter, we will discover what he is missing!

The SAM model was created in 1992, several other researchers referred to it to develop another model, for strategic alignment modeling, for assessing the coherence between the different domains of the SAM model, for evolution... but in the long term, we never find follow-up. The model gave no inability or real leads on the implementation of change and environmental flexibility. Nowadays, dynamism has become the trend; companies are faced with rapid and radical changes, making the organization's entities closely linked, agile and flexible.

Starting with the criticism that is characterized by the date of the model (1992), nowadays the model must integrate dynamism and not remain static by the weakness of the empirical results that it could produce by its referencing. The development of the SAM model was created during a rather stable economic period. Today, market uncertainty and instability are important for companies. Adaptability becomes a factor of competitiveness.

The complexity of the SAM model relationships is difficult to implement. In (Reix and al., 2016) they say that the world of practitioners has sought to tune the SAM model. He concludes that support is difficult to implement. This author also emphasizes the time dimension. In his book, he points out that "the model does not explicitly integrate time and history". In the face of environmental instability, organizations must be increasingly flexible and agile in their alignment process; there is no reference to time management.

Alignment between the different domains of the SAM model must be able to anticipate new strategies and technologies useful to the company and allow their adoption by synchronization over time. In the same context, it is worth mentioning the work of (Chan, 2002) they conclude that the SAM model is not applicable to concretely analyze real situations, in addition, this type of criticism would weaken strategic alignment.

Nowadays the acronym VUCA stands for volatility, uncertainty, complexity and ambiguity characterize the world in which we live and the circumstances in which we must make decisions. The acronym has been developed to all the uncertainties and unpredictability we confronted. In connection with the concept of VUCA, it helps us to developed strategies that support the effective progress of operations and can be applied to business success. Basically, all the requirements described above correspond to the principles of business IT alignment because it's necessary to work closely and interdisciplinary. Except the SAM model does not handle complexity or uncertainty. The strategy aspect ensures business success in a VUCA world; it becomes clear that IT produced a very important role in the planning and execution of individual measures. It is therefore essential to make companies aware of the skills and performance of computers so that IT can help to find the right answers to the questions of tomorrow. However, the SAM model does not evoke the quality of the information system next to the context of the company and its activity, nor the quality of the uses of technological tools neither the behavior of the actors and the operation of information systems.

The goal of the SAM model is that the four components must be aligned, i.e. the overall strategy, the IT strategy, the organizational infrastructure and processes, and finally, the technological infrastructure and the IT processes. This means that these four components must evolve so as to converge for the same goal. The model ignore in each of its perspectives a part of the coherence of alignment and there is unfortunately no continuity between the 4 perspectives which normally must have a common objective, therefore the model SAM does not generate the function synchronization between the entities of strategic alignment from business strategy to IT infrastructure and process. We will explain this synchronization in the following table 2:

Table 2. Synchronize The SAM Model-

<table>
<tr><td>1
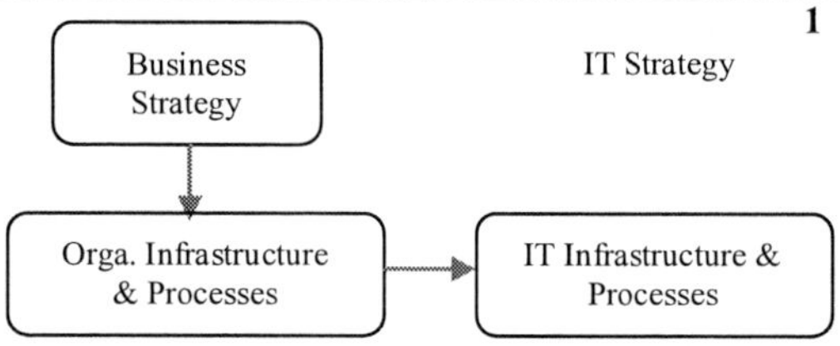
The alignment perspective is between business strategies, infrastructure and organizational processes and with IT infrastructure and processes that is incomplete without the IT strategy. The objectives of alignment will be different.</td><td>1
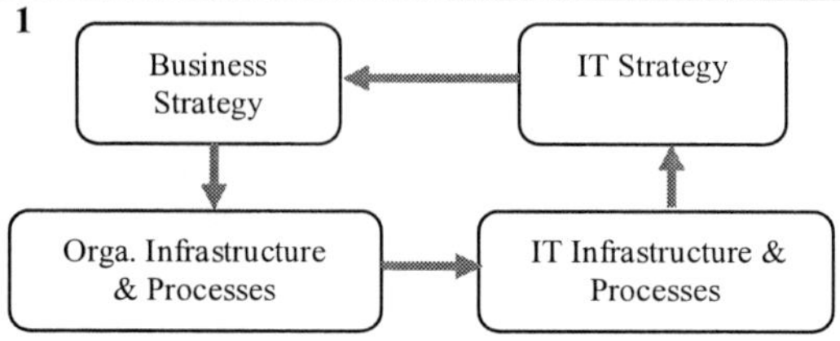
The new business and IT strategies will have the most impact on the SAM model alignment process, a synchronous perspective between the 4 domains.</td></tr>
<tr><td>2
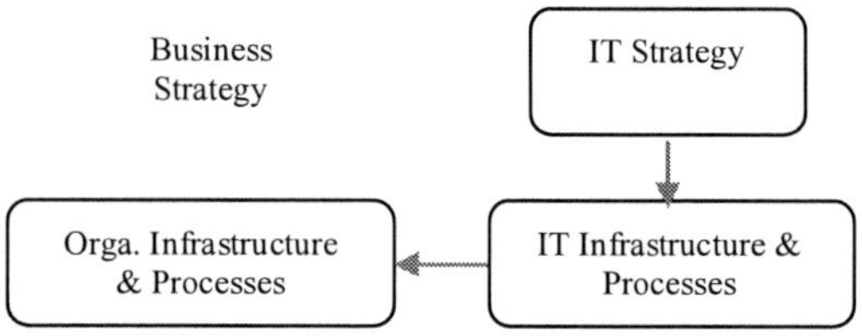
This perspective focuses on how to build the information system in the company, from IT strategy to organizational infrastructure, but without affecting the business strategy that complements the IT business alignment process.</td><td>2
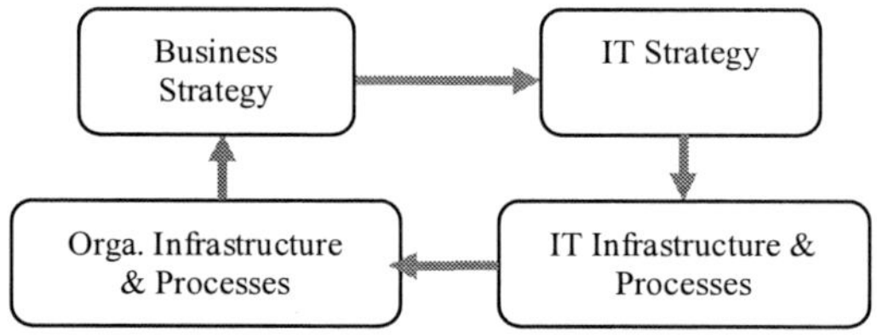
Good synchronization and continuity of the components of the strategic alignment model have been achieved based on the IT and business strategy that will impact the information technology of all stakeholders in a company.</td></tr>
<tr><td colspan="2">1+2
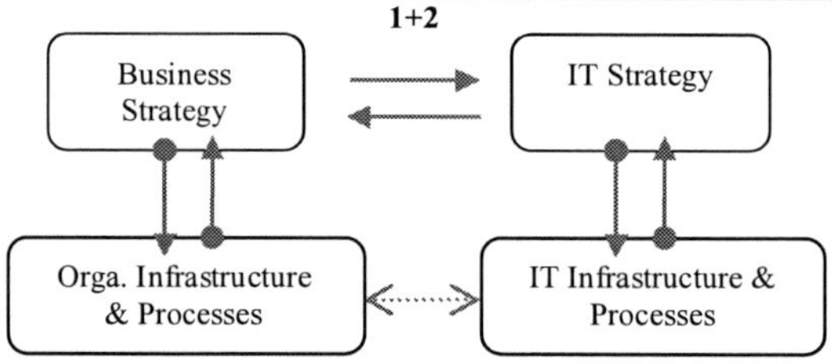
The two perspectives 1 and 2 will synchronize with each other to provide us with a single model with a single perspective that synchronizes the four levels of the SAM model. It is an ongoing process that helps the IT support structure remains relevant to the strategic goals and objectives of any organization.</td></tr>
</table>

To make the adjustment dynamics of each of the components, it is necessary to synchronize the different domains of the SAM model to remain attentive to the external / internal change of the environment and to make strategic alignment agile. The SAM model shows that the notion of alignment is not easy to grasp and that the purpose of alignment can go beyond the process between information technology and business and IT strategy. In the next part, we will define the revisited SAM model by synchronizing the different domains of the model to have an agile model.

4. SYNCHRONIZE A SAM MODEL

A lack of synchronization between business processes will lead to operational slowdowns within the company, errors and replication in data processing (HR, Finance, CRM, ERP, etc.). It is difficult to focus on all activities under these conditions until standards are established.

The company must provide its employees with quick and direct access to the most current information, at any time and from anywhere. Whatever the means and technologies used, if data integration has not been properly carried out, the collection of information dispersed over the enterprise can become truly complex, and it is therefore impossible in a company to "make changes at one level without affecting another, because everything is closely connected". Organizations must therefore reflect globally on their objectives.

The company's strategy is very important in information systems planning. The information system is developed to support the organization's strategic objectives, even in the near future. This is why the strategic role of the information system must be clearly defined in the scheduling processes. The information system is normally not dynamic enough to change significantly in order to be able to manage the changing needs of users. It is therefore expected that information systems will take into account all the eventualities related to the type of strategy, whether it is business or IT strategy.

Fundamentally, dynamism is important to support the Business and IT strategy with the development of information systems to enable the delivery of new strategic objectives that must be planned and adapted to each other while remaining scalable and constantly updated. It is an ongoing process that helps the information systems support structure to remain relevant to the strategic goals and objectives of any organization, to which the SAM model refers by adjusting some changes to obtain a synchronous model between the strategy that will verify the continuity of the acquired objectives between the strategy and the two levels (organizational and IT infrastructure).

All the elements that were presented and discussed in the previous sections are used to present a synchronous adaptation of the classic Strategic IT Alignment Model (SAM). Ensure that the strategic alignment model is revisited in a flexible way, which can at the same time take into account changes in the internal and external environment to obtain an update of the strategy that will be consistent with information technology with a synchronization that anticipates each time if there is a change to be made to renew the strategy and redo the Business IT Alignment. In Figure 2, we propose the SAM model revisited by correcting some of the limitations mentioned in the previous section.

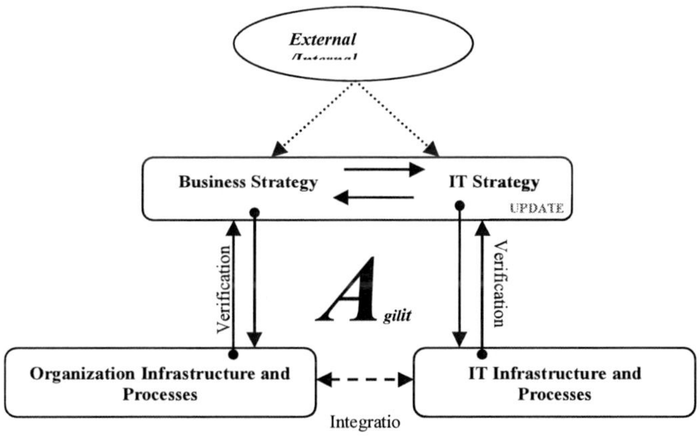

Figure 2. Revisited a SAM Model on a synchronization Model

Technology is becoming increasingly complex, and business processes are required to support the strategic objectives to maintain alignment between the four different levels of the SAM model including integration between technology and IT to be able to apply and return an appropriate response to the business and IT strategy, the infrastructure part must respond to the demands of constantly evolving strategic or operational business strategies in a cost-effective and dynamic manner.

5. CONCLUSION & FUTURE WORK

Despite the existence of many extensions of the SAM model, several limitations of this model emerge in relation to the external environment and the constant evolution of the activities. This document focuses on the limitations of the SAM model that were cited in previous sections showing that the SAM model is still limited and lacks several phases to achieve dynamic synchronization between the four domains of enterprise architecture. This is why we designed to revisit the SAM model by making it synchronous to the new objectives between strategy and information technology. To achieve this important step, organizations can follow a process that involves self-evaluation, strategy development, and business IT correlation. The IT function will be able to innovate and deploy the most appropriate simplification strategy to meet the company's specific needs.

The future objective of this study is to investigate how the assessment between all levels of the SAM model will be constituted to correct some limitations obtaining an instrument to measure both the agility between the level of alignment between the company and the IT, and the activities necessary for organizations to comply with it, following the work that was validated by (Imgharene & al., 2018).

REFERENCES

Avison, D., & al. 2004. Using and validating the strategic alignment model. J. Strateg. Inf. Syst. 13, 223–246.

Baets, W., 1992. Aligning information systems with business strategy. J. Strateg. Inf. Syst. 1, 205–213.

Bharadwaj, A.S., Sambamurthy, V., Zmud, R.W., 1999. IT capabilities: theoretical perspectives and empirical operationalization, in: Proceedings of the 20th International Conference on Information Systems. Association for Information Systems, pp. 378–385.

Bomarius, F., 2005. Product Focused Software Process Improvement: 6th International Conference, PROFES 2005, Oulu, Finland, June 13-18, 2005, Proceedings. Springer Science & Business Media.

Campbell, B., & al. 2005. Strategic alignment: a practitioner's perspective. J. Enterp. Inf. Manag. 18, 653–664.

Chan, Y.E., 2002. Why haven't we mastered alignment? The importance of the informal organization structure. MIS Q. Exec. 1, 97–112.

Chen, H.-M., Kazman, R., Garg, A., 2005. BITAM: An engineering-principled method for managing misalignments between business and IT architectures. Sci. Comput. Program. 57, 5–26.

Chung, S.H., Rainer Jr, R.K., Lewis, B.R., 2003. The impact of information technology infrastructure flexibility on strategic alignment and application implementations. Commun. Assoc. Inf. Syst. 11, 44.

Doumi, K., Baïna, S., Baïna, K., 2013. Strategic Business and It Alignment: Representation and Evaluation. J. Theor. Appl. Inf. Technol. 47, 41–52.

Fimbel, E., 2007. Alignement stratégique: Synchroniser les systèmes d'information avec les trajectoires et manoeuvres des entreprises. Pearson Education France.

Gerow, J.E., Thatcher, J.B., Grover, V., 2015. Six types of IT-business strategic alignment: an investigation of the constructs and their measurement. Eur. J. Inf. Syst. 24, 465–491. https://doi.org/10.1057/ejis.2014.6

Gutierrez, A., Orozco, J., Serrano, A., 2009. Factors affecting IT and business alignment: a comparative study in SMEs and large organisations. J. Enterp. Inf. Manag. 22, 197–211.

Henderson, J.C., Venkatraman, H., 1993a. Strategic alignment: Leveraging information technology for transforming organizations. IBM Syst. J. 32, 472–484.

Hinkelmann, K., n.d. A new paradigm for Continuous Alignment of Business and IT: Combining Enterprise Architecture Modeling and Enterprise Ontology 15.

Hirschheim, R., Sabherwal, R., 2001. Detours in the path toward strategic information systems alignment. Calif. Manage. Rev. 44, 87–108.

Imgharene, K., Doumi, K., Baina, S., 2018. Continuous Alignment Business IT by factor agility. CodiT.

Luftman, J., 2003. Assessing IT/business alignment. Inf. Syst. Manag. 20, 9–15.

Luftman, J., Brier, T., 1999. Achieving and sustaining business-IT alignment. Calif. Manage. Rev. 42, 109–122.

Maes, R., Rijsenbrij, D., Truijens, O., Goedvolk, H., others, 2000. Redefining business: IT alignment through a unified framework.

Oosterhout, M. van, Waarts, E., Hillegersberg, J. van, 2005. Assessing Business Agility: A Multi-Industry Study in The Netherlands, Business Agility and Information Technology Diffusion - IFIP TC8 WG 8.6 International Working Conference May 8-11, 2005, Atlanta, Georgia, USA, IFIP. Springer, pp. 275–294.

Reich, B.H., Benbasat, I., 1996b. Measuring the linkage between business and information technology objectives. MIS Q. 55–81.

Reix, R., Fallery, B., Kalika, M., Rowe, F., 2016. Systèmes d'information et management. Vuibert.

Silvius, A.G., 2007. Business & IT Alignment in theory and practice, in: System Sciences, 2007. HICSS 2007. 40th Annual Hawaii International Conference On. IEEE, pp. 211b–211b.

Tallon, P.P., Kraemer, K.L., 2003. Investigating the relationship between strategic alignment and IT business value: the discovery of a paradox. Creat. Bus. Value Inf. Technol. Chall. Solut. Hershey PA Idea Group Publ. 1–22.

vargas and al., 2007. Constructing a General Framework Definition of the Business and IT Alignment Concern through

Wegmann, A., Regev, G., Rychkova, I., Cruz, and J.D. de la, Julia, P., 2007. Business and IT Alignment with SEAM for Enterprise Architecture, in: 11th IEEE International Enterprise Distributed Object Computing Conference (EDOC 2007).

Wegmuller, M., Weid, J.P. von der, Oberson, P., Gisin, N., 2000. High Resolution Fiber Distributed Measurements With Coherent OFDR, in: Proc. ECOC'00. p. 109.

STRATEGIES TO IMPROVE QUALITY OF DATA DISSEMINATION WEBSITE: A CASE STUDY OF THE CENTRAL BUREAU OF STATISTICS

Betty Purwandari, Infaz Rizki Adawati, Puspa Indahati Sandhyaduhita and Iis Solichah
Faculty of Computer Science, Universitas Indonesia
Depok 16424, Indonesia

ABSTRACT

E-government facilitates the use of Information Technology to establish government public services. A common feature of e-government is a Website as public portal. One of prominent institutions in Indonesia, which is obliged to provide the Website is the Central Bureau of Statistics. However, a data requirement survey by the Central Bureau of Statistics in 2017 indicated a gap between user expectation and user satisfaction of the Website. Besides, an assessment by the Open Data Inventory (ODIN) indicated that the Website has not met the international Website quality criteria, especially data completeness and data openness measures. To address this problem, a research was conducted to investigate its shortcomings and propose strategies for improvement. The data were collected using questionnaires, which were grouped into the Importance Performance Analysis (IPA) matric quadrants. It was followed by literature studies and interviews with experts in statistical Website to propose improvement strategies. The priority of strategies was compiled using the Quality Functional Deployment (QFD). The results show that the Central Bureau of Statistics are required to optimize the Website code, redesign the Website layout, create statistical data forum, conduct statistical capacity building, and improve the data interoperability. Lesson learned from this research and its findings are potential to be adopted in other emerging economies, which strive to provide qualified data on e-government Websites to their citizens.

KEYWORDS

Website Quality, Importance Performance Analysis, Quality Functional Deployment

1. INTRODUCTION

E-government requires efforts to establish the government services by leveraging the Information Technology and the Internet (Parent, 2005). The use of Information Technology in e-government would ease both the service manager and the service user (Panagiotopoulos, 2012). Through e-government, the government could deliver better, efficient, transparent, and responsible services. Consequently, it will increase citizen participation and trust to the government (Panagiotopoulos, 2012; Parent, 2005).

The Indonesia government has the concern about the e-government, as stated in the President Instruction Number 3, 2003, in the e-government implementation policy and national strategy, that the government should improve the efficiency, effectivity, transparency, and accountability of the public services through e-government (Presiden RI, 2003). It is also stated in the Administrative and Bureaucratic Reform Ministry Regulations, Number 19, 2016, that the ministry supports the use of the Information Technology to improve the public services (Menpan RI, 2016). And it is also stated in the President Regulations, Number 95, 2018, about the electronic based government, that one of the strategy to improve the e-government, the electronic based and public oriented services, is by building a public service portal (Presiden RI, 2018).

In the international, the Open Data Watch (ODW) establishes some assessments to the National Statistics Office (NSO) in various countries (180 countries in 2017), to score the official national statistics as one of the e-government services, based on ten elements of coverage and openness. The resulted score for each country assessed are put in the ODIN (Open Data Inventory). For a country to get the higher score of coverage and openness, should pay attention to the ten elements assessed by the ODW. For Indonesia, the most important layer who is responsible about this score is the Central Bureau of Statistics. Therefore, Indonesia needs to put some efforts to enhance the e-government services of the Central Bureau of Statistics.

The Central Bureau of Statistics is a non-ministry agency whose responsible to establish the governmental works related to statistical data. the Central Bureau of Statistics provides some services to disseminate the statistical data to the data users in two ways: offline and online. The offline service enables users to drop in the Central Bureau of Statistics office to request the needed data offline. However, the online service is very important to support the e-government program. It enables non-staff users to access the statistical data via the Central Bureau of Statistics data dissemination Website and submit a data request via the online forum, while the Central Bureau of Statistics staff users could access the data via the Publication Information System, which is integrated with the Central Bureau of Statistics data dissemination Website. This study takes this Website as a case study to investigate strategies for required improvement to enhance data coverage and openness.

The Central Bureau of Statistics Strategic Plan 2015-2019 states that one of the Central Bureau of Statistics vision is "Improving the prime services to provide the statistical activity results" and that one of the strategic targets is "Improving the quality of user engagement" (Badan Pusat Statistik, 2015). One of the realizations is to disseminate the statistical data via the Central Bureau of Statistics Website. To support its vision, the Central Bureau of Statistics conducted the annual data requirement survey since 2005 to identify the needs and level of satisfaction of the data users, and finally to improve the data dissemination service. The user satisfaction level could be investigated by comparing the service quality to fulfill the user needs and the user expectations (Al-Hawary, S. I. S., 2016).

The data requirement survey measures the level of service importance and the level of user satisfaction using the 1 – 4 Likert scale. The survey results in 2017 (Table 1) shows a gap between the user expectations and the level of user satisfaction in the following aspects: easiness to find data, data completeness, communication between the user and the Central Bureau of Statistics staffs, easiness of Website access, and the tidiness of the Website layouts. It indicates that the Central Bureau of Statistics data dissemination Website still need some improvements to achieve the user expectations.

The ODW assessment also indicated that the Central Bureau of Statistics requires improvement as shown in Figure 1. The Indonesia's Central Bureau of Statistics Website was in the 27th rank of the 180 NSO Websites and in the 2nd rank in the Southeast Asia, after the NSO Singapore Website. Specifically, the Central Bureau of Statistics Website is in the 3rd rank after Singapore and Philippine in the data openness assessment category, in the Southeast Asia (Open Data Watch, 2017). We could conclude that the Central Bureau of Statistics Website has not yet fulfilled the assessment criteria of the ODW.

Similar problems were faced by public sectors in different countries (Hasan L., 2011). Therefore, this investigation was conducted to design strategies to improve quality of the Central Bureau of Statistics data dissemination Website. The processes and findings can be adopted in other countries with similar background to Indonesia. The assessment of a Website's quality is often challenging, as well as important to better meet citizen needs and satisfaction. The research question is then formulated as "How is the Central Bureau of Statistics data dissemination Website improvement strategy design to fulfill the user expectations and the international assessment criteria?"

Table 1. The data requirement survey in 2017 (Badan Pusat Statistik, 2017)

Assessment Aspects	User Expectation	User Satisfaction
Easiness to find the data	3.71	3.01
Public collections completeness	3.64	2.98
Easiness to communicate via email	3.60	3.02
Easiness to obtain the Central Bureau of Statistics products	3.66	3.08
Easiness to access the Central Bureau of Statistics Website	3.74	3.23
the Central Bureau of Statistics data is free from other parties' intervention	3.64	3.19
Easiness to search the publication collections	3.59	3.16
Easiness to communicate via telephone/faximile	3.59	2.99
The availability of complaints procedures	3.54	3.15
The products are tidy and formal	3.30	3.13

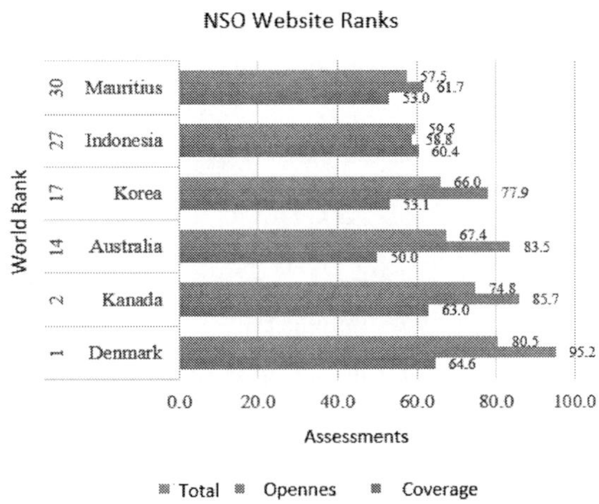

Figure 1. National Statistic Office Website Ranks, Open Data Watch 2017
(Open Data Watch, 2017)

The introduction to this investigation is discussed in section 1. It is followed by theoretical study in section 2 and research methods in section 3. The results are discussed in section 4 and concluded in section 5.

2. THEORETICAL STUDY

2.1 Importance Performance Analysis (IPA)

The Importance Performance Analysis (IPA) is a method of decision making by prioritizing the improvement strategies, determining which organization resources is the most needed by the users. This method is also used to enhance the competitiveness of the organization (Martilla, J.A., 1977; Azzopardi, E., 2013).

The IPA Matric classifies the research attributes into four quadrants:

1. Keep up the good work: The service attributes which lied in this quadrant are the main power of the organization and should be maintained. In this quadrant, the organization has put some amount of resources effectively to fulfill the users' needs.
2. Possible overkill: The service attributes which lied in this quadrant are considered less important by the users, but need some high efforts by the organization. This quadrant shows that the amount of resources in the service could be moved to the other more important services.
3. Low priority: The service attributes which lied in this quadrant are considered less important by the users, while the service quality is also not satisfactory. The organization could ignore these attributes.
4. Concentrate here: This quadrant contains the attributes with the highest priority and the most critical to the organization infestations, while the service quality is still not satisfactory. These attributes could be a threat to the organization if they are not improved. The organization should focus its improvement strategies on these attributes.

2.2 Quality Function Deployment (QFD)

The Quality Function Deployment (QFD) is a systematic design method to improve products, and to help the business to fulfill the users' needs (Chen, Y. T., 2011). It could transform the users' needs into a product or service characteristics specification. The QFD involves four matric in the house of quality which covers six types of needs as follows:

1. The user needs (The what).
2. The evaluation of needs (The why).

3. The technical needs (The how).
4. The relationship matric between the user needs and the technical needs (The what vs the how).
5. The correlation matric, i.e. the relationship matric among the technical needs (The how vs the how)
6. Technical achievements (The how much).

The formulated relationships are then ranked to obtain the highest priority user needs. The QFD could be combined with the other methods to get the better results (Khorshidi, H. A., 2016). The steps to compose the house of quality are as follows (Murali, S., 2016):

1. Identify the user needs (the whats). Obtained from the "concentrate here" and the "keep up the good work" quadrants of the IPA matric.
2. Form the prioritization based on the sum of the importance level values. The QFD scale value is obtained by calculating the average of the importance level values.
3. Identify the improvement strategies to fulfill the users' needs. This could be conducted by some brainstorming and interviews with the organization executives and the other parties involved in providing the services.
4. Develop the relational matric between the what and the how. The relationships between the what and the how are then assessed to identify the relationships between the user needs and the recommended improvement strategies. The strength of the relationship is shown in the value of 0-1-3-9 (from the weakest to the strongest relationship) (Fabiś-domagała, J., 2017).
5. Prioritize the strategies. The value of each of the strategy item is obtained by summing the relational matric result value with the relative weight of the user needs. The highest value is the most important strategy.

2.3 Theoretical Framework

The authors formulate a theoretical framework of this research as shown in Figure 2, containing the following items:

1. Comparing the existing Website quality measurement models

This step is conducted to identify the research dimensions and attributes. The models involved are: the ODIN (Open Data Watch, 2017), the webQual 4.0 (Barnes, S. J., 2005) and the e-GovQual (Papadomichelaki, X., 2012). The identified dimensions and attributes are then used to develop the research questionnaires. The used dimensions are: information quality (Napitupulu, D., 2017), reliability (Papadomichelaki, X., 2012), usability and service interaction (Barnes, S. J., 2005).

2. Regulations

The used dimensions and attributes are the one that is in line with the Central Bureau of Statistics dissemination regulations. Those regulations are:

a. The Law Number 16, 1997 about the statistics.
b. The Law Number 14, 2008 about the public information openness.

3. Data Processing using the IPA Matric.
4. Data Processing using the QFD method.

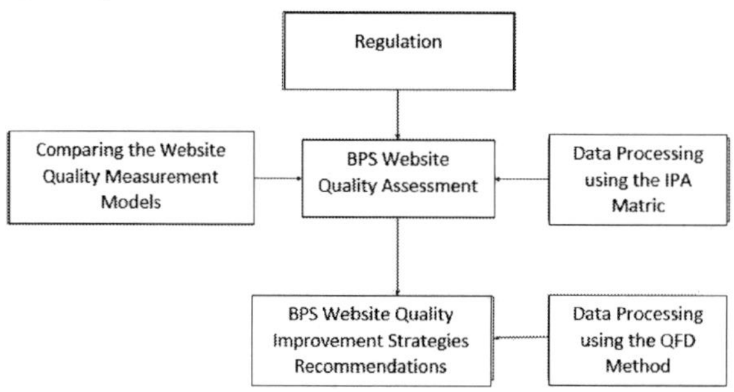

Figure 2. Research Theoretical Framework

3. RESEARCH METHODS

The research methodology in this study is depicted in Figure 3. This research was established by a continuous communication with the Statistics Dissemination Directorate, the Central Bureau of Statistics. The object of research is the Central Bureau of Statistics data dissemination Website. The respondents of this research are selected from the Website user community using the purposive sampling method. The data was collected online from November 23rd to 30th, 2018, using the online Google Forms features. The online questionnaires are distributed via the Email and WhatsApp groups. Several 2.350 user emails are contacted, which are obtained from the Central Bureau of Statistics Website admin.

The questionnaire consists of two main parts: respondent demography and Website quality measurement. The first part contains some questions about the respondent's profile, including some specific questions about their experience in accessing the Central Bureau of Statistics Website, to ensure that the respondents are really the Website users. The second part contains some questions about the following Website quality dimensions: information quality, reliability, usability, and service interaction. There are thirty 1 – 5 Likert scale questions in total. A reliability and validity test were conducted to make sure that all question items are valid.

The IPA Matric is used to create a prioritization of the Website attributes which lied in the "concentrate here" and "keep up the good work" quadrants, as the "what" of the IPA Matric. To produce the "how" of the IPA Matric, i.e. the improvement strategies recommendations, the authors conduct some document studies, literature studies (Kesuma, D. P., 2014), and study the discussions delivered by Head of the Central Bureau of Statistics (Suhariyanto, 2018) and Deputy of Statistics Information Methodology, the Central Bureau of Statistics (Nugraha, M. A., 2018) in the yearly coordination meeting.

The formulated solutions (the improvement strategies recommendations), i.e. "the how" of the QFD Matric are then validated by conducted some interviews with the executives, who are responsible in the Central Bureau of Statistics data dissemination Website management. The improvement strategies recommendations are then processed using the Quality Function Deployment (QFD) method to determine the prioritizations of the strategies. The Relationship and Correlation Matrices are composed by some brainstorming activities involving the authors and the Central Bureau of Statistics Website team.

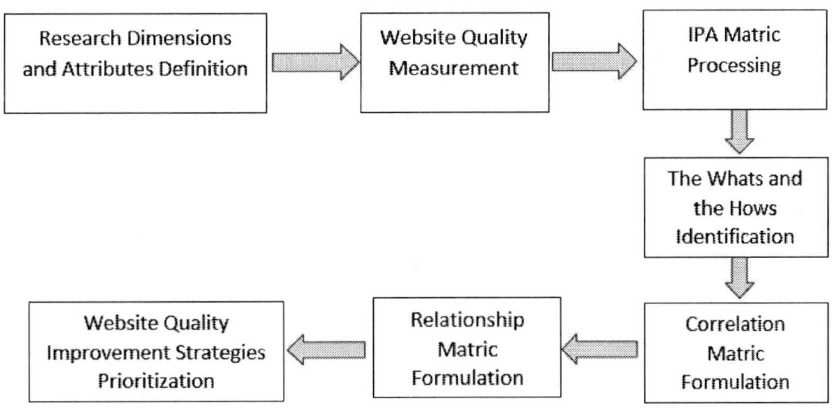

Figure 3. Research Methodology

4. RESULTS

The completeness and consistency of the collected answers from the respondents are investigated to filter which data to be included in the data processing step. Any incomplete, duplicated, or inconsistent data are excluded from the research. All valid answers about the service quality and the level of importance attributes are mapped into the IPA matric quadrants. The average value of each attributes is also calculated, to measure the quality of the Central Bureau of Statistics Website.

The next stage is to design the improvement strategy. The "what" of the IPA Matric as listed in Table 2 shows the Website attributes which need special attention from the Central Bureau of Statistics because those attributes lied in the "concentrate here" and the "keep up the good work" quadrants in the IPA matric. The "hows" of the IPA Matric as listed in Table 3 shows the strategies needed by the Central Bureau of Statistics to improve the quality of the attributes in the "what" part. The "what" and the "how" are treated as the input for composing the Relationship and Correlation Matrices to prioritize the strategies.

The produced Correlation Matric shows that there are some positive relations among the solutions, as follows:

1. "Introduce some statistical data forums" and "Improve the data interoperability"
2. "Introduce some statistical data forums" and "Establish some capacity building activities bringing the statistics topics"
3. "Improve the data interoperability" and "Establish some capacity building activities bringing the statistics topics"
4. "Improve the infrastructure supports" and "Integrate the system databases"
5. "Improve the infrastructure supports" and "Optimize the Website code"
6. "Integrate the system databases" and "Optimize the Website code"
7. "Redesign the Website user interface layout" and "Optimize the Website code"

The produced Relationship Matric as given in Table 4, gives the priorities among the strategies. The higher the value, the higher the priority of the strategy, and vice versa.

Table 2. The What of the IPA Matric Attributes

Dimension	The What Attributes
Information Quality	The format of the provided data is easy to be processed by the computer
	The provided data is complete to the user needs
	The provided data is accurate
	The provided data is easy to be understood
	The provided data is neutral
	The provided data is trusted
	The provided data is up to date
Reliability	The Website could be accessed well using the desktop browser
	The Website could be accessed well using the laptop browser
	The Website could be accessed well using the tablet browser
	The Website could be accessed well smartphone browser
	The Website always successfully appears in the browser in the first access to the www.bps.go.id
	The Website is available and could be accessed anytime it is needed
Usability	The Website is easy to use
	The Website has clear menus and easy to use
	The Website has an effective search feature to help searching certain data
Service Interaction	The user believes that his/her username and password is secure to download the statistics data
	The user believes that his/her private data entried to the Website is saved securely

Table 3. The Hows of the IPA Matric Attributes

Code	Improvement Strategies
TR1	Introduce some statistical data forums
TR2	Improve the data interoperability
TR3	Establish some capacity building activities bringing the statistics topics
TR4	Improve the infrastructure supports
TR5	Elaborate the possibility of using the open data portal in Indonesia
TR6	Establish some surveys on the users' data needs
TR7	Integrate the system databases
TR8	Put the user guideline in the Website
TR9	Optimize the Website code
TR10	Put a data security guarantee statement in the Website
TR11	Redesign the Website User Interface layout

Table 4. The Website Improvement Strategies Prioritization

Priority	Code	Value	Improvement Strategies
1	TR9	27.39	Optimize the Website code
2	TR11	26.28	Redesign the Website User Interface layout
3	TR1	11.44	Introduce some statistical data forums
4	TR3	9.84	Establish some capacity building activities bringing the statistics topics
5	TR2	5.43	Improve the data interoperability
6	TR5	4.93	Elaborate the possibility of using the open data portal in Indonesia
7	TR8	4.88	Put the user guideline in the Website
8	TR10	3.29	Put a data security guarantee statement in the Website
9	TR4	3.27	Improve the infrastructure supports
10	TR6	2.16	Establish some surveys on the users' data needs
11	TR7	1.09	Integrate the system databases

5. CONCLUSIONS

This research integrates the IPA and QFD methods to investigate the prioritization of the Website improvement strategies, by adopting the steps of research conducted by the (Murali, S., 2016) and adding the following improvements:

1. The Murali's research uses the value of 5-3.1-0 to determine the relationship between the problem (the what) and the solution (the how). While the authors use the value of 9-3-1-0, adopted them from the research of (Fabiś-domagala, J., 2017) to show the difference significance among the strategies.
2. The Murali's uses the brainstorming method to collect the how as the organization's technical solution. The brainstorming is conducted between the executive board and the service unit. While in this research, the authors conduct some literature and document studies and then validate the information by some interviews with the organization's experts: the executives, who are responsible in managing the Website.

Based on this research, some improvement strategies are suggested for the Central Bureau of Statistics data dissemination Website. Some suggestions (from the highest to the lowest priority) in the information quality dimension are as follow:

1. Introduce some statistical data forums to accommodate some discussions between the data provider and data users.
2. Establish some capacity building activities bringing the statistics topics.
3. Elaborate the possibility of using the open data portal.
4. Establish some surveys on the users' data needs.
5. Integrate the system databases.

Some suggestions (from the highest to the lowest priority) in the reliability dimension are as follow:

1. Optimize the Website code.
2. Redesign the Website User Interface layout.
3. Improve the supporting infrastructures.

Some suggestions (from the highest to the lowest priority) in the usability dimension are as follow:

1. Put the user guideline in the website.
2. Optimize the Website code.
3. Redesign the Website User Interface layout.

The first suggestion in the service interaction dimension is to show a formal statement from the Central Bureau of Statistics, which guarantees the security of the users' privacy data. The second one is to review and analyze the Website code to improve the Website security.

This study also suggests some recommendations for further related research:

1. Conduct a depth analysis to overcome the IPA quadrant's border determination problem. So far, the attributes which are lied on the border of two quadrants in the IPA matric are difficult to interpret (Azzopardi, E., 2013).
2. Include not only the government regulations which are related to data view, but also the one related to the government Website management.
3. Conduct some data triangulation to verify the validity of the experts' explanations in the interviews, and to enrich the research discussions.

This research is limited to the data dissemination Website of the Central Bureau of Statistics in Indonesia. However, the processes and findings have potential contribution to meet the gap of references on e-government Website quality advancement, especially in the developing world.

ACKNOWLEDGMENT

This publication is supported by the PIT 9 grant, Universitas Indonesia (NKB-0006/UN2.R3.1/HKP.05.00/2019).

REFERENCES

Al-Hawary, S. I. S., & Al-menhaly, S. M, 2016. The Quality of E-Government Services and its Role on Achieving Beneficiaries Satisfaction. *Global Journal of Management and Business Research: A Administration and Management*, 16(11).

Azzopardi, E., & Nash, R., 2013. A critical evaluation of importance-performance analysis. *Tourism Management*, 35, 222–233. https://doi.org/10.1016/j.tourman.2012.07.007

Badan Pusat Statistik, 2015. *Rencana Strategis (Renstra) Badan Pusat Statistik (BPS)* 2015-2019.

Badan Pusat Statistik, 2017. *Analisis Hasil Survei Kebutuhan Data*, XXXIII(2), 81–87.

Barnes, S. J., & Vidgen, R. T., 2005. Data triangulation in action: using comment analysis to refine web quality metrics. *Ecis*, (2005), 24.

Chen, Y. T., & Chou, T. Y. (2011). Applying GRA and QFD to Improve Library Service Quality. *Journal of Academic Librarianship*, 37(3), 237–245. https://doi.org/10.1016/j.acalib.2011.02.016

Fabiś-domagała, J., 2017. Quality function deployment method for selected Website usability analysis. *Czasopismo Techniczne*, 9, 165–171. https://doi.org/10.4467/2353737XCT.17.157.7169

Hasan, L., & Abuelrub, E., 2011. Assessing the quality of web sites. *Applied Computing and Informatics*, 9(1), 11–29. https://doi.org/10.1016/j.aci.2009.03.001

Kesuma, D. P., 2014. Integrating E-SERVQUAL and Kano Model into Quality Function Deployment to Improve Website Service Quality: An Application to University's Website, 35. https://doi.org/10.4018/978-1-4666-9764-5.ch003

Khorshidi, H. A., et al, 2016. Statistical process control application on service quality using SERVQUAL and QFD with a case study in trains' services. *TQM Journal*, 28(2), 195–215. https://doi.org/10.1108/TQM-02-2014-0026

Martilla, J. A., & James, J. C., 1977. Importance-Performance Analysis. *Journal of Marketing*, 41(1), 77. https://doi.org/10.2307/1250495

Menpan RI, 2016. Peraturan Menteri Pendayagunaan Aparatur Negara dan Reformasi Birokrasi Republik Indonesia Nomor 19 Tahun 2016, 1–20.

Murali, S., et al, 2016. Integration of IPA and QFD to assess the service quality and to identify after sales service strategies to improve customer satisfaction - A case study. *Production Planning and Control*, 27(5), 394–407. https://doi.org/10.1080/09537287.2015.1129463

Napitupulu, D., 2017. Analysis of Factors Affecting The Website Quality (Study Case: XYZ University). *International Journal on Advanced Science, Engineering and Information Technology*, 7(3), 792. https://doi.org/10.18517/ijaseit.7.3.1748

Nugraha, M. A., 2018. *Upaya Sinkronisasi Data Statistik Sektoral melalui Penerapan Prinsip-Prinsip Satu Data*. Jakarta: Badan Pusat Statistik

Open Data Watch, 2017. 2017 *Methodology Report of Open Data Inventory*. Akron, Inc.

Panagiotopoulos, P., et al, 2012. A business model perspective for ICTs in public engagement. *Government Information Quarterly*, *29*(2), 192–202. https://doi.org/10.1016/j.giq.2011.09.011

Papadomichelaki, X., & Mentzas, G., 2012. E-GovQual: A multiple-item scale for assessing e-government service quality. *Government Information Quarterly*, 29(1), 98–109. https://doi.org/10.1016/j.giq.2011.08.011

Parent, M., et al, 2005. Building citizen trust through e-government. *Government Information Quarterly*, *22*(4), 720–736. https://doi.org/10.1016/j.giq.2005.10.001

Presiden RI, 2003. Instruksi Presiden Republik Indonesia Nomor 3 tahun 2003. *Istr*, (Undang-Undang Informasi dan Transaksi Elektronik), 1–25.

Presiden RI, 2018. Peraturan Presiden Republik Indonesia Nomor 95 Tahun 2018 tentang Sistem Pemerintahan Berbasis Elektronik.

Suhariyanto, Kecuk., 2018. *Sambutan Kepala BPS dalam Rakor Pusdatin dan Diskominfotik*. Jakarta: Badan Pusat Statistik.

EXPLORING CONSULTANTS' ROLE IN ERP SYSTEMS IMPLEMENTATIONS

Raniin Chantel Baker and Moutaz Haddara
Department of Technology, Krisitiania University College
Chrisitian Krohgs gate 32, 0186 Oslo, Norway

ABSTRACT

This paper reviews the extant literature on Enterprise Resource Planning (ERP) systems consultants and investigates if their role change after their implementation in organizations. In ERP implementations, the consultant role is usually divided into different domains. For example, a financial and accounting functional consultants capture the clients' requirements and guide their clients on the best practices and ensure the compliance with standards and accounting principles, while the technical consultants help in the actual technical installation, integration and testing of the system. In general, the primary role of an ERP consultant is to lead an organisation through the transition to an ERP system environment. An ERP consultant is also a person who has various set of skills and expertise across different domains.
In this research, we investigate the under-researched area of consultants' roles in the ERP realm. Specifically, we attempt to investigate the changes in consultants' roles before, during, and post ERP adoptions.

KEYWORDS

ERP Systems, Adoption, Consultant Role, Literature Review

1. INTRODUCTION

For decades, the enterprise resource planning (ERP) systems have received substantial attention in the research community. ERP systems are large and complex systems, which require knowledge and expertise in many different domains and across various fields of business (Demi & Haddara, 2018). One of the major cost components in ERP systems are the consultants (Haddara, 2011), therefore it is important to understand their role in the process when a company embarks to deploy an ERP system. In the late 1800s, the consulting role grew with a main focus on technical research areas. After that, there was an increased demand for finance, strategy and organisation consultancy during the early 1900s (McKenna, 1995). By 1990s the consulting growth was primarily focused on both information technology (IT) and strategy development and advice (Wikipedia Contributors, 2019). During the dot-com bubble in 2001, the consulting industry stagnated for a short period and rose again after 2003 (McKenna, 2003). In our modern world, with the rise of social media, cloud-based implementations and Internet of thing (IoT) technology emergence, the consultant role has morphed and changed. Traditionally, the ERP consultants' role was mainly to technically implement systems that meet the organizations' demands, but now the consultant's role is more focused into guiding organizations on how to use these systems in the best practice possible (McKenna, 2003).

The objective of this paper is to review the consultants' role before, during and after ERP systems go-live through a focus on consulting history and change management and the role an ERP consultant plays in a radical redesign of an organisation. One of the most important benefits of an ERP consultant is the ability to transfer knowledge from consultant to staff, which if done correctly, will enable companies to become self-reliant. These topics were the most discussed in the selected literature chosen for this review. In order to increase the comprehension of the ERP consultant role, two interviews with two consultants in a leading international ERP vendor in Norway were conducted.

The rest of the paper is organized as follows. The next section presents the research methodology adopted in this research. Section 3 illustrates an overview of the selected articles. Section 4 demonstrates the main findings, followed by a discussion in section 5. Finally, a conclusion is provided in section 6.

2. RESEARCH METHODOLOGY AND ARTICLES OVERVIEW

In extant literature, a gap exists in research on post-ERP implementations in general (Haddara & Hetlevik, 2016), and specifically on the consultant's role before versus post the ERP go-live. The objective of this paper is to review the ERP consultant's role before, during and after the ERP system is up and running.

Literature reviews exemplify a well-established method for accretion of existing knowledge within a domain of interest. In this article we have adopted a systematic review method (Watson, 2015). This method is ruminated by implementing perspicuous procedures and conditions, which potentially minimize researcher's bias (Bryman, 2012). The search for papers included in this literature review was conducted using Google Scholar. At first, the searches in the databases were narrowed by looking at articles published in renowned journals in the field of information systems. The journals selected were primarily the basket of eight journals listed in the "Senior Scholars' Basket of Journals" published on the Association for Information Systems (AIS) website. The search keywords used when researching papers were "Consultant ERP", and "Consultant Enterprise Resource Planning System". In addition, other keywords were also used in conjunction with the previous key terms, like "implementation" "post-implementation", "Selection", "adoption", and "shakedown phase". In addition, only peer-reviewed articles written within the period 1995-2019 were included in this research. The mentioned criteria resulted in a very low number of articles. So, in order to broaden the scope of the literature review, we then extended the search keywords to include more broad combinations of terms like " Consultant Enterprise Systems", "Consultant role in Information Systems", "Consultant History" and others. After identifying some more articles, we have also scanned the references of these articles to pinpoint more research that we might have overlooked. This also made us able to review more studies, which some have been published in conferences/journals outside the IS field, like change management. This resulted in a significant number of article results that was more than 250 potential articles. The authors then glanced through the articles' abstracts and conclusions and have excluded various papers, which were not directly addressing the impact/role of consultants during ERP systems implementations. Thirty-two candidate articles remained after the first iteration. In the next phase, the authors read all of the 32 articles, which resulted in further exclusion of some papers, which the content turned out to be out of scope of this review. The authors then read the papers and classified them by their main topic in focus as shown in figure 1. It is important to note that some articles covered more than on topic or theme. In total, 18 articles were identified and reviewed in this research, including more general papers on the consultants' role in information systems' adoptions, and consultation history in organizations. As mentioned earlier, the focus of this research is on consultant role when a company embarks to deploy an ERP system. The consultant′ role in ERP implementation depends on the level of involvement of the consultant in a project. The more control a client company has, the less involved a consultant is (Heines and Goodhue, 2000). Having said that, it depends on the vendor, the client and the implementation partner, on how they can agree on the terms.

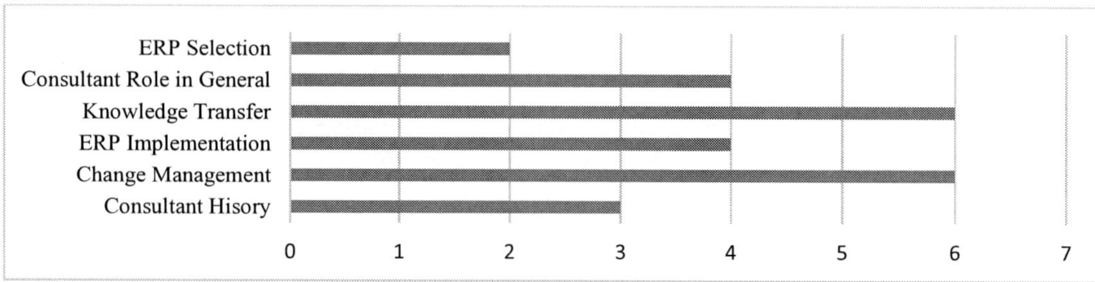

Figure 1. An Overview of Main Themes and Number of Reviewed Articles

Additionally, the first author conducted two qualitative interviews (Bryman, 2012) with two ERP consultants in an international ERP vendor in Norway. The interviews were digitally recorded, and transcribed, and relative sections were then included in this article. The participation of the ERP consultants aided in shedding more light on the modern ERP consultant role. The interview questions that were asked were mainly based on the ERP lifecycle model (Esteves & Pastor, 1999), and other topics like change management, and scope and commitment. The main questions that were asked were:

- What is the main role of ERP consultants?
- Does the consultant's role change after the ERP go-live?
- Do you help with the company's strategy? Alternatively, is it just training the system?
- Do you decide the role you undertake when starting a project or does the client decide your role?

3. FINDINGS

In general, the consultant's work is divided into different expertise and areas, like finance and accounting, human resources, technical implementation, and others. While ERP systems' literature is rich, however, papers focusing on the role of consultants in adoption projects are rare. Thus, identifying papers that could cover our review objectives was challenging regarding the limited literature about the topic. Our findings include the background history of consulting, the role of consultancy in different areas, and the role of consultancy in the ERP domain in specific. Table 1 presents our findings from the 18 sources in a chronological order from 1995 to 2018. The majority of the articles suggest that the role that consultants play is crucial as it is one of the success factors for implementing an ERP, but not much of these articles go in-depth on the exact role of these ERP consultants. However, the interviews provided more background information that compliments this paper.

Table 1. Overview of Articles and their Main Focus

Article	**Short Description**
McKenna (1995)	This paper describes the history of consulting, with a focus on management consulting. It also argues for the reasons that led to the growth of the consulting business after 1920.
Bessant & Rush (1995)	This article views the consultants' role regarding process transfer and the policy mechanism which enable it to proceed effective. It focuses on the role of consultancy in the innovation process within organizations. The authors present ten types of consultancy from the traditional consultancy aspect.
Canback (1999)	The article presents the history of consultancy and argues why management consulting is so important and explains it through the transaction cost theory. Moreover, the author develops illustrates potential scenarios for the future industry evolution and management consulting.
Esteves & Pastor (1999)	This paper presents a suggested ERP life-cycle model that includes 6 phases, which an organization goes through during the adoption of ERP systems. The paper also illustrates four dimensions in which they shed the light on the consultant's role during the implementation phase and change management efforts.
Westrup & Knight (2000)	This paper investigates how consultants´ change and shape the way in which ERP Systems are seen and implemented by viewing five types of organizational knowledge.
Adam & O'doherty (2000)	This article examines the key relationship between client organizations and their ERP implementing partners, in particular SMEs in Ireland.
Heines & Goodhue (2000)	The paper investigates the role of the vendor, the organization and the consultants in implementing an ERP system and the knowledge impact that these three parties have on the implementation.
Caldas & Wood (2000)	The paper discusses how consultants should enter the ERP world and how they would be a big part of ERP implementation. in the paper also presents the advantages and cons of ERP consultancy. In addition, the paper discusses whether ERP consultants should work on widening the project's scope to sell more services, or mainly focus on their main tasks.

Pereira (2001)	The article sheds light on five important roles that interplay between use of information systems and organizational change.
Askenäs & Westelius (2003).	The article examines five roles in the use ERP systems that provides organizational change. One of them is the consultant role in change management.
McKenna et al. (2003)	The article investigates modern management consulting activities in the era of globalization. They argue that some scholars claim that management consultants aid when there is a shortage of internal expertise within organizations. Otherwise, other researchers argue that consultants serve as scapegoats in situations that require difficult decisions, as a tool for risk sharing.
Zimmerman & Smedley (2006)	This article discusses the implementation of ERP systems and how organizations should adjust to changes. The paper focuses on the role of consultants in knowledge transfer and management.
Sturdy et al. (2009)	The article discusses consultancy and knowledge. Examines two dominant images of the role of consultants. The innovator and legitimating client knowledge.
Koh et al. (2009)	The paper argues about the necessity of investing in training and consultancy for reaching a successful implementation of ERP systems in SMEs.
Lunenburg (2010)	The article highlights the importance of consultants as change agents. It divides them into 4 types, with 3 roles and 10 characteristics.
Christensen et al. (2013).	The authors discuss how tech-disruption has caused changes in consultants' role. They also argue that the consultation industry is now faced with same disruption forces that are starting to impact the consulting industry, with intense implications for its future.
Haddara (2014)	This paper demonstrates the consultants' role during the ERP system selection phase within organizations. The article also provides evaluation criteria for ERP system selection.
Hustad et al. (2016)	The article presents a case study in which it demonstrates the role of functional consultants in ERP system customizations. In addition, the article discusses the impact of customizations on organization in case of misalignment with clients' requirements.
Haddara (2018)	The paper provides a case study on ERP selection efforts within a multinational organization. The paper argues on how international data exchange regulations (e.g. GDPR) can affect the consultants' selection process and criteria.

3.1 The Consultants' Role Throughout History

Greiner and Metzger (1983) defined consulting as an advisory service based on a contract and provisioned to organizations by experienced and qualified individuals who can aid clients in an objective and autonomous manner. Also, they assist client organizations in identifying their problems and requirements, recommend a solution to these problems, and aid in the enactment of solutions (Greiner & Metzger, 1983).

In specific, an ERP consultant is either an independent consultant or an employee who is employed in a company that is hired to do any of the following activities: select, implement, upgrade, or support an ERP system. The main role of an ERP consultant is to help organizations move from the current state to an ERP system. An effective ERP consultant is capable of understanding clients' business process, in order to establish where ERP systems would be most beneficial (King, 2012). Figure 2 below, depicts a timeline of the important events in the consulting world, gathered through the various articles that were reviewed in this paper. In general, the topics from the selected articles are much related to the general consultant's role within organizations. Often each vendor, consultancy firm or client agree on terms on the level of involvement from each partner regarding the modules to be implemented, implementing methodology, level of customization, and change management. Change management in particular was the focus of several papers in literature. Change management is required when an organisation is going through a radical redesign of their process and IT/IS infrastructure. This dimension refers to the body of knowledge that is used to guarantee that a compound change, like that associated with an implementation of a large system, obtains the right results, within the planned deadline, and at the estimated budget (Holland & Davis, 1998 in Esteves & Pastor, 1999). Opportunities for management consulting arise not only in IT-related consulting but also in change management (Miguel Caldas, 2000). The ERP consultant plays a large role in change management during ERP adoption projects (Lunenburg, 2010). An ERP consultant also helps with the planning, implementing and following-up changes in the ERP system during the project (Westrup and Knight, 2000). ERP projects are complex, and introduce changes in business processes and organizational structures. Thus, they require reliance on much different expertise, often found outside the client organisation (McKenna et al., 2003). In the ERP system adoption project, the environment of the project usually involves three parties: the client - the company that needs the ERP, the vendor, which sells the ERP software, and the consultant/the implementation partner. In some cases, the company does not need a partner; in which the vendor will provide consultants that could help with the implementation process in that case (Haddara, 2018). The need for consultants that can guide the company through the implementation process is critical, whether it comes from the vendor's or the implementation partner's side (Haddara, 2014).

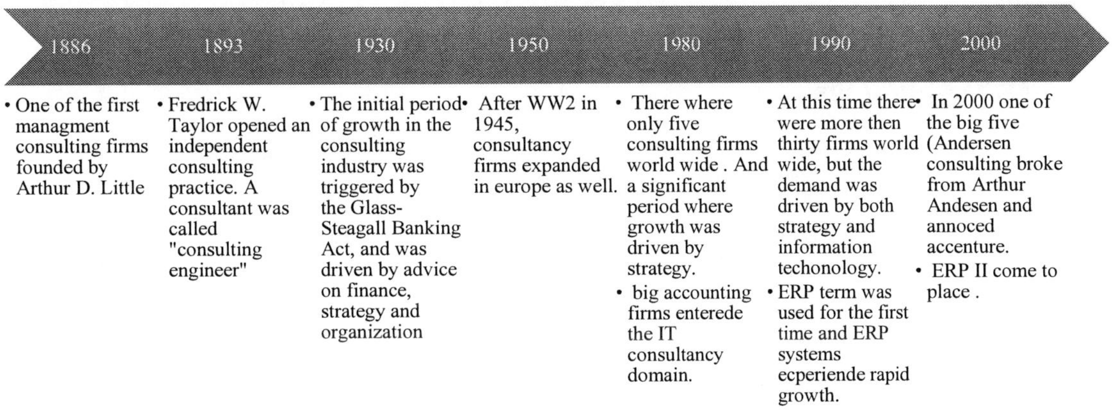

Figure 2. Milestones in the Consulting World's History

3.2 ERP Life Cycle Phases – Implementation- The Impact of the Consultant

When implementing an ERP system, it is necessary to adopt a life-cycle model. This is important for companies to know the status of the project, and to know which phase they are currently at, and also to be able to calculate the time, the needs and budget for consultants. The phases of the ERP life-cycle consist of several stages that an ERP system goes through during its whole life within the hosting organisation (Esteves and Pastor, 1999). One of them is the selection phase. The selection phase is the stage in which the organization evaluates the different ERP packages and vendors who meet its needs, budget, and requirements (Haddara, 2014). It is considered as a critical phase, as selecting the wrong ERP may lead to complete project failures or cancellations (Elragal & Haddara, 2013). Another important stage is the implementation phase, which is the actual installation of the system. This phase consists of the customisation or parameterisation and adaptation of the ERP package acquired according to the needs of the organisation. Usually, this phase is accomplished with the help of consultants who provide implementation methodologies, know-how, and adequate training (Esteves and Pastor, 1999). In the implementation phase, the impact of the consultant is imperative. Since an ERP project can take up to two years, especially large projects, the implementation partner usually has a "hands on" involvement. The consultants will solve issues regarding the ERP system and aid in ensuring that the implementation process is progressing as planned. Hence, the level of the consultants' experience and knowledge play a paramount role in applying this knowledge to the client organisation (Westrup and Knight, 2000).

3.3 Knowledge Transfer and Information Usage

Knowledge transfer in organization is a very important process during and post ERP implementations (Haddara & Hetlevik, 2016). Most of the studies reviewed discuss knowledge transfer in organizations and look at the consultant as knowledge transfer medium and catalyst. Knowledge management (KM) is the process of creating, sharing, using and managing knowledge and information of an organisation (Girard, 2015). It refers to a multidisciplinary approach to achieving organisational objectives by making the best use of knowledge, and can be achieved through different types of mechanisms, like communities of practice (Haddara & Hetlevik, 2016). Knowing how to create information that people can use and rely on is within an area that has come to be known as knowledge management (Zimmerman& Smedley, 2006). Similarly knowing how to transfer knowledge to others is an essential part of a consultant's role. From the KM perspective, consultants now work across different expertise when hired to help implement an ERP system, using for instance their IT- and financial skills so the client can benefit from using the ERP system in the best practice feasible. Zimmerman& Smedley (2006) support that argument and stress about the importance of the consultant's role in the implementation and post-implementation phases of the ERP system. The consultant should not only have knowledge concerning the system but also have communication skills, good language capability, industry knowledge and business analytical skills (Wong et al., 2005). Having and managing knowledge across these different domains help the consultant to perform in the best way possible.

3.4 Other Findings

The findings here are from the interviews conducted with two ERP consultants. One consultant was asked the main consultant role in ERP implementations. *"Before ERP adoptions, companies usually used multiple systems, and these may have functioned in isolation (like a silo) and therefore did not provide a comprehensive overview or overall image of the company's value chain. Now with ERP systems, one will be able to look at the entire company's value chain, so in this way, more consultants with different backgrounds and various expertise will be needed to implement a proper ERP system project."* (Consultant 1). Another question was if the consultant usually aids in the client's organization strategy. *"We do not help the in the company's strategy (as far as I know), but what we do is to emphasise that switching systems must be anchored from top management level and down to the users of the system. Since we have a standardised system, we map how the processes in the company work and what changes they should make in order to work optimised in our system. In addition to training, as I would say it is very important."* (Consultant 2). Traditionally, the consultant has served as a bridge between information and knowledge. Do you feel that this role is still existent during and post ERP implementations? *"I would say that this remains to some extent. Experienced consultants who work with us usually have the knowledge and previous experience with what works and what does not work. In this way, a consultant may in some cases act as a "counsellor" for any company that may need guidance or best practice advice."* (Consultant 2).

One of the consultants (Consultant 1) elaborated that *"each consultant gets assigned a module that they are going to specialise in. Those who work with payroll and accounting modules usually have a background in finance, but not all of them can advise on the economic situation of an organisation. While consultants who work with import and integration, as I do, could have a different area of expertise. However, since an ERP system is a standard database serving multiple functional areas in an organisation, basic financial skills are always an advantage."* Furthermore, both consultants explained that when initialling an agreement with an organisation, the client and the consultant work together from the implementation phase all the way to "go-live" phase. The consultant will also be the client's contact person as long as the customer relationship is active. However, this will vary from consultant level and area of expertise; often the principal consultant will participate in the entire journey. The presales consultants who are part of the sales phases will keep in contact with the client until the customer goes live. Part of the preparation for the presales consultant is how to precisely map out *what* is not working, *why* it is not working and *how* implementing the ERP system can solve it. Performance improvement is defined in many ways, but often a customer will get a lower cost, increased control and overview, and processes go faster than before, resulting in saved hours.

4. DISCUSSION

The objective of this paper was to examine the consultant's role in ERP adoption projects. Since the birth of consultancy in 1886, the consultant role in general did not face radical changes. Various articles view a consultant as an expert "outsider", helping organisations use internal information in the best way possible. Due to World War Two, and the growth of military contractors and the subsequent economic growth, the number of consulting firms grew from 400 – 1000, in 1940-1950. By 1950, and IT consulting grew as mainframe computers began to emerge (McKenna, 1995). A consultant's job was much involved in strategic planning, financial advice and accounting. The big five, now the big four entered the IT consulting arena around 1980. Even at that time IT consultants also were called "consulting engineers" and helped with system installations. Until 1999, there remained a certain doubt about the consultant growth, even though organisations such as the big five had adopted consulting in finance, strategy and IT consultancy domain. Canback (1999) argues that many sceptics were not sure if consultants did add real value, while some companies kept using consultants as outsider experts. However, in literature the consultancy is usually viewed as a critical success factor in ERP system implementations (Haddara, 2018).

So, what do ERP consultants actually do? According to our findings, ERP consultants aid organizations during the various ERP lifecycle phases. From the initial phases like the adoption and ERP selection phases, all the way to the post implementation phases. Hence, an ERP consultant should have different areas of expertise and also different set of skills. The skills set should include communication, conflict management, and analytical skills, among others. The role played by consultants in ERP implementations has also been questioned in some papers, and the reason for that might be that the tasks of a consultant could somehow be unclear in some situations, or sometimes the consultants are viewed as scapegoats for clients facing complex decision. In addition, there could be a mismatch between the client and the consultant, as demonstrated through the agency and transaction cost theories (Bahli & Rivard, 2003). As illustrated in the interviews, each consultant takes part in different phases. We could look at consulting as a cycle, which includes presales consultants that pitch the idea to a client, and other consultants involved in contracting, information gathering, analysis and reporting, action planning, and other serve as the implementation team (that is also divided by their area of expertise). It is important to keep in mind that an ERP consultant can be hired for an extended period, unlike the traditional management consultant. It is thus important for clients to choose the right implementation partner as choosing the ERP system that fits the company. Experienced consultants can play an essential role in improving organisations if both parties are entirely engaged in the process.

As for the consultant, they have to know that they are a part of a radical change that is about to happen for the client company. Consultants are expert outsiders with a new and fresh view, and their job is to make that change as sophisticated as possible. They are sitting with the knowledge, and the information about the system and it is their job to apply that knowledge and share that information in the best way possible.

5. CONCLUSION

There are different descriptions in the term *consultant,* to this date, the consultant's role has become more technical. Pre-ERP implementations, various department and divisions often had their systems and processes isolated. An ERP system in the broader definition, will integrate data and processes, and make information for the entire business available. As for an ERP consultant, it is not just about knowing technology, finance, or logistics. An ERP consultant also needs to be a ripple of change in the business processes in the company. Along with being a catalyst between business and technology, an ERP consultant should also need to manage knowledge transfer since implementing an ERP system can be a significant change for a company. During this research attempted to gain a better understanding on the various roles a consultant can play in the ERP systems life-cycle. Due to the scarce research in the ERP consultancy area, it is then recommended that other studies investigate the ERP consultancy domain in more depth, and also evaluate the impact of new technologies, like cloud ERP systems on the ERP consultants' roles.

REFERENCES

Adam, F., and O'Doherty, P. "Lessons from enterprise resource planning implementations in Ireland–towards smaller and shorter ERP projects." *Journal of information technology*15.4 (2000): 305-316.

Askenäs, L., and Westelius, A. "Five roles of an information system: a social constructionist approach to analyzing the use of ERP systems." *Proceedings of the twenty first international conference on Information systems.* Association for Information Systems, 2000.

Bahli, B., & Rivard, S. (2003). The information technology outsourcing risk: a transaction cost and agency theory-based perspective. *Journal of Information Technology*, *18*(3), 211-221.

Bessant, J., and Rush, H. "Building bridges for innovation: the role of consultants in technology transfer." *Research policy* 24.1 (1995): 97-114.

Bryman, A. Social research methods: OUP Oxford; 2012.

Caldas, M. P., and Wood, T. "How consultants can help organizations survive the ERP frenzy." *Paper submitted to the Managerial Consultation Division of the Academy of Management, Chicago* (1999).

Canback, S. "The logic of management consulting: Part 2." *Consulting to Management* 10.3 (1999): 3.

Christensen, C. M., Wang, D., and Bever, D. V. "Consulting on the Cusp of Disruption." *Harvard business review*91.10 (2013): 106-114.

Demi, S., & Haddara, M. (2018). Do Cloud ERP Systems Retire? An ERP Lifecycle Perspective. *Procedia Computer Science*, 138, 587-594.

Elragal, A., & Haddara, M. (2013). The impact of ERP partnership formation regulations on the failure of ERP implementations. *Procedia Technology, 9*, 527-535.

Esteves, J., and Pastor, J. "An ERP lifecycle-based research agenda." *1st International Workshop in Enterprise Management & Resource Planning*. 1999.

Greiner, L. E., & Metzger, R. O. (1983). *Consulting to management*. Prentice-Hall.

Girard, J., and Girard, J. "Defining knowledge management: Toward an applied compendium." *Online Journal of Applied Knowledge Management* 3.1 (2015): 1-20.

Haddara, M. (2011). ERP adoption cost factors in SMEs. *In European and Mediterranean Conference on Information Systems (EMCIS 2011)*, Athens, Greece.

Haddara, M. (2014). ERP selection: the SMART way. *Procedia Technology, 16*, 394-403.

Haddara, M. (2018). ERP systems selection in multinational enterprises: a practical guide. *International Journal of Information Systems and Project Management, 6*(1), 43-57.

Haddara, M, & Hetlevik, T. (2016). Investigating the Effectiveness of Traditional Support Structures & Self-organizing Entities within the ERP Shakedown Phase. *Procedia Computer Science*, 100, 507-516.

Heines, N. M., and Goodhue, L. D. ERP Implementations: "The role of implementation partners and knowledge transfer" Av Information Resources Management Association. International Conference (2000): 34-40.

Hustad, E., Haddara, M., & Kalvenes, B. (2016). ERP and organizational misfits: An ERP customization journey. *Procedia Computer Science, 100*, 429-439.

King, A. (2012). What is an ERP Consultant? *Retrieved from ERP Software Blog website*: https://www.erpsoftwareblog.com/2012/06/what-is-an-erp-consultant/

Koh, S. C. L., A. Gunasekaran, and J. R. Cooper. "The demand for training and consultancy investment in SME-specific ERP systems implementation and operation." *International journal of production economics* 122.1 (2009): 241-254.

Lunenburg, F. C. "Managing change: The role of the change agent." *International Journal of Management, Business and Administration* 13.1 (2010): 1-6.

McKenna, C. D. "The origins of modern management consulting." *Business and Economic History* (1995): 51-58.

McKenna, C., Djelic, M. L., & Ainamo, A. (2003). *Message and Medium: The Role of Consulting Firms in Globalization and its Load Interpretation* in: Globalization and Institutions, chapter 4 Edward Elgar Publishing.

Pereira, R. E. "An Action-Oriented Perspective of Information Systems in Organizations." *INFORMING SCIENCE*4.3 (2001): 105-114.

Sturdy, A., Clark, T., Fincham, R., and Handley, K. "Between innovation and legitimation—boundaries and knowledge flow in management consultancy." Organization 16, no. 5 (2009): 627-653.

Watson, R. T. (2015). Beyond being systematic in literature reviews in IS. Journal of Information Technology, 30(2), 185-187.

Werr, A. (2005). Consultant supported ERP implementation–a learning opportunity. Stockholm School of Economics. Stockholm. (SSE/EFI Working Paper Series in Business Administration, 2005: 3).

Westrup, C., and Knight, F. "Consultants and Enterprise Resource Planning (ERP) systems." ECIS 2000 Proceedings (2000): 178.

Wikipedia contributors. (2019, March 16). Management consulting. In Wikipedia, The Free Encyclopedia. Retrieved March 26, 2019, from https://en.wikipedia.org/w/index.php?title=Management_consulting&oldid=888089363

Wong, A., Chau, P. Y. K., Scarbrough, H., & Davison, R. (2005). Critical failure factors in ERP implementation. In *9th Pacific Asia Conference on Information Systems: I.T. and Value Creation, PACIS 2005*

Zimmerman, E., and Smedley, J. "ERP Implementations–a never ending story?." *IRIS 29, Paradigms Politics Paradoxes, 29th Information Systems Research Seminar in Scandinavia, August 12-15 2006, Helsingør, Denmark.* IRIS, 2006.

THE ROLE OF E-LEADERSHIP IN RELATION TO IT CAPABILITIES AND DIGITAL TRANSFORMATION

Pascal Ravesteijn and Guido Ongena
HU University of Applied Sciences, Research Group Process Innovation and Information Systems
Heidelberglaan 15, Utrecht, The Netherlands

ABSTRACT

In this research we examine the relationship between IT capability and digital transformation as well as the influence of digital leadership. A theoretical framework was developed to explain the effect of digital leadership. Subsequently this was tested using a survey of 127 respondents from firms across Western Europe. Consistent with our proposed model, this study finds that both IT capability and e-leadership positively influence digital transformation. However, there is mediating effect of e-leadership on the relation between IT capabilities and digital transformation.

KEYWORDS

Digital Leadership, IT Capability, Digital Transformation, e-Competence

1. INTRODUCTION

In today's digital society organizations can no longer ignore the range of new technologies that are available and can be used to improve or innovate its business (processes), products and/or services. Information technology capabilities can increase performance and be an enabler for innovation (Mithas, et al., 2011; Nwankpa & Roumani, 2016). Furthermore, IT capabilities can also improve an organization's digital transformation readiness (Anand, Oriani, & Vassolo, 2010; Nwankpa & Roumani, 2016). However, to meet the challenges related to digital transformation employees need the right e-skills, and according to Hüsing et al. (2013) many European organizations don't have the correct set of competences available. This is specifically true at the management and leadership level of organizations. Organizations need digital leaders that can develop a digital strategy which enables the organization to digitally transform. While, a large amount of research is available on the topic of digital leadership and also on IT capabilities and digital transformation, empirical research that combines these three concepts is very limited. Therefore, the objective of this research is to determine the influence of e-leadership related competences on IT capabilities and digital transformation readiness.

2. LITERATURE REVIEW

In this section the topics of e-leadership (including e-competences and more specifically the European e-competence framework), IT capabilities, and digital transformation are discussed. For this review the following academic search engines were used: EBSCO, AIS library, HUGO (cross-database search engine of our university) and Google Scholar. Search terms and keywords included: leadership, innovation leadership, eleadership, e-leadership, digital leadership, digital transformation, digital competence, e-CF, European e-Competence Framework, information technology, IT, IT and organization, IT capabilities, technology capability, and IT leadership. Finally, the number of papers was narrowed to articles that had ten or more citations.

2.1 e-Leadership

Definitions on e-leadership (also referred to as digital leadership) are commonly derived from definitions on leadership in general. Leadership is defined by Prentice (2004) as "*the accomplishment of a goal through the direction of human assistants. The man who successfully marshals his human collaborators to achieve particular ends is a leader*" (p.102). Based on this Avolio, Sosik, Kahai and Baker (2014) define e-leadership as "*a social influence process embedded in both proximal and distal contexts mediated by AIT that can produce a change in attitudes, feelings, thinking, behaviour, and performance*" (p.107), where AIT stands for Advanced Information Technology. Similarly, in the European eSkills VISION project Hüsing et al. (2013) propose that "*e-leadership is the accomplishment of a goal that relies on ICT through the direction of human assistants and uses of ICT*" (p.13).

What sets digital leaders apart from traditional leaders is that they aim for a digital strategy and a culture that enables the organization to digitally transform (Kane, et al., 2015). A strategic mindset is needed combined with the right behavior which leverages organization resources in order to create a meaningful and engaging culture to be able to turn investments in technologies and digital transformation into a competitive advantage (Sheninger, 2014; Westerman, et al., 2014b). However, Hüsing et al. (2013) found that many European organizations don't have the right set of competences which are needed to confront the challenges related to digital transformation. Both managers and employees need e-skills to "*to initiate and guide innovation utilizing ICT*" (Robinson, et al., 2015, p. 53) and therefore Robinson et al. propose the creation of a body of knowledge complemented with a set of competences that can be used to develop e-leadership curricula.

An important part of this body of knowledge is the European e-Competence Framework (e-CF). e-CF is a competency framework specifically developed for the IT domain. While there are other frameworks available for this domain (Plessius & Ravesteyn, 2016), it is a standard which is set by the European Committee for Standardization (CEN, 2016) and therefore needs to be implemented by all EU member states. e-CF consists of 40 competences that can be rated using five proficiency levels ranging from associate to principal (e-CF, 2014). In addition to e-CF 30 ICT role profiles have been developed (CWA 16458-1, 2018) in order to increase transparency of the European ICT Skills landscape. These profiles provide a generic set of roles that are performed by ICT Professionals in (ICT) business processes. For this study the *Digital Transformation Leader* role profile is used to research the impact on IT capabilities and digital transformation readiness. The digital transformation leader is responsible for "*the implementation of the digital transformation strategy of the organisation*" (CWA 16458-1, 2018, pg. 33). The necessary e-competences that are related to this role are derived from e-CF and are as follows: business plan development, architecture design, innovating, business change management, and governance.

2.2 IT Capabilities

Different studies find that strong information technology capabilities increases organizational performance and can be an important enabler for growth and innovation (Mithas, et al., 2011; Nwankpa & Roumani, 2016). Furthermore, Anand, Oriani, and Vassolo (2010) state that IT capabilities benefits digital transformation readiness. However, not everybody agrees with these findings. Coombs and Bierly (2006) state that researchers have not been able to consistently find empirical support for the relation between technological capability and organizational performance. According to Coombs and Bierly the reason for this is the multidimensionality of both technological capability and performance.

Bharadwaj (2000) defined IT capability as an organizations ability to organize and deploy IT-based resources in combination with other resources in the organization. Drnevich and Croson (2013) extended the notion of IT capability as 1) the firm's ability to mobilise and deploy IT based resources, "*creating value in combination with other resources and capabilities, and 2) the firm specific IT enabled knowledge and routines that improve the value of non-IT resources*" (p. 485). In many studies IT capability as a concept is further refined in different sub elements. Lu and Ramamurthy (2011) conceptualize IT capability as a latent construct reflected in three dimensions: IT infrastructure capability (the technological foundation), IT business spanning capability (business–IT strategic thinking and partnership), and IT proactive stance (opportunity orientation). In contrast, Chen and Tsou (2012) state that IT capability consist of four different resources: IT infrastructure, IT business experience, IT relationship resources, and IT human resources.

Nwankpa and Roumani (2016) agree with Lu and Ramamurthy and use their IT capability to research the relationship with firm performance including whether digital transformation influences this relationship (see figure 1).

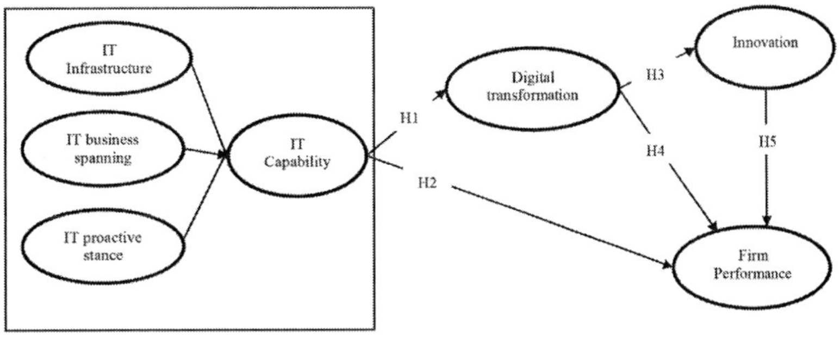

Figure 1. Research Model of Rwankpa & Roumani (2016)

2.3 Digital Transformation

The fast majority of participants in a global survey of managers and executives that is conducted by MIT Sloan Management Review and Deloitte stated that digital technologies will disrupt their business (Kane, Phillips, Kiron & Buckley, 2015). Despite this, only 44% found that their organisation is adequately prepared to face the challenges caused by these new technologies (Kane et al., 2015). Therefore, organizations should strive for additional value creation in their products or services by using new technologies (Matt et al., 2015). Furthermore, customer facing processes should be as digital as possible. Such a transformation towards digital "*constitutes a clear difference to process automation and optimization, since digital transformation strategies go beyond the process paradigm, and include changes to and implications for products, services, and business models as a whole*" (Matt et al., 2015). According to Libert at al. (2016) digital transformation is not about technology, such as cloud computing big data or others, but about the change in the organization based on new technology in business models and processes.

Furthermore, digital transformation is not limited to an organization but can also be viewed from the perspective of societies, industries, networks, economies and individuals (Ismail, Khater & Zaki, 2017). In this study however, the focus is on the organizational perspective. While there is a extensive amount of research on Digital Transformation, Henriette, Feki & Boughzala (2015, p. 10) find that a "rigorous theoretical frame" is lacking. Kutzner, Schoormann & Knackstedt (2018) concur by stating that a holistic structure for the digital transformation domain is still missing. However, according to Ismail et al. (2017) there is a general consent among scholars that digital transformation involves the application of technologies, in an effort to reach superior performance, related to three dimensions: external, internal and holistic (Ismail et al., 2017).

In this research we use the definition of digital transformation by Nwankpa & Roumani (2016) as they have already studied this concept in relation to IT capabilities. Nwankpa & Roumani define digital transformation as "*the changes and transformations that are driven and built on a foundation of digital technologies*" (p.4). Furthermore, in their research the digital transformation construct is specifically linked to technologies such as: big data, analytics, cloud, mobile and social media platform.

2.4 Conceptual Model

For this study a conceptual model is constructed (figure 2) consisting of three constructs. The IT capability and Digital Transformation constructs are based on the research by Nwankpa & Roumani (2016) as depicted in figure 1. Furthermore, an e-leadership construct is added, this is developed in line with the e-competences that belong to the *Digital Transformation Leader* role (CWA 16458-1, 2018, pg. 33) as is described in section 2.1. Derived from the conceptual model the following hypotheses are formulated:

H1: There is a positive relationship between IT capability and digital transformation.

H2: e-Competences are positively related to Digital Transformation.

H3: e-Competence positively moderates the relationship between IT Capability and Digital Transformation.

In the following section the research instrument and the process of data collection are described.

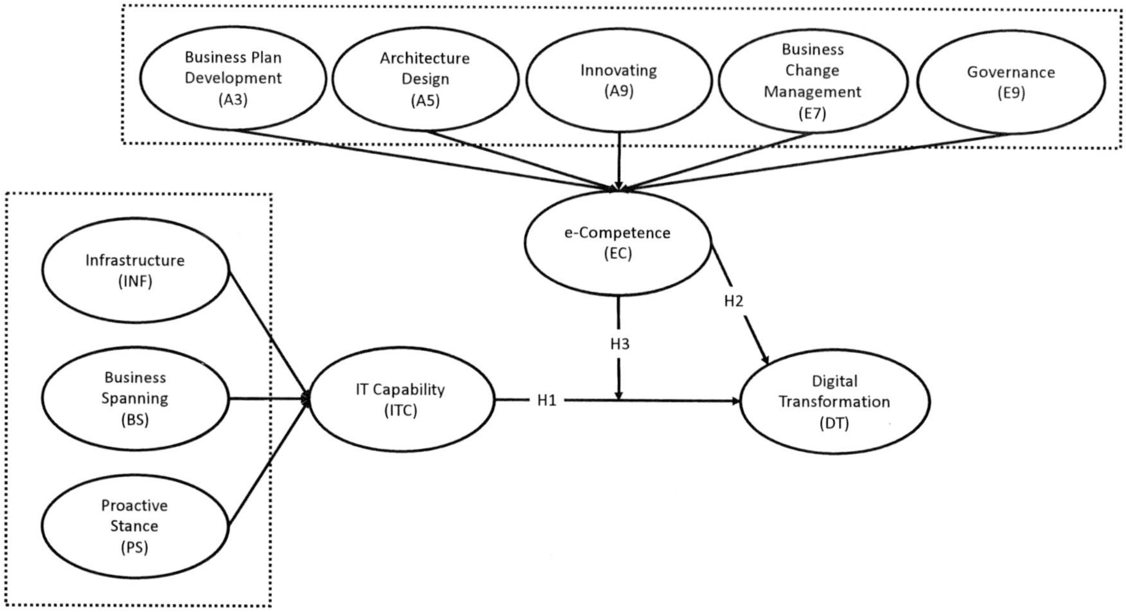

Figure 2. Conceptual Model

3. METHODOLOGY

This section discusses the research instrument that is used as well as the data collection process.

3.1 Measures

The constructs were measured with multiple indicators coded on a seven-point Likert scale. Digital Transformation is first operationalized by Nwankpa & Roumani (2016). We adopted their measures for this study. Additionally, we also utilized the measures they used in their study for IT Capability. These are based on prior information systems research (amongst others (Lu & Ramamurthy, 2011). Finally, we developed a set of questions to measure the e-competences related to digital leadership. The final set of measurement items used to determine scores for each construct and the original source of these measurement items can be received on request to the authors.

3.2 Sample and Procedure

Data is collected from June to September of 2018 by students of the Master of Business Studies (Innovation in European Business). The master diploma is awarded and partially delivered by Cork University College (Ireland) in partnership with HU University of Applied Sciences (Netherlands) and ISC Paris School of Management (France). The students surveyed organizations individually. For the purpose of this study, we pooled the data together which resulted in a set that comprised 127 respondents. For the greatest part, namely 118, these are organizations with 250 employees or less, thus SME's. Eight organizations have between 250 and 999 employees and one has more than 1000 employees. The organizations are active in four different industries: Accommodation and food service activities (25.2%), Information and communication (18.9%) Financial and insurance activities (19.7%), Professional, scientific and technical activities (36.2%).

4. RESULTS

Partial least squares (PLS) is used to test the model as it makes less demand on measurement scales (Gefen, et al., 2000; Hair, et al., 2011) and normal distribution (Chin, 1998). A bootstrap procedure was used to assess the statistical significance of the loadings and of the path coefficients (Ringle, et al., 2015). Bootstrapping is a non-parametric approach for estimation by re-sampling the original data with replacement to get an estimate for each parameter in the PLS model (Chin, 2001). Using the software SmartPLS (Ringle, et al., 2015), the measurement model is examined to assess reliability and validity before testing the structural model and thus test the hypotheses.

4.1 Measurement Model

Tables 1, 2, 3 and 4 present the measurement model results. The Cronbach's alpha values are between 0.834 and 0.936, the composite reliabilities of multi-item scales modeled with reflective indicators are 0.70 or greater, suggesting that the scales have a high level of internal consistency reliability (Hair, et al., 2009). The values of ρA are also acceptable as they are above 0.70 (Henseler, et al., 2016). Using the commonly applied criterion of average variance extracted (AVE) being at least 0.50 (Fornell & Larcker, 1981) the scores also demonstrate sufficient convergent validity of the constructs.

Table 1. Cronbach's Alpha, Composite Reliabilities and Average Variance Extracted (AVE)

	Cronbach's Alpha	ρA	Composite Reliability	AVE
A3	0.867	0.872	0.919	0.790
A5	0.887	0.888	0.930	0.815
A9	0.834	0.840	0.923	0.858
E7	0.894	0.894	0.934	0.825
E9	0.904	0.905	0.954	0.913
BS	0.928	0.928	0.949	0.823
INF	0.870	0.873	0.911	0.719
PS	0.936	0.938	0.955	0.840
DT	0.907	0.911	0.942	0.844

To assess discriminant validity, the latest guidelines are used (Henseler, et al., 2016). Following these guidelines, the Fornell-Larcker criterion (Fornell & Cha, 1994) is firstly examined. A latent construct should better explain the variance of its own indicator rather than the variance of other latent constructs. Therefore, the square root of each construct's AVE should have a greater value than the correlations with other latent constructs. Table 2 provides the results for our study. The results show insufficient discriminant validity as the correlation of IT Capability with e-Competence is higher than the square root of the AVE of e-Competence. However, to fully examine discriminant validity one should also assess the cross loadings.

Table 2. Correlations (off-Diagonal Elements) and Square Root of the AVEs (Diagonal Elements)

	e-Competence	Digital Transformation	IT Capability
e-Competence	*0.76*		
Digital Transformation	0.60	*0.92*	
IT Capability	0.81	0.59	*0.78*

Table 3 shows the cross loadings of the constructs as defined in the conceptual model. Taking a conservative threshold of 0.8 shows discriminant validity of the constructs. However, some loadings do exceed the threshold of 0.7, which is often used as cut-off value (Hair, et al., 2009).

Table 3. Cross Loadings

	A3	A5	A9	E7	E9	BS	INF	PS	DT
A3_1	0.86	0.58	0.51	0.5	0.4	0.58	0.34	0.54	0.38
A3_2	0.91	0.63	0.60	0.61	0.54	0.66	0.45	0.65	0.39
A3_3	0.90	0.59	0.52	0.58	0.47	0.65	0.46	0.58	0.42
A5_1	0.58	0.89	0.54	0.50	0.39	0.56	0.44	0.62	0.47
A5_2	0.59	0.92	0.59	0.51	0.44	0.62	0.47	0.67	0.47
A5_3	0.65	0.89	0.61	0.59	0.44	0.61	0.4	0.64	0.49
A9_1	0.62	0.65	0.93	0.67	0.50	0.62	0.42	0.61	0.48
A9_2	0.51	0.53	0.92	0.65	0.50	0.57	0.39	0.53	0.48
E7_1	0.59	0.49	0.67	0.90	0.57	0.57	0.41	0.52	0.51
E7_2	0.60	0.59	0.66	0.92	0.46	0.58	0.41	0.62	0.55
E7_3	0.53	0.53	0.62	0.90	0.54	0.54	0.44	0.56	0.46
E9_1	0.50	0.40	0.49	0.58	0.95	0.5	0.48	0.45	0.41
E9_2	0.52	0.50	0.54	0.52	0.96	0.54	0.44	0.46	0.39
BS_1	0.66	0.59	0.55	0.57	0.51	0.88	0.57	0.75	0.56
BS_2	0.70	0.62	0.60	0.53	0.48	0.93	0.48	0.66	0.49
BS_3	0.60	0.61	0.60	0.63	0.51	0.90	0.55	0.64	0.38
BS_4	0.62	0.57	0.59	0.52	0.47	0.92	0.53	0.69	0.45
INF_1	0.41	0.41	0.43	0.39	0.42	0.51	0.87	0.46	0.46
INF_2	0.39	0.40	0.42	0.47	0.43	0.46	0.84	0.52	0.34
INF_3	0.47	0.44	0.40	0.41	0.40	0.57	0.84	0.57	0.46
INF_4	0.32	0.37	0.22	0.28	0.37	0.45	0.83	0.39	0.36
PS_1	0.68	0.70	0.55	0.51	0.50	0.66	0.50	0.89	0.47
PS_2	0.64	0.65	0.58	0.53	0.41	0.73	0.53	0.94	0.49
PS_3	0.51	0.62	0.53	0.58	0.41	0.65	0.50	0.92	0.47
PS_4	0.61	0.64	0.62	0.66	0.43	0.73	0.57	0.92	0.59
DT_1	0.43	0.46	0.49	0.48	0.37	0.52	0.38	0.48	0.91
DT_2	0.44	0.52	0.52	0.56	0.41	0.46	0.50	0.53	0.95
DT_3	0.36	0.49	0.41	0.50	0.37	0.45	0.43	0.50	0.89

Additionally, following the latest guidelines, the heterotrait-monotrait ratio of correlations (HTMT) is also used to assess discriminant validity. Henseler Ringle and Sarstedt (2015) argued a strong case of using this approach. In order to clearly discriminate between two factors, the HTMT should be smaller than 0.90 (Henseler, et al., 2016). As Table 4 shows, all correlations comply to that criterion. Hence, discriminant validity is demonstrated by the heterotrait-monotrait ratio.

Table 4. Heterotrait-monotrait Ratio of Correlations (HTMT)

	A3	A5	A9	DT	E7	E9	BS	INF
A5	0.77							
A9	0.72	0.74						
DT	0.50	0.59	0.59					
E7	0.72	0.66	0.83	0.62				
E9	0.60	0.52	0.62	0.46	0.64			
BS	0.79	0.73	0.73	0.56	0.68	0.59		
INF	0.54	0.55	0.51	0.53	0.52	0.54	0.65	
PS	0.74	0.78	0.70	0.59	0.68	0.52	0.81	0.63

In sum, the data suffices for reliability and convergent validity, but displays mixed scores with regard to discriminant validity. For the purpose of this study, we continued with this data, but future research is needed to investigate the rationale behind this.

To test for multicollinearity, the variance inflation factors (VIFs) were computed (Kock, 2015). The values ranged from 1.97 and 4.89. Although some are a little bit high, they are found to be less than the conservative threshold of 5. Hence, this suggests that multicollinearity was not a major issue in the study.

4.2 Structural Model and Hypotheses Testing

In PLS analysis, examining the structural paths and the R-square scores of the endogenous variables, assess the explanatory power of the structural model. A bootstrapping procedure with 127 cases and 1000 subsamples was used to test the significance of all paths in the research model (Hair, et al., 2011). The results of the structural model are shown in Figure . The results suggest that the model is capable of explaining 40% of the variance of digital transformation. In support of hypothesis 1, IT Capability has a significant positive impact on digital transformation ($\beta = 0.296$, $p < 0.001$). Similarly, in support of hypothesis 2, e-Competence has a significant positive relationship with digital transformation ($\beta = 0.342$, $p < 0.001$). Hypothesis 3 states that digital transformation has a positive moderating effect on the relation between IT Capability and Digital Transformation. This hypothesis was not supported ($\beta = -0.047$, $p = 0.248$).

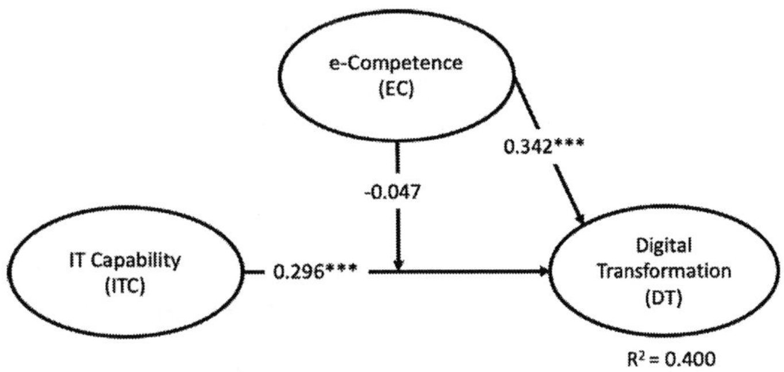

Figure 3. Hypothesis testing (*** $p < 0.001$)

5. DISCUSSION AND CONCLUSIONS

This study examined the mediating role of digital leadership in the relationship between IT capability and digital transformation, for this we introduced the concept of e-Competences. A theoretical framework explaining the effect of digital leadership was tested using a survey of 127 respondents from firms across

Western Europe. Consistent with our proposed model, this research finds that both IT capability and e-Competences positively influences digital transformation. The e-Competences related to the Digital Transformation Leader role do not moderate the relation between IT capabilities and digital transformation.

5.1 Implications for Theory and Practice

This study offers several theoretical implications. First, our study confirms prior research (e.g. (Nwankpa & Roumani, 2016) that found a significant positive relation between IT capabilities and digital transformation. Secondly, although prior studies have shown the influence of IT capability on digital transformation, less is known about the role of e-competences. To the best of our knowledge, this is the first study that empirically scrutinized the concept of e-competences in the role of digitally transforming businesses. The results of a significant relation between e-competences and digital transformation contributes to the theoretical development of determinants if this dependent concept.

Our research has also implications for professionals, e.g. managers. Specifically, the study will be of practical importance to managers and executives who are initiating plans to integrate digital technologies with their business processes. Practitioners should recognize that investments for digital transformation should be directed not only to IT capabilities, but also to e-competences. Enhancing personnel's leadership qualities as formulated in the European e-Competence Framework. More specifically, managers should pay attention to competences of business plan development, architecture design, innovating, business change management, and IS governance.

5.2 Limitations and Future Research

As any empirical study, this work has several limitations which should be recognized. First, our model comprised limited key constructs in relation to digital transformation. Other factors like financial resources or the culture of the organization potential influence the digital transformation. Future research could examine a more comprehensive model. Secondly, although the we utilized prior research for the operationalization of digital transformation, it is mainly focused on the use of technology. Anecdotal research however argues a more multidimensional approach of this concept. Westerman, Bonnet and McAfee (2014a) postulate three major building blocks of digital transformation, i.e. customer experience, operational processes, business models. This field of research should benefit from a validated operationalization of this construct for future references. Third, one must stipulate the representativeness of the sample. The limited number of respondents is not only skewed to SMEs, but also not well distributed over sectors. Hence, the conclusions must be interpreted with caution. Future research will extend the dataset with subjects in order to increase the reliability and validity of our study.

Despite these limitations we think this research contributes to the discussion of digital transformation and the factors that influence this, often radical, change that organizations are faced with.

REFERENCES

Anand, J., Oriani, R. & Vassolo, R. S., 2010. Alliance activity as a dynamic capability in the face of a discontinuous technological change. *Organization Science,* 21(6), pp. 1213-1232.

Avolio, B. J., Sosik, J. J., Kahai, S. S. & Baker, B., 2014. E-leadership: Re-examining transformations in leadership source and transmission. *The Leadership Quarterly,* 25(1), pp. 105-131.

Bharadwaj, A., 2000. A Resource-Based Perspective on Information Technology Capability and Firm Performance: An Empirical Investigation. *MIS Quarterly,* 24(1), pp. 169-196.

CEN, 2016. *The European Committee for Standardization, standard EN 16234- 1:2016,* Available from: https://standards.cen.eu.

Chen, J. S. & Tsou, H. T., 2012. Performance effects of IT capability, service process innovation, and the mediating role of customer service. *Journal of Engineering and Technology Management,* 29(1), pp. 71-94.

Chin, W., 1998. The partial least squares approach to structural equation modeling. In: G. Marcoulides, ed. *Modern Methods for Business Research.* Mahwah, N.J: Lawrence Erlbaum Associates, p. 1295–1336.

Chin, W. W., 2001. *PLS-Graph User's Guide.* Houston: C.T. Bauer College of Business, University of Houston.

Coombs, J. E. & Bierly III, P. E., 2006. Measuring technological capability and performance. *R&D Management,* 36(4), pp. 421-438.

CWA 16458-1, 2018. CEN, the European Committee for Standardization. *European ICT professionals role profiles 1-4.* CWA 16458. Retrieved from https://standards.cen.eu/dyn/www/f?p=CENWEB:84:::NO:::

Drnevich, P. L. & Croson, D. C., 2013. Information technology and business-level strategy: Toward an integrated theoretical perspective. *MIS Quarterly,* 37(2), pp. 483-509.

e-CF, 2014. *e-CF, the European e-Competence Framework, version 3.0,* Available from: http://www.ecompetences.eu.

Fornell, C. & Cha, J., 1994. Partial least squares. *Advanced Methods of Marketing Research,* Volume 407, p. 52–78.

Fornell, C. & Larcker, D., 1981. Evaluating structural equation models with unobservable measurement error. *Journal of Marketing Research,* 18(1), p. 39–50.

Gefen, D., Straub, D. & Boudreau, M., 2000. Structural equation modeling techniques and regression: Guidelines for research practice. *Communications of AIS,* 4(7), pp. 1-77.

Hair, J. et al., 2009. *Multivariate data analysis.* 7th ed. Englewood Cliffs, NJ: Prentice Hall.

Hair, J., Ringle, C. & Sarstedt, M., 2011. PLS-SEM: Indeed a Silver Bullet. *Journal of Marketing Theory and Practice,* 19(2), pp. 139-152.

Henriette, E., Feki, M. & Boughzala, I., 2015. The Shape of Digital Transformation: A Systematic Literature Review. In: *Proceedings of the Mediterranean Conference on Information Systems*. Samos: Greence.

Henseler, J., Hubona, G. & Ray, P., 2016. Using PLS path modeling in new technology research: updated guidelines. *Industrial Management & Data Systems,* 116(1), pp. 2-20.

Henseler, J., Ringle, C. M. & Sarstedt, M., 2015. A New Criterion for Assessing Discriminant Validity in Variance-based Structural Equation Modeling. *Journal of the Academy of Marketing Science,* 43(1), pp. 115-135.

Hüsing, T., Korte, W.B., Fonstad, N., Lanvin, B., Cattaneo, G., Kolding, M., Lifonti, R. & Van Welsum, D., 2013. eLeadership: e-Skills for Competitiveness and Innovation – Vision, Roadmap and Foresight Scenarios, Final Report, *Empirica – Gesellschaft für Kommunikations- und Technologieforschung mbH*, Bonn.

Ismail, M.H., Khater, M., & Zaki, M., 2017. Digital Business Transformation and Strategy: What Do We Know So Far?, *Cambridge Service Alliance*, Working Paper, 2017.

Kane, G. C. P. D., Phillips, A. N., Kiron, D. & Buckley, N., 2015. Strategy, not technology, drives digital transformation. *MIT Sloan Management Review and Deloitte University Press,* pp. 1-25.

Kock, N., 2015. Common method bias in PLS-SEM: A full collinearity assessment approach. *International Journal of e-Collaboration,* 11(4), pp. 1-10.

Kutzner, K., Schoormann, T., & Knackstedt, R., 2018. Digital Transformation in Information Systems Research: A Taxonomy-Based Approach to Structure the Field. In: *Proceedings of the 26th European Conference on Information Systems (ECIS)*, Portsmouth, UK

Libert, B., Beck, M., & Wind, Y., 2016. "7 Questions to ask before your next digital transformation," *Harvard Business Review*, July 2016

Lu, Y. & Ramamurthy, K., 2011. Understanding the link between information technology capability and organizational agility: An empirical examination. *MIS Quarterly,* 35(4), pp. 931-954.

Matt, C., Hess, T. & Benlian, A., 2015. Digital transformation strategies. *Business & Information Systems Engineering* 57 (5), pp. 339-343.

Mithas, S., Ramasubbu, N. & Sambamurthy, V., 2011. How information management capability influences firm performance. *MIS Quarterly,* 35(1), pp. 237-256.

Nwankpa, J. & Roumani, Y., 2016. *IT Capability and Digital Transformation: A Firm Performance Perspective.* Dublin, s.n.

Plessius, H. & Ravesteyn, P., 2016. *Mapping the European e-Competence Framework on the domain of Information Technology: a comparative study.* Bled, Slovenia, 29th Bled eConference: Digital Economy.

Prentice, W. C. H., 2004. Understanding leadership. *Harvard Business Review,* 82(1), pp. 102-109.

Ringle, C. M., Wende, S. & Becker, J.-M., 2015. *SmartPLS 3.* Boenningstedt: SmartPLS GmbH.

Robinson, S. L. et al., 2015. *New curricula for e-leadership skills. Guidelines and quality labels for new curricula for e-Leadership skills in Europe,* Available from: http://eskillsguide.eu/documents/.

Sheninger, E., 2014. *Digital leadership: Changing paradigms for changing times.* s.l.:Corwin Press.

Westerman, G., Bonnet, D. & McAfee, A., 2014a. The Nine Elements of Digital Transformation. *MIT Sloan Management Review.*

Westerman, G., Bonnet, D. & McAfee, A., 2014b. *Leading digital: Turning technology into business transformation..* s.l.:Harvard Business Press.

SCIENTOMETRICS-BASED STUDY OF COMPUTER SCIENCE AND INFORMATION SYSTEMS RESEARCH COMMUNITY MACRO LEVEL PROFILES

Erman Coşkun[1], Güzin Özdağoğlu[2], Muhammet Damar[2] and Büşra Alma Çallı[3]
[1]*Prince Mohammad Bin Salman College (MBSC) of Business & Entrepreneurship, Saudi Arabia*
[2]*Dokuz Eylül University, Turkey*
[3]*Sakarya University, Turkey*

ABSTRACT

This paper examines the current state and evolution of Computer Science (CS) and Information Systems (IS) research communities for the period of 2008 to 2019 by analysing Web of Science (WoS) core collection records. In order to compare and examine research outputs, the study period was divided into two time-periods. The first period included articles published between 2008 and 2013 and the second period included articles published between 2014 and 2019. Several analyses are presented in the scope of scientometrics regarding the (a) countries (b) historical occurrence-time (c) institutions (d) author collaboration (e) study topics-keywords (f) journals. This paper provides meta-analysis in different areas. We believe that our analysis results will shed a light for each area as well as interaction and intersection between both areas. As IS discipline and researchers we need to understand these intersections and interactions as well as understanding current trends in both disciplines.

KEYWORDS

Computer Science, Information Systems, WoS Publications, Macro Level Profiles, Scientometrics

1. INTRODUCTION AND BACKGROUND

Number of IS research and utilization of IS as reference discipline has been rising The Information Systems (IS) community has been developed significantly after its first emergence in the 1960s. A robust research tradition has been established and has guided IS to be grown into a scientific field. IS, as a reference discipline, is within the focus of researchers from other disciplines as well, which contributes to knowledge accumulation and growth of the field (Paré et al. 2014). Computer science is one of the major disciplines interacts and intersects with IS. Information Systems (IS), referring to Management Information Systems (MIS) and Computer Information Systems (CIS), integrates social and technical approaches with an interdisciplinary view. IS field has researchers from different backgrounds and disciplines (Alma et al., 2017). Terms of MIS, IS and CIS are often utilized interchangeably and different researchers have conceptualized the field in a different way.

Examining the state-of-the-art and evolution of academic discipline has been a traditional approach for observing the changes and developments within the field. Compared to other disciplines, IS is a new and fast developing discipline. Undoubtedly, examining the development of an academic field contributes the ongoing development of the discipline as it offers the opportunity of comparing past and present status of the research output, exploring research gaps, capturing trends and topics that have not been addressed and observing methodological issues (Serenko et al., 2008). Hence, some IS research have concentrated on theoretical overviews of the field and have examined theoretical IS research from numerous aspects (Abbasi et al. 2016; Banker & Kauffman, 2004; Cheon et al., 1993; Choi et al., 2011; Dickson, 1981; Palvia et al., 2003; Paré et al., 2014; Serenko et al., 2008; Shao et al., 2014).

This study, conducts several analyses in the scope of scientometrics for a sophisticated review of research and publication characteristics of IS research by encompassing a long-period of publication. Depending on the limited amount of research and aforementioned shortcomings of the previous review studies, this study contributes to evaluating the maturity of the field, trends and research gaps. To do so, a large-scale data set is analysed covering the research articles which were published between 2008 and 2019 and categorized under "Computer Science-Information Systems" within Web of Science(WoS) Core Collection. Studies in the scope of scientometrics facilitate this by exploring past and present status of the field by enabling analysing a wide range of publication characteristics in addition to subject trends. Furthermore, a huge amount of publication data extracted and gathered systematically facilitates conducting comprehensive analysis from a wide range of aspects. In order to compare the recent trends to the previous ones, the study period was divided into two time-periods. The first period included articles published between 2008 and 2013 and the second period included articles published between 2014 and 2019. Several analyses are presented in the scope of scientometrics regarding the countries, institutions, author collaborations, journals, and topics-keywords.

2. SHORT LITERATURE REVIEW

One of the earliest studies evaluating research in IS was performed by (Cheon et al., 1993) by synthesizing the associated research in order to evaluate the maturity of the field. Banker and Kauffman (2004) evaluated the IS literature within Management Science discipline for the last five decades by discussing major research streams within the field. Those research streams were identified as follows; "decision support and decision science", "the value of information, human-computer systems design", "IS organization" and "strategy and economics of IS and technology". Shao et al. (2014) conducted an overview of MIS literature with the aim of comparing domestic research in China with foreign research trends. In addition to research subjects, methodologies, journals and research output of MIS researchers were analysed and discussed. Abbasi et al. (2016) specifically focused on Big Data research in IS with concentrating on subjects and research gaps within the field. Choi et al. (2011) worked on the identification of the keyword patterns by analyzing MIS research publication data between 1999 and 2008. Rapid changing nature of the field was observed by means of network perspective. Interdisciplinary nature of the field was reflected by various concepts and areas emerged from a substantial combination of existing topics and concepts. Palvia et al. (2003) systematically reviewed top MIS journals covering a five-year publication period to analyse trends for subjects and methodologies. Paré et al. (2014) specifically reviewed the various review types published in top IS journals. Freitas et al. (2004) compared research characteristics in MIS for France and Brazil by focusing on particular domestic congresses. Evolution of subject in the 4-year period, number of citations and characteristics of congresses. Vessey et al. (2002) synthesized IS research papers published between 1995 and 1999 in five IS journals. Topics, research methodologies, and their evolution was analysed.

Most papers of the relevant literature conducted overview studies with mostly focusing on research trends and methodologies within IS / MIS research. A common aspect of papers was to cover a relatively short analysis period that constitutes limitations in anticipating actual trends, methodologies and research activities.

3. METHODOLOGY

3.1 Research Scope

This study mainly focuses on the area "Computer Science-Information Systems" to reveal information on following areas:

- Publication statistics,
- Country related statistics and collaboration analysis ,
- Institution related analysis,
- Research topic and area related analysis,
- Keywords and relevant topic analysis

By doing so, the study aims to present the leading countries, authors and research fields in the relevant literature with summary statistics, and to present the collaborations between the countries, the issues and their changes over time with advanced analyses based on scientometrics and visuals.

3.2 Data Source and Data Characteristics

The analyses were carried out through publications within the WoS database which has an important position in the international literature. Every publication covered by WoS Core Collection is assigned to at least one of 254 subject categories. There are seven categories, especially those relating to computer science and information systems, i.e. Computer Science, Artificial Intelligence (1); Computer Science, Cybernetics (2); Computer Science, Hardware & Architecture (3); Computer Science, Information Systems (4); Computer Science, Interdisciplinary Applications (5), Computer Science, Software Engineering (6); Computer Science, and Theory & Methods (7), respectively. The bibliometric dataset of original articles, which was tagged under these seven research categories, is included in the analyses.

The article search and data set extraction were conducted in 24.02.2019, and all original articles published from January 2008 to February 2019 were taken into consideration in the scope of the study. The main reason behind selecting only the original articles is the thought that the articles can be representative to reveal the major research patterns in the literature. During the analyses, the raw dataset was divided into two periods, 2008-2013 and 2014-2019, to be able to compare the trends and the characteristics in the related part of the literature. The first period consists of 57347 articles where the second period consists of 96219 articles.

3.3 Scientometrics and Related Techniques

The datasets were analysed through the techniques in the scope of scientometrics. Scientometrics is a concept in metrology as is the case in bibliometrics, informetrics or similar terms, which defines an old methodology, has been developed since 1960s, to reveal the characteristics of the particular literature over bibliometric datasets by using quantitative techniques (Glänzel & Schoepflin, 1994; Hood & Wilson, 2001; Garfield, 2009; Siluo& Qingli, 2017). In addition to the particular metrics and summary tables, the methodology utilizes advanced text and network analytics to extract clusters and networks for citations, co-citations, co-authorships, and co-occurrence networks through various attributes such as authors, countries, institutions, and journals (Sengupta 1992; Al 2008). All these analyses and networks shed light on the demographics, collaborations, and associations in the related literature, thus the visualizations reflect the academic social network of the related area over the selected publications as well as the publication performances and summary statistics. For example, in this study, the co-authorship analysis provided a vision of cooperation patterns between individuals and organizations and sometimes countries. Time dimension was added to see the change these collaborations over the years. Besides, keyword co-occurrences were extracted the keyword trends, associations, and densities over text clustering. The widespread use of scientometrics and its development have increased along with the developments in data science and software technologies. In this study, spreadsheets and VOSViewer application software (van Eck & Waltman, 2013) were used to obtain summary tables, to perform text analytics and to visualize the corresponding networks.

4. FINDINGS AND DISCUSSION

4.1 Publication Distributions over Years

The general status of all publications and the position of the articles in the publications are shown in Table 1. The number of publications in all types has increased during the second period. When we check yearly publication numbers from 2008-2019, we see a steady increase every year. However, after detailed analysis of two periods, we do not see the same steady increase in conference proceedings. The economic difficulties and crisis in the university system and in-country economies might be contributing to this by reducing participation in international conferences because of budgetary limitations. Or other reason might be an increasing number of journals in the area. Nevertheless, further in-depth research must be conducted to make certain judgment however the trend shows that along conference participations are staying at the same level while the number of journal publications is increasing.

Table 1. Document Types and Counts

Document Type	2008-2013 (1st Period)		2014-2019 (2nd Period)	
	No. of Publications	220529 %	No. of Publications	252010%
Proceedings Paper	160092	72.59	150585	59.75
Article	57347	26.00	96219	38.18
Editorial Material	3512	1.59	4111	1.63
Review	724	0.32	1687	0.66
Book Review	683	0.31	255	0.10
Correction	216	0.09	355	0.14
Others	267	0.21	539	0.21

In terms of language, approximately 98% of papers in both periods were written in English. Portuguese and Spanish are the most commonly used languages after English.

4.2 Country and Institution Related Analysis

In the light of the findings presented in Table 2 and Table 3, it can be revealed that the US and US university leadership in the first period has not continued in the second period and China and Chinese institutions were recently dominating the area based on the data we used. Our institution wise analysis, reveal that two Chinese institutions are leading in terms of publications in the area and only 1 US institution is staying in the top 10 list (comparing to 5 in the previous period). One important point is to recognize that Chinese universities outperformed others with significant increases. In terms of countries, not only China's outstanding performance but also developing countries such as India and Brazil is also getting attention by entering the list in the latest. Table 4 also presents the top institutions in each country contributing the field with the highest number of articles in addition to the most collaborative countries. We can conclude that China is a shining star for the second part and significantly dominating the discipline in terms of publications, and a number of institutions. Another important topic is collaboration and similar conclusions can be made however because of space limitations we will keep it for our presentation.

Table 2. Institutions

#	2008-2013 (1st Period)			2014-2019 (2nd Period)		
	Affiliations	N	%	Affiliations	N	%
1	University of California System (US)	1447	2.52	Chinese Academy of Sciences (CHINA)	3308	3.43
2	Chinese Academy of Sciences (CHINA)	1264	2.20	Beijing University of Posts Telecommunications (CHINA)	1459	1.51
3	Tsinghua University (CHINA)	778	1.35	Tsinghua University (CHINA)	1430	1.48
4	International Business Machines IBM (US)	736	1.28	University of California System (US)	1416	1.47
5	University of Texas System (US)	702	1.22	Xidian University (CHINA)	1256	1.30
6	Centre National De La Recherche Scientifique CNRS (FRANCE)	695	1.21	Centre National De La Recherche Scientifique CNRS (FRANCE)	1081	1.12
7	State University System of Florida (US)	638	1.11	University of Electronic Science Technology of China (CHINA)	1034	1.07
8	Nanyang Technological University (CHINA)	587	1.02	Shanghai Jiao Tong University (CHINA)	995	1.03
9	Nanyang Technological University National Institute of Education Nie Singapore (CHINA)	587	1.02	Zhejiang University (CHINA)	982	1.02
10	University System of Georgia (US)	563	0.98	Indian Institute of Technology System IIT System (INDIA)	941	0.97

In the first period, 14425 universities contributed to 57347 articles whereas in the second period 25029 universities contributed to produce 96219 articles. In both periods, the number of researchers having at least 20 articles are 960 and 1613 where the numbers of countries having at least 50 articles are 442 and 771 respectively. The institutions in China, US, and France have dominated the field in terms of their paper counts, however, in the second period India takes place as a new country with the papers produced by *the Indian Institute of Technology System.*

Table 3. The Top 10 Countries in the Related Area

#	2008-2013 (1st Period)				2014-2019 (2nd Period)			
	Country	N	TMCI	THC	Country	N	TMCI	THC
1	USA	15902	University of California System (1447)	China (1600)	China	32472	Chinese Academy of Sciences (3312)	USA (4609)
2	China	10345	Chinese Academy of Sciences (1264)	USA (1600)	USA	18570	University of California System (1419)	China (4609)
3	Japan	3865	Osaka University (281)	China (289)	South Korea	6277	Korea University (505)	USA (661)
4	South Korea	3778	Korea University (446)	USA (583)	India	4976	Indian Institute of Technology System IIT System (942)	USA (424)
5	Taiwan	3613	National Chiao Tung University (468)	USA (314)	England	4782	University of London (611)	China (1123)
6	Canada	3203	University of Waterloo (398)	USA (582)	Canada	4239	University of Waterloo (421)	China (1129)
7	England	2906	University of London (451)	USA (326)	Japan	4206	Osaka University (266)	China (607)
8	Germany	2659	Helmholtz Association (161)	USA (322)	Taiwan	3761	National Chiao Tung University (381)	China (517)
9	Spain	2567	Polytechnic University of Catalonia (323)	USA (175)	Australia	3709	University of Technology Sydney (443)	China (1,414)
10	France	2159	Centre National De La Recherche Scientifique CNRS (694)	USA (287)	Spain	3565	Polytechnic University of Catalonia (373)	USA (264)

*, ** *TMCI: The Most Contributing Institution, THC: The Highest Collaboration*

4.3 Analysis for Collaboration among Countries and among Authors

Co-authorship analysis is a bibliometric technique that is used to reveal the collaborations between authors or other demographics (Gmür, 2003). This study investigated the relationships between the countries regarding the co-authorships regarding minimum of 50 articles (Figure 1). In general, the networks indicate that there are four main country clusters in collaborations which are independent of the continental decomposition. In particular, the articles were produced by 135 distinct countries in the first period and 161 distinct countries in the second period. Figure 1 presents only 52 countries in the first period and 76 countries in the second period which have at least 50 articles in the related subject area.

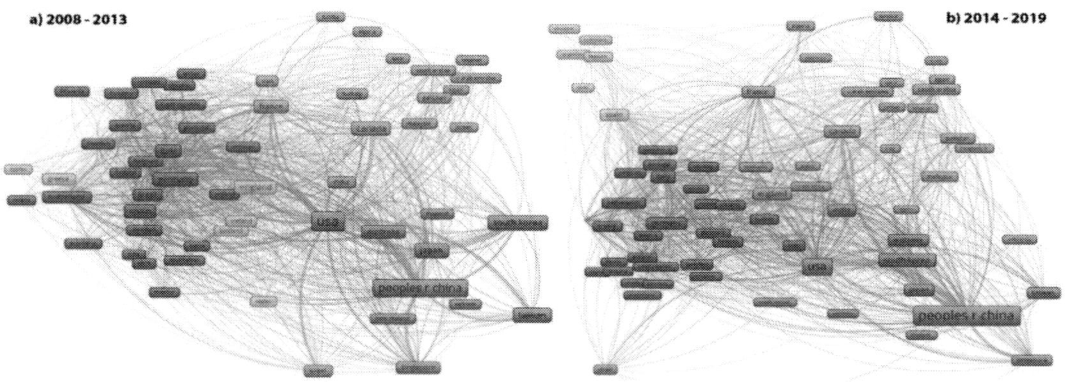

Figure 1. Co-authorship – Country Network (min 50 articles, left: 2008-2013; right: 2014-2019)

Further analysis of countries shows us that the US is still the main hub for this discipline. China is also becoming the main hub for collaboration. We also see that regional collaboration is still significant for most areas. For example England and surrounding countries Ireland, Scotland, Wales are creating a cluster. Also, Australia and East Asia countries are creating another cluster. This may be an indicator of different research streams and it should be analysed further. In terms of changes by the time, we can see that China is becoming more centralized and Israel's collaboration is shifting more toward European countries. Some countries are also showing shifts in their clusters. Many other significant analysis can be done.

4.4 Journal Analysis

Table 4 shows the journal rankings for both periods. We see that IEEE journals are significantly leading mediums for this discipline. From the IS discipline perspective, it is sad to see that leading IS journals cannot be seen in this top 10 journal list. They are located well below in this table and it might be an indicator of IS importance in computer systems area. Most of the journal in this list are technical side of computer science and we can conclude that IS is not a significantly important partner for computer scientists as of yet. Computer Science field is still dominated by technical and engineering related issues rather than the human and managerial side. As IS community, we have very strong ties with the CS field and we should increase our weight in this discipline. In terms of contribution to journals we see a similar picture and for most of the journals China and US are main contributors and other leading countries in the list are taking their place in top three countries data. Of course, further analysis is needed for detailed and more meaningful interpretations. When both periods are compared, we can say that journal list is significantly different and more multidisciplinary journals are becoming more popular for the area researchers. Journals with the highest impact factors are Information Sciences (4,378) and IEEE Access (4,199).

Table 4. Top 10 Journals in the Related Area

#	**2008-2013 (1st Period)**				**2014-2019 (2nd Period)**			
	Sources	**Top Two Countries**	**5IF**	**N**	**Sources**	**Top Two Countries**	**5IF**	**N**
1	IEEE Transactions on Information Theory	USA (1604); China (300)	2.76	2985	IEEE Access	China (6680); USA (1471)	4.199	10961
2	Information Sciences	China (787); Taiwan (278)	4.378	2374	Multimedia Tools And Applications	China (2026); South Korea (602)	1.471	4782
3	IEICE Transactions on Fundamentals of Electronics Communications and Computer Sciences	Japan (1492); South Korea (371)	0.303	2367	Information Sciences	China (1907); USA (399)	4.378	3825
4	IEICE Transactions on Information and Systems	Japan (1098); South Korea (436)	0.398	2092	IEEE Transactions On Information Theory	USA (1158); China (355)	2.76	2454
5	Journal of Chemical Information and Modelling	USA (536); Germany (235)	4.112	1566	International Journal of Distributed Sensor Networks	China (1217); South Korea (460)	1.646	2127
6	Computer Networks	USA (367); China (157)	2.589	1414	IEEE Latin America Transactions	Brazil (943); Mexico (352)	0.465	1960
7	Computer Communications	USA (261); China (222)	2.681	1328	IEICE Transactions on Information and Systems	Japan (955); China (590)	0.398	1894
8	Information Processing Letters	China (277); USA (198)	0.723	1272	IEICE Transactions on Fundamentals of Electronics Communications And Computer Sciences	Japan (1087); China (526)	0.303	1854
9	Journal of The American Society for Information Science And Technology	USA (435); China (101)	2.762	1090	KSII Transactions on Internet and Information Systems	China (905); South Korea (420)	0.543	1562
10	International Journal of Distributed Sensor Networks	China (581); South Korea (173)	1.646	1047	Computer Networks	China (350); USA (311)	2.589	1457

*, ** *5IF: Five-Year Impact Factor, JRD: Journal Research Domain*

4.5 Area Analysis

Each article in WoS can be assigned to more than one research areas, the area with the highest frequency is naturally the selected area where others follow this area (Table 5). Country contributions are also given in the second column of Table 1 highlighting the similar findings to Table 3 and Table 4. When both periods are examined, one can say that top-five research areas are exactly the same but rankings are different. The area information is also compatible with the top journals in the area as listed in Table 5.

Table 5. Research Areas

#	2008-2013 (1st Period)				2014-2019 (2nd Period)			
	Research Area	**Top-Two Countries**	**N**	**%**	**Research Area**	**Top- Two Countries**	**N**	**%**
1	Computer Science Information Systems	USA (15803); China (10320)	57.347	100.00	Computer Science Information Systems	China(32455); USA(18544)	96219	100.00
2	Engineering Electrical Electronic	USA (4143); China (3279)	16.262	28.35	Telecommunications	China (16352); USA (6074)	36103	37.52
3	Telecommunications	USA (4384); China (3023)	16.049	27.98	Engineering Electrical Electronic	China(15044); USA (5665)	34671	36.03
4	Computer Science Software Engineering	USA (2343); China (2110)	9.916	17.29	Computer Science Software Engineering	China(6325); USA (2500)	15816	16.43
5	Computer Science Hardware Architecture	USA (1823); Japan (1661)	7.396	12.89	Computer Science Theory Methods	China (3631); USA (1,380)	9722	10.10

4.6 Keywords, Clusters, and Topics

Co-occurrence analyses were conducted for keyword clusters, density, and keyword trends over time (Figure 2, Figure 3 and Figure 4). Figure 2 focuses on the potential topics over keyword clusters so this figure visualizes the results of the text clustering analysis. The colours in Figure 2 highlight the clusters which indicate a particular topic or issue handled in the studies in the field. Figure 3 represents the closeness of the keywords again where the colours show the use of the words over time. More recent words approach to red whereas old ones are getting blue to the earlier years. The densities of these keywords were emphasized in Figure 4 again via a heat map to distinct the most frequent ones.

In this context, nine clusters were obtained for both periods. In the first period, cryptology, privacy and security, sensors and networks, artificial intelligence, data mining, web services, enterprise systems, data mining, text mining whereas in the second period green computing, energy efficacy, internet of things, big data, artificial intelligence, sensors, security, machine learning, feature selection, cloud computing and related issues are the leading topics. It can also be seen from Figure 3 that the density of these topics varies from year to year even for the same topic.

When we look at the recurrence of keywords for two periods we see that between 2008-2013 the mostly worked areas are algorithms, wireless sensor networks, energy efficiency, information retrieval, authentication, performance measurement, and routing. For 2013-2019 most recurring words are privacy, IOT, authentication, security, wireless sensor networks, cloud computing, machine learning, energy efficiency, social media, ontology, algorithms, and clustering. These keywords are showing us that by the time research topics are shifting as well and more current issues such as privacy, security, IOT, big data, etc. are being studied widely by the researchers in this area. It also indicates that IS researchers might have an opportunity to collaborate or become more significant in this discipline since these are also most widely studied topics in IS.

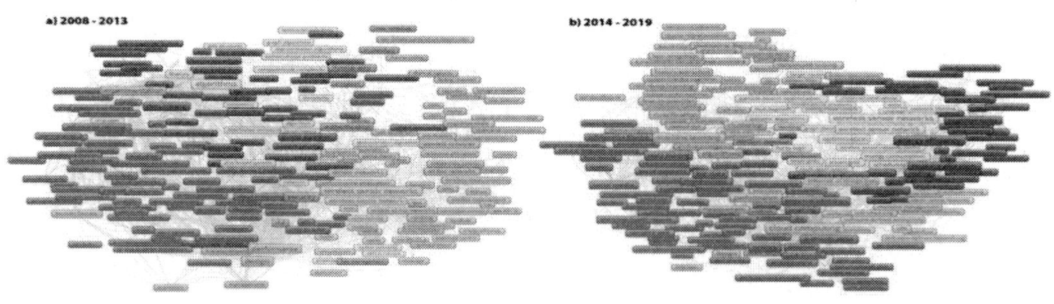

Figure 2. Co-occurrence-Author Keywords Network (min 40 keyword occurrences)

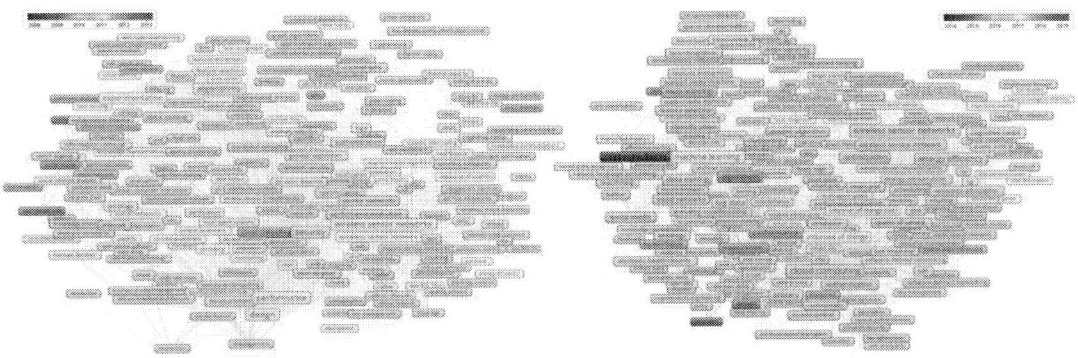

Figure 3. Co-occurrence-Author Keywords by Years (min 40 keyword occurrences)

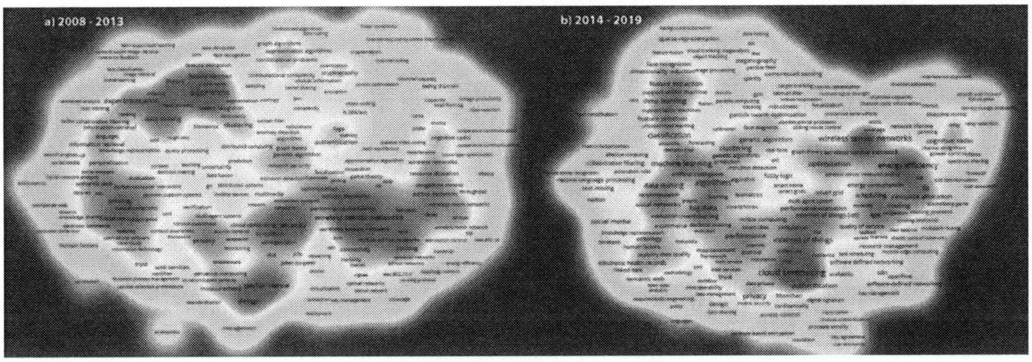

Figure 4. Co-occurrence-Author Keywords by Density (min 40 keyword occurrences)

5. CONCLUSION

This study revealed the particular characteristics of the literature regarding "Computer Science and Information Systems" over the articles categorized under the same title in WoS Core Collection. In this context, 57347+96219 articles were investigated through the related methods and techniques of scientometrics with respect to particular attributes such as countries, institutions, collaborations among the countries, journals, and topics. For each type of finding, several summary statistics, text and network analytics were used.

IS discipline and researchers need to understand the relationships and interactions, as well as understanding current trends in both disciplines for better collaboration CS and IS, should be completing each other with this mutual intersections and understanding. Thus, the findings may shed light on the future studies of the researchers in this field. For example, with co-authorship networks, the scientometrics studies provide author clusters which can help researchers to see idea and research groups from many countries and institutions in the corresponding research area. Keywords and topics over the keywords may indicate the current trends and the gaps in the area. We can see that the main topics have a lot of similarities, However, CS focuses on technical sides and IS should be focusing on human and managerial sides. Top journal list can be used while deciding about paper submissions regarding the country dimension, our significant finding is that China is becoming very dominant in this area by passing long term leader US. American and European universities that had high ranked in the first period have now been leaving their positions to Brazil, Spain, Taiwan, and Indian universities. Besides, there are particular country clusters showing the co-authorships. The researchers can use these findings to plan research visits or conference participations. Much more findings were obtained from the analyses, but could not be presented because of the manuscript limitations but will be included during our presentation.

REFERENCES

Abbasi, A., Sarker, S., & Chiang, R. 2016. Big Data Research in Information Systems: Toward an Inclusive Research Agenda. *Journal of the Association for Information Systems*, Vol.17, No.2, pp. I–XXXII.

Al, U. 2008. Evaluation of scientific publications: H-index and performance of Turkey. *Bilgi Dünyası*, 9(2), 263-285.

Alma, B., Koc, T., & Coşkun, E. 2017. Analysis of research characteristics of MIS discipline in Turkey. Americas Conference on Information Systems: A Tradition of Innovation, *AMCIS 2017*, 2017–Augus, pp.1–10.

Banker, R. D., & Kauffman, R. J. 2004. 50th Anniversary Article: The Evolution of Research on Information Systems: A Fiftieth-Year Survey of the Literature in Management Science. *Management Science*, Vol.50, No.3, pp. 281-298. https://doi.org/10.1287/mnsc.1040.0206

Cheon, M. J., Groven, V., & Sabherwal, R. 1993. The evolution of empirical research in IS. A study in IS maturity. Information and Management, Vol.24, No.3, pp.107–119. https://doi.org/10.1016/0378-7206(93)90060-7

Choi, J., Yi, S., & Lee, K. C. 2011. Analysis of keyword networks in MIS research and implications for predicting knowledge evolution. *Information and Management*, Vol.48, No.8, pp. 371–381. https://doi.org/10.1016/j.im.2011.09.004

Dickson, G. W. 1981. Management Information Systems: Evolution and Status. *Advances in Computers*, Vol. 20. https://doi.org/10.1016/S0065-2458(08)60494-5

Freitas, H., Luciano, M. E., & Testa, G. M. 2004. Research topics in Management Information Systems : a comparative study. *Colloque de l'AIM Systèmes d'information: Perspectives Critiques*, Vol.9.

Garfield, E. 2009. From the science of science to Scientometrics visualizing the history of science with HistCite software. *Journal of Informetrics*, *3*(3), 173-179.

Glänzel, W., & Schoepflin, U. 1994. Little scientometrics, big scientometrics... and beyond?. *Scientometrics*, *30*(2-3), 375-384.

Gmür, M. 2003. Co-citation analysis and the search for invisible colleges: A methodological evaluation. *Scientometrics*, Vol.57, No.1, pp.27-57.

Hood, W., & Wilson, C. 2001. The literature of bibliometrics, scientometrics, and informetrics. *Scientometrics*, *52*(2), 291-314.

Palvia, P., Mao, E., Salam, A. F., & Soliman, K. S. 2003. Management Information Systems Research: What' s There in a Methodology? *Communications of the Association for Information Systems*, Vol.11, No.March, pp. 289–209. Retrieved from http://aisel.aisnet.org/cais/vol11/iss1/16/

Paré, G., Trudel, M. C., Jaana, M., & Kitsiou, S. 2014. Synthesizing information systems knowledge: A typology of literature reviews. *Information and Management*.

Sengupta, I. N. 1992. Bibliometrics, informetrics, scientometrics and librametrics: An overview. *Libri*, Vol.42, No.2, pp.75-98.

Serenko, A., Cocosila, M., & Turel, O. 2008. The state and evolution of information systems research in Canada: A scientometric analysis. *Canadian Journal of Administrative Sciences*, Vol.25, No.4, pp. 279–294. https://doi.org/10.1002/cjas.73

Shao, P., Wu, L., & Zhou, B. 2014. A Comparative Study on MIS Research at Mainland China and Abroad (2002-2010). In Association for Information Systems AIS Electronic Library (AISeL) *WHICEB 2014 Proceedings Wuhan* (Vol. Summer 6-1).

Siluo, Y., & Qingli, Y. 2017. Are Scientometrics, Informetrics, and Bibliometrics different?. In *Conference: The 16th International Conference on Scientometrics & Informetrics (ISSI2017).*

van Eck, N., & Waltman, L. 2009. Software survey: VOSviewer, a computer program for bibliometric mapping. *Scientometrics*, *84*(2), 523-538.doi:10.1007/s11192-0090146.

Vessey, I., Ramesh, V., & Glass, R. L. 2002. Research in information systems: An empirical study of diversity in the discipline and its journals. *Journal of Management Information Systems*, Vol.19, No.2, pp. 129–174. https://doi.org/10.1080/07421222.2002.11045721

REGRESSION ANALYSIS OF NATIONAL ELECTIONS IN JAPAN USING SOCIAL LISTENING

Hisaki Goto[1] and Yukiko Goto[2]
[1]*Nagoya Gakuin University, Nagoya, Japan*
[2]*Enconnect Inc., Fukuoka, Japan*

ABSTRACT

In this study, results predictions on Japan's national elections are made by analyzing data obtained through social listening. The amount of information sent by end users has become enormous as expressed as "information explosion", and social media is a representative source of such information. Social listening on national elections after the internet campaign became available in 2013 was conducted in this study, and a new finding in results predictions that could replace a conventional prediction method, especially in the proportional representation system, was made.

KEYWORDS

Social Listening, Internet Election, Internet Election Campaign, Election Results Predictions, Regression Analysis

1. INTRODUCTION

A conventional method used for election results predictions in Japan is RDD (Random Digit Dialing), in which media randomly call landline telephones to gather statistics. However since people nowadays have mobile phones and those especially under 40 years of age choose not to own landline phones, the RDD method has become less effective for predictions. Although research methods using mobile phones have been sought, mobile phones in Japan do not have area codes which make it impossible to obtain regional information through mobile phones.

As an alternate method of the RDD social listening has drawn attention. Through social listening, which tracks conversations about specific topics, keywords, phrases, products, etc. posted in social media, it is possible to collect massive data that was not available previously, and with that prospect social listening plays an important role in society. For example, under the conventional method, marketing research is conducted by gathering information at the scene or by survey using a certain number of samples for product development, marketing and management. In contrast, social listening makes it possible for companies to listen to numerous opinions from consumers and society through SNS (Social Network Service); as a result consumers and society can be put in the center for product development, marketing and management.

SNS such as Facebook and Twitter is quite actively used in Japan. Especially Twitter is exceedingly popular enough for Twitter Inc. to portray Japan's love of Twitter as "insane". This research is to look into the effectiveness of SNS as a tool for election results predictions by collecting data through social media after the ban on Internet campaigns was lifted in Japan in 2013. It is found that results predictions of Japan's national elections using social media is possible for nationwide proportional representation.

2. BACKGROUND OF STUDY

In this chapter social listening and Internet elections in Japan are discussed as the background of the study.

2.1 Internet Election Campaigns in Japan

Election campaigns using the Internet had not been available in Japan due to the Public Offices Election Laws which regulate various campaign activities such as door-to-door canvassing, pre-election campaigns and distribution of documents to protect the fairness and equality of elections. Among them is the prohibition of distribution of documents and drawings (such as post cards, placards or flyers), and the Supreme Court decided that the contents displayed on computer screens or cell phones are also considered documents or drawings; therefore, election campaigns using the Internet had not been available. However election campaigns which utilize the IT era had been discussed, and "The Act for Amending Part of the Public Offices Election Law related to Permission for Internet Election Campaigns" was passed in 2013, through which election campaigns using social media became available. The Japanese national elections have two types; the Lower House elections and the Upper House elections. The Lower House election consists of 289 single-member districts and 11 proportional representation electoral districts for176 seats. The Upper House election consists of 47 districts for 73 seats and 48 seats by proportional representation on the national level.

2.2 Social Media in Japan

A social network service that holds the largest number of accounts in Japan (total population 126,937,000 as of November 1, 2016) is LINE with 68 million users, followed by Twitter and Facebook with 40 million and 27 million users respectively. However, LINE could be called a closed social media because LINE is to exchange messages between friends and family members, and the size of the network is quite small compared to Twitter. Thus, Twitter and Facebook are appropriate for this study. Twitter Inc. portrays Japan's love of Twitter as "insane". The world record for the number of tweets per minute is 618,725 tweets right after the match between Argentina and Germany during the 2014 Soccer World Cup, and the world record for the number of tweets per second is 143,199 during the Japanese animated adventure film "Laputa: Castle in the Sky" broadcast on August in 2013. In addition, Japan dominates high ranking positions in the number of tweets per second.

3. LITERATURE REVIEW

Analysis of elections using social media have been conducted in many countries such as by Tumasjan, A. et al. (2010) and Jungherr, A. et al. (2012) that focused on the number of tweets. Tumasjan, A. et al. (2010) and Jungherr, A. et al. (2012) both analyzed a German Federal election using 100,000 tweets, and they found contradictory results. This may have been caused by an insufficient number of twitter users in Germany as Doerner S. (2014) indicated. The research by Daniel G. et al. (2011) and Jessica C. et al. (2011) using emotion analysis from 240,000 data found contradictory results as well.

In Japan Nasuno et al. (2013 and 2014) and Yoshimi (2016) published studies focusing on social media to analyze Japanese elections after the ban on Internet campaigning was lifted. Nasuno et al. (2013 and 2014) analyzed the 23rd Upper House regular election using 42,645 tweets by 287 candidates and 368,694 of re-tweets of them. Also Yoshimi (2016) targeted 30,941 tweets posted on their official accounts by 537 candidates running from five major political parties in the 47th Lower House general election. The above three studies only show a tendency due to the scarce amount of data.

On the other hand, this study takes advantage of the Japanese insane love of Twitter, through which anonymous online support groups are created. As Goto (2015) found the predictions in small constituencies at national elections were not possible due to the scarce number of postings. Our research found that for other candidates several hundred to one thousand tweets is the line to win, but that data shows tendencies only. The same thing can be said for candidates who rely on organized votes[1]. For example, Yoshifumi

[1] Votes cast for specific candidates or parties by various groups or organizations. Large units of professional office workers (such as self-defense army or police), industry groups, labor unions, interest groups, religious groups are applied to those groups or organizations. A political party Komei was founded based on Sokagakkai, a Buddhist religious corporation, to achieve moderate political influence and wins seats by organized votes.

Takushoku earned the largest number of votes of 429,002 at the 23rd Upper House general election in spite of the fact that the number of postings containing his name was only 8. He is a former head of the national association of postmasters and received organized votes from postal businesses. Thus, with this research method it is difficult to analyze parties or individual candidates in small constituencies or who rely on organized votes. However, analysis by party name in the proportional representation system is effective. For this study 956,268 tweets and Facebook postings that contained political party names for the 23rd Upper House regular election were collected. Furthermore, 1,287,982 tweets for the 47th Lower House general election and 1,777,724 tweets during the 24th Upper House general election were collected. With this overwhelmingly large volume of data compared to other research performed in Japan or other countries this study is distinguished from others.

4. RESEARCH METHOD

A regression analysis using data collected via social listening was performed for this study. In this chapter the methods for social listening and analysis are discussed.

4.1 Methods for Social Listening

Social listening data regarding Japanese national elections are collected through Yahoo! Japan real-time search. The Public Offices Election Law allows an election campaign only between a candidate's registration on the date of a public announcement and a day before a voting date. Campaigning in another period such as pre-election campaign before a candidate registration is prohibited. Therefore, the period for social listening is between the date of public announcement and a day before a voting date.

The media such as press and TV station conduct a sample survey using RDD during election campaigns to predict the election results. Through social listening more precise information can be collected by taking advantage of information generated via Twitter in a spontaneous manner during the same period.

As Goto (2015) previously noted, the number of tweets by candidates name in small constituencies were too scarce to use for the analysis of elections. Also the same can be said of candidates who rely on organized votes. Therefore, social listening was conducted by party names in the proportional representation system using Yahoo! Japan Real-time Search. Some parties cannot be identifiable; for example, although at the 23rd Upper House regular election 12 registered parties' official and official abbreviated names were extracted, the official names of "Your party", "New Party DAICHI", "People's Life Party", "Green Wind", "Green Party" and "Happiness Realization Party" whose official abbreviated names are "You", "DAICHI", "Life", "Midori (note that 'midori' is the Japanese translation of green), "Green" and "Happiness" respectively could not be identified. Since those unidentifiable parties by party name have lesser power, and also the amount of data collected via Yahoo! Japan real-time search is small, only official names of those parties were used for data gathering. Also, since tweets on Liberal Democratic Party, a majority party, included Democratic Party of Japan, another major party, some procedures were used to distinguish tweets between those two parties.

4.2 Analysis Method

Goto (2015) has analyzed a correlation between the total number of postings containing party names on social media during a campaign period and the number of votes each party obtained in the proportional representation system. At the 23rd Upper House regular election held in 2013 R2 is 0.857, and a strong correlation between the number of postings that contained a party name and the party-list votes in the proportional representation system is found. Also, at the 47th Lower House general election in 2014 R2 is 0.880, and Pearson correlation coefficient is 0.938 which is 1% level and is significant (both sides); thus a strong correlation between the number of tweets containing party name and the total party-list votes in each constituency in the PR system is found. Further, at the 24th Upper House regular election in 2016 R2 is 0.891, and Pearson correlation coefficient is 0.944 which is 1% level and is significant (both sides); thus a strong correlation between the number of tweets that contained a party name and the total number of party-list votes in each constituency in the proportional representation system is found as well.

In this study, a regression analysis is performed to the above three elections to find the correlation between social media postings and election results.

5. ANALYSIS

In this chapter the past three national elections after the ban on internet election campaign was lifted are analyzed using the methods described in the previous chapter.

5.1 Analysis of the 23rd Upper House Regular Election

The terms of office for the Upper House members elected in 2007 expired on July 28, 2013, and 121 seats (73 for constituencies and 48 for the proportional representation system by open list) were included in the election on July 21, 2013. This was the first election where the internet campaign was allowed, and public announcement was made on July 4.

Table 1. Each registered party's total number posted during the 23rd Upper House election

	Jul.4	Jul.5	Jul.6	Jul.7	Jul.8	Jul.9	Jul.10	Jul.11	Jul.12	Jul.13	Jul.14	Jul.15	Jul.16	Jul.17	Jul.18	Jul.19	Jul.20	Total	Nr. Of votes
YP	1,586	2,311	2,102	1,803	1,891	1,534	1,791	1,661	1,767	1,586	2,709	2,132	2,628	2,079	2,171	2,031	2,115	33,897	4,221,422
DPJ	7,924	11,024	10,497	12,014	8,863	9,436	9,982	9,652	10,817	8,715	7,595	9,711	12,255	12,352	12,181	11,938	11,357	176,313	4,827,158
NPD	141	2,744	844	413	327	220	369	327	1,065	427	396	376	710	297	433	353	546	9,988	398,848
SDP	1,683	3,002	1,902	2,957	2,325	1,629	1,809	1,995	1,663	1,459	1,492	1,871	1,516	1,631	1,761	2,088	2,051	32,834	983,227
PLP	1,006	2,701	2,190	2,216	2,128	1,721	1,719	1,912	1,927	2,492	2,405	2,781	2,284	2,499	3,110	3,151	2,714	38,956	723,987
GW	970	1,470	1,034	935	899	808	837	849	748	803	1,135	1,426	1,542	1,338	1,276	1,404	1,501	18,975	319,630
LDP	9,577	24,012	33,144	25,220	19,431	17,485	16,506	14,894	15,498	15,643	15,934	18,407	18,437	22,023	30,730	28,149	30,409	355,499	14,080,143
JCP	1,212	3,348	3,112	3,211	2,971	2,734	2,484	2,815	2,998	2,637	2,446	2,890	3,285	3,372	3,838	4,146	4,726	52,225	4,647,765
KOMEI	1,285	3,805	3,054	3,311	3,413	2,855	2,457	2,639	2,587	2,334	2,957	3,247	3,752	3,961	4,237	4,325	4,303	54,522	3,333,142
GP	1,144	1,839	2,720	2,010	1,496	1,695	1,733	2,580	2,405	2,591	2,509	2,931	3,647	4,075	3,578	3,556	3,985	44,494	242,460
JRP	2,845	5,463	5,144	5,463	5,786	6,919	6,263	6,220	5,044	6,791	8,591	7,096	5,538	5,897	6,242	6,177	7,023	102,502	5,191,563
HRP	935	1,730	1,248	1,288	1,482	1,502	1,447	2,031	2,340	2,242	2,383	2,398	2,807	3,405	2,648	2,793	3,384	36,063	153,296

Table 1 shows the number of postings containing party names on Twitter and Facebook, (note that the number of postings in this section is the total from Twitter and Facebook), total number of postings and the votes each party received in the proportional representation system between the day of the official announcement and the day before a voting date. A regression analysis2 was performed with the total number of postings containing a party name as an independent variable and with the total number of votes those parties each obtained as a dependent variable. A regression line is given by Y (votes gained)=37.402×x(number of postings)+279687.511 with t-ratio=7.443, p-value= 0.000, R2=0.874, and F=55.403. Figure 1 shows a scatter plot. And as Figure 2 of scatter plot standardized residuals shows, standardized residuals is within ±2.

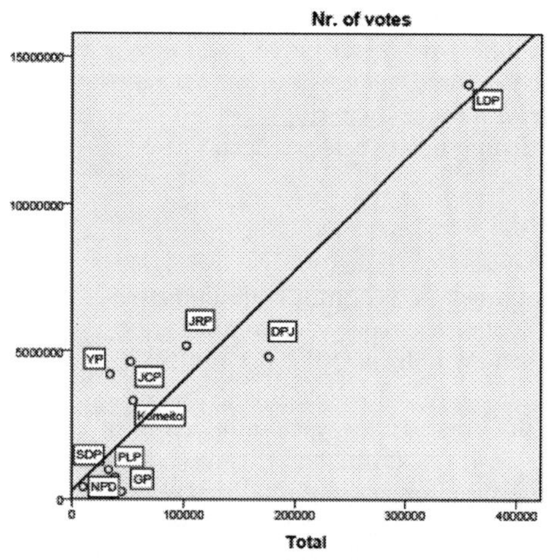

Figure 1. Scatter plot

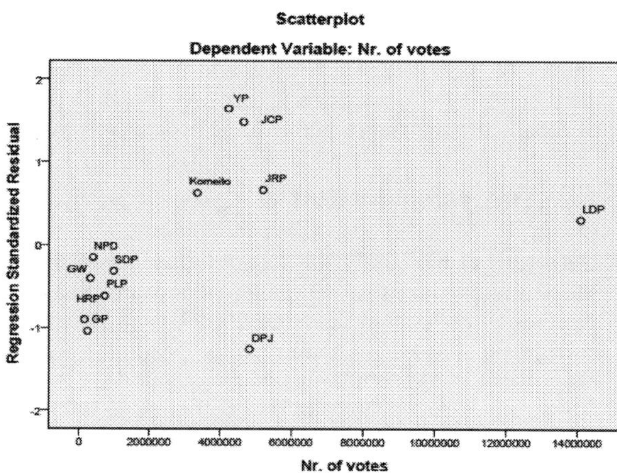

Figure 2. Scatter plot of standardized residuals

---

2 SPSS Ver.24 was used.

A seats prediction can be calculated by multiplying the ratio of the number of postings on each party and 48 seats in the proportional representation, and the comparison with actual election results is made in Figure 3. The prediction errors are 0 for Liberal Democratic Party of Japan, 2 for Democratic Party of Japan, 4 for Komeito, 1 for Japan Restoration Party, and 2 for Japanese Communist Party. Except for Komeito, which relies on organized votes and has a large error, errors are within two seats; therefore, it is suggested that election results predictions in the proportional representation system are correctly made.

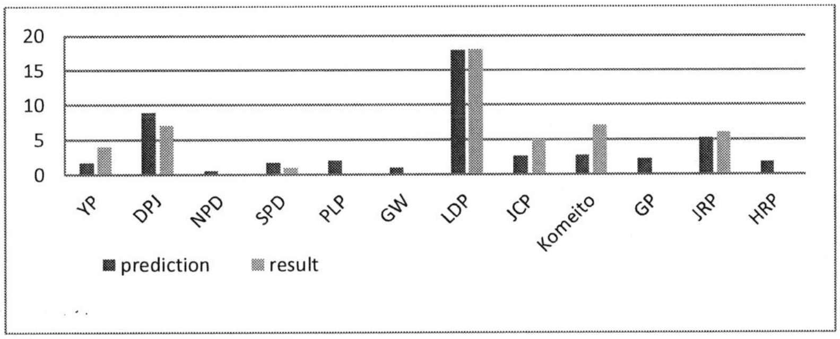

Figure 3. Results predictions in PR system by social media and actual results

5.2 47th Lower House General Election

Due to the dissolution of the Lower House on November 21, 2014, a national election was called for 475 seats (295 for small constituencies and 180 for proportional representation system by fixed list). The election was publicly announced on December 2 and voted on December 14.

The number of tweets containing party name (the number of postings on the 47th Lower House general election is from Twitter only), total number of tweets and total number of votes each party gained in 11 electoral districts (Hokkaido, Tohoku, Kitakanto, Minamikanto, Tokyo, Hokurikusinetsu, Tokai, Kinki, Chugoku, Shikoku, Kyushu) are shown in Table 2. Also Table 3 shows the same items after the "emotion analysis" through Yahoo! Japan real-time search was made.

Table 2. Each registered party's total number posted during the 47th Lower House election

	Dec. 2	Dec. 3	Dec. 4	Dec. 5	Dec. 6	Dec. 7	Dec. 8	Dec. 9	Dec. 10	Dec. 11	Dec. 12	Dec. 13	Total	Votes
LDP	28,543	24,607	40,095	32,825	34,458	35,868	39,460	37,649	37,557	37,335	41,140	55,762	445,299	17,658,916
NRP	363	237	170	171	116	159	96	95	78	75	101	202	1,863	16,597
DPJ	19,958	15,786	21,535	17,870	18,922	21,622	21,734	21,862	24,073	22,613	21,637	25,699	253,311	9,775,991
KOMEI	8,801	7,367	9,006	9,845	9,577	8,589	11,713	10,662	10,493	8,853	8,417	11,726	115,049	7,314,236
SPD	3,562	3,001	2,891	2,497	2,608	2,771	2,772	3,887	3,872	3,733	3,981	5,609	41,184	1,314,441
JRP	5,760	5,638	6,777	5,301	5,937	6,743	7,159	6,761	7,417	6,647	6,633	10,241	81,014	8,382,699
HRP	1,376	130	867	929	904	956	967	975	1,014	996	1,222	1,417	11,753	259,060
PLP	1,612	1,311	1,604	1,557	1,996	1,711	2,263	2,226	2,297	2,374	2,200	2,928	24,079	1,028,721
JCP	12,408	10,663	13,568	11,589	12,508	14,572	14,388	19,064	17,317	22,283	20,205	23,997	192,562	6,062,962

Table 3. Each registered party's total number posted excluding negative postings during the 47th Lower House election

	Dec. 2	Dec. 3	Dec. 4	Dec. 5	Dec. 6	Dec. 7	Dec. 8	Dec. 9	Dec. 10	Dec. 11	Dec. 12	Dec. 13	Total	Votes
LDP	12,273	11,565	19,246	14,771	15,506	15,782	17,362	16,189	16,901	16,801	18,924	24,535	199,855	17,658,906
NRP	225	142	136	125	86	121	65	76	76	51	68	127	1,298	16,597
DPJ	8,981	8,051	11,629	8,399	9,083	10,811	10,650	10,712	12,518	12,211	11,684	12,850	127,579	9,775,991
KOMEI	4,753	3,978	5,043	5,513	5,842	4,896	7,613	6,717	6,611	5,046	4,882	6,449	67,343	7,314,236
SPD	2,030	1,681	1,677	1,498	1,591	1,552	1,552	2,332	2,478	2,314	2,468	3,702	24,875	1,314,441
JRP	3,110	3,101	3,863	2,863	3,325	3,844	3,937	3,516	4,228	3,589	3,847	5,530	44,753	8,382,699
HRP	867	87	555	632	579	669	600	624	659	657	880	1,006	7,815	259,060
PLP	1,225	1,009	1,283	1,199	1,617	1,317	1,833	1,759	1,907	1,828	1,738	2,313	19,028	1,028,721
JCP	5,584	5,012	6,648	5,679	6,004	7,286	6,906	9,341	8,659	10,919	10,709	11,999	94,746	6,062,962

A regression analysis was performed with the total number of postings containing a party name as an independent variable and with the total number of votes those parties each obtained as a dependent variable. A regression line is given by Y (votes gained) = 89.935×x (number of postings) + 279959.002 with t-ratio=7.555, p-value= 0.000, R^2=0.880, and F=55.403. Figure 4 shows a scatter plot. And as Figure 5 of scatter plot standardized residuals shows, standardized residuals is within ±2.

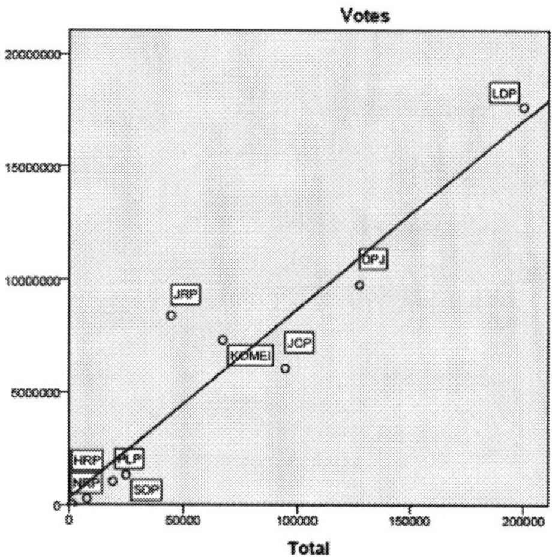

Figure 4. Scatter plot

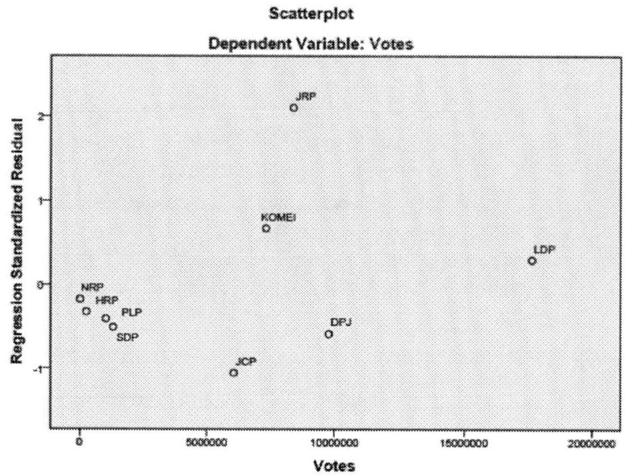

Figure 5. Scatter plot of standardized residuals

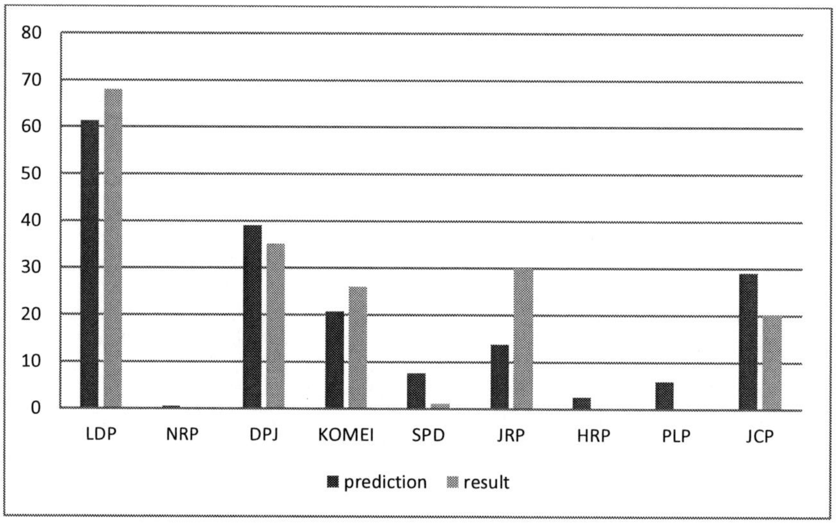

Figure 6. Results predictions in PR System by social media and actual results

A seats prediction can be calculated by multiplying the ratio of the number of postings on each party and 180 seats in proportional representation, and the comparison with actual election results are made in Figure 6. The prediction errors were 7 for Liberal Democratic Party of Japan, 4 for Democratic Party of Japan, 5 for Komeito, 7 for Japan Restoration Party, and 9 for Japanese Communist Party. Those errors are considered to be caused by the complicated Lower House electoral system, under which the number of seats in the Lower House is over three times the number of seats in the Upper House, candidates win by sekihairitsu (best loser calculation), some parties do not list candidates in the proportional representation system in some of the 11 constituencies, etc.

5.3 24th Upper House Regular Election

On July 25, 2016, the terms of office for the half of the Upper House members elected in 2013 expired, and a national election was called for 121 seats (73 for constituencies and 48 for proportional representation system by open list). The election was publicly announced on June 22 and voted on July 10.

Table 4. Each registered party's total number posted during the 24th Upper House election

	Jun.22	Jun.23	Jun.24	Jun.25	Jun.26	Jun.27	Jun.28	Jun.29	Jun.30	Jul.1	Jul.2	Jul.3	Jul.4	Jul.5	Jul.6	Jul.7	Jul.8	Jul.9	Total	Votes
LDP	27,538	24,232	24,842	22,508	24,459	27,703	31,894	34,280	28,446	28,787	30,068	29,865	29,581	37,151	40,998	36,696	38,962	63,885	581,895	20,114,788
DPJ	19,682	11,984	13,977	13,286	16,200	14,136	17,575	13,718	14,135	13,214	12,854	18,935	14,963	15,155	17,242	13,320	17,718	19,343	277,437	11,751,015
JCP	13,233	12,070	13,935	14,018	25,614	23,242	26,066	25,379	16,889	14,646	15,689	18,190	17,490	19,392	20,096	20,416	20,711	26,136	343,212	6,016,194
KOMEI	5,407	5,025	5,115	5,624	6,204	6,108	6,393	5,919	6,304	5,945	6,642	7,668	7,304	7,312	7,867	7,971	8,299	11,073	122,180	7,572,960
SDP	2,793	2,267	2,284	2,341	2,895	3,171	4,355	4,258	3,067	3,491	4,021	4,119	2,757	2,940	3,320	3,643	3,360	4,626	59,708	1,536,238
ORP	4,807	4,598	4,393	5,139	4,994	4,596	4,308	4,182	4,083	4,191	4,556	5,437	6,046	6,157	6,637	7,679	7,403	9,587	98,793	5,153,584
AVP	348	282	196	190	197	274	236	290	332	671	350	284	316	278	285	583	587	784	6,483	466,706
HRP	853	713	572	500	490	494	691	655	857	877	1,287	844	1,133	834	853	1,677	2,344	4,238	19,912	366,815
NRP	661	727	335	448	398	405	330	444	473	629	345	428	473	450	457	709	1,455	1,064	10,231	580,653
PJK	1088	772	1016	1050	1184	920	904	728	569	709	794	1219	1026	1470	1,630	2,034	2,046	3,587	22,746	734,024
PLP	1126	803	1054	895	898	1006	1118	1253	943	1115	1186	1512	1473	1810	1,581	1,732	2,229	3,217	24,951	1,067,300

The number of tweets on each party posted (the number of postings on the 24th Upper House regular election is from Twitter only), total number of tweets and total number of votes each party gained during the campaign (between the day of public announcement and the day before the voting) are shown in Table 4.

A regression analysis was performed with the total number of postings containing a party name as an independent variable and with the total number of votes those parties each obtained as a dependent variable. A regression line is given by Y (votes gained) =89.935×x (number of postings) + 27.775 with t-ratio=8.565, p-value= 0.000, R2=0.891, and F=73.362. Figure 7 shows a scatter plot. And as Figure 8 of scatter plot standardized residuals shows, standardized residuals is within ±2.

A seats prediction can be calculated by multiplying the ratio of the number of postings on each party and 48 seats in proportional representation, and the comparison with actual election results are made in Figure 9. The prediction error is 1 for Liberal Democratic Party of Japan, but prediction errors widen because, in this election, the same individuals tweeted the same content many times.

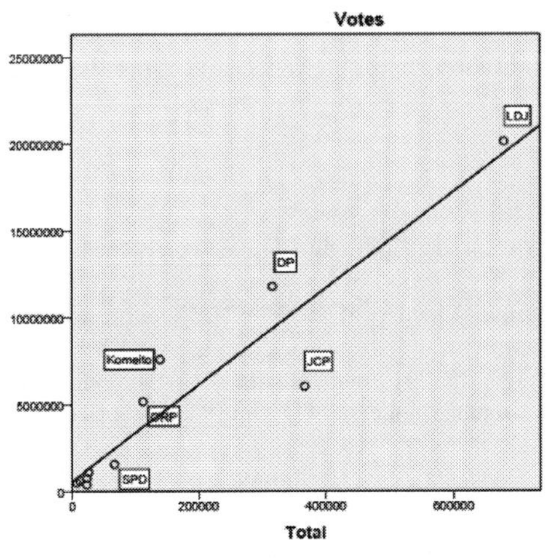

Figure 7. Scatter plot

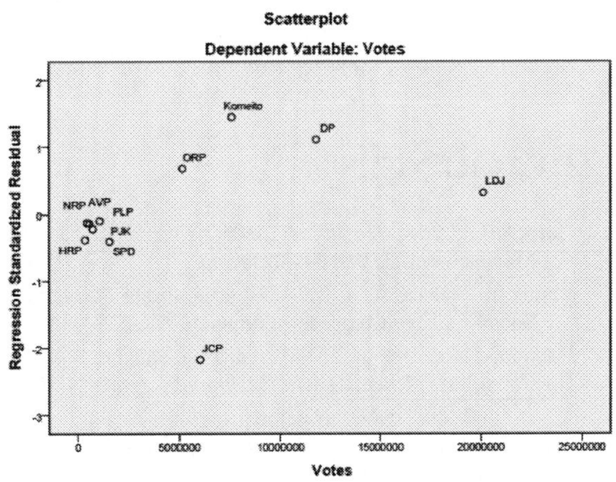

Figure 8. Scatter plot of standardized residuals

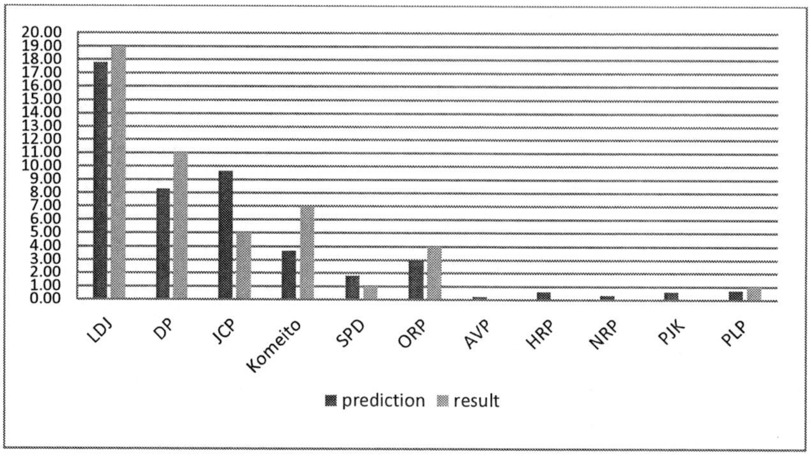

Figure 9. Results predictions in PR system by social media and actual results

6. CONCLUSION

In this research, it is found that results predictions of Japan's national elections using social media is possible in a more frequent manner at lower cost with higher accuracy compared to the conventional research through RDD. As described in Chapter 3, Literature Review, although it is difficult to make predictions on parties or candidates in small-constituency districts or who rely on organized votes, election results predictions using social listening in the proportional representation system are effective. Especially the predictions for the proportional representation system in Upper House elections, which is voted nation-wide, were more precise than those in Lower House elections in which the nation is divided into 11 districts. In addition, adding variables such as the number of party members would make more precise predictions possible than through the conventional methods.

In the era of the "Information Explosion", social listening or big data such as IoT, or a combination of both are essential tools for not only business management but also for problem solving or prediction-making.

REFERENCES

Goto, Hisaki 2015 A study of Elections using Social Media and the Internet Journal of Japan Society for Information and Management, *35 (4),* 34-42(Japanese)

Jungherr, Andreas. et al 2012 Why the Pirate Party Won the German Election of 2009 or The Trouble with Predictions Social Science Computer Review *30 (2)*, 229-234

Nasuno, Kaoru. et al 2013 Predicting Japanese General Election in 2013 with Twitter: Considering Diffusion of Candidates' Tweets *IECE Technical Report.* NLC, Natural language understanding and models of communication, *11113 (338)*, Japan, 25-28

Nasuno, Kaoru. et al 2014 Considering Diffusion of Candidates' Tweets *The 28th Annual Conference of the Japanese Society for Artificial Intelligence, Japan*, 1-4 (Japanese)

Yoshimi, Kenji 2016 Usage Tendencies of Social Media by Each Political Party during Election Campaign — A Study on Twitter Use in the 47th General Election — *Socio Informatics, 4 (3), Japan*, 16-29 (Japanese)

Tumasjan, Andranik. et al 2010 Predicting Election with Twitter: What 140 Characters Reveal about Political Sentiment *Proceedings of the Fourth International AAAI Conference on Weblogs and Social Media*, 178-185

APPLYING DATA MINING AND DATA VISUALIZATION WITHIN THE SCOPE OF AUDIO DATA USING SPOTIFY

Marika Apostolova Trpkovska, Arbesa Kajtazi, Lejla Abazi Bexheti and Arbana Kadriu
South East European University
Ilindenska n.335, 1200, Tetovo, Macedonia

ABSTRACT

The aim of this research is to put forward an overview of applying data mining and data visualization within the scope of audio data from a dataset of Spotify. The research starts by presenting background information of these two fields and their influence on music industry. The paper includes explanation of the most essential concepts and their role. The research is concentrated on analysis of audio features of the tracks of Spotify's Top Songs in 2017 playlist and tries to highlight the common patterns behind the audio features of these songs. For the purposes of this research, Spotify datasets are used as practical scenario. For this reason, more detailed information is given about songs features, what are they, what do these top songs have in common and why do people like them. The result of the study showcase how singers and song makers can leverage the power of data visualization and data mining to help trying to predict one audio feature based on the others, look for patterns in the audio features of the songs and see which features correlate the most.

KEYWORDS

Data Mining, Data Visualization, Audio Data, Patterns, Spotify

1. INTRODUCTION

In the recent years, we started witnessing Big Data. This trend has influenced all industries. More and more data is generated and stored in different formats. There are many challenges we face with these exaggerated volumes of data, starting from the step of capturing them till properly displaying valuable information. "Data is the new oil. It's valuable, but if unrefined it cannot really be used. It has to be changed into gas, plastic, chemicals etc. to create a valuable entity that drives profitable activity; so data must be broken down, analyzed for it to have value". Big data comes with big promises. However consisting of only 1s and 0s the data is imperceptible to the public. For organizations to excel in their work, sometimes conducting only an analysis of data is not enough, therefore effective dissemination of the information is required.

The merit of data mining and visualization here is that they, together, utilize and make sense of the data. Since both fields are emerging, research on how to best combine these two areas is conducted every day. The field of music industry can benefit a lot from this synthesis. As new technology rapidly is being developed, the way of storytelling is changed by integrating data visualization tools.

The purpose of this research is to see what these songs have in common and why people like them by using big data analytics. Hopefully, with the new knowledge, it can contribute to the prediction of audio features based on others. To achieve this purpose, it is used a Spotify dataset where the audio features where extracted using the Spotify Web API and the Spotify Python library. The credit goes to Spotify for calculating the audio feature values. In doing so, this research will be of interest for the field of music industry where the organizations are trying to adapt to changes in the industry and for the scholars wanting to expand their knowledge in the application forms of data mining and data visualization.

2. BACKGROUND

Data mining is new powerful technology enhances the value of existing data by automating the process of extracting knowledge from it. By Rieger, massive databases are analyzed in minutes which enable users to conduct more studies in shorter amount of time and at the same time helps understand complex data. Data mining often is used as synonym for knowledge discovery from data (KDD), but in fact, it only depicts a step of that process.

Hidden patterns are found following various techniques and implementing the corresponding algorithms. Most popular techniques that provide diverse insights are: classification analysis, association rule learning, anomaly detection, clustering analysis and regression analysis. Data mining offers a solution to the problem by intelligently analyzing the present data in the database. This process often includes discovering patterns among data, finding specific connection between them that will be used for prediction of further actions.

The importance of data mining as resource is that it elucidates the hidden knowledge in large datasets. Applying data mining has proved to lead to new insights, better decision making and sometimes bring competitive advantage to companies. Data mining is interdisciplinary computer science field with broad implementation in other fields as well.

In scope of this, also the application of visualization provides unique perspective on the information and is often associated with coordinated system, points, lines, tables, charts or graphs. Additionally, it can be viewed as a form of humanizing statistics. The capability of combining data visualizations with stories gave birth to new form of storytelling known as "narrative visualization". Data visualization plays perhaps one of the most important roles in successfully communicating information. From human-computer interaction perspective, it has an ability to capture the attention of the human eye and brain. Ware explains the crucial role that it has by proclaiming that "Visual displays provide the highest bandwidth channel from the computer to the human. We acquire more information through vision than through all of the other senses combined. The 20 billion or so neurons of the brain devoted to analyzing visual information provide a pattern-finding mechanism that is a fundamental component in much of our cognitive activity.".

The two main reasons to use visualization as a form of presentation in stories by Goldman are: (1) exploratory: to understand what is present in the data; (2) communicative: to display and discuss visualizations with the public by telling stories based on the data and the facts.

Surprisingly, the question of "Why we like or not a particular song?" has received little attention from music psychology. Although music preference is recognized as a central aspect of modern identities, the field is "still in its infancy". The issue of liking per se is indeed difficult to study directly, and music psychologists have traditionally focused on less elusive, more directly measurable phenomena such as memorization, recognition or learning.

In our context, a central issue in trying to explain music hits is exposure, that is, the simple fact of listening to a musical piece. What is the effect of exposure on preference or liking? Studies on exposure show that there is indeed an impact of repeated exposure on liking, but also that this impact is far from simple. Parameters such as the context, type of music or listening conditions (focused or incidental), seem to influence the nature of this impact, and many contradictory results have been published. The popular idea that repeated exposure tends to increase liking was put forward early and was confirmed experimentally in a wide variety of contexts and musical genres. The so-called mere exposure effect, akin to the familiarity principle, or perceptual fluency, is considered by many psychologists to be a robust principle, pervading many facets of music listening.

However, as noted by Schellenberg, this increase in liking may be restricted to musically impoverished or highly controlled stimuli. Indeed, other studies have shown a more subtle effect of repeated exposure. The study by Siu-Lan et al. showed different effects of exposure on intact and patchwork compositions. An inverted U-curve phenomena was observed in particular by Szpunar et al. and Schellenberg in his journal article, it explained in large part by the "two factor model". In this model, two forces compete to build up liking: (1) the arousal potential of the stimulus (the music), which decreases with repeated listening, thereby increasing liking (with the habituation to this arousal potential), and (2) familiarity, which tends to create boredom. These two forces combined produce typical inverted U-shapes that have been observed in many studies of preference. This model is itself related to the famous "Wundt curve". The Wundt curve describes the typical experience of arousal as being optimal when achieving a compromise between repetition/boredom and surprise.

Yet, other studies performed by Witvliet showed in contrast a polarization effect, whereby repeated exposure does not influence initial likings but makes them stronger, both positively and negatively. At last, Loui et al. studied exposure effects by considering exotic musical temperaments, to study the relation between learning and preference. They showed that passive exposure to melodies built in an entirely new musical system led to learning and generalization, as well as increased preference for repeated melodies.

This work emphasizes the importance of learning in music preference. These psychological experiments show that a relation between exposure and liking exists, but that this relation is complex and still not well understood, in particular for rich, emotionally meaningful pieces. It is therefore impossible to simply consider, from a psychological point of view, that repeated exposure necessarily increases liking: it all depends on a variety of factors.

Big data is a term that reflects the amount of information people generate. Some estimate that today, humans generates more information in one minute than in every moment from the earliest historical record through 2000. Unsurprisingly, harnessing this data has shaped music industry in radical new ways. With data becoming easier to acquire and analyze, it has now become possible to crunch large numbers and predict audience preference and buying tendencies. Whereas in the past, the industry relied primarily on sales and how often a song was played on the radio, they can now see what specific songs people are listening to, where are they hearing it and how they are consuming it. Big Data is being integrated into nearly every field. It should be no surprise that the multi-billion dollar music industry wants in. There are two major ways big data is already influencing the music industry; music creation and music selection.

There is a certain circular quality to pop music. The more you are forced to listen to that inescapable new song, the more you like it. You liking means more music of the same type will be produced. Data, however, is making the new era of music one of the most populist. For example; in our case Spotify knows what listeners like and want. The ability to listen to music is only the most basic feature of Spotify. They constant compile data and create algorithms to suggest new music to listeners.

3. PROBLEM STATEMENT

The music industry is in the middle of something new and bold, thanks to digital technology. Traditional distribution venues have already been replaced with digital ones and this has surprisingly boosted the popularity of artists. Instead of slowing things down, downloads and media streaming have helped artist mount more successful tours and sold out concerts than ever before. This is a positive example of what digital (data-driven) innovations and bold ideas can do.

From a global music currency to virtual multi-camera recording setups, there are a lot of ways that technology is helping the music industry grow. Fifteen years ago, Steve Jobs introduced the iPod. Since then, most music fans have understood this has radically changed how they listen to music. Data from what we download and listen to can now be mined to create and promote future songs. Less understood are the ways that raw information – accumulated via downloads apps and online searches – is influencing not only what songs are marketed and sold, but which songs become hits.

Decisions about how to market and sell music, to some extent, still hinge upon subjective assumptions about what sounds good to an executive, or which artists might be easier to market.

Increasingly, however, businesses are turning to big data and the analytics that can help turn this information into actions. But, the big question raised in this research is: Can someone predict whether your recently produced song will become a hit?. Any pop song composer would probably laugh at this question and respond: How could someone predict the success of what took so much craft, pain, and immeasurable creativity to produce?. This question raises a recurring fantasy in every culture: wouldn't it be thrilling to understand the "laws of attraction" that explain how this sort of preference system of music in human beings works, to the point of being able to predict the success of a song or any other cultural artifact before it is even released? This fantasy is elaborated in detail in Malcom Gladwell's story "The Formula". In this fiction, a system is able to predict the success of movies by analyzing their script in automatic way. The system is even smart enough to propose modifications of the script to increase the success of the movie, with a quantified estimation of the impact in revenues.

This process is also true for music: what makes us like a song or not probably has to do with a complex combination of micro-emotions, themselves related to our personal history, to the specifics of the song and too many other elusive elements that escape our direct understanding.

However daring, we challenged this assumption by precisely undertaking the task of making these kinds of predictions. Researches with similar background of a predictive analysis with data visualization could not be found just some of them were only researches without including data mining and data visualization. There is one project on Kaggle in python that is really close to this research but, that used different kind of techniques for an attempt to build a classifier that can predict whether or not he likes a song.

4. METHOD

For this research, a traditional knowledge discovery process was used: first the data was gathered, pre-processed and cleaned, analyzed and at the end the results were visualized. The general system architecture followed is presented in Figure 1.

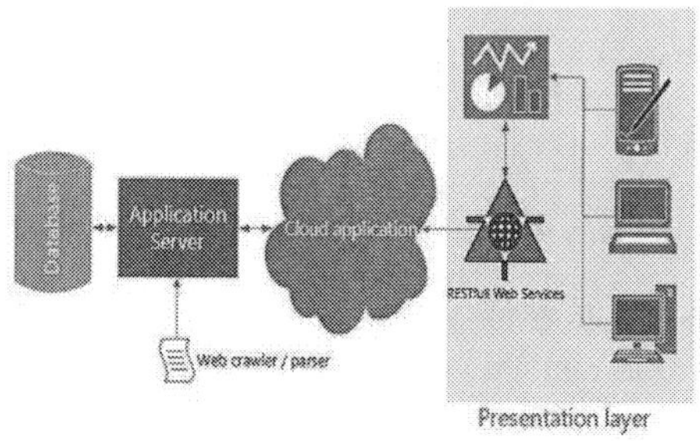

Figure 1. General system architecture

Even though the data is open and free, there are costs associated with the process of getting the dataset as a resource. Often the data should be converted into specific format, annotated or by necessity a certain metadata to be created. All of this requires human resources with specialized skills to do the work and technology resources (both hardware and software).

Spotify has developed a workflow manager, Luigi, which it is open source. Luigi is a Python framework for data flow definition and execution. Luigi is used to crunch a lot of data. Most of the data is user-centric data, such as billions of log messages that allows Spotify to provide music recommendations or select for example the next song heard on the radio. The data however is also used in decision-making, providing forecasting information and business analytics. So, the dataset was taken from Kaggle. The dataset contains the daily ranking of the 200 most listened songs in 53 songs from 2017 and 2018 by most Spotify users. It contains more than 2 million rows, which comprises 6629 artists, 18598 songs for a total count of one hundred five billion streams count. The data spans from 1st January 2017 to 9th January 2018 and will be kept up-to-date on following versions. It has been collected from Spotify's regional chart data.

For manipulating with data and visualizing the results, RStudio as integrated development environment (IDE) for R was used. R is designed to read entire datasets into memory and work with them there. The dataset imported in RStudio was of .csv format. For some of the cases, it was necessary to read the data into a data frames and use that data frame to conduct further manipulations. Data visualization was possible with the use of ggplot2 and plotrix package. This plotting system of R allows customization of the diagram and offers different built-in functions. Combination of data, aesthetic mappings and geom (geometric object) are specified for every diagram. The details of how data values are translated into visual representation were controlled by changing the scales, limiting the values of the axes, modifying labels and legend and adding theme to the plot.

4.1 Results

First of all the duration is converted in seconds for the need to simplify the analysis (Figure 2). Here we create a variable where we get the column "duration_ms" and convert it into seconds with a name of "duration_s".

```
features_data$duration_ms <- round(features_data$duration_ms/1000)
colnames(features_data)[15] <- "duration_s"
```

Figure 2. Converting the Duration in Seconds

On the next step the bar graph on Figure 3 shows "top artists based on their appearance and songs" and the R code.

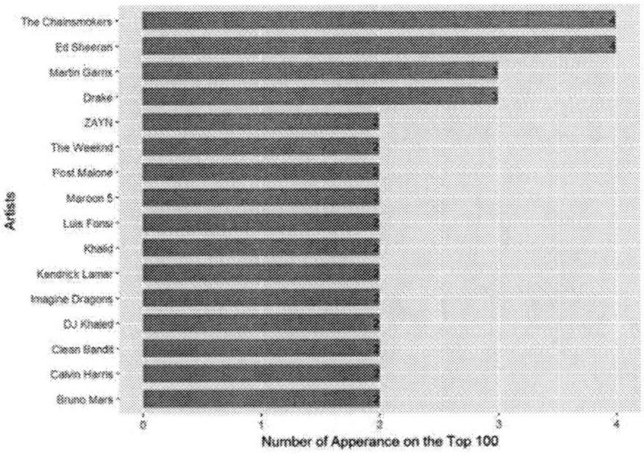


```r
top_artists <- features_data %>%
    group_by(artists)  %>%
    summarise(n_apperance = n()) %>%
    filter(n_apperance > 1) %>% # In decreasing order
    arrange(desc(n_apperance))

top_artists$artists <- factor(top_artists$artists, levels = top_artists$arti
sts[order(top_artists$n_apperance)])
# in order to visualise the list in descending order we create a vector with
 levels by their apperance and this vector later will be used to plot into
graph(also for classification)

ggplot(top_artists, aes(x = artists, y = n_apperance)) +
    geom_bar(stat = "identity",  fill = "steelblue3", width = 0.7 ) +
    labs(x = "Artists", y = "Number of Apperance on the Top 100") +
    theme(plot.title = element_text(size=10,hjust=-.3)) +
    geom_text(aes(label=n_apperance), hjust = 1, size = 3, color = 'BLACK')
+
    coord_flip()
```

Figure 3. Top Artist Based on their Appearance and the R Code

Here firstly we create a variable top artists and took the dataset features_data to group all the artists where and summarize all the appearance in the data set of the artist and filter them in descending order.

For creating the graph we used ggplot where we use the list top artists we created and with two axes, x which equals to artists and y which equals the appearance of an artist. Then we use the R studio features to design the graph with the colors and other features we like.

The graph on Figure 4 below shows the Top Artist in Central Europe by playing time.

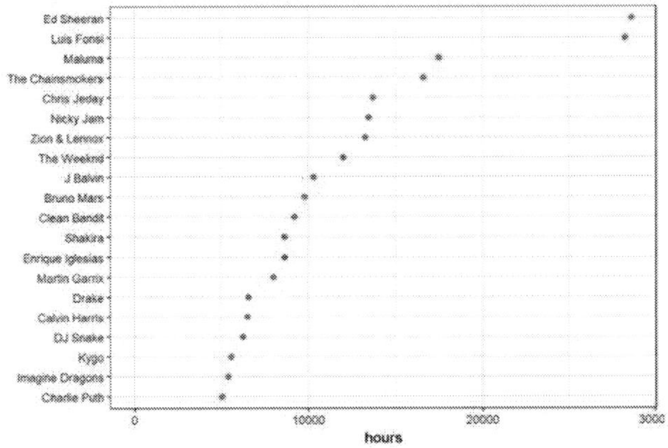


```r
ec_spotify_data <- spotify_data %>%
  filter(Region == "ec") %>%
  group_by(`Track.Name`) %>%
  summarise(total_streams = sum(Streams))

names(ec_spotify_data)[1] <- paste("name")

top_by_playtime <- features_data %>%
  left_join(ec_spotify_data,by = "name") %>%
  select(name,artists,duration_s,total_streams) %>%
  mutate(total_time = duration_s * total_streams/60000)
```

Figure 4. Top Artists in Central Europe by Paying Time and the R Code

As we can see on the above graph the artist Ed Sheeran was played the most by the users, reaching nearly 30000 hours played, followed by artist Luis Fonsi and so on going down. From the graph we can see that artists like Lois Fonsi and Maluma and Chris Jeday now started to be on top of the list.

For Top Artist by playing time in this case we used the "Streams" variable of Spotify_data and "duration" of features_ data, data sets.

Here at the first code we create a new list with the name top20_by_playtime, by using the list top_by_playtime we group by the artist's name, create a variable n_time where we save the sum from the total_time and arrange by descending order.

In the below graph (Figure 5) we visualized finding the relationship between the variables of the features_data dataset.

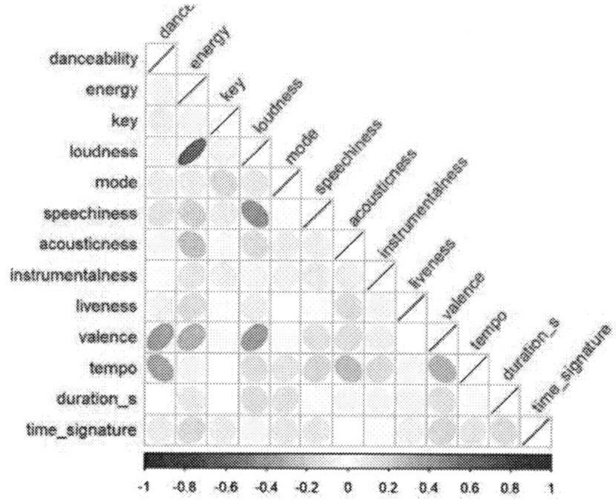


```
library(corrplot)
features_data_num <- features_data[,-(1:3)]
mtCor <- cor(features_data_num)
corrplot(mtCor, method = "ellipse", type = "lower", tl.srt = 50)
```

Figure 5. The Relationship between the Variables and the R Code

After finding the relationship between the variables we can conclude that "energy" and "loudness" are highly positively correlated. Also "valence" is more correlated with "danceability, energy and loudness". The variable "loudness" and "speechness", "tempo" and "danceability", "tempo" and "valence" are negatively correlated.

Here we used the library corrplot for visualizing the relationship between the variables. Will create a new variable fetures_data_num and will avoid the three first columns because the first columns are not numeric and include the name of the artist, song etc. And then we will use the method "ellipse" of type "lower". On Figure 6 is shown the distribution of the above 3 variables and how are they distributed among top 100 songs.

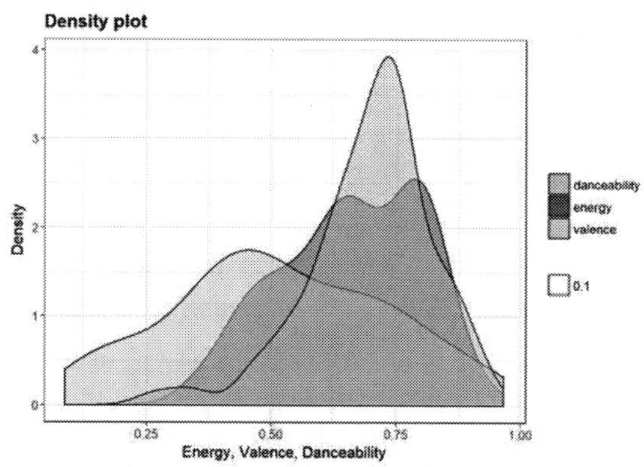


```
correlated_density <- ggplot(features_data) +
  geom_density(aes(energy,fill = "energy", alpha= 0.1))+
  geom_density(aes(valence,fill = "valence", alpha= 0.1))+
  geom_density(aes(danceability,fill = "danceability", alpha= 0.1))+
  scale_x_continuous(name="Energy, Valence, Danceability") +
  scale_y_continuous("Density")+
  ggtitle("Density plot")+
  theme_bw() +
  theme(plot.title = element_text(size = 14, face = "bold"), text = element_
text(size = 12))+
  theme(legend.title = element_blank())+
  scale_fill_brewer(palette="Paired")
correlated_density
```

Figure 6. The distribution of Energy, Valence and Danceability and the R code

We created a variable correlated_density where this variable contains the ggplot of features_data datasets then we find the density of the variables energy, valence and danceability and we use the R studio features to design the graph depending on our preferences.

Among all the 13 Keys that were appeared on this top 100 songs in Spotify by users we counted the amount of time each key song appeared the most (Figure 7).

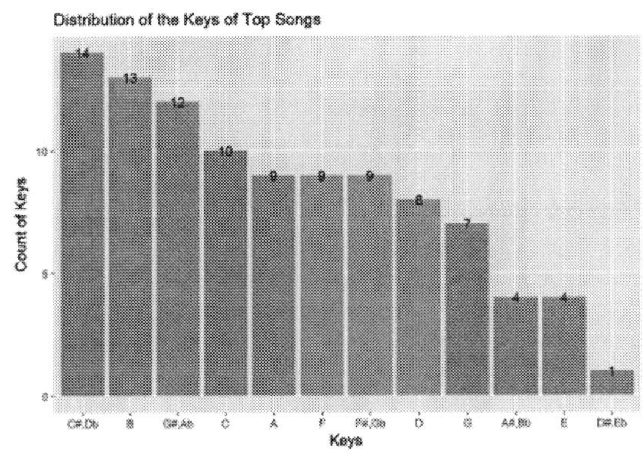


```
features_data$key <- as.character(features_data$key)
###since we made the keys from numerical to character type we can now change
 them
features_data$key <- revalue(features_data$key, c("0" = "C", "1" = "C#,Db",
"2" = "D", "3" = "D#,Eb", "4" = "E", "5" =  "F", "6" = "F#,Gb","7" = "G","8"
 = "G#,Ab","9" = "A","10" = "A#,Bb","11" = "B"))
###http://www.zebrakeys.com/lessons/beginner/musictheory/?id=12 referenced t
o convert key notes

song_keys <- features_data %>%
  group_by(key) %>%
  summarise(n_key= n()) %>%
  arrange(desc(n_key))

song_keys$key <- factor(song_keys$key, levels = song_keys$key[order(song_key
s$n_key)]) # in order to visualise the keys in descending order

ggplot(song_keys, aes(x = reorder(key,-n_key), y = n_key, fill = reorder(key
,-n_key))) +
    geom_bar(stat = "identity") +
    labs(title = "Distribution of the Keys of Top Songs", x = "Keys", y = "C
ount of Keys") +
    geom_text(aes(label=n_key)) +
    theme(plot.title = element_text(size=13), axis.title =element_text(size=
12))+
    theme(legend.position = "none")
```

Figure 7. Distribution of the Keys of Top Songs and the R Code

For the benefit of analysis, we converted the keys into their original symbols. First, here we create a variable fetures_data$key where we convert the keys into their original symbols. After that we create another variable where we summarize all the keys and arrange by descending order. We then use the ggplot to show the distribution of the keys and here from the graph we can see that the note C# was the one that appeared the most on the top 100 list of Spotify songs played by users.

On the graph presented on Figure 8 we used a Decision tree analysis to see which of the songs have the highest chances to be on the top 100 list played by users.

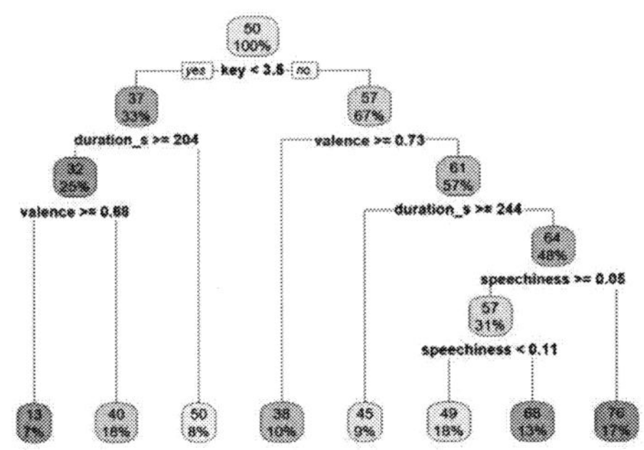


```
library(rpart)
library(rpart.plot)
features_data_num$standing <- c(1:100)
tree_model<-rpart(standing ~ ., data = features_data_num)
rpart.plot(tree_model, box.palette = "GnBu")
```

Figure 8. Decision Tree and the R Code

First, for conducting a decision tree analysis we need two libraries rpart and rpart.plot. Then, create a list features_data_num$standing with all top 100 songs and then, create a variable tree model where we generate the decision tree model.

5. CONCLUSION

The main purpose of this research was to put forward an overview of applying data mining and data visualization within the scope of audio data from a dataset of Spotify. The paper presented explanation of the most essential concepts and their role in this field. By the analysis of audio features of the tracks of Spotify's Top Songs in 2017 playlist were highlighted the common patterns behind the audio features of these songs.

A practical scenario was detailed explained. The results of the study showed how singers and song makers can leverage the power of data visualization and data mining, supporting the prediction of one audio feature based on the others, looking for patterns in the audio features of the songs and seeing which features correlate the most. We can conclude that the songs on which the key values are less than 3.5 ('C', 'C#', 'D', 'D#', 'Eb'), Duration is more than 204 seconds and Valence is more than 0.68 have highest chance to be around the Top 100 list.

REFERENCES

Rieger, A., 2011. *Large scale data analysis and predictive modeling in data mining.* Bosch ConnectedWorld Blog, [online] available at: https://blog.bosch-si.com/developer/large-scale-data-analysis-and-predictive-modeling-in-data-mining/

Gladwell, M., 2006. *The formula.* The New Yorker, [online] available at: https://www.newyorker.com/magazine/2006/10/16/the-formula

Goldman, W., 1983. *Adventures in the Screen Trade.* Warner Books, New York.

Loui, P., et al, 2010. Humans rapidly learn grammatical structure in a new musical scale. *Music Perception*, 25(5), pp. 377– 388.

Spotify Charts, 2018. [online] available at: https://spotifycharts.com/regional

GeorgeMcIntire, 2017. *Spotify Song Attributes | Kaggle.* [online] available at: www.kaggle.com/geomack/spotifyclassification/data

Schellenberg, E.G., 2008. *The role of exposure in emotional responses to music.* Behavioral and Brain Sciences.

Schellenberg, E.G. et al, 2008. Liking for happy- and sad-sounding music: Effects of exposure. *Cognition and Emotion Journal*, 22(2), pp. 218–237, 2008.

Siu-Lan, T. et al, 2006. The effects of repeated exposure on liking and judgments of musical unity of intact and patchwork compositions. *Music Perception: An Interdisciplinary Journal*, Vol. 23 No. 5, pp. 407–421.

Szpunar, K.K. et al, 2004. Liking and memory for musical stimuli as a function of exposure. *Journal of Experimental Psychology: Learning, Memory, and Cognition*, 30(2), pp. 370–381.

Ware, C., 2013. Information Visualization: Perception for Design. Third Edition, Elsevier.

Witvliet C.V.O., et al, 2007. Play it again Sam: Repeated exposure to emotionally evocative music polarizes liking and smiling responses, and influences other affective reports, facial EMG, and heart rate. *Cognition and Emotion Journal*, 21(1), pp. 3–25.

Wundt, W., 1897. *Outlines of Psychology.* Englemann, Leipzig, Taylor & Francis Group, LLC

VALIDATING THE FIRM TECHNOLOGY ADOPTION MODEL (F-TAM)

Joshua Kofi Doe[1], Rogier Van de Wetering[2], Ben Honyenuga[3] and Johan Versendaal[2]
[1]Open University, The Netherlands
[2]Faculty of Management, Science & Technology, Open University of the Netherlands
[3]Ho Technical University, Ghana

ABSTRACT

The revised firm technology adoption model (F-TAM), developed through the Delphi interviews and focus group discussions, was a remarkable turning point in technology adoption studies. This study aims to test the F-TAM, using data collected from Ghanaian SMEs. Data was collected from 400 SMEs in the Greater Accra Region of Ghana, using purposive sampling. Partial least squares structural equation modeling (PLS-SEM) was used for the data analysis. Data showed that, while employee factors can lead to firm adoption, firm factors of adoption do not lead to adoption if societal factors, characteristics of the innovation, and employee factors do not moderate that relationship. Societal factors do not lead to firm adoption if employee factors do not mediate it. A theoretical relevance of this study is that it challenges the idea that firm adoption of innovation will be realized, without reference to other domains of factors. This positioning of the F-TAM model is a significant departure from earlier models. For industry practitioners, these findings illustrate the essence of putting a premium on recruiting technologically savvy employees if the firm intends to adopt digital technologies.

KEYWORDS

Mobile Technologies, Firm Technology Adoption Model (F-TAM), SMEs, Adoption, Developing Countries

1. INTRODUCTION

Theoretical models that study individual-level technology adoption (Rogers, 2010) have been the most developed group of scholarship among the diffusion and adoption-related studies (Venkatesh et al., 2007). There have been very few models that focus on organizational/firm or societal levels (Rogers, 2010). Examples of studies that used such models include the Technology Organization and Environment (TOE) framework (Yeboah-Boateng & Essandoh, 2014), Task Technology Fit (TTF) (Goodhue & Thompson, 1995), the Perceived Electronic Readiness Model (PERM) (Molla & Licker, 2005). Various researchers have tested these earlier models in different contexts such as developing counties and on different technologies. Tobin and Kuwornu (2011), for instance, studied the adoption of mobile money in Ghana at the individual level, adapting constructs from the Technology Acceptance Model (TAM) model and Diffusion of Innovation (DOI) theory. They, however, posited behavioral intention to use innovation as a mediator between the antecedents and actual adoption. One dominant idea in the many research streams that studied adoption of innovations at the individual, firm or societal level of adoption is the impression created in the models that the antecedents of behavioral intention to adopt an innovation are enough to lead to adoption; an idea that has been questioned when contextual issues are taken into consideration (Data, 2011).

Furthermore, some researchers reported that user satisfaction is a more applicable dependent variable in adoption rather than behavioral intention (Brown, Massey, Montoya-Weiss, & Burkman, 2002; Brown, Venkatesh, Kuruzovich, & Massey, 2008). One major implication of the contextual argument in Datta (2011) and Brown et al. (2008) is that further studies on adoption in developing countries need to develop models and instruments, with the contexts as a major consideration. This argument for context relevant models and instruments is on the premise that the need to ground research in context is as strong as the need to ground research in the international scientific discourse (Röling, Hounkonnou, Offei, Tossou, & Van Huis, 2004). It is also premised on the idea that adopters' choices regarding adoption are based on rationality embedded in culture and the context of adoption rather than persuasion (Agarwal, 1983; Dewan & Kraemer, 2000; Shih, Venkatesh, Chen, & Kruse, 2013; Amoako, Doe, & Deheer, 2014).

The quest for context relevant factors that lead to the adoption of innovation in developing countries has therefore been on-going since Data (2011). In Ghana, this drive increased, owing to the recent discussion of factors that explain the rapid growth of mobile technologies (Attopley, 2016; Tagoe, 2016; Bank of Ghana, 2016). Doe et al. (2018) refined the F-TAM model (Doe et al., 2017), which sought to explain the adoption of mobile innovations at the SME level relying on qualitative data (focus group interviews). This contribution was a significant departure from the earlier norm of adapting constructs (Data, 2011; Brown et al., 2008). This new path of measuring firm level adoption while accounting for the influence of other levels of adoption, and with the model developed from the socio-cultural context of adoption, set forth a new stream of adoption studies. Paramount among such new streams of studies include the development of measuring instruments, quantitatively testing of the instrument in similar contexts, and final validation of the model with data across countries. This study, therefore, aims to *quantitatively test one of such current context relevant models, the revised firm technology adoption model (F-TAM), using data collected from Ghanaian SMEs.*

2. THEORETICAL BACKGROUND

2.1 Previous Literature on Adoption of Innovations

Various theories of models used in studying innovations at the personal, organizational, and societal levels include Theory of Reasoned Action (TRA) (Fishbein & Ajzen, 1975), Theory of Planned Behaviour (TPB) (Ajzen, 1985), Decomposed Theory of Planned Behavior (DTPB) (Taylor & Todd, 1995), Integrated Model of Technology Acceptance (IMTA) (Venkatesh, Speier & Morris, 2002), TAM (Venkatesh & Bala, 2008), UTAUT 1 & 2 (Venkatesh, Thong & Xu, 2012), and Dynamic Use Diffusion Model (DUDM) (Shih, Venkatesh, Chen, & Kruse, 2013), for the study of individual adoption of technology. Models developed for the study of societal level adoption include Culture, Policy & Technology Framework (CPT) (Bajaj & Leonard, 2004). At the firm level, models such as Technology, Organization and Environment Framework (TOE) (Tornatzky, Fleischer & Chakrabarti, 1990), Task-Technology Fit (TTF) (Goodhue & Thompson, 1995), and Perceived Electronic Readiness Model (PERM) (Molla & Licker, 2005). Varying results, however, were reported when these models were applied to developing country contexts (Datta, 2011). The varying results highlight the need for a model that is developed with data from a developing county context.

In the recent scholarly discussion of digital technologies such as data mining, cloud computing, social media, cybersecurity, and mobile applications, a strong emphasis has been on adoption studies (Doe et al., 2018; Masocha & Dzomonda, 2018; Asongu, 2018; Adjei & Odei-Appiah, 2018). Examples of such studies in Ghana includes Adadevoh (2018), Adjei and Odei-Appiah (2018) and Ansong and Boateng (2018). Similar studies in other developing countries include Chaouali, Souiden, and Ladhari (2017), Asongu (2018) and Masocha and Dzomonda (2018). It is worth noting, however, that apart from Doe et al. (2018), none of these studies was done with a model initially developed from developing country contexts. Following the groundbreaking study of Doe et al. (2018), an F-TAM measuring instrument (Doe et al., nd) was subsequently developed to aid researchers to measure or study firm technology adoption among SMEs.

2.2 F-TAM

The revised F-TAM (Doe et al., 2018) was a contextual validation of the initial F-TAM (Doe et al., 2017) through two rounds of Delphi panel interviews of both academics and industry experts. To understand the model refinement process, a highlight of the Delphi process in that study is worth mentioning here. In the first round of interviews, ten industry expert were purposively sampled (Saunders et al., 2007; Yin 1994) from an industry awards list, showing the firms that introduced the most adopted mobile digital innovations. The participants were completely anonymous. Five academic participants were sampled using a snowballing technique of academics who had a Ph.D. and were published in the area of study. Academic membership was therefore not entirely anonymous. The respondents commented on the original variables and relationships of the F-TAM model (Doe et al., 2017). New variables and relationships discovered were added as part of the second round of interviews. In the second round, respondents commented on the revised variables, restricting the comment to an agreement, disagreement, and neutrality. Researchers role in the process was restricted to that of a planner, facilitator, recorder and reviewer or synthesizer of the data (Avella, 2016).

Delphi interviews were administered orally and recorded, or sent by email. Voice data was transcribed into text, using, content analysis and pattern matching (Yin, 2013, Ezzy, 2002),) to scan out the main issues being discussed and to confirm, add to or subtract from the original model. Cross-case analysis was conducted using the concept-centric approach (Webster & Watson, 2002) to assemble the discussion into building blocks or themes that refine the existing model with pattern matching (Yin, 2013). A variable index was developed in that study and used to determine the weight of consensus for each variable or relationship agreed upon by the end of the second round (Doe et al. 2018).

These validation processes captured new constructs and propositions that refined the original F-TAM. The relevance of the original F-TAM, as well as the revised F-TAM, is that it posits antecedents of firm-level adoption while accounting for the influence on the individual (employee) adoption and societal adoption. Thus the revised F-TAM proposes that employee level variables of *Perceived Ease of Use, Perceived Usefulness, Perceived Indispensability, Perceived Social Influences*, *Trial Feedback*, and *Employee Self Enhancement Motives* will taken collectively, lead to firm adoption, and influence firm factors. Following the model's logic, Doe et al. (2018) proposed the following hypotheses:

H1: Personal level factors lead to firm adoption;
H2: Personal level factors influence firm factors.

At the firm level, organizational factors such as *Technological Readiness Managerial Innovativeness, Organizational Readiness, Strategic Fit with Operations, Ease of Support, and Organizational Culture,* in addition to industry factors such as *Customer Needs/demand, Competitive Pressure,* and *Partner Requirement* will combine at the firm level to influence firm adoption. Doe et al. (2018) hypothesized this as follows:

H3: Firm factors lead to firm adoption.

Societal level factors proposed in the revised F-TAM (Doe et al., 2018) are *Government Policy, Government Championship, Government Laws, Innovation Infrastructure, Opinion Leadership* and *Successive Government Commitment* to promoting the diffusion of the innovation will, taken together, lead to firm adoption, influence employee factors, influence firm factors and moderate the relationship between firm factors and firm adoption. These particular relationships are hypothesized as follows:

H4: Societal level factors influence personal level factors;
H5: Societal level factors influence firm-level factors;
H6: Societal level factors lead to firm adoption.

Rogers (1962) theorized how the characteristics of innovation affect its adoption. Later theories and models that focused on technology adoption did not anticipate this construct of technology characteristics. The revised F-TAM, however, has placed great emphasis on the technology characteristics as a strong influence on individuals, firms, and society at large. These technology characteristics are *Observability, Flexibility, Complexity* and *Relative Advantage.* They are hypothesized in this study as follows:

H7: Technology factors influence employee factors;
H8: Technology factors influence firm-level factors;
H9: Technology factors influence societal factors.

3. METHODOLOGY

Data for the study was collected from 400 SMEs, purposively sampled (Straits & Singleton, 2017) from the Greater Accra Region of Ghana. Trained data collectors were engaged to collect data. The data collection instrument was designed and validated an evaluation process of self-review, expert review of four experts, and focus group discussion involving twelve academics (Leeux et al., 2008). Question items in the instrument were either adapted from relevant previous studies related to the purpose of this study or crafted and taken through the evaluation process. During the evaluation process, the authors checked for length (Holbrook et al., 2006; Fink, 2003) grammar (Donyei, 2003; Leeux et al., 2008); simplicity (Bhandari & Wagner, 2006);

social desirability (Brace, 2004); double-barreled questions (Leeux et al., 2008); and question order (Baker, 2003). The instrument was also taken through a field test (Leeux et al., 2008), with a sample size of 25 respondents (Fowler, 1995, Converse & Presser, 1986, Sheatsley, 1983, Sudman, 1983, Converse & Presser, 1986). The instrument was found to be valid and reliable (see Doe et al. nd) in testing SME for the F-TAM model of technology adoption at the firm level. Steiger (1988) emphasizes that the exact statistical tools used in the quantitative analysis must be reported to support a reliable replication of a study. Partial least squares structural equation modeling (PLS-SEM) was used (SmartPLS Release: 3.2.7) (Ringle et al., 2015) for the data analysis. Except for firm adoption, constructs are measured reflectively, because the individual items were similar and correlated well such that the deletion of some items will not significantly affect the definition of the construct. Model indicators are suggested by the underlying construct and have positive and desirably high intercorrelations (Coltman, Devinney, Midgley, & Veniak, 2008).

4. DATA ANALYSIS

4.1 Assessment of The Measurement Model

Confirmatory factor analysis tests of convergence and discriminant validity for the reflective constructs (Lings & Greenly, 2010; Hair et al., 2016) are relevant for structural equation models. The minimum Cronbach's alpha recommended for adequate convergent validity is 0.6 for exploratory studies (Hair et al., 2016; Chin, 2010). The recommended minimum composite reliability and average variance extracted (AVE) estimates are 0.7 and 0.5 respectively (Hair et al., 2016). Guided by these recommendations, we show the convergent validity test for the measurement model in table 1. An examination of the initial loadings showed that ***Personal Factors*** was measured using six constructs, with three items under various constructs loading below the minimum threshold. ***Firm Internal Factors*** was measured using six constructs with two items under different constructs loading below the minimum threshold. ***Firm External Factors*** was measured using three constructs, with two items under *organization partner requirement*, two items under *needs of customers*, and one item under *competitive pressure* all had loadings below the minimum threshold. We measured ***Societal Factors*** with six constructs, with two items under *government championship*, and four other items under various constructs all had loadings below the minimum threshold (Hair et al., 2016). ***Technological Characteristics*** was measured using four constructs, with four items under various constructs loading below the minimum threshold. All items with loadings below the minimum threshold (all had loadings below the minimum threshold of 0.6 (Hair et al., 2016) were deleted and the model re-run to obtain acceptable loadings. Therefore, following recommendations by Hair et al. (2016) and Chin (2010) convergence validity has been met for the six constructs under personal factors, six constructs under firm internal factors, three constructs under firm external factors, six constructs under societal factors, and four constructs under technological characteristics.

4.2 Discriminant Validity Assessments

Discriminant validity is about the uniqueness of a construct. Hair et al. (2016) and Hensler et al. (2015) recommend assessing the Fornell-Lacker criterion, item cross-loadings, and the heterotrait-monotrait ratio (HTMT) criterion to test discriminant validity. Henseler et al. (2015) argued that cross-loadings of indicators explain zero percent of discriminant validity while Fornell-Larcker and HTMT criterions explained 20.82 percent and 97 to 99 percent of discriminant validity respectively. This study therefore examines the discriminant validity of the reflective constructs using Fornell-Larcker and HTMT criteria.

Discriminant Validity- Fornell-Larcker Criterion- The square root of the average variance extracted estimates for each of the 25 reflective constructs is higher than the inter-construct correlations between them (Fornell & Lacker, 1981; Hair et al., 2016). Thus each construct is distinct and differs from the other measurement constructs in the model hence discriminant validity is met, as shown in table 1.

Table 1. Convergence & Discriminant Validity of Reflective Constructs
(Square root of AVEs in diagonal bold)-Fornel & Lacker Criterion

Constructs	CA	CR	AVE	1	2	3	4	5	6	7	8	9	10	11	12	13	14	15	16	17	18	19	20	21	22	23	24	25	26
1. Firm Level Adoption	NA	NA	NA	NA																									
2. Perceived Ease of Use	0.61	0.79	0.56	0.37	**0.75**																								
3. Perceived Usefulness	0.62	0.80	0.57	0.41	0.37	**0.76**																							
4. Perceived Indispensability	0.74	0.84	0.56	0.29	0.22	0.33	**0.75**																						
5. Perceived Social Influences	0.69	0.81	0.60	0.17	0.15	0.24	0.50	**0.77**																					
6. Trial Feedback	0.66	0.81	0.59	0.22	0.25	0.24	0.36	0.42	**0.77**																				
7. Employee Self Interest	0.74	0.84	0.56	0.36	0.18	0.41	0.51	0.47	0.45	**0.75**																			
8. Technological Readiness	0.73	0.83	0.54	0.25	0.15	0.24	0.46	0.46	0.44	0.52	**0.74**																		
9. Managerial Innovativeness	0.62	0.78	0.54	0.17	0.17	0.16	0.36	0.42	0.44	0.46	0.48	**0.74**																	
10. Org. Readiness	0.67	0.81	0.59	0.28	0.18	0.23	0.43	0.44	0.52	0.51	0.58	0.44	**0.77**																
11. Strategic Fit with Ops.	0.74	0.84	0.56	0.25	0.20	0.23	0.41	0.51	0.56	0.54	0.50	0.50	0.57	**0.75**															
12. Ease of Support	0.80	0.87	0.62	0.30	0.22	0.35	0.49	0.41	0.30	0.54	0.45	0.32	0.41	0.43	**0.79**														
13. Organisational Culture	0.71	0.81	0.52	0.30	0.24	0.30	0.37	0.36	0.31	0.43	0.43	0.46	0.39	0.44	0.46	**0.72**													
14. Org. Partner Requirement	0.67	0.81	0.59	0.19	0.09	0.24	0.47	0.49	0.35	0.47	0.49	0.38	0.47	0.43	0.59	0.49	**0.77**												
15. Competitive Pressure	0.65	0.81	0.58	0.18	0.15	0.27	0.41	0.45	0.43	0.52	0.43	0.43	0.47	0.51	0.42	0.47	0.48	**0.76**											
16. Needs of Customers	0.62	0.80	0.57	0.23	0.19	0.26	0.44	0.41	0.34	0.39	0.39	0.39	0.38	0.40	0.43	0.51	0.54	0.55	**0.75**										
17. Govt. Championship	0.77	0.83	0.56	0.13	0.21	0.18	0.46	0.46	0.41	0.40	0.35	0.43	0.35	0.43	0.41	0.46	0.51	0.47	0.47	**0.75**									
18. Government Policy	0.63	0.80	0.57	0.26	0.20	0.23	0.37	0.43	0.28	0.32	0.39	0.34	0.30	0.29	0.41	0.36	0.35	0.37	0.43	0.41	**0.75**								
19. Govt. Regulation/ Laws	0.61	0.79	0.55	0.34	0.23	0.28	0.35	0.39	0.40	0.43	0.29	0.34	0.40	0.44	0.34	0.39	0.28	0.40	0.43	0.33	0.55	**0.74**							
20. Innovation Infrastructure	0.68	0.83	0.61	0.15	0.19	0.11	0.19	0.26	0.26	0.20	0.29	0.27	0.28	0.25	0.19	0.27	0.26	0.32	0.38	0.32	0.45	0.52	**0.78**						
21. Opinion Leadership	0.69	0.80	0.51	0.17	0.08	0.24	0.34	0.44	0.24	0.37	0.38	0.31	0.39	0.41	0.46	0.39	0.52	0.46	0.50	0.46	0.55	0.46	0.47	**0.71**					
22. Successive Govt Commit.	0.76	0.86	0.66	0.21	0.19	0.15	0.33	0.47	0.42	0.37	0.36	0.46	0.38	0.49	0.30	0.42	0.39	0.53	0.46	0.54	0.50	0.51	0.53	0.58	**0.81**				
23. Flexibility	0.65	0.81	0.59	0.18	0.21	0.20	0.21	0.32	0.32	0.20	0.19	0.18	0.25	0.29	0.22	0.29	0.23	0.36	0.39	0.45	0.42	0.38	0.51	0.45	0.53	**0.76**			
24. Observability	0.72	0.83	0.63	0.18	0.16	0.17	0.26	0.41	0.43	0.26	0.26	0.31	0.37	0.48	0.36	0.37	0.41	0.47	0.45	0.47	0.43	0.45	0.46	0.50	0.58	0.60	**0.79**		
25. Complexity	0.70	0.83	0.62	-0.12	-0.21	-0.23	-0.34	-0.45	-0.36	-0.38	-0.36	-0.32	-0.35	-0.45	-0.41	-0.39	-0.48	-0.48	-0.39	-0.38	-0.33	-0.37	-0.34	-0.47	-0.46	-0.31	-0.44	**0.79**	
26. Relative Advantage	0.67	0.82	0.60	0.33	0.28	0.28	0.33	0.40	0.42	0.46	0.33	0.38	0.41	0.43	0.42	0.42	0.44	0.51	0.48	0.50	0.46	0.50	0.47	0.44	0.58	0.49	0.57	-0.48	**0.77**

All correlations are positive and mostly significant. Source: Field Data (2018)

Discriminant Validity- Heterotrait-Monotrait Ratio- Although Henseler et al. (2015) provided three HTMT criteria: HTMT specificity ratio of 0.90, HTMT specificity ratio of 0.85 and HTMT inference score ranging from -1 to 1 (-1 < HTMT < 1) as an indication of distinctiveness, they argued that HTMT.85 is the most conservative criterion. HTMT inference is the most liberal whilst HTMT0.9 lies in between the two extreme categories in terms of specificity rates. The authors, therefore, adopt the 0.9 ($HTMT_{0.9}$) as a criterion for assessing discriminant validity (Gold et al., 2001; Teo et al., 2008; Henseler et al., 2015). The HTMT result presented in this study shows that none of the correlations exceeded 0.9 thus confirming discriminant validity for the 25 reflective constructs in the model.

4.3 Structural Model

The structural model examines the construct relationships within the context of the conceptual framework or hypotheses/propositions to be tested. This study examines the relationships between the higher-order constructs (independent variables) and firm-level adoption. Since the structural model involved higher-order constructs, the following procedures were applied based on recommendations by Hair et al. (2016) and Becker, Klein, and Wetzels (2012).

Personal factors were measured using six constructs. Personal factors were modeled as a reflective-formative type II construct (Becker, Klein, & Wetzels, 2012) with the six first-order reflective indicators. Firm internal factors were measured using six first-order constructs. Firm external factors were measured using three first-order constructs. General firm-level factors were modeled as a reflective-formative type II construct (Becker et al., 2012) with nine first-order reflective indicators. Societal factors were measured using six constructs. Societal factors, thus, were modeled as a reflective-formative type II construct (Becker et al., 2012) with six first-order reflective indicators. Technological characteristics were measured using four constructs. Technological characteristics were modeled as a reflective-formative type II construct (Becker et al., 2012) with six first-order reflective indicators. A correlation matrix of the five high-order constructs (table 2.) shows significant (strong) positive correlations between firm adoption, personal factors, firm-level factors, societal level factors and technology characteristics ($p<0.01$ in all cases). Even though some of the indices are closer to 0.8, several authors argue that correlation values alone are not conclusive to establish multicollinearity. The Variance Inflation Factors, tolerance, collinearity, and conditional indices are additional analysis that are relevant and were done (Hair et al., 2014, Hair et al., 2016). The results show that all the variance inflation factors (VIFs) are lower than 5, which is recommended to prove the absence of collinearity problems (Hair et. al. 2014). Therefore, the five high-order construct model does not present a collinearity problem.

Table 2. Correlation Matrix for Second/high-order Constructs

High level Constructs	**1**	**2**	**3**	**4**	**5**
Firm-level Adoption	1				
Personal Level Factors	0.368***	1			
Firm Level Factors	0.278***	0.776***	1		
Societal Level Factors	0.246***	0.617***	0.733***	1	
Technology characteristics	0.276***	0.334***	0.416***	0.592***	1

Note: ***Correlation is significant at 0.01 level of significant

Source: Field Data (2018)

Table 3 provides a summary of the hypotheses test and conclusions made in this study. Of the nine study hypothesis, five are supported by the data.

Table 3. Summary of Hypotheses Assessment

Propositions	Definition	Standard Beta	Bootstrap t-value	Hypothesis results
P1	Personal level factors lead to firm adoption	0.480***	4.900	Supported
P2	Personal level factors influence firm factors	0.524***	12.190	Supported
P3	Firm factors lead to firm adoption	-0.029	0.229	Not Supported
P4	Societal level factors influence personal level factors	0.646***	14.265	Supported
P5	Societal level factors influence firm level factors	0.410***	7.633	Supported
P6	Societal level factors lead to firm adoption	-0.131	1.141	Not Supported
P7	Technology characteristics influence employee factors	-0.049	0.950	Not Supported
P8	Technology characteristics influence firm-level factors	-0.001	0.029	Not Supported
P9	Technology characteristics influence societal factors	0.592***	14.660	Supported

Note: ***Significant at $p<0.01$; **Significant at $p<0.05$; *Significant at $p<0.10$

The hypotheses test results are explained as follows:

***H 1**: Personal level factors lead to firm adoption.* A positive and significant association exists between personal level factors and firm adoption of mobile money innovations (β=0.480, t=4.900, $p<0.01$). Therefore, hypothesis 1 (*H1*) is supported in the present context. These outcomes suggest that the attitudes and perceptions of employees in a firm (SME) towards mobile money innovation, drive adoption of mobile money innovations, confirming a proposition of Doe et al. (2018).

***H2**: Personal level factors lead to firm factors.* A positive and significant association exists between personal level factors and firm-level factors (β=0.524, t=12.19, $p<0.01$). Therefore, hypothesis 2 (*H2*) is supported in the present context. This means employees attitudes and perceptions in a firm (SME) drive firm-level factors, confirming another proposition of Doe et al. (2018).

***H3**: Firm factors lead to firm adoption.* The relationship between firm-level factors and firm adoption of mobile payment innovations was not statistically significant (β=-0.029, t=0.229, $p>0.05$). Therefore, hypothesis 3 (*H3)* is not supported in the present context. This outcome means that firm-level factors do not necessarily drive adoption. This contradicts a proposition of Doe et al. (2018) that suggested that firm factors will lead to firm adoption. A significant indication of the findings in hypothesis H1, H2, and H3 is that they challenge earlier models such as PERM model and TTF that suggest that firm factors lead to firm adoption. Perhaps, if those studies had decoupled employee factors from other firm-level factors, the results of those studies would have been different.

***H4**: Societal level factors influence personal level factors.* A positive and significant association exists between societal level factors and personal level factors (β=0.646, t=14.265, $p<0.01$). Therefore, hypothesis 4 (*H4*) is supported in the present context. This means societal level factors drive personal level factors, confirming another proposition Doe et al. (2018).

H5**: Societal level factors influence firm-level factors.* A positive and significant association exists between societal level factors and firm-level factors (β=0.410, t=7.633, $p<0.01$). Therefore, hypothesis 5 (H5***) is supported in the present context. This outcome suggests that societal level factors drive firm-level factors, confirming Doe et al. (2018) propositions.

***H 6**: Societal level factors lead to firm adoption.* The relationship between societal level factors and firm adoption of mobile payment innovations was not statistically significant (β=-0.131, t=1.141, $p>0.05$). Therefore, hypothesis 6 (**H**6) is not supported in the present context. This means societal level factors do not necessarily drive adoption. Juxtaposing this finding with *H1,* the evidence demonstrates that societal level factors rather drive personal level factors which subsequently drive adoption. This finding also contradicts a proposition of Doe et al. (2018) that societal factors will drive firm adoption. It also contradicts propositions in other models such as the Culture, Policy and Technology framework (Bajaj & Leonard, 2004)

H7**: Technology factors influence employee factors.* The relationship between technological factors and personal/employee factors was not statistically significant (β=-0.049, t=0.950, $p>0.05$). Therefore, proposition 7 (P7***) is not supported in the present context. This means technological factors do not necessarily influence personal/employee factors as contrarily suggested by Doe et al. (2018).

H 8: Technology factors influence firm-level factors. The relationship between technological factors and firm level factors was not statistically significant (β=-0.001, t=0.029, p>0.05). Therefore, proposition 9 (***H8***) is not supported in the present context. Again, this means technological factors do not necessarily drive firm-level factors, as contrarily suggested by Doe et al. (2018)

H 9: Technology factors influence societal factors. A positive and significant association exists between technological factors and societal level factors (β=0.592, t=14.660, p<0.01). Therefore, proposition 9 (***H9***) is supported in the present context. This means technological factors drive societal level factors, confirming another proposition in Doe et al. (2018).

4.4 Additional Study Observations

The structural model presented in figure 1 suggests a direct effect of technology characteristics on firm adoption as well as possible mediational effects of personal and societal factors. Likewise, we discovered that technological characteristics moderate the relationship between firm-level factors and firm adoption.

This study discovered that a positive and significant association exists between technological characteristics and firm adoption (β=0.165, t=1.984, p<0.05). This means technological characteristics drive firm adoption, confirming Rogers' (1962) diffusion theory as still being relevant in the adoption of any innovation. This study also discovered that technological factors moderate the relationship between firm-level factors and firm adoption (β=0.12, t=2.242, p<0.05). Thus even though firm factors did not lead to firm adoption, technological factors strengthen the relationship between firm-level factors and firm adoption.

Next to the observation, we discovered some remarkable mediation effects. First, we discovered that personal factors fully mediate the relationship between societal factors and firm adoption. Therefore, contrary to hypothesis 6 (H6) societal factors instead have an indirect effect on firm adoption.

We also found that societal level factors fully mediate the relationship between technological characteristics and firm-level factors. Therefore, contrary to hypothesis 8 (H8) of this study, technological characteristics rather have a significant indirect effect on firm-level factors through societal level factors.

Finally, we found that Societal level factors fully mediate the relationship between technological factors and personal factors. This implies that technological characteristics have a significant indirect effect on personal factors through societal level factors. Therefore, contrary to hypothesis 7 (H7) of this study, which proposes a direct effect of technological characteristics on personal factors, the effect is an indirect one.

5. SUMMARY, CONCLUSION, AND DISCUSSION

This paper sought to test the F-TAM, with associated hypotheses, using data collected from Ghanaian SMEs. The hypotheses were tested using PLS-SEM. The study found a positive and significant relationship between personal factors and adoption, personal factors and firm-level factors, societal level factors and personal factors, societal level factors and firm-level factors, technological factors and societal level factors, and technological factors and firm adoption.

Furthermore, societal level factors, personal factors, and technological factors were all found to moderate the association between firm-level factors and firm adoption. As a result, five of the nine hypotheses of the study are supported in the present context. The study also found a mediating effect of personal level factors on the relationship between societal level factors and adoption, a mediation effect of societal factors on the relationship between technology factors and firm-level factors, and also between technology factors and personal factors. It is important to note that, if this study had examined the effect of firm-level factors alone on adoption, we would have found a significant relationship as earlier studies had found. However, disaggregating personal level factors exposes the flaw in that idea.

Our findings confirm most of the hypothesis in the revised F-TAM version (Doe et al., 2018), at the same time challenging some propositions in other models such as the CPT framework, PERM, TOE models. Striking revelations from this study that calls for further studies include the following:

While employee factors can lead to firm adoption, firm factors of adoption, mainly posited by models such as the PERM model and TTF do not lead to adoption if societal factors, characteristics of the innovation, and employee factors do not moderate that relationship.

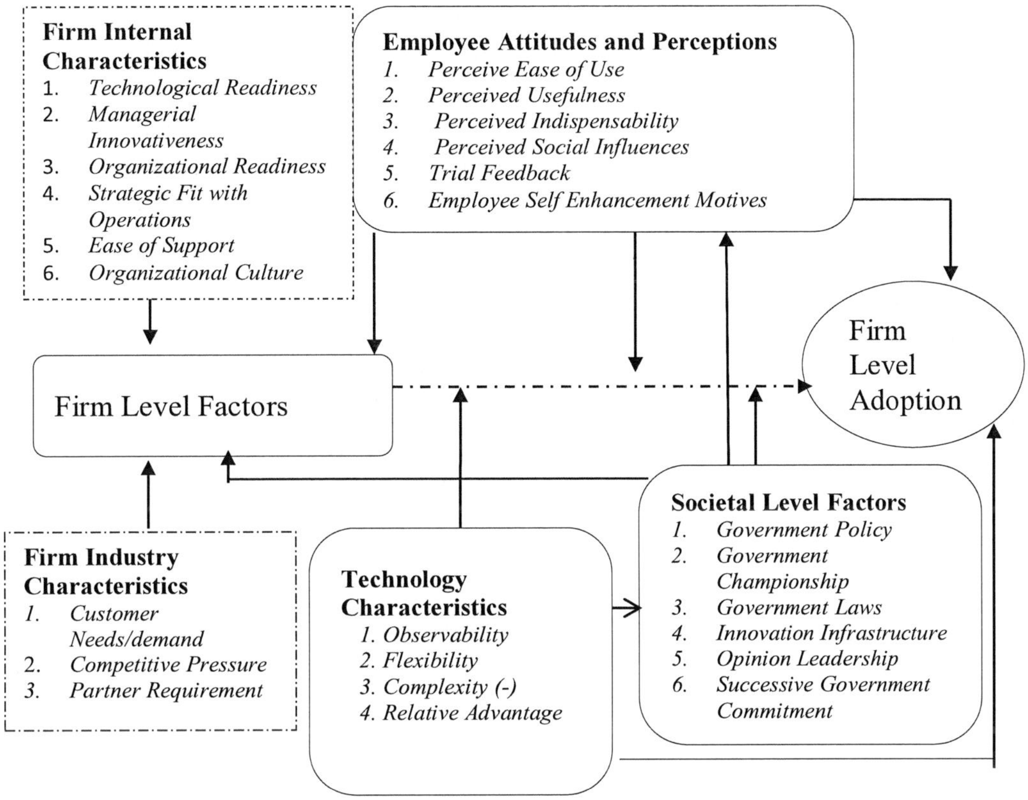

Figure 1. Survey Tested Technology Adoption Model (F-TAM)

Societal factors do not lead to firm adoption if employee factors do not mediate this relationship. These findings make employee factors probably the most significant construct in the pool of factors that engender adoption. The findings seem to challenge all models that posit that firm factors alone will lead to firm adoption. Studies that classify employees as part of the firm factors may not face this challenge.

Irrespective of government efforts concerning laws, discussions, policies, and championships made towards the adoption of an innovation, innovation will not generally be adopted if employees are not at the center of the adoption drive. Technology factors do not influence employee factors. Thus an innovation could be flexible, easy to use, give some advantages and be easy to observe. However, if its employees do not perceive the innovation as such through the lenses of the employee factors, particularly self-enhancement motives, the innovation may not be adopted. These findings may challenge models such as the DOI, wherein technology characteristics alone is suggested to lead to adoption.

This study is theoretically relevant because the study challenges the concept that any particular level of factors will lead to adoption, without reference to the adoption ecosystem. Thus for firm adoption, all dimensions of factors must be aggregated before the real factors that engender adoption can be uncovered. Our current contribution with the F-TAM, therefore, is a significant departure from earlier models. For industry practitioners, these findings illustrate the essence of putting a premium of recruiting technologically savvy employees if the firm intends to adopt digital technologies.

6. LIMITATIONS

This study has some limitations that future research should seek to address. First, this study employed purposive sampling (Straits & Singleton, 2017) in data collection in order to reach small firms that have adopted and used mobile payment technology innovation. The downside of this sampling technique is that studies that employ this technique do not generally lend themselves to a statistical representation of the whole population. Given that the initial adopters of new technologies tend to be technology-savvy, and in most of the firms, the owner-managers lead the adoption, the findings of this study may appear to be more tailored to technologically savvy SMEs. The results may, therefore, have some minor variations for SMEs who are not technologically savvy. Again, the adoption is assumed to be a voluntary adoption process as opposed to mandatory adoption. For instance, in several government championships and policy drives, there are issues of mandatory adoption imposed on adopters. When this model is applied to SMEs who may have adopted out of mandatory adoption, varied results may be reported under such circumstances. Secondly, we took samples from the capital of the Greater Accra Region, which is assumed to be the most developed region in Ghana. The generalizability of these findings on other regions may realize minor variations. Finally, this study is based on the F-TAM model with firm adoption as the dependent variable. Although our results support the use of F-TAM in measuring the adoption of mobile digital innovations at the firm level, other satisfactory models can be applied to firm technology adoption. Any such model, however, must factor all four domains of the construct into the adoption equation. We recommend future studies with larger samples taken across the whole country and different countries. We also recommend the application of this model in mandatory adoption situations.

REFERENCES

Andersson, L.M. & Bateman, T. S. (1997). Cynicism in the workplace: Some causes and effects. *Journal of Organizational Behavior, 18* (5), 449-469.

Acheampong, P., Zhiwen, L., Antwi, H. A., Otoo, A. A. A., Mensah, W. G., & Sarpong, P. B. (2017). Hybridizing an Extended Technology Readiness Index with Technology Acceptance Model (TAM) to Predict E-Payment Adoption in Ghana. *American Journal of Multidisciplinary Research*, *5*(2).

Adadevoh, C. K. (2018). Factors That Influences the Adoption of E-Commerce in the Ghanaian Banking Industry. *International Journal of Innovative Research and Development*, *7*(2).

Adjei, J. K., & Odei-Appiah, S. (2018). Mobile Financial Services in Emerging Countries: Technology, Adoption, and Regulatory Issues. In *Mobile Technologies and Socio-Economic Development in Emerging Nations* (pp. 109-128). IGI Global.

Afutu-Kotey, R. L., Gough, K. V., & Owusu, G. (2017). Young entrepreneurs in the mobile telephony sector in Ghana: From necessities to aspirations. *Journal of African Business*, *18*(4), 476-491.

Agarwal, B. (1983). Diffusion of rural innovations: some analytical issues and the case of wood-burning stoves. *World Development*, *11*(4), 359-376.\

Amoako, G. K., Doe, J. K., & de Heer, F. (2014). Innovation and marketing in Africa - a Ghanaian perspective. *International Journal of Technology Marketing*, *9*(4), 356-375.

Ansong, E., & Boateng, R. (2018). Organisational adoption of telecommuting: Evidence from a developing country. *The Electronic Journal of Information Systems in Developing Countries*, *84*(1), e12008.

Asongu, S. A. (2018). Conditional determinants of mobile phones penetration and mobile banking in Sub-Saharan Africa. *Journal of the Knowledge Economy*, *9*(1), 81-135.

Brown, S. A., A. P. Massey, M. M. Montoya-Weiss, & J. R. Burkman (2002). Do I really have to? User acceptance of mandated technology. *European Journal of Information Systems* (11) 4, 283-295.

Barclay, D., Thompson, R., & Higgins, C. (1995). The Partial Least Squares (PLS) Approach to Causal Modeling: Personal Computer Adoption and Use an Illustration. *Technology Studies* (2:2), 285-309.

Brown, S. A., Venkatesh, V., Kuruzovich, J., & Massey, A. P. (2008). Expectation confirmation: An examination of three competing models. *Organizational Behavior and Human Decision Processes* (105) 1, 52-66.

Chaouali, W., Souiden, N., & Ladhari, R. (2017). Explaining adoption of mobile banking with the theory of trying, general self-confidence, and cynicism. *Journal of Retailing and Consumer Services*, *35*, 57-67.

Chin, W. W. (1998). The partial least squares approach to structural equation modeling. Modern Methods for Business Research, 295(2), 295-336.

Chin, W.W. (2010), "How to write up and report PLS analyses", in Esposito Vinzi, V., Chin, W.W.,Henseler, J. and Wang, H. (Eds), *Handbook of Partial Least Squares: Concepts, Methods and Application*, Springer, Berlin, pp. 645-689.

Chin, W. W., & Newsted, P. R. (1999). "Structural Equation Modeling Analysis with Small Samples Using Partial Least Squares," in *Statistical Strategies for Small Sample Research*, Rick Hoyle (ed.), Thousand Oaks, CA: Sage Publications, 1999, pp. 307-341.

Cohen, J. (1988). Statistical power analysis for the behavioral sciences (2nd ed.). Hillsdale, NJ: Erlbaum

Efron, B., & Gong, G. (1983). A leisure look at the bootstrap, the jackknife, and cross validation. *The American Statistician, 37*(1), 36-48.

Fornell, C., & Larcker, D. F. (1981). Evaluating structural equation models with unobservable variables and measurement error. *Journal of Marketing Research, 18*(1), 39-50.

Hair, J. F.J., Anderson, R.E., Tatham, R.L., & Black, W.C. (1998). *Multivariate Data Analysis*, Prentice-Hall, Upper Saddle River, NJ.

Hair, J. F.J., Ringle, C. M., & Sarstedt, M. (2011). PLS-SEM: Indeed a silver bullet. *The Journal of Marketing Theory and Practice, 19*(2), 139-152.

Hair J.F.J., Sarstedt, M., Hopkins L., & Kuppelwieser, V.G. (2014). Partial least squares structural equation modeling (PLS-SEM) An emerging tool in business research. *European Business Review, 26* (2), 106-121.

Hair, J. F., Hult, G. T. M., Ringle, C. M., & Sarstedt, M. (2016). A Primer on Partial Least Squares Structural Equation Modeling (PLS-SEM) . 2nd edition. Thousand Oaks, CA: Sage.

Harman, H. H. (1967). *Modern Factor Analysis*, 2nd ed. University of Chicago Press, Chicago, IL.

Henseler, J., Ringle, C. M., & Sinkovics, R. R. (2009). The use of partial least squares path modeling in international marketing. In R. R. Sinkovics & P. N. Ghauri (Eds.), Advances in International Marketing (Vol. 20, pp. 277-319). Bingley, UK: Emerald Group.

Kazi, A. K., & Mannan, M. A. (2016). Factors affecting adoption of mobile banking in Pakistan: Empirical Evidence. *International Journal of Research in Business and Social Science (2147-4478), 2*(3), 54-61.

Kock, N., & Hadaya, P. (2018). Minimum sample size estimation in PLS-SEM: The inverse square root and gamma-exponential methods. *Information Systems Journal, 28*(1), 227-261.

Ledden, L., Kalafatis, S.P., & Mathioudakis, M. (2011). The idiosyncratic behaviour of service quality, value, satisfaction, and intention to recommend in higher education: An empirical examination. *Journal of Marketing Management, 27*(11–12), 1232–1260.

Lee, K.-H., Yang, G., & Graham, J.L. (2006). Tension and trust in international business negotiation: American executives negotiating with Chinese executives. *Journal of International Business Studies, 37*(5), 623–641.

Lings, I. N., & Greenley, G. E. (2010). Internal market orientation and market oriented behaviours. *Journal of Service Management, 21*(3), 321-343.

Marumbwa, J., & Mutsikiwa, M. (2013). An analysis of the factors influencing consumers' adoption of mobile money transfer services (MMTS) in Masvingo urban Zimbabwe. *Br J Econ Manag Trade, 3*, 498-512.

Masocha, R., & Dzomonda, O. (2018). Adoption of Mobile Money Sevices and the performance of Small and Medium Enterprises in Zimbabwe. *Academy of Accounting and Financial Studies Journal, 22*(3)

Nijssen, E.J., & Douglas, S.P. (2008). Consumer world-mindedness, social-mindedness and store image. *Journal of International Marketing, 16*(3), 84–107.

Nitzl, C., Roldan, J. L., & Cepeda, G. (2016). Mediation analysis in partial least squares path modeling: Helping researchers discuss more sophisticated models, *Industrial Management & Data Systems, 116* (9), 1849-1864

Podsakoff, P. M., MacKenzie, S. B., Lee, J. Y., & Podsakoff, N. P. (2003). Common method biases in behavioral research: A critical review of the literature and recommended remedies. *Journal of applied psychology, 88*(5), 879.

Röling, N.G., Hounkonnou, D., Offei, S.K., Tossou, R., & Van Huis, A. (2004). Linking science and farmers' innovative capacity: diagnostic studies from Ghana and Benin. *NJAS - Wageningen Journal of Life Sciences, 52*(3–4), 211-235.

Ringle, C. M., Wende, S., & Will, A. (2005). SmartPLS 2.0 (M3) beta, Hamburg: http://www.smartpls.de.

Straits, B. C., & Singleton, R. (2017). *Social research: Approaches and fundamentals.* Oxford University Press.

Suárez, S. L. (2016). Poor people' s money: The politics of mobile money in Mexico and Kenya. *Telecommunications Policy, 40*(10-11), 945-955.

Tortosa, V., Moliner, M. A., & Sanchez, J. (2009). Internal market orientation and its influence on organisational performance. *European Journal of Marketing, 43*(11/12), 1435-1456.

Yeboah-Boateng, E. O., & Essandoh, K. A. (2014). Factors influencing the adoption of cloud computing by small and medium enterprises in developing economies. *International Journal of Emerging Science and Engineering, 2*(4), 13-20.

RELATION BETWEEN BUSINESS PROCESS MANAGEMENT MATURITY AND INNOVATION IN THE FINANCIAL SECTOR

Harmen Gerrit (Harold) van de Kamp[1], Kobus Smit[2] and Pascal Ravesteijn[2]
[1]*e-office, The Netherlands*
[2]*HU University of Applied Sciences, The Netherlands*

ABSTRACT

To survive in the increasing globalization competition, companies are required to continuously increase their productivity and enhance innovation. To realize this enhanced productivity, Business Process Management (BPM) maturity models are often used to analyze, improve and manage business processes across the organization. Literature suggests that a relation between BPM maturity and innovation could exist and recommends more research in specific sectors. Specifically, the financial sector is facing a fintech revolution, putting an enormous pressure on how they deal with technology innovation, process disruption and service transformation. Therefore, the objective of this research is to determine the relation between business process management maturity and innovation in the financial sector. Data was collected using a survey at a large financial enterprise in Europe, resulting in sixty-eight responses. Regression analysis shows that 20.6% of the variance in innovation can be explained by BPM maturity.

KEYWORDS

Business Process Management, BPM-Maturity, Innovation, Innovation Value Chain, Innovation Adoption

1. INTRODUCTION

We are living in an increasingly globalizing world (Steger, 2017). This process of globalization generates increased competition between organizations, forcing them to boost their productivity on one hand, and to innovate on the other (Sanders Jones & Linderman, 2014; Tidd & Bessant, 2013). Therefore, existing processes need to be continuously managed and improved in line with strategic aims (Hung, 2006). For this Business Process Management (BPM) can be used. BPM includes activities to analyze, improve and manage organizational processes (Rosemann & De Bruin, 2005b). In recent years, BPM gained broader attention (Plattfaut, Niehaves, Pöppelbuß, & Becker, 2011; Ravesteyn, Zoet, Spekschoor, & Loggen, 2012; Rosemann & vom Brocke, 2010). Several studies identified a positive relation between BPM and competitive advantage (Ravesteijn, Smit, & McGuinness, 2016; Tang, Pee, & Iijima, 2013). Aside from managing efficiency and time-to-market, innovation is a key factor to remain competitive in the contemporary market (Porter, 2008; Roberts, 1998). In the financial sector, organizations are facing a fintech revolution which includes three forces: technology innovation, process disruption and service transformation (Gomber, Kauffman, Parker, & Weber, 2018). Fintech describes an emerging financial services sector in the 21st century and includes any technological innovation in this sector (Investopedia, 2018). According to Gomber et al. (2018), this is changing financial service operations in dramatic ways. To cope with this, organizations need to focus on BPM and innovation. However, it is unclear how both concepts relate to each other. BPM can be important for enabling innovation and a positive relation was already identified, although sector-specific research was suggested (Cats & Ravesteyn, 2017). Since the financial sector is facing a fintech revolution, both BPM and innovation are important topics in this sector. Therefore, this study investigates the relation between these two topics at a large financial enterprise located in Europe. This leads to the main research question: "What is the relation between business process management maturity and innovation in the financial sector?".

2. LITERATURE REVIEW

In this section the main constructs of this study are briefly explained, as well as the conceptual model.

2.1 Business Process Management Maturity

Although organizations have many business processes, they differ in how they manage business processes and incorporate these in their departments. Companies that use a BPM methodology have a process-based instead of a siloed department-based view on the activities they execute for their customers (Van Looy, De Backer, Poels, & Snoeck, 2013). Furthermore, organizations implementing BPM have a competitive advantage (Fisher, 2004). Additionally, business users are expected to be more engaged in setting up, changing and measuring the running business when undertaking BPM (Craggs, 2010; Miers, Harmon, & Hall, 2005).

Models exist to assess the maturity of an organization implementing BPM (Fisher, 2004; Ravesteyn et al., 2012; Rosemann & De Bruin, 2005a). This list of BPM-maturity (BPMM) models is rapidly increasing, but the validity and use of these models is still limited (Tarhan, Turetken, & Reijers, 2016). Several of these BPMM models use levels to describe the maturity plateau of an organization, such as Shafiei and Hajiheydari (2014). In contrast to one-dimensional BPMM models there are multi-dimensional BPMM models, consisting of different dimensions that influence the BPMM level of an organization. For example, the Business Process Maturity Model by Rosemann & De Bruin (2005b), consisting of the dimensions factor, maturity stage, organizational entity scope, time scope, coverage and proficiency. Additionally, Ravesteyn et al. (2012) presented a BPMM model based on the Capability Maturity Model Integrated (CMMI) and previous models (Rosemann & De Bruin, 2005b; Rosemann, De Bruin, & Hueffner, 2004; Rosemann, De Bruin, & Power, 2006). This BPMM model consists of seven dimensions, which are:

- **Process awareness**: Refers to a clear relation between the strategy and goals of the organization and business processes, with active involvement of both (executive) management as well as employees.
- **Process description**: Includes whether processes are transparent by capturing them in process models, defining roles, tasks, responsibilities and guidelines in relation to the strategy.
- **Measurement of processes**: Covers that for each process in- and outputs are defined, key performance indicators (KPIs) are known, and responsibilities for the process KPIs are clear.
- **Management of processes**: Relates to the fact that it is clear who is responsible for how process design, analyses, implementation, execution, and improvement is done.
- **Process improvement**: Relates to the fact that the organization strives to continuously improve processes and actively plans and manages the improvement process.
- **Process resources and knowledge**: Covers that the right people (with required competencies) and resources (money, facilities, systems) are provided to execute or improve a process according to its goals.
- **Information Technology**: Covers whether appropriate information systems support the BPM lifecycle.

Because the BPMM model of Ravesteyn et al. (2012) was used and validated in several studies (Cats & Ravesteyn, 2017; De Waal, Valladares, & Ravesteyn, 2017; Roslyakova & Ravesteyn, 2017; Widmann, de Waal, & Ravesteyn, 2018), it has been selected to form the BPM-maturity construct in the conceptual model of this research.

2.2 Innovation

Innovation is often confused with invention, according to Tidd and Bessant (2013). They state that invention is having a new idea, whereas innovation is the process of turning an idea into reality to capture value from it. This innovation process can focus on introducing something new and improving existing solutions (Kirchmer, 2017a; Rothwell & Gardiner, 1985; Tidd & Bessant, 2013). However, innovation relates to the adoption of innovations as well (Rogers, 2003). These two views on innovation are discussed in the following sections.

2.3 Innovation Value Chain

The innovation value chain (IVC) focusses on innovation as a production process. IVC is a sequential set of stages related to innovation, and although several studies in the literature mention innovation stages, they have their own perspective on this topic. An example IVC is presented by Van Horne et al. (2006) and is based on Porter's generic value chain (Porter, 1985). Porter's value chain describes the activities an organization undertakes to deliver value for its customers. In other IVC related studies, innovation is described from a knowledge perspective, consisting of knowledge sourcing, transformation and exploitation (Ganotakis & Love, 2012; Roper, Du, & Love, 2008).

IVC as a more generic model towards innovation is presented by Hansen and Birkinshaw (2007), which is a tailored, end-to-end approach for generating, converting and diffusing ideas. Their IVC starts with the idea generation phase, where novel ideas are born inside the company or with parties outside the company. The second phase, idea conversion, covers selecting the ideas and translating them into solutions. During diffusion in the final phase, the result is spread across the organization. Furthermore, Hansen and Birkinshaw (2007) proposed a questionnaire to rate the IVC of a company. Because of the comprehensiveness of the IVC of Hansen and Birkinshaw (2007), it is selected as part of our innovation construct in the conceptual model.

2.4 Innovation Adoption

Through the years, the adoption of innovation was studied widely resulting in many related theories. The Theory of Reasoned Action (TRA) is an important Innovation adoption (IA) model mentioned in the literature, which focuses on an individual's voluntary behavior (Ajzen & Fishbein, 1980; Fishbein & Ajzen, 1975). An extension of the TRA is the Theory of Planned Behavior (TPB), which describes the relation between someone's intention and behavior (Ajzen, 1991). Although the TRA and TPB were outstanding in explaining the individuals behavior in general, it lacked specific knowledge on the implementation of information technology solutions. Therefore, Davis Jr. (1985) introduced the Technology Acceptance Model (TAM), an IA model for empirically testing new end-user information systems. Although the TAM is focused on the attitude of an individual towards new technology, it doesn't take social factors into consideration. Therefore, the Diffusion of Innovation Theory (DOI) of Rogers (2003) describes how the adoption of innovation is dispersed among a group.

Based on TPB (Ajzen, 1985) and DOI (Rogers, 2003), Tan and Teo (2000) investigated the factors influencing the adoption of internet banking (FAIB). The results of this study is the FAIB framework that shows that attitudinal and perceived behavioral control factors, rather than social influence, play a significant role in influencing the intention to adopt Internet banking. Because the FAIB is an extended version of the renowned existing TPB and DOI models, its factors were selected to be used in the conceptual model of this study.

2.5 Conceptual Model

Based on the two main topics discussed in the previous sections, a conceptual model was constructed to investigate the relation between BPMM and innovation (see Figure 1). The first part of the conceptual model is the BPMM model of Ravesteyn et al. (2012), including the seven BPMM dimensions. The other part of the model is innovation (the dependent variable), which is based on the previously described IVC (Hansen & Birkinshaw, 2007) and IA (Tan & Teo, 2000). IVC contains the Idea generation, Idea conversion and Idea diffusion dimensions (Hansen & Birkinshaw, 2007). IA consists of three dimensions, namely attitude to innovation, subjective norms and perceived behavioral control (Tan & Teo, 2000).

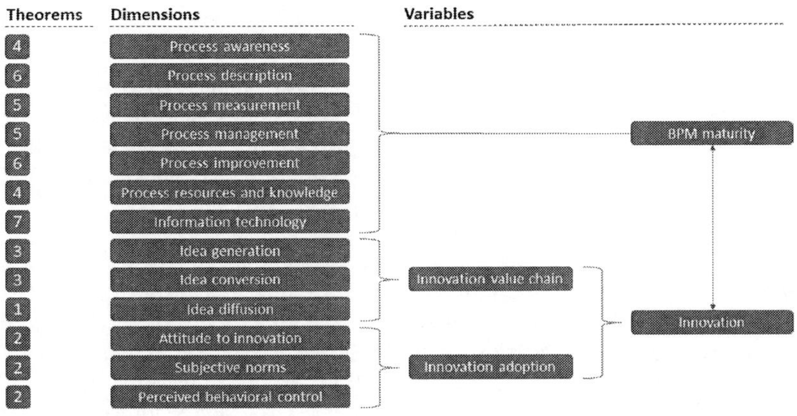

Figure 1. Conceptual Model - Relation between BPM Maturity and innovation (Cats & Ravesteyn, 2017)

Seven hypotheses were defined, which are depicted in Figure 2. The hypotheses are:

H1. There is a significant positive relation between process awareness and innovation.
H2. There is a significant positive relation between process description and innovation.
H3. There is a significant positive relation between process measurement and innovation.
H4. There is a significant positive relation between process management and innovation.
H5. There is a significant positive relation between process improvement and innovation.
H6. There is a significant positive relation between process resources and knowledge and innovation.
H7. There is a significant positive relation between information technology and innovation.

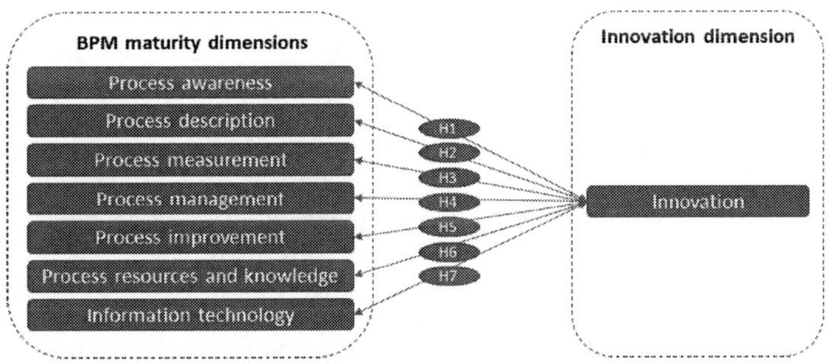

Figure 2. Hypotheses between BPM Maturity Dimensions and Innovation Dimensions

3. RESEARCH METHOD

This study is a cross-sectional exploratory research (Bryman & Bell, 2015). To get more knowledge on the relation between BPMM and innovation within the financial sector, a large financial enterprise located in Europe was willing to participate in this study by allowing data collection within their organization. The collected data was analyzed using IBM SPSS Statistics version 25 and included descriptive statistics, data validation analysis, factor analysis, correlation analysis and regression analysis.

3.1 Data Collection

For this study, data was collected using a survey. Approximately 500 employees from the contributing financial organization were invited, resulting in 68 valid responses. No missing responses were received, because all the questions in the survey were required before it could be submitted. This resulted in 68 cases used for analysis.

3.2 Questionnaire

The questionnaire was based on an existing validated questionnaire (Roslyakova & Ravesteyn, 2017). Respondents were provided with an introduction on the study, the questionnaire setup, an ethical statement and the invitation to participate. Subsequently, organization specific questions meant for descriptive analysis purposes were given, followed by questions on the respondents view on BPM definitions and their BPM knowledge level. Finally, the current situation within the organization related to process maturity and innovation was asked.

3.3 Measurement and Validation

Data validation analysis was conducted to verify the internal consistency of the dimensions based on the collected data. To verify this, the distribution of the 50 Likert scale measured theorems on the BPMM and innovation dimensions was validated by calculating the Cronbach's alpha for each set of questions (Cronbach, 1951; Nunnally & Bernstein, 1994; Tavakol & Dennick, 2011), see table 1.

Table 1. Reliability Analysis on the BPMM and Innovation Dimensions

Dimension	Cronbach's alpha	Number of items
Process Awareness	0.692	4
Process Description	0.747	6
Process Measurement	0.807	5
Process Management	0.773	5
Process Improvement	0.782	6
Process Resources and Knowledge	0.462	4
Information Technology	0.692	7
Innovation Value Chain	0.780	7
Innovation Adoption	0.595	6

Considering the analyzed dimensions, most of the BPMM sub-dimensions had a Cronbach's alpha score greater than 0.7, which implies an acceptable or good internal consistency (Tavakol & Dennick, 2011). Both the process awareness and information technology dimension were indicated as questionable but close enough to be acceptable. Although process resources and knowledge was identified as unacceptable (α=0.462), the BPMM dimensions were previously identified as reliable (Cats & Ravesteyn, 2017; De Waal et al., 2017) and therefore used for further analysis. The poor and questionable alpha score of IA (α=0.595) was expected to be related to the innovation statements setup in the questionnaire (Cats & Ravesteyn, 2017; Widmann et al., 2018).

3.4 Analysis Techniques

Correlation analysis was used to determine the relationship between the main dimensions of this study, namely BPMM and innovation, and its sub-dimensions (Field, 2013). Because a scatter plot displayed a linear cohesion between the variables, the strength of the cohesion was calculated using Pearson's correlation and interpreted (Evans, 1996). Subsequently, to identify to what extent innovation could be predicted by the BPM-maturity level, regression analysis is conducted (Field, 2013) with innovation, IVC and IA as dependent variables and the BPMM dimensions as the independent variables.

4. FINDINGS AND DISCUSSION

Between BPMM and innovation a moderate positive relation was identified (r=0.454; p=0.000), which was observed in previous studies as well (Ravesteijn et al., 2016; Widmann et al., 2018), see table 2. Of all the BPMM dimensions, process awareness had the strongest relation to innovation and the sub-dimensions IA and IVC. Process awareness had a moderate relation with innovation in general (r=0.545; p=0.000), followed by a moderate positive relationship with IVC (r=0.529; p=0.000) and a weak relation with IA (r=0.274; p=0.024). The moderate relation between process awareness and innovation implies that organizations who understand the relation between strategy and goals of business processes and who have everyone actively involved, are good in developing and adopting new ideas. This correlation was identified in previous studies as well (Ravesteijn et al., 2016; Widmann et al., 2018), and confirms hypothesis 1. Between the IVC and BPMM a moderate positive relation was identified (r=0.459; p=0.000), in accordance with the results observed in previous studies (Ravesteijn et al., 2016; Widmann et al., 2018). Furthermore, all BPMM dimensions except information technology were identified as having a significant positive relation with IVC, which was in accordance with the study of Widmann et al. (2018). This implies that companies where BPMM disciplines are executed, better understand how to generate, convert and diffuse ideas. Kirchmer (2017b) endorsed this result by mentioning BPM as a method for the structured setup of a company's innovation discipline.

Process awareness compared to the other BPMM dimensions was identified as having the strongest relation to the IVC dimensions. These process awareness relations were respectively moderate when related to idea generation (r=0.441; p=0.000), moderate related to idea conversion (r=0.432; p=0.000), and to idea diffusion a weak relation was identified (r=0.398; p=0.001). These findings imply that organizations willing to generate and distribute new ideas and considering investing in BPM, should start with increasing process awareness. This increase of process awareness requires organizations to deeply connect their strategy and goals to their business processes, and furthermore make sure everyone in the company is involved in these processes. However, this implication is not supported in the study of Tang et al. (2013), because they found no significant relation between the process view of an employee and employee innovativeness.

The correlation analysis on the IA sub-dimensions revealed that only perceived behavioral control had a significant positive relation with BPMM (r=0.382; p=0.001). Furthermore, four out of seven BPMM sub-dimensions were identified as significant positive related to perceived behavioral control. Consequently, a significant positive relation between BPMM and perceived behavioral control implies that organizations who are aware of their described processes, their employees stronger belief they have control over the external and personal factors that may facilitate or constrain the innovation use. However, continuously improving processes and having the right resources and knowledge, does not necessarily mean that employees belief they have control over the external and personal factors that may facilitate or constrain the innovation use.

Table 2. Correlation analysis on the BPMM vs. innovation, IVC and IA dimensions.

		Innovation dimensions		Innovation Value Chain dimensions			Innovation adoption dimensions		
	Innovation	Innovation Value Chain	Innovation Adoption	Idea Generation	Idea Conversion	Idea Diffusion	Attitude To Innovation	Subjective Norms	Perceived Behavioral Control
BPM Maturity	0,454**	0,459**	0,206	0,367**	0,400**	0,316**	-0,058	0,088	0,382**
Process Awareness	0,545**	0,529**	0,274*	0,441**	0,432**	0,398**	-0,063	0,134	0,480**
Process Description	0,372**	0,315**	0,244*	0,265*	0,249*	0,250*	-0,007	0,142	0,360**
Process Measurement	0,325**	0,355**	0,115	0,319**	0,285*	0,229	0,000	0,007	0,226
Process Management	0,245*	0,269*	0,086	0,209	0,243*	0,175	-0,138	0,084	0,215
Process Improvement	0,419**	0,425**	0,188	0,381**	0,357**	0,236	-0,068	0,118	0,325**
Process Resources And Knowledge	0,361**	0,436**	0,076	0,379**	0,358**	0,290*	-0,144	-0,067	0,351**
Information Technology	0,204	0,205	0,095	0,034	0,277*	0,170	0,053	0,002	0,143

**p<0.01; *p<0.05

A summary of the regression analysis is shown in table 3. In relation to the dependent variables (innovation, IVC and IA variable) only significant BPM dimensions are listed.

Table 3. Regression Analysis between the Innovation Dimensions and the BPMM Dimensions

Dependent variable	Predictor	*B*	*SE B*	β	*t*	*P*	r^2
Innovation	BPM Maturity	0.431	0.104	0.454	4.142	0.000**	0.206
	Process Awareness	0.312	0.103	0.498	3.040	0.004**	
Innovation Value Chain	BPM Maturity	0.586	0.140	0.459	4.198	0.000**	0.211
	Process Awareness	0.368	0.138	0.437	2.658	0.010*	
Innovation Adoption	BPM Maturity	0.250	0.146	0.206	1.710	0.092	0.042

**p<0.01; *p<0.05

The results from the regression analysis show that 20.6% of the variance in innovation can be explained by changes in BPMM (r^2=0.206). However, 79,4% of the variance in innovation is not explained by changes in BPMM. This implies organizations improving innovation are expected to partially realize this by investing in BPM capabilities.

Process awareness is the only BPM dimension being statistically significant for innovation (β=0.498; *p*=0.004) and IVC (β=0.437; *p*=0.010). These moderate strong relationships (Cohen, 1988) confirm the previous findings on the correlation of process awareness. This implies that organizations who want to improve on innovation, can predict 49.8% of this change by providing a clear relation between their organizations strategy, goals and business processes, and having all employees actively involved. Additionally, organizations improving their procedure of idea generation, conversation and diffusion, can explain 43.7% of this variance from process awareness.

5. CONCLUSIONS AND RECOMMENDATIONS

The objective of this research was to determine the relation between BPMM and innovation in the financial sector. Therefore, the main research question was: "What is the relation between business process management maturity and innovation in the financial sector?". To answer this question seven hypotheses were formulated. Table 4 lists whether these hypotheses were supported.

Table 4. Hypotheses Testing Results of the Relation between BPMM and Innovation

Hypothesis	Correlation coefficient	Test result
H1. Significant positive relation between process awareness and innovation	0.545**	Supported
H2. Significant positive relation between process description and innovation	0.372**	Supported
H3. Significant positive relation between process measurement and innovation	0.325**	Supported
H4. Significant positive relation between process management and innovation	0.245*	Supported
H5. Significant positive relation between process improvement and innovation	0.419**	Supported
H6. Significant positive relation between process resources and knowledge and innovation	0.361**	Supported
H7. Significant positive relation between information technology and innovation	0.204	Not Supported

**p<0.01; *p<0.05

Based on the correlation analysis a moderate positive relation between BPMM and innovation is identified. Between BPMM and IVC a moderate positive relation is identified. Overall, no significant relation is identified between BPMM and IA, only significant relations between BPMM sub-dimensions and sub-dimensions of IA are found. Furthermore, to predict whether changes in innovation are related to changes in BPMM, regression analysis was conducted. 49.8% of the variance in innovation was predicted from process awareness, 43.7% of the variance in IVC was predicted from process awareness.

The findings imply that organizations willing to improve their innovation process, are advised to invest in increasing their BPM maturity. The most important part of this investment is making people aware of the processes. Remaining investments should focus on describing, measuring, managing and continuously improving business process. Finally, they should make sure the right people and resources are in place. However, based on this study we find that investing in BPM is not enough to increase the innovation capability of the organization.

Because this study was set up as a cross-sectional research, data was collected using a snapshot in time which is a limitation to the study. Another limitation is the data being collected from only one large financial enterprise with its head office located in The Netherlands. Because the respondents were mostly located in The Netherlands (82.4%) and worked for the IT department of the organization (51.5%), generalization of the results can only be done conservative.

Based on data validation, subsequent research is suggested to improve the process resources and knowledge dimension. Also, based on the factor analysis, future research to improve the innovation part of the conceptual model is suggested. Considering 79.4% of the variance in innovation was not explained based on the model of this study, future research is advised to be conducted regarding BPMM and innovation to constitute a better understanding of the relation between these dimensions. Furthermore, because regression analysis showed that process awareness was the only BPMM dimension being statistically significant for innovation, future research is suggested to identify which activities make this relation that strong. Combining data from previous studies regarding the relation between BPMM and innovation is recommended for conducting advanced analysis such as structural equation modeling. Finally, additional research is suggested on this main topic for different organizations and sectors.

REFERENCES

Ajzen, I. (1985). From Intentions to Actions: A Theory of Planned Behavior. In *Action Control* (pp. 11–39). Berlin, Heidelberg: Springer Berlin Heidelberg.

Ajzen, I. (1991). The Theory of Planned Behavior. *Organizational Behavior and Human Decision Processes*, *50*(2), 179–211.

Ajzen, I., & Fishbein, M. (1980). *Understanding attitudes and predicting social behaviour*. Prentice-Hall.

Bryman, A., & Bell, E. (2015). *Business research methods* (4th ed.). Oxford University Press.

Cats, T., & Ravesteyn, P. (2017). The Relation Between Process Management and Innovation – A comparison of the IT and Manufacturing industries. In *30th Bled eConference* (pp. 1–13).

Cohen, J. (1988). *Statistical power analysis for the behavioral sciences* (2nd ed.). Taylor & Francis.

Craggs, S. (2010). *Comparing BPM from IBM, Software AG and Pegasystems.*

Cronbach, L. J. (1951). Coefficient alpha and the internal structure of tests. *Psychometrika*, *16*(3), 297–334.

Davis Jr., F. D. (1985). *A technology acceptance model for empirically testing new end-user information systems: Theory and results*. B.S., Industrial Engineering, Wayne State University.

De Waal, B. M. E., Valladares, R., & Ravesteyn, P. (2017). BPM Maturity and Process Performance: The case of the Peruvian Air force Full Paper. In *Twenty-third Americas Conference on Information Systems* (pp. 1–10).

Evans, J. D. (1996). *Straightforward statistics for the behavioral sciences*. Pacific Grove: Brooks/Cole.

Field, A. P. (2013). *Discovering statistics using IBM SPSS Statistics* (4th ed.). SAGE Publications Ltd.

Fishbein, M., & Ajzen, I. (1975). *Belief, Attitude, Intention, and Behavior: An Introduction to Theory and Research*. Addison-Wesley Pub. Co.

Fisher, D. M. (2004). The Business Process Maturity Model: A Practical Approach for Identifying Opportunities for Optimization. *BPTrends*, *September*, 1–7.

Ganotakis, P., & Love, J. H. (2012). The Innovation Value Chain in New Technology-Based Firms: Evidence from the U.K. *The Journal of Product Innovation Management*, *29*(5), 839–860.

Gomber, P., Kauffman, R. J., Parker, C., & Weber, B. W. (2018). On the Fintech Revolution: Interpreting the Forces of Innovation, Disruption, and Transformation in Financial Services. *JMIS*, *35*(1), 220–265.

Hansen, M. T., & Birkinshaw, J. (2007). The Innovation Value Chain. *Harvard Business Review*, *85.6*(June 2007), 121–130.

Hung, R. Y.-Y. (2006). Business Process Management as Competitive Advantage: a Review and Empirical Study. *Total Quality Management & Business Excellence*, *17*(1), 21–40.

Investopedia. (2018). Fintech Definition. Retrieved July 9, 2018, from https://www.investopedia.com/terms/f/fintech.asp

Kirchmer, M. (2017a). *High Performance Through Business Process Management: Strategy Execution in a Digital World* (3rd ed.). Cham: Springer International Publishing.

Kirchmer, M. (2017b). Innovation: Enabled by Process Management. In *High Performance Through Business Process Management* (pp. 29–46). Cham: Springer International Publishing.

Miers, D., Harmon, P., & Hall, C. (2005). The 2007 BPM suites report. *Business Process Trends: Version, 1.*

Nunnally, J. C., & Bernstein, I. H. (1994). *Pychometric Theory* (Third Edit). McGraw-Hill.

Plattfaut, R., Niehaves, B., Pöppelbuß, J., & Becker, J. (2011). Development of BPM Capabilities–Is Maturity the Right Path? In *European Conference on Information Systems (ECIS)* (pp. 1–13).

Porter, M. E. (1985). *Competitive Advantage: Creating and Sustaining Superior Performance.* Free Press.

Porter, M. E. (2008). *Competitive Strategy: Techniques for Analyzing Industries and Competitors.* Simon and Schuster.

Ravesteijn, P., Smit, J., & McGuinness, B. (2016). A study on the relation between business process management maturity and innovation. *22nd Americas Conference on Information Systems*, 1–10.

Ravesteyn, P., Zoet, M., Spekschoor, J., & Loggen, R. (2012). Is There Dependence Between Process Maturity and Process Performance? *Communications of the IIMA*, *12*(2), 65–80.

Roberts, R. (1998). Managing innovation: The pursuit of competitive advantage and the design of innovation intense environments. *Research Policy*, *27*(2), 159–175.

Rogers, E. M. (2003). *Diffusion of Innovations* (5th ed.). Free Press.

Roper, S., Du, J., & Love, J. H. (2008). Modelling the innovation value chain. *Research Policy*, *37*(6–7), 961–977.

Rosemann, M., & De Bruin, T. (2005a). Application of a Holistic Model for Determining BPM Maturity. *BPTrends*, *February*, 1–21.

Rosemann, M., & De Bruin, T. (2005b). Towards a Business Process Management Maturity Model. In *ECIS 2005 Proceedings of the Thirteenth European Conference on Information Systems.* Regensburg.

Rosemann, M., De Bruin, T., & Hueffner, T. (2004). A Model for Business Process Management Maturity. In *Australasian (ACIS)* (p. 7).

Rosemann, M., De Bruin, T., & Power, B. (2006). A model to measure business process management maturity and improve performance. *Business Process Management*, 299–315.

Rosemann, M., & vom Brocke, J. (2010). The Six Core Elements of Business Process Management. In *Handbook on Business Process Management 1* (pp. 107–122). Berlin, Heidelberg: Springer Berlin Heidelberg.

Roslyakova, L., & Ravesteyn, P. (2017). Relation between Business Process Management Maturity and Innovation. In *13th European Conference on Management, Leadership and Governance: ECMLG 2017* (pp. 434–443).

Rothwell, R., & Gardiner, P. (1985). Invention, innovation, re-innovation and the role of the user: A case study of British hovercraft development. *Technovation*, *3*(3), 167–186.

Sanders Jones, J. L., & Linderman, K. (2014). Process management, innovation and efficiency performance: The moderating effect of competitive intensity. *Business Process Management Journal*, *20*(2), 335–358.

Shafiei, A., & Hajiheydari, N. (2014). Developing a business process management maturity model: A study of 300 Iranian superior companies. *International Journal of Engineering and Technical Research (IJETR)*, *2*(10), 231–242.

Steger, M. B. (2017). *Globalization: A very short introduction* (Vol. 86). Oxford University Press.

Tan, M., & Teo, T. (2000). Factors Influencing the Adoption of Internet banking. *Journal of the Association for Information Systems (JAIS)*, *1*(5), 1–42.

Tang, J., Pee, L. G., & Iijima, J. (2013). Investigating the effects of business process orientation on organizational innovation performance. *Information & Management*, *50*(8), 650–660.

Tarhan, A., Turetken, O., & Reijers, H. A. (2016). Business process maturity models: A systematic literature review. *Information and Software Technology*, *75*, 122–134.

Tavakol, M., & Dennick, R. (2011). Making sense of Cronbach's alpha. *International Journal of Medical Education*, *2*, 53–55.

Tidd, J., & Bessant, J. (2013). *Managing Innovation: Integrating Technological, Market and Organizational Change* (5th ed.). John Wiley & Sons.

Van Horne, C., Frayret, J.-M., & Poulin, D. (2006). Creating value with innovation: From centre of expertise to the forest products industry. *Forest Policy and Economics*, *8*(7), 751–761.

Van Looy, A., De Backer, M., Poels, G., & Snoeck, M. (2013). Choosing the right business process maturity model. *Information & Management*, *50*(7), 466–488.

Widmann, V., de Waal, B. M. E., & Ravesteyn, P. (2018). How Do BPM Maturity and Innovation Relate in Large Companies? In *World Conference on Information Systems and Technologies* (pp. 87–96). Springer.

TOWARDS A STRATEGIC CLOUD COMPUTING FRAMEWORK: A SOUTH AFRICAN CONTEXT

Andrian Wilby Twala[1] and Ray M Kekwaletswe[2]
[1]*Graduate School of Business Leadership, University of South Africa, Midrand, South Africa*
[2]*School of Economic and Business Sciences, University of the Witwatersrand*
Johannesburg, South Africa

ABSTRACT

This paper covers the current research about cloud computing in the context of South African information technology professionals. The main question is how should cloud computing be strategically adopted and used sensitively to the South African context. In this paper, the research argument is that, there is a need for a framework that would assist to strategically adopt and use cloud computing in a uniformed and coordinated manner. To help understand the adoption and use of cloud computing, the stakeholder theory (Freeman, 1984) and contingency theory (Blanton, Watson, & Moody, 1992) are used as research lenses. This study follows an interpretivism philosophy. The adoption and use of cloud computing will be understood through interviews. The findings from this paper proposed a strategic cloud computing framework that will provide guidance for adoption and use of cloud computing in general. The framework will be analysed based on cloud computing factors, stakeholders, and contingency variables.

KEYWORDS

Cloud Computing, Strategic Framework, South Africa, Stakeholders, Contingency Theory

1. INTRODUCTION

Cloud computer is an internet based computing in which users can share information technology resources in a secure and efficient system(Hayes, 2008). In South Africa, organizations are faced with the challenges of mounting costs in keeping the existing hardware and software. Researchers such as (Varia, 2010;Chang, Walters and Wills, 2011) agrees that, cloud computing offers benefits such as, fast provisioning of hardware space, reduced costs for hardware and software, high availability, virtualization, data protection and sharing resources. Cloud computing is defined as the delivery of information technology resources or service via the internet (Mell & Grance, 2011). The cloud computing model is delivered to organization as pay as you use, where organization consume resources via the internet that are provided by the cloud service provider with guarantees offered via service level agreements (SLA) (Yang and Tate, 2009). South African organizations can benefit from a technology such as cloud computing, where they can leverage on its ability to offer a flexible resource that is scalable to the needs of the organization, which are accessible from anywhere at whatever time. This paper uses the stakeholder theory and contingency theory to understand, how should cloud computing be strategically adopted and used sensitive to the South African context. The paper conceptualizes a strategic cloud-computing framework in the context of South African information technology professionals. The next section discusses the theoretical foundations.

2. THOERETICAL FOUNDATIONS

This section discusses the theories that grounded this study. This study underpinning by theories of stakeholder theory by Freeman (1984) and contingency theory (Blanton, Watson, & Moody, 1992).

2.1 Stakeholder Theory

Stakeholder theory is viewed as a tool for understanding the relation between management , stakeholders and the organization's behavior towards the stakeholders (Freeman,1984). The stakeholder theory is widely used in previous studies, including information systems and management studies. According to Freeman (1984) stakeholders are defined as "any group or individual that can affect or is affected by the achievements of the organization's objectives". Clarkson (1995) defines stakeholders as "persons or groups that have claimed ownership, rights, or interests in a corporation and its activities, past, present, or future." The stakeholder theory asks managers to communicate the value that is being created when stakeholders working together. The focus of the stakeholder theory is to answer two main questions(Freeman, 1984). The first question asks is, "What is the purpose of the firm?" This encourages leaders of an organization to communicate the value that is being created by stakeholders working together, to produce outstanding performance. The second question asks is, "What responsibility does management have to stakeholders? "The stakeholder theory was originally presented as a map with the firm in the center of the wheel and the stakeholders around the rim. The stakeholder map is presented in figure 1. According to figure 1, there are various stakeholders influencing the firm when adopting and using innovation.

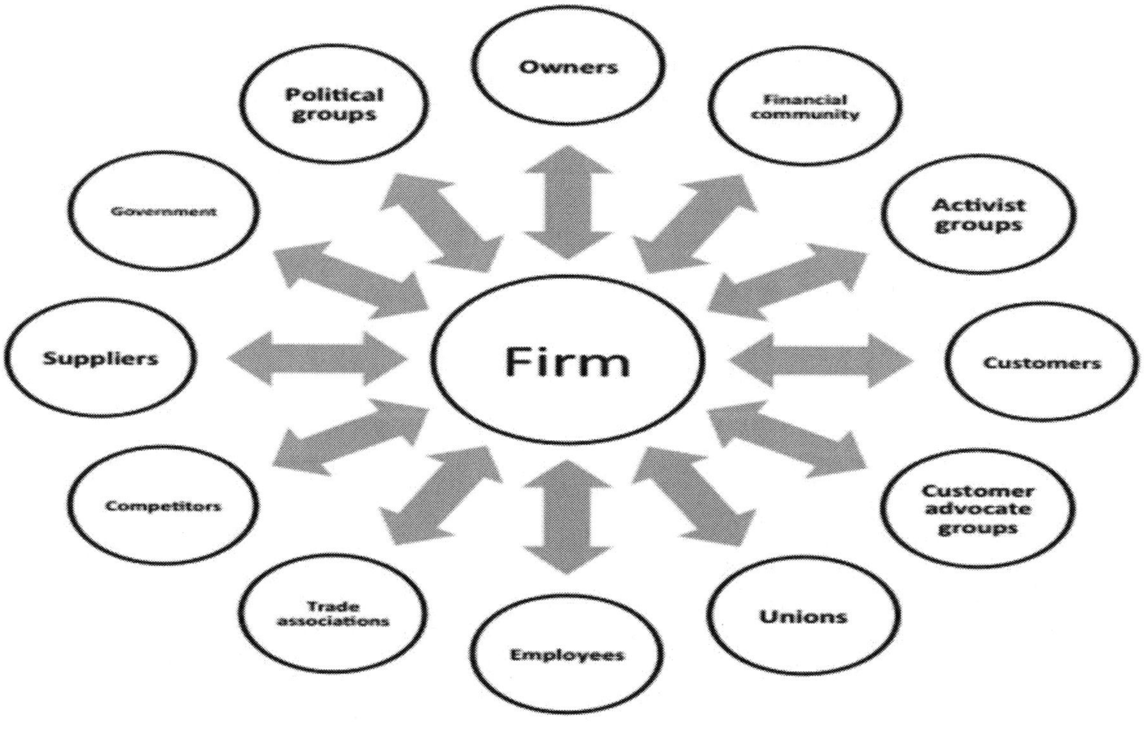

Figure 1. Stakeholder Map (Freeman, 1984)

2.2 Contingency Theory

The contingency theory is used to view organizations as a whole. The contingency theory assumptions are that there is no one best way of organizing. According to Donaldson (2001), contingency theory is defined as "a variable that moderates the effect of organizational characteristics on organizational performance." The basis of contingency theory is that organizational performance is dependent on the organizational characteristics such as a structure that reflects the situation of an organization (Donaldson, 2001). The organizational performance depends on the matching fitted between organizational structure and the contingencies. The key contingencies that have been suggested are environmental uncertainty, organizational strategy, and technology. The organizations are seeking to design their organizational characteristics that can handle uncertainties in the contingencies to achieve high performance and avoid any losses due to misfit when contingencies changes. The contingencies represent any variable that moderates the effect of an organizational characteristic of its performance. Researchers such Blanton et al. (1992) used the components: structure, environment, strategies and environment as illustrated in figure 2, to explain how an organization would require its structures to create strategies to improve the organization's economic stance in the market, thus ensuring the organization (performance) creates a profit.

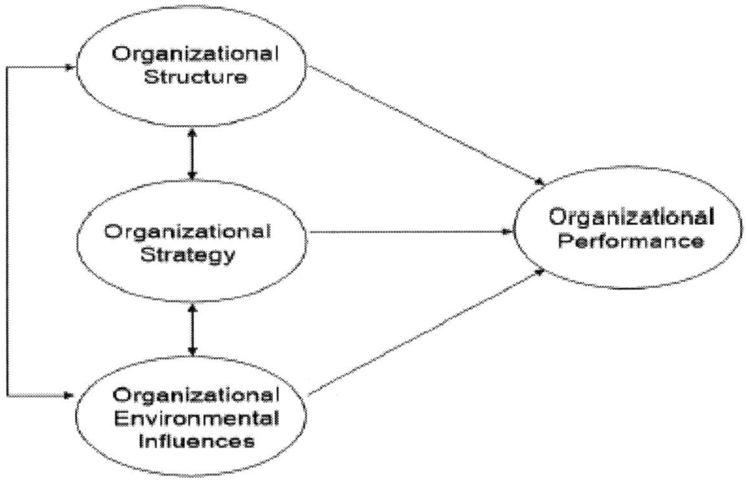

Figure 2. Contingency Theory (Blanton *et al.*, 1992)

The contingency components are briefly explained as follows:

- An environment is a place that allows its employees to work in favourable conditions. Employees, embracing the same vision, should be able to complete a task easily by freely accessing various procedures and processes.
- The structure is the foundation of each organization that explains how tasks can be shared or how to delegate responsibilities in different departments to maintain the processes within the organization. It also allows decision making to sustain workflow.
- The strategy is the core of the organization. It directs the functions of the organization in the long term. It allows the organization to be sustainable towards its competitors.
- Performance is defined as the past, present and future accomplishment of a given organizational task against pre-set standards of accuracy, completeness or whether cloud computing delivers value or not.

3. BACKGROUND TO THE RESEARCH PROBLEM

This section discusses the knowledge gaps and problem statement.

3.1 Knowledge Gaps

The knowledge gaps are discussed into theoretical knowledge gaps, methodological knowledge gaps, context and study location.

3.1.1 Theoretical Gaps

The review of literature on cloud computing has highlighted knowledge gaps that need to be addressed by this study. Previous studies on cloud computing were reviewed and the technology-organization-environment (Tornatzky, Fleischer and Chakrabarti, 1990)(TOE) is mostly used as a research lens. The TOE framework is an organisation level theory that explains the three elements that influence technology adoption decisions. The TOE framework elements are the organisational context, technological context and environmental context. The literature seems to be consistent of the three factors suggested by the TOE framework. Empirical research that combines stakeholder theory and contingency theory has not yet researched in the context of the South African information technology professionals. Therefore, this study is underpinned by stakeholder theory and contingency theory as the research lens that will bridge the theoretical knowledge gap.

3.1.2 Methodological Gaps

Previous studies on cloud computing has highlighted knowledge gaps with regard to methodology. The studies reviewed, used the survey methods as a research strategy. The methodological findings indicate that, there are fewer qualitative studies that have contributed to the understanding of cloud computing. The case study method is considered the most appropriate and viable for its in-depth approach. According to Yin (2016) a case study research strategy allows the researcher a deep understand of a phenomenon. In the context of this study, the study used the case study as research strategy.

3.1.3 Context and Study Location

Organizations in South Arica have seen an exponential increase in the use of information technology, specifically the use of the internet. The use of information technology in the organizations has increased the budget expenditure on IT infrastructure, software licensing, support, and maintenance costs. Considering these challenges, there is a need for cost-effective alternative technology. Cloud computing can be seen as an alternative technology. In the context of this study, the practical gap is bridged by developing a conceptual framework that combined key stakeholders' views on cloud computing. The stakeholders included executives, senior managers, middle managers, experts, and the users of cloud computing in their private capacity. South Africa as the location of the study. South Africa or the republic of South Africa is situated in the southern country in Africa. The paper conceptualizes a strategic cloud computing framework in the context of South African information technology professionals

3.2 Problem Statement

Against the aforementioned literature review, it is evident that the adoption and use of cloud computing in the context of South African is necessary for the organizations to realise maximum value from cloud computing investments and to improve operational efficiency. How cloud computing may be strategically used or adopted has not been adequately addressed in the literature. The following observations further supported that, there are still some knowledge gaps in realising the value of cloud computing in the South African context.

- Lack of literature that address the cloud computing adoption and use in the context in the context of South African information technology professionals.
- Lack of a theoretical framework that describes the drivers of cloud computing for different stakeholders.
- The conceptual framework that describes the adoption and use of cloud computing in the South African context.

Hence, this study will bridge the identified knowledge gap by developing a strategic cloud computing framework for the adoption and use of cloud computing in the South African context. This study is set out to determine how cloud computing could be strategically adopted and use sensitively to the South African context. The next section discusses the theoretical framework.

4. RESEARCH METHODS

This section discusses the research methodology that will be followed to develop a strategic cloud computing framework in the context of South African information technology professionals. This study attempts to obtain deep, rich data on cloud computing adoption and use from individuals. This study follows an interpretivism paradigm. Interpretive researchers believe that the reality to consists of people's subjective experiences of the external world (Saunders, Lewis and Thornhill, 2016). The interpretivism paradigm, gives the researcher the best way to understand the phenomena of cloud computing in South Africa context with the views and experiences of South African information technology professionals. This study used a qualitative research method. The reason for choosing the qualitative research method is to collect primary data from individuals with working experience and knowledge of cloud computing. This will help in understanding of how should cloud computing be strategically adopted and used sensitive to the South African context. The nature of this study is interpretive and research approach is qualitative research approach that is inductive in nature.

4.1 Research Strategy

The case study is a preferred research strategy, given the interpretive position and the nature of research questions. According to Yin (2016) a case study research strategy allows the researcher a deep understand of a phenomenon. This study uses a case study strategy. A case study approach is selected to obtain data from managers, professional, cloud experts, consultants, and user through semi-structured interviews. The reasons for conducting interviews is to obtain rich information about how cloud computing can be strategically adopted and user in the context of South African information technology professionals.

4.2 Research Design

4.2.1 Participants

This study attempts to obtain deep rich data on cloud computing adoption and use from individuals. The adoption and use of cloud computing will be understood through interviews. The study anticipates conducting interviews with IT professionals, including senior managers, middle managers, cloud experts, consultants, and users of cloud computing who have working experience and knowledge of cloud computing adoption and use, including those who take decisions about cloud computing technology

4.2.2 Data Collection Techniques

This study is a qualitative study and the following data collection techniques will be followed to collect empirical evidence for the study.

- **Interviews:** for this study, semi-structured interviews will be used to collect primary data. This study is set out to determine how cloud computing could be strategically adopted or used sensitively to the South African context. The face to face interviews will be conducted with individuals.
- **Observations:** for this study, the researcher as a participant-observer will be observing how the participant's behavior when answering questions. The observations will support the outcomes of the interviews

5. STRATEGIC CLOUD COMPUTING FRAMEWORK

This section discusses the conceptual research framework. The framework is developed from stakeholder theory by Freeman (1984), contingency theory (Blanton, Watson, & Moody, 1992) and technology-organization-environment (Tornatzky, Fleischer and Chakrabarti, 1990) which was used as the research lenses. The high-level view of the conceptual framework is made of environmental, stakeholder, contingencies, organizational and technological. Figure 3 is the proposed strategic cloud framework.

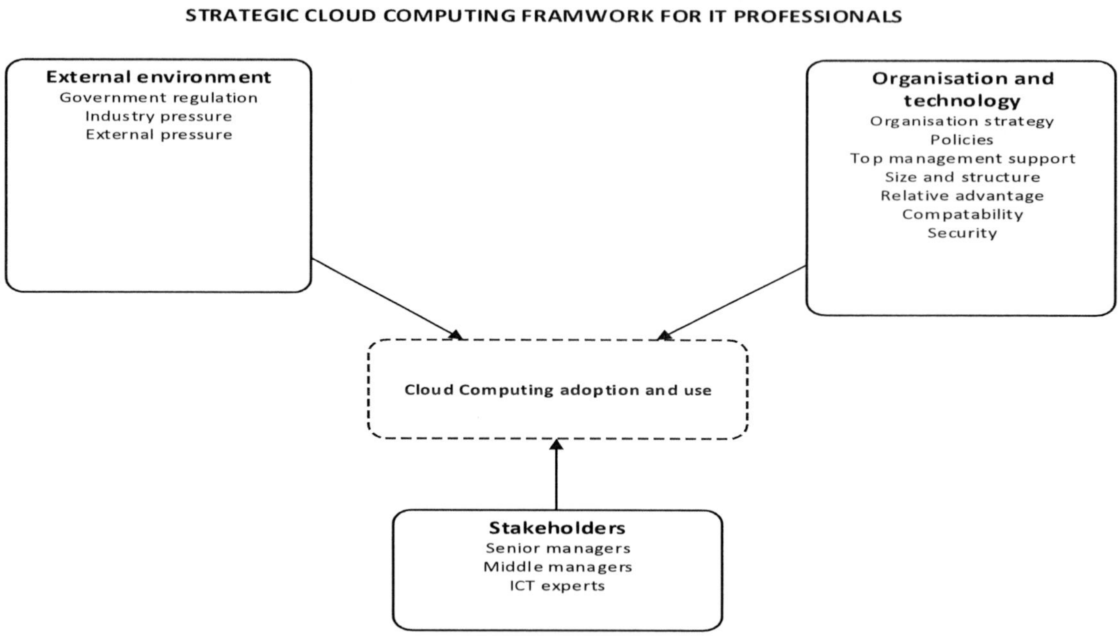

Figure 3. Strategic Cloud Computing Framework (Researcher)

The framework components are briefly explained

1. **External environment** – the environmental factors look at how the organization operates. For this study, the conceptual framework included the following environmental constructs:
   - Government regulation - government regulation refers to the support given by a government authority to encourage the adoption of cloud computing within the South African context.
   - Competitive pressure - competitive pressure refers to the pressure felt by the organizations from industry competitors.
   - Trade partner pressure - trade partner pressure refers to the pressure felt by the organization from business partners with whom the business is conducted.

2. **Stakeholders** - in this study the conceptual framework, stakeholders will include the following stakeholders, senior managers/executives, middle managers, ICT experts, and consultants.

3. **Contingencies** - for this study the conceptual framework, contingencies for analyzing cloud computing are as follows:
   - Size and structure - size refers to the size of an organization in terms of number of employees and the organization structure.
   - Strategy - strategy is defined as the direction and scope of an organization over the long-term required to achieve organizational goals and objectives.

4. **Organization** - for this study, the conceptual framework will use the following organizational constructs:
   - Policies – organization policies that may enable or hinder the adoption and use of cloud computing.
   - Management support – refers to top management support for the adoption of cloud computing
   - Relative advantage – refers to the benefits and advantages that can be gained by using cloud computing over the traditional way

5. **Technological factors -** for this study, the conceptual framework will use the following technological constructs:

- Compatibility – refers to the degree in which existing infrastructure can be used with cloud computing technology.
- Security – refers to how secure is the cloud computing environment.

6. CONCLUSION

The paper showed how cloud computing could be strategically adopted and use sensitively to the South African context. The paper conceptualizes a strategic cloud computing framework for the adoption and use of cloud computing in the South African information technology professional's context. To help understand the adoption and use of cloud computing in the context of South African information technology professionals, the stakeholder theory (Freeman, 1984) and contingency theory (Blanton, Watson, & Moody, 1992) are used as research lenses. The paper envisages that a strategic cloud computing framework will help to position the cloud computing adoption and use sensitively to South African organizations strategically, to address the needs of different stakeholders. Furthermore, the framework would assist to strategically adopt and use cloud computing in a uniformed and coordinated manner.

ACKNOWLEDGEMENT

The author would like to Prof Ray Kekwaletswe for his support during this research and Unisa Graduate School of Business Leadership (SBL).

REFERENCES

Blanton, J. E., Watson, H. J. and Moody, J. (1992) 'Toward a Better Understanding of Information Technology Organization: A Comparative Case Study', *MIS Quarterly*, 16(4), p. 531. doi: 10.2307/249735.

Chang, V., Walters, R. J. and Wills, G. (2011) 'Review of Cloud Computing and Existing Frameworks for Cloud Adoption', *IEEE Security & Privacy*, (2014), p. 35. doi: DOI: 10.4018/978-1-4666-8210-8.ch001.

Clarkson, M. B. . (1995) 'A Stakeholder Framework for Analysing and Evaluating Corporate Social Performance', *Academy of Management Review*, 20(1), pp. 92–117. doi: 10.5465/AMR.1995.9503271994.

Freeman, R. E. (1984) *Strategic Management: A Stakeholder Approach*, *Analysis*. doi: 10.2139/ssrn.263511.

Hayes, B. (2008) 'Cloud computing', *Communications of the ACM*, 51(7), p. 9. doi: 10.1145/1364782.1364786.

Mell, P., Grance, T. and Grance, T. (2011) 'The NIST Definition of Cloud Computing Recommendations of the National Institute of Standards and Technology', *National Institute of Standards and Technology, Information Technology Laboratory*, 145, p. 7. doi: 10.1136/emj.2010.096966.

Saunders, M., Lewis, P. and Thornhill, A. (2016) 'Research Methods for Business Students', in *Research methods for business students*, p. 649. doi: 10.1017/CBO9781107415324.004.

Tornatzky, L. G., Fleischer, M. and Chakrabarti, A. K. (1990) *The processes of technological innovation*. Lexington Books. Available at: https://openlibrary.org/books/OL2207473M/The_processes_of_technological_innovation (Accessed: 30 March 2018).

Varia, J. (2010) 'Migrating your existing applications to the AWS cloud', *A Phase Driven Approach to Cloud Migration*.

Yang, H. and Tate, M. (2009) 'Where are we at with Cloud Computing?: A Descriptive Literature Review', in *Australasian Conference on Information Systems*. doi: 10.17705/1CAIS.03102.

Yin, R. K. (2016) *Qualitative research from start to finish*, *Qualitative research from start to finish*. doi: 10.1007/s13398-014-0173-7.2.

Short Papers

TOWARDS AN INTEGRATED PLATFORM FOR DECISION SUPPORT IN WATER UTILITY MANAGEMENT

Cédric Grueau[1], André Antunes[1], Bruno Ferreira[2], Miguel Gonçalves[1], João Gomes[1] and Nelson Carriço[2]
[1]Setúbal School of Technology, Instituto Politécnico de Setúbal
Campus do IPS, Estefanilha, 2910-761 Setúbal, Portugal
[2]Barreiro School of Technology, Instituto Politécnico de Setúbal,
Rua Américo da Silva Marinho, s/n, 2839-001 Lavradio, Portugal

ABSTRACT

The pressure on water supply systems is a real challenge for water utilities, which are entrusted with the responsibility to manage and operate those systems. Water utility engineers and managers make decisions based on data that are obtained from several information systems (IS), such as geographic information systems (GIS), billing, asset operation and maintenance or accounting. Most of the time, these IS result in data silos as a consequence of lack of machine communication protocols, common data formats or common meaning of exchanged content. On the other hand, the diversity of IS is a challenge to water utilities which struggle with data consistency and interoperability. In this context, water utility engineers and managers make decisions based on data which are often incomplete, inaccurate or out-of-date. In this paper, we present an IT platform that integrates data from different information systems, including tools to support decision-making on water supply systems (e.g., performance indicators, water, and energy balances). This platform, developed in collaboration with a representative set of Portuguese water utilities, allows water utilities to integrate their data and perform analysis of their systems. With this approach, we provide water utilities and water supervision agencies with the possibility to compute a unified set of metrics whatever the IS they use.

KEYWORDS

Water Utility Management, Web Services, Data integration, Decision Support System, Information Systems

1. INTRODUCTION

In recent decades the percentage increase in water use on a global scale has exceeded twice that of population growth (Cosgrove and Loucks, 2015). Water utility companies, under pressure from consumers and regulators alike, are transforming and adapting their management models to improve water quality and increase supply while protecting water sources. Those organizations often rely on a vast software eco-system to manage the board set of data generated by utility's activity. Substantial investments are being carried out by water utility companies in several Information Systems (IS), namely, Enterprise Resource Planning system (ERP), Geographic Information System (GIS), Customer Relationship Management (CRM) or Supervisory Control and Data Acquisition System (SCADA). These IS generate data that ranges several areas of utility activity, namely, billing and accounting data, GIS data, time series of water volume, pressure, discharge, tank levels, consumption and water quality parameters, such as chlorine, pH and temperature, infrastructure and user characteristics and meteorological data (Carriço et Al., 2018).

The daily control, operation, management and current or future planning carried by water utility companies often resort on several analysis techniques (e.g., calculation of performance indicators or simulation of hydraulic behaviour, as well as more complex Artificial Intelligence (AI) techniques). These different analysis techniques require data that is produced by utility's multiple IS and is often distributed across several decentralized databases, where little interaction occurs between.

The required interoperability and integration between the different utility's IS habitually face many barriers. Systems often don't share information, creating data silos that leave various departments without a holistic view of operations or customer behaviour. The dispersion and variety of data sources and formats is pronounced, resulting from diverse software, systems and departments, as well as the use of outdated technological trends (i.e., use of old technologies based in spreadsheets).

Considering the lack of machine communication protocols, common data formats or common meaning of exchanged content, the access to data from a particular IS or department can be a time-consuming task, typically involving several individuals, multiple file formats and several intermediate processes. Thus, the application of information and communication technologies in water utilities is often restricted, foreclosing the ability to share data and knowledge, and hence interoperate across people and software involved (Howell et Al., 2016).

2. RELATED WORK

Geographical Information Systems (GIS) play a very important role in managing spatial data within the network infrastructure. (Meyers, 2005). Each GIS uses its own data model in order to represent the water facility and provides toolboxes to perform network analysis tools and planning. For this reason, if one wants to compare different systems, he will eventually need to convert data from a system to the GIS solution to perform the comparison.

Several solutions have been developed to solve the data integration and analytics problem in water utilities. The development of this type of solutions may start within the utility itself, which has the necessary resources to develop a system suited to their needs, or through the development of commercial software.

Two Portuguese utilities developed their data integration and analytics problem through GIS driven solution, as a mean of integration between their diverse IS. As such, through this solution it is possible to easily access data related to infrastructures, fleets, water demands, billing, among others (Silva et Al. 2017, Sousa et Al. 2017). H2Porto is a platform developed by a Portuguese utility aiming at integrating data gathered from different sources (i.e., sensors, GIS, equipment automation signals, among others), as well as results from hydraulic simulation models, aiming ultimately at predictive models of network hydraulic behaviour and decision support tools (Vieira et Al., 2018). Nonetheless, the use of both of these platforms is restricted to the utility itself.

Baseform and WaterSmart are commercial software that claim to provide comprehensive, actionable analytics to assist in water utilities specific efficiency issues and key business outcomes. Nonetheless, even if integration of real sensor data is possible with these solutions, integration of raw data from the scattered data sources may not be possible and the processing treatment required to import and integrate data may not be justified. On the other, if these solutions allow the analysis of a single system, they are not prepared to integrate utilities with different levels of maturity and encompassing different management models.

A dashboard is visual display of the most information needed to achieve one or more objectives which fits entirely on a single computer screen so it can be monitored at a glance (Few, 2006). Various providers such as Tableau or DataHero provide solutions to build dashboards. These solutions implement predefined powerful visualisations that can be combined into a dashboard. To get more flexibility, it is also possible to use visualisation libraries such as D3 JS or Bokeh to create building blocks for a dashboard. These libraries are more suited for the creation of specific visualisations that can cope with the specificity of our domain.

3. METHODOLOGICAL CONCEPT AND SYSTEM DESIGN

In the context of the DECiDE project, a new platform has been designed from scratch. To cover this wide range of utilities, a set of five Portuguese water supply utilities was selected, ranging from small to medium size and from countryside to coastal utilities, encompassing different management models (i.e., Direct municipal management and Autonomous water services of a municipality). These five utilities form a representative sample of the diversity of IS and data gathering methods among Portuguese utilities. As an example, one of these utilities is able to collect consumption data at the costumer level every hour, while the remaining obtain the consumption by manual readings every two months.

3.1 Concept

For improved decision making, water management companies need to compute a set of metrics that help to manage the physical system and the commercial operation. The Portuguese Water and Waste Services Regulator (ERSAR) published several technical guides (ERSAR, 2019), outlining a water supply service quality assessment system based on metrics. A set of sixteen metrics was selected by the five case studies, reflecting the real needs of utilities for systems' performance assessment. The calculation of these metrics resort on data from different IS. Water and energy balances are also carried on a regular basis by the utilities, in order to assess the water supply system's efficiency, both in terms of water losses (Alegre et al., 2000) and energy use (Mamade et al. 2017). Nonetheless, these balances resort on a broad set of data (i.e., input volumes and energy consumption, billed and unbilled consumptions, elevations, amongst others). If sectorial balances are meant to be calculated, the complexity of data collection and management carried by the utility manager can be overwhelming.

As such, water utilities need a system to assess and compare the performance of its water supply systems. The basic question therefore to answer is: how can we provide a unified approach to integrate and compare data organized and stored in a plethora of IS?

Thus, the aim of this platform is to implement a set of services to upload water utilities data and parse those data into a unified database where data from all water utilities are stored. Using web services capabilities, the system design in Figure 1 creates a platform for Spatial and Consumption Data through the use of webservice RESTful API. One of the API is dedicated to serve the values of management metrics for each utility. Another of the API serves the dashboard application that is used by decision makers to visualize and analyse metrics from each water supply system.

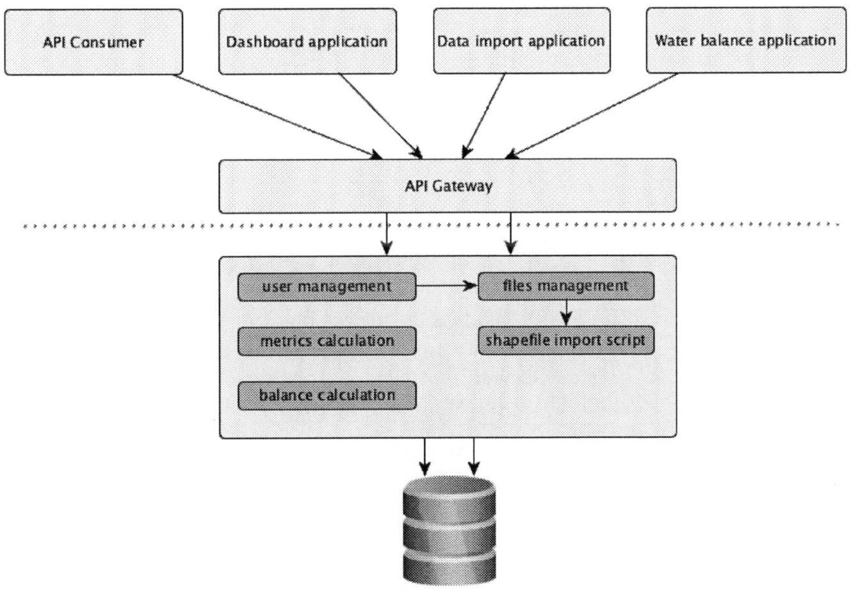

Figure 1. System architecture for the DECiDE web-based decision support platform for water utility management

The dispersity of data in the various utilities' information systems, as well as the high number of performance metrics related to water supply systems, motivate the need of a system that can graphically represent this type of data in order to facilitate the decision-making process.

The dashboard is one of the tools that is intended to facilitate the decision-making process, based on user-defined filtering (e.g. analysis area, data type and time period), it is possible to represent a set of data with different types of graphical representation (e.g. bar chart, pie chart, timeline chart, bullet chart, map). The system evaluates the best types of representation for each data set.

3.2 System Design

The first challenge to overcome was to design a domain model that could represent all the concepts present in the different water utilities. Due to the heterogeneity of IS and data models used by those utilities, we followed a Domain Driven Design in order to map the domain concepts into software. It was necessary to intensively involve domain expert (researchers and engineers from water utilities) into the process of domain modelling, in order to resolve ubiquitous language, establish a common vocabulary and draw the context boundaries. The result of the expert participation is a domain model that has been enriched with a set of sixteen management metrics about water supply systems, as well as a set of recommendations regarding data management in order to assess the performance of their systems.

3.3 System Overview

After a registration process, water utilities upload their infrastructural data from their own GIS data and their consumption data into the cloud platform using a Web application. The file format required for geographical data is shapefile, a format used as a standard by GIS community. Data are parsed and stored into a database. A set of services, built in the platform, uses data from the physical network and from clients' consumption to compute performance and sustainability metrics about the network, as well as water and energy balances. This information is organized and made available to the decision maker of each water utility through a dashboard. Using this dashboard, managers can assess the health and performance of their systems by comparing metrics for different time periods. The values of those metrics are also made available to public through a REST API. This makes it possible for the regulator to compare the performance of different water utilities at a regional scale, increasing the relevance of the proposed platform.

For the implementation, we decided to use MySQL technology for the database. We wanted to build a flexible system that could be used by utilities with different levels of maturity. Consequently, it was a requirement to be able to upload incomplete data to the platform. With relational databases it is easier to check if a given data is missing, i.e., what columns (attributes) exist for a given row. The API server technology was implemented using Django, a free and open source Python Web framework, in order to obtain a fast developed, scalable and secure platform. We used Django REST framework toolkit that supports Authentication to build the first version of the Web API. The API exposes the endpoint for the frontend application. The client application on the frontend of the framework uses D3 JS library. D3 offers a wide range of possibilities to define the specific visualization that were needed to represent the water and energy balances as well as the dashboard components to represent the metrics.

The platform architecture offers a set of directly accessible services. Figure 2 represents the requests reaching the backend platform services. In the figure, there are three servers (implemented with docker containers), which contain an Apache Service that runs a frontend client application (i.e. import app and dashboard app); the Django backend API application and the MySQL database.

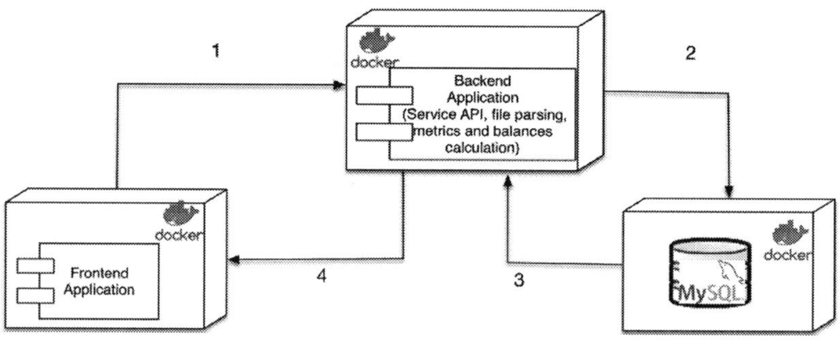

Figure 2. Platform Architecture

3.4 Data Import into the Platform

The data import process is challenging due to the disparity between utilities own information systems and their data storage methods and formats.

The DECiDE platform allows registered entities to upload their updated data files. Each file is registered in the system and placed in a distinct entity folder. Files can be in multiple formats and content organization is not consistent. Our platform must be able to parse uploaded files and update the database with the parsed data. The challenge was to implement a file parsing mechanism allowing a common interface, semi-automatic process and minimum user intervention. File parsing starts by trying to determine file content. Identification is based on file extension and content analysis. Previous knowledge obtained by analysis of partner entities sample data files is included in the detection algorithm. After detecting file type and content, we are able to identify the related data model elements, database tables and formats to target.

An initial mapping is created between data model elements and file content. The user is allowed to correct and/or validate the detected mapping. The validated mapping is registered in the system and used the next time a similar file from that entity is uploaded. After validation, the importation process starts. Data can be converted as needed to be validated in the platform data model.

The data model is prepared to maintain an historical record of infrastructure and other time-sensitive data. When updating such data elements, the previous state is timestamped and kept in database allowing historical analysis of data evolution. To validate the data import process, a specific web-based application has been developed. It includes the calculation of control values about the GIS imported from a shape file.

4. DISCUSSION

Many services and API for the DECiDE platform have already been implemented. The application built to validate the import process have allowed us to highlight the necessity of implementing a two-steps import process. The first step will consist in the importation of all the necessary files to integrate the GIS data and the data related to water consumption. After the parsing of all these data, the user will be informed about the possible missing information, necessary to calculate the set of metrics. He will be notified about the metrics that can be calculated from the uploaded information and the one that cannot. He will then have the possibility to validate or to complete the missing data. This two steps validation process will help water utilities with fewer data to continue to take advantage of the platform even though they cannot provide all the information.

5. CONCLUSIONS AND FURTHER WORK

We have presented the first step towards a platform for decision support in water utility management. Web service technologies were utilized to develop applications on both client and server side, as well as to integrate data from different IS. With our approach, data integration and metric calculation, required to support the decision-making process, is easily achieved by the utility. This approach will also be useful for any regional or national utilities resorting on data integration for combined analysis, such as sanitation services or state irrigation projects. Future work will be carried out towards improving the dashboard application with water utilities' users and developing the water balance and energy balance applications.

ACKNOWLEDGEMENT

The work presented in this paper is part of DECiDE project - SAICT-POL/24135/2016 | LISBOA-01-0145-FEDER-024135 | ALT20-03-0145-FEDER-024135 - which is funded by FCT – Fundação para a Ciência e a Tecnologia, through Programa Operacional Regional Lisboa 2020 and Programa Operacional Regional Alentejo 2020, via FEDER.

REFERENCES

Alegre, H., Hirner, W., Baptista, J.M., Parena, R. (2000). *Performance indicators for water supply services*, 1st edition, Manual of Best Practice Series, IWA Publishing, London, ISBN: 1 900222 272 (160 p.).

Carriço N., Ferreira B., Monteiro L., Mendes A., Grueau C., Covas D., Santos J., Figueira, J., Baio M., Barreira R., Silvestre I., Isidro R., Mestrinho J., Faím J., Traitolas S., Chaveiro P., 2018. "Multicriteria decision platform for urban water infrastructures", In: *Proceedings of 18thENASB*, Porto, Portugal.

Cosgrove, W. J., Loucks, D. P., 2015. Water management: Current and future challenges and research directions. *Water Resources Research*, 51(6), 4823–4839. American Geophysical Union (AGU). Retrieved from http://dx.doi.org/10.1002/2014WR016869

Few, S., 2006, *Information Dashboard Design*, O'Reilly Media, CA, USA.

Howell, S.K. , Rezgui, Y. , Beach, T., Zhao, W. , Terlet, J., Li. H., 2016. Smart Water System Interoperability: Integrating Data and Analytics for Demand Optimized Management through Semantics, *ICCCBE 2016*, pp. 1-9.

Mamade, A., Loureiro, D., Alegre, H., Covas, D. (2017). A comprehensive and well tested energy balance for water supply systems, *Urban Water Journal*, DOI: 10.1080/1573062X.2017.1279189

Meyers, J. R., 2005. GIS in Utility, In: *Geographical Information Systems: Principles, Techniques, Management and Applications*, 2nd Edition, Abridged, [available online, last accessed on 3/1/2019]. http://www.geos.ed.ac.uk/~gisteac/gis_book_abridged/files/ch57.pdf,

Silva M. H., Vilela J., Morais M. (2017). Interconnection of information systems in SMAS Sintra - contribution in providing quality public service (In Portuguese). In: *Proceedings of ENEG 2017*, Évora, Portugal.

Sousa C., Marques A., Fernandes J. (2017). The contribution of GIS information for an integrated and efficient management systems (In Portuguese). In: *Proceedings of ENEG 2017*, Évora, Portugal.

Vieira P., Costa F., Cunha R., Marques R., Fernandes M. (2018). Technological platform for the urban water cycle. From concept to implementation (In Portuguese). In: *Proceedings of 18thENASB*, Porto, Portugal.

SUCCESS PATTERNS FOR THE DIGITAL TRANSFORMATION OF B2B COMMERCE

Matthias Lederer and Jan-Gerd Bruns
ISM International School of Management, D-Karlstraße 35, 80333 Munich, Germany

ABSTRACT

Various companies in different industries face a variety of new technological opportunities, often referred as digital transformation. This research collects and classifies successful cases for digital transformation in the business-to-business (B2B) commerce. The initial qualitative analysis of 80 cases results in the derivation of eight potential patterns. For example, it can be concluded from the dataset that B2B companies are enriching their web shops with personal service, data-driven features or individual media. Some companies transform their B2B product portfolio to connected smart solutions and newly also sell to end-consumers. Moreover, it seems that offline and online services as well as sales and communication channels are combined in innovative ways to be prepared for a digital future.

KEYWORDS

Digital Transformation, B2B Transactions, E-Business Models, Best Practices

1. MOTIVATION

The economic potential of digitization in B2B (business-to-business) transactions is considered to be strong, but has not been completely analyzed in the scientific and practical discourses on digital transformation (Pagani & Pardo, 2017; Marketing Leadership Council, 2015). For example, in public discourses, the various applications of the "GAFA" players (Google/Alphabet, Amazon, Facebook, Apple) are dominant. Many of the digital innovations focus on marketing-oriented issues (e.g., individualized advertising on Facebook, increasing customer experience with AmazonWebServices, etc.). Available applications are widely used to enhance B2C (business-to-consumer) commerce (e.g., Amazon Echo and Apple as a platform for innovative sales applications, Google as an advertising partner in the customer journey, etc.) (Horovitz, 2017).

Nonetheless, the potential for digital solutions in B2B commerce, understood as the sale of goods and services to professional customers using the Internet, is tremendous (Lindh & Nordman, 2018). Depending on the industry, the degree of digitization in B2B is even less than 40 percent (Bughin et al., 2017). The overall digital maturity of B2B providers is increasing, but is on average lower than at B2C companies (Catlin et al., 2016). So far, the major focus of B2B projects in digital transformation, understood as the application of digital technologies to improve design parameters of a company, was on internal processes like production (e.g., smart factory), back-office workflows (e.g., automation of services) and resource planning (e.g., predictive technologies) (Statista, 2017; Lingqvist, 2015).

According to statistics, B2B commerce is growing steadily worldwide with a growth rate of about five to ten percent (global gross merchandise volume in 2013 was 5.826 and 7.661 billion U.S. dollars in 2017) (Statista, 2017; Lingqvist, 2015). Traditional small and medium-sized (SME) B2B companies seem still to be a long way from a comprehensive digitalization of their transactions or from disruptive innovations in e-commerce. Nevertheless, they need to adapt to the dynamic conditions of concentrated online and digital markets in order not to risk their competitive position (Lässig, 2016). At the same time, they will not be able to prevail against new digital global players (e.g. Alibaba).

This work-in-progress collects cases, in which B2B companies succeeded in implementing new digital techniques, processes, services and products in order to increase their economic success. The question of how success of digital transformation projects can be measured and compared, is currently the subject of various studies. Typically, they use or combine insights from existing research fields such as process management, innovation management or accounting, or from the functions concerned by the transformation (such as marketing, purchasing, sales, etc.). Comparing recent surveys of companies and theoretical work, the turnover of new/additional products and services, the extent of optimized processes as well as classic productivity and profitability figures are often mentioned. It is noteworthy that more frequently the extraction and analysis of data (business analytics) is seen as success parameter (e.g. survey by IDC, 2018).

In this article, *digital transformation* is understood as a comprehensive and sustainable change process of transactions or business models that is enabled by newly available digital technologies (Lankshear & Knobel, 2008; Heinze et al., 2018). Collected cases are examined according to common significances. Significant patterns to be identified are understood as possibly imitative behaviors of companies that can increase the respective business success (Streuer et al., 2016). As a summary, the aim of this research is to answer the following question:

Which patterns can be drew from B2B commerce cases, which successfully carried out a digital transformation?

2. METHODOLOGY

The methodology of this research follows a multi-case design (Herriott, 1983) combined with an integrative review (Kornmeier, 2007). For this documentation, the approach should be documented in four steps:

- **Search and selection**: In order to ensure a scientific basis and to not use any self-marketing or consulting publications, only documents from scientific databases (e.g., EBSCO) have been used to identify cases. The two central limiting parameters ("digital transformation" and "B2B" transactions; including synonyms) designed the search string.
  After reviewing more than 3,000 documented cases, only those were considered that fulfill an explicit proof of business success (for example with key figures) as well as supplementary quality standards (for example completeness, correctness, still existing business models). Since many forms of success are discussed (see above), one concrete proof is sufficient in the classical views on successful company developments (resource, capability, leadership and process) (Muller et al., 2005).
- **Coding**: For the 80 cases so far, a total of 26 attributes for each was coded to determine the transformation approaches. In addition to metadata (e.g., name, company size, industry, sales areas) and the actual business model/model change (parts of the Business Model Canvas), the orientation within recognized classifications (e.g., the St. Gallen business model navigator) and some other attributes (e.g., success measures) were extracted from the cases.
- **Analysis**: So far, a qualitative analysis was carried out by deducing general theses in the dataset (Lee, 2002). The qualitative content analysis overall followed the recommended approach of (Mayring, 2014). Based on the research question, the deductively generated criteria were semantically analyzed with their relative distribution. Based on the formal analysis, suitable cases were structured inductively. Both the contained criteria as well as the common content of the cases lead to explicitly formulated patters as interpreted summary of transformation approaches.
- **Documentation**: Patterns identified so far have been described and interpreted in a standard template for Best Practices documentation (including for example key changes, risks, opportunities, performance measures and sample companies). The specified number (n) of each pattern indicates in the following section how many of the 80 cases fall into the described type of digital transformation.

3. PRELIMINARY RESULTS

Based on the previous qualitative analysis, eight patterns in the digital transformation of B2B commerce could be identified. They will be shortly introduced using examples:

- **B2B companies conquer the B2C markets** (n=11): Established B2B companies are increasingly acquiring private end-customers. Most of these companies come from the fast-moving consumer goods industry. By omitting wholesalers and retailers through digital channels, these companies realize lower prices and gain a better customer understanding.
For example, Flexfire LED, a manufacturer of indoor and outdoor lighting, nowadays generates 20% of sales in the end-consumer sector.
- **Marketplaces organized by large-sized companies** (n=8): Four companies (Amazon Business, Alibaba, Klöckner and Mapudo) predominantly organize transactions on digital B2B marketplaces. It can be concluded from the dataset, that the creation and sustainable operation of such platforms with a critical mass goes hand in hand with large investments only large companies can afford.
- **B2B companies transfer physical to digital goods** (n=9): Many companies enrich their traditional product portfolio by connectivity und smartness. The actual added value is more perceived by its new digital possibilities.
Smart farming, as offered for example by Claas, means that farmers profit from agricultural management systems including integrated harvester and connected stock cabins.
- **From online service to offline service or multi-channel offers** (n=19): A lot of companies still rely on offline services (e.g. personal on-site advice) although they aim to reduce transaction cost. Personal support is needed to handle complex products or orders of considerable investment, but it is now often part of a cross-channel solutions.
For example, the tool manufacturer Hilti placed a new contact possibility for personal help (e.g. video chat) on its B2B online shop page. So called "Hilti Center" offer stationary help for online customers.
- **Digital channels reduce transaction costs** (n=38): The most frequent focus of B2B transactions of standard products is reducing transaction costs through digital channels (e.g. Electronic Data Interchange [EDI]). Tendencies can be observed, which go away from classical interface standardization (e.g. EDIFACT).
Hirschmann Automotive for example speeded up the order process by offering free digital samples. If engineers and developers are convinced, they have access to all internal planning processes (advanced interface) to optimize their own scheduling.
- **Modern mass Customization** (n=8): Especially manufacturers were successful in adapting products to the individual needs of customers at the price of mass production.
At Zeppelin Cat, excavators can be pre-configured and ordered including a real-time support by digital consultants. Goin, as another example, sells furniture for restaurants using an online configurator. It offers a 3D room planning showing the furnishing concept including service routes for the operating staff.
- **Added value through experience selling** (n=23): Some B2B providers offer their customers a new shopping experience. In addition to the pure sale, companies tend to new forms of product and service impressions with emotional attraction or technical richness.
The e-bikes manufacturer Riese & Müller, for example, launched a dealer portal displaying about 1.2 million configuration options with real-time pricing. While increasing the orders, the number of support requests was reduced due to media items (e.g. video guidelines) available for all configurations.
- **SMEs acquire new customers** (n=19): It become clear that especially SMEs often take the chance of their flexibility to adapt to new market conditions and are thus able to gain new customers in existing segments.
Lex & Hesse, a wholesaler of spare parts for buses and rail vehicles employing about 30 people, has for example been able to generate a 500% increase in turnover by the introduction of a new B2B shop. It focuses on very specific requirements such as automated transfer of orders.

4. CONCLUSION AND IMPLICATIONS

The analysis shows that successful digital transformations in B2B commerce in principle follow generic patterns. They can serve as a set of templates for the creation of digital innovations especially in traditional companies. At the same time they can now be used to further investigate detailed obstacles and beneficial factors. The patterns derived can serve as a basis for discussions with researchers from multiple fields. The various identified example cases are suitable for concrete discourses with practitioners. Especially against the background that in the context of digital transformation, often only general trends, rough ideas and exaggerated scenarios are described (Mertens & Barbian, 2016), an extended analysis of this dataset might give specific answers for the future of B2B transactions. Although some of the identified patterns are known in established literature, the dataset has the potential to provide answers and applicable solutions for the digital transformation of B2B commerce. The attributes documented for each successful case show specifics for the different types of transactions and business models (e.g., complex vs. standard products, focus on new vs. old customer groups, own vs. third-party development, etc.). In particular, the detailed analysis may provide new insights into the clever combination of sales media, which is occasionally discussed under the term omni-channel.

After this initial qualitative analysis, the authors extend the dataset in current research by adding further cases. The aim is to substantiate the patterns with quantitative proofs and further analyzes (exact dependencies of the attributes) early next year. In ongoing case studies, the authors are also about to examine the applicability of previously documented patterns in German SMEs.

REFERENCES

Bughin, J. et al, 2017. The digital reinvention, *McKinsey Quarterly*, Vol. 02/2017.

Catlin, T. et al, 2016. *How B2B digital leaders drive five times more revenue growth than their peers*. McKinsey, New York.

Heinze, A. et al, 2018. Knowledge exchange partnership leads to digital transformation at Hydro-X Water Treatment. *Global Business and Organizational Excellence*, Vol. 37, No. 4, pp. 6-13.

Herriott, R.E. and Firestone, W.A., 1983. M*ultisite Qualitative Policy Research: Optimizing Description and Generalizability*. Educational Researcher Vol. 12, No. 2, pp. 14-19.

Horovitz, B., 2017. Impacting Consumers, Upending Retail: Why Amazon, Apple, Facebook and Google rule. *Stores Magazine*. Vol. 99, No. 8, pp. 38-40.

IDC 2018. *Digital Transformation KPIs to Enable Systems of Accountability*. IDC PlanScape, 09/2018.

Kornmeier, M., 2007. *Wissenschaftstheorie und wissenschaftliches Arbeiten*. Physica, Mannheim.

Lankshear, C. and Knobel, M., 2008. *Digital literacies*. Zirndorf: Peter Lang Publishing.

Lässig, R. et al, 2016. *Die digitale Zukunft des B2B-Vertriebs*. Google/Roland Berger, New York.

Lee, A. S., 2002. A Scientific Methodology for MIS Case Studies. In Myers, M. D. and Avison, D., 2002. *Qualitative Research in Information Systems*. SAGE, London.

Lindh, C. and Nordman, E., 2018. New Service Development and Digitalization: Synergies of Personal Interaction and IT Integration. *Services Marketing Quarterly*, Vol. 39, No. 2, pp. 108-123.

Lingqvist, O. et al, 2015. Do you really understand how your business customers buy?, *McKinsey Quarterly*, Vol. 05/2015.

Marketing Leadership Council, 2015. *The digital Evolution in B2B Marketing – Research Studies*. The Corporate Executive Board Company, Washington.

Mayring, P., 2014. *Qualitative content analysis*. Belt, Klagenfurt.

Mertens, P. and Barbian, D., 2016. *Digitalisierung und Industrie 4.0*. Friedrich-Alexander-University, Nuremberg.

Muller, A. et al. 2005. Metrics for innovation: Guidelines for developing a customized suite of innovation metrics. *Strategy & Leadership*, Vol. 33, No. 1, pp. 37-45.

Pagani, M. and Pardo, C., 2017. The impact of digital technology on relationships in a business network. *Industrial Marketing Management*. Vol. 67, No. 11, pp. 185-192.

Statista, 2017. *B2B e-Commerce 2017 - Digital Market Outlook*. Statista Trend Report, Hamburg.

Streuer, M. et al, 2016. Profit Driving Patterns for Digital Business Models. *Proceedings of International Society for Professional Innovation Management Conference*. Worsley, pp. 1-14.

CONCEPTUAL DESIGN OF A TOOL SUPPORTING THE "LAST MILE" LOGISTICS IN HOSPITALS

Davide Aloini[a,1], Elisabetta Benevento[b] and Alessandro Stefanini[a]
[a]*University of Pisa, Italy*
[b]*University of Rome Tor Vergata, Italy*

ABSTRACT

This work reports preliminary outcomes from the LINFA project, which aims to develop a technological, information and organizational system for improving the procurement process of medicines and medical devices within healthcare organizations. Accordingly, the paper presents insights from a real case study within an Italian Hospital where the project team has gone through-out the phases of process discovery, modelling and use-cases identification and analysis to devise an integrated tool for supporting logistic decisions and operations. Findings provide readers with a complete identification and formalization of the conceptual requirements of such tool for supporting pharmaceutical last-mile logistic within a hospital.

KEYWORDS

Healthcare, Pharmaceutical Logistics, Last-mile, Hospital Information System, LINFA Project

1. INTRODUCTION

Logistics function has gained a strategic role in the management of hospitals. As a matter of fact, hospital material management has been identified as one key cost driver to cope with steadily increasing healthcare costs in industrialized countries (Volland et al., 2017). This is particularly true for pharmaceutical logistics where supply chain management has become more and more complex in the last decades since it has to meet life-saving interests at sustainable costs. Solving this trade-off requires to enable the collaboration of different stakeholders such as pharmaceutical manufacturers, wholesalers, distributors, customers, information service providers and regulatory agencies.

'Last-mile' of logistics in this context refers to the challenge of the final movements of goods and services to the delivery or consumption point. The 'last-mile' of pharmaceutical goods tends to be less efficient and most problem-prone. One side this is due to the variability and unpredictability of the patient profile and the high demand for care (Wieser, 2011; Bourlakis et al., 2011), on the other to the high process fragmentation and the increasing touch-points that are often related to additional costs and complications. Nevertheless, emerging IT tools (such as Radio Frequency Identification, Enterprise Resource Planning), vertical organizations as well as the new disruptive technologies for last-mile logistics solutions (e.g., drones, automatic guided vehicles) have risen consistent expectations of reducing the costs of distribution while guaranteeing adequate service levels. In such an evolving context, scholars and practitioners widely agree that hospitals must pay close attention to the inventory and information technology system used to manage their daily operations (Kritchanchai et al., 2017). As a matter of fact, technological progress and Information flows management are a prominent source of improvement of the hospital practices (Mazzocato et al., 2010). Definitely, they can enable communication and process coordination supporting the information sharing between the partner institutions (laboratory, blood transfusion center, etc.). Internal and external integration is therefore the new challenge for hospitals (Krichanchai and MacCarthy, 2017).

[1]Corresponding author - davide.aloini@unipi.it

This work aims to report a practical experience from the LINFA project which objective is to develop a technological, information and organizational system for improving the procurement process of medicines and medical devices within health care organizations. The system is developed through models of forecast analysis and process optimization, advanced logistics practices, increased traceability with the use of RFID technologies and health and administrative data flows. Accordingly, the paper presents a real case study within an Italian Hospital where the project team has gone through-out the phases of process discovery, use-cases identification and analysis to devise an integrated tool for supporting logistic operation (Niranjan et al., 2012; Govindan, 2013). Results provide readers with a complete identification and formalization of the conceptual requirements of such tool for supporting pharmaceutical last-mile logistic within a hospital or hospital network setting.

2. THE LINFA PROJECT AND RELATED OBJECTIVES

LINFA is a research project funded by the Region Tuscany and carried out jointly by companies and research organizations with a focus on the regional drug logistics at the hospital level. The idea originating the project is to provide decision support tools to facilitate the task of operators, who deal with the replenishment orders and inventory management in hospital departments, while developing methodologies, practices and cooperation tools oriented to their extension and scale up.

Exploiting the availability of historical information about drugs and patients, the development of forecasting methods, together with optimization algorithms integrated in a shared technological platform, the project aims to deliver a technological, information and organizational system for improving the procurement process of medicines and medical devices within healthcare organizations. In so doing, it will make possible to move towards the minimization of stocks and the effective and efficient management of medicines, with a consequent reduction in healthcare expenditure.

Specifically, the LINFA system aims to integrate models for demand forecast and process optimization systems with advanced logistics practices, increased traceability with the use of RFID technologies by exploiting health and administrative data flows. To this purpose, LINFA would make available and shares information about departmental stocks, hospital stocks and the actual availability of drugs at regional central warehouses. LINFA also proposes an innovative approach for managing safety stocks by enabling a unitary virtual warehouse based on the real stocks stored in the several hospital departments and permitting the transfer of drugs between them.

Summarizing, LINFA aims to provide a tool:

- To monitor the current drugs stock and support medical staff in the re-ordering process;
- To keep under control the expiring date of drugs;
- To support more efficient reorders thanks to the demand forecasting and optimization algorithms;
- To share stock information among the different hospital departments to deal with emergency orders;
- To record drugs withdrawals and exchanges between different departments.

3. METHOD

To discover and formalize functional requirements for the LINFA System and to fully understand the hospital staff needs, we accomplished a case study within an Italian Hospital. It goes through the following three phases:

1. ***Analysis of the drug management process:*** This phase aimed at understanding the current procedures of drugs procurement and inventory management and identifying potential criticalities and bottlenecks within the process. The analysis was carried out within an Italian Hospital by means of field observations and interviews with hospital staff. The resulting process model was represented through the BPMN language- see Chinosi & Trombetta (2012) for methodological details about this notation - and validated with hospital staff.
2. ***Primary users' and functional requirements identification:*** The aim of this phase was to identify the stakeholders of LINFA system users and to collect key information from their field experience. Identifying who will be involved in the information gathering process is important due to the input these

individuals can provide regarding technological needs. The collection of functional requirements was conducted through interviews and focus groups with hospital staff. In so doing, we focused on two main questions: (i) How can the LINFA system contribute to the operational goal of each user? (ii) What features are desirable for achieving such result? The outcome of this step was a set of functional requirements written in natural language.

3. ***Formalization of functional requirements for the LINFA system:*** In this step, we formalized the functional requirements previously identified, by using the UML (Unified Modelling language) language (Rumbaugh et al., 2017). In so doing, it was possible to automated traceability of requirements in the subsequent phases of LINFA system development. Specifically, we translated conceptual requirements into UML use case diagrams representing the relationships between primary users and system functionalities. Each use case was accompanied by text explaining the purpose of the use case as well as what functionality is accomplished when it is executed. The use cases can capture the intended behavior of the system being developed without specifying how the behavior is implemented.

4. RESULTS

4.1 Analysis of the Drug Management Process

The drug management process includes the following sub-phases: inventory management, drug procurement, drug receipt and storage, and control and reporting (reported in fig 1). Each sub-phase is detailed below.

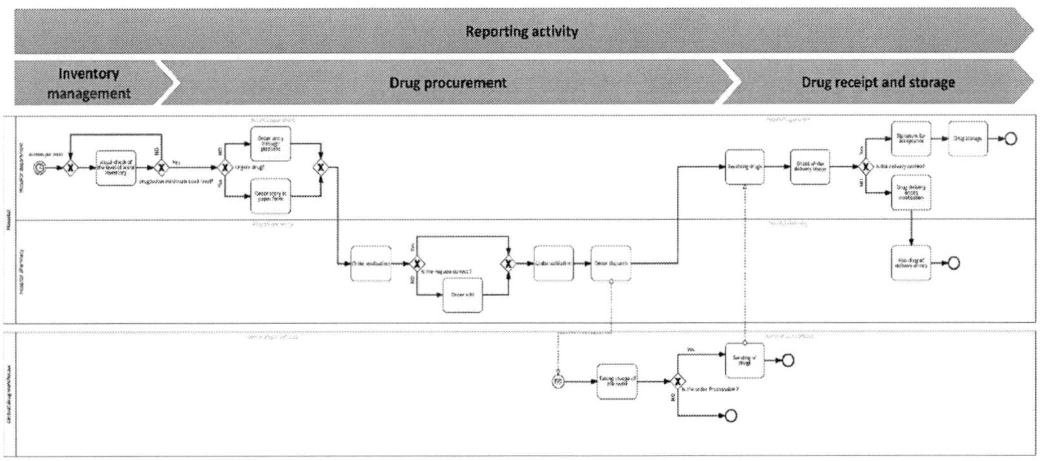

Figure 1. Drug Management process: a BPMN Diagram

- *Inventory Management*: At fixed intervals and independently by prescription, the head nurse or nurses check the ward inventory level, manage drug's expiration dates, and quantify the drug needs. Such monitoring is usually carried out by a visual check. In addition, the evaluation of the quantity of drugs to be reordered is based on nurse personal experience;
- *Drug procurement*: Regular requests for drugs are executed by the head nurse through a specific IS platform. On the other hand, urgent drug requests are drawn up in paper form. Each type of request is validated by the hospital pharmacy and sent to a central drug warehouse;
- *Drug receipt and storage*: Once drugs arrive in the ward, the head nurse checks the delivery status and signs for acceptance on the bill of delivery. Specifically, each delivery is checked against the relevant purchase order and each container physically verified. The storage of drug packages on the appropriate shelves is handled by nurses and nursing assistants. The order criteria may vary from ward to ward. In the case of incomplete or incorrect delivery, the pharmacy has to define a new replenishment request;
- *Control and Reporting*: The hospital pharmacy periodically monitors and measures the performance of hospital departments as concerning the drugs management.

Interview with participants have shown that the drug management process suffers from several criticalities. The lack of control over actual consumptions, together with the unpredictability of the demand for healthcare services, causes high levels of ward inventory and, then, considerable holding costs, obsolescence risk, and a negative effect on the hospital service level. In addition, drug replenishment requests are usually independently from real needs and quantities are determined based on nurse personal experience. This often results in oversized and too frequent orders. Drugs are often stocked without a standard codification and may be placed in different positions, thus determining an inefficient space utilization and code retrieval. Consequently, applying First-In-First-Out (FIFO) picking rule is also difficult. Accordingly, nurses and nursing assistants tends to be overly involved in logistics duties, reducing the time available for medical activities.

4.2 Primary Users' and Functional Requirements Identification

Primary users within the hospital who will be using the LINFA system include: *Hospital pharmacy*, *Doctor*, *Head nurse*, and *Nurse*. We defined a set of 17 functional requirements according to the aforementioned primary users. For sake of brevity, table 1 shows just an excerpt of such list.

Table 1. An Excerpt of the Functional Requirements List

Functional requirement	Description
Drug stocks visualization	The system must provide real-time information about the quantity and type of drugs in stock, keeping track of the batch number and the expiration date.
Drug stocks update	The system must allow the updating of the drugs in stock, as a result of drug loading (storage of drugs) and unloading (administration to patients).
Notification of new availability of a drug	The system must notify the unavailability of the requested drug and the failure to process the order, indicating a potential date for drug availability.

4.3 Formalization of Functional Requirements for the LINFA System

The overall use case diagram including all functional requirements identified in the previous step is shown in figure 2. Some use cases, such as *drug stocks update* and *order status display*, incorporate the behavior of other use cases as fragments of their own behavior. On the other hand, others (e.g., *order edit*) are an incremental extension to a base use case (e.g., *order validation and dispatch*). Each use case was also translated into structured textual specification format to identify the temporal sequence of behaviors and the state of the system and of the actors before and after the execution of that use case. As an example, the textual specification of the use case "*Notification of urgent drug availability*" (Table 2) is given below.

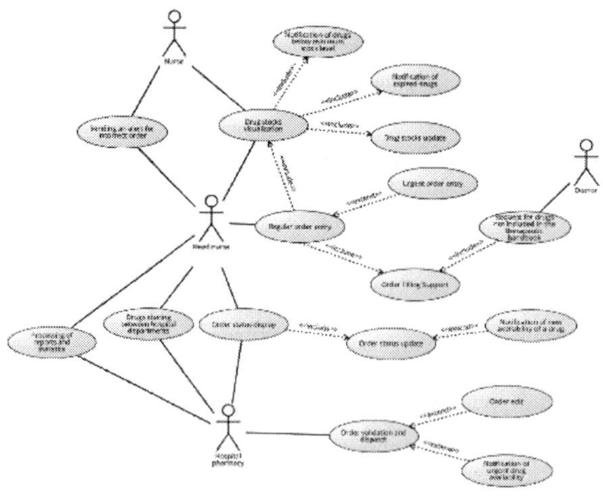

Figure 2. Overall Use Case Diagram

Table 2. Textual Specification of the Use Case "Notification of Urgent Drug Availability"

Use case name	**Notification of urgent drug availability**
Actor	Hospital Pharmacy
Pre-conditions	The operator must be logged into the system. The system must have notified an urgent order
Basic flow of events	1) The operator displays order items; 2) The operator selects the drug code and enters it in the search field; 3) The system shows the list of the wards where the drug is available with the related quantity;
Extensions	2.a The system is not able to find any correspondence with the parameters entered; 2.a.1. The operator checks the text correctness in the search field. 3.a The system shows a null result for the search 3.a.1 The system shows the appropriate message and terminates the operation.
Post-conditions	The system shows the list of hospital departments with drug availability

5. CONCLUSION

This work reports some preliminary outcomes from the LINFA project. Final expected benefits from the project include:

- reduction of errors and delivery times for drugs reorders;
- reduction of expiring drugs in hospital departments;
- improvement of the overall procurement and cost awareness at every level of the supply chain;
- support to monitoring and quick identification of anomalous situations;
- optimization of transit points from the central warehouse to the hospital departments;
- reduction of drugs stock costs and needed space in hospital departments.

Future project steps will concern the design and test of demand forecasting and optimization algorithm, conceptual architecture design, design of the interfaces, development of a test version, field testing.

ACKNOWLEDGEMENT

This work has been partially supported by LINFA (Logistica INtelligente del FArmaco) project, funded by Regione Toscana under the call PAR FAS 2007-2013, LINEA D'AZIONE 1.1 - BANDO FAR FAS 2014

REFERENCES

Bourlakis, M., F. Clear, and L. Patten. 2011. "Understanding the UK Hospital Supply Chain in an Era of Patient Choice." Journal of Marketing Management 27 (3–4): 401–423. doi:10.1080/0267257X.2011.547084.

Chinosi, M., & Trombetta, A. (2012). BPMN: An introduction to the standard. Computer Standards, 34(1), 124-134.

Govindan, K. (2013). Vendor-managed inventory: a review based on dimensions. International Journal of Production Research, 51(13), 3808-3835.

Krichanchai, S., & MacCarthy, B. L. (2017). The adoption of vendor managed inventory for hospital pharmaceutical supply. The International Journal of Logistics Management, 28(3), 755-780.

Kritchanchai, D. & Hoeur, S. & Engelseth, P. (2017). Develop a strategy for improving healthcare logistics performance. Supply Chain Forum: An International Journal. 19. 1-15.

Mazzocato et al., 2010 Mazzocato, P., C. Savage, M. Brommels, H. Aronsson, and J. Thor. 2010. "Lean Thinking in Healthcare: A Realist Review of the Literature." Quality and Safety in Health Care 19 (5): 376–382.

Niranjan, T. T., Wagner, S. M., & Nguyen, S. M. (2012). Prerequisites to vendor-managed inventory. International Journal of Production Research, 50(4), 939-951.

Rumbaugh, J., Booch, G., & Jacobson, I. (2017). The unified modeling language reference manual. Addison Wesley.

Volland, J., A. Fügener, J. Schoenfelder, and J. O. Brunner. 2017. "Material Logistics in Hospitals: A Literature Review." Omega 69: 82–101.

Wieser, P. 2011. "From Health Logistics to Health Supply Chain Management." Supply Chain Forum: An International Journal 12 (1): 4–13.

REFLECTIONS ON SOCIAL MEDIA USE ALONG THE ACADEMIC RESEARCH LIFE CYCLE

Anand Sheombar
HU University of Applied Sciences Utrecht, The Netherlands

ABSTRACT

This short paper argues for the need for discussion on the role social media could have in the research life cycle, particularly for Information Systems (IS) scholars. ICTs are pervasive, and their societal impact is profound. Various disciplines including those of social sciences are present in the online discourse and join the public debate on societal implications of ICTs and scholar are familiar with web tools for publishing. Information Systems scholars could not only further explore the possibilities for joining that online discourse, but also could explore the potential social media may have for activities related to the research life cycle. In this paper we do not focus solely on social media as a data collection source but regard their merits as a channel for scholarly communication throughout the whole research life cycle, from the start of getting inspired to conduct a research, finding collaboration partners or funding, through suggestions for literature, to the stage of research dissemination and creating impact beyond the own scientific community. This paper contributes an original approach to research communication by combining the research life cycle with practical insights of how social media can be applied throughout each phase of that lifecycle. We conclude with some questions debating the stance that (future) IS scholars are prepared to become the digital scholar that can manoeuvre well on social media for scholarly communication.

KEYWORDS

Social Media, Scholarly Communication, Research Communication, Open Science, Academic Research Life Cycle

1. INTRODUCTION

Social media may change the academic research life cycle. What implications it has on scholarly communication is not clear (Mas-Bleda et al., 2014), but the younger generation of scholars is more used to use those technologies in their personal life and eventually for academic activities. “As researchers adopt new tools and are increasingly encouraged by institutions and funders to reach wider audiences, science communication is changing. In some ways, these new media formats are replicating previous systems, and in other ways, these tools present profoundly new ways of communicating”, Mollett et al. (2017) argue. The potential for IS scholars is evident.

When we discuss research communication via social media, we first have to outline the concepts involved. The terms social media, social networks (SNSs), and web 2.0 are often interchanged in usage (Parameswaran, 2007, Iriberri and Leroy, 2009, Zuniga and White, 2009). For this research, social media is defined as a techno-social system for participatory culture, having characteristics like openness, participation, conversation, connectedness, and community. This definition relies heavily on the ideas set forward by Fuchs (2013) and Mayfield (2008). Scholarly communication is defined as "the system through which research and other scholarly writings are created, evaluated for quality, disseminated to the scholarly community, and preserved for future use. The system includes both formal means of communication, such as publication in peer-reviewed journals, and informal channels, such as electronic listservs." (ACRL, 2016).

Research or scholarly communication is often depicted as a lifecycle documenting the steps involved in the creation, publication, dissemination, and discovery of a piece of scholarly research. Lugovic et al. (2015) provide an overview of theoretical models of scientific communication systems beginning with the UNISIST model the UN developed in the 1970s, via the lifecycle model of the scientific communication process by Björk (2005), up to more recent models that socio-technical or information system lens for scientific communication. They suggest a theoretical model distinguishing “primary and secondary experience of subjects and objects acting to produce and communicate scientific knowledge" (Lugovic et al., 2015). The academic research life cycle describes the cyclical research process, from idea to implementation to dissemination and back to the idea (Gessner et al., 2017). The academic research life cycle encompasses all activities of academic scholars, which of course include the research and publication activities usually associated with scholarly communication, but also includes, for example, pre-scholarly communication explorative activities, social networking, or teaching activities. In the next section, we elaborate on the use of social media throughout the research life cycle and for what purpose IS scholars could use social media.

2. SOCIAL MEDIA ACROSS THE RESEARCH LIFE CYCLE

The CIBER research group conducted a major international questionnaire survey that investigated the use of social media in the research workflow (CIBER, 2012). For their study, they surveyed more than 2000 researchers. They conclude that social media has an impact on all points of the research lifecycle, from identifying research opportunities to disseminating findings at the end. When asked about the use in research of eight categories of social media tools (social networking, blogging, microblogging, collaborative authoring, social tagging and bookmarking, scheduling and meeting tools, conferencing, or image or video sharing), a vast majority (63.4%) of researchers responded that it use tools in only one or two categories, and only a few researchers are using the full spectrum of social media tools (Nicholas and Rowlands, 2011). Collaborative authoring is by the most popular tool, followed by conferencing, and scheduling meetings, while social tagging and microblogging are the least popular. As main reasons for drivers of social media use in research were mentioned in this study: personal initiative, the technological developments and the need for speed, while the main perceived benefits of social media use in research are an international collaboration, faster dissemination and collaboration of people outside academia. Evidence supports the argument that an online social media presence may influence the researcher's citations (Terras, 2012).

Goodier and Czerniewicz (2013) have adapted the functional building blocks of social media by Kietzmann et al. (2011) to create a diagram to present goals for academics' online presence consisting of seven building blocks of the networked scholar. These building blocks are presence (extent to which you as the scholar are visible to others), sharing (extent to which you allow users to exchange your information), connections (the relevance and appeal of your work to others), identity (the extent to which others can identify you online as a scholar), conversations (extent to which others engage with you and vice versa), groups (the extent of your engagement with communities), and reputation (your online standing and the extent to which you influence others). Together they provide a useful overview of social media for research activities. Ortega (2015) observes disciplinary differences in users and use of social media platforms by scientists. Humanists and social scientists massively populate Academia.edu, while ResearchGate is more popular with natural sciences. These scientific, social networks intend to increase the flow of research information by offering new reputation metrics Rinaldi (2014) argues. These new metrics, part of the various alt-metrics, may be used by grant-awarding agencies or hiring committees. Shuai et al. (2012) observed a correlation between Twitter mentions of publications and increase of the preprints on Arxiv of those papers as well as an increase of early citations. This effect or impact may not be that evident for other social media platforms and activities that are related to alt-metrics (e.g. Facebook likes, blog posts, LinkedIn posts and so forth), cf. Thelwall et al. (2013). This paper avoids exaggeration of the potential of research communication but focuses on the benefit it may bring to the communication activities of scholars.

Kell and Czerniewicz (2017) argue that social media communication "offers new affordances for changing research communication practices". The model they present consists of four stages, starting with (1) conceptualisation, then (2) data collection and analysis, followed by (3) articulation of findings and finally (4) translation and engagement. Within each stage, the forms of scholarly communication may change due to social media communication. We suggest adopting a practical model while considering scholarly communication a subset of the academic research life cycle (Figure 1). For this, we adopt the research life cycle approach from Mollett et al. (2017) for its comparative advantages for understanding the role of social media in a research context. "The framework captures the complexity of science communication today and offers a new way to understand research's relevance to society", Mollett et al. (2017) argue. Their life cycle model, although similar but with fewer stages than the life cycle model used by Nicholas and Rowlands (2011), or less detailed than for example the scientific communication process model provided by Björk

(2005), is useful for its explanatory power. The research life cycle described by Mollett et al. (2017) builds on previous models and developments in communication and the research process (Weller, 2011, Kramer and Bosman, 2015), and consists of six 'phases' of the research: Inspiration, Collaboration, Primary Research, Dissemination, Engagement and Impact. The authors argue that research has always been a social process, but in the advent of digital technologies, academic researchers are collaborating more with each other and with a broader audience than ever before thereby exploring the use of social media.

Taking the six phases as described in the research life cycle model from Mollett et al. (2017) we can illustrate each phase with social media uses and the reason for those activities (Figure 1). This model states that after the Impact phase a new Inspiration phase starts, so a new cycle starts. We have to emphasise the non-linear and iterative nature of scholarly research (Cooper, 2018) which in practice means that not all stages of the life cycle have the same duration and often scholars go back and forth between those stages. Kramer and Bosman (2015) provide an up-to-date overview of tools used for scholarly communication categorised per phase of the academic research life cycle.

The first phase, called Inspiration initiates the research. Exploring ideas is the primary function in this phase. Social media provide a useful online communications channel for encountering new ideas and having a conversation with a global audience. After having established the research idea, in the second phase, the quest for Collaboration partners may be supported by for example social networks dedicated to researchers.

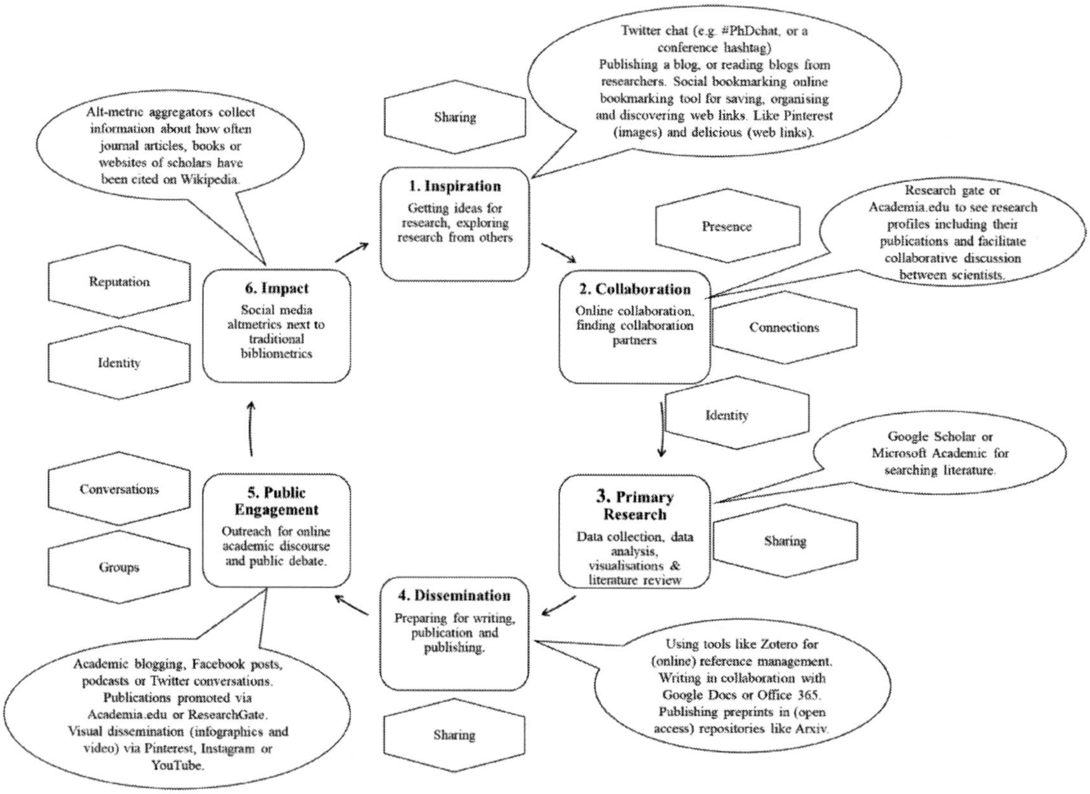

Figure 1. Amalgamation of the phases of the academic research life cycle adapted from Mollett et al. (2017) combined with the most prominent networked scholar building blocks per phase from Goodier and Czerniewicz (2013) depicted as hexagonal tiles, and examples of social media use illustrated by the oval callouts

During the third phase of the primary research activities, the use of online data analysis tools may facilitate collaboration with remote partners. In the fourth phase, writing and preparing for publication are supported with tools for reference management and collaborative writing. In the next phase of public engagement outreach with academic and non-academic audiences can be leveraged with blogs, social networks for researchers or conversations on microblogging platforms. Academic blogging is considered part of an elaborate online academic attention economy which is having a positive impact to readership Thomson and Mewburn (2013) argue. In the final phase of impact, tools for measuring social media altmetrics can provide information on impact and outreach. Although a formal definition for altmetrics (short for "alternative metrics") is not available various descriptions are available that elucidate the actual intent of this alternative to traditional bibliometrics. Where bibliometrics as a measure of scholarly output is statistically and mathematically derived from the number of publications, citations and amount of peer reviews (cf. Gingras (2016)), altmetrics are similarly derived from social media activities. Priem et al. (2015) define altmetrics as a diverse group of activities that reflect and transmit scholarly impact on social media which forms a composite trace of impact far richer than traditional bibliometrics. Priem et al. (2015) argue that these altmetrics reveal online scholarly activities and provide alternative or additional means of measuring scholarly impact. A comparison between traditional bibliometrics and altmetrics is illustrated by (Libguides, 2017). After going through all these phases, the academic life cycle starts again with phase 1 where new ideas lead to new research activities and so forth. "Social media affords opportunities for researchers to explore the research process in more social ways, which may in turn help to connect research with its core social remit and commitment", Mollett et al. (2017) argue. The IS researcher can add social media practices to the repertoire needed as a digital scholar. This cycle is complemented with the networked scholar building blocks as suggested by Goodier and Czerniewicz (2013), where the prominent building blocks are assigned to the relevant phase. These building blocks are presence (extent to which you as the scholar are visible to others), sharing (extent to which you allow users to exchange your information), connections (the relevance and appeal of your work to others), identity (the extent to which others can identify you online as a scholar), conversations (extent to which others engage with you and vice versa), groups (the extent of your engagement with communities), and reputation (your online standing and the extent to which you influence others) (Goodier and Czerniewicz, 2013).

As we have discussed the possibilities for scholarly activities and communication by using social media throughout the academic research life cycle, one cannot ignore some of the disadvantages of social media. Online harassment is occurring on the Internet and researchers are not exempt from that kind of harassment. As with private use of the Internet and social media, the professional academic use needs some precautions for protection against online harassment. Furthermore, other disadvantages to being considered are social media considered as time-consuming, distracting, or concerns of too much self-promotion by oneself or by others (Lupton, 2014), or a possible suppressing culture in the academic institution where university managers may try to dictate what is considered acceptable online communication, cf. Bothwell (2019). Supporting information on how to start and choose social media for scholarly online communication are provided by for example Goodier and Czerniewicz (2013), Bik and Goldstein (2013), and Rinaldi (2014).

3. CONCLUSION

This paper has contributed an original approach to the field of research communication by combining the research life cycle with insights of how social media can be applied throughout each phase of that lifecycle.

Furthermore, the need for research communication by IS scholars is addressed. We conclude that social media provide additional opportunities for the IS scholar in the academic research life cycle. Of course, there are not only opportunities. There are aspects of social media that need to be prepared for such as online harassment or fear for (online) reputation damage. Many are scholars are well aware of the intricacies of ICTs but being part of the audience and debate in public may be daunting. This paper provides a short overview of possibilities to situate social media in the academic research workflow activities. The paper wants to reflect on the potential of social media for research. Social media is a techno-social environment where the digital IS scholar is not a separate observer but acting participant of the ecosystem. We conclude with a question for future research. Are (next generation) IS researchers as digital scholars well prepared and equipped with the necessary skills to effectively make use of social media for research and scholarly communication in a dynamic society? The impact and (questioning of) value of scientific knowledge are causing public debates where scholars should be prepared for. These become evident in for example the issues arising around digital surveillance and privacy on social media, or the impact of machine learning algorithms and possible embedded bias on society which are of interest for IS researchers. The researcher's voice can then be (additionally) heard in the online public sphere accessible to a broader audience that the traditional publication channels for scientific output.

REFERENCES

ACRL. 2016. *Scholarly Communication Toolkit: Scholarly Communication Overview* [Online]. Association of College and Research Libraries, a division of the American Library Association. Available: https://acrl.libguides.com/scholcomm/toolkit/ [Accessed].

Bik, H. M. & Goldstein, M. C. 2013. An introduction to social media for scientists. *PLoS Biology,* 11, e1001535.

Björk, B. C. 2005. A lifecycle model of the scientific communication process. *Learned Publishing,* 18, 165-176.

Bothwell, E. 2019. *Call for sector guidelines on academic freedom on social media* [Online]. Imes Higher Education (THE). Available: https://www.timeshighereducation.com/news/call-sector-guidelines-academic-freedom-social-media [Accessed].

CIBER 2012. Social media and research workflow.: CIBER, University College London, Emerald Group Publishing Ltd.

Cooper, D., & Rieger, O. Y. 2018. Scholars ARE Collectors: A Proposal for Re-thinking Research Support.

Fuchs, C. 2013. *Social Media, A Critical Introduction*, SAGE Publications Ltd.

Gessner, G. C., Eldermire, E., Tang, N. & Tancheva, K. 2017. The Research Lifecycle and the Future of Research Libraries.

Gingras, Y. 2016. Bibliometrics and research evaluation: an overview. Cambridge MA: MIT Press.

Goodier, S. & Czerniewicz, L. 2013. Academics' online presence guidelines: A four step guide to taking control of your visibility. University of Cape Town, South Africa.

Iriberri, A. & Leroy, G. 2009. A life-cycle perspective on online community success. *ACM Computing Surveys,* 41, 1-29.

Kell, C. & Czerniewicz, L. 2017. Visibility of Scholarly Research and Changing Research Communication Practices: A Case Study from Namibia. *Research 2.0 and the Impact of Digital Technologies on Scholarly Inquiry.* IGI Global.

Kietzmann, J. H., Hermkens, K., McCarthy, I. P. & Silvestre, B. S. 2011. Social media? Get serious! Understanding the functional building blocks of social media. *Business Horizons,* 54, 241-251.

Kramer, B. & Bosman, J. 2015. 101 Innovations in Scholarly Communication - the Changing Research Workflow. Poster presented at Force 2015 https://www.force11.org/meetings/force2015.

Libguides. 2017. *Research Impact & Visibility: Traditional and altmetrics* [Online]. University Library Utrecht University. Available: http://libguides.library.uu.nl/researchimpact [Accessed].

Lugovic, S., Dunđer, I. & Horvat, M. 2015. The Secondary Experience of an Information System Enabling Scientific Communication.

Lupton, D. 2014. 'Feeling better connected': Academics' use of social media.

Mas-Bleda, A., Thelwall, M., Kousha, K. & Aguillo, I. F. 2014. Do highly cited researchers successfully use the social web? *Scientometrics,* 101, 337-356.

Mayfield, A. 2008. *What is Social Media?* [Online]. Available: http://www.icrossing.co.uk/fileadmin/uploads/eBooks/What_is_Social_Media_iCrossing_ebook.pdf [Accessed].

Mollett, A., Brumley, C., Gilson, C. & Williams, S. 2017. *Communicating Your Research with Social Media: A Practical Guide to Using Blogs, Podcasts, Data Visualisations and Video*, SAGE Publications.

Nicholas, D. & Rowlands, I. 2011. Social media use in the research workflow. *Information Services and Use,* 31, 61-83.

Ortega, J. L. 2015. Disciplinary differences in the use of academic social networking sites. *Online Information Review,* 39, 520-536.

Parameswaran, M. 2007. Social computing: an overview. *Communications of the Association for Information Systems,* 19, 762-780.

Priem, J., Taraborelli, D., Groth, P. & Neylon, C. 2015. *Altmetrics: a manifesto; 2010* [Online]. Available: http://altmetrics.org/manifesto/ [Accessed].

Rinaldi, A. 2014. *Spinning the web of open science*.

Shuai, X., Pepe, A. & Bollen, J. 2012. How the Scientific Community Reacts to Newly Submitted Preprints: Article Downloads, Twitter Mentions, and Citations. *PLOS ONE,* 7, e47523.

Terras, M. 2012. Is blogging and tweeting about research papers worth it? The Verdict. *Melissa Terras' blog*.

Thelwall, M., Haustein, S., Larivière, V. & Sugimoto, C. R. 2013. Do Altmetrics Work? Twitter and Ten Other Social Web Services. *PLOS ONE,* 8, e64841.

Thomson, P. & Mewburn, I. 2013. Why do academics blog? An analysis of audiences, purposes and challenges. *Studies in Higher Education,* 38, 1105-1119.

Weller, M. 2011. *The Digital Scholar: How Technology Is Transforming Scholarly Practice,* London, Bloomsbury Academic.Zuniga, L. & White, N. 2009. Module Web 2.0 and Social Media for Development. *Information Management Resource Kit (IMARK).* FAO.

A SYSTEMATIC REVIEW ON SMART CITY SERVICES AND IOT-BASED TECHNOLOGIES

Firat Bestepe and Sevgi Ozkan Yildirim
Middle East Technical University, Turkey

ABSTRACT

Due to the technological developments, Internet of things (IoT) has become a real phenomenon. Accordingly, many IoT-based smart concepts appeared in our daily lives such as smart home, smart healthcare and smart city. There are several factors accelerating or hindering the adoption of such new services and concepts. So, the acceptance of IoT-based smart services is critical and should be analyzed carefully. In this study, we aimed to prepare a proper starting point for future studies on end user acceptance of smart city services and IoT technologies by presenting a comprehensive systematic review of literature. We got 34 articles focusing on the adoption of IoT-based services with a model-based approach among initially resulted 237 papers. Our findings indicate that the adoption of smart services is getting more and more popular in recent years, especially in Asian countries. We also see that most reviewed studies prefer to develop integrated adoption models and deploy the factors of technology acceptance model (TAM). Additionally, our review results show that the researchers studying on this field generally use demographics in adoption models, mostly as control variables. This paper presents valuable findings lightening up the way of researchers who want to develop an adoption model for IoT-based smart services.

KEYWORDS

Internet of Things, Smart Services, User Acceptance, Adoption, Systematic Literature Review

1. INTRODUCTION

Cost-effective technologies, broad access to wireless networks and mobility are changing our lives rapidly. Almost all physical objects such as vehicles, home appliances, buildings, embedded with sensors, gain connectivity to collect and exchange data(C.L. Hsu & Lin 2018). Accordingly, smart healthcare, smart home and smart city concepts are emerged based on solutions with internet of things (IoT) technology. Due to IoT, it is expected to reach 24 billion devices connected by 2020(Gubbi et al. 2013). However, highly digitized structure based on large volumes of digital data due to many physical objects connected bring out many challenging issues such as security, privacy, interoperability, scalability, adaptability, standardization and so on(Atzori, Iera, & Morabito 2010). These open issues, which are the main barriers to extensive usage of IoT-based smart services, still wait feasible solutions. Besides, IoT based smart concepts cover some other disruptive technologies such as cloud computing and big data. Such a deep change potential of IoT and attached technologies on daily routines would also affect end users' intention to use smart services. So, acceptance of IoT-based services by end users become an issue to be evaluated by IT companies and city administration. The success of investments made to make the cities smarter and improve the quality of life depends on whether or not people adopt these smart services in their daily routines. There are many factors analyzed in the literature accelerating or hindering the adoption of such new technologies and concepts. However, the adoption of smart city services and IoT technologies were not reviewed systematically in the literature much in detail. In this study, we reviewed the academic literature systematically in order to prepare a proper starting point for future studies on end user acceptance of smart city services and IoT technologies. We also aim to fill the gap in information systems (IS) literature on IoT adoption. By this means, the researchers thinking to study adoption of IoT based smart solutions could get our study as a first step and see the potential research fields.

2. SEARCH METHODOLOGY

This literature review study was performed based on 3-stage Kitchenham methodology: planning, conducting and reporting(Kitchenham 2004). In the planning phase, we defined the research criteria and search databases. Then keyword searches were conducted in the specified databases. After the results were managed and assessed, we reported the findings in a systematic manner. The defined search keywords were as follows: ("Smart City" or "Internet of Things") and (Technology or Service) and (Acceptance or Adoption). In order to confine the search scope, only the journal papers written in English and published in between January 2008 – March 2018 in Web of Science, IEEE Xplore, ScienceDirect (Elsevier) and Emerald online libraries were covered. The articles in press, conference proceedings, textbooks, unpublished papers and academic thesis were excluded from the scope of this review. Initially, the search resulted 397 papers. After eliminating irrelevant and duplicated papers, the number of papers reduced to 237.

3. REVIEW STATISTICS

72 out of remaining 237 papers are about user acceptance of new technologies, mostly IoT based. 34 papers in this group have a model-based approach for adoption of IoT based technologies and smart services (smart healthcare, smart home/building and smart city). Among these 34 journal papers; 14 studies analyze the adoption of general IoT based services including wearable sensors, RFID (Radio Frequency Identification) sensors and so on. There are 7 papers for each, smart healthcare services and smart home (or building) applications, and they are analyzing adoption issue from end users' perspective. Only 6 out of 34 articles directly study the acceptance and adoption of smart city services with a model-based approach (Figure 1). As seen in Figure 2, the number of academic studies on adoption and acceptance of IoT based technologies and services have been increasing dramatically in last three years (note: just first quarter of 2018 is covered). This indicates that adoption of IoT based smart services is getting more popular rapidly. Especially in Asian countries, there are much more studies on user acceptance matters than other parts of the world (Figure 3).

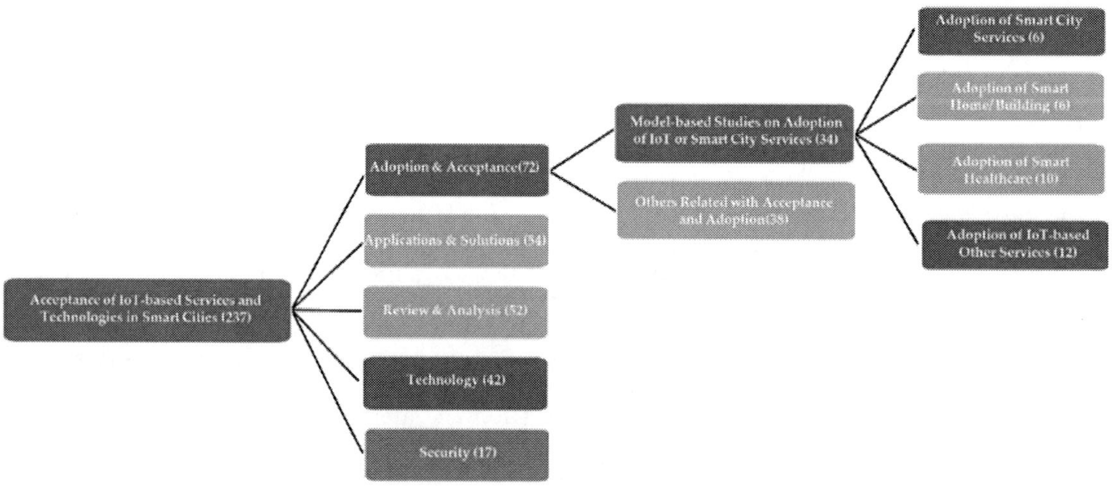

Figure 1. Classification of Reviewed Papers

When looking at the research methodologies, questionnaire is the most preferred survey method in model-based adoption studies (31 out of 34) to get the intentions of users or potential users. Just three of them have conducted expert interview or focus group technique while analyzing end user adoption issue. Most questionnaires (13) are solely online, however, 5 studies preferred to use both online and paper-based surveys. Totally, 58% of reviewed studies have employed online surveys. Just 16% of them (5 out of 34) have conducted fully paper-based surveys. In 8 studies, there isn't any specification about survey method. Average number of respondents in surveys is 373. The maximum and minimum number of sample size are 1091 and 76, respectively. There are several statistical techniques used in the reviewed papers such as

First-Generation Multiple Regression Analysis, Kruskal-Wallis H Test, Back Propagation Neural Network Analysis and etc. However, most of the researchers (74% - 23 out of 31 studies) have employed Structural Equation Modelling technique to test the hypothesis and validate the proposed models statistically. Smart PLS is the most preferred statistical tool (29% - 9 of the studies). Other popular tools are AMOS and LISREL. 11 studies (35%) do not say anything on statistical tool used.

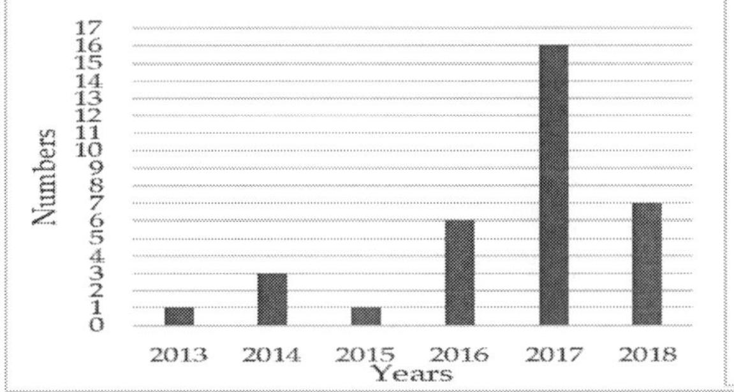

Figure 2. Distribution of Papers Over Years

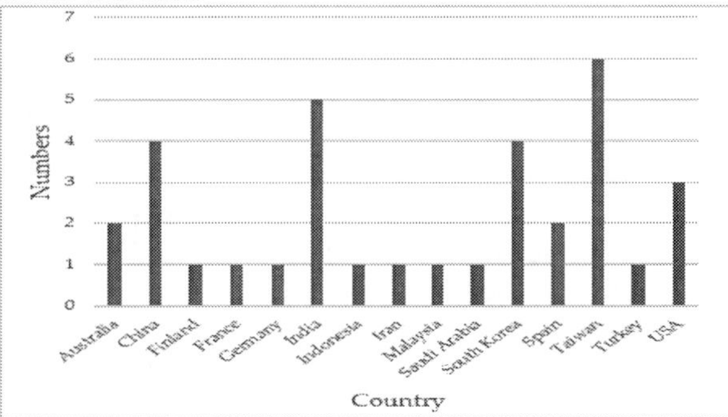

Figure 3. Distribution of Papers by Countries

4. REVIEW RESULTS

In 6 out of 34 articles, the researchers have studied the acceptance of smart city services such as smartcards, municipal Wi-Fi, mobile sensing and e-government applications from the citizens' perspective (Yeh 2017; Susanto, Diani, & Hafidz 2017; Leao & Izadpahani 2016; Sheshadri Chatterjee & Arpan Kumar Kar 2017; Gracia, Ariño, & Rueda 2015; Ylipulli et al. 2014). Smart home or smart building term implies a complete solution based on IoT to monitor, control and manage connected electronic or non-electronic devices used in a home. In this literature review, we get 6 papers studying the acceptance of smart home or smart building applications (Saeidi, Tajfar, & Vahdat 2017; Y. Kim, Park, & Choi 2017; E. Park et al. 2017; Dong et al. 2017; Bao et al. 2014; Srikanth Beldona, Zvi Schwartz, & Xian Zhang 2018). Reduced cost of technology and communication have triggered the digital revolution. Relatedly, by embedding IoT-based technologies into the healthcare systems and applications, smart healthcare phenomenon is emerged. During this literature review, we get 10 papers studying the adoption model of smart healthcare products (Marakhimov & Joo 2017; Papa et al. 2018; Martínez-Caro et al. 2018; D. Pal et al. 2018; Karahoca, Karahoca, & Aksöz 2017; Alaiad & Zhou 2017; Chong et al. 2015; S. Kim & Kim 2017; Liu, Chen, & Tzeng 2017; Canhoto & Arp 2017). Smart solutions implementing automated services under the concept of IoT could provide more efficient business processes and increased quality of life. So, IoT-based smart services and their adoption are critical matters for end user, so as for researchers. The results of our review have yielded 12 papers on end user acceptance of IoT-based services (Hsu & Lin 2018; Mital et al. 2017; Hsu & Lin 2016; Gao & Bai 2014; Tsai et al. 2017; Singh, Gaur, & Ramakrishnan 2017; Mani & Chouk 2017; Tu 2018; Yildirim & Ali-Eldin 2018; Shin 2017; Roy et al. 2018; Hsu & Yeh 2017). Our review has showed that many different adoption factors are deployed in user acceptance studies according to relevant core technology and preferred model. By comprehensive analysis of each factor deployed in each adoption model reviewed, we have defined adoption factors used in different models but having similar or same meaning. According to our findings, there are 50 different factors used in adoption models of IoT based smart services. The most preferred factors are perceived usefulness (PU) and perceived ease of use (PEOU) which were introduced by Davis (Davis 1989). This is not an unexpected finding because Davis's Technology Acceptance Model (TAM) has a broad usage area in the literature because of its simplicity and relevance for the technology acceptance. Social influence or subjective norm is another commonly used adoption factor which is strongly taken part in the literature with Theory of Reasoned Action (TRA) model (Fishbein & Ajzen 1975; Ajzen 1991). Interestingly, the privacy concern is the third most preferred factor. When considering the increased security threats and user awareness on privacy risks recently, this finding is quite reasonable. The other common factors are cost, attitude, trust, perceived behavioral control and perceived enjoyment. In most studies, researchers have evaluated the demographics of the respondents, as well (74.2%). In just 8 of 31 studies (25.8%), there is no statement about the demographics of the users. The most used ones are gender, age and education. Income and use experience are other commonly preferred demographic features surveyed.

5. CONCLUSION

The smart services based on interconnected devices such as wireless sensors, smart cards and mobile phones allow users to interact with smart environments connected to the internet (i.e. home, office, building, even city). Many daily life activities such as transportation, shopping, education, even healthcare services could become more efficient thanks to the smart services. However, the users should embed these smart services into their daily routines properly and effectively. Therefore, user acceptance of such services and technologies is very critical. For this reason, in this study, we have reviewed the literature on the adoption of IoT based smart services in between 2008 – 2018 (till the end of the first quarter) systematically. We have aimed to present the state of the art and trending research areas for the adoption of IoT based smart services.

The quantitative results of this review show that the number of academic studies on adoption and acceptance of IoT based technologies and services have been increasing dramatically especially in last three years and Asian countries are much more concerned about the technology adoption and user acceptance matters than other parts of the world. The literature on the adoption of smart city services looks a bit poorer than smart home and smart healthcare. However, all these smart concepts are mostly based on IoT technology. So, adoption studies on different smart concepts can easily feed each other. By examining the papers in detail, we have provided the most preferred adoption factors in IoT acceptance literature.

Our study is not a meta-analysis, so we have just reviewed the papers relevant to our search objective and analyzed acceptance factors and demographics used in adoption models. As a limitation, most reviewed studies are examining the intention to use rather than the actual use. In future studies, with the increased usage of IoT-based smart services, it should be useful or even necessary to analyze the actual use of such services. Also, longitudinal studies should be conducted rather than cross-sectional studies in order to understand continuous use of IoT-based smart services properly. Finally, because of our search criteria, we might have missed some valuable studies in the field, as well.

REFERENCES

Ajzen, I. (1991). The Theory of Planned Behavior. In *Organizational Behavior and Human Decision Processes*, 179–211.

Alaiad, A., & Zhou, L. (2017). Patients' Adoption of WSN-Based Smart Home Healthcare Systems: An Integrated Model of Facilitators and Barriers. *IEEE Transactions on Professional Communication* 60 (1): 4–23.

Atzori, L., Iera, A., & Morabito, G. (2010). The Internet of Things: A Survey. *Computer Networks* 54 (15): 2787–2805.

Beldona, S., Schwartz, Z., & Zhang, X. (2018). Evaluating Hotel Guest Technologies: Does Home Matter? *International Journal of Contemporary Hospitality Management*, March.

Bao, H., Chong, A.Y.L., Ooi, K.B., & Lin, B. (2014). Are Chinese Consumers Ready to Adopt Mobile Smart Home? An Empirical Analysis. *International Journal of Mobile Communications* 12 (5): 496–511.

Canhoto, A.I., & Arp, S. (2017). Exploring the Factors That Support Adoption and Sustained Use of Health and Fitness Wearables. *Journal of Marketing Management* 33 (1–2): 32–60.

Chatterjee, S. & Kar, A.K. (2017). Effects of Successful Adoption of IT Enabled Services in Proposed Smart Cities of India: from User Experience Perspective." *Journal of Science and Technology Policy Management*, December.

Chong, A.Y.L., Liu, M.J., Luo, J., & Keng-Boon, O. (2015). Predicting RFID Adoption in Healthcare Supply Chain from the Perspectives of Users. *International Journal of Production Economics* 159 (January): 66–75.

Davis, F.D. (1989). Perceived Usefulness, Perceived Ease of Use, and User Acceptance of Information Technology. *MIS Quarterly* 13 (3): 319–40.

Dong, X., Chang, Y., Wang, Y., & Yan, J. (2017). Understanding Usage of Internet of Things (IOT) Systems in China Cognitive Experience and Affect Experience as Moderator. *Information Technology & People* 30 (1): 117–38.

Fishbein, A. & Ajzen, I. (1975). *Belief, Attitude, Intention and Behavior: An Introduction to Theory and Research*. Vol. 27.

Gao, L. & Bai, X. (2014). Unified Perspective on the Factors Influencing Consumer Acceptance of Internet of Things Technology. *Asia Pacific Journal of Marketing and Logistics* 26 (2): 211–31.

Gracia, D.B., Ariño, L.V.C., & Rueda, A.P. (2015). Determinants of Multi-Service Smartcard Success for Smart Cities Development: A Study Based on Citizens' Privacy and Security Perceptions. *Government Information Quarterly* 32 (2): 154–63.

Gubbi, J., Buyya, R., Marusic, S., & Palaniswami, M. (2013). Internet of Things (IoT): A Vision, Architectural Elements, and Future Directions. *Future Generation Computer Systems* 29 (7): 1645–60.

Hsu, C.W., & Yeh, C.C. (2017). Understanding the Factors Affecting the Adoption of the Internet of Things. *Technology Analysis & Strategic Management* 29 (9): 1089–1102.

Hsu, C.L., & Lin, J.C.C. (2016). An Empirical Examination of Consumer Adoption of IoT Services: Network Externalities and Concern for Information Privacy Perspectives. *Computers in Human Behavior* 62 (September): 516–27.

Hsu, C.L., & Lin, J.C.C. (2018). Exploring Factors Affecting the Adoption of Internet of Things Services. *Journal of Computer Information Systems* 58 (1): 49–57.

Karahoca, A., Karahoca, D., & Merve Aksöz. (2017). Examining Intention to Adopt to Internet of Things in Healthcare Technology Products. *Kybernetes* 47 (4): 742–70.

Kim, S., & Kim, S. (2017). User Preference for an IoT Healthcare Application for Lifestyle Disease Management. *Telecommunications Policy*.

Kim, Y., Park, Y., & Choi, J. (2017). A Study on the Adoption of IoT Smart Home Service: Using Value-Based Adoption Model. *Total Quality Management & Business Excellence* 28 (9–10): 1149–65.

Kitchenham, B. (2004). *Procedures for Performing Systematic Reviews*. 33.

Leao, S., & Izadpahani, P. (2016). Factors Motivating Citizen Engagement in Mobile Sensing: Insights from a Survey of Non-Participants. *Journal of Urban Technology* 23 (4): 85–103.

Liu, Y., Chen, Y., & Tzeng, G.H. (2017). Identification of Key Factors in Consumers' Adoption Behavior of Intelligent Medical Terminals Based on a Hybrid Modified MADM Model for Product Improvement. *International Journal of Medical Informatics* 105 (September): 68–82.

Mani, Z. & Chouk, I. (2017). Drivers of Consumers' Resistance to Smart Products. *Journal of Marketing Management* 33 (1–2): 76–97.

Marakhimov, A. & Joo, J. (2017). Consumer Adaptation and Infusion of Wearable Devices for Healthcare. *Computer in Human Behavior* 76 (November): 135–48.

Martínez-Caro, E., Cegarra-Navarro, J.G., García-Pérez, A., & Fait, M. (2018). Healthcare Service Evolution towards the Internet of Things: An End-User Perspective. *Technological Forecasting and Social Change*.

Mital, M., Chang,V., Choudhary, P., Papa, A., & Pani, A.K. (2017). Adoption of Internet of Things in India: A Test of Competing Models Using a SEM Approach. *Technological Forecasting and Social Change*.

Pal, D., Funilkul, S., Charoenkitkarn, N., & Kanthamanon, P. (2018). Internet-of-Things and Smart Homes for Elderly Healthcare: An End User Perspective. *IEEE Access* 6: 10483–96.

Papa, A., Mital, M., Pisano, P., & Giudice, M.D. (2018). E-Health and Wellbeing Monitoring Using Smart Healthcare Devices: An Empirical Investigation." *Technological Forecasting and Social Change*.

Park, E., Cho, Y., Han, J., & Kwon, S. J. (2017). Comprehensive Approaches to User Acceptance of Internet of Things in a Smart Home Environment. *IEEE Internet of Things Journal* 4 (6): 2342–50.

Roy, S.K., Balaji, M.S., Quazi, A., & Quaddus, M. (2018). Predictors of Customer Acceptance of and Resistance to Smart Technologies in the Retail Sector. *Journal of Retailing and Consumer Services* 42 (May): 147–60.

Saeidi, M., Tajfar, A.H., and Vahdat, D. (2017). Assessing of the Effective Factors in the Acceptance of Internet of Things Technology in Smart Buildings *Journal of Fundamental and Applied Sciences* 9 (1, SI): 1102–16.

Shin, D.H. (2017). Conceptualizing and Measuring Quality of Experience of the Internet of Things: Exploring How Quality is Perceived by Users. *Information & Management* 54 (8): 998–1011.

Singh, G., Gaur, L., & Ramakrishnan, R. (2017). Internet of Things - Technology Adoption Model in India. *Pertanika Journal of Science and Technology* 25 (3): 835–46.

Susanto, T.D., Diani, M.M., & Hafidz, I. (2017). User Acceptance of E-Government Citizen Report System (a Case Study of City113 App). *Procedia Computer Science*, 124 (January): 560–68.

Tsai, Y.T., Wang, S.C., Yan, K.Q., & Chang, C.M. (2017). Precise Positioning of Marketing and Behavior Intentions of Location-Based Mobile Commerce in the Internet of Things. *Symmetry-Basel* 9 (8).

Tu, M. (2018). An Exploratory Study of Internet of Things (IoT) Adoption Intention in Logistics and Supply Chain Management: A Mixed Research Approach. *The International Journal of Logistics Management* 29 (1): 131–51.

Yeh, H. (2017). The Effects of Successful ICT-Based Smart City Services: From Citizens' Perspectives. *Government Information Quarterly* 34 (3): 556–65.

Yildirim, H. & Ali-Eldin, A.M.T. (2018). A Model for Predicting User Intention to Use Wearable IoT Devices at the Workplace. *Journal of King Saud University - Computer and Information Sciences*.

Ylipulli, J., Suopajarvi, T., Ojala, T., Kostakos, V., & Kukka, H. (2014). Municipal WiFi and Interactive Displays: Appropriation of New Technologies in Public Urban Spaces." *Technological Forecasting and Social Change* 89 (November): 145–60.

THE IMPACT OF SECURITY AND CUSTOMIZATION ON CONTINUANCE INTENTION OF M-BANKING

Mousa Albashrawi
King Fahd University of Petroleum and Minerals
Dhahran 31261, Saudi Arabia

ABSTRACT

User satisfaction is crucial to reinforce continued usage intention of m-banking. Since banking industry considers satisfaction and loyalty as bottom-line goals, antecedents of such consequence need to be investigated. Prior research has focused more on m-banking behavioral intention rather m-banking continuance intention nevertheless the latter shows more strategic and economic value. Secondly, the role of customization and security, though its importance, has been overlooked in m-banking research. Technology acceptance model (TAM) with extended expectation-confirmation model in IT (ECM-IT) are employed to evaluate the factors influencing satisfaction, which in turn influences continuance intention of m-banking. Structural equation modeling (SEM) will be used to analyze the data and test the developed hypotheses. This research in progress has potential contributions to both academia and industry.

KEYWORDS

Customization, Security, M-banking, Continued Usage Intention, TAM, and ECM-IT

1. INTRODUCTION

The rapid pace of advancements in the world of technologies has imposed many challenges on organizations, especially those in FinTech industry. M-banking, a FinTech tool, enables customers to conduct financial transactions in a faster and easier fashion. This tool is defined as the use of mobile device (e.g. Smartphones) to perform many functions on the go, such as making payment, transferring fund, checking balance, etc. M-banking derives its popularity from the easy access to bank's services at anytime and anywhere. This type of convenience has been considered a big factor in increasing the adoption rate of m-banking. However, m-banking comes with challenges that may burden banks and other financial institutions, for example, providing customized services, secure environment, higher promotion, etc.

M-banking adoption has been amply examined in IS research (Riquelme & Rios, 2010; Lin, 2011; Oliveira et al. 2014). A few other studies have been developed to explore continued IT usage intention such as Hong et al. (2006) who used technology acceptance model (TAM), expectation-confirmation model (ECM-IT) and extended ECM-IT to examine the continuance intention of mobile internet. Yuan et al. (2014) and Mohammadi (2015) used TAM also for examining m-banking continuance intention. However, prior research has not paid much attention to the impact of customization and security in m-banking although their importance has been emphasized in online environment (Devaraj et al., 2006) and in banking sector (Coelho & Henseler, 2012). This has motivated us to explore this area through our research question: How customization and security influence continuance intention of m-banking. We believe that TAM would be appropriate to be used in our study because previous research has indicated that TAM is a good fit to study continued usage intention of experienced IT users (Hong et al., 2006).

This study can contribute to theory and practice. First, extending TAM with overlooked but important factors in the context of m-banking is our main contribution that can enrich theoretical knowledge in m-banking research. Second, this research can reveal the role of customization and security in m-banking and hence enable banks to take advantage of the study's insights by implementing a proper action.

2. RELATED WORK

Many research studies have mainly focused on adoption and behavioral intention of m-banking, for example, Chung & Kwon (2009) used TAM with its two factors of perceived usefulness and perceived ease of use, and proposed that technical support positively moderates the relationship between TAM's two pillars and adopting m-banking. Riquelme & Rios (2010) also used TAM to explore m-banking adoption, but with gender as a moderating factor. Another study found that multidimensional trust and multi-faceted risk perceptions can influence behavioral intention to use m-banking (Luo et al., 2010). Lin (2011) studied how attitude and behavioral intention to use m-banking can be impacted by knowledge-based trust and innovation attributes. Recently, Oliveira et al. (2014) integrated three models; technology-task fit (TTF), unified theory of acceptance and use of technology (UTAUT), and initial trust model (ITM) to provide a holistic framework that determine m-banking adoption among Portuguese university students. Hanafizadeh et al. (2014) also used the student sample and expanded TAM with trust, credibility, and compatibility with life style to investigate their effects of on m-banking behavioral intention. As well, Pavithran et al. (2014) utilized TAM to examine m-banking adoption in the context of a developing country.

M-banking continuance intention has been underlined in IS literature to be more important than behavioral intention because it can provide a good indication to customer's loyalty (Hew et al., 2016). A few studies, though, have paid attention to continuance intention of m-banking; for instance, Zhou & Liu (2014) combined ECM-IT and flow theory to investigate continuance intention of m-banking users in China. Likewise, Yuan et al. (2014), Mohammadi (2015), Albashrawi & Motiwalla (2017) examined continuance intention of m-banking users in China, Iran, and USA, respectively through extending TAM with different factors such as risk, awareness, resistance, privacy, gender, subjective norms, and personal innovativeness. Despite its economical value, m-banking continuance intention has scant studies in IS literature and hence further research in this area is needed to increase the understanding and advance theoretical knowledge.

Security and customization are two embedded factors in most information systems and have been plentifully highlighted in prior research to understand satisfaction and continued usage intention of IT users (Coelho & Henseler, 2012; Guo et al., 2012; Ozer et al., 2013), but not explored yet in m-banking context especially as interaction effects. From an industry perspective, 70% of banks have shown their concerns regarding security as the biggest barrier to move forward with m-banking (Crowe et al., 2015). While customizing user experience with adding special tools in m-banking may increase satisfaction and generate more revenue (Townsend, 2014). Since academic research and industry reports have emphasized the importance role of security and customization, we integrate them to our theoretical model.

3. HYPOTHESES AND RESEARCH MODEL

TAM has two pillars; perceived usefulness in which described as an assessment of how IT can improve job performance and perceived ease of use in which described as an assessment of how IT can be effortless (Davis, 1989). Bhattacherjee (2001) determined that perceived usefulness has a positive influence on satisfaction. Likewise, Joo et al. (2011) concluded that both TAM pillars are significant predictors of satisfaction in online university environment. Accordingly, we hypothesize that:

H1: *Perceived ease of use is positively related to customer satisfaction of m-banking.*
H2: *Perceived usefulness is positively related to customer satisfaction of m-banking.*

Customization in m-banking describes the adjustments made to m-banking services based on customer needs and wants. Once m-banking provides customized services according to the users' preferences, the users may show a higher satisfaction towards it. Prior research showed a theoretical support of this relationship (Coelho & Henseler, 2012). In addition, Devaraj et al. (2006) found that when online store provides personalized and customized services, the customers tend to be satisfied. Besides IS literature, we think that once m-banking enables customization, the users may perceive the services to exhibit a higher level of friendly use and provides more productivity, which in turn leads to a higher level of satisfaction.

On the other hand, security describes to what extent m-banking users feel safe and not vulnerable to online attacks. Shen et al. (2010) emphasized that m-banking provides convenience as a main advantage, but is attached with security as a main disadvantage. Guo et al. (2012) suggested that a higher level of security can generate a higher customer satisfaction in online shopping environment. It can be argued that when security is reinforced in m-banking, its embedded services could be seen to be more usable and useful, leading to a higher level of satisfaction among the users. From a practical side, banks are most likely to be interested to understand the role of customization and security in having more satisfied users of m-banking. According to the above, customization and security as moderating variables are worthy to investigate and thus hypothesized below as:

H3: *The higher level of customization, the greater positive relationship between perceived ease of use and customer satisfaction of m-banking.*
H4: *The higher level of customization, the greater positive relationship between perceived usefulness and customer satisfaction of m-banking.*
H5: *The higher level of security, the greater positive relationship between perceived ease of use and customer satisfaction of m-banking.*
H6: *The higher level of security, the greater positive relationship between perceived usefulness and customer satisfaction of m-banking.*

Bailey & Pearson (1983) defined customer satisfaction as: "satisfaction in a given situation is the sum of one's feelings or attitudes toward a variety of factors affecting that situation". Bhattacherjee (2001) used ECM-IT model and proposed that continued IT usage intention is predicted by user satisfaction. In the same vein, Hong et al. (2006) extended ECM-IT and suggested that IT usage intention is determined by customer satisfaction. In essence, when a customer is satisfied with IT product or service, he/she will be more willing to continue using it. Since m-banking is no exception, the above can lead us to hypothesize that:

H7: *Customer satisfaction is positively related to continued usage intention of m-banking.*

As per the hypothesized relationships, a research model is developed from TAM and depicted in Figure 1. The model shows TAM's two pillars are independent variables; customization and security are moderating variables; customer satisfaction and continued m-banking usage intention are dependent variables.

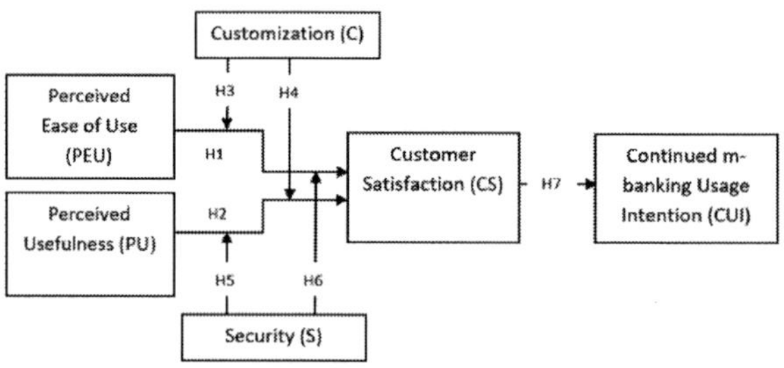

Figure 1. Research Model

4. RESEARCH METHOD

Our sample will be collected from a mid-sized US bank's customers who use m-banking. We will use SurveyMonkey to invite m-banking users to complete the questionnaire online. A 7-point, Likert-type scale is implemented to measure the survey items with a range of 1, "strongly disagree" to 7, "strongly agree". Structural equation modeling (SEM) will be employed to test the hypothesized relationships in the research model. We will control for other variables that could influence m-banking continuance intention, for example, age, gender, and education.

Study's constructs were adapted from literature in a similar area and modified to m-banking context as shown in Table 1 below. Perceived usefulness and perceived ease of use were adapted from Davis (1989). Customization was adapted from Suki (2011) and Coelho & Henseler (2012) whereas security was adapted from Shen et al. (2010). Customer satisfaction was adapted from Fornell et al. (1996) and Thong & Tam (2006). Continued m-banking usage intention was adapted from Hong et al. (2006).

Table 1. Constructs Operationalization

Construct	Item Code	Lead Questions
Perceived Usefulness	PU1	Q1. Overall, I find mobile banking to be useful.
	PU2	Q2. Using mobile banking enables me to process financial transactions quickly.
	PU3	Q3. Using mobile banking improves my performance in conducting financial transactions.
	PU4	Q4. Using mobile banking enhances my productivity with financial transactions.
Perceived Ease of Use	PEU1	Q5. Overall, I find mobile banking to be easy to use.
	PEU2	Q6. Mobile banking is easy for doing what I want to do.
	PEU3	Q7. My interactions with mobile banking are clear and understandable.
	PEU4	Q8. I find that mobile banking is flexible to interact with t is easy to become skillful at using mobile banking.
	PEU5	Q9. It is easy to become skillful at using mobile banking.
Security	S1	Q10. Overall, I find mobile banking to be secure.
	S2	Q11. I am suspicious of security techniques used in mobile banking.
	S3	Q12. I am concerned that other people may steal my account information when using mobile banking.
	S4	Q13. I am confident that mobile banking provides adequate security.
	S5	Q14. I think that there is a higher security risk associated with mobile banking compared to branch banking.
	S6	Q15. I think that there is a higher security risk associated with mobile banking compared to internet (online) banking.
	S7	Q16. I feel that mobile banking is a safe environment for conducting my financial transactions
	S8	Q17. I think that mobile banking will be more secure if it sends all transactions confirmations to my personal email.
Customization	C1	Q18. Overall, I find mobile banking is customized to my personal needs.
	C2	Q19. I feel that mobile banking offers me services that satisfy my specific needs.
	C3	Q20. I find that mobile banking provides me with services according to my preference.
	C4	Q21. Mobile banking with Enterprise Bank offers services that I could NOT find in other banks.
	C5	Q22. If I changed to another bank, I would NOT obtain services as customized as I have now.
Customer Satisfaction	CS1	Q23. Overall, I am satisfied with my mobile banking experience.
	CS2	Q24. Mobile banking experience meets my expectations.
Continued M-Banking Usage Intention	CUI1	Q25. I intend to continue using mobile banking services in the future.
	CUI2	Q26. I intend to increase my time spent using mobile banking in the future.
	CUI3	Q27. I intend to increase my use of various services provided by mobile banking in the future

5. CONCLUSION

This research in progress explores the interaction effect of customization and security on continuance intention of m-banking. It is important to divert the research focus from behavioral intention to continuance intention because the latter has been scarcely studied in m-banking. Secondly, m-banking continuance intention has a greater value to practice due to its direct impact on customer loyalty. However, this study is limited with the use of survey, which is a self-reported tool that may generate bias. Thus, future studies in m-banking should seek to employ a longitudinal design to better reflect causality among the relationships.

REFERENCES

Albashrawi, M. & Motiwalla L., 2017. Privacy and Personalization in Continued Usage Intention of Mobile Banking: An Integrative Perspective. *Information Systems Frontires*, pp. 1-13.

Bailey, J.E. & Pearson, S.W., 1983. Development of a Tool for Measuring and Analyzing Computer User Satisfaction. *Management Science*, Vol. 29, No. 5, pp. 530-545.

Bhattacherjee, A., 2001. Understanding Information Systems Continuance: An Expectation Confirmation Model. *MIS Quarterly*, Vol. 25, No. 3, pp. 351-370.

Chung, N. & Kwon, S.J., 2009. The Effects of Customers' Mobile Experience and Technical Support on the Intention to Use Mobile Banking. *Cyberpsychology & Behavior*, Vol. 12, No. 5, pp. 539-543.

Coelho, P.S. & Henseler, J., 2012. Creating Customer Loyalty through Service Customization. *European Journal of Marketing*, Vol. 46, No. 3/4, pp. 331-356.

Crowe, M., Tavilla, E. & McGuire, B., 2015. Mobile Banking and Mobile Payment Practices of US Financial Institutions: Results from 2014 Survey of FIs in Five Federal Reserve Districts, *Federal Reserve Boston*, pp. 1-66.

Davis, F.D., 1989. Perceived Usefulness, Perceived Ease of Use, and User Acceptance of Information Technology. *MIS Quarterly*, Vol. 13, No. 3, pp. 319-340.

Davis, F.D. et al, 1989. User Acceptance of Computer Technology: A Comparison of Two Theoretical Models. *Management Science*, Vol. 35, No. 8, pp. 982-1003.

Devaraj, S. et al, 2006. Examination of Online Channel Preference: Using the Structure-Conduct-Outcome Framework. *Decision Support Systems*, Vol. 42, No. 2, pp. 1089-1103.

Fornell, C. et al, 1996. The American Customer Satisfaction Index: Nature, Purpose, and Findings. *Journal of Marketing*, Vol. 60, pp.7-18.

Guo, X. et al, 2012. Evaluating Factors Influencing Consumer Satisfaction towards Online Shopping in China. *Asian Social Science*, Vol. 8, No. 13, pp. 40-50.

Hanafizadeh, P. et al, 2014. Mobile-Banking Adoption by Iranian Bank Clients. *Telematics and Informatics,* Vol. 31, No. 1, pp. 62-78.

Hew, J.J., et al, 2016. Mobile Social Commerce: The Booster for Brand Loyalty?. *Computers in Human Behavior*, Vol. 59, pp 142-154.

Hong, S.-J. et al, 2006. Understanding Continued Information Technology Usage Behavior: A Comparison of Three Models in the Context of Mobile Internet. *Decision Support Systems*, Vol. 42, pp. 1819-1834.

Joo, Y.J. et al, 2011. Online University Students' Satisfaction and Persistence: Examining Perceived Level of Presence, Usefulness and Ease of Use as Predictors in a Structural Model. *Computers & Education*, Vol. 57, No. 2, pp. 1654-1664.

Lin, H.F., 2011. An Empirical Investigation of Mobile Banking Adoption: The Effect of Innovation Attributes and Knowledge-Based Trust. *International Journal of Information Management*, Vol. 31, pp. 252-260.

Luo, X., et al, 2010. Examining Multi-Dimensional Trust and Multi-Faceted Risk in Initial Acceptance of Emerging Technologies: An Empirical Study of Mobile Banking Services. *Decision Support Systems*, Vol. 49, pp. 222-234.

Mohammadi, H., 2015. A Study of Mobile Banking Loyalty in Iran. *Computers in Human Behavior*, Vol. 44, pp. 4435-47.

Oliveira, T. et al, 2014. Extending the Understanding of Mobile Banking Adoption: When UTAUT meets TTF and ITM. *International Journal of Information Management,* Vol. 34, No. 5, pp. 689-703

Ozer, A., et al, 2013. The Effect of Mobile Service Quality Dimensions on Customer Satisfaction. *Procedia-Social and Behavioral Sciences*, Vol. 99, pp. 428-438.

Pavithran, R., et al. 2014. An Empirical Investigation of Mobile Banking Adoption in Developing Countries. *International Journal of Enterprise Information Systems*, Vol. 10, No. 1, pp. 76-93.

Riquelme, H.E. & Rios, R.E., 2010. The Moderating Effect of Gender in the Adoption of Mobile Banking. *International Journal of Bank Marketing*, Vol. 28, pp. 328-341.

Shen, Y.C., et al, 2010. A Benefit–Cost Perspective of the Consumer Adoption of the Mobile Banking System. *Behaviour & Information Technology*, Vol. 29, No. 5, pp. 497-511.

Suki, N.M., 2011. A Structural Model of Customer Satisfaction and Trust in Vendors Involved in Mobile Commerce. *Int. Journal of Business Science and Applied Management*, Vol. 6, No. 2, pp. 17-30.

Townsend, Z., 2014. Era of Mass Customization in Banking. *Bank Innovation*, retrieved from: https://bankinnovation.net/2014/04/era-of-mass-customization-in-banking/

Yuan, S., et al, 2014. An Investigation of Users' Continuance Intention towards Mobile Banking in China. *Information Development*, Vol. 32, No. 1, pp. 20–34.

Zhou, T. & Liu, Y., 2014. Examining Continuance Usage of Mobile Banking from the Perspectives of ECT and Flow. *International Journal of Services Technology and Management*, Vol.20, No. 4-6, pp. 199-214.

INNOVATION AND KNOWLEDGE MANAGEMENT IN PRECISION FARMING

Natalia Bakhtadze[1], Evgeny Maximov[1], Danila Donchan[1], Lamara Kozlovskaya[2] and Natalia Maximova[1]

[1]*V.A.Trapeznikov Institute of Control Science, 65, Profsoyuznaya street, Moscow, Russia*

[2]*Russian Timiryazev State Agrarian University, Russia*

ABSTRACT

This paper is devoted to the development of information systems for precision farming, which make it possible to use fertilizer and fuel more efficiently on the basis of information technologies and intelligent predictive models, which reduces the cost of production and increases the efficiency of agricultural production. In addition, a long-term agronomic and ecological effect can be achieved due to more careful tillage and reduced use of nitrogen fertilizers.

Description of the creating a knowledge base and models of grain yield depending on the mode of mineral fertilizer application based on intelligent associative search algorithms describes.

KEYWORDS

Precision Farming, Soft Sensors, Predictive Models, Knowledge Management

1. INTRODUCTION

Currently, in different countries, integrated systems for the differential application of nitrogen fertilizers are used quite widely (Jordan et al., 2004; Aubert et al., 2012) . However, these systems are costly and provide no means all the possible information about the dynamics of the properties of the field pieces, affecting the growth of productivity and determining the application rate. No less costly and time consuming is an approach based on extracting data from multiple sensors, with subsequent processing using specialized software (Ehlert et al., 2009).

Recently, new information technologies and intellectual methods of analysis have become more and more popular (Pavon-Pulido et al., 2017; Biomax, 2018; IBM, 2018). An alternative could be the development of information systems and so-called *soft sensors* - virtual analyzer to build a predictive model of indicators for the fields of land, based on the intelligent analysis of already available measurement of current and historical data and knowledge base Bakhtadze et al., 2007, 2012, 2015).

Knowledge refers to the laws that are extracted from data analysis, refined as information accumulates. On the basis of predictive models, not a specific control algorithm should be implemented, but a certain strategy, within which not only parameters can change, but also the structure of the system. This approach is significantly less costly and technologically efficient. To build the model, a temporary database of archival and current technological information is formed. After determining the forecast for the output based on the current state of the object, this virtual base is destroyed without memorization. The algorithm does not adjust the approximating model of the real process — it builds a new model for each point in time, and the parameter estimates at any time point are the best in terms of the minimum of the root-mean-square error.

The associative search algorithm is a procedure based on data mining, in particular, clustering methods are used. On the basis of these methods, a set of inputs (in the general case, multidimensional) close to the current input vector in the sense of a certain criterion is selected from the data archive at the time studied. The criterion is called the associative pulse and can be both a functional and a logical or fuzzy function. Further, on the basis of the classical (non-recurrent) least squares method (OLS), the output value is determined at the next time point. Under the assumption that input actions satisfy Gaussian-Markov conditions, the estimates obtained by the least squares method are consistent, unbiased statistically effective.

The advantage of this approach is that it allows you to build locally linear models for objects characterized by the most different types of non-linearities. The construction of virtual predictive models by the method of associative search is an automated procedure for generating a control action based on the image of the situation being analyzed. The algorithms have demonstrated highly accurate results for non-linear non-stationary objects in industry and energy. The use of such algorithms in Agromanagement systems allow to synthesize the effective management solutions in precise (coordinate) farming systems.

Thus, the article presents methods for creating high-performance innovative systems for supporting the management of differential fertilizer application based on data mining. The proposed methods have no analogues in the world scientific literature, and, at the same time, are due to practical significance.

2. CREATING A KNOWLEDGE BASE, AND MODEL BUILDING

The yield forecast, for example, of wheat for a specific field is based on the analysis of the dynamics of several indicators. We analyzed both natural factors and indicators defined farming mode.

The following factors were selected for the study and construction of the forecast model:

• Soil-climatic zone.

• Climate characteristic for the last 10 years: monthly precipitation, average daily air temperature monthly.

it is planned to take into account: the moisture reserve in the soil layer is up to 1 m at the critical phases of grain development: sowing – seedlings, tillering-booting, earing – pouring

• Field history for the last 7-10 years:

• Preceding and currently cultivated crops

• Crop yield (it is planned to take into account also the quality of grain)

• Amount (doses) of the applied mineral fertilizers for the previous crop and for the cultivated crop, including the frequency and doses of nitrogen fertilizers.

It is also planned to take into account in the model for further research:

• Soil characteristic of the field, including: soil difference, humus content, texture, and pH acidity (for sod-podzolic and gray forest soils),

• The field relief, including the steepness of the slopes, the exposure of the slopes, the closure of the relief elements,

• Provision of soil with nutrients: phosphorus, potassium (in the arable layer) - once every 5 years or after harvesting the previous culture and nitrogen - every spring, before applying nitrogen fertilizers at the beginning of the growing season in the upper soil layer (up to 60 cm).

Figure 1 presents the database structure. The experimental database contains information from 30 agricultural enterprises.

Further the Base of inductive knowledge was developed. Under the knowledge in the system refers to patterns that are identified on the basis of data analysis of the real functioning of the object, the model of which is built. Patterns can be formalized by a set of "inputs" and corresponding to these sets of "outputs" of the model.

Further, using the statistical analysis, and application of the associative search algorithms, the analysis was made on the influence of various factors yields of main crops. The main purpose of the analysis was to assess whether the impact of the mode of application of mineral fertilizers on crop yields.

To provide the analysis process with the necessary data from the knowledge base, a software module was developed that samples data using SQL queries and then performs the necessary software processing so that the data can be correctly processed by associative search algorithms.

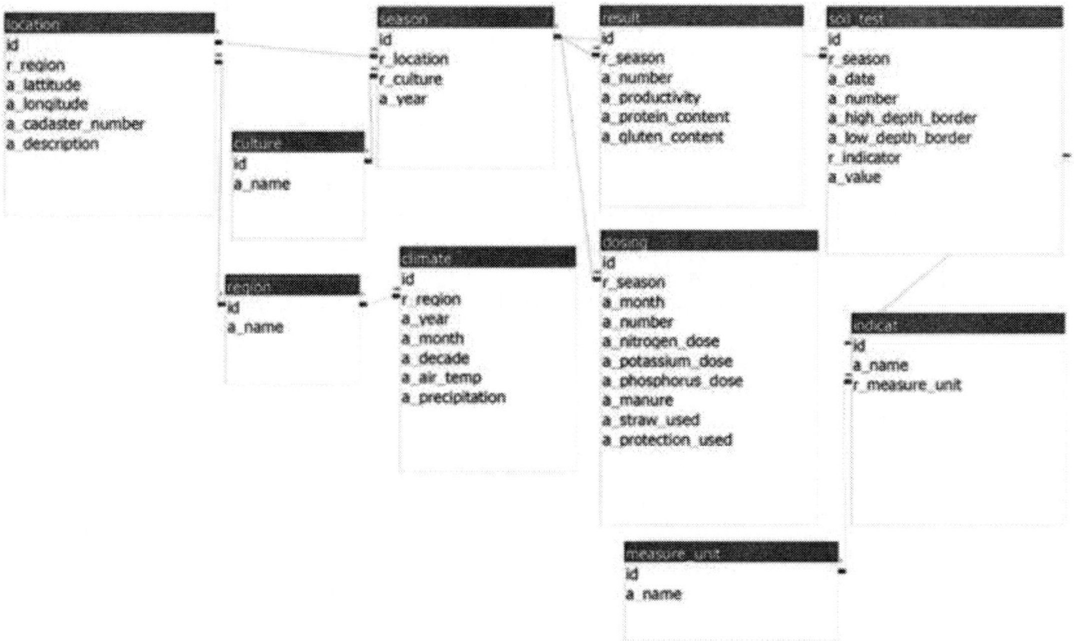

Figure 1. Database Structure

3. ASSOCIATIVE SEARCH TECHNIQUE

Algorithms based on knowledge revealed from process history (inductive knowledge, persistently enriched) implement an intelligent approach to constructing identification models. The intelligence is applying knowledge (*Knowledge Based*) revealed from historical data on the basis of their analysis (*Data Mining*).

The process of knowledge processing in the intelligent system is reduced to recovering (associative search of) *knowledge* over its fragment. Meanwhile, the *knowledge* may be interpreted as associative connections between *images*. As an image, we will use "sets of indicators", that is components of input vectors, input variables.

The criterion of closeness between images may be formulated in very different manners. In the most general case, it may be a logic function, the predicate. In a particular case, when sets of indicators are vectors in n-dimensional space, the criterion of closeness may be a distance in this space.

The associative search process may be implemented either as a process of recovering the image over partially given indicators (or recovering a knowledge fragment under the conditions of incomplete information; as a rule, just this process is simulated in different models of the associative memory), or as a process of searching another images that are associatively connected with the given one, respecting to other time instants.

In (Bakhtadze et al., 2007) an approach to form the support of decision making on the control is proposed, based on dynamic modeling the associative search procedure. Results of adoption of the associative search algorithms developed by the authors for industrial processes of the chemical and petroleum manufacturing, processes of control in intelligent power networks (smart grids), trading processes, transport logistic processes.

The method of the *associative search* consists in constructing *virtual* predicting models. The method assumes constructing predicting model of a dynamic plant, being new under each t, by use of a set of history data ("associations") formed at the stage of learning and adaptively corrected in accordance to certain criteria, rather than approximating real process in the time. Within the present context, linear dynamic model is of the form:

$$y_N = \sum_{i=1}^{m} a_i y_{N-i} + \sum_{j=1}^{r_s} \sum_{s=1}^{S} b_{j,s} x_{N-j,s}, \qquad \forall j = \overline{1,N}, \tag{1}$$

where: y_N is the prediction of the plant output at the time instant N, x_N is the vector of input actions, m is the memory depth in the output, r_s is the memory depth in the input, S is the dimension of the input vectors, a_i and $b_{j,s}$ are the tuned coefficient, meanwhile $x_{N-j,s}$ are selected disregarding the order of the chronological decreasing, have been referred as the *associative pulse.*

Let us note that this model is not classical regression one: there are selected certain inputs in accordance to a certain criterion, rather than all chronological "tail". The algorithm of deriving the virtual model consists in constructing at each time instant an approximating hypersurface of the space of input vectors and single-dimensional outputs. To construct a virtual model, corresponding to a certain time instant, from the archive, there are selected input vectors being in a certain sense close to the current input vector. An example of selecting the vectors is described below. The dimension of this hyper-surface is selected heuristically. Again, by use of classical (non-recursive) least squares (LS) method there is determined the output value (modeled signal) in the next time instant. Meanwhile, each point of the global non-linear surface of the regression is formed in the result of using linear "'local" models, in each new time instant.

Unlikely to classical regression models, for each fixed time instant from the process history, there are selected input vectors being close to the current input vector in the sense of a certain criterion (rather than the chronological sequence as it is done in regression models). Thus, in equation (1) r_s is the number of vectors from the archive (from the time instant 1 to the time instant N), selected in accordance to the associative search criterion. At each time segment $[N-1, N]$ there is selected a certain set of r_s vectors, $1 \le r_s \le N$. The criterion of selecting the input vectors from the archive to derive the virtual model in the given time instant over the current plant state may be as follows.

Let us introduce as a distance (a norm in $\Re^S$) between points of the S-dimensional space of inputs the value:

$$d_{N,N-j} = \sum_{s=1}^{S} \left| x_{N,s} - x_{N-j,s} \right|, \forall j = \overline{1,N}, \tag{2}$$

where $x_{N,s}$ are components of the input vector at the current time instant N. By virtue of a property of the norm («the triangle inequality», we have:

$$d_{N,N-j} \le \sum_{s=1}^{S} \left| x_{N,s} \right| + \sum_{s=1}^{S} \left| x_{N-j,s} \right|, \qquad \forall j = \overline{1,N}, \tag{3}$$

To derive an approximating hypersurface for the vector x_N let us select from the archive of the input data such vectors x_{N-j}, $j = \overline{1,N}$ that for a set D_N the condition will hold:

$$d_{N,N-j} \le d_N + \textstyle\sum_{s=1}^{S} \left| x_{N-j,s} \right| \le D_N, \ \forall j = \overline{1,N}, \text{ where } \ \textstyle\sum_{s=1}^{S} \left| x_{N,s} \right| = d_N. \tag{4}$$

where D_N may be selected, for instance, from the condition:

$$D_N \ge 2 d_N^{max} = 2 \max_j \sum_{s=1}^{S} \left| x_{N-j,s} \right|. \tag{5}$$

Under the assumptions that the input actions meet the Gauss-Markov conditions, the estimates obtained via the LS method are unbiased and statistically effective.

4. CASE STUDIES

The yield of calculated by the model was compared with the real yield for different regions of the Russian Federation.

Model. Experimental fields of the Nizhny Novgorod Research Institute of Agriculture from 2008 to 2016.

When building this model, data were used not only from the Nizhny Novgorod Research Institute of Agriculture, but also from other regions of the middle zone with similar climatic conditions. The following influencing factors were identified: temperature in April – August; precipitation in April; precipitation in August

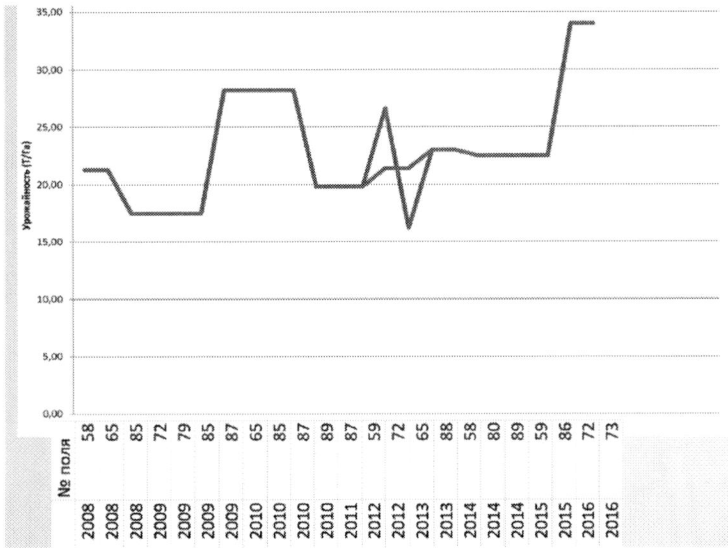

Figure 2. Dynamics of wheat yield – and forecast – using the associative search method in the fields of Nizhny Novgorod Research Institute of Agriculture (Russian Federation)

The accuracy of the model was high. KMK (coefficient of multiple correlation) by the model is 0.95.

5. PERSPECTIVE RESEARCH

Along with the yield forecast, some agrochemical indicators could be useful. For fields with similar characteristics (soil type, water-holding properties) from regions with a similar climate, it is possible to predict the concentration of certain chemical elements and compounds in the soil after applying fertilizers.

The input parameters of the forecast model will be statistical data of previous periods, as well as climatic indicators, under the influence of which chemical processes take place in the soil, contributing to (or hindering) the absorption of fertilizers by plants. In addition to mineral fertilizers, other chemicals also get into the soil - means of protection against pests, etc. They may contain compounds that can affect the values of agrochemical parameters. This factor will also be taken into account in the model. For the cultivation of various crops by agricultural enterprises, technological maps are formed in which, taking into account the climatic zone, the recommended scenarios of the work of agricultural producers are given, which make it possible to achieve a given yield.

For the best assimilation of minerals contained in the soil, different cultures need to moisture and temperature of the air were in certain ranges, beyond which the metabolism slows down. If we trace the dependence of the dynamics of the amount of various trace elements in the soil on the amount of precipitation and temperature (i.e., determine the rate at which plants absorb minerals found in the soil or coming in with fertilizers for different values of climatic indicators), we can determine the required amount of fertilizers applied depending on the region's climate (it may be necessary to apply less fertilizer, because the climate does not allow the plants to assimilate all the mineral substances introduced, or on the contrary, plants may need additional feeding during the season). The input parameters of the model will be air temperature and rainfall, and output - agrochemical indicators, which can be used to determine in dynamics the extent to which plants absorb minerals from the soil. Similarly, you can choose the recommended type and number of means of protection, taking into account the indicators of crop rotation, climate, soil characteristics, desired yield. As a result, in essence, technological maps will be developed that more accurately take into account the specifics of a particular field. To determine the need for additional irrigation and its volumes, data on the content of productive moisture in the soil are needed. Based on the dependence of indicators of soil moisture on precipitation, you can make a forecast that allows you to calculate the time and amount of artificial irrigation required. Fields are sampled by culture (possibly also by variety and reproduction), taking into account water permeability and moisture capacity. Then the input parameter will be the amount of precipitation, the output - the content of productive moisture in the soil.

6. CONCLUSIONS

The article presents the results on the development of field plots models and methods to support the management of differential fertilization.

The knowledge-based identification and simulation algorithms developed in the framework of this work have demonstrated highly accurate results. The use of such algorithms in Agromanagement systems allow to synthesize the effective management solutions in precise (coordinate) farming systems.

REFERENCES

Aubert B. A, A. Schroeder, J. Grimaudo, 2012. IT as enabler of sustainable farming: An empirical analysis of farmers' adoption decision of precision agriculture technology. *Decision Support Systems*, v.54, p.510–520

Bakhtadze, N. and Sakrutina, E., 2015. The Intelligent Identification Technique with Associative Search. *International Journal of Mathematical Models and Methods in Applied Sciences* 9, pp. 418-431.

Bakhtadze, N., Kulba, V., Lototsky, V. and Maximov, E. Identification-based approach to soft sensors design. *Proceedings of IFAC Workshop of Intelligent Manufacturing Systems*. Alicante, Spain (2007), pp. 86-92.

Bakhtadze, N., Lototsky, V., Vlasov, S., and Sakrutina, E., 2012. Associative Search and Wavelet Analysis Techniques in System Identification. *IFAC Proceedings*, Volumes 45(16), pp. 1227-1232.

Biomax. Agriculture IoT System, 2018. Available online: http://www.biomax.com.tw/en/product/ Agriculture-IoT-System/agriculture_iot_system.html (accessed on 16 April 2018).

Ehlert D., Adamek R., Horn H.J. Vehicle based laser range finding in crops. Sensors, 2009, pp. 3679–3694. doi: 10.3390/s90503679. [PMC free article] [PubMed] [CrossRef].

IBM. IBM Research Precision Agriculture. 2018. Available online: https://www.ibm.com/us-en/ marketplace/agri-resrch-innov (accessed on 16 April 2018).

Jordan C., Shi Z, Bailey J.S., Higgiris A., 2004. Sampling strategies for mapping 'within-field' variability in the dry matter yield and mineral nutrient status of forage grass crops in cool temperature climates. *Precision Agriculture* 4, pp. 69-86.

Pavon-Pulido N., Lopez-Riquelme J.A., Torres R., Morais R., Pastor J.A., 2017. New trends in precision agriculture: A novel cloud-based system for enabling data storage and agricultural task planning and automation. Precis. Agric. 18, pp.1038–1068. doi: 10.1007/s11119-017-9532-7. [CrossRef].

THE INFLUENCE OF BLOGGERS ON CONSUMER PURCHASE

Zehra Serman and Julian Sims
Birkbeck, University of London
Malet Street, London WC1E 7HX, UK

ABSTRACT

This paper evaluates the impact of online blogging on buying intentions of customers. It begins by offering an overview of digital marketing. Next, it analyses the process of e-commerce and its relevance to modern business. Then there is an overview of digital marketing and the manner in which it has affected contemporary business. The paper then offers an insight into the construct of online blogging and how it is used by contemporary organizations. The paper also examines the manner in which blogs are being used for search engine optimization and content marketing to influence the buying behavior of consumers. Finally, the paper concludes by identifying a literature gap and the need to conduct further research work in this area.

KEYWORDS

Online Blogging, Customer Buying Behavior, SEO Optimization, Content Marketing, Marketing

1. INTRODUCTION

Business has undergone substantial change brought about by innovative technologies and globalization (Kannan 2017). The process of globalization can be seen as the single most important factor to change the nature of business (Urban, Gosline and Lee 2017). Contemporary businesses are increasingly engaging in internationalization and globalization. This has enhanced business competition by increasing the number of choices available to consumers (Kingsnorth 2016) and businesses are increasingly attempting to mitigate competition (Baltes,2015). Business prospects depend on the kind of strategies organizations deploy (Ho et al. 2015). Digital marketing strategies have a prominent role and firms are increasingly using digital marketing (Patrutiu-Baltes 2016).

This paper evaluates blogging as a form of digital marketing and the manner in which blogs influence consumer behavior. It highlights how blogging is used as a form of digital marketing. The paper suggests that effective use of blogging can aid promotion of products or services, contributing to firm success.

2. MARKETING AND ITS IMPORTANCE

The processes of marketing and promotion determine firm success or failure (Hsiao, Chang and Tang 2016). Firms deploy different kinds of marketing and promotional strategies to cascade the right kind of information to consumers. This act of offering relevant information to consumers is important: if consumers do not have appropriate information regarding products or services they are less likely to choose them (Ukpabi and Karjaluoto 2017). Consumers count on reliable and reputable sources while making purchase decision. Alsaleh (2017) finds that reputable bloggers with good social relations can establish a positive reputation that impacts consumer purchasing attitudes.

Blogs and social media tools positively affect consumers' purchase intentions. They help marketers to engage with customers and build strong customer relationships (Alsaleh 2017). In the past, firms used newspapers, radio and other means (Cheung, Xiao and Liu 2014), but these days many firms use digital marketing (Stephen 2016). This creates new opportunities, reducing costs and recent research suggests digital marketing leads to greater chances of success than traditional marketing (Lim, Cheah and Wong 2017).

3. E-COMMERCE AND ONLINE SHOPPING

E-commerce creates more choice for customers (Schafer 2001). Having more choice increases the amount of information that customers need before they make purchase decisions. One way to overcome information overload is recommendations which provide: personalized product information; summarized community opinion; community critiques of products. Recommendations give customized personal experience (Schafer 2001). Reviews by existing customers, and the brand image of organizations and their products or services, plays a pivotal role in determining consumer buying decisions (Zhou et al. 2017).

4. DIGITAL MARKETING

The use of social media, Internet and other digital tools for marketing and promotion is cost effective compared to traditional forms of marketing and promotion (Cano, Doyle and Zhang 2018). Uzunoglu (2014) defines bloggers as “digital influencers” that have an impact on members of particular communities gathered around similar interests. Many studies find that face to face communication is not the only determinant of personal interaction: bloggers are also online opinion leaders (Uzunoglu 2014). Uzunoglu applies the two-step flow theory (Katz & Lazarsfeld 2017) which suggests opinion leaders act as intermediaries in the web of social attraction: opinion leaders interpret the data they receive than pass it to others. This flow of information increases the influence among customers compared to mass media (Weimann 1994). Consequently, firms increasingly resort to digital marketing to enhance brand and online image, which in turn is directly related to the sale of products and services (Laroche et al. 2012).

5. BLOGGING

Blogging can be defined as the process by which individuals express their opinion over online media (Cheng and Fang 2015). Alsaleh (2017) defines blogs as writer’s comments, brief texts, images and links structured in sequential order. Singer (2019) claims that approximately 900,000 articles are posted by bloggers every day. Twitter, Instagram and Facebook are examples of micro-blogging tools (Alsaleh 2017). Micro blogging increased by up to 62% between 2009 and 2011 (Alsaleh, 2017). Customer experience affects purchasing intentions due to information accountability, and information accountability plays a vital role in enhancing consumer experiences: hence strengthening purchase intentions (Hsu Tsou, 2011).

Micro-blogs offer an overview of the reasons why consumers should choose products or services, and the key benefits they are likely to receive. Professional blogs also offer detailed information regarding products or services that firms will be launching in the future (Hwang and Jeong 2016). E-Commerce is expected to flourish in the future with the help of blogging and online reviews (Barrett, Oborn and Orlikowski 2016) and cross blog reviews by product experts of famous brands is another emerging marketing tool (Barret 2016).

6. BLOGGING, SEO OPTIMIZATION, CONTENT MARKETING

Content marketing is an important digital marketing strategy (Urban, Gosline and Lee 2017). There are two kinds of content marketing blogs: sponsored blogs and unsponsored blogs (Hsiao, Chang and Tang 2016). Firms publish sponsored blogs to promote their goods or services (Ukpabi and Karjaluoto 2017), enumerating the positive aspects. They help in the SEO optimization (Ho et al. 2015): the more positive reviews a firm has the better will be its online presence or brand image.

Bloggers of unsponsored blogs are not paid for the blog they write. They offer an unbiased or unprejudiced viewpoint (Liljander, Gummerus and Söderlund 2015). However, they also indirectly help in the process of content marketing (Hernández-Méndez, Muñoz-Leiva and Sánchez-Fernández 2015). For example, the greater number of keywords or product or service name one has in a directory, the higher that name will appear in Google search engine when consumers look up the name of the product, service or firm (Kim and Johnson 2016). This is important as many customers judge brand image on the basis of its position on the Google search list. Thus, the various kinds of online blogs directly influence the buying behavior of consumers by means articulating the positive and negative aspects of products and services, but also by helping search engine optimization.

7. CUSTOMER BUYING BEHAVIOR

Customer buying behavior can be defined as the conglomeration of the customer's preferences, attitudes, demands, needs and other attributes (Cheung, Xiao and Liu 2014). The business prospect of an organization depends on the effectiveness and efficiency with which it is able to take into consideration the attributes of the customer demographic on which they are focusing (Chen and Lin 2015). Thus firms regularly conduct marketing surveys and analysis to understand the needs of consumers (Lim, Cheah and Wong 2017).

Various theories and models relating to customer behavior have gained prominence. The "Theory of Reasoned Action" (Fishbein & Ajzen 1975) is used to analyze consumer behavior (Baker, Donthu and Kumar 2016). According to this theory, individuals may develop beliefs by referring to information from normative practices of groups and peers. These beliefs influence individual behavior (Alsaleh 2017). Consequently, it can be hypothesized that "perceived usefulness of blogger recommendations will positively affect blog readers' attitudes toward purchasing products/services" (Alsaleh 2017).

"Motivation-Need Theory" (Maslow 1943) is also used for analysis of consumer behavior (Erkan and Evans 2018). Maslow's theory suggests that the primary motivation for consumers to opt for products or services is the extent to which the products or services are able to fulfill their requirements (Lu, Chang and Chang 2014). Blogs aspire to shed light on positive and negative aspects of products and services. Thus, regardless of the kind of blog, they take into consideration one kind of customer behavior theory or the other.

8. IMPACT OF BLOGGING ON CUSTOMER BEHAVIOR

The number of options available to consumers has increased due to number of firms offering similar products or services (Zhou et al. 2017). This has not only increased competition, but also made consumers more fickle than was previously the case. Consumers often opt for products or services which are best in quality and available at the lowest possible price (Chen et al. 2016), unlike earlier buying behavior when products or services were chosen on the basis of quality, customer loyalty or customer satisfaction.

Bloggers are very influential: 81% of consumers read recommendations through social websites before purchasing a product (Wegert 2010). Thus bloggers become opinion leaders. People can obtain knowledge about products and services, but also new trends in shopping and new places to visit. Consumers may be reviewing and checking the same blog daily over and over again (Alsaleh 2017). Alsaleh found 54% of students reviewed blogs more than 10 times per day (Alsaleh 2017). This high level of commitment can be explained as a result of trust and reputation towards bloggers. Further studies verified that trust and reputation influence consumer purchase intentions to shop online (Chu Kamal 2008).

Consumers are influenced by online reviews written by bloggers as well as existing customers (Hsiao, Chang and Tang 2016). Firms use content marketing and SEO optimization to try to keep only the positive reviews on their official website and delete the negative (Liljander, Gummerus and Söderlund 2015). Recent research suggests this has a profound impact on consumer buying behavior (Patrutiu-Baltes 2016).

The decision of consumers to repeatedly opt for the products or services offered by a particular business depends on the kind of satisfaction offered to consumers (Urban, Gosline and Lee 2017). This in turn is directly related to the loyalty of consumers towards the products or services and organization. However, because of increasing competition, consumer loyalty has substantially decreased (Patrutiu-Baltes 2016). Firms are use blogs and bloggers to enhance their brand image because consumers opt for products or services of firms which have a positive brand image. It is precisely here that blogs become indispensable for firms as they are used for posting positive aspects of their organizations. Negative reviews or blogs also help (Ho et al. 2015) as they highlight the negative aspects or the drawbacks of the products or services, but also help content marketing and SEO optimization (Hsiao, Chang and Tang 2016). Thus, it can be said that blogs not only help firms influence consumer buying intention but also determine business prospects.

9. LITERATURE GAP

Customer buying behavior and digital marketing has formed the central lacuna of numerous research works, but the concept of blogging and its use for influencing consumer buying intentions is a nascent one and there has been very little research on this topic. This paper evaluates the manner in which blogging can be utilized by firms to influence consumer behavior and serves as a framework for further research. The impact on buying behavior of negative perceptions from reading blogs also needs further study. With or without out real experience of a product, bloggers have the power to influence consumer perceptions and persuade them to buy or not buy products. Existing literature does not shed much light on these issues.

10. CONCLUSION

Consumer buying behavior has undergone substantial change in recent times due to the plethora of choices available to them, thus firms are using of different marketing strategies: one of the most important is blogging. Blogs offer various benefits to firms: SEO optimization, content marketing, highlighting positive aspects of products and services. These in turn have enabled organizations to positively affect the consumer buying behavior.

REFERENCES

Alsaleh,D (2017). Understanding the Role of Blogger Recommendations on Consumer Purchasing Behavior. The Journal of Business Inquiry 2017,17, Issue 1 (Special Issue), 23-40

Baker, A.M., Donthu, N. and Kumar, V., 2016. Investigating how word-of-mouth conversations about brands influence purchase and retransmission intentions. Journal of Marketing Research, 53(2), pp. 225-239.

Baltes, L.P., 2015. Content marketing-the fundamental tool of digital marketing. Bulletin of the Transilvania University of Brasov. Economic Sciences. Series V, 8(2), p. 111.

Barrett, M., Oborn, E. and Orlikowski, W., 2016. Creating value in online communities: The sociomaterial configuring of strategy, platform, and stakeholder engagement. Information Systems Research, 27(4), pp. 704-723.

Beck, K. and Ralph, J., 1994. Patterns Generates Architectures. Proceedings of European Conference of Object-Oriented Programming. Bologna, Italy, pp. 139-149.

Cano, M.B., Doyle, S. and Zhang, Y., 2018. Do Fashion Blogs Influence Vintage Fashion Consumption? An Analysis from the Perspective of the Chinese Market. In Vintage Luxury Fashion (pp. 167-183). Palgrave Macmillan, Cham.

Chen, J., Teng, L., Yu, Y. and Yu, X., 2016. The effect of online information sources on purchase intentions between consumers with high and low susceptibility to informational influence. Journal of Business Research, 69(2), pp. 467-475.

Chen, S.C. and Lin, C.P., 2015. The impact of customer experience and perceived value on sustainable social relationship in blogs: An empirical study. Technological forecasting and social change, 96, pp. 40-50.

Cheng, R.J. and Fang, W., 2015. Blog intention based on fashion involvement and trust. International Journal of Electronic Commerce Studies, 6(1), pp. 19-36.

Cheung, C.M., Xiao, B.S. and Liu, I.L., 2014. Do actions speak louder than voices? The signaling role of social information cues in influencing consumer purchase decisions. Decision Support Systems, 65, pp. 50-58.

Daunt, K.L., Greer, D.A., Pancer, E., McShane, L. and Poole, M., 2017. The Dark Side of Marketing. Journal of Marketing Management, 33(15-16).

Ebru Uzunoglu, S. M. (2014). Brand communication through digital influencers: Leveraging bloggerengagement. Izmir: International Journal of Information Management 34.

Erkan, I. and Evans, C., 2018. Social media or shopping websites? The influence of eWOM on consumers' online purchase intentions. Journal of Marketing Communications, 24(6), pp. 617-632.

Fishbein, M., & Ajzen, I. Belief, attitude, intention andbehavior: An introduction to theory and research.Reading, Mass.: Addison-Wesley, 1975

Hernández-Méndez, J., Muñoz-Leiva, F. and Sánchez-Fernández, J., 2015. The influence of e-word-of-mouth on travel decision-making: consumer profiles. Current issues in tourism, 18(11), pp. 1001-1021.

Ho, C.H., Chiu, K.H., Chen, H. and Papazafeiropoulou, A., 2015. Can internet blogs be used as an effective advertising tool? The role of product blog type and brand awareness. Journal of Enterprise Information Management, 28(3), pp. 346-362.

Hsiao, C.H., Chang, J.J. and Tang, K.Y., 2016. Exploring the influential factors in continuance usage of mobile social Apps: Satisfaction, habit, and customer value perspectives. Telematics and Informatics, 33(2), pp. 342-355

Hsu, C.L., Chuan-Chuan Lin, J. and Chiang, H.S., 2013. The effects of blogger recommendations on customers' online shopping intentions. Internet Research, 23(1), pp. 69-88.

Hwang, Y. and Jeong, S.H., 2016. "This is a sponsored blog post, but all opinions are my own": The effects of sponsorship disclosure on responses to sponsored blog posts. Computers in Human Behavior, 62, pp. 528-535.

Kannan, P.K., 2017. Digital marketing: A framework, review and research agenda. International Journal of Research in Marketing, 34(1), pp. 22-45.

Katz, E., Lazarsfeld, P. F., & Roper, E. (2017). *Personal influence: The part played by people in the flow of mass communications*. Routledge.

Kim, A.J. and Johnson, K.K., 2016. Power of consumers using social media: Examining the influences of brand-related user- generated content on Facebook. Computers in Human Behavior, 58, pp. 98-108.

Kingsnorth, S., 2016. Digital marketing strategy: an integrated approach to online marketing. Kogan Page Publishers.

Laroche, M., Habibi, M.R. and Richard, M.O., 2013. To be or not to be in social media: How brand loyalty is affected by social media?. International Journal of Information Management, 33(1), pp. 76-82.

Laroche, M., Habibi, M.R., Richard, M.O. and Sankaranarayanan, R., 2012. The effects of social media based brand communities on brand community markers, value creation practices, brand trust and brand loyalty. Computers in Human Behavior, 28(5), pp. 1755-1767.

Liljander, V., Gummerus, J. and Söderlund, M., 2015. Young consumers' responses to suspected covert and overt blog marketing. Internet Research, 25(4), pp. 610-632.

Lim, X.J., Cheah, J.H. and Wong, M.W., 2017. The Impact of Social Media Influencers on Purchase Intention and the Mediation Effect of Customer Attitude. Asian Journal of Business Research, 7(2), p. 19.

Lu, L.C., Chang, W.P. and Chang, H.H., 2014. Consumer attitudes toward blogger's sponsored recommendations and purchase intention: The effect of sponsorship type, product type, and brand awareness. Computers in Human Behavior, 34, pp. 258-266.

Maslow, A. H. (1943). A theory of human motivation. *Psychological review*, *50*(4), 370.

Ngai, E.W., Tao, S.S.and Moon, K.K., 2015. Social media research: Theories, constructs, and conceptual frameworks. International Journal of Information Management, 35(1), pp. 33-44.

Patrutiu-Baltes, L., 2016. Inbound Marketing-the most important digital marketing strategy. Bulletin of the Transilvania University of Brasov. Economic Sciences. Series V, 9(2), p. 61.

Ryan, D., 2016. Understanding digital marketing: marketing strategies for engaging the digital generation. Kogan Page Publishers.

Schafer, J. B. (2001). E- commerce Reccomandation Applications. Data Mining and Knowledge Discovery,5 115-153.

Stephen, A.T., 2016. The role of digital and social media marketing in consumer behavior. Current Opinion in Psychology, 10, pp. 17-21.

Ukpabi, D.C. and Karjaluoto, H., 2017. Consumers' acceptance of information and communications technology in tourism: A review. Telematics and Informatics, 34(5), pp. 618-644.

Urban, G.L., Gosline, R. and Lee, J., 2017. The Power of Consumer Stories in Digital Marketing. MIT Sloan Management Review, 58(4).

Weimann, G. (1994). The influentials: People who influence people. SUNY Press.

Zhou, X., Song, Q., Li, Y.Y., Tan, H. and Zhou, H., 2017. Examining the influence of online retailers' micro-blogs on consumers' purchase intention. Internet Research, 27(4), pp. 819-838.

ESCALATION OF COMMITMENT IN NPD AND COST SAVING IT PROJECTS

Mark van der Pas and Niels van der Pas
European Center for Digital Transformation, Maastricht University
Tongersestraat 53, Maastricht, The Netherlands

ABSTRACT

Stopping non promising projects as early as possible saves resources that can be allocated to more relevant investments or be saved to improve the bottom line of an organisation. Gated processes are in use in numerous organisations to decide on proceeding or cancelling a project. This study examines the consequences of the setup of the gatekeepers, the managers deciding on the gates, in these processes. Gatekeepers deciding on two consecutive gates are, according to the escalation of commitment theory, tended to confirm their initial decisions. They hold a higher approval rate for the consecutive decision as compared to a setup where the gates are approved by different gatekeepers. In this paper we present the results of, as far as we know, the first natural experiment on the escalation of commitment using 820 new product development and cost saving IT projects over a time span of 4.5 years. We found empirical evidence that escalation of commitment, as predicted in theory, leads to a higher approval rate of the consecutive gate. Organisations can mitigate this by changing the setup of the governance by avoiding the approval of two consecutive gates by the same gatekeeper. Furthermore, the data showed that large investment projects hold a significantly larger possibility to receive approvals (after an initial approval) than small investment projects. This indicates the importance of the initial gate approval. Finally, we studied the difference between cost saving and new product development projects and found no differences in their mortality rate nor in the approval rate of the consecutive gate.

KEYWORDS

Escalation of Commitment, IT Decision Making, Stage-Gate Process

1. INTRODUCTION

People are creative beings that come up with numerous ideas for new product development (NPD) or cost saving IT projects. Where some of these ideas are a straight success, a lot of them are (painful) failures. Failures because they never earned back their investment after they were launched or failures since they were aborted before launch. Whatever the type of failure, these projects have consumed resources that could have been reallocated towards successful new products, alternative improvements like process optimisation or bluntly be saved to improve the organisations' bottom-line.

In 2004 Cooper et al. claimed that products fail at an alarming rate; amongst others they found that only 21% of businesses' total NPD efforts meet their project objectives. In a more recent study Van der Pas and Furneaux (2015) found that 43% of new products deliver at least 80% of the expected revenue whereas 26% of new products never earned back more than the cost they occurred and thus delivered a negative bottom line value. On cost saving projects the results were better as 69% of the projects delivered at least 80% of the expected benefits and 7% of these projects generate a negative profit and loss effect.

The StageGate® process to manage ideas through key steps into launched products is an instrument to organise decision making and is used to evaluate, select or cancel projects (Cooper 2008). The StageGate® process is focused on the development of new products, this kind of processes are also used for other project types like cost saving or security improvements (see for an overview Van der Pas 2017). Decision points separating the phases are known as 'gates', 'milestones' and 'tollgates' (Cooper 2001, Chao and Ishii 2005) and determine whether a project migrates into the next stage or is terminated. These processes are described as Stage-Gated Processes in this paper.

Optimising decision making within the Stage-Gated process could significantly improve the impact of cost saving and NPD projects. If we focus on project cost avoidance then the cost of each failed new product or IT project is not the same, nevertheless it is generally accepted that projects that need to be stopped are to be cancelled as early as possible (Unger et al., 2012). The Stage-Gated process can be used for this purpose and in this paper we focus on one specific aspect of decision making: escalation of commitment. Eliens et al. (2018) described escalation of commitment as the unwillingness of a gatekeeper to let go of a fruitless new product development project. Escalation of commitment occurs when two consecutive gates are approved by the same gatekeeper and postpones the cancellation of failing projects. Although defined as an issue within NPD we study this for both NPD as well as cost saving IT projects. Several cancellation rates are published (Barczak et al., 2009; Hossain & Islam 2015). Unlike this paper they did not study escalation of commitment.

This paper describes a natural experiment within an organisation that switched their gatekeeper structure. In one period the organisation used a structure that avoided escalation of commitment by assigning different gatekeepers to the first gates. In the other period the gates were approved by the same gatekeeper which could lead to escalation of commitment. We found clear evidence of escalation of commitment in organisation and provided suggestions to improve the performance of NPD and cost saving IT projects.

2. THEORY AND HYPOTHESES

Cancelling unpromising projects as early as possible turned out to be challenging in daily practice (Sarangee et al. 2014; Schmidt and Calantone, 2002). The gates of the Stage-Gated process could be used to stop or cancel projects. The managers deciding on the gates are called the gatekeepers (Cooper et al. 1994). As claimed by Staw and Ross (1987) 'individuals may have the tendency to become locked into a course of action, throwing good money after bad money'. For that, escalation of commitment could occur when two consecutive gates are approved by the same gatekeeper. In taking the second decision the gatekeeper should ignore sunk cost as they are irrecoverable, nevertheless the gatekeeper is, whilst deciding on the second decision, biased by his first decision. By confirming his earlier approval on the previous gate he would consciously or unconsciously confirm the correctness of his initial decision. The effect would be a delay of the cancellation of an unpromising project. Based on this we expect a higher approval rate of the consecutive gate in case both gates are approved by the same gatekeeper. This is tested in the first hypothesis.

H1. The approval likelihood of a gate is higher when the preceding gate was approved by the same gatekeeper

Not all projects hold the same investment volume. The larger the project size the higher the sunk costs for stopping a project. Based on this it can be expected that the reconfirmation of the second gate is higher for large investments than for smaller. On the other hand, the larger the investment size, the better a gatekeeper is expected to consider the approval of the second gate and for that to overcome the escalation of commitment. We expect the forces to balance and to find no difference for the approval of a preceding gate for large as compared to smaller investments.

H2. Investment size holds no influence on the approval likelihood of the second gate by the same gatekeeper

IT projects related to new product development hold higher risks than cost saving projects. E.g. Bower (1986) found that cost saving projects deliver on average 110% of the expected value whereas NPD projects deliver 10% of that value. The time during the Stage-Gated process enables an organisation to gain additional information that can be used to reevaluate the risk. Knowing that NPD investments hold a higher risk and that additional information on risks is found during the Stage-Gated process, we expect a higher mortality rate for NPD than for cost saving projects.

H3. New product development IT projects hold a higher mortality rate than cost saving IT projects

In case two consecutive gates are to be approved by the same gatekeeper and this leads to a higher approver rate of the second gate, then this could reduce the mortality rate over those gates. A lower mortality rate indicates that the disadvantage of escalation of commitment could be higher for NPD than for cost saving IT projects. Knowing this difference could trigger gatekeepers of NPD projects to be more conscious about escalation of commitment and for that mitigate it. Based on interviews with practitioners and the modest knowledge in organisations on escalation of commitment we expect organisations not to leverage this knowledge and for that we expect no difference between the two project categories. This leads to H4:

H4. Escalation commitment does not differ between NPD and cost optimizing IT projects

In the next section we describe the methodology to test these hypotheses; then the results are described.

3. METHODOLOGY

The data used for this study comes from a European telecommunication organisation with an annual revenue of more than 2 billion Euros and capital investments exceeding 100 million Euro per anno. The organization offered data for all projects that were managed over the process from November 18th 2014, as it implemented the current gated structure upto March 1st 2019. The gates and stages of the process did not change during that timeframe and the process was used for IT projects. The process holds in total 6 gates; the third gate is the go on implementation and on average 79.8% of the project resources are spend after that gate. The last three gates are technical readiness, commercial launch and project closure.

As from October 2016 the first two gates are approved by one gatekeeper. From November 2014 up to October 2016 the first gate was approved by a different gatekeeper than the second gate. Based on this set up a lower escalation of commitment is expected on the first period (up to October 2016) than in the second period.

For H1 we used 820 projects with an approval for the first gate; 633 of these projects were implemented and 187 were cancelled. 712 of the 812 projects also received an approval for the second gate (86.7%). In case a gate was initially rejected but in a later request approved then the rejection was excluded from our analysis and the gate counted as an approved gate. We compared the percentage of these projects that got an approval for the second gate in the first period with the same percentage for the second period. We tested H1 and all hypotheses by comparing datasets with each other. The comparison is made using a t-test.

The size of the project for H2 was determined based on the budget. We allocated the 320 projects in the period with expected escalation of commitment into three classes. E.g. 192 projects held an investment volume of less than or equal to 25,000 Euro and 128 held a higher investment volume (see table 1).

Table 1. Allocation of the Projects into Investment Categories

Definition of 'large project	Amount of small projects	Amount of large projects
> 25,000 Euro	192	128
> 50,000 Euro	215	105
> 100,000 Euro	240	80

In H2 we tested for each of the three categories the difference of the approval rate of the second gate.

For H3 we split the dataset of 820 projects into two project categories by using the project initiator. The marketing and sales-initiated (and financed) projects are allocated to the NPD category whereas all other projects initiated by e.g. operations, HR, finance and technology are allocated to the cost saving category. This is a very broad clustering where e.g. sales enhancements and sales channel investments such as e- or m-commerce are allocated to the new product development category. Investments in technology, scalability, architecture, security etc. are all allocated to the brought cost saving category. The mortality rate was calculated based on all projects that received an approval for the first gate. It was defined as the ratio of cancelled projects as compared to all projects.

The dataset from the period with possible escalation of commitment was also used for H4 and we studied the difference between the approval rate of the consecutive gate for NPD projects and compared that to the same approval rate for cost saving projects.

4. RESULTS

In the first period 320 projects received an approval for the first gate 72.8% of these also received an approval of the second gate. 95.6% of the 501 projects in period two received an approval for the first two gates. Due to the large difference in variance (0.20 and 0.04) we used a two-sample t-test assuming different variances and tested whether the difference of means of these two datasets is 0. This was rejected with an extremely low p-value (9.55 E-17). Based on this we accept H1.

Large projects hold a stronger likelihood of approval of the consecutive gate than smaller projects. 96.1% of projects over 25,000 Euro received an approval for the second gate whereas 57.6% of the projects with an investment volume below 25.000 Euro received an approval for that gate. Also, the variance differs strongly (0.25 and 0.04). The p-value of the t-test for equal means assuming inequal variances generated a low p-value (1.72 E-19). Also, the other investment size categories held a low p-value (6.32 E-16 for 50,000 Euro and 5.55 E-13 for 100,000 Euro). Based on this H2 was rejected.

The mortality rate of both NPD and cost saving IT projects in the studied data was 0.23 meaning that on average 77 of the 100 projects with a first gate approval are finished. Not only the means, but also the variances are identical (0.18), this leads to a high p-value of 0.42 indicating no differences to the mortality rate of NPD and cost saving IT projects. We reject H3.

95.5% of cost saving IT projects received an approval of the consecutive gate (variance 0.04); whereas 95.7% of the NPD IT projects received such an approval (variance 0.04). The two-sample t-test assuming equal variance for a mean difference of 0 returned a one-tail p-value of 0.45. The lack of difference between both data sets allowed us to accept H4.

5. CONCLUSION

In this study we found a clear correlation between the likelihood of approval of a consecutive gate and governance of the Stage-Gated process. In a set up where one gatekeeper is empowered to approve two consecutive gates for a project the likelihood of approving the second gate is significantly higher than in case the setup uses two different gatekeepers. This indicates that a sharp mortality rate can be created by using a governance where consecutive gates are not approved by the same gatekeeper.

A strong confirmation rate of initial decisions as found in the set up where a gatekeeper is empowered to approve multiple gates, strengthens the importance of the initial gate approval. In case the setup cannot be changed, performance improvements of the process should be focused on that first gate.

Furthermore, we found that large investment projects hold a higher possibility to receive an approval for the second gate in case the gatekeeper approved the first gate too. This supports the idea that an increase in the sunk cost reduces the likelihood to cancel a project.

Finally, we found no difference between cost saving and NPD IT projects. Escalation of commitment seems independent from the project category despite their completely different risk structure.

6. LIMITATIONS AND SUGGESTIONS FOR FUTURE RESEARCH

This study is based on data of one organisation, other organisations or even other agents within the same organisation could show different results. Generalising the conclusions for other organisations, especially organisations in different branches, different continents and different sizes should be done with utmost care. Since the setup of this study is now known it can be easily repeated by organisations knowing the required input data. Replicating this study and performing a meta-analysis on those studies would increase the robustness of the findings as well as the level at which they can be generalised.

The differences found could also be explained by intermediate variables. These variables are not known to the authors but could be studied in future research. Furthermore, we illustrated correlations, the statistical methods used did not study the causality of these relations.

This study focused on the approval of two consecutive gates in the Stage-Gated process and used for H3 the information whether a project was cancelled or finished. Future research should enhance this by including the expected profitability as well as the realised profitability of the IT project. Using more than the two investment categories from this study, NPD and cost saving IT projects, such as strategic, sales expansion or legally obliged investments could also be studied in future research.

We furthermore suggest a study to the awareness of escalation of commitment in Stage-Gated processes. Perhaps the Theory of Planned Behavior (Ajzen 1991) can be used to study behavior, intention as well as attitude, subjective norm and perceived behavioral control on neglecting sunk costs in future Stage-Gated Process decisions.

Finally, we suggest studying the usage of machine learning to support gatekeepers in deciding on the gates. Machine learning could be used to increase the 'objectiveness' of decision making and by doing so be a counter action against escalation of commitment.

ACKNOWLEDGEMENT

The authors wish to thank the participating organisation for allowing us to study their data. Furthermore, they wish to thank the team developing the portfolio management tooling which delivered the data for this study 'at the push of a button'.

REFERENCES

Ajzen, I., 1991. *The theory of planned behavior.* Organizational behavior and human decision processes: a journal of fundamental research and theory in applied psychology, 50: 179-211.

Barczak, G., A. Griffin, and K.B. Kahn, 2009. *Perspective: Trends and Drivers of Success in NPD Practices: Results of the 2003 PDMA Best Practices Study*. Journal of Product Innovation Management 26(1): 3-23.

Bower, J. L., 1986. *Managing the Resource Allocation Process.* Boston: Harvard Business School.

Chao, L.P. and K. Ishii, 2005. Design process error proofing, benchmarking gate and phased review life-cycle models. IDETC/CIE 2005, Long Beach, CA, USA, September 24-28.

Cooper, R. G., 1994. *Third-generation new product processes.* Journal of Product Innovation Management 11 (1): 3-14.

Cooper, R. G., 2008. *Perspective: The stage-gateVR idea-to-launch process-update, what's new, and Nextgen systems.* Journal of Product Innovation Management 25(3): 213-232.

Cooper, R. G., S. J. Edgett, and E. J. Kleinschmidt, 2004. *Benchmarking best NPD practices I.* Research-Technology Management 47: 31-43.

Cooper, R.G., 2001. *Winning at new products: accelerating the process from idea to launch*. Cambridge Massachusetts: Perseus publishing.

Eliens, R., K. Eling, S. Gelper and F. Langerak, 2018. *Rational versus intuitive gatekeeping: escalation of commitment in the front end of NPD.* Journal of Product Innovation Management 35(6): 890-907.

Hossain, M., and K. M. Z. Islam. 2015. *Generating ideas on online platforms: A case study of "My Starbucks Idea."* Arab Economic and Business Journal 10(2): 102–11.

Pas, van der M. and B. Furneaux, 2015. Improving the Predictability of IT investment Business Value. *European Conference on Information Systems 2015*, paper 190, http://aisel.aisnet.org/ecis2015_cr/190/

Pas, van der M., 2017. Speeding up time-to-market of it investments. *10th IADIS International Conference on Information Systems 2017*, full paper: 155-162.

Sarangee, K. R., J. L. Woolley, J. B. Schmidt, and E. Long, 2014. *De-escalation mechanisms in high-technology product innovation.* Journal of Product Innovation Management 31(5): 1023-1038.

Schmidt, J. B., and R. J. Calantone, 2002. *Escalation of commitment during new product development.* Journal of the Academy of Marketing Science 30(2): 103-118.

Staw, B.M., and J. Ross,1987. Behavior in Escalation Situations: Antecedents, Prototypes and Solutions, in *Research in Organizational Behavior*, Eds. L.L. Cummuings and Barry M.Staw Greenwich, CT: JAI: 39-38.

Unger, B.N., A. Kock, H.G. Gemünden, and D. Jonas, 2012. *Enforcing strategic fit of project portfolios by project termination: An empirical study on senior management involvement.* International Journal of Project Management 30(6): 675-85.

TOWARDS THE CASE FOR INTRODUCING ENTERPRISE RESOURCE PLANNING AT NATIONAL OIL CORPORATION (NOC) OF LIBYA: A CASE STUDY

Naser Aniba[1], Jawed Siddiqi[2] and Mohamed Elmosbahy[1]
[1]*International Marketing Department, National Oil Corporation, Libya*
[2]*School of Computing, Sheffield Hallam University, UK*

ABSTRACT

Enterprise Resource Planning (ERP) systems provide an integrated view of core business processes operating in real-time over the web so it can track its resources, manage its back-office functions and facilitate customer and supplier relationship in an efficient and cost-effective manner that can lead to improved planning and decision quality, and a smoother coordination between business units, resulting in higher efficiency and a quicker response time to customer demands and inquiries. We argue that for the Oil sector the goals to be achieved for a successful ERP deployment are to streamline business processes, compliance with the regulatory environment but at the same time increase profitability This paper aims to contribute to develop a better understanding of the transition required by focusing on objectives, constraints, and the implementation process of ERP in this sector and provide guidelines from lessons learnt. It reports work in progress to share our experiences so that we might benefit from early feedback from those that have already trodden this path as well those that are currently thinking of doing so.

KEYWORDS

NOC, ERP Implementation, Oil Industry

1. INTRODUCTION

The oil industry has been for some time a highly volatile and turbulent market, which is difficult to characterise, however some of the key characteristics of complexities involved in managing in a visible and efficient manner are: the enormous levels of investment in equipment and capital, the process of discovering, extracting and delivering oil, the organisational supply chain etc.

For these reasons alone, it is not surprising that Enterprise Resource Planning (ERP) is essential business management software and therefore is frequently present in the sector to effectively manage the day to day operations.

The novelty in the paper is that it sets out the case for introducing an Enterprise Resource Planning (ERP) System at National Oil Corporation (NOC) of Libya.

2. ERP SYSTEM FOR THE OIL INDUSTRY?

To develop a sound understanding of the goals to be achieved for a successful ERP implementation a prerequisite is the need to consider the forces that shape the energy sector particularly within the oil industry. Three primary forces shape the oil industry: highly volatile and turbulent markets, a challenging regulatory environment and significant lack of trust from its end customer base. Therefore, the goals to be achieved for a successful deployment are to streamline business processes, compliance with the regulatory environment but at the same time increase profitability.

A key requirement of the oil industry is to accurately and efficiently channel its resources yet comply with the demanding regulations of the extraction industry. An ERP system enable organization to view, understand, process and deliver results via real-time snapshots of the entire operation and therefore focus collective insight on issues that are currently trapped in information silos at different levels and structures of the organisation.

Currently company practice is to use hardcopy field ticket methods which are highly prone to be subject to increased costs, can have unknown financial ramifications and certainly lengthy reporting processes. As mentioned previously more recent innovations in ERP systems provide the ability to access live activity updates from the field using mobile devices and real-time reporting and therefore decision making is both better informed and timely

Some specific challenges that an oil company could be facing are: a lack of a consolidated of overview of inventory or assets globally, absence of management of rigs that are constantly changing location as well as their constant need for spare parts and the requirement to automate communication via barcode and mobile devices.

An ERP System, in an oil industry, can lead to:

1. Increased improved visibility of key assets because of gains in the efficiency of key inventory processes and visibility of the entire inventory lifecycle.
2. Enabled the ability to drive efficiencies and increased visibility up and down the supply chain.
3. Leverage automated data collection technology where applicable thereby improving ability to locate inventory at various locations (Warehouse & Rigs).
4. ERP systems are more secure, all enterprise data is centralized leading to an improved management of globally dispersed resources.
5. Provide the most current and future-proof integration leveraging web services.

3. NATIONAL OIL CORPORATION LIBYA: A CASE STUDY

3.1 An Overview of NOC Libya: Profile, Products and Services

Libya is a member of the Organization of Petroleum Exporting Countries (OPEC) and holds the largest proven oil reserves in Africa about 46.5 billion barrels (7.38×10^9 m^3) as of 2010. Oil production was 1.65 million barrels per day (262×10^3 m^3/d). About 80% of Libya's proven oil reserves are located in the Sirte Basin Province, which accounts for 90% of the country's oil output.

The National Oil Corporation (NOC) was established in November 1970 to assume the responsibility for the operation of the oil sector in area of petroleum, supporting the national economy through increasing, developing and exploiting the oil reserves and operating and investing in those reserves to realize optimum returns.

NOC is carrying out exploration and production operation through its own affiliated companies marketing operations of oil and gas, locally and abroad. NOC also has participation agreements with specialized international companies. NOC owns refining, and oil and gas processing companies. NOC also owns national service companies, which carry out oil well drilling and work over operations, provide all drilling material and equipment, lay and maintain oil and gas pipelines, build and maintain oil and gas storage tanks and carry out related technical and economic studies.

3.2 Enterprise Resource Planning: A Three Step Strategy for NOC Libya

3.2.1 Expectations

To define clear set of expectations it is important to agree the three most important high-level considerations: *in-house development or third part buy in*, *time frame* and *budget*. In relation to first consideration it was important to decide this at the outset as this would have a direct bearing on the latter two. In relation to the latter two reports of variances that have occurred in the past for even modest projects the time frame can typically take 50% or more than initially estimated whilst the variance can typically exceed three times the initial estimate. These factors will have a direct bearing, but they may well determine the choice in the first consideration. Due to these interdependencies in practice meeting these expectations is an iterative process.

3.2.2 Business Requirements

Before exploring the scope of the business requirements, it was essential to ensure that we had the support of the senior management team to support this venture and as it was initiated by the senior management team this hurdle had been cleared. Furthermore, from the start we were assured that strong motivation would be matched with a strong budget to fulfil the requirements.

In developing a business requirements document for introducing ERP and possibly an ERP "system" the goal here was to provide NOC with an integrated view of its core business activities for all departments so this would provide the visibility for all staff involved in these activates, especially for senior management of all the important processes, across various departments of NOC. In our initial discussions with key stakeholders it became clear that the main functions are, exploration, production, transport, storage, exportation, industrialisation and commercialisation.

For our purposes, we agreed with clients that the main functions of the company could be categorised as:

Onshore and Offshore Drilling Operations: Logistics Management responsible for providing logistics support in terms of transportation of products and equipment.

Technical: Providing technical support to the operations function, field development, maintenance, services and engineering and projects.

Commercialisation: this is essentially Business and Administration support. The former focuses on commercial activities such as marketing procurement, inventory, tendering, finance etc. and the latter includes human resources.

The client wished the primary focus to be on the drilling operations required for exploration on both onshore and offshore areas; this has successfully played an important role in the discovery of oil.

For commercialisation, the client decided that marketing was to be the primary focus. In our conversations, we discovered that the current level of automation is such that most department within these functions are operating either manually or at best using spreadsheets. However, it was important to note that the finance department is attempting to use Oracle and therefore any decisions on our choices had to consider the work and data flows of these and the interoperability of any systems to be recommended with potential implementation that finance might choose.

3.2.3 ERP Selection

This requires deciding between the following two options either: a *single ERP* (vendor selection) or *best of breed* (selecting the best module for each functional area).

Our initial thoughts favoured the former approach however given that the client has chosen to incorporate ERP in an incremental manner the latter approach seemed more attractive. In fact, at present we have decided to take a hybrid approach in that many ERP vendors are willing to implement functions in an incremental manner. The next question was which vendor to choose potential candidates include SAP and Oracle particularly as these two ERP packages were amongst the most popular choices in that industrial sector and region.

Discussions are currently taking place as to whether to hire a consultant to study the company's requirements and propose a particular ERP system or to carry out the task in-house. As ever there is a trade-off between the options the in-house option has its obvious benefits provided there is sufficient in-house expertise which of course the consultant option offers; however, additional time is required for the tendering process itself could take several months as well as the additional cost.

At present, we are conducting market research to find out the range of costs and timeframe. The initial data collected appeared not very encouraging as the minimum cost identified was USD 8 million (software license, hardware and implementation cost). The average implementation time ranged from 18 months to 3 years; which was beyond the initial estimations, as the company was aiming to complete the transition in 12 months. However, our decision to proceed incrementally means that these figures are not representative, and we will be able to control the time frame and budgets in an incremental manner.

4. CONCLUSIONS

In conclusion, in presenting work in progress we are looking to share our experience so that we might benefit from early feedback from those that have already trodden this path as well those that are currently thinking of doing so. Additionally, we are seeking potential partners from the vendor community to provide initial guidance and outline proposals of what they have to offer.

REFERENCES

Ceylon Petroleum Storage Terminals Limited has decided to implement SAP. Available online at: http://www.cpstl.lk/sap.html accessed on 05.12.2018.

Chang, M. K., Cheung, W., Yeung, J. H. Y. (2008) Understanding ERP System Adoption from the User's Perspective, International Journal of Production Economics, vol. 113(2), 928-942.

Kimberling, E. Lessons Learned From Oil and Gas ERP Implementations August 13, 2014 .Available online at: http://panorama-consulting.com/lessons-learned-from-oil-and-gas-erp-implementations/. Accessed on 05.12.2018.

Laughlin, S.P. (1999) An ERP game plan, Journal of Business Strategy, 20(1), 32-37.

Mendelson, H. (1999) ERP Overview: Stanford Business School, Mimeo (1999).

Mishra, A. and Mishra, D. (2009) ERP System Implementation: An Oil and Gas Exploration Sector Perspective, F. Bomarius et al. (Eds.): PROFES 2009, LNBIP 32, 416-428.

Mishra, A. and Mishra, D. (2011). ERP project implementation: evidence from the oil and gas sector. Acta Polytechnica Hungarica, 8(4), 55-74.

Srivastava, M. and Gips, B.J. (2009) Chinese cultural implications for ERP implementation. Journal of technology management & innovation, 4(1), pp. 105-113.

ICT ADOPTION IN SMEs: DETERMINANTS, LEVELS, AND INFLUENCE ON THE ORGANIZATIONAL INNOVATIVENESS

Büşra Alma Çallı[1], Erman Coşkun[2] and Mehtap Özşahin[3]
[1]*Sakarya University, Turkey*
[2]*Prince Mohammad Bin Salman College (MBSC) of Business & Entrepreneurship, Saudi Arabia*
[3]*Yalova University, Turkey*

ABSTRACT

While ICT adoption and utilization are essential for all kind of companies for various reasons, it could be especially essential for SMEs for their sustainability and innovativeness. ICT awareness and perception is the main determinants of ICT adoption and utilization. In SMEs, ICT adoption and utilization will be dependent on a) owner/manager's individual characteristics, b) owner/manager's ICT awareness c) company related features. Thus, this study aims to investigate: (1) effects of company characteristics, owner/manager's individual characteristics and ICT awareness on ICT adoption and utilization (2) how the extent of ICT adoption and utilization influences different aspects and types of innovativeness. Mixed approach combining quantitative and qualitative research methods is used for gaining insight related to subject and the studied phenomenon. Data gathered from semi-structured interviews, and a developed questionnaire applied to SMEs are synthesized to reveal findings regarding the determinants of ICT adoption and utilization levels of SMEs.
The developed model is being tested in Turkish SMEs. Moreover, the effects of ICT adoption and utilization levels on the components of organizational innovativeness are investigated comprehensively in this study.

KEYWORDS

ICT adoption, ICT awareness, Organizational innovativeness, SMEs

1. INTRODUCTION

Small and medium enterprises (SMEs) are drivers of the economy by constituting a major role in creating employment opportunities and developing innovations, because of agile and flexible processes. In OECD countries, SMEs constitute a remarkable part of the total enterprises, and make the greatest contribution to the economy (Scupola, 2009, as cited in Awa, Ojiabo, & Emecheta, 2015). Concentrating on SMEs, associated literature has highlighted several advantages of adopting ICT from the point of cost savings, enhancement of services, creation of new opportunities, improved access to market information, increased organizational performance and competitiveness (Giotopoulos et al., 2017; Quinton et al., 2018). Consequently, digital technologies have shifted the way in which organizations interact with the environment and their solutions to problems stemming from the business environment. Growing utilization of ICTs is the major driver of the knowledge economy (Kossaï & Piget, 2014). ICTs compromising a broad range of technological implementations, digital and telecommunication technologies and digital information facilities, are promising for advancement of SMEs (Ismail et al., 2011, as cited in Ibrahim et al., 2016). Although digitalization is not a recent concept, SMEs might not get full benefits from digitalization due to limited financial, technical resources, skilled and knowledgeable workers and adequate experience. They have considerable barriers in front of technology adoption (Dahnil et al., 2014). Nguyen, Newby and Macaulay (2015) mentioned non-existence of proper business and ICT strategies, insufficient research and planning, inadequate project management, and missing top management support as barriers in front of successful ICT adoption. Similarly, Makiwa (2018) put emphasis into insufficient organizational strategies, limited guidance and inadequate policies.

2. CONCEPTUAL BACKGROUND

Theories including "Technology Acceptance Model" (Davis, 1985) and "Diffusion of Innovation" theory (Rogers, 1983) and "Technology-Organization and Environment" (TOE) (Tornatzky & Fleischer, 1990) framework have been widely adopted to examine adoption process and decision-making in different contexts. Diffusion and Innovations Theory and TOE framework focus on both organizational and individual level characteristics. TOE, furthermore, emphasizes the remarkable role of environment by considering competitors, government and industry in which the firm operates (Giotopoulos et al., 2017). Depending on these theories, this study proposes a conceptual model by incorporating individual and organizational characteristics in terms of ICT awareness of owners/managers, organizational innovativeness and some particular demographic characteristics in order to examine ICT adoption at SMEs. ICT adoption behavior is evaluated by means of a framework that emphasizes ICT infrastructure and ownership, the extent of internal and external integration, utilization of Internet and e-business activities.

2.1 Determinants of ICT Adoption and Utilization

Adoption of ICT, its determinants and consequences have been topic of numerous studies. Awa et al. (2015) investigated e-commerce adoption of SMEs and its determinants associated with technology, organization and environment. Kusumaningtyas & Suwarto (2015) examined ICT adoption with regard to some demographical factors of owners / managers. Age and education level were significantly determined differences in ICT adoption, use and skills, while gender did not demonstrate significant effect. Thong (1999) mentioned CEO characteristics and IS characteristics in addition to organizational and environmental factors (as cited in Taylor, 2015). In this context, the following assumption is developed:

A1: *Demographic characteristics of owners/managers of SMEs in terms of age, education level and training field affect the ICT adoption level of SMEs.*

Kim, Jang and Yang, (2017) specifically focused on the adoption of Software-as-a-Service (SaaS). Perceived benefits and risks within technological, organizational and environmental contexts were investigated with regard to their influence on intention to adopt SaaS. Ramayah et al., (2016) focused on the level of web adoption and antecedents were determined as follows: innovativeness of CEO, perceived advantages, cost and attitudes towards information technologies. Al Isma'ili, Li, Shen and He (2016) examined cloud-computing adoption at SMEs. Technological factors compromising "cost reduction, compatibility, relative advantages and trialability", organizational factors including "size, organizational innovativeness, information systems knowledge and top management support" were explored as significant predictors of cloud computing adoption. Giotopoulos et al. (2017) discovered that innovative activities and research & development, qualified employees, proper guidance and leadership, and decentralization of decision-making enhances adoption of up-to-date technologies in SMEs. Esmaeilpour et al. (2016) focused on e-commerce adoption at SMEs and found that all kind of barriers (organizational, technical and environmental barrier), had significant effect on perceived usefulness and ease of use, which significantly determined intention to use e-commerce. As been indicated in most of earlier researches, the characteristics and perceptions of top management play a great role in ICT adoption of organizations. In this respect, it is proposed that:

A2. *ICT awareness of owners/managers of SMEs affects the ICT adoption level of SMEs.*

Sin Tan et al. (2010) investigated the demographic characteristics of SMEs as antecedents of ICT adoption. ICT benefits and perceived barriers were focused on so as to determine differences among companies based on industry type, size, size in terms of annual sales and years of internet experience. There were significant differences in terms of perceptions of benefits and barriers based on demographic properties of companies. For instance, relative advantage and perceived benefits were mentioned by (Iacovou et al., 1995; Merthens et al., 2001; Premkumar & Roberts, 1999, as cited in Taylor, 2015). Relative to large-scale organizations, SMEs view the implementation expensive, risky and complicated procedure, which constitutes an important barrier in front of adoption (Dahnil et al., 2014). Accordingly, researchers propose that:

A3. *Organizational features of SMEs in terms of size, lifespan, industry and annual revenue affect the ICT adoption level of SMEs.*

2.2 ICT Adoption - Organizational Innovativeness

Martins and Terblanche (2003) conceptualized organizational innovativeness based on: behaviour towards encouragement, strategy, support mechanisms and structure (as cited in Jaakson et al., 2019). Martínez-Román and Romero (2017) examined innovativeness of SMEs from the aspects of product, process, marketing and organization. Based on earlier studies, Wang and Ahmed (2004) conceptualized OI with five dimensions including strategic, product, process, behavioral and market innovativeness. The relationship between innovativeness and ICT adoption examined by numerous studies. For instance, Adeniran and Johnston (2015) examined impact of innovativeness within dynamic capabilities of organizations and their ICT adoption on achieving competitiveness. Similarly, Giotopoulos et al. (2017) investigated the influence of organizational innovations as technological competency on ICT adoption. On the other hand, Neirotti and Pesce (2019) argued that, ICTs offer opportunity of performing various innovation activities as a result of facilitating automation, information processing and providing mechanisms for complex product development. Moreover, Valdez-Juárez et al. (2018) explored that ICT had significant effect on innovation, KM and profitability. Parallel to Neirotti and Pesce (2019) and Valdez-Juárez et al. (2018), our study also emphasizes the effect of ICT adoption level on organizational innovativeness. Wang and Ahmed (2004) conceptualized market and product innovativeness as externally-focused and market-based inter-twins; whereas, behavioral and process innovativeness as internally-focused inter-twins, which emphasizes the need for product and market innovativeness. On the other hand, strategic innovativeness captures the features of both sides as it emphasizes the organization's ability to match external opportunities with internal capabilities in order to introduce innovative products and exploit new markets. In this respect, it is expected that ICT adoption levels influence different types of innovativeness in different ways. Based on these, the following assumptions were developed;

A4: Different levels of ICT adoption affect different components of organizational innovativeness.

$A4_a$: Basic communication, basic ICT utilization and internal integration levels of ICT adoption affect behavioral and process innovativeness significantly.

$A4_b$: External integration and inter-organizational integration levels of ICT adoption affect market and product innovativeness significantly.

$A4_c$: Strategic integration level of ICT adoption affect strategic innovativeness significantly.

Based on all these assumptions and literature review we constructed our research model in Figure-1.

3. METHODOLOGY

Purpose: This study aims (1) to investigate the effect of individual characteristics -in terms of demographic factors and ICT awareness of owners/managers of SMEs-, and organizational factors -in terms of organizational features of SMEs- on ICT adoption level, and (2) to examine how the extent of ICT adoption influences different aspects of innovativeness. ***Research Method and Sample:*** This survey is currently being conducted on SMEs, operating in Marmara Region-Turkey. This research follows a mixed methodology by integrating both qualitative and quantitative research methods. In the case of qualitative approach, semi-structured in depth interviews are used to understand and reflect entrepreneurs' views, and to synthesize findings with the quantitative results for gaining deep insight into phenomenon. The researchers, using convenience-sampling technique, targeted entrepreneurs, who are owners or managers in SMEs. On the other hand, in the case of quantitative research method, questionnaire survey is being executed on SMEs. Besides the owner/manager of the SME, two other employees are asked to fill out the questionnaire. Hence, three participants from each SMEs are targeted to fill out questionnaire to achieve more reliable and valid results. ***Measures:*** In in-depth interview questions are based on literature findings, and included f 8 open-ended and 5 closed-ended questions. In context of quantitative research, questionnaire form is composed of two parts. First part includes the questions related to demographic characteristics of participants (e.g. age, education level, gender of participant) and enterprises (e.g., establishment year, size, annual revenue, industry). Second part includes the questions about ICT awareness, ICT adoption and innovativeness of SMEs. All scales at second part are adopted from literature (ICT awareness from Sin Tan et al. 2010; ICT adoption from Alma et al, 2018; innovativeness from Wang and Ahmed, 2004), and based on five point Likert Scale. ***Analysis Plan:*** As a part of qualitative research analysis, the responses of 50 entrepreneurs to the in-depth interview questions are coded, and analyzed by three researchers based on triangulation strategy. Moreover, data obtained from quantitative survey, will be analyzed through SPSS statistical package program. To test the model, regression analysis will be performed.

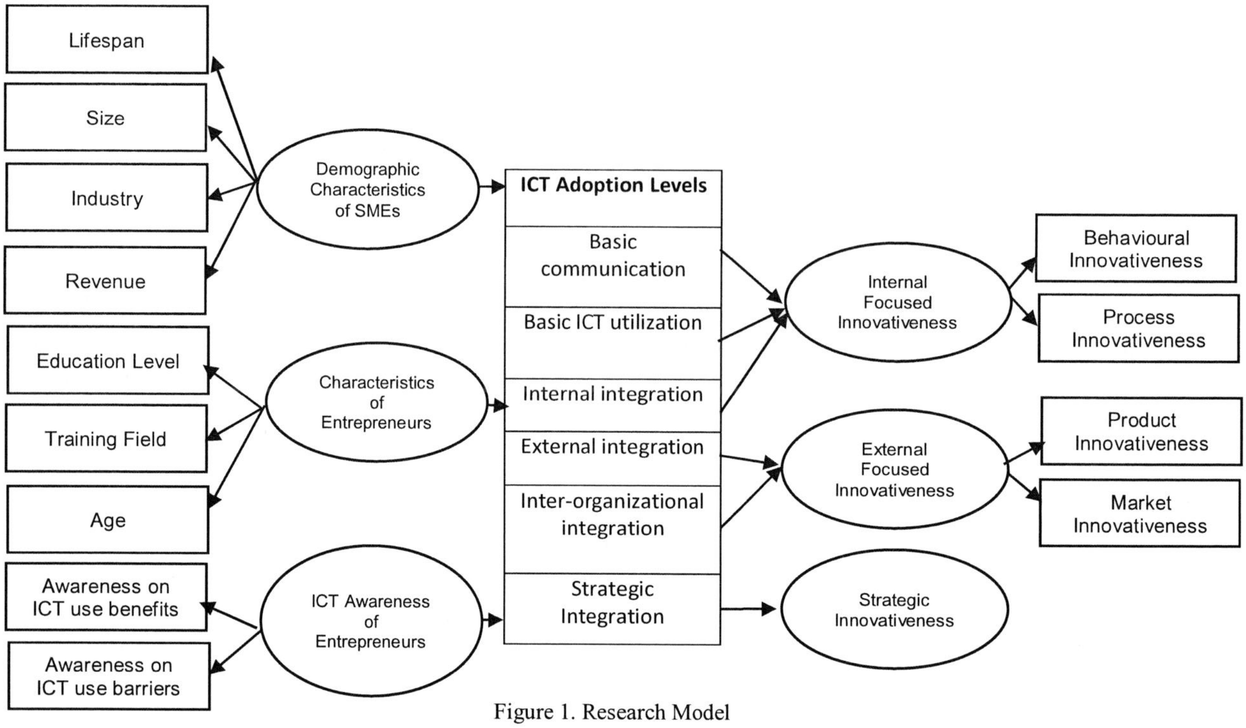

Figure 1. Research Model

4. CONCLUSION

This study, aiming to explore determinants of ICT utilization in SMEs and influence of ICT utilization on innovativeness is expected to provide the following contributions. Firstly, qualitative analysis results are expected to reveal some detailed and context specific findings on the ICT awareness and competency of entrepreneurs, and ICT adoption capability and innovativeness level of their firms. Secondly, quantitative survey conducted to reveal the effects of individual factors, and organizational factors on ICT adoption & utilization level of SMEs is expected to provide statistical evidence for answering one aspect of the research phenomenon. In this respect, quantitative analyses' results are expected to produce proof of evidence on determinants of ICT adoption levels of SMEs within a developing country context. Thirdly, the effects of ICT adoption and utilization levels on the components of organizational innovativeness are investigated comprehensively through this quantitative research. Although a remarkable number of research have focused on the impact of ICTs on product and process innovation (Neirotti & Pesce, 2019), to the best of our knowledge, the effects of ICT adoption & utilization levels in terms of *basic communication, basic ICT utilization, internal integration, external integration, inter-organizational integration and strategic integration* on the components of organizational innovativeness- *behavioral innovativeness, process innovativeness, market innovativeness, product innovativeness and strategic innovativeness* are examined comprehensively for the first time in this study, which constitutes the main contribution of the study.

REFERENCES

Adeniran, T. V., & Johnston, K. A. (2015). The impacts of ICT utilisation and dynamic capabilities on the competitive advantage of South African SMEs. International Journal of Information Technology and Management, 15(1), 59.

Al Isma'ili, S., Li, M., Shen, J., & He, Q. (2016). Cloud computing adoption determinants : an analysis of Australian SMEs. Pacific Asia Conference on Information Systems 2016, 1–17. Retrieved from http://ro.uow.edu.au/cgi/viewcontent.cgi?article=6855&context=eispapers

Alma, B., Coşkun, E., & Ozsahin, M. (2018). A Framework Proposal for Examining the Effect of ICT Adoption Level on Innovativeness in SMEs. In Twenty-fourth Americas Conference on Information Systems (pp. 1–10). New Orleans.

Awa, H. O., Ojiabo, O. U., & Emecheta, B. C. (2015). Integrating TAM, TPB and TOE frameworks and expanding their characteristic constructs for e-commerce adoption by SMEs. Journal of Science & Technology Policy Management, 6(1), 76–94.

Dahnil, M. I., Marzuki, K. M., Langgat, J., & Fabeil, N. F. (2014). Factors Influencing SMEs Adoption of Social Media Marketing. Procedia - Social and Behavioral Sciences, 148, 119–126.

Davis, F. D. (1985). a Technology Acceptance Model for Empirically Testing New End-User Information Systems: Theory and Results. MASSACHUSETTS INSTITUTE OF TECHNOLOGY.

Esmaeilpour, M., Hoseini, S. Y., & Jafarpour, Y. (2016). An empirical analysis of the adoption barriers of e-commerce in small and medium sized enterprises (SMEs) with implementation of technology acceptance model. Journal of Internet Banking and Commerce, 21(2).

Falahat, M., Tehseen, S., & Van Horne, C. (2018). Entrepreneurial innovativeness and ITS impact on smes' performances. International Journal of Entrepreneurship, 22(3), 1–9.

Giotopoulos, I., Kontolaimou, A., Korra, E., & Tsakanikas, A. (2017). What drives ICT adoption by SMEs? Evidence from a large-scale survey in Greece. Journal of Business Research, 81(December 2016), 60–69.

Ibrahim, A. M., Salleh, M., Hassan, H., Gambo, D., & Yusuf, S. (2016). Influence of ICT Adoption on Agro-Enterprises: Conceptual Framework and Structural Model. Jurnal PengaJian Media Malaysia / Malaysian Journal of Media Studies, 18(2), 37–54.

Jaakson, K., Aljaste, H., & Uusi-Kakkuri, P. (2019). Dimensions of organisational innovativeness and company financial performance in the biotechnology sector. International Journal of Manpower.

Kim, S. H., Jang, S. Y., & Yang, K. H. (2017). Analysis of the Determinants of Software-as-a-Service Adoption in Small Businesses: Risks, Benefits, and Organizational and Environmental Factors. Journal of Small Business Management, 55(2), 303–325.

Kossaï, M., & Piget, P. (2014). Adoption of information and communication technology and firm profitability: Empirical evidence from Tunisian SMEs. Journal of High Technology Management Research, 25(1), 9–20.

Kusumaningtyas, N., & Suwarto, D.H.(2015). ICT Adoption, Skill and Use Differences among Small -Medium Enterprises Managers Based on Demographic Factors. Procedia-Social and Behavioral Sciences, 169(August 2014), 296–302.

Makiwa, P. J. (2018). Developing and validating an ict adoption framework for smes in developing countries: A case of Zimbabwe. University of Pretoria.

Martínez-Román, J. A., & Romero, I. (2017). Determinants of innovativeness in SMEs: disentangling core innovation and technology adoption capabilities. Review of Managerial Science, 11(3), 543–569.

Neirotti, P., & Pesce, D. (2019). ICT-based innovation and its competitive outcome: the role of information intensity. European Journal of Innovation Management, 22(2), 383–404.

Nguyen, T. H., Newby, M., & Macaulay, M. J. (2015). Information technology adoption in small business: Confirmation of a proposed framework. Journal of Small Business Management, 53(1), 207–227.

Quinton, S., Canhoto, A., Molinillo, S., Pera, R., & Budhathoki, T. (2018). Conceptualising a digital orientation: antecedents of supporting SME performance in the digital economy. Journal of Strategic Marketing, 26(5), 427–439.

Ramayah, T., Ling, N. S., Taghizadeh, S. K., & Rahman, S. A. (2016). Factors influencing SMEs website continuance intention in Malaysia. Telematics and Informatics, 33(1), 150–164.

Rogers, E. M. (1983). Diffusion of Innovations. New York: Free Press.

Sin Tan, K., Chong, S. C., Lin, B., & Eze, U. C. (2010). Internet-based ICT adoption among SMEs: Demographic versus benefits, barriers, and adoption intention. Journal of Enterprise Information Management, 23(1), 27–55.

Taylor, P. (2015). The Importance of Information and Communication Technologies (Icts): an Integration of the Extant Literature on Ict Adoption in Small and Medium Enterprises. International Journal of Economics, Commerce and Management, III(5), 274–295. Retrieved from http://ijecm.co.uk/

Tornatzky, L. G., & Fleischer, M. (1990). The Processes of Technological Innovation. Lexington: Lexington Books.

Valdez-Juárez, L. E., García-Pérez-de-Lema, D., & Maldonado-Guzmán, G. (2018). ICT and KM, Drivers of Innovation and Profitability in SMEs. Journal of Information & Knowledge Management, 17(01), 1850007.

Wang, C. L., & Ahmed, P. K. (2004). The development and validation of the organisational innovativeness construct using confirmatory factor analysis. European Journal of Innovation Management, 7(4), 303–313.

COGNITIVE INFORMATION SYSTEMS – ARTIFICIAL INTELLIGENCE & MANAGEMENT DECISIONS

Bálint Molnár and Dóra Mattyasovszky-Philipp
Information Systems Department, Eötvös Loránd University, ELTE,
Pázmány Péter Sétány 1/C, Budapest, Hungary

ABSTRACT

We investigate the interlink between the management decisions and Artificial and Computational Intelligence (ACI) in the context of Cognitive Information Systems (CIS). The analysis is focused on the current trends of application of ACI within the realm of Information Systems (IS) for supporting management decision. One of the research issues is whether there is a difference between CIS and IS based on Artificial Intelligence (AI). Is there any chance to distinguish them from each other? If yes, we should locate the subtle differences and similarities between them. There are various definitions for the recent and the future AI, there are approaches to circumscribe the concept of CIS. The research issue is how the Cognitive Architecture, Science, IS and AI can be reconciled for management information systems (MIS) to support decision making.

KEYWORDS

Cognitive Information Systems, Enterprise Information Systems, Cognitive Architecture, Artificial Intelligence, Computational Intelligence, Management Decision

1. INTRODUCTION

MIS, Enterprise Resource Planning Systems (ERP) and their spin-offs - as Customer Relationship Management Systems (CRM) etc. - play important role within enterprises for supporting the management in decision making whereby these systems occupy an important position within Management Sciences as well. The most recent trends in ACI, Machine Learning (ML), Data Science, which are placed under one hood of AI, provide enormous selection of tools for exploiting data, content that are stored in IS. However, there are preconditions for both using and understanding of data (Rasmussen, 1980), (Mattyasovszky-Philipp & Molnár, 2018) ."Three important concepts help make a system cognitive: contextual insight from the model, hypothesis generation (a proposed explanation of a phenomenon), and continuous learning from data across time." (Hurwitz, 2015.) Extending Hurwitz (2015) definition of CIS, the ideal CISs, other than the above predefined details, should impact the carbon agent cognition in a positive way, improving it, leveraging the synergy originated form he interactions between silicon and carbon agent. This synergy generated leverage expressed via cognitive resonance, where the cognitive resonance orienting the entire process to the automated data understanding, meanwhile extracting the semantic information, which supporting the interpretation of the understanding. The concept of cognitive resonance is one of the attempts that try to make sense of the modelling activities in the most recent world of data analytics that uses tools out of data science (Mattyasovszky-Philipp & Molnár, 2018). CIS related information and the knowledge is limited, the lack of information generates misunderstandings, that has to be clarified for further explanation. Therefore the aim and the expected contribution of the research is to find a model, and combine the available knowledge considering CIS and management decision, and then to analyse the gap within silicon and carbon agent interaction from management decision prospective, to support the understanding, therefore support the enterprise operation using CIS. The research methodology that were applied during the research analyses and assessment of the available (limited) publications pursued by the comparative study pattern, i.e. studying and comparing the results published in articles, then a case study paradigm has been used for observing and monitoring the work with a CIS during daily operation (Molnár & Mattyasovszky-Philipp, 2018).

2. MODEL FOR DECISION MAKING IN CIS

A model is a representation of a system of "relevant" properties assumes an *oracle*. The system may consist of one or more entities and their relationships that are the relevant entities that should own at least two distinctly definable properties that can and should be related to each other (Muller et al., 2012).

Definition: Models in computer science and informatics aim to capture semantic properties of a domain of discourse by syntactic representations for the pragmatic benefits of users. A model is a tuple $M = (W, R, I: W \rightarrow R)$, (1) where W is the modeled system (domain of discourse); (2) R is the representation of modeled system W; (3) I is an interpreter that determines the semantic properties of W in terms of syntactic expressions of R. To build up a model M means to specify W, R, I and to define the mapping $W \rightarrow R$. To describe R means to determine the purpose of the model that it should serve (i.e. to acquire knowledge of the structure, of patterns, of behavior, of functionality of the system); furthermore, the representation R defines the entities that constitute the model and the set of relationships thereby the significant parameters of the properties can be identified. The interpreter I assists the human being, the carbon agent to understand the meaning of the syntactical expressions, data, bit strings, signs. Basically, the interpreter I can evaluate logical formulae whether they are true or false then more complex and meaningful description can be constructed from these elementary statements for understanding (see Herbrand Universe. (Coppin, 2004)).

2.1 Interaction between Managers and Cognitive Systems

In a Business Cognitive Information Systems, we meet *two types of models*. One model is that describes the *human computer interaction*, i.e. information exchange between silicon agent and carbon agent. The other type of models is that is built up for training through the available data and the model is associated to a certain algorithm belonging to the realm of ACI and ML. Such models out of data science approaches are the subject of interaction between humans and machines. In the environment of CIS, one of the helping hand for modeling the interaction between the carbon agent and silicon agent is the cognitive resonance (Ogiela, 2010). The services for data science and data analytics that are offered are based on the following pattern: (1) Creation of data collections of historical data. (2) The data set will become the basis for training the selected algorithm. (3) The problem should be defined, and experiments should be started to seek the proper models and algorithms measured in appropriate metrics whether it fits to purpose. (4) Afterward the models should be finalized so that it should yield good approximation on the training data set and according to the pre-defined accuracy metrics. (5) Finally, the models could be used for prediction and prescription for the enterprise (Wirth & Hipp, 2000), (Clarke et al., 2009). The MIS environment can be characterized by the notion of "Big Data" and "AI." Disregarding hype, there are serious problems that should be handled within the modeling of manager-CIS interactions. Modeling carbon agent - silicon agent information interchange means that two sets of parameters on both sides should be clearly defined, the two sets of parameters embodying single models should be related to each other. The parameters implicitly formalize *models* on both sides, in data science and analytics context means that the data that are required for decision making should be organized into *analytics base table* (*ABT*). The well-formed ABT integrate the disparate data and information sources that are available within the IS of the enterprise and the ABT will be the subject of the various algorithms that may produce predictions and IS prescriptions for the organization. The ABT and a set of algorithms together form the model. However, the parameters on the silicon agent side are defined with respect to the symbolic representation of the interface, and this model described by parameters does not reflect the representation of underlying structure within the machine. Since, there are lots of alternative user interfaces that represent the underlying *data science models* whose parameters at interface levels should be mapped and correlated to parameters that are apt to the human abilities. In a CIS environment, carbon agents are components of the system during the man-machine communication. The carbon agent should build up a representation of *data science models*' structure and acquire understanding the function and algorithms of the models with respect to a set of tasks connected to decision making. The carbon agent should learn the description language of the data science model, i.e. the symbols, signs, denotations that are employed, the syntactical rules, the essence of operations and algorithms that belong to these elements, those operators that can be used to invoke services for manipulating the models. The sequences of operations are related to tasks and subtasks of business processes in the enterprise. The cognitive model within the mind of carbon agent is a mapping of a *virtual machine* that is a contracting map of components that embrace the user interface with operations, the data science models along with data structure and algorithms, and the computing machinery.

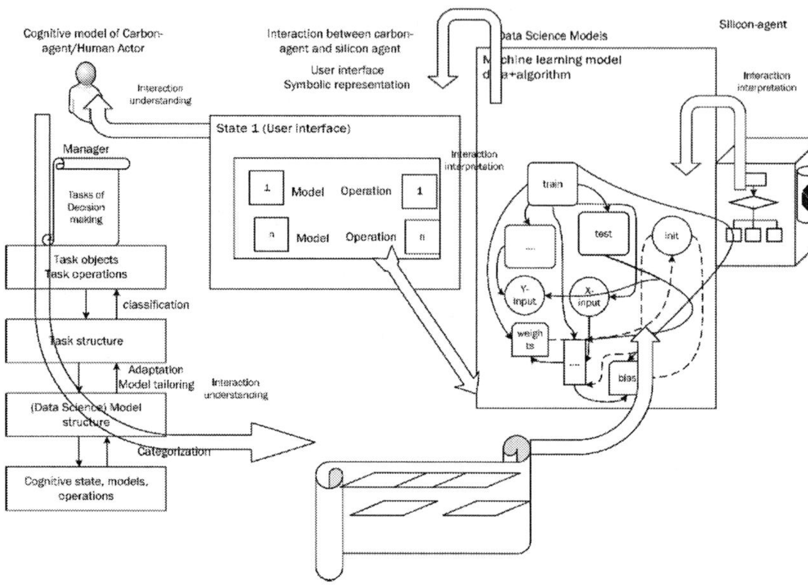

Figure 1. Model for the Interaction between Carbon Agent and Silicon Agent

The most important phenomena for the end-users are the relationships between tasks within business processes and the services of silicon agent including user interface, data science model and the underlying complex IS. On modeling the carbon agent and silicon agent information interchange, the system should take into account the symbolic representation of data science models, cognitive models of carbon agent, the mental models in the mind of the end-users, and the complex relationships among them (Figure 1).The symbolic representation of the *virtual machine* consists of the following elements: (1) objects that are manipulated by operations, (2) operations that are depicted by symbols and their syntactic rules and cause changes states of the systems, (3) states of the system that can be characterized by the permitted operations and set of significant parameters. The cognitive model that captures the mental representation of the environment within the mind of carbon agent contains the following constituents: (1) objects, (2) operations, (3) states and state transitions, (4) architecture (business, information, application system), (5) tasks and their structure of business processes.

2.2 Strategic Management Decision & CIS

The process of the decision making a consist of multiple perceptions and many other, sometimes the result of the decision leads in the mistaken way. Boulding (1994) try to close the gap between the actual and normative managerial behavior researching the strategic decision process. Strategic managerial decision messier, they occur in a complex environment difficult or expensive to reverse and the outcomes are to a greater degree contingent, that are influenced by individuals and impacted by the organization's behavior, and often substantially alters the internal and external relationships. The viability of the decision depends on the knowledge about the current status and about the expected reactions. Management's decision in its surrounding environment, while this environment surrounds the organization (Boulding, 1994). The decision making starts with a trigger, which before the outcome could originate a start new decision process. the model highlights two questions, *"what"* and *"how"*? The framework measuring the manager knowledge and his believes about the current economic environment, which determinates the value assigned to the decision. *"What"* knowledge determines the value that manager assigns to the mental market model, which represents the facts. The *"how "* as a manager mapping function represents his/her current believes about the market behavior. *"How"* impacted by multiple factors, external and internal, from price sensitivity to the personal relationship etc., meanwhile the manager *"What"* and *"how"* decision and knowledge about the situation linked to the *"if-than"* decision rule. The *"if-than"* knowledge, must be at least implicitly generate by some managers *"how"* knowledge. *"What"*, and *"how"* contains, the anticipated outcome as a believe of the manager, because the manager maps the context and the anticipated reaction within his/her mind. There are highlighted tree major reasons, when *'what"* may differ to the actual situation: (1) Wrong mental (market) model: wrong variables and/or functional forms etc., (2) Omitted variables (unobserved, ignored facts), (3) Wrong weights included into the decision model. All of them might have a significant impact on the outcome of the decision. Context and the it's change impact the relative sensitivity of the trigger mechanism. These contextual factors influence the overall mental model of the manager, therefore the decision process impacted thru the outcome. Managers might learn from the decision process, which does not imply better or the right decision. Meanwhile, because of the confusing strategic decision-making process it is possible that the managerial knowledge deteriorates rather than increase over the time. According to the decision research the problem decomposition increase the quality of the decision (Boulding, 1994). Managers are humans, sometimes, the decision taking is correct, but might happen it's opposite. The technology is able to mimic the human decision-making process in general, however there is an uncertainty whether the individual decision-making remains always individual process, considering the above "mental" model. We examine what we could expect from those systems and how we could use them to support the management decision. Those are the questions to be answered to be able to better understand CIS in the light of the "mental" model, considering the process of strategic decision making. **"What":** (1) *CIS is capable to (after appropriate coding and programming) use the correct "mental" (market) model.* (2) *CIS never omits variable or ignore available data or facts, and it apply the weights coded.* (3) *Advanced technology ensures the learning cycle, a supervised learning ensure the highest possible accuracy of the collected knowledge, which impact the system output.* **"How":** (1) *CISs are not yet trained to consider the part of anticipation of reactions, which is included into the human strategical decision process.*

Silicon and carbon agent interaction with supervised learning is one possible solution, however the anticipation related to the reaction is still to be built in to CIS, to empower CIS to mimic the human strategical decision-making process. Potential development as the carbon agent is learning from the previous decision process, might be included for one scenario, but in a different situation - stating that the subject of the prediction is different - this learned adds in is not available, therefore this gap in the decision-making process seems to be standard. That causing a chain of chains as iterations, to a continuous process. It may be simple, but this process could be repeated as many times as a difference occurs from the original concept, i.e. the anticipated reaction. This would appear weighted in the result obtained; as changing one's expectations on one side, approaching the "ideal of final" anticipation would shape the ending output. On the other hand, carbon agent repeats any mistakes resulting from a previous decision-making. Most probably the above described exercise to train any CIS to be able to consider expectations is not affordable, from time prospective. Any change in the environment might re-trigger a need of new training, that takes further form the acceptable output. *(Acceptable result is key during managerial decision, due to various limitations exits in the business environment.)* However, the complexity might be managed easier, speed of the environment change might impact negatively the learning cycle -lack of time to re-train, therefore the decision/output might not be accurate. To this end, it is closely related to the fact that the delegation levels associated with each job role are not accidentally defined within an organization.

2.3 Research & CIS with Cognitive Resonance

We consider that cognitive resonance is an additional feature of CIS, due to speed up the expert knowledge of CIS, support management decision with the newly learned information, and it improves during iteration by iteration providing new aspects in line with the decision taken. The current research in AI related in knowledge representation focuses on restricted logics that guaranty the efficient processing, meanwhile there are less flexibility and power that found in the human reasoning (Langley, 2015). *Our view the focus of the restricted logic is extended, balanced and corrected in sense of quality improvement and improvement of the features of CIS during the cognitive resonance. The power ensured by the cognitive resonance as a" power" or knowledge transfer via learning cycle.* During the problem solving and planning relies on extensive search and emphasize processing speed, and bears little resemblance to flexible problem solving in humans" (Langley, 2015). *The carbon-silicon cooperation strictly focuses on the problem solving, meanwhile narrows and synthesizes the area of search, which supports the existence of cognitive resonance.* Researches in case of Natural Language Processing the current trend of the AI research focus on statistical methods with few links to psycho/linguistics and emphasis on tasks like information retrieval and extraction (Langley, 2015). *The already solved problems utilizing the synergy originated via cognitive resonance, where stored as a "personalized" knowledge in relation to the already learned problem, therefore all inputs and outputs including all search result are available for the future as a "template" rules of the problem solution, which significantly improve the speed of the data and information elaboration for further problem solving. The expert based supervised learning supports the template (pattern) generation, speed up the problem solving to exclude all not appropriate, or necessary data.* Considering ML, the trend is focuses on statistical techniques that learn far more slowly than humans and almost exclusive focus on classification and reactive control (Langley 2015). *The silicon carbon collaboration, speeds up the learning cycle, the understanding and the implementation of any statistical technique, as the classification and the reactive control as well. Our proposal is that these research emphases should be supplemented and evaluated together with the interpretation of cognitive resonance.*

3. CONCLUSION

We have overviewed the most recent literature on CISs related to business administration and decision making. The definition of CISs refers to the cognitive architectures, data processing, models for insights hypotheses for new phenomenon and opportunity for the silicon agents for the continuous learning. The cognitive resonance provides a kind of interpretation framework for describing the information interchange between human and automated systems. Although, the ideas of economic analysis are superficial from point of operating enterprises where the management and IS should solve in tandem serious problems. Hence, the research has plenty to do on defining the idea of CISs in economics, in business administration as a management decision support system, and in the organization science to leverage the tools of data science for business efficiency and effectiveness during decision process.

ACKNOWLEDGEMENT

The project has been supported by the European Union, co-financed by the European Social Fund (EFOP-3.6.3-VEKOP-16-2017-00002).

REFERENCES

Boulding, W. e. a., 1994. Understanding managers' strategic decision-making process. Marketing Letters, 5(4), pp. 413-426.

Clarke, B., Fokoue, E. & Zhang, H. H., 2009. Principles and theory for data mining and machine learning. Dordrecht Heidelberg London New York: Springer Science & Business Media.

Coppin, B., 2004. Artificial intelligence illuminated. Sudbury, MA, US: Jones and Bartlett Publishers.

Hurwitz, J. K. M. B., 2015. A Cognitive Computing and Big Data Analytics., 10475 Crosspoint Boulevard Indianapolis, IN 46256.: John Wiley & Sons, Inc.

Langley, P., 2015. Introduction to Interactive Cognitive Systems, Auckland: University of Auckland.

Mattyasovszky-Philipp, D., 2018. Research on Cognitive Information Systems in Enterprise Environment. Moscow, Russia, CEUR, pp. 232-237.

Mattyasovszky-Philipp, D. & Molnár, B., 2018. Cognitive Enterprise and Cognitive Information Systems. Szeged, Hungary, Polygon Publisher, p. 64.

Molnár, B. & Mattyasovszky-Philipp, D., 2018. Cognitive Information Systems and Enterprise Engineering. Luxembourg, CEUR Vol-2229.

Muller, P.-A., Fondement, F., Baudry, B. & Combemale, B., 2012. Modeling modeling modeling. Software & Systems Modeling, 11(3), pp. 347-359.

Ogiela, L., 2010. Cognitive informatics in automatic pattern understanding and cognitive information systems. In: Advances in Cognitive Informatics and Cognitive Computing. Berlin, Heidelberg: Springer, pp. 209-226.

Rasmussen, J., 1980. The human as a systems component. In: Human interaction with computers. London: London Academic Press, pp. 67-96.

Wirth, R. & Hipp, J., 2000. CRISP-DM: Towards a standard process model for data mining. Manchester, UK, Practical Application 2000, pp. 29-39.

METRICS AND TOOLS THAT ARE AVAILABLE FORTESTING SCALABILITY

Anila Umar, Muhammad Abbas and Saad Rehman
National University of Sciences & Technology (NUST), Islamabad, Pakistan

ABSTRACT

Scalability covers the ability of an application to cope up with heavier processing load as desired. Other than that, it also covers how small one can start a system. Testing scalability is a very challenging task among all the other quality attributes i.e. performance, reliability, usability, accessibility and security. However empirically there is not much research work done on this specific domain. The focus of this study is to identify the all the metrics and tools that are in practice for measuring the scalability of a specific system. Moreover, finding out the challenges that are being faced while performing these measurement practices.
To collect information regarding the identification of metrics and tools for testing scalability, a systematic mapping study was conducted. Through this method we tried to get a generalized data from many resources over the internet.

KEYWORDS

Scalability, Metrics, Tools, Testing, Systematic Mapping Study

1. INTRODUCTION

Scalability plays a very vital role in the design of parallel and distributed systems. Generally, scalability is the measure of a system that keeps its performance when its size is scaled up. In proper terms it is defined as "Scalability is a desirable property of a system, a network or a process which indicates its ability to either handle growing amounts of work in a graceful manner or to be enlarged" (Wikipedia).

In other terms "Scalability is a characteristic of a system, model or function that describes its capability to cope and perform under an increased or expanding workload. A system that scales well will be able to maintain or even increase its level of performance or efficiency when tested by larger operational demands." (Investopedia). Testing scalability is a very challenging task among all the other quality attributes i.e. performance, reliability, usability, accessibility and security. In research domain several research work has been carried out and a number of metrics and tools are proposed so far for measuring scalability. However, there is still lack of an effective mapping that can help the testers to find out which are the best metrics and tools so far which can be used for measuring scalability to get better results.

2. LITERATURE REVIEW

(Serdar Dogan, 2014) tried to identify the tools and metrics available for testing different applications specifically web applications. He also identified these metrics based on the criteria of cost effectiveness. (Xiaokai Xia, 2010) focused on explaining some of the metrics and tools considered while testing. He mainly proposed to analyze and evaluate different attributes of web applications. He proposed in his model the issues that left unidentified during the phase of testing. (Gupta., 2015.) worked mainly on addressing the tools, types and methods used for testing different kinds of applications. In his research he also focused on explaining some metrics related to performance. (J. Križanic, 2010) attempted to conduct a systematic study to evaluate the testing tool Grinder. Other than that, he also finds out some of the other tools related to performance testing. (Wang., 2010) worked on a framework by integrating the basic functionalities of the tools like Selenium and JMeter together. This work concentrates mainly on different sort of testing Backend testing, load testing and UI testing etc. (N, 2009) worked on comparing web application for two different technologies .NET and Java by using different testing tools and metrics. In their work both the technologies are evaluated in terms of response time and throughput. They find out in their research that the Java technology performs better than that of the .Net in web applications. (Arora., 2015) performed a case study on different automated tools available for testing performance and other attributes. As a part of their research they also focused on literary survey and find out 18 different automated tools. (Vahid Garousi, 2013) performed a systematic mapping study to find out the tools available for web testing. They have also identified few tools along with the factor availability of the tool. (Rina., A Comparative Study of Performance Testing Tools. , 2013) worked on comparison of some of the testing tools in terms of some metrics available. They have also evaluated in their research work the testing tools by conducting experiments to make selection for suitable tools for conducting testing.

The metrics used for testing are not fixed for a application, but they vary from one organization to the other. Some organizations are small while others are large. These organizations face severe problems in selecting metrics for their testing activities due to constrains they have regarding resources like cost and time etc. There is a very little amount of research work done in this specific domain i.e. the selection of metric in different organizations by the software testing team (Tanjila Kanij, Performance assessment metrics for software testers, 2012). As in literature these drawbacks are also not particularly provided. Also, the new set of features that the testers want to have in their tools. All these identified issues represent the gap in the research work so far, hence providing basis and motivation for our problem domain. We in our work focused on a systematic mapping of the metrics and tools available and tested so far for measurement of scalability by the testers.

3. METHODOLOGY

A systematic mapping study is conducted to identify the metrics and tools available for the measurement of scalability. A systematic mapping is a type of study in which an overview of the topic is provided to the researchers for their research study. It also gives the research the number of publications available in their specific research area. As in our case we used systematic mapping study to get the data regarding the tools and metrics for the measurement of scalability. To conduct systematic mapping study the guidelines provided by (Kai Petersen, 2008) are followed.

3.1 Systematic Mapping Study Protocol

To conduct systematic study a protocol is designed and made selection of the key words related to our domain:

3.1.1 Selection of Keywords

Table 1. Keywords Selection

Category ID	Category	Keywords
C1	Quality Attributes	Scalability, Scalable, Scale up, Scale down.
C2	Testing	Verify, verification, validation, validate, testing
C3	Tool	Tool, tools, framework
C4	Metric	Metric, Metrics, Measure, Measures, evaluation, evaluate.

3.2 Formation of the Search String

To form search string, we have used 2 Boolean operators, i.e. AND & OR operators. The search string is formed as:

```
((Scalability)OR(scalable))AND((Assess)OR(Assessment)OR(Evaluate)OR(Evaluating)OR(Measure)OR(Measurement)OR(Metric)OR(Metrics))AND((Quality)OR(Attributes))
```

After having a search string, we have further two important steps.

3.2.1 Selection of Scientific Library or Database

We have selected 5 scientific libraries over the web. These includes: INSPEC, IEEE, SCOPUS, ACM, WILLEY.

3.2.2 Study Selection Criteria

Literature regarding scalability, metrics and tools. Literature that is in English language Literature from year 2000 to 2017.

3.3 Execution of the Search String

The search string is than executed in all the 5 databases mentioned above keeping in view the selection criteria given. All the results that are duplicated or are irrelevant to our selection criteria is excluded from the final gathered results. The following table shows our findings

Table 2. Results after String Execution

Database	Tools		Metrics	
	Total Searched Articles	Selected Articles	Total Searched Articles	Selected Articles
INSPEC	133	43	120	35
IEEE	140	47	135	32
SCOPUS	97	29	87	34
ACM	66	37	59	10
WILEY	40	2	92	5

In total 969 articles were obtained from all the databases. In which only 274 were selected keeping in view the selection criterion. Similarly, some of the articles were part of more than one database which were also merged to get the selected total.

3.4 Selected Literature for our Study

After studying the abstract of the 274 articles we have selected only 25 articles which were more specific and relevant to our study. During screening of the articles, the relevancy of the articles to our problem is thoroughly examined.

3.5 Studying and Assessing the Articles

The selected 25 articles are carefully studied to identify the metrics and tools that are used to measure the scalability of different applications. In all these articles important points are highlighted for further analysis.

3.6 Data Extraction Strategy

From all the highlighted points' data is extracted in the form of a table. This table gives the overview of our systematic study.

Table 3. Extracted Data

Author Name	Quality Attr.	Tools	Metrics
Fei Wang, Wencai Du (Du., 2012)	Scalability	Provided	Not Provided
Osama Hamed, Nedal Kafri (N, 2009)	Scalability	Provided	Provided
Qinglin Wu, Yan Wang (Wang., 2010)	Scalability	Provided	Provided
Zao-Bin GAN, Varadharajan (Varadharajan., 2005)	Scalability	Provided	Provided
G. Ruffo, R. Schifanella, & M. Sereno (G. Ruffo, 2004)	Scalability	Provided	Provided
Jordi Guitart, Vicenç Beltran, (Jordi Guitart, 2005)	Scalability	Provided	Provided
Tiantian Gao, Gongxin Wu (Wu Gongxin Jinlong Gao, 2010)	Scalability	Provided	Provided
Lakshmi S.Iyer, B. Gupta, N. Johri (Gupta., 2015.)	Scalability	Not Provided	Not Provided
Niclas Snellman , Adnan Ashraf(Niclas Snellman, 2011)	Scalability	Provided	Provided
R. Aganwal, B. Ghosh, S. Banerjee (R. Aganwal, 2000)	Scalability	Provided	Provided
Sandhya,Kiran,AkshyansunMohapatra (S. Kiran, 2015)	Scalability	Provided	Provided
Jörg Zinke, Jan Habenschuss, (J Zinke, 2012)	Scalability	Provided	Provided
B.M.Subraya, C.Ravi (B. M. Subraya, 2001)	Scalability	Provided	Provided
M. Kalita, S. Khanikar, T. Bezboruah (M. Kalita, 2011)	Scalability	Provided	Provided
Shraddha Mungekar, Dhanashree (taas., 2015)	Scalability	Provided	Provided
Arabi Keshk, Amal Ibrahim (Ibrahim, 2007)	Scalability	Provided	Provided
Hidam Kumarjit, Tulshi Bezboruah (Bezboruah., 2015)	Scalability	Provided	Provided
Manish Rajendra Dhote, G.G. Sarate (Sarate., 2013)	Scalability	Not Provided	Provided
Ana Cavalli, Gerardo Morales (Ana Cavalli, 2007)	Scalability	Provided	Provided
Hashemian, Martin Arlitt (Arlitt Martin Hashemian, 2012)	Scalability	Provided	Provided
Kai Lei1, Yining Ma, Zhi Tan (Kai Lei, 2014)	Scalability	Provided	Provided
Martti Vasar, Marlon Dumas (Martti Vasar, 2012)	Scalability	Provided	Provided
Breno Lisi, Romano (Breno Lisi Romano, 2009)	Scalability	Provided	Provided
Kalita1, T. Bezboruah (M. Kalita, 2011)	Scalability	Provided	Provided
Sebastian Lehrig (Sebastian Lehrig, 2015)	Scalability	Provided	Not Provided

4. RESULTS AND DISCUSSION

After we are done with all the steps of our systematic mapping study we resulted in two tables. One for the determined metrics for measurement of scalability in testing an application while the other for the tools for measuring scalability. In both tables not only, the names are listed but also their frequency count in the articles taken under consideration.

Table 4. Results for Scalability Metric

Scalability Metric	Frequency Count	Scalability Tool	Frequency Count
Response time	22	Tsung	5
Throughput	20	WebLOAD	5
Number of concurrent users	18	Silk performer	4
CPU utilization	16	QA load	3
Number of hits per second	14	CloudTest	3
Memory utilization	13	TestComplete	3
Disk I/O (access)	8	MBPeT	2
Latency	8	Pylot	2
Number of connections per second (user)	6	Testmaker	2
Disk queue length (request)	5	Application Center Test	1
Number of transactions per second (http)	4	Selenium WebDriver	1
Disk space	1	BrowserMob	1
CPU model	1	Zabbix	1
CPU clock	1	Nagios	1

5. CONCLUSION

This study was conducted to identify all the metrics and tools available and are in practice by the testers for the measurement of scalability of a system. We accomplished our objective by following steps of systematic mapping study. To have the required information for making our task done we have used 5 scientific libraries databases and through these databases we were able to get our desired articles that resulted in the final analysis and extraction of data.

Based on these results obtained we identified all the metrics that are available and are in practice for measuring scalability. We observed that the metrics response time and throughput are most commonly in practice. We also observed that there are very limited number of tools available for testing scalability as compared to other quality attributes like performance and reliability. Though we succeeded in refining a few of them that are successfully in practice, i.e. Tsung, Webloader and Silk Performer. Through this study we were successfully able to generate 2 lists, one for tools and the other for metrics. These lists can be helpful for the software testers to gain knowledge regarding testing scalability of different applications.

REFERENCES

Ana Cavalli, S. M. (2007). Regression and performance testing of an e-learning web application. *Dotlrn Proceedings-International Conference on Signal Image Technologies and Internet Based Systems, SITIS.*

Arlitt Martin Hashemian, K. (2012). Overcoming web server benchmarking challenges in the multi-core era. *Proceedings - IEEE 5th International Conference on Software Testing, Verification and Validation.*

Arora., I. (2015). A Brief Survey on Web Application Performance Testing Tools Literature Review. *International Journal of Latest Trends in Engineering and Technology.*

B. M. Subraya, S. V. (2001). A new model to bridge the gap between user and designer perceptions. *25 th Annual International Confernece on Computer Software and Applications, COMPSAC.*

Bezboruah., H. K. (2015). Performance metrics of a customized web application developed for monitoring sensor data. *IEEE 2nd International Conference on Recent Trends in Information Systems (ReTIS).*

Breno Lisi Romano, G. B. (2009). Software testing for web applications for non-functional requirements. *6th Intenational Conference on Information Technology ITNG.*

Du.,]. F. (2012). A test automation framework based on WEB. *IEEE/ACIS 11th International conference on Computer and Information Science, ICIS.*

G. Ruffo, R. S. (2004). A tool for evaluating web application performance in Quantitative Evaluation of Systems. *First International Conference QEST 2004*.

Gupta., D. D. (2015.). Performance testing and evaluation of web applications using wapt pro. . *International Journal of Innovative Research in Computer and Communication Engineering*.

H.M.a Aguiar, J. S. (2010). Profiling of real-world web applications. *International Workshop on Parallel and Distributed Systems: Testing, Analysis, and Debugging.*

Ibrahim, A. K. (2007). Ensuring the Quality Testing of Web Using a New Methodology. *IEEE International Symposium on Signal Processing and Information technology*.

J Zinke, J. H. (2012). Generating representative workloads for web server benchmarking. *Simulation Series, 44*.

J. Križanic, A. G. (2010). Load testing and performance monitoring tools in use with ajax based web applications. *MIPRO*.

Jordi Guitart, V. B. (2005). Characterizing secure dynamic web applications scalability. *19th IEEE International Parallel and Distributed Processing Symposium.*

Kai Lei, Y. M. (2014). Performance comparison and evaluation of web development technologies in php, python and node. js. *IEEE 17th Interntional Conference on Computational Science and Engineering (CSE)*.

Kai Petersen, R. F. (2008). Systematic mapping studies in software engineering. *12th international conference on evaluation and assessment in software engineering.*

M. Kalita, S. K. (2011). Investigation on performance testing and evaluation of PReWebN: A Java Technique for Implementing Web Application. . *IET.*

Martti Vasar, S. N. (2012). Framework for monitoring and testing web application scalability on the cloud. *Proceedings of the WICSA/ECSA.*

N, H. O. (2009). Performance testing for web based application architectures (.NET vs. Java EE). *1st International Conference on Networked Digital Technologies, NDT 2009*.

Niclas Snellman, A. A. (2011). Towards Automatic Performance and Scalability Testing of Rich Internet Applications in the Cloud. *37th EUROMICRO Conference on Software Engineering and Advanced Applications.*

R. Aganwal, B. G. (2000). Ensuring website quality: a case study. In Management of Innovation and Technology. *IEEE International Conference on ICMIT.*

Rina., T. (2013). A Comparative Study of Performance Testing Tools. *International Journal of Advanced Research in Computer Science and Software Engineering.*

S. Kiran, A. M. (2015). Experiences in performance testing of web applications with unified authentication platform using jmeter. *Technology Management and Emerging Technologies (ISTMET), An International Symposium.*

Sarate., M. R. (2013). Performance testing complexity analysis on ajax-based web applications. *IEEE Conference*.

Sebastian Lehrig, H. E. (2015). Scalability, Elasticity, and Efficiency in Cloud Computing: A Systematic Literature Review of Definitions and Metrics. *Proceedings of the 11th International ACM SIGSOFT Conference on Quality of Software Architectures.*

Serdar Dogan, A. B.-C. (2014). Web application testing: A systematic literature review. *Journal of Systems and Software*.

taas., S. M. (2015). An architecture of website analysis in a cloud environment. *1st International Conference on Next Generation Technologies (NGCT)*.

Tanjila Kanij, R. M. (2012). Performance assessment metrics for software testers. *5th International Workshop on Cooperative and Human Aspects of Software Engineering, CHASE.*

Vahid Garousi, A. M. (2013). A systematic mapping study of web application testing. *inernational journal of Information and Software Technology.*

Varadharajan., V. (2005). Evaluating the Performance and Scalability of Web Application Systems. *Third International Confernce on Information and Technology and Applications.*

Wang., Q. W. (2010). Performance testing and optimization of J2EEbased web applications. *2nd International Workshop on Education Technology and Computer Science*.

Wu Gongxin Jinlong Gao, T. (2010). A Reactivity-based Framework of Automated Performance Testing for Web Applications. *Ninth International Symposium on Distributed Computing and Applications to Business, Engineering and Science.*

Xiaokai Xia, Q. P. (2010). Multi-level logs based web performance evaluation and analysis. *International Conference on Computer Application and System Modeling, Proceedings, 4(Iccasm)*.

FROM BA TO BQA: INCREASING ROLE OF ANALYSTS IN IMPROVING PRODUCT QUALITY IN AGILE ENVIRONMENTS

Faizan Ahmed, Irtaza Tarar and Muhammad Abbas
National University of Sciences and Technology (NUST), Islamabad, Pakistan

ABSTRACT

Quality Software is one of the most sought out commodity in the digital world. Different quality standards like GQM, FURPS, ISO 9126 etc. have been proposed over the years and are continued to be used by companies as per their quality requirements, quality goals, kind of products, services and development processes. While traditional development practices place responsibility of Quality goals with Quality Engineers, Testers etc. recently there has been an increase in talks of integrating Business Analysts (BAs) role in defining and validating quality requirements especially in Agile based software developments, so much so as to suggestions of creating a BQA (BA/QA) role; integrating functional responsibilities of two in a single role in Agile frameworks. Proponents of this philosophy backs BAs for this challenging role because of their familiarity with both business and technological needs of clients, as well as knowledge of in-house products and services. Using statistics from a global SAAS based company; this paper provides valuable insights that such roles have started to exist in our Industry with good effect while bringing a positive impact on product quality and ultimately increase in customer satisfaction.

KEYWORDS

BAs (Business Analysts), QAs (Quality Analysts), BQA (Business Quality Analyst), Software as a Service (SaaS), Agile, Scrum, Software Quality

1. INTRODUCTION

Forbes defines Subject Matter Experts (SMEs) as among the top 10 business trends that will drive customer success in 2017 and 2018. As more and more companies embrace technology to automate their business processes, SMEs work hand in hand with BAs (at times as BAs) to ensure the delivery of correctly conceived solutions. With IT industry fast moving towards Service based Architecture (SaaS) - commonly via Agile based product centric approach - and Businesses putting high focus on quality and timely delivery, the intermediary role of BAs is evolving into one that has a direct impact on Product Quality. As agents of change, and being in a position where they can understand both business and technical needs of to be developed services, BAs are well placed to identify problems beforehand and highlight key quality matrices, ensuring product quality and clients satisfaction are always met. Starting with a brief overview of existing literature that directly/indirectly calls for such a role (next section), this paper provides a numerical analysis on how a key US based Software company has practically embraced this new BQA position in their Agile environment to improve product maturity and quality, and how other enterprises can follow suit.

2. NEED FOR A BUSSINGESS QUALITY ANALYST (BQA)

Feldman (2005) and Vinod (2015) stresses that Quality assurance is not a one-time activity in software projects but it is an ongoing process. During the software development, there is always a miscalculated cost for the unpredicted repeated actions. One of these actions is reopening of the user stories. User stories are reopened due to the errors committed at four major fronts; developers, quality analyst (QA), business analysts (BA) and environment issues. Since a Business analyst (BA) is responsible for analyzing and receiving the user requirements and then developing the user stories while a Quality analyst (QA) works as testers of user stories. So if these two positions can be integrated, the reopening of user stories can be avoided to decrease the additional costs faced during the software development cycle.

Daneva et al. (2013) in their exploratory study discuss role of Software Architects (SAs) in dealing with Quality Requirements (QRs) in context of large component based SAAS projects. Their findings reflect that by involving SAs with QRs leads to better definitions, better designs and hence better results in terms of customer satisfaction and product quality. Their study discusses direct impact that SAs have in QRs discovery, documentation, quantification, and in later stages, validation. It stresses that with SAs involvement: QRs are approached the same way as functional and architecture design requirements, ownership of QRs is proactively embraced, quantification is specialized as per specific subfields e.g. response time, availability etc., prioritization is handled keeping costs, values and benefits in focus with help of clients, and QRs validation is taken as a social activity rather than a method-centric checklist process.

Bennett et al. (2013) suggests role revamp of REs by allowing them to handle data, quality and security requirements in addition to their existing requirement gathering role. Quality criteria that they focus include performance, reliability and maintainability requirements. They stress that since requirement changes are an inherent part of RE process, continuous interfacing between customer stakeholders and REs puts them in an ideal place to forecast quality values for clients.

Herrmann et al. (2013) study focuses on existing disparity between the theoretical role of REs and the industry wide practiced role. Based on empirical analysis of job advertisements and interviews conducted from RE practitioners between 2009 - 2012, his study concludes that RE mostly exists as an Ad Hoc role with focus on experience, soft skills and solution design as key characteristics and that REs spend nearly 1/3rd (approx. 31.3%) of their total time in quality assurance activities.

Hruschka et al. (2012) propose Quality Driven Software Architecture (QDSA) by putting SA in center of development activities to ensure software products have key quality characteristics of Maintainability, Scalability, and Modularity etc. covered. He stresses that by assigning Quality ownership to SA would result in well negotiated, precise, and quantifiable quality goals that would ensure project goals (ownership of project manager) go hands in hand with Quality goals and conflicts are discussed and resolved proactively.

Karre et al. (2016) proposes heuristic based approaches of Defect dependency, CFGs, and Feature correlation to study defects in large scale integrated software solutions e.g. CBDs. They propose using Defect Dependency Metric to improve overall quality and track defect dependency in such complex systems. Atish et al. (2017), based on similar lines, discusses bipartite relationship between Analysts and CBDs for modelling business systems. Their research concludes that: Analysts develop accurate models by reusing components, and because of their simplicity and compactness, CBDs allow Analysts even with less industry experience perform at par with more experienced ones without effecting quality and costs.

Hareton (1997) stresses that user acceptance testing, where the system is tested in actual usage environment and gathers real time inputs, is another vital cog for success of software projects. Jennifer Biewer (2017) proposes that finding a quality analyst with the business knowledge would be very helpful in successful completion of this crucial stage of the software development. He goes on to say that by teaming up quality analysts with the experienced business analysts we can certainly produce very good results; alternatively we should encourage the integration of these two positions to find optimized results.

Ritesh Kaul (2015) discusses the problems faced by large scale software enterprises where multiple teams which are often geographically sparse work on the same project. He says that while these companies have multiple teams with different quality (at times even conflicting) goals, absence of a central collaboration framework (personnel) often delays effectiveness of agile development timelines. He suggests that by integrating the quality analyst and business analyst roles these companies can resolve Multivendor outsourcing strategies and agile development issues. He stresses that this integration model is much more efficient as it places same person on both ends of the development and helps create better understanding.

3. PROPOSAL FOR PROCESS IMPROVEMENT VIA BQA

3.1 Definitions and Process

Industry wide, IT companies continue to employ Business Analysts, System Analysts, Solution Analysts, Business Architects, Solution Architects, and Requirement Engineers etc. for nearly similar roles. While technically distinct definitions exists in literature for each of these roles, practical implications like size of company, kind of business and time/resource constraints often means that all of these roles are often merged into a single person. At their core, these people are responsible to interact with all of the involved stakeholders and bring answer to a key question: What do the systems need to do, and how do they do it?

Hence, by definition, an Analyst has following key roles and responsibilities:

- Interacting with business stakeholders for requirement elicitation, analysis, and prioritization
- Translate and document business needs as functional, non-functional, domain requirements
- Creating design prototypes for requirement, architecture, solution validation
- Act as liaison between in-house developers and outside clients

3.2 Case Study

While there are increasing direct/indirect calls of formal role integration of a BQA in Agile framework, no numerical data (as per our findings) currently exists to support potential benefits of such a leap. To bridge this gap, this paper is a small step in that direction. Based in US, Z Technologies (Company name has been kept anonymous to protect confidentiality of data) is a SAAS based multinational software company that deals with Customer Communication Management (CCM) based solutions and services. Over the past 30 years, the company's global clientele includes key players from healthcare, insurance and telecom industry.

The company is a key proponent of Agile framework and uses integration of Confluence with Jira for streamlining of development activities like user stories, sprints, tasks, bug reporting and resolution etc. Because of the nature of their products and services they provide, Analysts in Z Tech. were found to be practical examples of BQAs. Being in close contact with customers allows them to play dual role of product champions and naysayers, e.g. Quality Engineers or Quality Analysts.

3.3 Data Analyses

Based on analysis of Bug reporting/resolution and Enhancement Requests (ERs) data of Z Tech. from 2013-2017, we are in a position to numerically evaluate the benefits of a BQA in Agile framework for large companies that provide SAAS based solutions by coming up with following two hypothesis.

Hypothesis # 1: *Bugs reported by Analysts are critical for product quality and its overall acceptance and hence should receive high priority for defect resolution.*

As true representative of client expectations and being both aware of their immediate business needs as well as products current capabilities, Analysts are not only responsible to capture and convey quality characteristics to those involved in development and decision making, but are also responsible to validate (both before and after development) and prioritize these through project managers.

The quality covering efforts they put in include: Regression Testing of customer solutions against each new release, End to End workflow testing ensuring all components are interfaced correctly, Functional Testing including Installation Testing, Relevant Non-functional testing e.g. Performance measures, Localization etc., Root Cause Analyses of customer reported defects.

During these testing efforts - in principal with normal defect reporting/resolution cycle - Analysts report all encountered defects after verification with defect severity, defect priority and acceptance criteria. Defect severity and customer priority are two key factors that determine early resolution of reported defects. Once appropriate corrective actions are implemented by relevant teams, Analysts validates defect correction.

Table 1. Summary of bugs reporting and fixed

	Total Bugs (A)	BAs Reported (B)	Total Fixed (C)	BAs Fixed (D)	Total Not Fixed (E)	Analysts Not Fixed (F)
Avg. Count	2036.4	495.2	1449.2	413.8	587.2	81.4
Ratios	**B/A**	**D/B**	**C/A**	**D/C**	**E/A**	**F/B**
Percentages	24.3	83.6	71.1	28.6	28.8	16.4

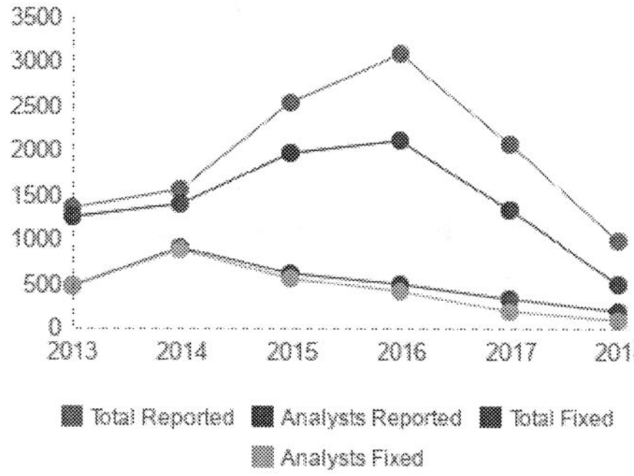

Figure 1. Bugs reported vs. bugs fixed

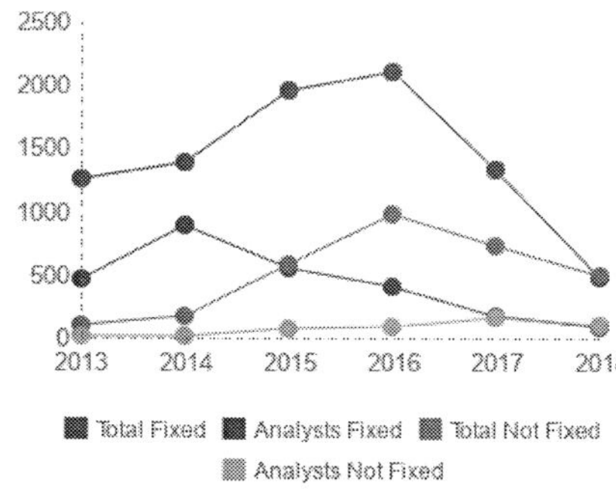

Figure 2. Bugs fixed vs. not fixed

From Table 1and Figures 1 and 2, we can draw following conclusions:

- Analysts are playing a key role in defect reporting and resolution process. As Figure **1.** Bugs reported vs. bugs fixed shows, from 2013-2018, they reported nearly a quarter (25%) of total reported defects (**B/A**), and were responsible for resolution of nearly a third (30%) of total fixed defects (**E/A**).
- Bugs reported by Analysts are of critical nature for both product quality and acceptance and hence receive higher priority for resolution. From Figure **2.** Bugs fixed vs. not fixed, it is evident that while overall Defect Reporting to Defect Fixation ratio (**C/A**) is about 71%, the same fixation ratio for Analysts reported defects (**D/B**) is nearly 84%.

Hypothesis # 2: *ERs reported by Analysts are a representative of customer immediate needs and hence gets prioritized accordingly.*

Being in direct contact with customer representatives allows Analysts to have a deeper understanding of client business needs as well as potential pain points. This knowledge helps them translate those business needs into product technological needs and hence identify and prioritize development of key features (for each sprint) by involving relevant stakeholders e.g. Project Manager, Product Owner, Scrum Masters etc.

While traditionally ERs are considered responsibility of Project Managers, putting Analysts in the mix allows them to timely forecast and advocate for customer needs.

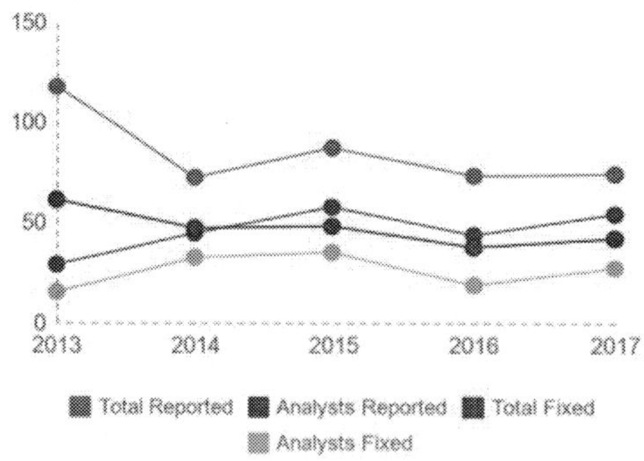

Figure 3. ERs requested vs. fixed report

Table 2. Summary of ERs reported vs. fixed

Years (2013 - 2018)	Total ERs (A)	BAs Reported (B)	Total Fixed (C)	BAs Fixed (D)
Avg. Count	84.6	45.4	47	25.4
Ratios & Percentages	B/A	53.66	D/B	55.94

A quick analysis of Figure 3 and Table 2 reveals strong support for above made claims with following key findings:

- As the processes mature, more and more ERs get requested by Analysts. From Figure **3**. ERs requested vs. fixed report the decreasing vertical distance between Lines Blue and Green from Years 2013 (29/117) to 2017 (54/74). Overall, Analysts requested for more than half of total reported ERs **(B/A)** i.e.54% during the past 5 years.
- More than half of reported ERs by Analysts **(D/B)** i.e. 56% get fixed in earliest Sprints (Line Yellow) as per client's priority. (While rest of these are either deferred for future releases, or are added to backlog for further discussion, while a few gets rejected.)

4. CONCLUSION

From the available data and shared hypothesis, it can be argued that with their Business and Technical knowledge, integrating BA and QA into a single role BQA in agile environments, can help large scale enterprises achieve better quality results. A BQA can guarantee successful delivery of quality solutions by proactively taking part in both requirement definitions and validations. A properly elicited set of requirements, with clear cut quality expectations and acceptance metrics, later validated against same established metrics by the same person is bound to buffer information gaps that can otherwise exist between different parties, and eventually help deliver a cost effective, quality focused solution. With focus of IT companies shifting towards large scale, customizable products and service based architecture, BQAs can play an important part in delivery of value based, and quality focused services to clients.

Possible limitations of this study include non-applicability of a BQA in a traditional software development environment and lack of existing data to numerically evaluate benefits of this role integration.

REFERENCES

Atish P. S.et al, 2017. Reusing business components and objects for modelling business systems: The influence of decomposition characteristics and analyst experience. *Journal of Systems and Software*, Vol. 131, pages 550-569.

Bennett-Therkildsen A. et al, 2013. *Redefinition of the Requirements Engineer Role in Mjølner's Software Development Process. In: Doerr J., Opdahl A.L. (eds) Requirements Engineering: Foundation for Software Quality.* Vol. 7830. Springer, Berlin, Heidelberg

Daneva M.et al, 2013. Software Architects' Experiences of Quality Requirements: What We Know and What We Do Not Know? In: Doerr J., Opdahl A.L. (eds) Requirements Engineering: Foundation for Software Quality. Vol. 7830. Springer, Berlin, Heidelberg.

Feldman. S, 2005. Quality Assurance: Much More than Testing. Magazine: Queue - Quality Assurance ,Vol. 3 No. 1, pp. 26-29, ACM, New York, USA.

Hareton K. N.et al, 1997. A study of user acceptance tests. *Software Quality Journal,* Vol. 6 No. 2, pp 137-149.

Herrmann A, 2013. *Requirements Engineering in Practice: There Is No Requirements Engineer Position. In: Doerr J., Opdahl A.L. (eds) Requirements Engineering: Foundation for Software Quality.* Vol. 7830. Springer, Berlin, Heidelberg

Hruschka P, 2012. Quality Driven Software Architecture. In: Biffl S., Winkler D., Bergsmann J. (eds) Software Quality. Process Automation in Software Development. Vol. 94. Springer, Berlin, Heidelberg.

Jennifer Biewer. 2017. *Value of a Partnership Approach to User Acceptance Testing*, https://www.fisglobal.com/

Karre S.A.et al, 2016. *Heuristic Approaches to Improve Product Quality in Large Scale Integrated Software Products. In: Maciaszek L.A., Filipe J. (eds) Evaluation of Novel Approaches to Software Engineering*. Communications in Computer and Information Science, Vol. 599. Springer, Cham.

Ritesh Kaul, 2015. *Integrating BA and QA in Healthcare IT* , https://www.emids.com/how-baqa-integration-supports-agile-adoption/

Robin Poston.et al, 2014. Managing User Acceptance Testing of Business Applications, *International Conference on HCI in Business, HCIB 2014: HCI in Business*, pp 92-102, Springer.

Vinod Kumar Chauhan, 2015. How to reduce user story reopen count in Scrum development? *2nd International Conference on Computing for Sustainable Global Development (INDIACom)*, pages 2204 – 2208, IEEE.

Reflection Papers

UNDERSTANDING CHANGE PROCESS AND ORGANISATIONAL PERFORMANCE ASSOCIATED WITH ENTERPRISE SYSTEM IMPLEMENTATION

Wallayaporn Techakriengkrai
ICL Graduate Business School, New Zealand

ABSTRACT

The enterprise system implementation process is considered to be a complex process that impacts organisations, processes, tasks, knowledge and skills, and relationships with clients and suppliers. Organisations that implement an enterprise system are required to make changes in their business, modify their business processes, and restructure their organisations to obtain the benefits of the new system. Past research on enterprise system has largely focused on organisational initial adoption decisions on an enterprise system. However, there has been little research concerning the continued use of an enterprise system and the associated change process in the post-adoption stage. Therefore, this proposed research will attempt to fill the gap in knowledge by examining the post-adoptive change and organisational performance resulting from organisational enterprise system implementation. The research questions are: (1) How do organisational changes unfold in enterprise system implementation? (2) How do enterprise systems shape organisational performance in the post-adoption stage of enterprise system implementation? This research will adopt the qualitative interpretive case study method to examine the change process and organisational change associated with enterprise system implementation in organisations. This study will employ the embedded multiple-case design. Semi-structured interviews will be conducted in this study. The proposed research will develop new knowledge based on how an integrated theoretical perspective using institutional logics and a socio-technical perspective can inform changes in organisations. The findings will assist organisations in providing appropriate resources and support for successful enterprise system implementation in the post-adoption stage.

KEYWORDS

Post-Adoption, Enterprise System Implementation, Organisational Change, Organisational Performance, Socio-Technical Perspective, Institutional Logics

1. INTRODUCTION

This proposed research will focus on enterprise system implementation. Enterprise systems are commercial software packages that include Enterprise Resource Planning (ERP), Customer Relationship Management (CRM), Supply Chain Management (SCM), and others (Markus & Tanis, 1999). The enterprise system implementation process is considered to be a complex process that impacts organisations, processes, tasks, knowledge and skills, and relationships with clients and suppliers (Wognum et al., 2004). Organisations that implement an enterprise system are required to make changes in their business, modify their business processes, and restructure their organisations to obtain the benefits of the new system (Davenport, 1998). Past research on enterprise system has largely focused on organisational initial adoption decisions on an enterprise system. However, there has been little research concerning the continued use of an enterprise system and the associated change process in the post-adoption stage (See et al., 2019). At the post-adoption stage, individuals commence using the enterprise system to support and accomplish work tasks. In this study, post-adoptive behaviour is regarded as that which occurs after the enterprise system has been installed in the organisations. There are continuous adjustments and improvisations in IS use. In other words, users can adapt and change their behaviours in IS use (Sun, 2012). Therefore, this proposed research will attempt to fill the gap in knowledge by examining the post-adoptive changes resulting from organisational enterprise system implementation. CRM and ERP systems are considered as particular types of an enterprise system. CRM implementation has shown to have a 63% fail rate based on a survey in the US by Merkle Group Inc (2018), while ERP implementation has had a 75% fail rate (Gartner, 2018). These failures can potentially be attributed to organisations tending to focus on the system itself without being concerning with the issues of integrating culture, processes, people, and technology within and across the organisational context (Finnegan & Carrie, 2010). It is argued that technical issues are not the most important issues in enterprise system implementation (Finnegan & Willcocks, 2007). The main issues of enterprise system implementation are related to organisational change and disruption, changes in the business (Schwartz, 2002), and technology misfit (Finnegan & Willcocks, 2007). Lack of appropriate technology use is one of the failure factors of enterprise system implementation (Zablah, Bellenger, & Johnston, 2004). Therefore, the enterprise system is an interesting context in which to examine change in the post-adoption stage of enterprise system implementation. From the organisation's perspective, new enterprise system implementation helps to improve efficiency, effectiveness, and employees' job performance in organisations (Davis, 1993). However, the introduction of a new system tends to include disruptive workplace changes (Orlikowski, 2000), requiring changes elsewhere in the organisation. These include changes in work processes, work practices, relationships between different professional work groups, roles, skills, capacities of the system users (Clegg & Shepherd, 2007), and balance of identities (Schilhavy & Iyer, 2007). This study will focus on change process associated with the disruptive change of implementing a new enterprise system in an organisation.

2. THEORETICAL BACKGROUND AND FOUNDATION

In this research, the researcher will develop new knowledge based on how an integrated theoretical perspective using institutional logics and a socio-technical perspective can inform changes in organisations. A socio-technical system consists of two subsystems: the social system and the technical system. The social system consists of two components include actor and structure such as culture, norms, skills, and values (Cummings, 1978). The technical system consists of tasks and technology (Kwon & Zmud, 1987). According to Leavitt (1964), there are four components of a socio-technical system include actors (e.g., project participants and stakeholders) and their characteristics and attributes; tasks which refer to what and how work is accomplished; structure which represents institutionalised rules and arrangements; and technology including hardware, software and tools. Previous IS research that has adopted a socio-technical perspective has allowed researchers to understand change through the interactions of the four socio-technical components after implementing new IS systems, leading to the modification of organisational structures and work processes. A socio-technical perspective is useful to understand an emergent process of change and socio-technical components that affect organisational changes after new enterprise system implementation. Institutional theory can be used as a theoretical lens to "develop a more structural and systemic understanding for how technologies [enterprise systems] are embedded in complex interdependent social, economic, and political networks, and how they are consequently shaped by such broader institutional influences" (Orlikowski & Barley, 2001). Institutional logics will be used to investigate the interaction between enterprise systems and organisations' structures and processes as well as to identify and explain misalignment problems in enterprise systems implementation (Svejvig, 2009).

3. RESEARCH OBJECTIVES AND QUESTIONS

The main objective of this study is to provide a better understanding of the change process in enterprise system implementation and how this change shapes organisational performance. To achieve this, the research explores the change process associated with enterprise system implementation. This research will focus on the post-adoption stage of enterprise system implementation. Specifically, the objectives set out for this study are: (1) To reveal change process in the post-adoption stage of enterprise system implementations and (2) To investigate organisational performance in the post-adoption stage of enterprise system implementations. This proposed study aims to investigate the change process and organisational performance in enterprise system implementation. Institutional theory, and a socio-perspective are used to ground the empirical enquiry on changes in organisations from enterprise system implementation. The main research questions guiding this study are: (1) How do organisational changes unfold in enterprise system implementation? and (2) How do enterprise systems shape organisational performance in the post-adoption stage of enterprise system implementation?

4. RESEARCH METHODOLOGY AND APPROACH

This research will adopt the qualitative interpretive case study method to examine the change process associated with enterprise system implementation in organisations. An interpretive approach is an appropriate approach to develop a rich understanding of the changes and organisational performance associated with new enterprise system implementation in the organisational context. Interpretive case study research aims to understand the nature of phenomena from the point of view of participants and seeks to elicit meanings from behaviour in the social context (Cavaye, 1996). Case study allows researchers to discover an event, an activity, and a process from participants. The case study strategy consists of three main steps: case study design, case study selection, and case study analysis. Case study design involves identifying the unit of analysis, identifying criteria for case selection, determining an appropriate number of cases, selecting an appropriate data collection method, and designing data collection instruments. The case study design involves the decision to use multiple case studies and the preparation of interview questions. This study will employ the embedded multiple-case design (Yin, 2003). A multiple-case design is regarded as more appropriate than a single-case design because a single case approach is suitable for testing the boundaries of well-formed theory or examining an extreme or a unique case. The benefits of adopting a multiple-case design in this study are related to the need to identify a variety of socio-technical changes according to different organisational contexts. Two case studies will be conducted in New Zealand. The unit of analysis is an organisational level. For case study selection, the researcher will adopt a theoretical sampling strategy. Participants will be selected based on their knowledge and expertise in the CRM applications. The last step is case analysis. Within-case and cross-case analysis will be conducted. The researcher will use thematic analysis to analyse data (Braun & Clarke, 2006). In this study, Nvivo software will be used as a tool to organise and analyse data.

5. CONCLUSION

In this research-in-progress paper, the author is in the process of finding appropriate organisations to participate in the study. Two organisations from different industries will be selected to identify a variety of changes and organisational performances according to different organisational contexts. This research will contribute to an understanding of change process in enterprise system implementation. The results will be useful to reveal changes in response to new enterprise system implementation in organisational contexts. In addition, this research will reveal the results in terms of how new enterprise systems shape organisational performance in the post-adoption stage of enterprise system implementation. The proposed research will develop new knowledge based on how an integrated theoretical perspective using institutional logics and a socio-technical perspective can inform changes in organisations. This study will provide practical contributions in several ways. Firstly, the findings will assist organisations in providing appropriate resources and support for successful enterprise system implementation in the post-adoption stage. Secondly, the findings will enable organisations to become aware of unanticipated events and consequences that may occur after enterprise system implementation. Lastly, the results will support IT developers in preparing a good implementation plan for successful implementation.

REFERENCES

Braun, V. and Clarke, V., 2006. Using thematic analysis in psychology. *Qualitative research in psychology*, Vol. 3, No. 2, pp 77-101.

Cavaye, A. L., 1996. Case study research: A multi-faceted research approach for IS. *Information Systems Journal*, Vol. 6, No. 3, pp 227-242.

Clegg, C. and Shepherd, C., 2007. The biggest computer programme in the world… ever!: Time for a change in mindset? *Journal of Information Technology*, Vol. 22, No. 3, pp 212-221.

Cummings, T. G., 1978. Self-regulating work groups: A socio-technical synthesis. *Academy of Management Review*, Vol. 3, No. 3, pp 625-634. doi:10.5465/amr.1978.4305900

Davenport, T. H., 1998. Putting the enterprise into the enterprise system. *Harvard Business Review*, Vol. 76, No. 4, pp 1-11.

Davis, F. D., 1993. User acceptance of information technology: System characteristics, user perceptions and behavioral impacts. *International journal of Man-Machine Studies*, Vol. 38, No. 3, pp 475-487.

Finnegan, D. and Currie, W. L., 2010. A multi-layered approach to CRM implementation: An integration perspective. *European Management Journal,* Vol. 2, No. 2, pp. 153-167.

Finnegan, D. and Willcocks, L., 2007. *Implementing CRM: From technology to knowledge*. John Wiley & Sons, West Sussex, UK.

Gartner, 2018: 75% of all ERP projects fail – But why? Retrieved from http://officeoffinance.com/gartner-75-of-all-erp-projects-fail-but-why

Kwon, T. H. and Zmud R. W., 1987. *Unifying the fragmented models of information systems implementation. In R. J. Boland & R. A. Hirschheim (Eds.), Critical issues in information sys-tems research (pp. 227-251).* John Wiley & Sons, New York, USA.

Leavitt, H. J., 1964. Applied organization change in industry: Structural, technical and human approaches. *New Perspectives in Organizational Research*, pp 55-71.

Markus, L. and Tanis, C., 1999. *The enterprise systems experience – from adoption to success. In R. W. Zmud (Ed.), Framing the domains of IT research: Glimpsing the future through the past. Pinnaflex Educational Resources*, Ohio, USA.

Merkle executive survey, 2018: 7 Must-Know CRM Adoption Statistics and What They Mean for Your CRM. Retrieved from https://www.business2community.com/customer-experience/7-must-know-crm-adoption-statistics-mean-crm-02023236

Orlikowski, W. J., 2000. Using technology and constituting structures: A practice lens for studying technology in organizations. *Organization Science*, Vol. 11, No. 4, pp 404-428.

Orlikowski, W. J. and Barley, S. R., 2001. Technology and institutions: What can research on information technology and research on organizations learn from each other? *MIS Quarterly*, Vol. 25, No. 2, pp 145-165.

Schilhavy, R. and Iyer, L., 2007. Exploring the information effects of identity and information transparency in reputation systems. *Presented at the DIGIT Workshops*, Montreal, Canada.

Schwartz, S. J., 2002. In search of mechanisms of change in identity development: Integrating the constructivist and discovery perspectives on identity. *International Journal of Theory and Research*, Vol. 2, No. 4, pp 317-339.

See, B. P., Yap, C. S. and Ahmad, R., 2019. Antecedents of continued use and extended use of enterprise systems. *Behaviour & Information Technology*, Vol. 38, No. 4, pp.384-400.

Sun, H., 2012. Understanding user revisions when using information system features: Adaptive system use and triggers. *MIS Quarterly*, Vol. 36, No. 2, pp 453-478.

Svejvig, P., 2009. Literature review of enterprise systems research using institutional theory: Towards a conceptual model. *Qorking Paper*

Wognum, P. et al, 2004. Improving enterprise system support: A case-based approach. *Advanced Engineering Informatics*, Vol. 18, No. 4, pp 241-253.

Yin, R. K., 2003. *Case study research: Design and methods (3rd ed.).* Sage Publications, California, USA.

Zablah, A. R. et al., 2004. Customer relationship management implementation gaps. *Journal of Personal Selling and Sales Management*, Vol. 24, No. 4, pp 279-295.

PREPROCESSING STRATEGY IN WEB-MINING: RECOMMENDED OR INEVITABLE?

Dror Ben-Ami
Zefat Academic College, Zefat, Israel

ABSTRACT

Web-browsing users' behavior is one of the fascinating, attractive and interesting subjects, specially from socio-technological perspectives. Companies and learning-organizations are investing huge human resources, efforts and capital to follow their users' behavior, trying to find out and plot their users' profiles. Knowing, understanding and predicting users' tangible and intangible behavior help these organizations to focus on users' needs and interests. Thus, companies and learning-organizations can generate significant intellectual capital and use this asset efficiently and effectively later. The intellectual capital asset can target into business-based and knowledge-based activities, such as pointed-newsletters, targeted markets, crystalizing pricing policies and much more. The users' profiles usually categorized into different classifications, such as social aspects, personality traits, purchase behavior, cognitive behavior, and more. The raw data for this research was collected from web users. Around one hundred thousand internet-society users from one the OECD countries were the basis of the research population. The research examines users' behavior through the net, after collecting wide range of data elements during few months period, using progressive data analysis tools and techniques, afterwards. The case study relies of real work (project), conducted from July-2018 till Feb-2019. The purpose was to recover and re-analyze the collected data after performing improper and incorrect analysis procedures by the original staff. The paper deals with the possible missteps which can happen during the data preprocessing steps in data-intensive projects and tries to understand the consequences of those early missteps can have on the end result. Specifically, the paper recounts those missteps based on real experience during a web mining project. The paper presents a guide on the procedures and decisions which should be taken to avoid or at least minimize critical mistakes during the data preprocessing step.

KEYWORDS

Internet-society, Data/Web Mining, Preprocessing, Machine Learning, I2K (Information to Knowledge)

1. INTRODUCTION

The internet-society is a global worldwide community. It consists of internet users from different continents, different countries, different cultures and different browsing habits. This case study research was arranged in one European internet-society population; trying to explore and plot the following:

a) Socio-technological behavior aspects of the internet-society.
b) Follow communication and collaborations between internet users, from within a specific sub-group.
c) Follow the population's relationships with the global worldwide internet-society community.

The case study is focused on the scientific data analysis continuous process, from its inter-organizational working process and procedures, and NOT focus in the Internet-Society itself. Specifically, the following pinpoints the sub *data-preprocessing* stage. A large data sets were assembled and monitored for few months during the research project. More than one hundred thousand internet users take part in this project. Fifteen to twenty different web browsing attributes and traits were collected, arranged and categorized, separately and within sub-groups categories. Ten research variables were the basis of the research data analysis process, after collecting, arranging and classifying the relevant data elements.

2. WEB MINING MODEL

The purpose of the researches' team was clearly defined: to explore and learn wide range of data behavior aspects, discover behavioral patterns and reinforce known paradigms and templates. The staff was interested to establish data-mining methods and techniques, rather than using the standard and conventional statistical analytical tools. The preference of data mining tools, as scientifically powerful analysis environment, rely on the facts that descriptive and predictive data mining models (Awad et al) (Dunham) can find out wide, deep, tangible and intangible data aspects, by using systematic machine learning rule-based, rather than those offered by the conventional data analysis tools, which are limited (Sivakumar et al) (Fauset). At first glance and based on this assumption, it seems clear and simple. Well-known and well-defined straight-forward process was approved; according to this scheme (Uwe).

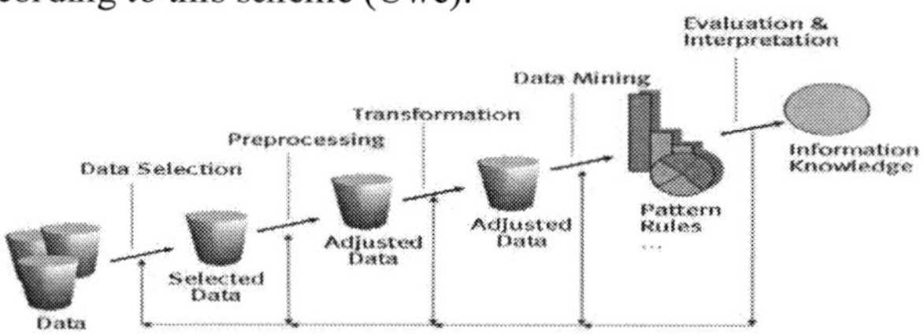

Figure 1. Data Mining – Information to Knowledge Process

One of the main and central mile-stones in the DM general model is the preprocessing stage. Critical faults and significant mistakes were discovered and recognized in the *Preprocessing* stage. These, as expected, affected all the next data analysis stages. Wide range of references covers the issue of DM-preprocess stage/s from different points of view, but from one common significant angle: *the necessity to establish correct and proper step by step methodology, in order to increase the ability to analyze the data on the best way*; to achieve real valuable KNOWLEDGE, in the entire Information to Knowledge [I2K] continuous process. Kaur et al, refer in their article to effective pre-processing methodology, which involves field extraction, significant attributes selection, data selection, and data cleaning. Krell et al, focus on data selection strategies which limit the size of the stored training data by different inclusion, exclusion, and further dataset manipulation criteria. Similar reference can be found at Hatzi, et al. They emphasize that DM is long-continuous process, which sometimes might be cumbersome task, which requires expert knowledge, concerning preprocessing of data, selection of algorithms, appropriate configuration, feature identification and result comprehension. Two more such references are mentioned in the following articles and books. The first is specifically to the web-mining preprocess (Valesquez et al), and the second notes relevance for any data-mining analysis application, in general (Lawrence et al) (Michael et al). Feelders et al specify: "Despite the predominant attention on analysis, data selection and pre-processing are the most time-consuming activities, and have a substantial influence on ultimate success."

All the references express in different words, the required methodology and the accurate-proper preprocess "must-be-done" sub-activities. The project which relies on these articles' recommendations and inevitable steps, exposes few issues which cause to wrong process. Something went wrong along the socio-technological project. What was it? why? and could it be recovered and fixed up? Databases can include missing data elements, noisy data, inconsistent and/or multiple data elements and such. These all generate low-quality of the explored data, in general. Specifically, in this project – it affected the DM process and cause damage to activate the next DM analysis procedures well.

3. RELATED TERMS AND PREPROCESSING STAGES

Each selected data mining processing model is based on few critical data analysis aspects, which must be defined and categorized properly: data characteristics, level of detailed data and the data scope, environment of the research field, accuracy level of the data and type of the implementation to be managed. The DM world offers and equipped us with two different model types: descriptive and predictive, as mentioned (Dunham)(Han). Each approach has few leading root models and branched models for almost each root model. So, what is the preferred model which is best-fit for our mission? Activating suitable array of decisions can eliminate immediately the improper models and ensure that we are in the "correct" and "right" environment, in our way to make the final decision for our best-fit model selection. Different kinds of DM models are proposed to us, according to these wide range of pre-checks, preprocess estimations and evaluations we need to make, to be sure that the results would be maximized: reliable and validated **scientifically**. The preprocessing stages is a strategy. It is not a recommended set of what essential or not essential to do. It is a set of MUST-BE-DONE and inevitable set of procedures, instructions, and how to-do detailed information. Just small range of degrees of freedom is permitted. Any small exception may lead to incorrectness. The article backups and presents one typical mistake, which was recognized during the research. It shows that even professional companies and development teams are not always "immune" from making such mistakes. Wrong model selection leads, of course, to total wrong results: false-distorted results, erroneous results which may cause to improper results' interpretation. In addition, confusion, distrust and mental negative aspects accompanied the entire implementation process. The line below describes the complete and proper preprocessing 4-stages, regarding the data elements. (1)Cleaning → (2)Integration → (3)Reduction → (4)Transformation & Discretization. Briefly, the *data cleaning* includes completion of missing values, removing outliers and resolve inter-consistencies. The *data integration* stage merger multiple databases and/or data cubes into one central integrated data structure. Next, the *data reduction* sub-procedure copes with data and dimensions reductions, without damaging the data properties. Finally, the data transformation & discretization procedures are required to customize the data for the next data analysis DM models, for a proper, convenient and effectively working procedures (Han et al, chapter 3). In addition, few more data mining aspects must be considered, in order to achieve a complete wide efficient way to analyze the entire data and in order to establish a correct DM model. These aspects cover the following accepted terms: Overfitting, Outliers, High Dimensionality, Integration (Dunham, p.15-16). Overfitting: Once a DM model was established, it must fit future database states. Overfitting occurs when the model does not fit future states (Dunham, p.14, p.77). Outliers: These are all the data elements which do not fit the data fields format from few possible reasons: invalid experimental error or any other validity in the measurement process. In addition, wide range of reasons can cause "noise" to the entire data set, like: range (less/greater than specific values), type (string instead of numeric values), missing values, duplicated values etc. These all cause "noise" to the entire data set and cause data distortion, which finally decrease the accuracy level of the data analysis process. High Dimensionality: conventional DB schema may be composed of many different attributes. NOT all these attributes are always needed for the main data analysis process that we want to implement. This may lead into dimensionality curse, which means that we need to specify correctly the precise attributes' set (Dunham, p. 15). Integration: Knowledge Data Discovery requests may be treated as special, unusual or one-time needs. These make them inefficient and ineffective. DM integration into traditional DBMS is certainly a desirable goal (Dunham, p.15). The data mining researchers must be aware prominently and consistently that the attribute selection can be critical to the entire analysis process. Wrong or even unintentional distinguishing between nominal and numerical attributes data objects (Han et al, p.40), from within the specific data mining models – affects immediately the results, and cause data distortion. This part is based on *attribute selection and pattern evaluation* (Han et al, p. 336, 224, 40, 264, respectively.)

4. THE FINDINGS

Can predefined array of MUST-BE-DONE actions and activities can ensure reduction and reducing the estimated error/s on one hand, and increase certainty of the results on the second hand? The answer is 'simple' BUT complicated: YES, it can be done – for sure. BUT very professional step-by-step systematic and consistent stages MUST be done. JUST very professional and experienced staff must lead and manage such projects. The staff skipped over some critical professional issues, from uncertain and uncleared reasons, which navigate into improper professional process. Part of the mistakes have been done from within the web-mining model itself, as well. In wide perspective, it seems that in spite that, the major problems were caused by skipping over the preprocessing rather that the mistakes in the web-model itself. The list below summarizes precisely the necessary practical-implemental conclusions:

1) The DM preprocessing methodology requires step-by-step of proper, accurate, rechecked and monitored all the data elements in the research field. We have to "stick" to the preprocessing methodology.

2) The need of using normalized data is essential. Some of the models must have their input as normalized data, on the range (0,1). Otherwise – it may be ineffective to continue with the next DM-process.

3) Distinguishing between parameters' types is critical. Specially, the distinguishing between nominal and numerical values may affect the DM-process (Han et al, p. 40), and lead to total unexpected results. The analysis rulers (such as Gini Index, CART, Gain ratio) are based on this distinguishing (Han et al).

4) Cross-checking of few models' results can leverage and increase significantly the entire correctness and preciseness of the entire project. These are important as well, in the entire pre-process array decisions and considerations, and at the end, whilst all the models' work was completed, and results should be interpreted (Fauset) (Krell et al). For example, established the classification model with regression, beside neural-network model/s. This was a critical issue; a conceptual mistake, which has been done by the staff, which decided to concentrate only on one model.

5) From managerial point of view – Knowledge expert must follow ALL the project stages carefully, with measures steps; "heel to toe" (Chipman et al). This part was basically not implemented well during the project. Project manager with wide knowledge about DM aspects can cover and solve out this point. Regarding to this point, it is recommended to appoint a specific data expert – to the preprocessing stage itself. Thus, another cover of "two-eyes" professional programmer – would prevent such mistakes, as mentioned.

6) It is recommended that an expert in web-mining will be the project manager. This expert should manage the entire project work, side by side with sociologist and with information-technology. The sociologist should cover the sociology aspects, and the information-tech should cover the DM side.

7) Finally, the cost of the total project was significantly much higher than the expected, approximately 20% of the planned budget. The reason was the necessity to fix-up the data elements, and reactivate the DM analysis models, in order to interpret the results. "Think before you act, act proactively". Investing much THINKING at the beginning and more planning – saves a lot of money and means. Always correct, but sometimes we skip it, without meaning to.

REFERENCES

Awad, M. and Thuraisingham, B. and Wang, L., 2009. *Design and Implementation of Data Mining Tools*, CRC Press.

Chipman, S. and Meyrowitz, A., 1993, *Foundations of Knowledge Acquisition, cognitive Models of Complex Learning*, Kluwer Academic Publishers.

Dunham, M.H., 2003. Data Mining: Introductory and Advanced Topics, Prentice Hall, Pearson Education Inc.

Fauset, L.V., 1994. *Fundamentals of neural networks, architectures, algorithms, and applications*, Prentice Hall.

Feelders, A. and Daniels, H. and Holsheimer, M., 2000. *Information & Management*, Methodological and practical aspects of data mining, Elsevier, Vol. 37, Issue 5, pp. 271-281.

Han, J., and Kamber, M., 2011. *Data Mining: Concepts and Techniques*, 3rd Edition, Morgan Kaufmann.

Hand, D. and Heikki, M. and Padhraic, S., 2001. *Principles of Data Mining*, MIT press.

Hatzi, O., and Zorbas, N. and Nikolaidou, M. and Anagnostopoulos, D., 2014. Panhellenic Conference on Informatics, *An intelligent tool for expediting and automating data mining steps*, ACM International Conference Proceeding.

Kaur, J. and Garg, K., 2019. Advances in Intelligent Systems and Computing, *Efficient management of web data by applying web mining pre-processing methodologies*, Vol. 731, pp. 115-122.

Krell, M. and Wilshusen, N, and Seeland, A., and Kim, S.K., 2017. Journal of Neural Engineering, *Classifier transfer with data selection strategies for online support vector machine classification with class imbalance,* Vol.14, Issue 2.

Lawrence, K.D. and Kudyba, S., and Klimberg, R.K., 2008. *Data Mining Methods and Applications*, CRC Press.

Michael J.A.Berry and Gordon L., 2011. *Data Mining Techniques: For Marketing, Sales and Customer Support*, John Wiley& Sons, 1st Edition.

Sivakumar, P., and Prakash, M., and Singaravel, G., 2015. International Journal of Applied Engineering Research, *Efficient methods for distinction preclusion in data mining,* Vol. 10, Issue 55, pp. 2212-2215.

Uwe, L., 2012. PowerPoint presentation, *Artificial Neural Networks and Data Mining*, Hochschule Wismar University of Technology, Business and Design, (slide: Table1).

Velasques, J.D. and Lakhmi, C.J., 2010. *Advanced Techniques in Web Intelligence – I*, Springer, SCI, Vol. 311.

Poster

CONFIDENCE INFORMATION SETS

Manish Aggarwal[1] and Madasu Hanmandlu[2]
[1]*IIM Ahmedabad, India*
[2]*MVSR Engineering College, Hyderabad, India*

ABSTRACT

A new data structure for the representation of an agent's assessment of an information source value, along with the associated confidence degree is presented. The proposed structure is termed as confidence information set (CIS). It gives multiple information values, as perceived, corresponding to an information source value, along with the associated confidence degree. The usefulness of the proposed CIS in multi criteria decision making is shown through illustrative examples.

KEYWORDS

Information Set, Confusion, Imprecision, Decision Making

1. INTRODUCTION

The fuzzy set theory (Zadeh, 1965) represents in-exactness, ill-definedness in an information source value. However, it has its own difficulties (Aggarwal, 2016). The fuzzy concepts are the linguistic expressions, and hence limited by the words in the daily language (Zimmerman ,1983). Human thinking and feelings that conjure the uncertainty in a given situation, have certainly more comprehensions and concepts than the words in the daily language. Therefore, it is often difficult to guarantee, unequivocally, a one to one mapping between the uncertainty perceived and its depiction by means of a membership function. Moreover, a membership grade is always relative without an explicit consideration of the associated information source value. Resultantly, the interpretation of a membership grade depends on the onlooker agent. For instance, an agent's evaluation of a person as highly knowledgeable conveys only a little information and it means different for each interpreting agent. Inspired by these drawbacks of a membership function, in this work, we develop alternate structures for the representation of uncertainty.

To address this, the concept of information set is proposed in (Aggarwal,2016). It gives a linked representation of an information source value and its evaluation (termed as agent), computed through the Hanman-Anirban entropy function (Hanmandlu, 2011). Such entropy values are referred to as the information values, and collectively comprise an information set. These entropy values are easier to interpret and deal with, as shown in (Aggarwal, 2016). Since, agent is a function of a combination of parameters and an information source value, it can take many forms, including those of the commonly used membership functions like Gaussian, triangular, or trapezoidal etc.

These features of information set theory make it quite useful in any application where an agent (a DM, etc.). Besides, it is especially useful in representing vague or subjective assessment of the decision-maker (DM), in multi criteria decision making (MCDM). However, when the values are ill-defined (or vague), the agent inevitably faces confusion. That is, often (s)he may have multiple possible perceptions for the same information source value. To address this, the concept of information set has been extended as hesitant information set (HIS) in (Aggarwal M, 2019), inspired by the concept of hesitant fuzzy set. A HIS gives a set of all the perceived values that an agent may have for an information source value.

HIS provides an excellent data structure to address confusion in the information set theory. However, the confusion of an agent may manifest not only in the form of multiplicity of perceived values, but also in the form of varying confidence degrees. For instance, an agent witnesses a fast-moving car. In the absence of a ready device to know the objective speed of the car, (s)he would at best try to express the perceived value for the same, but (s)he may have some confusion about the accuracy of his/her expression of the perceived speed of the car. In such a situation, the agent may find it more convenient to associate the perceived value (information value) with a degree of confidence, in place of giving multiple perceived values, as required in the case of HIS. This extra piece of information could be vital in the decision making application. For instance, if the agent has witnessed the car from very far distance, and therefore has a very vague idea of the real speed, he would have very low degree of confidence. In the absence of a provision to have this confidence degree of the agent, this perceived value given by the agent is very much likely to be considered as the true speed value, in contrast to what it would have been considered with a low confidence value. To address this, we are motivated to extend the concept of information set with the confidence degree of the agent. The data structure, so formed, is termed as confidence information set. The rest of the paper is organized as follows. Section 2 gives the background for the study. In Section 3, we introduce the concept of confidence information set. Section 4 concludes the paper.

2. BACKGROUND

2.1 Information Set

Let $U = \{u_1, \ldots, u_m\}$ denote the reference set with each u_i described by a set of attributes E. The value an attribute e ∈ E takes for $u_i$is termed as information source value, and is denoted by $I_e(u_i)$. The collection of all such information source values is shown as: $I_e = \{I_e(u_i) \mid \forall u_i \in U\}$ (1)

I_e in (1) can be seen as an information function $I_e : U \to I_e(u_i)$, and $I_e(u_i)$ refers to a normalized information source value in the interval [0, 1]. The information gain function is given as:

$$g_e(u_i) = e^{-(a_e(I_e(u_i))^3 + b_e(I_e(u_i))^2 + c_e(I_e(u_i)) + d_e)^{\alpha_e}} \quad (2)$$

where $g_e(u_i)$ gives the desirability for the value that attribute e takes for alternative u_i; and a_e, b_e, c_e, d_e and α_e are the free parameters, specific to e, i.e. $\{I_e(u_i)\}, \forall u_i \in U$. These parameters lead to different forms of $g\_e(\cdot)$. A set of parameters therefore uniquely represents the evaluation pattern of a DM.

The parameter values can also be the moments such as mean and standard deviation of the distribution of the information source values. This results into generation of a generalized Gaussian function. For instance, let $a_e = 0, b_e = 0, c_e = \frac{1}{\sigma x}, d_e = -\frac{m_e}{\sigma_e}$ (where m_e refers to the mean value $\frac{1}{n}\Sigma_i I_e(u_i)$), then we obtain $g_e(\cdot)$ as:

$$g_e(u_i) = e^{-\left(\frac{I_e(u_i) - m_e}{\sigma_e}\right)^{\alpha_e}} \quad (3)$$

where, α_e is termed as a DM's utilitarian parameter for attribute e which uniquely specifies a DM's evaluation behaviour. Different values of $\propto_e = 0.5, 1, \ldots, 5$ correspond to different shapes of $g_e = 2$ shown in Figure 1. A Gaussian function is obtained at $\alpha_e = 2$.

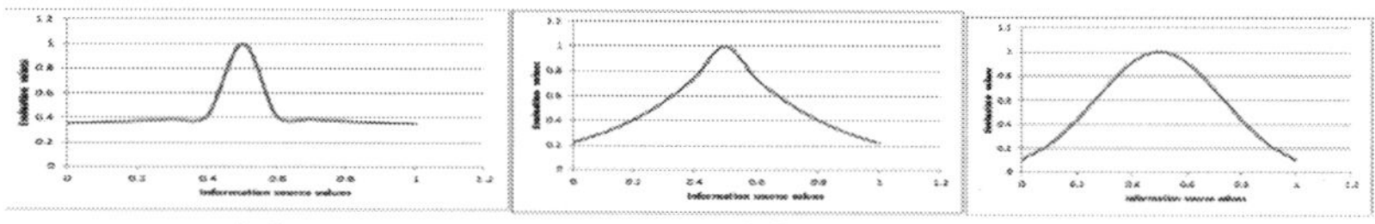

(a) $\alpha = 0.1$ (b) $\alpha = 1.0$ (c) $\alpha = 2.0$

Figure 1. The evaluation values of the form $g_e(u_i)$, as obtained with information gain function, shown in (3)

The uncertainty in $\{I_e(u_i)\}, \forall u_i \in U$, as evaluated by $g_e(\cdot)$ is given as: $Q_e = \sum I_e(u_i)\, g_e(u_i)$ (4) where $I_e(u_i)\, g_e(u_i)$ gives $I_e(u_i)$, as perceived by the agent. The set $\{I_e(u_i) g_e(u_i)\}$ constitutes an information set S_e, shown as: $S_e = \{I_e(u_i)\, g_e(u_i)\}, \forall u_i \in U$ (5)
Each element of S_e is expressed as: $S_e(u_i) = I_e(u_i)\, g_e(u_i)$ (6), which is an entropy (information) value.

3. CONFIDENCE INFORMATION SET

The information set is generalized as confidence information set (CIS) by having the confidence degrees associated with each of the information values in the information set. A confidence information set C over soft universe (U,C), with $\ominus$ as a vector of the confidence values, is a set defined by a mapping $F: C \to S \times \mathbb{R}$, and $\ominus: C \to \mathbb{R}$. The confidence information set is formed from the sets of ordered pairs of

$F(e_i)$ and $\theta(F(e_i))$, and shown as: $\mathrm{C} = \{(Fe_i) \mid \theta(Fe_i)))\}, \forall e_i \in C$, where $\theta\,(F(e_i))$indicates the evaluator's confidence in his assessment of an alternative against e_i, and $\ominus = \{\theta(F(e_i))\}, \forall e_i \in C; F(e_i) \in P(U); \theta(F(e_i)) \in [0,1]$. We denote each element of confidence information set as $S(e_i) = (F(e_i)|\theta(F(e_i)))$. Each element of the proposed CIS is a tuple of the agent's perceived value along with the agent's confidence in the same. This allows to consider the confidence degrees, often associated with the agent's perceived values in MCDM problems.

Example 3.1. Let the universal set $U = \{u_{1,}\, u_2, u_3, u_4\}$, where u_i refers to as an alternative each of which is defined by the criteria $C = \{e_1, e_2\}$. The conventional information set is then shown as: $S = \{S_1, S_2\}$, where s_i refers to the information value corresponding to e_i. Let the confidence of the expert in his evaluation be $\theta(e_1) = (0.8)$ and $\theta(e_2) = (0.3)$. Then the corresponding confidence information set is $\mathrm{C} = \{(S_1|0.8), (S_2|0.3)\}$. The confidence values are indicated in the bold, and are reflected in the final decision outcome. A few basic operations on the proposed CIS are presented as follows. Let C^1 and C^2 be two CISs defined over (U, C). Then C^1 is a *subset* of C^2, *i.e.* $\mathrm{C}^1 \subseteq \mathrm{C}_2$ *iff* i. $\theta(F^1(e_i)) \leq \theta(F^2(e_i))$, $\forall e_i \in C$; ii. $F^1(e_i) \subseteq F^2(e_i)$, $\forall e_i \in C$. The *complement* of C, denoted by , $\bar{\mathrm{C}}$ is defined as $\bar{\mathrm{C}} = \{\bar{S_\iota}\, |\bar{\theta_\iota} = 1 - \theta_i)\}, \forall e_i \in C$ (13). The complement of a CIS can be seen as an evaluation, just opposite to that of the given CIS. The union of C_1 and C_2, denoted by $\mathrm{C}^1 \cup \mathrm{C}^2$, is defined as $\mathrm{C}^1 \cup \mathrm{C}^2 = \{{S_i}^1 \cup {s_i}^2 \mid {\theta_i}^1 \cup {\theta_i}^2)\}, \forall e_i \in \mathrm{C}$. The intersection of C^1 and C^2 is: $\mathrm{C}^1 \cap \mathrm{C}^2 = \{{S_i}^1 \cap {s_i}^2 \mid {\theta_i}^1 \cap {\theta_i}^2)\}, \forall e_i \in \mathrm{C}$. The *union* and *intersection* of C and C_1 is :

$$\mathrm{C} \cup \mathrm{C}^1 = \{S_1 \cup {S_1}^1 |\, \mathbf{0.8}), (S_2 \cup {S_2}^1 \mid \mathbf{0.3})\};\ \mathrm{C} \cap \mathrm{C}^1 = \{S_1 \cap {S_1}^1 |\, \mathbf{0.1}), (S_2 \cap {S_2}^1 \mid \mathbf{0.2})\}$$

3.1 Properties

Let C be a CIS defined over (U, C), then

i) $\mathrm{C} \subseteq (\mathrm{C} \cup \mathrm{C})$ ii) $(\mathrm{C} \cap \mathrm{C}) \subseteq \mathrm{C}$ iii) $\mathrm{C} \cup \mathrm{C}_0 = \mathrm{C} \cap \mathrm{C}_0 = \mathrm{C}_0$ iv) $\mathrm{C} \cup \mathrm{C}_1 = \mathrm{C} \cap \mathrm{C}_1 = \mathrm{C}$

4. CONCLUSION

The proposed confidence information set (CIS) provides a convenient data structure to represent the perceived values for an information source value, along with the corresponding confidence value. It is inspired from the fact that an agent often faces confusion, or lack of a complete confidence, in the assessment of imprecise values. The proposed structure provides a useful provision for the agent(s) to provide this crucial information to qualify the evaluations. In contrast to a hesitant fuzzy set, it is easier for the agent to give his/her degree of confidence for the evaluations given by him/her. Besides, the proposed CIS are compact and easier to operate with, in comparison to a hesitant information set. CIS finds a good potential in multi criteria decision making in providing evaluations qualified by their associated degrees of confidence. As a future work, the arithmetic and geometric aggregation operators for CIS can be explored, which can add to their usefulness as a datastructure in MCDM. Besides, it can also be extended to the domains of type-2, rough sets, ignorance functions, and intuitionistic fuzzy sets, to present multi-faceted uncertainty. CIS can also be conveniently fitted with learning systems such as a neural network.

REFERENCES

Aggarwal M. (2019): Hesitant information sets and application in group decision making. *Appl. Soft Compu.*, 75, 120–129.

Aggarwal M. (2016), and Hanmandlu, M.: Representing Uncertainty With Information Sets. *IEEE Trans. on Fuzzy Systems*, 24(1), 1–15.

Hanmandlu M. (2011) and Das, A.: Content-based Image Retrieval by Information Theoretic Measure. *Defence Science Journal*, 61(5), 415–430.

Zadeh L. A. (1965): Fuzzy sets. *Information and Control*, 8 (3), 338–353.

Zimmerman H. (1983). J.: Using fuzzy sets in operational research. *European Journal of Operational Research*, 13(3), 201–216.

AUTHOR INDEX